# The Great Jazz Guitarists

Also by Scott Yanow

*Swing*
*Bebop*
*Classic Jazz*
*Trumpet Kings*
*Afro-Cuban Jazz*
*Jazz On Film*
*Jazz On Record: The First Sixty Years*
*Duke Ellington*
*Jazz: A Regional Exploration*
*The Jazz Singers*

# The Great Jazz Guitarists

## *The Ultimate Guide*

Scott Yanow

Backbeat
Books
An Imprint of Hal Leonard Corporation

Published in 2013 by Backbeat Books
An Imprint of Hal Leonard Corporation
7777 West Bluemound Road
Milwaukee, WI 53213

Trade Book Division Editorial Offices
33 Plymouth St., Montclair, NJ 07042

Printed in the United States of America

Book design by Snow Creative Services


Library of Congress Cataloging-in-Publication Data

Yanow, Scott.
    The great jazz guitarists : the ultimate guide / by Scott Yanow.
      pages cm
    Includes bibliographical references, discography, and filmography.
    ISBN 978-1-61713-023-6
1. Guitarists. 2. Jazz musicians. 3. Guitar music (Jazz)—History and criticism.  I. Title.
    ML399.Y358 2013
    787.87'1650922—dc23
    [B]
                                                                    2012050685


www.backbeatbooks.com

# CONTENTS

# ACKNOWLEDGMENTS

In addition to the 154 guitarists who took the time and trouble to answer a detailed questionnaire that I sent, I was assisted in small and large ways by these 20 people, who often suggested or helped track down specific guitarists. I want to thank (in alphabetical order) Ron Anthony, Jeffrey Andrew Caddick, Anders Chan-Tidemann, Christophe Deghelt, Jim Eigo, Gary Fukushima, Joanie Henderson, Tamm E. Hunt, Jon-Erik Kellso, Judi K, Jack Leitenberg, Mundell Lowe, Jenny McVie, Robert Nolting, Red O'Sullivan, Ali Ryerson, Brooke Vigoda, Dory Yanow, Doug Yoel, and Barry Zweig.

I also want to express my appreciation to Steve Subrizi, the tireless copy editor of this book, and the staff at Backbeat Books, including Mike Edison and Jessica Burr, for their belief in the project.

A special thank you goes out to Brian Ashley who, as editor of *Record Review*, got me started writing about jazz 37 years ago. And most of all, a heartfelt thanks and love to Dory Yanow (to whom this book is dedicated), whose love, consistently great ideas, enthusiasm and desire to always cheer me on made the completion of this long project possible.

# INTRODUCTION TO THE JAZZ GUITARISTS

The guitar has always had an odd position in the jazz world. While it is difficult to imagine a rock group, a blues band with over three pieces, a folk singer, or a bluegrass ensemble not having at least one guitar, many of the most important jazz bands have gotten along fine without a guitarist. There were no guitars in the original Benny Goodman Quartet, the Charlie Parker Quintet, the Birth of the Cool Nonet, either of Miles Davis' classic quintets, or the famous John Coltrane Quartet. The role of the guitar (is it a member of the rhythm section or part of the frontline with the horns?) was ambiguous and uncertain for decades. It would not be too much of an oversimplification to say that if no guitarist had ever played jazz, the history of the music would not be drastically different. That certainly cannot be said about the trumpet, saxophone or piano.

So why write a book about jazz guitarists? Skipping over the fact that the guitar is the world's most popular instrument (having succeeded the piano), it has had an intriguing history in jazz and spawned an assortment of colorful personalities. Its battle with the banjo for supremacy, the development and grudging acceptance of the electric guitar, its use in fusion of the 1970s, and the countless number of approaches that have been created since that time make this a story worth telling. More than any other instrumentalists in jazz, guitarists have been influenced by other idioms, from blues and rock to world music. That can make it a little difficult to decide whom to include in a book of this type, certainly much more than deciding whom to feature in *Trumpet Kings*. I believe that the 342 on whom I settled represent the most significant jazz guitarists, past, present and future. Undoubtedly, a new earth-shattering guitarist will emerge on the scene a week after this book is published, but at least I was able to cover the jazz guitar world of 1920–2010, with updates made in 2012.

In addition to the 342 greats, there are short mentions of 218 other guitarists (44 deceased and 175 active) who came close. Some of the 175 could make it to the upper ranks in the future. There is also a section on 36 performers famous for other activities who have also played jazz guitar.

When I started listening to jazz at the beginning of the 1970s, among the first guitarists who I heard were George Benson, Wes Montgomery, Herb Ellis, Barney Kessel and Al Di Meola. A few years later, I acquired a double-LP of Charlie Christian performances with Benny Goodman. It caused a light to

go on in my head, and I remarked, "Ahh, now it makes sense. It all connects together." I hope that reading *The Great Jazz Guitarists* will give readers the motivation to connect all of the dots.

## A Brief History of the Banjo in Jazz

First there was the guitar, then the banjo, and then the guitar.

While guitarists were part of some of the very first New Orleans jazz bands, by the time jazz was recorded, the banjo was the dominant string instrument. The origin of the banjo is not positively known, but the chances are that it was originally derived from the African ngoni instrument, which slaves recreated in a slightly different form in the Southern United States.

One of the first to popularize the instrument was Joel Sweeney, a white man, who led the Virginia Minstrels in minstrel shows as early as the 1830s. The instrument was frequently used in minstrel shows of the next 80 years due to its volume and portability. It has a ringing metallic sound that makes it easy to hear and allows the performer to function as a one-man band when it fits the situation. Several different variations of the banjo were developed, with the number of strings usually being four or five.

By the time jazz was being recorded in the 1920s, three types of banjos were utilized. The plectrum banjo (essentially a five-string banjo with one string removed) and the tenor banjo (a bit higher pitched and tuned like a mandolin or violin) both use four strings. They differ in their tuning and the size of their necks, with the plectrum being much taller and having more frets. The six-string guitar-banjo allowed musicians to create denser chords, and it led the way to the guitar's future dominance.

During the ragtime era (1899–1915), one would have expected that many of the recordings of rags would have been made by pianists. But due to the primitive recording techniques of the period, the piano did not pick up particularly well on records, and in ensembles it tended to be inaudible. However, the banjo, which was much louder than the acoustic guitar, proved to be ideal, and Vess Ossman (1868–1923) was the perfect musician for the time. His solos on the five-string banjo were quite popular. He first recorded in 1893 and was featured on a variety of instrumentals in his career, including syncopated rags and marches. He went on tours, recorded in England, and for a time had his own dance band. He was among the first to record "Maple Leaf Rag," and was also featured on "The Stars And Stripes Forever." Ossman made his last recordings in 1917 and was never heard in a jazz setting, but he remained active up until his death in 1923 from a bad heart.

Fred Van Eps (1878–1960) idolized Ossman and by the late 1890s had become his main competitor. He began recording in 1897 and had a similar repertoire as Ossman, mixing together rags with popular tunes of the time. During 1912–22 he led the Van Eps Trio, a ragtime-oriented group that at times included Nathan Glantz or Rudy Wiedoeft on saxophone and Felix Arndt or Frank Banta on piano. In 1921, his band made one of the very first sound films, a short called *The Famous Van Eps Trio Plays A Bit Of Jazz*. That short can be considered the first near-jazz sound film. Van Eps, like Ossman, made around 1,000 recordings; the exact number is not known. With the rise of jazz, his popularity started to drop and he stopped recording after 1937. Van Eps attempted a comeback in the 1950s, recording for his own 5 String Banjo label as late as 1956. His son, George Van Eps, played banjo at first before mastering the guitar. It is a great pity that father and son never recorded together. And it is also surprising that few recordings by Vess Ossman or Fred Van Eps are currently available, and just as part of sampler CDs. A complete issuance of their work is long overdue.

The first jazz recordings were by the Original Dixieland Jazz Band in 1917, a group that did not include a banjo or a guitar. However, by the early 1920s, the banjo had found its place in most working jazz groups. Due to the still-primitive quality of recordings, the guitar and the string bass were not used because they were considered to be inaudible, while drummers were restricted to using a few percussion instruments (such as a cow bell and a cymbal) so as not to overwhelm the ensembles. The rhythm was largely kept by a pianist and a strumming banjoist, with the latter generally stating each beat. While a tuba was sometimes used so there would be some bass notes, since musicians needed to take breaths, tuba players were only able to play on every other beat (the first and third beat). A banjoist was almost as indispensable as the pianist.

Only one banjoist in the 1920s could approach and even top the virtuosity of Vess Ossman and Fred Van Eps. Ironically, the first instrument of Harry Reser (1896–1965) was the guitar. As a youth, he also played violin, cello, piano, marimba, trumpet and saxophone. At 16, he began to dedicate himself to the banjo, and was inspired by the recordings of Ossman and Van Eps. Reser, who was from Ohio, worked in local dance bands before moving to New York in 1921. He immediately became greatly in demand

for studio work, recording with virtually all of the most significant studio orchestras and with all types of groups. At the same time, starting in 1922 with his recording of "Kitten On The Keys," he waxed a series of incredible banjo features that found him playing with the virtuosity, complexity and speed of the top pianists. Reser recorded more than 20 novelty rags, which still sound wondrous today; 14 are on *Banjo Crackerjax 1922–1930* (Shanachie).

But most of Reser's work in the 1920s was with hot dance groups. He led the radio band the Cliquot Club Eskimos (they appeared onstage dressed in eskimo suits) during 1925–35 while recording with similar groups under a wide variety of pseudonyms. Among the names that his band used on records were the Blue Kittens, the Bostonians, the Campus Boys, the Four Minstrels, the High Hatters, the Jazz Pilots, Earl Oliver's Jazz Babies, the Parlophone Syncopators, the Plantation Players, the Rounders, the Seven Rag Pickers, the Seven Wild Men, the Six Hayseeds, the Six Jumping Jacks, the Victorian Syncopators, and the Seven Little Polar Bears.

After the 1920s faded into history and the Cliquot Club Eskimos ended their decade on the radio, Reser went back to being a freelance studio musician. He wrote ten instruction books for the banjo, ukulele and guitar, and was active until his death in 1965.

The other banjoists of the 1920s were generally sidemen who simply kept the rhythm steady behind other musicians, taking occasional brief solos. Mike Pingatore, a member of Paul Whiteman's orchestra for 25 years, had occasional feature numbers (such as "The World Is Waiting For The Sunrise") but was mostly in the supporting cast. Elmer Snowden (1900–73) was the original leader of the Washingtonians in 1923 but lost his leadership role and his band in a dispute over money; it became the Duke Ellington Orchestra. While Snowden led other bands later in the decade, they did not record. He spent many years as a music teacher before making a comeback as a player in the 1950s and '60s, when he was viewed as a link to the past.

Ikey Robinson (1904–90) should have been a big star, for he was not only a fluent banjo soloist but a versatile singer who could also play guitar, clarinet and piano. He sounded great on records with Jabbo Smith's Rhythm Aces in 1929 and made a few worthy sessions of his own, included on *"Banjo" Ikey Robinson* (RST 1508), but he spent decades in obscurity in Chicago, where he moved in 1934.

Johnny St. Cyr (1890–1966) is famous for playing his guitar-banjo on the recordings of Louis Armstrong's Hot Five and his Hot Seven during 1925–27. A decent soloist, St. Cyr was most significant as a rhythm player. He was part of the New Orleans jazz scene as early as 1905 and along the way worked with Kid Ory, Fate Marable, Freddie Keppard and, in the 1920s, on records with King Oliver, Doc Cook, and Jelly Roll Morton.

Other fine banjoists of the classic jazz era include Charlie Dixon (with Fletcher Henderson's orchestra during 1921–28), Dave Wilborn (with McKinney's Cotton Pickers in 1928–31), Steve Washington (with the Washboard Rhythm Kings during 1931–32), Lee Blair, Buddy Christian, Bud Scott (with King Oliver in 1923 and particularly effective on trumpeter Willie Hightower's 1927 session), Fred Guy (Duke Ellington's banjoist starting in 1924), and Howdy Quicksell, who played with Bix Beiderbecke in Jean Goldkette's big band of 1927.

But two events resulted in the end of the banjo's prominence in jazz. In 1925, Eddie Lang emerged as jazz's first major guitarist. And with the development of electrical recording during 1925–27, suddenly the guitar could be heard in ensembles. It was no longer necessary to use the banjo, which was louder and, when played by most banjoists other than Reser, had a repetitive and clanging sound. Although the banjo was still a major instrument in 1927, by 1929 the guitar was taking over, by 1931 most banjoists were doubling on guitar, and by 1934 banjoists were largely extinct other than Mike Pingatore. The instrument might be trotted out for nostalgia purposes, but the banjo was no longer taken seriously in jazz. One would be hard-pressed to name a single rhythm banjoist in swing era big bands.

The banjo did find a place in other kinds of music. While it was never that major in the blues (Papa Charlie Jackson was the only significant blues banjoist in the 1920s), Eddie Peabody was a colorful and popular performer who for a time was the world's most famous banjoist, although his flashy performances were mostly outside of jazz. The banjo found a home in country music, bluegrass, folk, Irish music and New Orleans jazz. While the Dixieland-oriented groups of the 1930s usually used rhythm guitar, the banjo was thought of as more "authentic" by many of the revivalists of the 1940s, despite the fact that the acoustic guitar was there at the beginning of jazz. By the 1950s, the banjo was an expected part of most New Orleans jazz–style bands, and it has had a similar role up to the present day, with very little musical evolution having taken place.

Clancy Hayes (1908–72) was a fine banjoist who played with Lu Watters' Buena Vista Jazz Band in the 1940s and later Bob Scobey, but much of his fame was due to his singing. Such banjoists as George Guesnon, Lawrence Marrero, Emanuel Sayles and Narvin Kimball were featured with New Orleans bands ranging from George Lewis to the Preservation Hall Jazz Band. Their style was primarily rhythmic, and they were more significant for helping hold the ensembles together than for any solos that they took. Danny Barker returned to the banjo from rhythm guitar when he returned to New Orleans in 1965, becoming a significant teacher and an inspiration in general to younger musicians. Banjoists active today include Eddy Davis (who often plays with Woody Allen's band), Jimmy Mazzy, Cynthia Sayer, and Eddie Erickson (who doubles on guitar). Also worth mentioning is Howard Alden, who, although he has spent most of his life playing guitar, recorded *Plays The Music Of Harry Reser* (Stomp Off 1200), a remarkable recreation of Reser's banjo solos.

But outside of New Orleans jazz, the banjo quickly disappeared from jazz after 1932. While most of the guitarists who rose to prominence in the 1930s had started on banjo (including Django Reinhardt) or at least doubled on it earlier in their careers, the ones in the 1940s rarely did unless they were also studio musicians. There were no significant banjo soloists in the bop movement, in cool jazz, hard bop, or even the avant-garde of the 1960s.

But surprisingly, there was one banjoist whose eclectic repertoire and combination of styles made him the world's only fusion banjoist. Bela Fleck (b. 1958) came to jazz through bluegrass. As a teenager attending the High School of Music and Art, he was one of the first to adapt bebop for the banjo. He picked up experience with several groups and during 1982–90 was part of the New Grass Revival, using bluegrass instruments to play a variety of different kinds of music, including some jazz. By 1990, he was leading the Flecktones, a unique band consisting of Howard Levy on harmonica, electric bassist Victor Wooten and Roy "Future Man" Wooten on the electronic drum called the drumitar. Although Levy eventually dropped out, the Flecktones have stayed together up until the present time, with Fleck's banjo being featured in fusion, modern jazz, blues, world music, and other idioms. He has even recorded a duet album with Chick Corea, and in 2012, he recorded and performed with the Marcus Roberts Trio.

But Bela Fleck stands alone and has yet to influence guitarists to switch to banjo. The guitar's future seems pretty secure.

## A Brief History of the Jazz Guitar

The history of the guitar in jazz can be divided into three separate struggles: the battle to become part of jazz, to be audible, and to find its own role in the music. It took some time, but the jazz guitar won all three battles and is now in its golden age.

While it is tempting to say that the jazz guitar began with Eddie Lang in 1925, the guitar was used in jazz groups from the very beginning. Most early New Orleans bands had a guitarist, and in fact, one of the first bands to be considered a bit jazz-oriented was led by guitarist Charlie Galloway as early as 1889. Galloway led a string band that by the mid-1890s also had brass and woodwind players, including pioneer cornetist Buddy Bolden, shortly before Bolden put together his own group in 1895. Bolden's bands of 1895–1906 usually had a guitarist, including Galloway, Brock Mumford (who was with Bolden during 1897–1905 and is in the only photograph ever taken of the cornetist) and Lorenzo Staulz. Other early jazz guitarists (none of whom had the chance to record) include Dominick Barocco, Joe Guiffre, Coochie Martin and Rene Baptiste. Louis Keppard (1888–1986), cornetist Freddie Keppard's older brother, led the Magnolia Orchestra (his sidemen included King Oliver, trombonist Honoré Dutrey and bassist Pops Foster) around 1910. While he worked with other New Orleans bands and visited Chicago as early as 1917, Keppard spent his life in New Orleans, and his only recordings were with Wooden Joe Nicholas in 1949.

A feature on the New Orleans music scene from around 1890–1920 was string bands that usually consisted of guitar, bass, and mandolin or violin. String bands played for dances and parties in which quieter and more polite music was desired rather than brass bands. While several string bands recorded, none of the ones that appeared on record before 1917 could be considered jazz groups. Eventually cornets, clarinets and other instruments were added, and by the mid-1920s, this type of string band had passed into history.

Although the guitar preceded the banjo into jazz groups, by the time jazz was starting to be recorded, the guitar (which was considered inaudible by recording engineers) was largely absent in favor of the louder banjo. Prior to 1925, not only was Nick Lucas the most significant jazz guitarist, but, at least on records, he was practically the only one. Lucas, who recorded test cylinders as early as 1912, began making records in 1921. His "Pickin' The Guitar" and "Teasing The Frets" from 1922 are the earliest examples of unaccompanied solo guitar. Lucas fought to record on guitar with studio orchestras at a time when banjos were becoming commonplace. But due to the popularity of his singing, by the mid-1920s his guitar playing had become secondary to his vocals.

Eddie Lang played both guitar and banjo with Red McKenzie's Mound City Blue Blowers during 1924–25 and then became a very significant New York studio musician. Due to the sophistication and versatility of his playing and the steady improvement in recording techniques, during 1925–29 the guitar won its battle over the banjo to be accepted in jazz. The guitar was found to be a much more flexible instrument, and while still felt more than heard in dense ensembles, it gradually became an indispensable instrument in larger ensembles and big bands, keeping the rhythm steady and stating chords.

While guitar soloists were very common in blues recordings from the mid-1920s on, they were a rarity in jazz for quite some time. Although the acoustic guitar could now at least be heard, it rarely had the commanding presence needed to be a solo instrument. Even Lang was mostly featured as a supportive player who took very brief solo breaks on most recordings on which he appeared. There were some special occasions, including dates where he was accompanied by just a pianist, and brilliant duet guitar sessions with Lonnie Johnson and Carl Kress, but even sessions that he co-led with violinist Joe Venuti mostly had Lang supplying the accompaniment. The same was true of such superb late 1920s/early '30s studio guitarists as Carl Kress, Dick McDonough and George Van Eps.

The top guitar soloist of the 1930s (and possibly of all time) was Django Reinhardt. He overcame the difficulty in being heard by performing with the premiere swing string group, the Quintet of the Hot Club of France, which featured him joined by violinist Stéphane Grappelli, two rhythm guitars and string bass. A strong influence in Europe during the era, Reinhardt was overshadowed by the arrival in 1939 of Charlie Christian and the electric guitar, and few today realize that by the late 1940s he had developed into one of the top bop-oriented guitarists.

Django Reinhardt aside, few jazz guitarists of the 1930s had much solo space and, due to their instrument being so quiet, were restricted to keeping the rhythm behind other soloists. While the rhythm guitar is an art form in itself, and nearly every big band of the swing era included a rhythm guitarist in its lineup (Freddie Green with Count Basie and Allan Reuss with Benny Goodman were among the best), it was a frustrating role for those who wanted to solo and be on an equal footing with horn players. As early as the 1920s, there were experiments that sought to amplify the guitar, including those by Les Paul and George Barnes in the early-to-mid-1930s. An amplified guitar was patented by George Beauchamp as early as 1931, and some were built the following year, but they were not considered very efficient. An amplified Hawaiian guitar was used by musicians who played Hawaiian music, including Andy Iona as early as 1933. But it was not until March 1, 1938, when George Barnes recorded two songs on an electric Spanish guitar on a date with Big Bill Broonzy, that the electric guitar made its debut in jazz. Fifteen days later, Eddie Durham recorded on electric guitar with the Kansas City Five (a group of Count Basie–associated musicians). That year, several acoustic guitarists began to experiment with the electric guitar, including Charlie Christian.

When Christian was discovered by producer John Hammond and joined Benny Goodman in 1939, it changed the history of the guitar. For the first time, a guitarist could compete on the same level (both artistically and in volume) with a horn player. Christian was influenced not so much by Lang and Reinhardt as by Lester Young, Coleman Hawkins and Louis Armstrong. His phrases and catchy riffs became the main source of the vocabulary of guitar soloists for the next 25 years. His influence on guitarists was similar to that of Charlie Parker on horn players a few years later. In fact, the early history of the guitar can be divided into two periods: before Charlie Christian and after Charlie Christian.

Christian's early death in 1942 kept him from exploring bebop, but he set the stage for what was to come on his instrument. With only a few exceptions, the jazz guitarists who emerged during the 1940s, '50s and at least the first half of the '60s were following closely in Charlie Christian's footsteps. Even the ones who developed their own approach to bebop sounded like close relatives. Tiny Grimes, Al Casey, Oscar Moore and Slim Gaillard were among the first to be influenced by Christian. The bop era included some fine guitarists (including Barney Kessel, Remo Palmieri, Chuck Wayne, Billy Bauer and Bill DeArango) but none had the impact of a Dizzy Gillespie or Miles Davis. In the 1950s, Jimmy Raney was the best of the cool jazz guitarists, Johnny Smith was greatly admired, Tal Farlow could not be beat at fast tempos, Herb Ellis avoided being buried by Oscar Peterson (a difficult feat), and Kenny Burrell pioneered the guitar-bass-drums trio. The Chico Hamilton Quintet featured such guitarists as Jim Hall, John Pisano and Dennis Budimir. The guitar became an integral part of soul-jazz organ groups, interacting with organ, drums and sometimes a tenor-sax.

The 1960s brought to fame Wes Montgomery, Grant Green and George Benson. But still to a large extent, nearly all of the jazz guitarists of the time were strongly influenced by Charlie Christian. Even Montgomery, whose mastery of octaves and brilliance put him on the level of the very best ever, and Green, who stuck exclusively to single-note lines and considered his main influences to be horn players, were followers of Christian even as they developed their own individual voices within that style. Joe Pass brought the solo bop guitar to an unprecedented level in the 1970s. But few, other than the Brazilian guitarist Laurindo Almeida and Charlie Byrd (inspired by Django Reinhardt, classical music and Brazilian players), were able to forge new paths for the instrument. While the guitar had succeeded in being part of jazz, and it was very audible, there was no equivalent to John Coltrane or Miles Davis. No guitarist was blazing a new path in jazz, much less influencing players of other instruments, at least not yet.

That all changed by the end of the 1960s. First there were some new individualists who were much less influenced by Christian. Larry Coryell, who can be considered the first fusion guitarist, brought the influence of mid-1960s rock and electric blues into jazz. Gabor Szabo, playing with Chico Hamilton and his own groups, brought in his Eastern European heritage. Derek Bailey and Sonny Sharrock came up with two very different ways of playing avant-garde jazz.

But it was the arrival of John McLaughlin, who brought the sound, power and energy of rock along with a superb technique and a constantly fertile imagination, that opened up infinite possibilities for jazz guitarists. No longer did guitarists have to compete with or play a subservient role to horn players. They could be the leaders and the main stars, and they could play in any style that they desired, or have an approach beyond any style.

Since the early 1970s, the evolution of the jazz guitar has gone in many different directions. John McLaughlin went in several directions by himself, playing fusion, Indian music, straight-ahead jazz and unclassifiable post-bop. Al Di Meola went from fusion to other forms of creative jazz strongly influenced by world music. Larry Coryell has covered fusion and bop, and all three of these guitarists have spent a lot of time exploring the acoustic guitar. Other adventurous guitar greats of the past 40 years have included Pat Martino (who slightly preceded McLaughlin), John Abercrombie, Philip Catherine, Allan Holdsworth, Scott Henderson, Steve Khan, Terje Rypdal, Ralph Towner (mostly on acoustic guitar) and Mike Stern.

That only scratches the surface of the present state of the jazz guitar. The "big three" of modern jazz guitar—Pat Metheny, John Scofield and Bill Frisell—while all saying that they were inspired to a degree by the still very active Jim Hall, each have their own sounds and musical personalities, playing music beyond any simple classification. There are also many guitarists around who play mainstream jazz or creatively in historic styles, including Marty Grosz, Howard Alden, Peter Bernstein, Joe Cohn, Russell Malone and Duke Robillard. Pop/jazz is well represented by Larry Carlton and Lee Ritenour, both Stanley Jordan and Charlie Hunter have come up with new techniques to express themselves in straight-ahead and funky jazz, and Earl Klugh shows how pretty a guitar can sound. In addition, the rise of "gypsy jazz," first in Europe and more recently in the United States, has resulted in many guitarists exploring the musical legacy of Django Reinhardt, often on acoustic guitar. These include Biréli Lagrène, Stochelo Rosenberg, Jimmy Rosenberg, Dorado Schmitt, and Angelo Debarre among many others.

Whether played by Kurt Rosenwinkel or Julian

Lage, Anthony Wilson or Eugene Chadbourne, the potential of the jazz guitar is limitless and the current scene is full of giants.

## Other Significant Guitarists

Unlike the trumpet and the saxophone, the jazz guitar has consistently been strongly influenced by events on its instrument from other worlds of music, whether it is Segovia or Jimi Hendrix.

The guitar has had a long history. It had many ancestors among string instruments that were plucked, and could be said to have been invented over 3,000 years ago, but it all depends on how one defines a guitar. A stone carving from around 1300 B.C. depicts an instrument that looks like a guitar. Preceded by the *oud* and the six-string Scandinavian *lut* (or lute), the guitar began to really develop in Spain in the 1400s, when it had four pairs of strings. In 1546, the earliest known music for the guitar was published, *Tres Libros De Musica En Cifras Para Vihuela* by Alonso Mudarra. A century later, many guitars had five double strings, although by the mid-1700s the guitar dropped the double strings and became a six-string instrument. It was first taken seriously in classical music in the 1800s, and around 1850 the guitar (which was originally a very small instrument) was increased in size by Antonio de Torros Jurado, who developed the acoustic guitar that is around today. Many different variants have been used since that time, but the modern guitar can be said to have been around for over 150 years.

While the guitar was originally not considered suitable for classical music, in the early 1800s composer Fernando Sor (1778–1839) wrote many classical pieces for the guitar, promoting it as a legitimate instrument. Dionisio Aguado (1784–1849) was considered one of the first classical virtuosos on guitar, performing at pioneering concerts. Still, for many years the guitar was primarily associated with Spain, where it was played in taverns and bars, usually by gypsies. But decades after Sor, the Spanish composer Francisco Tarrega (1852–1909) did a great deal to get the guitar into classical music, writing quite a few guitar pieces, as did Mario Castelnuovo-Tedesco (1895–1968) and Heitor Villa-Lobos (1881–1959).

Andrés Segovia (1893–1987), who was only a teenager when Tarrega died, was the classical virtuoso whom Tarrega probably dreamt of. Segovia was at the top of his small field in the 1920s, and his 1928 American debut in New York was seen by Eddie Lang and other jazz musicians of the period. It was an important event that pronounced that the guitar was a "legit" instrument. Segovia transposed music from other instruments to the guitar, and there were also many classical pieces written specifically for him. He did more than any other musician to get the guitar accepted in classical music and taught in schools. Even if the guitar is still not as associated with classical music as the violin or piano, Segovia stands as a major figure who inspired such current-day classical guitarists as Julian Bream (1933– ), John Williams (1941– ), Christopher Parkening (1947– ) and Sharon Isbin (1956– ), plus a few classical guitarists who have also played jazz, most notably Laurindo Almeida and Carlos Barbosa-Lima (1944– ).

While it was a battle to get the guitar accepted in classical music, it never had any problem becoming part of the blues world, where it has reigned supreme from the beginning. Even the banjo was never a serious contender. Whether it was the street guitarist who inspired W.C. Handy to write "St. Louis Blues" (which he copyrighted in 1914) or other long-forgotten performers from the 1890s on, the history and development of the blues is inconceivable without the guitar. Lonnie Johnson was among the blues-oriented guitarists who were performing in New Orleans during the teens. The first significant blues guitarist to be recorded was Sylvester Weaver (1897–1960), who on November 7, 1923, recorded "Guitar Blues" and "Guitar Rag." Although these were not the first unaccompanied guitar solos to be documented (Nick Lucas beat him to records by a year), they briefly made Weaver the first blues guitar hero. But while he lived until 1960, Weaver made no recordings after 1927 and was long forgotten.

Because the acoustic guitar is such an expressive instrument, very portable, and it can be used by those functioning as a one-man blues band or in a group, it flourished in the blues before it emerged as a major solo instrument in jazz. Among the major blues guitarists of the 1920s and '30s were Blind Lemon Jefferson (1893–1929), Blind Blake (circa 1893–1933), Tampa Red (1904–81), Charlie Patton (circa 1887–1934), Robert Johnson (1911–38), Memphis Minnie (1897–1973), Blind Willie McTell (1898–1959) and Big Bill Broonzy (1898–1958). Most of these guitarists had careers that were independent from jazz, such as the country blues greats Blind Lemon Jefferson, Charlie Patton, Memphis Minnie and the short-lived Robert Johnson. Several of the others could have been successful jazz guitarists if that had been their goal. Blind Blake used clarinetist Johnny Dodds on one of his hotter sessions, Tampa Red's goodtime hokum music (where practically every song seemed to be a variation of "It's Tight Like That") from the late 1920s/early '30s was close to jazz, and Blind Willie McTell certainly had the technique to play jazz, although he never did. Big Bill Broonzy sometimes crossed over into jazz, particularly in his late 1930s Chicago recordings, although he stayed tied to blues and folk music. Leadbelly (1888–1949) was the ultimate early folk singer, included blues in his repertoire, and in the 1940s sometimes appeared at jazz concerts (including with Bunk Johnson) as a symbol of the roots of jazz.

Jazz and country music overlapped most often during the 1930s and '40s when Western swing was at its height. Since Western swing is a form of jazz, some of its best guitarists are included in the main entries. One of the main instruments of many country groups has been the steel guitar. While a few of the pioneering steel guitarists (particularly the Hawaiian players of the 1920s) are in the main entries along with bandleader Alvino Rey and Roy Smeck, in general steel guitarists are outside the scope of this book since it is a different instrument. Andy Sanella (1900–62) appeared on a countless number of recordings in the 1920s, playing very effective jazz clarinet and alto. His steel guitar playing added an exotic sound to many of the records, and his fluidity and creativity on that instrument made him second to Roy Smeck among the part-time steel guitarists of the era. An early death kept Sam Ku West (1907–30) from being ranked among the best Hawaiian steel guitarists, but his recordings show that he was close. Among the steel guitarists who set the standard for Western swing and country music were Leon McAuliffe (1917–88), Noel Boggs (1917–74), Herb Remington (1926– ), Joaquin Murphey (1923–99), Speedy West (1924–2003), and Doug Jerigan (1946– ). Bob Dunn (1908–71) was particularly jazz-oriented, as can be heard on the superb two-CD set *Master Of The Electric Steel Guitar 1935–1950* (Origin Jazz Library 1004). Probably the most jazz-oriented of the Nashville steel guitarists of the past half century is Buddy Emmons (1927– ), who recorded an album called *Steel Guitar Jazz* (Verve 542536) in 1963 and sometimes collaborated with Lenny Breau.

Sticking for a moment with instruments related to the guitar, the Spirits of Rhythm in the 1930s was a hot jive group that featured Douglas Daniels, Wilbur Daniels and drummer Leo Watson (best known as an innovative scat singer) on the *tiple*, a small guitar similar in size to a mandolin although with a lower-pitched sound. All of the group's recordings are available as *The Spirits Of Rhythm* (Retrieval 79004).

While the mandolin has a colorful history of its own—as a descendant of the lute and an integral part of bluegrass (starting with Bill Monroe) and in the folk musics of many countries, including Italy, England, Scotland, Ireland, Portugal, Greece, Brazil and Japan—it has only been utilized in jazz on rare occasions. The Harlem Hamfats, a blues/jazz group from Chicago in the 1930s, had Charlie McCoy taking mandolin solos. Tiny Moore (1920–87) of Bob Wills' Texas Playboys played an electric five-string mandolin. Jethro Burns (1920–89) was a superior jazz mandolinist, although jazz was only part of what he played. While there have been several mandolinists who have played jazz in more recent times, including Mike Marshall (1960– ), Dave Grisman (1945– ) is in his own category. His background was in bluegrass but he has always been interested in swinging jazz and crossing stylistic boundary lines. Part of the "new acoustic" movement, Grisman (who calls his open-ended style "dawg music") has often recorded swing, including *Hot Dawg* (A&M 75021-3292), which teams him with guitarist Tony Rice and guest Stéphane Grappelli.

With the rise of the electric guitar, by the early 1940s the blues world had its Charlie Christian in T-Bone Walker, whose music sometimes crossed over into swinging jazz. Walker was an influence on the most famous guitarist in rock and roll of the 1950s, Chuck Berry (1926– ), who took some of his licks directly from Walker. Berry's background was in the blues before he gained great commercial success. Walker was also an inspiration for the most popular of all blues performers, B.B. King (1925– ), whose illustrious career often found him performing at both blues and jazz festivals. King resisted any temptation to play jazz (although he loves Charlie Christian and other key jazz guitarists) other than occasional salutes to Louis Jordan and jamming on uptempo instrumental blues.

Two of the major blues artists to have an impact in the 1950s were much further away from jazz than T-Bone Walker and the always-accessible B.B. King. John Lee Hooker (1912–2001) was both primitive in his playing (looking back to the earliest country blues) and futuristic. Hooker was playing one-chord jams a decade before Ornette Coleman, and his tonal distortions predated the more adventurous rock guitarists of the late 1960s. Muddy Waters (1913–83) defined Chicago blues of the 1950s, leading the way to rock and roll while remaining deep in the blues, both as a guitarist and as a highly influential singer.

Pee Wee Crayton (1914–85) and Mickey Baker (1925– ) were both originally jazz guitarists who found it much easier to make a living playing in the studios and straddling the worlds of blues and R&B. In the late 1950s/early '60s, with the folk and blues revival, many of the surviving blues artists of the 1920s and '30s were rediscovered and recorded. One of the very best was Rev. Gary Davis (1896–1972), a brilliant guitarist whose repertoire included ragtime-style tunes along with blues and spirituals.

While jazz and rock mostly stayed very separate during 1955–65, and very few in the jazz world took Chuck Berry all that seriously as a guitarist, the quality of rock guitarists began to rise sharply after the mid-1960s, and the younger generation of jazz guitarists listened closely. Of all the rock guitarists, Jimi Hendrix (1942–70) was the most innovative, a musician who, like John Coltrane, broke the sound barrier. After gaining experience playing with a wide variety of rock and R&B groups during 1962–66, Hendrix recorded *Are You Experienced* in 1967. He gained notoriety for his wild shows (which included playing a guitar with his teeth and setting his guitar on fire) but is today most significant for his virtuosity and ability to create a wide range of intense and dramatic sounds on the guitar. His *Live At Monterey* DVD of his historic performance at the 1967 Monterey International Pop Festival is still remarkable. Late in his short life, Hendrix was reportedly discussing with Gil Evans the possibility of a joint recording. Since Miles Davis was also a fan, it is possible that had he lived, Hendrix would have recorded with Davis sometime in the 1970s and possibly become involved in fusion. As it is, some of his recordings are of blues and he hints at jazz in his more abstract improvisations. *Are You Experienced* (MCA 9007), *Axis: Bold As Love* (Universal 5301383), *Electric Ladyland* (Universal 91387), and *Band Of Gypsys* (Capitol 96414) are his main musical legacy, although there have been a countless number of posthumous discoveries and collections.

Jimi Hendrix not only changed rock guitar and was an influence on fusion and avant-garde jazz but was also very important in the evolution of the blues. Buddy Guy (1936– ), who was already a major blues player, has utilized some of Hendrix's sounds in his own vocabulary. Stevie Ray Vaughan (1954–90), who is arguably the most recent and possibly the last of the blues innovators, built up his style where Hendrix left off, showing just how intense and powerful the blues guitar can sound.

Among the other guitarists of the rock world who have been admired by jazz guitarists are Michael Bloomfield (1943–81), who was a master of blues rock in the 1960s and '70s; Eric Clapton (1945– ), whose lengthy solos as part of Cream sometimes bordered on jazz (although at heart he is a bluesman); Carlos Santana (1947– ), a master of Latin rock who has flirted with jazz without ever crossing over; and Jeff Beck. While an influence on both blues and heavy metal guitarists, during 1975–76 Beck recorded a pair of superior instrumental fusion albums, *Blow By Blow* (Sony 5021819) and *Wired* (Sony 33849), that show that he could have been a major jazz guitarist if he had stuck to that course. Instead, it was up to John McLaughlin, Al Di Meola and others in the 1970s to use what they learned from Jimi Hendrix and his contemporaries plus their own imaginations to move the jazz guitar to a different dimension.

Today's modern jazz guitarists draw inspiration not only from their predecessors in jazz and those listed in this article but also from other unclassifiable guitarists, some of whom have very fresh approaches

to playing the acoustic guitar. Leo Kottke (1945– ) brought folk music to a new level, Michael Hedges (1953–97) and Will Ackerman (1949– ) were two of the best New Age guitarists (although both stretched beyond that idiom), and Paco de Lucía (1947– ) is a master of flamenco music who held his own during tours with John McLaughlin, Larry Coryell and Al Di Meola.

It is thanks to the inspiration of all of these guitarists and the jazz innovators that the jazz guitar now occupies its own special world of music.

## So Who Are the Jazz Guitar Giants?

In this book, I have full-length entries on 342 great jazz guitarists. But who were the most significant ones? The guitarists listed below, due to the combination of virtuosity, originality, influence on others, and body of work, are the ones that I would rank at the top. Of course, the list is open to debate, but these are my top 30, listed roughly in chronological order.

Eddie Lang
Carl Kress
Dick McDonough
George Van Eps
Django Reinhardt
Les Paul
Charlie Christian
Barney Kessel
Tal Farlow
Jimmy Raney
Jim Hall
Charlie Byrd
Wes Montgomery
Grant Green
Joe Pass
George Benson
Pat Martino
Derek Bailey
Sonny Sharrock
John McLaughlin
Al Di Meola
Pat Metheny
John Scofield
Howard Alden
Bill Frisell
Mike Stern
Russell Malone
Stanley Jordan
Biréli Lagrène
Charlie Hunter

## Introduction to the Entries

Here are some quick statistics: Of the 342 jazz guitarists in the main entry to the book, 239 are alive at this point, while 103 are deceased. One hundred fifty-four of the living guitarists answered the questionnaires I sent them, while the others did not respond to requests or were untraceable. Three hundred thirty of the guitarists are males, while just twelve are females. Sorry, I wish there were more, but that is how it is. The guitarists represent virtually every jazz style, with some of the players stretching the definition of jazz a bit.

The length of each entry does not necessarily convey the importance of the guitarist, so do not measure their significance by counting the number of words. The length often has much more to do with how interesting their answers were in the questionnaire or how colorful a life they have led.

Their quotes are, unless stated otherwise, taken from the questionnaire and are often just excerpts of their full response. I put a guitarist's birth name in parentheses if it differs drastically from the name by which they are best known. The recommended lists of CDs are not meant to form complete discographies, although that is true in the cases of some guitarists. The albums are listed loosely in chronological order and usually do not include samplers, best-of collections, or limited-edition box sets from the Mosaic label. Due to the always-strange recording industry, not all of the CDs are in print at the moment, but nearly all can be acquired with a bit of luck.

All of the guitarists who have entries in the main portion of this book, plus most of the ones listed in other sections, deserve to be heard. The jazz guitar has had a very interesting history, and I truly hope that this book does justice to each guitarist's story.

# THE 342 GREAT JAZZ GUITARISTS

## Rez Abbasi
b. August 27, 1965, Karachi, Pakistan

A highly original guitarist who infuses post-bop jazz with his Pakistani heritage, Rez Abbasi would never be mistaken for anyone else. Born in Pakistan, Abbasi was four when he moved with his parents to Los Angeles. He began on the guitar when he was 11. Abbasi worked with rock bands for a few years as a teenager before discovering jazz and classical music when he was 16. "They both gave me a reason to use my mind and become a scientist of music, as opposed to moving from band to band looking for fame. A friend of mine took me to see a concert of Joe Pass and Ella Fitzgerald and showed me the Omni book that contains Charlie Parker solos."

In the 1980s, he attended the USC guitar program and earned a degree in jazz from the Manhattan School of Music, graduating in 1989. "All of my teachers in college were very helpful in setting a path. When I graduated, one of them, Rodney Jones, had me sub for him at the New Orleans Jazz & Heritage Festival with Ruth Brown. After we played, Charles Lloyd's Fish out of Water group was on. That kind of playing still resonates with me till this day."

Two months spent in India, where he studied tabla with Ustad Alla Rakha, also had a strong effect on Abbasi, awakening his interest in music from India and Pakistan. He has since worked with Kenny Werner (studying with the pianist and using him on one of his record dates), Tim Hagans, Billy Hart, Marvin "Smitty" Smith, Gary Thomas, Rick Margitza, D.D. Jackson, Dave Liebman, Dave Pietro, Sunny Jain, Tony Malaby, Ron Horton and other creative musicians.

As a leader, Rez Abbasi's adventurous guitar has been featured on six albums. Freedance is a quartet with altoist John O'Gallagher, bassist David Phillips and drummer Tony Moreno, and he also has a very unique organ quartet that features Gary Versace, Dan Weiss and Kiran Ahluwalia.

"Other than recording and performing with my groups, I've been an integral part of Rudresh Mahanthappa's Indo-Pak Coalition as well as his group called Dakshani. Also, I play and arrange music for singer Kiran Ahluwalia's project. Her music, as well as Rudresh's and my own, can be considered hybrid music. We are influenced by both Western and Indian musical ideas and concepts. And I also did a wonderful recording with saxophonist Dave Pietro called *The Chakra Suite*, which incorporates Brazilian and Indian music with jazz. My goal is to create a world-based music steeped in jazz."

**Recommended CDs:** Each of Rez Abbasi's nine recordings as a leader are of strong interest and display their own personalities. 1995's *Third Ear* (Cathexis 4) can be considered lyrical fusion. *Modern Memory* (Cathexis 3) has Abbasi on both electric and acoustic guitar, introducing a variety of colorful originals. *Out Of Body* (Feroza 480) has Abbasi exploring post-bop jazz. *Snake Charmer* (Arabesque 0166) has Abassi doubling on sitar-guitar and leading a trio with organist Gary Versace and drummer Danny Weiss (also heard on tabla) with guests soprano-saxophonist Dave Liebman and the haunting voice of Kiran Ahluwalia (the guitarist's wife). *Bazaar* (Zoho 200613) builds on *Snake Charmer*'s success, utilizing Versace, Weiss, Ahluwalia, altoist Rudresh Mahanthappa, Marc Mommaas on tenor and soprano, and percussionist Gautuam Siram. *Things To Come* (Sunnyside 281236) is even stronger, featuring Mahanthappa, pianist Vijay Iyer, bassist Johannes Weidenmuller, Weiss and Ahluwalia. Is it Indian music, post-bop jazz, soul jazz or world fusion? It is all of them and none of them. *Natural Selection* (Sunnyside 1264) with his acoustic quartet features Abbasi's mastery of acoustic guitar. *Suno Suno* (Enja 9575) was his follow-up to *Things To Come*, while *Continuous Beat* (Enja) is an intimate trio set with bassist John Hebert and drummer Satoshi Takeishi.

**Website:** www.reztone.com

## John Abercrombie
b. December 16, 1944, Port Chester, NY

Although he has been a significant guitarist since the 1970s, John Abercrombie is a perfect symbol for modern jazz guitarists of the 21st century. While he has recorded some standards albums and occasional projects that could be considered soul jazz, hard bop or fusion, his playing and music are usually beyond any accurate categorization. He sounds like himself in every situation, is very versatile, and performs music that tends to be a bit unpredictable while always being creative jazz no matter what the setting. His playing may be difficult to write about, but it is always stimulating to hear.

Abercrombie, who grew up in Greenwich, Connecticut, began playing guitar when he was 14. "My first influence was the rock music of the '50s, including Chuck Berry, Mickey Baker (of Mickey and Sylvia), Fats Domino, Elvis Presley and others. My earliest gigs were with little rock bands, playing the music of the day at school dances, record hops and country clubs." He was introduced to jazz by friends and through records by Dave Brubeck, Barney Kessel and Miles Davis.

The young guitarist attended the Berklee School of Music during 1962–65. By then, Jim Hall, Wes Montgomery and Bill Evans were influences, but Abercrombie already had a sound of his own. He played locally while in school and, during 1967–69, picked up important experience working with organist Johnny "Hammond" Smith. "We played standard tunes and blues, usually in a trio setting. I really had to play on a professional level and be consistent night after night." Abercrombie next worked with the Brecker Brothers as part of their group Dreams and he was with Chico Hamilton's band during 1970–72. As a busy session player, he also recorded with Gil Evans, Gato Barbieri and Barry Miles. As a member of Billy Cobham's group, Abercrombie began to gain a lot of attention in the fusion world.

But that was not the direction that he really wanted to go. "The turning point for me was getting to meet Manfred Eicher and record for ECM." His *Timeless* album (a trio date with Jan Hammer and Jack DeJohnette) and *Gateway* (with DeJohnette and Dave Holland) set the stage for his career as early as 1975. Abercrombie recorded three albums as the leader of a quartet also featuring Richie Beirach, George Mraz and Peter Donald. He played guitar synthesizer for the first time while leading a trio with Marc Johnson and Peter Erskine, had reunions with the Gateway Trio in 1995, and teamed up with organist Dan Wall for a few projects. Other associations include Michael Brecker, Charles Lloyd (in the late 1990s), Jan Garbarek, Andy Laverne (with whom he has recorded on a few occasions for the Steeplechase label), a quintet with violinist Mark Feldman and Joe Lovano, and duet projects with Joe Beck, John Scofield and Ralph Towner.

In recent times, John Abercrombie has led an organ trio with Gary Versace and Adam Nussbaum,

and a quintet with Mark Feldman, Joey Baron, Marc Johnson or Thomas Morgan, and Marc Copland or Andy Laverne. He continues recording for ECM (and occasionally elsewhere) nearly four decades after *Timeless* and is an influential force on the modern jazz scene.

**Recommended CDs:** *Timeless* (ECM 1047), *Gateway* (ECM 1061), *Sargasso Sea* (ECM 1080) with Ralph Towner, *Gateway 2* (ECM 1105), *Characters* (ECM 1117), *Arcade* (ECM 1133), *Abercrombie Quartet* (ECM 1164), *M* (ECM 1191), *Night* (ECM 1272), *Current Events* (ECM 1311), *Getting There* (ECM 1321), *Abercrombie/Johnson/Erskine* (ECM 1390), *Animato* (ECM 1411), *Witchcraft* (Justin Time 16) with Don Thompson, *While We're Young* (ECM 1489), *November* (ECM 1502), *Speak Of The Devil* (ECM 1511), *Gateway: Homecoming* (ECM 1562), *In The Moment* (ECM 1574), *Now It Can Be Played* (Steeplechase 31314), *Tactics* (ECM 1623), *Open Land* (ECM 1683), *Cat 'N' Mouse* (ECM 1770), *Timelines* (Steeplechase 31538), *Three Guitars* (Chesky 248) with Larry Coryell and Badi Assad, *Class Trip* (ECM 1846), *A Nice Idea* (Steeplechase 31571), *Structures* (Chesky 317), *Third Quartet* (ECM 1993), *Topics* (Challenge 70137), *Wait Till You See Her* (ECM 2102), *Within A Song* (ECM 2254).

**Website:** www.johnabercrombie.com

## Morris Acevedo
*b. April 8, 1966, El Paso, TX*

A versatile guitarist whose main influence is Jim Hall, Morris Acevedo has long been interested in all eras of jazz guitar, from Eddie Lang to Al Di Meola. "I started on rock guitar when I was 12 years old in the late 1970s. I enjoyed heavy rock like Led Zeppelin, but I also had a big interest in progressive rock like Yes and Genesis. The guitarists in those bands had jazz, classical and country influences, so that pointed me to a way of being a guitarist that was not just blues/rock based." He heard early Pat Metheny and that led him into jazz and exploring other guitarists, including Wes Montgomery and Charlie Christian.

Acevedo's first professional performance was after high school when he played with Arnett Cobb. He attended the University of North Texas and earned a degree in Jazz Composition and Arranging at Berklee. While based in the Boston area for over a decade, he had opportunities to play with Joshua Redman, Jim Black, Ken Vandermark, the Either Orchestra, the Charlie Kolhase Quintet, the organ trio Be-3, and Matt Wilson, plus some R&B and rock bands. "I was quite proud of a group I had in New York from 2004–07 called Quartet Doloroso with altoist Dave

Pietro. We performed the music of the Paul Desmond Quartet, the one with Jim Hall on guitar. We took their concept of playing melodically rather than bebop lines. It's been an approach that I've continued to use in many different styles of music as well."

After moving to the San Francisco Bay area, Acevedo played with Richie Cole's Alto Madness Orchestra, drummer Scott Amendola's group and Ann Dyer, and led his trio Dam East (with bassist Jon Christensen and drummer Kevin Stevens). He is currently the head of the music department at Cardinal Newman High School in Santa Rosa, California, conducting a 50-person guitar orchestra, teaching improvisation, and leading a jazz big band. "As far as my own music goes, I've been composing some instrumental music for guitar trio that uses all the jazz improvisation tools that I use in modern jazz, but the music has more of an almost rock groove. Also, I formed a group called the Plectrum Duo with another guitarist, Cody Anderson. We play acoustically and concentrate on the duet music that was played in the 1930s by guys like Carl Kress, Eddie Lang and Dick McDonough."

**Recommended CDs:** Quartet Delarosso recorded *Any Other Time* (Evander 042) in 2007. Acevedo's Electric Trio and Plectrum Duo have yet to record, although CDs are planned. Obscure recordings made with Dam East in the late 1990s will be reissued in the near future.

## Bernard Addison
*b. April 15, 1905, Annapolis, MD; d. December 18, 1990, Rockville Centre, NY*

Bernard Addison's chordal solo and accompaniment on "Toledo Shuffle" in 1935 (from a session co-led with trumpeter Freddie Jenkins) is so explosive and inventive that it is surprising that he never became famous or grew more in demand as a soloist. Addison started off playing violin and mandolin in his native Annapolis before becoming a banjoist. He moved to Washington, DC, in 1920, co-leading a group with pianist Claude Hopkins and working with Oliver Blackwell's Clowns. A few years later, he relocated to New York, picking up experience with Sonny Thompson, the Seminole Syncopators (with whom he made his recording debut in 1924), Harry's Happy Four and Ed Small's band (1925–28).

Switching to guitar in 1928, he began a decade of notable associations. Addison worked with Louis Armstrong, Bubber Miley's Mileage Makers, Milton Senior, Art Tatum (in Toledo during 1931–32 before Tatum made his move to New York), Russell Wooding, Fats Waller, the Fletcher Henderson Orchestra (1933–34) and Adelaide Hall. In addition to Armstrong, Miley and Henderson, Addison recorded with Mamie Smith (1924), Sara Martin, Jelly Roll Morton (including "Fussy Mabel"), Henry "Red" Allen, Coleman Hawkins, the Wabash Trio, Bennett's Swamplanders, and Horace Henderson. His six titles with Freddie Jenkins, particularly "Toledo Shuffle," show how powerful an acoustic guitarist he could be.

When John Mills, Jr., who was not only one of the singing Mills Brothers but also their guitarist, passed away suddenly in 1936, Addison became the vocal quartet's guitarist for two years. He toured with the group around the US and Europe, recording frequently with the Mills Brothers and on a London date with Benny Carter, also taking a day off to record with Mezz Mezzrow. When Addison left the Mills Brothers in 1938, he was greatly in demand, working with Stuff Smith (1939) and Sidney Bechet; recording with Billie Holiday (including "Them There Eyes"), Zutty Singleton, Willie "The Lion" Smith, Red Allen; working on the famous session in 1940 that teamed together Louis Armstrong and Sidney Bechet; and playing an all-star date with Hawkins, Carter and Roy Eldridge.

Addison briefly led his own group before being drafted during World War II. After his discharge, the guitarist continued working, although he had a much lower profile. He gigged with Snub Mosley, freelanced in Canada for a few years, was part of the Fletcher Henderson Reunion Band of 1957, and was the guitarist with the Ink Spots in the late 1950s. After appearing with Eubie Blake at the 1960 Newport Jazz Festival and leading his only album, Addison was primarily a guitar teacher in his last decades. It seems odd that he did not perform with the many all-star trad and swing groups of the 1950s and '60s, but perhaps by then he preferred a quieter and more stable lifestyle.

**Recommended CDs:** The complete Freddy Jenkins session with "Toledo Shuffle" has not been available coherently since a Barney Bigard/Albert Nicholas RCA Vintage LP from the 1960s, but "Toledo Shuffle" pops up on a few CDs, including the grab-bag set *1927–1941: Legendary Jazz Guitarists* (Allegro/Jazz Legends 4003). *Louis Armstrong 1940–1942* (Classics 685), while mostly featuring Satch's big band recordings of the period, also has the four titles from the Armstrong-Bechet session, which includes some spots for Addison's guitar.

**LPs to Search For:** *Pete's Last Date* (77 SEU 12/52) reissues Bernard Addison's one album as a leader although under altoist Pete Brown's name. It was one of Addison's few opportunities to stretch out during the later part of his career, and he sounds fine on standards and basic originals in a quintet.

## Steve Adelson

*b. March 3, 1952, Brooklyn, NY*

A master of the Chapman Stick in addition to being a fine post-bop guitarist, Steve Adelson leads a group that he calls the Sticktet. Adelson did not begin playing guitar until he was 17, when he was a chemical engineering major at City College. "All of my friends played folk and rock tunes of the time. Someone showed me a G Major chord, and I was hooked. I would practice constantly and probably had the guitar in my hands 8–12 hours a day." He soon discovered jazz through his teacher Charlie Didier, studied music at Brooklyn College, and worked at local clubs and restaurants, including with pianist Kenny Barron, baritonist Cecil Payne and guitar duos at Peppers that teamed him with Jimmy Ponder, Attila Zoller, Jack Wilkins and Mark Elf. In 1977, he founded a music school, the Guitar Workshop.

In 1983, Adelson saw Emmett Chapman playing the Stick at a guitar expo, and it changed his musical life. Within a year, he had purchased a Stick, and that has been his main focus ever since. "The Stick is a twelve-string fingerboard, covering the guitar and bass range and played with the tapping (hammering) technique. I do clinics worldwide and have written an instruction book and a tutorial DVD package about the Stick. It has been very rewarding being involved in the growth process of the Stick and its music."

Adelson has worked regularly at a restaurant in duos with vibraphonists, most notably Bryan Carrott. "I'm playing a unique and revolutionary instrument, one that needs exploration and documentation. It has been remarkable to produce music on Emmett's invention and be part of a new instrument's history."

**Recommended CDs:** *Adventures In Stickology* (available from his website) is the best all-round showcase for Steve Adelson's Stick playing. Originally, it was to be a duet recording with guitarist Steve Howe of Yes. But when Howe went on the road, Adelson put together duets/trios with nine different guitarists, including Ben Lacy, Chieli Minucci, Dean Brown, Phil deGruy, and Tony Levin, plus occasional drums or percussion. *The Answer's Inside* (Jazzheads 1143) features Adelson's Stick with a quintet (piano, guitar, Stick, drums and percussion) and guest Larry Coryell on some funky and easy-listening selections.

**Website:** www.steveadelson.com

## Dan Adler

*b. July 8, 1959, Tel Aviv, Israel*

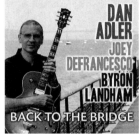

Although he has only led one CD so far, Dan Adler has shown himself to be a superior bop-based guitarist with a potentially significant musical future. Born and raised in Israel, he started having classical guitar lessons when he was ten. After a period of playing rock guitar, he got a jazz teacher, Avry Sharon, who had studied with Jim Hall and Chuck Wayne. "In high school, I started going to hang out at the only jazz club that existed back then in Israel. Soon, I became good enough to sit in and get my own gigs. It was hard to find jazz records in Israel back then, so I would subscribe to *Downbeat*, read the reviews, and based on that I had to special-order the records I wanted. When I first discovered jazz guitar, I listened to all of the great players. But it was Joe Pass who spoke to me on a different emotional and intellectual level. Everything he played made perfect sense to me."

Adler worked a regular weekly gig in Israel in a quartet with Ilan Mochiach (an arranger who played vibes and tenor) and also had a chance to play with tenor-saxophonist Steve Grossman. He moved to New York City in 1986 but has never been a full-time musician, earning graduate degrees in computer science and electrical engineering. "I have always worked outside of music, first as a microchip designer and then as a software designer and architect. I consider myself very lucky not to have to teach music or play non-jazz gigs for a living as many professional musicians are forced to do given the state of the jazz industry. I consider playing music as my reward for doing everything else."

Dan Adler studied privately with a variety of guitarists in New York (most significantly Jack Wilkins), played guitar duets with Joe Giglio, and has worked with small groups in the years since, including dueting with pianist Richard Samuels, leading an organ trio, and playing with tenor-saxophonist Grant Stewart. Throughout his gigs, he has helped to keep the legacy of bebop jazz guitar alive.

**Recommended CDs:** Dan Adler's debut recording, *All Things Familiar* (Emdam 820 360 13602), teams him with Grant Stewart and Richard Samuels. The quintet performs swinging versions of four standards and six of Adler's originals, including "If I

Were A Jazz Man." *Back To The Bridge* (Emdam 820 360 244325) features him in top form in a trio with organist Joey DeFrancesco and drummer Byron Landham.

**Website:** www.danadler.com

## Ron Affif
*b. December 30, 1964, Pittsburgh, PA*

A powerful and passionate bop-oriented guitarist, Ron Affif never seems to take an uninspired chorus. When he was 12, Affif received a record player, discovered the guitar, and received his first guitar lessons from his uncle, Ron Anthony. "My world was completely overwhelmed. That feeling is still the same, 34 years later." Affif started his career playing in small bars in the Pittsburgh area. Encouraged by his parents, both of whom loved music, and older brother Mark, he developed quickly. Although he had private lessons, Affif never went to music school and learned his most important lessons onstage.

When he was 18, Affif moved to Los Angeles, making his first record, taking lessons from Joe Pass and working with Dick Berk, Dave Pike, Pete Christlieb and Jack Sheldon. Five years later in 1988, he relocated to New York. "Playing with Essiet Essiet and Jeff Watts really helped me find my voice. There are so many great musicians in New York, you can't help but grow."

Ron Affif, who recorded some notable albums for Pablo during 1993–99, played regularly at the Zinc Bar (which he founded) on Monday nights starting in 1996 and throughout New York in addition to touring Europe and Asia. He has generally been featured with his trio, although he toured with Claudia Acuña during 2006–07 and has worked at the Carlyle Hotel for three years with the Loston Harris Trio. An enthusiastic soloist who also enjoys playing in ensembles, Affif says, "I love to play somewhere every night."

**Recommended CDs:** Ron Affif led five albums for Pablo: *Ron Affif* (Pablo 2310949), *Vierd Blues* (Pablo 10954), *52nd Street* (Pablo 10958), *Ringside* (Pablo 10962), and *Solotude* (Pablo 10965); the latter features a full set of Affif creating beautiful unaccompanied solos. Surprisingly, he has only led one CD since that time, the lesser-known *Affif, Valihora, Griglak* (Hevetia 6165).

## Noël Akchoté
*b. December 7, 1968, Paris, France*

An avant-garde guitarist who is nevertheless familiar with all jazz styles, Noël Akchoté has been creating important music in his native France. He started on guitar when he was eight, taking lessons from a friend's grandfather who ran a local music store. Akchoté also took basic classical guitar lessons in school. "Guitar became an obsession for me. I played all the time at home, carrying my nylon string guitar everywhere from my room to the living room, to dinner and in front of TV in the evening. By the time I was ten, I played all the time in any sort of styles with records, from jazz to rock, classical to chansons. Jazz was always around in France. The first time I was really totally blown away by jazz guitar was at age 10 when I was taken to a Baden Powell solo concert in Paris and some months later to a club where Jimmy Gourley was featured."

Akchoté played in bars, hotels and restaurants (often in guitar duos) five nights a week, four to five hours a night, from the time he was 14 until he was 18. He was so busy that it is not surprising that he dropped out of school when he was 16. In addition to standards, he occasionally slipped in some Ornette Coleman and Albert Ayler tunes, playing them quietly and disguising them as Dixieland. He also doubled on bass and learned drums.

Akchoté—who played with Chet Baker, Barney Wilen and René Urtreger in his early days and took guitar lessons at workshops from Tal Farlow, Mickey Baker and Philip Catherine—eventually became a teacher himself. By the 1990s, he got even busier, working with Henri Texier, Daniel Humair, Aldo Romano, Louis Sclavis, Michel Portal, Glenn Ferris, Lol Coxhill, Sam Rivers and Joey Baron. Akchoté, who started the Rectangle Ltd. label in France in 1993, was in the free-funk group Trash Corporation and the acoustic trio the Recyclers. He played post-bop and free improvised music with Derek Bailey, Eugene Chadbourne, Fred Frith, Evan Parker, Lol Coxhill, Tim Berne, George Lewis, Herb Robertson, Phil Minton, Marc Ducret, Christian Escoudé, Marc Ribot and Ingrid Jensen. In addition, he wrote for a variety of magazines about different topics and has been an actor in films.

Akchoté became a founding member of the group Big Four in 2001, a band that also includes saxophonist Max Nagl, trumpeter Steven Bernstein and bassist Bradley Jones. In addition to touring with Big Four, in recent times he has played a lot of solo concerts, various shows with Han Bennink and top European musicians, and duets with guitarists Tetuzi Akiyama and Adam Levy.

"My practice has always been to cross many styles and approaches without any judgments as to what is 'better' or more 'advanced.' To me, there is a huge and obvious common root that guitar music has embraced and that unifies blues, swing, jazz, gospel, early rock and most of what came out of it."

**Recommended CDs:** *Lust Corner* (Winter & Winter 19) has intriguing and eccentric duets with either Marc Ribot or Eugene Chadbourne. *Noël Akchoté & Bruno Meillier* (SMI 209) teams Akchoté in duets with the reeds of Meillier. *Rien* (Winter & Winter 57) features Akchoté interacting with a turntablist and a manipulator of computers to achieve otherworldly sounds. *Alike Joseph*, *Simple Joseph* and *Perpetual Joseph* (all put out by Rectangle Ltd.) are unusual sets of accompanied guitar solos. *Adult Guitar* (Blue Chopsticks 13) has Akchoté playing 20 short pieces, including a few standards. *Sonny Vol. 2* (Winter & Winter 108) is a tribute to Sonny Sharrock. *Toi-Même* (Winter & Winter 910146) is with a larger group, and *Big Four Live* (Hatology 637) is an exciting set full of fire.

# Howard Alden
*b. October 17, 1958, Newport Beach, CA*

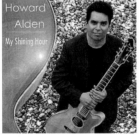

When he first rose to prominence in the 1980s, Howard Alden was part of a new generation of players who revived and revitalized small-group swing, along with tenor-saxophonist Scott Hamilton, cornetist Warren Vaché and trombonist Dan Barrett. Since then, he has stretched himself into bop, Thelonious Monk, Bill Evans, Herbie Nichols, and more modern tunes, but Alden is still a master of pre-bop styles.

"I was ten years old when I started playing a tenor (four-string) guitar that was in our closet and had belonged to my uncle. Shortly after that, I started taking lessons in a local Huntington Beach music store from Charles Shortino. He was an old tenor banjo player from St. Louis who taught me right away to read music, play tunes, and play melodies with chords. After a few weeks, when I mentioned there was also a tenor banjo at home, he had me playing that, learning a lot of the old tunes from the '20s. On my own, I started improvising and playing a little jazz on the banjo. A couple of years later at a banjo club meeting, I met a part-time guitarist named Jim Elsaas, who introduced me to recordings of many of the classic jazz guitarists, including Barney Kessel, Charlie Christian, Django Reinhardt, Tal Farlow, George Van Eps, Jim Hall, Kenny Burrell, as well as Joe Pass/Herb Ellis (the first Concord LP), Charlie Byrd and Chuck Wayne/Joe Puma. I made tapes of as many of these as I could; I was particularly smitten by Barney Kessel, who was a major influence on my guitar style. I got a six-string guitar and started learning to play it, adapting my knowledge from the tenor banjo tuning."

Alden played banjo in a Long Beach pizza parlor, the Village Inn, as a teenager. He also worked at a different pizza parlor, Blinky's, when he was 16, learning from the pianists whom he played with. During the summers of 1976 and '77 (and part of '78), he played banjo at Disneyland, enjoying hearing the many jazz bands that were employed at Disney during the era. Alden attended Cal State Fullerton for two semesters, where he studied classical guitar. He also studied during 1977–78 at the Guitar Institute of Technology. He played Dixieland gigs with Dan Barrett, worked with Jake Hanna, and, in 1979, played guitar with Page Cavanaugh at a club in Encino. Singer Mavis Rivers heard him playing with Cavanaugh and recommended him to Red Norvo. In 1979, Alden worked with Norvo's vibes-guitar-bass trio for three and a half months during the summer in Atlantic City. He spent a few more years in Southern California, joined Joe Bushkin at the Cafe Carlyle in 1982, recorded with Bud Freeman, and moved to New York in 1983.

Since then, Howard Alden has performed with both swing veterans and the great players of his generation. His associations include Dan Barrett (with whom he co-led a notable quintet during 1985–95), Milt Hinton, Joe Williams, Woody Herman's small group (1984), Ruby Braff, Flip Phillips, Dick Hyman, Kenny Davern, Benny Carter, Dizzy Gillespie, George Van Eps (recording four CDs in the 1990s), Ken Peplowski, Ray Brown, Charlie Byrd, Carol Sloane, Mel Powell, Maxine Sullivan, Rosemary Clooney, Jack Wilkins, Bucky Pizzarelli, Warren Vaché, and George Wein's Newport All-Stars, plus a countless number of all-star groups. For the Woody Allen film *Sweet And Lowdown*, he played most of the guitar solos and taught actor Sean Penn (who played a guitarist inspired by Django Reinhardt) how to play guitar. Alden has led his own record dates since 1986 (starting with an impressive string for Concord), has appeared at many jazz festivals, parties and cruises, and has symbolized swing guitar for the past 25 years while keeping an open mind toward other jazz styles.

In recent times, in addition to touring with the Newport All-Stars (including an appearance at the 2010 Monterey Jazz Festival), Howard Alden has worked in New York City on weekly gigs with singer Jeanne Gies and on duo collaborations with Jack

Wilkins, Bucky Pizzarelli, Anat Cohen, Warren Vaché and Ken Peplowski. He has also appeared with many acoustic ensembles at Djangofest concerts and spends six months of the year performing in Europe. "I enjoy the adventure of playing with musicians all over the world. I also continually work to develop my potential on the seven-string guitar (acoustic and electric). A new goal of mine is to lead and travel with my own group and explore a wider range of musical ideas."

**Recommended CDs:** *Plays The Music Of Harry Reser* (Stomp Off 1200) is a stunning series of banjo solos originally recorded by Reser in the 1920s. *My Shining Hour, Take Your Pick* and *Your Story* have been cited by the guitarist as personal favorites, but all of Howard Alden's recordings are quite worthy, certainly including *Swing Street* (Concord 4349) with Dan Barrett, *The ABQ Salutes Buck Clayton* (Concord 4395), *Snowy Morning Blues* (Concord 4424), *No Amps Allowed* (Chiaroscuro 303), *Misterioso* (Concord 4487), *A Good Likeness* (Concord 4544), *Your Story: The Music Of Bill Evans* (Concord 4621), *Encore* (Concord 4654), *Concord Jazz Guitar Collective* (Concord 4672) with Jimmy Bruno and Frank Vignola, *Full Circle* (Concord 4788), *Hot Club Of 52nd Street* (Chesky 271), *Take Your Pick* (Concord 4743), *My Shining Hour* (Concord 4841) and *In A Mellow Tone* (Concord 2207) with Bucky Pizzarelli. Alden has also recorded extensively with a sideman, including with Ruby Braff (for Concord and Arbors); as co-leader with George Van Eps: *Thirteen Strings* (Concord 4464), *Hand Crafted Swing* (Concord 4513), *Seven & Seven* (Concord 4584), *Keepin' Time* (Concord 4713); with Scott Hamilton: *Race Point* (Concord 4492), *Groovin' High* (Concord 4509); with Ken Peplowski: *Live At Maybeck Recital Hall* (Concord 4556); and with Dick Hyman: *Cheek To Cheek* (Arbors 19155).

**Website:** www.howardalden.com

## Johnny Alegre
*(Juan Bautista H. Alegre III)*
*b. June 4, 1955, Pasay City, Greater Manila, Philippines*

Johnny Alegre has become increasingly significant during the past decade as a jazz guitarist from the Philippines. He grew up listening to American pop music, rock, Motown and British blues. "I taught myself to play an acoustic guitar when I was 15, and after, with money saved up, I bought a secondhand semi-hollow electric guitar and an amplifier, joining my first rock 'n' roll garage band." Alegre started his career as a folk singer-songwriter, meeting a lot of musicians and making important contacts.

He frequented the Thomas Jefferson Cultural Center and Library, which was run by the US Information Services in Manila. Alegre discovered jazz through the library's huge record collection and became a record collector. Alegre attended the University of the Philippines' College of Music, studying composition and enrolling in the jazz program, playing in the university's jazz ensemble. "My first concerts as a teenage musician are the obvious choices for turning points in my career, particularly the one when I first played in my first college jazz recital. After that, the high points would be my first participation in a Philippine movie soundtrack (1977), my first residency in a jazz bar (1980), my first stint as a record producer (1985), and my launch as a solo recording artist (2005)."

Alegre worked in many aspects of the music business in the Philippines as a musician and record producer. In 2002, he formed his own quintet, Affinity, which is considered one of the Philippines' finest jazz combos. Their first album gained a lot of attention in the Philippines and was released on the Candid label as *Jazzhound* in England. "My third album, *3*, which I made with Ron McClure and Billy Hart on MCA Music, best represents my playing style." Johnny Alegre holds his own with the Americans, becoming an influential force in the Philippines jazz scene.

**Recommended CDs:** Johnny Alegre's three jazz CDs as a leader are *Jazzhound* (Candid 79842); *Eastern Skies* (Candid 6006), which has Allegre accompanied by the Global Studio Orchestra; and *Johnny Alegre 3* (MCA 75320). A recording in a quartet with percussionist Susie Ibarra, *Humanfolk*, has not yet come out as of late 2012.

**Website:** www.johnnyalegre.com

## Oscar Alemán
*b. February 20, 1909, Resistencia, Argentina; d. October 14, 1980, Buenos Aires, Argentina*

Oscar Alemán was, in some ways, the Sonny Stitt of the guitar. Stitt was branded as a Charlie Parker imitator in the late 1940s but always claimed that he developed his style independently of Parker. By doubling on tenor, he managed to develop his own musical personality while not compromising his mastery of bebop. Alemán emerged in Europe in the 1930s sounding almost exactly like Django Reinhardt. Ironically, he was 11 months older than Django, but Reinhardt dominated the European jazz scene. While Alemán worked steadily and was also a singer and a dancer, the only way that he could eventually escape the comparison was to return to his native Argentina and continue to grow.

Oscar Alemán danced and sang with his family's group, the Moreira Sextet, from the time he was six. He was already playing the ukulele at that time, soon switching to guitar. After his parents' death four years later, the orphan often performed in the streets. He developed quickly as a guitarist and, by 1924, was working with Brazilian guitarist Gastón Bueno Lobo as part of Les Loups. They recorded in Buenos Aires during 1927–28, and when they added a violin in 1929, they were called Trio Victor. Alemán moved to Spain in the late 1920s and Paris in 1931. By then, he had discovered the jazz of Joe Venuti and Eddie Lang. He was hired by Josephine Baker and became the leader of her backup band, the Baker Boys. He soon was acquainted with Django Reinhardt and they became friends.

After leaving Baker, Alemán worked with Freddy Taylor's Men from Harlem during 1933–35. He led a nonet in Paris, making records with trumpeter Bill Coleman and clarinetist Danny Polo. While visiting Denmark in 1938, he appeared on two recordings with violinist Svend Asmussen in addition to recording a pair of unaccompanied guitar solos ("Nobody's Sweetheart" and "Whispering"). In Paris in mid-1939, Alemán cut four titles for the Swing label in a trio with a rhythm guitarist and bassist-singer Wilson Myers. Around this time, critic Leonard Feather visited France and was soon saying that Alemán was a greater jazz guitarist than Django Reinhardt, a viewpoint that he never varied from. In reality, Django was the innovator, while Alemán was a talented interpreter of swing music.

In 1941, World War II resulted in Oscar Alemán returning to Argentina. He stayed in his homeland for the rest of his life, apparently never visiting the United States except possibly in 1944. Although largely forgotten outside of Argentina, Alemán stayed very active as a guitarist and entertainer. He recorded regularly, was a constant in nightclubs, and appeared in a few movies that found him playing guitar, scatting a bit like Leo Watson, and dancing. Unlike Reinhardt, he never seems to have seriously explored either bebop or the electric guitar (except on rare occasions), continuing to perform in the timeless swing style.

Oscar Alemán recorded as late as 1974 and stayed active until his death in 1980 at the age of 71.

**Recommended CDs:** *Swing Guitar Masterpieces* (Acoustic Disc 29) is a definitive two-CD set that includes Alemán's two dates as a leader in Europe plus 44 selections dating from 1941–54, mostly with his Argentinian sextet, which also included piano, violin, rhythm guitar, bass and drums. Many more of his recordings are long overdue to be reissued and made available in the United States.

## Laurindo Almeida
*(Laurindo Jose de Araujo Almeida Nobrega Neto)*
b. September 2, 1917, Prainha, Brazil; d. July 26, 1995, Van Nuys, CA

Laurindo Almeida was the first in several areas. The first important Brazilian to make an impact on the American jazz scene, Almeida was a pioneer in bossa nova (playing a similar type of music years before it even had a name), he was nearly the only young jazz guitarist in the late 1940s not to sound like Charlie Christian, and he introduced the acoustic classical guitar to jazz.

Part of a musical family, Almeida had piano lessons from his mother but was self-taught on the guitar, starting when he was nine. At 12, he moved with his brother to São Paulo, and at 15, he fought in a civil war, getting wounded but recovering. In 1935, Almeida began to work on the radio in Rio with singer-guitarist Nestor Amaral, as a guitarist, arranger and songwriter. He stayed busy with the radio work, playing in clubs (including heading a group at the Casino da Urea for five years), and recording. In 1936, after performing on a cruise ship for months, Almeida had an opportunity to meet Django Reinhardt in France. His song "Johnny Peddler," which he wrote in 1940, was recorded in the United States by several acts, including Jimmy Dorsey, Les Brown, and the Andrews Sisters.

Almeida, who had a strong reputation in Brazil, surprised many locals by moving to California in 1947. He appeared on the soundtrack of *A Song Is Born*, a film starring Danny Kaye and a variety of top swing stars. As a member of the Stan Kenton Orchestra during 1947–48 and 1950–51, Almeida was well featured, including on "Lament" and his own "Amazonia." His Spanish classical guitar added a new sound to the Kenton arsenal. After leaving Kenton, Almeida's playing became a regular in films, appearing on over 800 soundtracks. He also wrote the scores for at least ten films.

In 1953, Almeida teamed up with Bud Shank to record two pioneering Brazilian jazz albums that hint strongly at bossa nova a few years before Antonio Carlos Jobim got started. He was quite prolific throughout his career, whether working in the studios, performing solo works for his classical guitar, starring on a classic album with the Modern Jazz Quartet, or making appearances with jazz artists including Stan Getz and Herbie Mann. During 1974–82, Almeida reunited with Bud Shank to perform Brazilian jazz with the L.A. Four. In addition, he wrote over 1,000 compositions, led a series of easy-listening recordings in the 1960s, collaborated late in life with Charlie Byrd, and led a guitar trio, Guitarjam, that also featured Larry Coryell and Sharon Isbin.

Laurindo Almeida, who was active until his death at age 77, never tired of performing jazz, Brazilian pieces and Western classical music, usually in a soft-spoken manner. He was a unique voice in jazz and music history.

**Recommended CDs:** *Brazilliance Vol. 1* (World Pacific 96339) has the legendary 1953 recordings with Bud Shank, bassist Harry Babasin and drummer Roy Harte, while *Brazilliance Vol. 2* (World Pacific 96102) has a similar 1958 reunion with Shank. Almeida's 1960s recordings, which are often bossa nova–oriented, are mostly out of print, although *Guitar From Ipanema* (Toshiba EMI 53721) is available in Japan. A good sampling of his later jazz recordings include *Chamber Jazz* (Concord 4084); *Brazilian Soul* (Concord 4150), which is the first of four collaborations with Charlie Byrd; *Artistry In Rhythm* (Concord 4238); *Tango* (Concord 4290), which is also with Byrd; and *Outra Vez* (Concord 4497). There are also eight recordings made with the L.A. Four, all of which are rewarding: *The L.A. Four Scores* (Concord 8), *Concierto De Aranjuez* (Concord 4018), *Watch What Happens* (Concord 4063), *Live At Montreux* (Concord 4100), *Zaca* (Concord 4130), *Montage* (Concord 4156), *Just Friends* (Concord 4199) and *Executive Suite* (Concord 4215). *Collaboration* (Collectables 6911) is the very memorable recording with the Modern Jazz Quartet, highlighted by a classic version of "One Note Samba."

# Peter Almqvist
*b. July 17, 1957, Lund, Sweden*

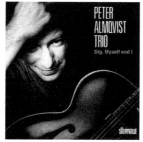

A fine hard-bop guitarist from Sweden, Peter Almqvist has held his own with American jazzmen and the top Swedish players. Almqvist started playing the guitar at seven, inspired by the Beatles. He heard jazz early on through his father's jazz guitar records. While in high school, he decided that music was his life. "Guitarist Ike Isaacs was a big influence and a great teacher. I took lessons from him while he lived in London. I also learned that jazz is very honest and direct."

In 1980, he formed Guitars Unlimited, an acoustic guitar duo that co-starred Ulf Wakenius. The group became quite popular, appearing on Swedish television regularly and touring throughout Europe. Almqvist had opportunities to play with violinist Svend Asmussen during 1982–83, toured with an all-star Brazilian jazz band in 1986, and two years later formed his own trio. The group was featured with Art Farmer on a pair of Scandinavian tours (1995–96) and also recorded with pianist Horace Parlan.

These days, Peter Almqvist still performs with his trio but has also been heard occasionally giving solo guitar recitals.

**Recommended CDs:** Peter Almqvist's inventive guitar solos should be of strong interest to fans of straight-ahead jazz guitar. He has recorded a trio of worthy CDs for Storyville: *Dig Myself And I* (Storyville 4201), *Peter Almqvist Trio With Horace Parlan* (Storyville 4205), and *My Sound: Solos And Duets* (Storyville 4236); the latter features Almqvist unaccompanied and in overdubbed duets.

**Website:** www.myspace.com/peteralmqvist

# Tuck Andress
*b. October 28, 1952, Tulsa, OK*

Tuck Andress has spent nearly his entire career touring and performing with his wife, singer Patti Cathcart, as Tuck and Patti. His father and older sister played piano, although not professionally. Andress took classical piano lessons from the age of seven until he was 14. After playing piano in a neighborhood rock band, he switched to guitar, playing in his high school band. Wes Montgomery was an early influence as was George Benson, in addition to the blues and rock guitarists of the era. After a semester at Stanford in 1970, he moved to Los Angeles and became a session musician, working on the Sonny and Cher television series. But because commercial music did not interest him, Andress quit the scene, alternating between taking classes at Stanford and playing in Tulsa with the Gap Band. After finishing at Stanford in 1974, he worked in a variety of soul bands in the San Francisco Bay area and also with a few rock and top-40 groups. During this period, he practiced from 8 to 14 hours a day, figuring out a system for playing every possible voicing of every chord.

In 1978, Tuck Andress met Patti Cathcart as she auditioned for a band that he was in. They realized immediately that they were a perfect match, at first musically and then personally. They began performing together and were married in 1983. After many performances and plenty of offers to record, they made their first album in 1987 and have been a popular attraction ever since.

Most of Tuck Andress' performances have been in the role of being an accompanying orchestra for the singer. His mastery of chords has always come in handy, and he takes many concise solos during their performances in a repertoire that ranges from jazz to folk music and includes pop, R&B and originals. The sparse setting of their duets has given the guitarist a great deal of freedom, and he has long had his own style.

**Recommended CDs:** Tuck and Patti have been very consistent in their recordings, which include *Tears Of Joy* (Windham Hill 0111), *Love Warriors* (Windham Hill 0116), *Dream* (Windham Hill 0130), *Learning How To Fly* (Epic 64439), *Paradise Found* (Windham Hill 11336), *Taking The Long Way Home* (Windham Hill 11507), *Chocolate Moment* (T&P/33rd Street 3310), *A Gift Of Love* (T&P/33rd Street 3331), and *I Remember You* (Universal 174402), which was their first set of standards. Tuck Andress has also recorded two albums as an unaccompanied soloist without his wife: *Reckless Precision* (Windham Hill 0124) and his Christmas album *Hymns, Carols And Songs About Snow* (Windham Hill 10135). It would be particularly interesting to hear the guitarist playing with a full group, but that has not happened yet on record.

**Website:** www.tuckandpatti.com

## Ron Anthony

*b. December 16, 1933, Pittsburgh, PA*

A tasteful and melodic guitarist long active in the Los Angeles area, Ron Anthony has the ability to blend into any setting and is particularly skilled at working with other guitarists. Anthony was originally a singer when he was 12, doing vocal impersonations of Nat Cole, Billy Eckstine and Frankie Laine. After three months on clarinet, he started playing guitar when he was 16. "My influences were originally the George Shearing Quintet with Chuck Wayne and Oscar Moore with Nat Cole's Trio. Later, they became Jimmy Raney, Tal Farlow, Andrés Segovia and, above all, Miles Davis' trumpet solos. His romantic lyricism and economy really got to me."

Anthony started working professionally at 18, playing in the Pittsburgh area until 1955, when he entered the Army, becoming a member of the 7th Army Jazz Band in Germany. After his discharge, he attended Duquesne University but after a year moved to New York. "My first important job was with the George Shearing Quintet in 1962 for two years. I later rejoined George in 1971 for another four. Shearing's harmonic sense was very important in my development as a player." After leaving Shearing the first time, Anthony moved to Los Angeles, where he became a busy studio musician who also played jazz clubs with a variety of groups. Another important association was working with Frank Sinatra during 1986–95.

In recent times, Ron Anthony, who is the uncle of Ron Affif, has taught privately and in Los Angeles at Pierce College in addition to playing locally. He accompanies singers, plays solo and often teams up with fellow guitarist Barry Zweig.

**Recommended CDs:** Of his recordings, Ron Anthony's favorites are a duet set that he did with the late bassist Dave Carpenter (*It's Always 4 A.M.*) and a quintet date from 1993 with trumpeter Conte Candoli (*Same Time, Same Place*). Both have been privately issued and are available through his website.

**Website:** www.ronanthonyjazz.com

## Irving Ashby

*b. December 29, 1920, Somerville, MA; d. April 22, 1987, Perris, CA*

A tasteful swing guitarist, Irving Ashby had a high-profile association with the Nat King Cole Trio but did relatively little as a leader. Ashby began playing the acoustic guitar when he was nine. He gained early experience working locally in Massachusetts, switched to electric guitar, and was with the early Lionel Hampton big band during 1940–42, including being on the hit recording of "Flying Home." After a few years of living in Los Angeles and freelancing, Ashby replaced Oscar Moore in the Nat King Cole Trio in 1947. He was on many recordings with Cole and became influential on younger guitarists who enjoyed his clean sound and melodic solos. Ashby was also on jazz dates during the second half of the 1940s with Erroll Garner, Nellie Lutcher, Lester Young, Illinois Jacquet, Benny Carter, Buck Clayton, Woody Herman, Gerald Wilson, Helen Humes and Wardell Gray.

After 1949, Cole de-emphasized his piano playing and the trio in favor of vocals and orchestral recordings. Moore departed in 1951 and was a member of the Oscar Peterson Trio for a moment the following year, recording nine selections with Peterson on January 26, 1952. A month later, Barney Kessel was in the spot.

Ashby spent much of the 1950s as a studio player, including at MGM and 20th Century Fox. Although he appeared on record with Charlie Parker, most of his sessions were in an anonymous role in the pop and rock-and-roll worlds, including with the

Ernie Freeman Combo, Sandy Nelson, B.B. King, Pat Boone, Amos Milburn and Perez Prado. By the 1960s, he was mostly teaching privately in Perris, California, and at the University of California at Riverside, publishing a guitar instruction book. In his later years, Ashby popped up on occasional records, including a brief reunion with Oscar Peterson (*History Of An Artist Vol. 1*), Mundell Lowe's *California Guitar*, and two projects with Count Basie on Pablo (*Basie Jam* and *Bosses*, which also features Big Joe Turner). But Irving Ashby spent most of his career out of the spotlight despite his talents and was long forgotten by the time of his 1987 death.

**Recommended CDs:** Most of Irving Ashby's recordings with Nat King Cole are on *1947 Vol. 3* (Classics 1135), *1947–1949* (Classics 1145), *1949* (Classics 1196) and *1949–1950* (Classics 1305).

**LPs to Search For:** Other than a few singles, Irving Ashby's only date as a leader resulted in the obscure album *Memoirs* (Accent 5091) in 1976. The easy-listening swing set is with a quartet that also features pianist Jimmy Rowles.

## Dave Askren
*b. November 17, 1955, Milwaukee, WI*

Dave Askren has been an important contributor to the jazz and Latin music scenes in Los Angeles. Born in Milwaukee but raised in Raleigh, North Carolina, and Dayton, Ohio, Askren started on 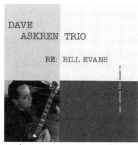 guitar when he was 12 after stints on piano, clarinet and saxophone. "Although I was playing rock, blues, and R&B in the '70s as a teenager, many of the musicians were open-minded. My drummer friends turned me on to a lot of jazz." At 15, he was working at school dances, parties and occasional clubs. Askren attended Berklee during 1976–80, later earning a master's in music from Cal State L.A. in the mid-1990s. In the early 1980s, he taught at Berklee and played jobs with Antonio Hart, Delfeayo Marsalis and Bob Moses.

After moving to Los Angeles in the 1990s, Askren worked with a variety of pop artists (including Marilyn McCoo and La Toya Jackson) and soul vocal groups. "All of this taught me a lot about being a professional musician and how to 'groove' with a rhythm section, which applies to jazz as well. All great music has a groove and a lot of soul." Since

that time, Askren has worked with Eddie Resto, the Banda Brothers, Sal Cracciolo, Jimmy Branly, Gary Foster, Mike Vax, Linda Hopkins and most recently Trio Nuevo.

**Recommended CDs:** Dave Askren has thus far led three very different but equally rewarding CDs: *Re: Bill Evans* (String Jazz 1029), *Some Other Things* (Sea Breeze 3077), and *Trio Nuevo +* (Daway Music 30255).

**Website:** www.daveaskren.com

## Badi Assad
*b. December 23, 1966, S.J. Boa Vista, São Paulo, Brazil*

A major performer from Brazil, Badi Assad is best known as a singer, but her accompanying of her own vocals reveals a brilliant guitarist. Her two brothers, Sergio and Odair, became famous in Brazil as  the Duo Assad. "I was 14 years old when my father asked: 'Do you want to play with me?' I didn't resist the invitation." She had been studying piano since the age of eight but, at her father's suggestion, switched to the guitar to accompany his playing of chorinhos on the bandolim. Badi Assad attended the University of Rio de Janeiro and debuted in 1986 as a member of the Guitar Orchestra of Rio de Janeiro. That year, she acted and sang in a musical, *Mulheres De Hollanda*.

In 1987, she performed in Brazil, Israel, and Europe with guitarist Françoise-Emmanuelle Denis as Duo Romantique. The following year, Assad starred in a solo performance act called "Antagonism." She made her recording debut as a leader in 1989 with *Dança Dos Tons*, which was originally released only in Brazil. After moving to New York, Assad gained a lot of recognition with 1993's *Solo* and a series of performances and recordings that followed throughout the decade.

Health problems (a motor skills disability that affected her guitar playing) resulted in Assad moving back to Brazil. Fortunately, she fully recovered, recording *Three Guitars* in 2003 with Larry Coryell and John Abercrombie, which she names as one of her personal favorite recordings.

"I hope to record a children's project with my own material and also release a CD with my songs. Music for me is a way to experience true freedom. The technique is just a way to make it possible for you to be free. After that, you have to let it go and just be the music."

**Recommended CDs:** *Dança Dos Ondas* (GHA 120653) is a reissue of Badi Assad's debut recording. *Solo* (Chesky 99) fully showcases Assad's talents as a guitarist and singer. *Rhythms* (Chesky 137), the instrumental *Echoes Of Brazil* (Chesky 154); *Chameleon* (Polygram 539889); *Three Guitars* (Chesky 248), which finds Assad holding her own with Coryell and Abercrombie on acoustic guitar; *Verde* (Universal 477523); and *Wonderland* (Deutsche Grammophon 153) display the evolution and constant surprises heard in the music of Badi Assad.

**Website:** www.badiassad.com

## Derek Bailey

*b. January 29, 1930, Sheffield, Yorkshire, England;*
*d. December 25, 2005, London, England*

Derek Bailey, the most radical guitarist in this book, could be considered the Cecil Taylor of the guitar in some ways. However, while it is always obvious that Taylor is playing a piano, Bailey's free improvisations and wide range of sounds sometimes disguised the fact that he was playing a guitar or (as some detractors might say) music at all!

Bailey was born into a musical family; his grandfather and uncle were musicians. He studied guitar from the age of ten, and by 1950, he was playing jazz and dance music in British pubs. The turning point in his musical evolution occurred when he teamed up with bassist Gavin Bryars and drummer Tony Oxley in a trio called Joseph Holbrooke (after a recently deceased classical composer) during 1963–66. The group quickly evolved from a straight-ahead jazz group to one that featured totally free improvisations. Bailey never looked back from that point on.

After moving to London in 1966, the guitarist teamed up with like-minded musicians (including Evan Parker, Kenny Wheeler and Dave Holland) in John Stevens' Spontaneous Music Ensemble. His playing became even freer during this time, not just in his choice of notes but also in his very wide array of sounds. While Bailey always reacted quickly to his fellow musicians, his playing was so abstract that one either loved or hated his music.

Derek Bailey played with Tony Oxley in a sextet (1968–73), formed the Music Improvisation

Company with Evan Parker (1968–71), played in the trio Iskra 1903 with bassist Barry Guy and trombonist Paul Rutherford starting in 1970, and had a free improvisation ensemble called Company from 1976 on. The latter group constantly changed its personnel and at times included Steve Lacy, Anthony Braxton, George Lewis, Misha Mengelberg, Lol Coxhill, Leo Smith, Eugene Chadbourne, Henry Kaiser and John Zorn among others. Bailey was also heard in a countless number of combinations with musicians (including a very dissonant three-CD set with Pat Metheny) and sometimes played unaccompanied solos.

While some may think that Derek Bailey's playing was haphazard and random, he wrote a book, *Improvisation: Its Nature And Practice*, that explained his methods and those of other improvisers. Many of his groundbreaking recordings are on the Incus label, which he founded in 1970 with Evan Parker and Tony Oxley; Parker and Oxley left due to musical and personal differences a few years later.

Derek Bailey never compromised his music. Although he gave many solo concerts and would seem to be most at home in that setting, he actually preferred to play off of other musicians, and he was eager for new collaborations up until the time shortly before his death at age 75.

**Recommended CDs:** There is no shortage of Derek Bailey recordings. *Pieces For Guitar* (Tzadik 7080) has Bailey's earliest solo guitar records (from 1966–67) on a set not originally issued until 2002. A few of the most intriguing Bailey releases through the years are 1968's *Karyobin* (Paratactile 2001) by the Spontaneous Music Ensemble, *Music Improvisation Company* (Incus 12), *Eighty-Five Minutes Part 1* (Quintessence 1), *Eighty-Five Minutes Part 2* (Quintessence 2), *First Duo Concert* (Emanem 4006) with Anthony Braxton, *Royal Vol. 1* (Incus 43) also with Braxton, *Improvisation 1975* (Cramps 062), *The London Concert* (Incus 16), *Domestic And Public Pieces* (Emanem 4001), *Time* (Incus 34), *Aida* (Incus 40), *Notes* (Incus 48), *Pleistozaen Mit Wasser* (FMP 16) with Cecil Taylor, *Lace* (Emanem 4013), *One Time* (Incus 22), *Playing* (Incus 14), *Wireforks* (Shanachie 5011) and *Takes Fakes & Dead She Dances* (Incus 31). Unexpected and unusual are Derek Bailey's late-period treatments of older songs on *Ballads* (Tzadik 7607) and *Standards* (Tzadik 7620). Bailey's match-up with Pat Metheny on *The Sign Of 4* (Knitting Factory Works 197) is so consistently noisy as to be a bit of a disappointment.

**LPs to Search For:** Historically significant but difficult to find are *So, What Do You Think?* (Tangent 118), *The Topography Of The Lungs* (Incus 1) from 1970, *Iskra 1903* (Incus 3/4), *Company 1* (Incus 21), and *Fables* (Incus 36).

## Sheryl Bailey
*b. May 20, 1966, Pittsburgh, PA*

Sheryl Bailey is a superior guitarist with a blazing style who keeps the melody in mind even during her wildest improvisations. "I came from a family of classical pianists, so I had to study piano as a young  child. When I was 13, I begged my mother for a guitar from the JC Penney's catalog: a Harmony Strat and Amplifier. I got completely into heavy metal and blues and started my own garage bands. By age 15, I was playing classic rock in bars. But then I stumbled across a small renegade radio station, WYEP. I heard Wes Montgomery, Kenny Burrell and George Benson. I was so intrigued by the sounds and rhythms and it really spoke to me. At the same time, my mother wanted me to study, so she found a teacher from the University of Pittsburgh, John Maione. He in turn made recordings of Jimmy Raney, Herb Ellis, and Joe Pass for me and we dove into playing the repertoire of the early players." She also studied with Mark Koch (a disciple of Pat Martino), and in college she really loved the playing of John Abercrombie and Ralph Towner.

Bailey went to Duquesne University in Pittsburgh for one year and Berklee for three in the 1980s. She was in the house band at Wally's Jazz Club in Boston the summer after graduating. Bailey worked with Gary Thomas (touring Japan), in Baltimore with Gary Grainger (1993–96), and in Washington, DC, with drummer Harold Summey (1994–98). Other important associations since then include Dwayne Burno, George Garzone, Richard Bona (2002–04), David Krakauer's Klezmer Madness (since 2002), Jack Wilkins, Howard Alden and Ingrid Jensen.

Sheryl Bailey formed her own trio in 2001 with organist Gary Versace and drummer Ian Froman. "We've had a regular residency at the famed 55 Bar in NYC over the years. I also started my own label, PureMusic Records, in 2001, have produced four recordings, and built an audience and a launching pad for some of my more recent releases. I have two other projects: the Sheryl Bailey 4 (a straight-ahead and traditional bop project) with pianist Jim Ridl, bassist Gary Wang and drummer Shingo Okudaira, and Jazz Guitars Meet Hendrix with fellow guitarist Vic Juris, which is a jazz homage to the great Jimi." Bailey also teaches regularly at Berklee and appears as a guest in a variety of settings.

"Jazz is the music of the moment. You have to be fully awake and aware to play it. It is an extended meditation."

**Recommended CDs:** *Little Misunderstood* (Oasis 6990); a set of guitar duets with Chris Bergson called *Reunion Of Souls* (Orchard 801676); *The Power Of 3*, which is the recording debut of her organ trio (Pure 21402); *Bullseye* (Pure 21403); *Live At The Fat Cat* (Pure 21404); *A New Promise* (MCG Jazz 1028); and *For All Those Living* (PureMusic Records 616 892 151 869) all have passionate and exciting playing by Sheryl Bailey.

**Website:** www.sherylbailey.com

## Duck Baker
*(Richard Royall Baker IV)*
*b. July 30, 1949, Washington, DC*

Duck Baker is an unusual fingerstyle jazz guitarist in that all eras of the music interest him. He has recorded everything from swing and blues to free improvisations, along with most idioms that fall in  between. Baker grew up in Warsaw, Virginia. "My father gave me a ukulele for my 14th birthday, and then I wanted a guitar for Christmas." After playing rock and folk music, he decided that he wanted to discover much more, introducing himself to jazz. "I had gotten some Jimmy Smith records and listened to the Jazz Crusaders a bit. But then I felt like I needed to understand the real stuff, so I bought records by Miles (*Four And More*) and Monk (*Misterioso*). The Monk did it. Within about 30 seconds, I was hooked, at age 16."

Baker was self-taught on guitar, learning about music and stride pianist Buck Evans. "Buck turned me on to ragtime at a time when no one knew about it, as well as early jazz. He also got me to understand that there was not any essential difference between that stuff and the blues I was listening to. Sure saved me a lot of time, learning that at age 16. It pointed me towards arranging everything I could, from fiddle tunes to folk blues to ragtime and swing, for fingerstyle guitar. I never felt that this was essentially different from working on free jazz, or when I got a bit further along, modern jazz."

By 1974, Baker was playing swing duets with guitarist Thom Keats in San Francisco and recording for the Kicking Mule label. He also joined a bluegrass band to expand his horizons. Baker worked with Eugene Chadbourne during 1977–81 and, through Chadbourne, met and worked with John Zorn (1978–81). Baker spent 1978–86 living in Europe. "Being in London brought me into contact with both the London free improv scene and also the Irish trad scene, extending my musical world in both directions." In addition to jazz recordings, he recorded solo guitar albums of Irish and Scottish music. Baker traveled the world extensively before returning to San Francisco in 1987.

During the next 17 years, he worked in a wide variety of idioms, including swing in a trio with violinist Tony Marcus and guitarist Bob Wilson, free duets with bassist Mark Dresser, guitar duets with Jamie Findlay, and a stimulating trio with clarinetist Ben Goldberg and violinist Carla Kihlstedt. Baker's 1997 recording of Herbie Nichols compositions, *Spinning Song*, gained him recognition and some acclaim. "Making *Spinning Song* opened a lot of doors for me. I got to know Roswell Rudd doing that, and the things you pick up working with someone like Ros you can't get anywhere else. It was also very important to realize that people like Roswell and Steve Lacy thought I was doing something worthwhile with the music. The acoustic guitar world can get weird. You're always trying to adopt different musical styles on the instrument, and there can be a nagging feeling that it isn't the real thing."

Since moving back to Europe in 2004, Duck Baker has had a trio with clarinetist Alex Ward and bassist Joe Williamson; a duo with bassist Michael Moore; a free-jazz quartet with Ward, bassist Simon Fell and drummer Steve Noble; and a trio dedicated to Irish and American trad music, and has performed solo concerts. "I want to keep doing as many different things as I can. I've started work on another solo project for John Zorn that involves the music of the forgotten piano genius Hasaan Ibn Ali. I'd also like to do a solo Monk record and finally finish a project I've been working on for years involving jazz arrangements of folk tunes.

"I'd like to add some advice for aspiring jazz guitarists. One thing that would apply for any musician is something Steve Lacy said: Don't listen to bad music if you can possibly help it; it hurts your musical mind. Make an excuse and leave a bad concert, or ask people to turn off stupid pop music on the radio. Another thing is don't limit yourself as a listener to jazz and especially not to jazz guitar. Challenge yourself to listen to things that seem strange. Musical systems from very different cultures can teach us so much about how to hear and construct music. And remember that the guitar in jazz history is less important than saxophones, trumpets, and pianos.

So listen to all of them and steal every note that you can, and then make it yours. Don't just borrow it, steal it!"

**Recommended CDs:** There is quite a bit of diversity to be heard on *There's Something For Everyone In America* (Sonet 116); *When You Wore A Tulip* (Sonet 123); *The King Of Bongo Bong* (Sonet 137); *The Art Of Fingerstyle Jazz Guitar* (Shanachie 98005/6); *Opening The Eyes Of Love* (Shanachie 97025); *Spinning Song* (Avant 040), which is Baker's set of Herbie Nichols songs; *Do You Know What It Means To Miss New Orleans* (Day Job); *The Roots And Branches Of American Music* (Les Cousins 010); *Everything That Rises Must Converge* (Mighty Quinn 1117); *Out Of The Past* (Day Job) with Jamie Findlay; *The Waltz Lessons* (Les Cousins 011); *The Ducks Palace* (Incus 59); and *Amnesia In Trastevere* (Les Cousins 014). Duck Baker has said that his favorite personal recording is his Christmas record, *The Salutation* (Day Job).

**Website:** www.duckbaker.com

## Dave Barbour

b. May 28, 1912, Long Island, NY; d. December 11, 1965, Malibu, CA

A solid guitarist and a skilled songwriter, Dave Barbour is best remembered for his work with his wife, Peggy Lee. Barbour began as a banjoist, playing with Adrian Rollini (1933) and Wingy Manone. He switched to guitar shortly before the swing era began. Barbour worked with Red Norvo (1935–36) and then became busy in the studios, including with orchestras headed by Lennie Hayton and Raymond Scott. Barbour, who recorded with Artie Shaw (1939), Louis Armstrong, Lil Armstrong, Bunny Berigan, Teddy Wilson, Mildred Bailey and Glenn Miller, joined Benny Goodman's orchestra on electric guitar in the summer of 1942. After he broke Goodman's rule of getting involved with the female singer, marrying Peggy Lee, Barbour was fired.

In 1943, Peggy Lee retired from music, and Dave Barbour supported his new wife. But soon, Johnny Mercer had them working as a songwriting team for his Capitol label, Lee began recording regularly, and the retirement proved short-lived. With Barbour usually leading the backup band and contributing guitar solos, Peggy Lee became a star. They co-wrote such songs as "It's A Good Day," "I Don't Know Enough About You," "Mañana," and "What More Can A Woman Do?" In addition to his work with Lee, Barbour continued recording dates as a sideman, including with Charlie Barnet, Kay Starr and Woody Herman.

Unfortunately, Dave Barbour was an alcoholic, the marriage fell apart, and he was divorced from Lee in 1952. The remainder of his career and his life were anticlimactic. As Peggy Lee's fame continued to grow, Dave Barbour was largely forgotten, and his drinking continued. He occasionally played, including recording an album with Benny Carter and Ben Webster in 1962. But when he passed away in 1965, he was only 53. Dave Barbour's skills as a guitarist can be best experienced by seeing the Snader Transcriptions (shorts filmed for television during 1950–51) that feature him lovingly interacting with Peggy Lee.

**Recommended CDs:** Dave Barbour can be heard in a prominent role throughout the four-CD Peggy Lee set *Miss Wonderful* (Proper Box 108).

# Danny Barker

*b. January 13, 1909, New Orleans, LA; d. March 13, 1994, New Orleans, LA*

Danny Barker was a fine rhythm guitarist who was also an important force in the 1930s and '40s, and later, in his native New Orleans, as a banjoist, singer, lyricist, author and educator. Barker began playing banjo as a youth with the Boozan Kings (a kids' band) in the streets of New Orleans. While a teenager, he toured Mississippi with Little Brother Montgomery. In 1927, when he was 18, he married Louisa Dupont, who was just 13. That marriage worked, and Louisa later became known as the singer Blue Lu Barker.

In 1930, Danny Barker moved to New York, switched to guitar, and, during the next eight years, worked with Jelly Roll Morton, Sidney Bechet, Fess Williams, Albert Nicholas, James P. Johnson, the Lucky Millinder Big Band and Benny Carter's orchestra. A steady rhythm guitarist, Barker gained fame for his wife when, in 1938, he got her a record date and supplied the lyrics to four songs, including the big hit "Don't You Feel My Leg." Barker was guitarist with Cab Calloway's orchestra during 1939–46, often being part of a great rhythm section with pianist Bennie Payne, bassist Milt Hinton and drummer Cozy Cole.

During 1946–49, Barker recorded more sessions with his wife, contributing witty lyrics. He also wrote "Save The Bones For Henry Jones." In his post-Calloway years, he switched back to banjo, was part of the Dixieland revival movement, and, in 1965, moved home to New Orleans. Barker worked as the assistant curator of the New Orleans Jazz Museum, wrote his memoirs (*A Life In Jazz*), led the Onward Brass Band, and was a teacher and inspiration for many younger players.

**Recommended CDs:** In addition to his recordings with Cab Calloway and Blue Lu Barker, along the way Danny Barker made records with many jazz all-stars, including Wild Bill Davison, Bunk Johnson, Paul Barbarin, Sidney Bechet, Tony Parenti, Coleman Hawkins, Henry "Red" Allen, Lionel Hampton, Billie Holiday, Benny Carter, Roy Eldridge, Ethel Waters, Jelly Roll Morton, Jonah Jones, Mezz Mezzrow, and even Wynton Marsalis (*The Majesty Of The Blues*) and Charlie Parker (his date with Sir Charles Thompson). Barker was rarely heard as a leader, but his 1988 release *Save The Bones* (Orleans 1018) is a delight.

# Everett Barksdale

*b. April 28, 1910, Detroit, MI; d. January 29, 1986, Inglewood, CA*

A versatile studio musician, Everett Barksdale was a fine jazz soloist and accompanist for decades. He began on bass and banjo before becoming a full-time guitarist. Raised in Detroit, Barksdale moved to Chicago in the early 1930s, where he worked with Erskine Tate's orchestra and during most of 1931–39 with violinist Eddie South. Barksdale made his recording debut with South's group, appearing on eight selections during 1931–33. After moving to New York, he was with the Benny Carter Big Band, recording with Carter, Una Mae Carlisle and Sidney Bechet during 1940–41. He soon became very busy working for CBS in the studios and on radio.

During the next 25 years, Barksdale played with a countless number of musicians and in nearly every style, including swing, pop music, doo-wop groups and rock and roll, such as the Mickey & Sylvia hit "Love Is Strange." From the jazz standpoint, he is perhaps best known for being with Art Tatum's regular trio on and off from 1949 until Tatum's death in 1956. Barksdale was also musical director of the Ink Spots for a time, occasionally played bass (including electric bass on an album with Louis Armstrong in 1967), and was in the ABC/Paramount house band in the 1950s and '60s, performing on recordings behind many stars, including Dinah Washington and Sarah Vaughan.

Everett Barksdale stayed active until he retired in the early 1970s.

**Recommended CDs:** Everett Barksdale never led a record date of his own. His work with Art Tatum, eight trio selections from 1952 that also include bassist Slam Stewart, are reissued as part of Tatum's *The Complete Capitol Recordings Vols. 1 & 2* (Capitol 92866 and 92867), and he is on Eddie South's *1923–1937* (Classics 707).

## Junior Barnard
*(Lester Robert Barnard)*
*b. December 17, 1920, Coweta, OK; d. April 15, 1951, Fresno, CA*

One of the top guitarists featured with Bob Wills' Texas Playboys, Junior Barnard was an aggressive player who rarely played it safe. He often distorted his tone, an innovation in the 1940s when the electric guitar was still in its early days, and his playing was both jazz- and blues-oriented, yet fit comfortably into country music while hinting at rock and roll.

Born into a musical family where his father and uncle played fiddles at dances and parties, Junior Barnard sometimes accompanied his dad on guitar. By the time he was 15, he was playing acoustic guitar with local bands in Tulsa, had his own radio show, and was working as a staff musician. He played briefly with Art Davis' Rhythm Riders before being hired by Bob Wills to work with the Lonestar Rangers, a band led by his father, Uncle John Wills. Barnard also worked with Wills' cousin Son Lansford in the Sons of the West for a year.

Back in Tulsa in 1937, he switched to electric guitar and worked with Dave Edwards' Original Alabama Boys. During the next few years, Barnard occasionally subbed with Bob Wills' Texas Playboys but mostly played with Johnnie Lee Wills (Bob's brother) in the Rhythmaires and back with Uncle John Wills. During World War II, he was in and out of music, sometimes working as a welder at a defense plant. In 1943, he relocated to Southern California and appeared in a few films, including a short with Bob Wills, *Frontier Frolic*. As a member of the Texas Playboys, Barnard is featured on Bob Wills' recordings of the period and also the extensive series of radio transcriptions cut for Tiffany. His "Fat Boy Rag" is his most famous recording and feature number. His guitar was the group's main jazz solo instrument during this period, taking the place of horns.

Barnard took some time off in 1946 to work and record with Luke Wills and his Rhythmbusters (where he made some of his most extroverted recordings) before returning to the Playboys. During the next few years, Bernard, who was often restless, was sometimes back with the Playboys but also worked with bands led by Tommy Duncan and Jesse Ashlock. During 1949–51, he mostly led his own group, the Radio Gang (which featured his brother Gene Barnard on second guitar) in Fresno.

But it all came to an end when Junior Barnard, a passenger in a car driven by his brother-in-law, was killed in an accident. He was just 30.

**Recommended CDs:** Junior Barnard was featured with Bob Wills during 1946–47. His blend of jazz, country, hints of rockabilly and even early rock and roll perfectly fit with the pacesetting Western swing band and can be heard throughout Bob Wills' box set *The Tiffany Transcriptions* (Collectors' Choice 991).

## George Barnes
*b. July 17, 1921, South Chicago Heights, IL; d. September 5, 1977, Concord, CA*

George Barnes, who was a pioneering electric guitarist, was one of the few major swing guitarists still active in the 1970s. Barnes was taught the acoustic guitar by his father (also a guitarist) when he was nine. A year later, in 1931, his brother built him a primitive pickup and amplifier, leading to Barnes' credible claim years later that he was the first electric guitarist, an accomplishment that Les Paul also claimed for himself. A professional by the time he was 13, Barnes was always interested in using the guitar as a solo instrument. He considered his main influences to be horn players rather than other guitarists. He headed his own quartet in the Midwest during 1935–37, a period in which guitar-led jazz groups were very rare.

On March 1, 1938, George Barnes became the first to record on electric guitar, making his debut on "Sweetheart Land" and "It's A Low-Down Dirty Shame" on a session led by blues guitarist Big Bill Broonzy. It took place 15 days before Eddie Durham recorded on electric guitar with the Kansas City Five. Barnes worked with clarinetist Jimmie Noone and made sideman recordings during 1937–38 with such blues performers as Curtis Jones, Washboard Sam, Jazz Gillum, Louis Powell, Blind John Davis, Merline Johnson and Hattie Bolton as a house guitarist and arranger for the Decca label, and he became a member of the staff of NBC when he was still just 17.

After serving in the Army, Barnes was a staff musician at ABC for years, just playing jazz on an occasional basis. He made some notable radio transcriptions in 1946 at the head of an octet and headed a few albums for Mercury in the 1950s. But it was not until 1961, when he formed a guitar duo with Carl Kress, that Barnes was heard in a prominent role playing jazz. The duets, with Barnes playing single-note lines and Kress sticking to chords, were classic and happily out of place in the jazz world of 1961–65.

After Kress' death, Barnes continued in the studios. He collaborated with Bucky Pizzarelli during

1969–72, sometimes played with old friend Bud Freeman, and performed with Joe Venuti at the 1976 Concord Jazz Festival. Most notable was his co-leading a brilliant quartet with cornetist Ruby Braff during 1973–75 (usually with Wayne Wright on rhythm guitar and bassist Michael Moore), which resulted in quite a few excellent recordings.

George Barnes stayed active until shortly before his 1977 death at the age of 56, 39 years after he had paved the way for all electric guitarists.

**Recommended CDs:** George Barnes' pioneering session on electric guitar with Big Bill Broonzy, along with a slightly later four-song date, are included on Broonzy's *Volume 7 1937–1938* (Document 5129). Two songs that George Barnes recorded as a leader in 1940 ("I Can't Believe That You're In Love With Me" and "I'm Forever Blowing Bubbles") and eight selections from Keynote sessions in 1946 are pretty scarce. For the fun of it, Barnes wrote arrangements and was the main soloist with a unique octet that made some radio transcriptions during 1946–51. The two-CD set *The Complete Standard Transcriptions* (Soundies 4122) and *The Uncollected: George Barnes And His Octet 1946* (Hindsight 106) feature the unusual group, which includes four woodwind players; Barnes is the only improviser. *Two Guitars (And A Horn)* (Jass 636) features the brilliant Barnes-Kress duo with tenor-saxophonist Bud Freeman making the group a trio on a few numbers. Barnes and Kress are also in excellent form on *Guitars, Anyone?* (Audiophile 87). *The Ruby Braff–George Barnes Quartet: Live At The New School* (Chiaroscuro 126) is a greatly expanded reissue of that group's second recording. Also containing plenty of the Braff and Barnes magic are *Plays Gershwin* (Concord Jazz 6005) and *Salutes Rodgers And Hart* (Concord Jazz 6007). From Barnes' last period, *Swing Guitars* (Audiophile 87); *Gems* (Concord 6014), which matches the guitarist with Joe Venuti; *Plays So Good* (Concord 4067); and *Don't Get Around Much Anymore* (Acoustic Disc 52) find him playing with undiminished abilities and enthusiasm.

**LPs to Search For:** In 1951, George Barnes used multi-tracking to record himself on several guitars à la Les Paul. The resulting album, *Guitars . . . By George!* (Decca 8658), is a true obscurity. The guitar duo of Barnes and Carl Kress is featured on *Town Hall Concert* (United Artists 6335). Barnes and Bucky Pizzarelli are heard on part of *Historic Town Hall Concert* (Columbia 31045) and all of *Guitars Pure And Honest* (A&R 7100/007). The Braff-Barnes Quartet is showcased on *The Best I've Heard* (Chiaroscuro 121) and *To Fred Astaire With Love* (RCA 8442). Barnes' 1976 live recording with Joe Venuti,

*Live At The Concord Summer Festival* (Concord 30), also awaits discovery and reissue.

## Jeff Barone
*b. April 2, 1970, Syracuse, NY*

Inspired by Jack Wilkins, Jeff Barone is a creative straight-ahead guitarist based in New York. Barone started playing guitar after receiving one for Christmas when he was seven or eight. He had extensive lessons on classical guitar. "In seventh grade, I was invited to a jazz ensemble rehearsal and the guitar part had a performance note that said 'play à la Joe Pass.' I went out and bought my first jazz record, Joe Pass' *Virtuoso*."

Barone started playing professionally at 16 with the Syracuse Parks and Recreation All-Star Band led by Stan Colella. "In addition, I was playing in clubs, big bands, wedding bands, and touring shows that would come through Syracuse. I was fortunate that I had people who thought enough of my potential to call me for work at an early age." He also had opportunities to work with the Syracuse Symphony Orchestra and Al Martino.

Barone attended Onondaga Community College (1988–90), Ithaca College (1990–93) and the Manhattan School of Music (1993–95), where he earned a master's in jazz performance. After moving to New York City in 1993, he worked with trumpeter Charles McGee, singer Evelyn Blakey (Art Blakey's daughter), organist Jimmy "Preacher" Robins, Mel Davis and for five years with Reuben Wilson. During this period, he also studied with Jack Wilkins and Rodney Jones. Jack Wilkins has been an important part of Jeff Barone's life, performing with the younger guitarist in a variety of settings and recommending him for gigs, including with the Vanguard Orchestra, the Mingus Epitaph Orchestra and vibraphonist Warren Chiasson. He also persuaded him to record his debut CD, *Crazy Talk*.

In recent times, Jeff Barone has worked with Tom Harrell and Joe Magnarelli in addition to leading his own groups. He has also been active as a record producer, working on dates for altoist Mike Dubaniewicz, Jim Silberstein and Wilkins.

"I continue to learn something new every day about my instrument, music and life. I've devoted my life to music and look forward to those moments when all of the elements are in place; this leads to a true spiritual experience. That's the reward."

**Recommended CDs:** Jeff Barone's two CDs, *Crazy Talk* (String Jazz 1032) and *Open Up* (Jazzed Media 1033), are both excellent outlets for his cool-toned yet heated guitar playing. He is also well featured on Mike Dubaniewicz's *Drive Time* (Jazzed Media 1039).

**Website:** www.jeffbarone.com

## John Basile
b. March 5, 1955, Boston, MA

A lyrical and tasteful guitarist who makes every note count, John Basile is a melodic improviser and a superb accompanist. Basile started playing guitar when he was 12, having been drawn to a version of "Organ Grinder's Swing" that featured Jimmy Smith and Kenny Burrell. He gained early experience playing with R&B show bands in the Boston area. But after working with some organ groups, Basile was with Red Norvo for three months, which led him toward jazz. He attended Berklee and graduated from the New England Conservatory of Music in 1979.

Basile moved to New York in 1980. "I remember a tour with the Great Basie 8, a group that included Red Mitchell and Sweets Edison. I was playing the part of Freddie Green, and the combination of the music and the hang was unforgettable." Basile became well known as an accompanist, working with such singers as Peggy Lee, Sylvia Syms, Rosemary Clooney, Mark Murphy, and Tony Bennett. He also worked in instrumental settings with clarinetist Brad Terry (1985–90), John Abercrombie, George Mraz and Tom Harrell. "For me the highlights have been getting to know and play duos with Jim Hall, Michael Brecker and Red Mitchell."

And in a second career, John Basile is in the field of medical imaging as an MRI technologist and educator.

**Recommended CDs:** John Basile has yet to record an unworthy album. He can be heard in excellent form on his *Very Early* (Sea Breeze 2024), *Quiet Passage* (Pro Jazz 627), *Sunnyside Up* (Pro Jazz 641), *John Basile/Brad Terry Duo* (Music Masters 51244), *For All Time* (Philology 214W103) and *The Desmond Project* (Chesky 165). For his own Underhill Jazz label, Basile recorded *It Was A Very Good Year* (Underhill Jazz 001), *Animations* (Underhill Jazz 002), *Time Will Reveal* (Underhill Jazz 003), and *No Apologies* (Stringtime Jazz 001), which features the guitarist in a soulful trio with organist Pat Bianchi and drummer Carmen Intorre. His most recent

recording is a set of unaccompanied guitar solos, *Amplitudes* (Stringtime Jazz 002).

**Website:** www.johnbasile.net

## Billy Bauer
(William Henry Bauer)
b. November 14, 1915, New York, NY; d. June 17, 2005, Melville, NY

One of the most promising guitarists of the bebop era, Billy Bauer was flexible enough to fit in perfectly with both Woody Herman's First Herd and Lennie Tristano. Bauer, who first played in public in 1928, started out on banjo before switching permanently to the guitar in the early 1930s. He gained experience working with the big bands of Jerry Wald, Carl Hoff (with whom he made his recording debut in 1941), Dick Stabile and Abe Lyman. Bauer joined the Woody Herman Orchestra in 1944 and stayed for two years. During that period, he proved to be both an expert rhythm guitarist and an important early electric guitar soloist with Herman's First Herd. While influenced by Charlie Christian, Bauer had a forward-looking style and was very open to the innovations of bebop.

After working with Benny Goodman and Jack Teagarden, during 1946–49 Bauer was associated with pianist Lennie Tristano, playing and recording with Tristano's drumless trio and with the famed sextet that also featured altoist Lee Konitz and tenor-saxophonist Warne Marsh. Bauer's cool tone and ability to play long melodic lines was a perfect match with Tristano, as was his ability to improvise freely, which can be heard on the first two recorded jazz free improvisations, "Intuition" and "Digression." Due to those recordings, he could very loosely be considered the first avant-garde jazz guitarist. He became a major influence on the cool jazz guitarists to follow.

In the 1950s, Bauer was increasingly employed by the studios, being a member of the staff at ABC. He won both the *Downbeat* and *Metronome* polls as best jazz guitarist during 1949–53 and recorded with such all-stars as Konitz (with whom he cut "Duet For Saxophone And Guitar"), the J.J. Johnson–Kai Winding quintet, trumpeter Cootie Williams, tenor-saxophonist Charlie Ventura, Billie Holiday, Stan Getz, pianist Tony Aless, Benny Goodman (with whom he played in Brussels in 1958), Dinah Washington, Coleman Hawkins, and cornetist Bobby Hackett.

After running his own jazz club on Long Island for a few years in the early 1960s, Bauer mostly worked as an educator, organizing and teaching at the Billy Bauer Guitar School for over 35 years and publishing guitar instructional books. A serious ear infection slowed down his playing schedule quite a bit after 1975. His autobiography, *Sideman*, was published in 1997.

**Recommended CDs:** *Let's Have A Session* (Fresh Sound 516) has Billy Bauer's only two albums as a leader. Actually, the 1953 session (*Let's Have A Session*) is a "music minus one" album of limited interest, with Bauer and a rhythm section leaving lots of space for unheard beginning musicians. The second album, *Plectrist* from 1956, is a conventional quartet session in which Bauer gets to stretch out a bit. *Anthology* (Interplay 8603) has some private recordings, including a trio date from 1969, and unaccompanied solos from 1959–60 and 1969. In addition, Bauer is featured occasionally with Woody Herman on the double-CD *Blowin' Up A Storm: The Columbia Years 1945–47* (Sony 65646); with Lennie Tristano on *Complete Lennie Tristano On Keynote* (Mercury 830921), *Intuition* (Blue Note 52771), which has the most vital Bauer recordings with Tristano along with an unrelated set by Warne Marsh, *Wow* (Orchard 7946) and *Live At Birdland* (Orchard 7939); and with Lee Konitz on *Subconscious Lee* (Original Jazz Classics 186) and *Lee Konitz With Warne Marsh* (Koch 8502).

## Billy Bean
b. December 26, 1933, Philadelphia, PA; d. February 6, 2012, Philadelphia, PA

A superior bop-oriented guitarist who was most active in jazz for a few years on the West Coast, Billy Bean was under-recorded throughout his career but highly respected by his fellow musicians. Bean's parents played music (his mother was a pianist and his father a guitarist), and his sister worked as a singer. Bean began playing the guitar when he was 12. After moving to New York in the mid-1950s, he worked with Charlie Ventura and Red Callender, making recordings with both. Relocating to Los Angeles in 1958, Bean worked with Bud Shank, John Pisano, Hal Gaylor, Paul Horn and Buddy Collette. In the early 1960s, he recorded and toured with Herbie Mann.

After working in the studios, Bean eventually moved back to Philadelphia, retiring in the 1980s. Today, Billy Bean is primarily remembered by guitarists, including Pat Martino and Larry Coryell, both of whom consider him an early influence. He is well worth discovering.

**Recommended CDs:** *Makin' It Again* (String Jazz 1003) teams Bean with John Pisano, while *West Coast Sessions* (String Jazz 1006) has Bean joined by Pisano and John Budimir. *On The Trio Rediscovered* (String Jazz 1007), he co-leads a trio with Walter Norris on piano and Hal Gaylor on bass and cello. In addition, Billy Bean recorded as a featured sideman with Charlie Ventura, Red Callender, Buddy DeFranco and Herbie Mann. Throughout each of these sessions, the guitarist adds class and swing to the proceedings along with a clear tone and a melodic improvising style.

**LPs to Search For:** *Take Your Pick* (Decca 9212) has Bean and John Pisano both playing at their best.

## Gerry Beaudoin
b. August 6, 1954, Waltham, MA

A fine jazz and blues guitarist who enjoys interacting with other guitarists, Beaudoin is often heard at his best in swing-oriented settings. "I was ten or twelve years old and wanted to try to play guitar after listening to Chet Atkins and Johnny Cash. My dad had a wide taste in music and he would listen to country, Segovia, Satchmo and Basie. I had an older cousin Paul who took me to see Roomful of Blues with Duke Robillard when I was a sophomore in high school. I got blown away by Duke and the horns. Little did I realize that I would spend a good portion of my career performing and recording with Duke and some of the guys in the band." Beaudoin had his first gigs when he was 15, playing in a country group and also in an Italian wedding band. He worked in rock and blues bands throughout high school, sometimes playing electric bass.

Beaudoin attended Berklee (1972–77) and remembers meeting Bucky Pizzarelli in 1973. "I wandered into a club called PS 77, and Bucky and his seven-string just amazed me. I realized that I wanted to play like that. One night he let me sit in and I was in heaven. We have been good friends over the years and played on gigs and recordings together." In the early 1980s, Beaudoin worked with Ronnie Earl and Roomful of Blues, getting to play regularly with both Eddie "Cleanhead" Vinson and Jay McShann.

Other important associations have been drummer Alan Dawson, who played in Beaudoin's Boston Jazz Ensemble; altoist Fred Lipsius; clarinetist Dick Johnson; and mandolinist David Grisman, with whom he recorded in 1992 (*Minor Swing*). After meeting rock guitarist Jay Geils in 1992, they sat in with each other's groups and, in 1997, formed the New Guitar Summit with Duke Robillard. "When we first started playing together, Jay got me to reach back to the roots (Christian, Eddie Lang, and Louis Armstrong) and play simpler and with more finesse but still be myself." The group, with Howard Alden sometimes in Robillard's place, has continued on a part-time basis to the present time.

Gerry Beaudoin, who has been an adjunct professor of music at Quincy College since 2000, currently plays with Jay Geils in an acoustic quintet called Kings of Strings; leads the Angel Street Band; has brought back the Boston Jazz Ensemble, which features his writing for four horns; and performs frequently in the Boston area in a guitar duo with Teddy Lavash and with a quartet that has his son Gerard Beaudoin on vibes. "I hope my music touches people and adds a bit of beauty to their lives."

**Recommended CDs:** *Minor Swing* (North Star Music 47) features Dave Grisman. *A Sentimental Christmas* (North Star Music 53) has Beaudoin playing Christmas music with the Boston Jazz Ensemble, while the same group also plays standards on *In A Sentimental Mood* (North Star 39) and *Sentimental Over You* (North Star Music 49). Bucky Pizzarelli, David Grisman and Duke Robillard are strong assets to Beaudoin's swinging *Just Among Friends* (Linn 5002). The New Guitar Summit provides plenty of musical excitement on *Retrospective* (Q&W Music 1002) and *Shivers* (Stony Plain 1328).

## Joe Beck

b. July 29, 1945, Philadelphia, PA; d. July 22, 2008, Woodbury, CT

A brilliant guitarist whose mastery of electronics and invention of the alto guitar resulted in an original style and sound even when playing standards, Joe Beck had an episodic career filled with high points. Beck was born in Philadelphia and raised in New Jersey and the San Francisco Bay area. At five or six, he discovered a banjo in the attic of his family's house and enjoyed fooling around with it. But a year later, after hearing Andrés Segovia on the radio, he decided that playing guitar was what he really wanted to do, and he persuaded his parents to get him an instrument. He had just six guitar lessons and was otherwise self-taught.

Joe Beck started playing professionally at 14. After graduating from high school, he worked at Chuck's Compository in New York for 18 months with a trio that had bassist Don Payne and several pianists, including Don Friedman. It proved to be the perfect place for the young guitarist to be discovered. Soon, he was making a lot of money doing commercials for television and radio, not only playing guitar but also working as a composer, arranger and conductor while he was still a teenager. He also worked and recorded with Gil Evans. In 1967, Beck received a phone call from Miles Davis, who asked him to rehearse with his quintet. While Davis had no idea how he wanted to use the guitarist, and while the resulting recordings (issued decades later as "Circle In The Round" and "Water In The Pond") were considered unsuccessful at the time, it was Miles' first tentative steps toward creating a new fusion music.

Under constant pressure and feeling a bit inadequate musically for all of the opportunities he was receiving, Beck dropped out of music during 1968–70, buying a dairy farm. In 1971, he returned, and four years later he recorded a popular album with David Sanborn called *Beck And Sanborn*. He had a very busy musical life during the 1970s and '80s, playing a countless number of studio sessions and recording jazz whenever the opportunity arose. Beck worked and/or recorded with Esther Phillips, Herbie Hancock, Buddy Rich, Paul Desmond, Maynard Ferguson, Woody Herman, Stan Getz, Larry Coryell, Blue Mitchell, Gene Ammons, Antonio Carlos Jobim, Houston Person, Roger Kellaway, Joe Farrell, Gato Barbieri, Michael Brecker, Frank Sinatra, and even James Brown and Paul Simon, among many others.

A second period as a dairy farmer (1989–91) was followed by Beck's decision to cut back on the studio work, put together a band, and play jazz much more often. In his later years, he was often heard dueting with alto flutist Ali Ryerson. Beck invented the alto guitar, an instrument that allowed him to be a one-man band when he wanted, creating all types of sounds through the guitar. His last project was a duet album with singer Laura Theodore. Joe Beck passed away from lung cancer a week before his 63rd birthday.

**Recommended CDs:** *Beck And Sanborn* (Mosaic Contemporary 5014) is a pretty good mid-1970s crossover album. *Empathy* (Jazz Heritage) has Beck and bassist Red Mitchell stretching out for 90 minutes in 1980 on 11 jazz standards and one original. *Joe Beck & Friends* (DMP 446) teams Beck with Michael Brecker in 1984. Among Beck's other straight-ahead jazz albums are *Relaxin'* (DMP 444), *Just Friends* (Whaling City Sound 18) and *Trio* (Whaling City Sound 37), while *Back To Beck* (DMP 464), *The Journey* (DMP 481) and *Finger Painting* (Wavetone 8634) find him straddling post-bop jazz and fusion with style and passion. Joe Beck and Ali Ryerson always made for a perfect team, as can be heard on *Alto* (DMP 521) and *Django* (DMP 20013). Among the guitarist's most rewarding special projects of his later years are a collaboration with Jimmy Bruno on *Polarity* (Concord 4888), fireworks shared with John Abercrombie on *Coincidence* (Whaling City Sound 40), and Beck's final recording, a very inventive tribute to Peggy Lee and Dave Barbour with singer Laura Theodore, *Golden Earrings* (Whaling City Sound 49).

# David Becker

*b. October 20, 1961, Cincinnati, OH*

David Becker first gained recognition as a top fusion/contemporary jazz guitarist and the leader of the David Becker Tribune. Since relocating to Europe, he has continued growing in versatility and creativity without ever losing his fire. After a stint on drums, at 12 he started studying trumpet. An early influence was his junior high school music teacher Ted Dechter, who had the school band playing Maynard Ferguson arrangements and featured Becker as a soloist at concerts with the school's choir. At 15, he took up the guitar. "At first, rock and roll pulled me there, but within a short time I gravitated back to jazz, which I had played on the trumpet. It was hearing Grant Green on the radio when I was 16 that made me want to play jazz guitar."

Becker played gigs as a teenager, attended the Guitar Institute of Technology in 1980, and was inspired by Joe Diorio and Pat Martino. "When I was a student at G.I.T., I knew exactly what I wanted to do: compose my own tunes and play in a trio with my brother Bruce on drums." The Dave Becker Tribune, with several players on electric bass (including Jim Donica, Bob Mair and, later on, Tom Lilly), was founded in the early 1980s and, during 1986–91, recorded two albums apiece for MCA and Blue Moon. "During that time, I was performing all over the US and Europe with the DBT. I kind of skipped the sideman routine, although I took every opportunity to sit in with other musicians." Best known as a fiery and creative electric guitarist, Becker also played acoustic guitar, sometimes unaccompanied, whenever he had the chance.

The Becker brothers moved to Europe in 1992, and although their profile in the US has been low, the Dave Becker Tribune has been quite active, recording three CDs during 2001–08 and touring regularly, traveling over 60,000 miles in the past year. In addition, Becker recorded the solo *Euroland* and a duet set with Joe Diorio, *The Color Of Sound*.

"I have always considered my quest in music to be exploring the jazz guitar trio format with the borders wide open. Too many musicians today stay in a very narrow scope of a certain style and try to define it by giving it a certain name and never really going beyond that. Jazz is and has always been about taking the traditions that have been set and trying to find new and different ways to address it. Each time you begin to play or compose, it is like a new world is opening up. The challenges that come with it make it so enjoyable."

**Recommended CDs:** The four early recordings by the David Becker Tribune, *Long Peter Madsen* (MCA 5865), *Siberian Express* (MCA 42159), *Third*

*Time Around* (Blue Moon 79155) and *In Motion* (Blue Moon 79167), contain many fine examples of Becker's guitar playing. The music was called "contemporary jazz" at the time, having playing reminiscent of Pat Metheny and Larry Carlton but also including explorations of such pieces as "Days Of Wine And Roses," John Coltrane's "Central Park West" and McCoy Tyner's "Passion Dance" along with the originals. The obscure *Nevsky Prospekt* (Pinorrekk 5019) was the group's first European recording and was followed by 2001's *Germerica* (Silverline 81044). *Where's Henning?* (Paras 1140), with Tom Lilly on bass, features five standards and seven originals with the group moving toward postbop improvising. *Euroland* (Cool Springs 2303) has Becker as the only performer, while *The Colour Of Sound* (Acoustic Music 31912622) teams the guitarist with his former teacher Joe Diorio. 2008's *Leaving Argentina* (Acoustic Music 31913852), with Bruce's older brother Ed Becker on bass, has a variety of originals that reflect the Tribune's visits to 17 countries and is full of colorful music.

**Website:** www.davidbeckertribune.com

# Roni Ben-Hur

*b. July 9, 1962, Dimona, Israel*

A masterful bop-based guitarist from Israel, Roni Ben-Hur adapted quickly to the American jazz scene after moving to the US in 1985. He started playing guitar when he was 11 and discovered jazz through a friend's records in high school. "In Israel I had some small jazz gigs in the clubs. I joined a band that played weddings and bar mitzvahs for a couple of years. That helped me save money to pay my way to come to New York. It was mostly a drag of a gig, but the interesting part was that we had to play a lot of ethnic music, since the population in Israel at that time was mostly immigrants."

After moving to New York City in 1985, Ben-Hur often attended Barry Harris' Jazz Cultural Theater during the next two years, learning from older musicians. He continued studying privately with Harris during 1987–90 and became part of the pianist's group. "We performed in many festivals and had a yearly engagement at Birdland." Among his other significant associations have been Chris Anderson (1991–99), Walter Booker, Leroy Williams, Earl May, Santi Debriano, Nilson Matta, Cecil Payne, Rufus Reid, Gene Bertoncini, Clark Terry, Jimmy Heath, Slide Hampton, Charles McPherson and Etta Jones. He is also an author (*Talk Jazz Guitar*) and a jazz educator, directing the jazz program at Kaufman Center's Lucy Moses School since 1994.

Roni Ben-Hur, who is married to singer Amy London, mostly leads his own groups these days. "I hope that when people listen to my music, they hear that it is not just jazz but rather a bridge between cultures using the discipline of jazz."

**Recommended CDs:** *Backyard* (TCB 95902) from 1995 has Roni Ben-Hur joined by the Barry Harris Trio. Other rewarding sets include *Sofia's Butterfly* (TCB 98802); *Anna's Dance* (Reservoir 167); *Signature* (Reservoir 181) with John Hicks; *Keepin' It Open* (Motéma 10) with a sextet; *Fortuna* (Motéma 28); *Mojave* (Motéma 64); *Our Thing* (Motéma 76), which features Brazilian and Panamanian music in a jazz context; and a collaboration with Gene Bertoncini, *Smile* (Motéma 18).

**Website:** www.ronibenhur.com

# George Benson
*b. March 22, 1943, Pittsburgh, PA*

In the mid-1960s, George Benson emerged as one of the top new guitarists in jazz. As with Nat King Cole, Benson broke through to a huge non-jazz audience when he had an unexpected vocal hit. Although

he still plays guitar and is capable of greatness at a moment's notice, it has literally been decades since he has challenged himself as an instrumentalist.

Few know that George Benson's very first recordings, four numbers made in 1954 when he was 11, were made as a singer. By then, he had already been a performer for three years. He was taught the guitar by his stepfather and started playing in nightclubs when he was eight, although no recordings exist to show how he sounded as a child in 1951.

Benson played rock for a period as teenager, but by the time he joined organist Jack McDuff's band for a two-year stint in 1962, his main influences were Charlie Christian and, to a lesser extent, Wes Montgomery. Benson earned a strong reputation while with McDuff, sounding particularly strong at burning tempos. He competed well with Montgomery and Grant Green during that era. He first recorded an album as a leader in 1964, started his solo career the following year, and made two notable albums for Columbia (*It's Uptown* and *The George Benson Cookbook*) with a quartet that also featured baritonist Ronnie Cuber and organist Lonnie Smith. While these include a few short vocals, the sets are most notable for their fiery instrumentals.

Benson recorded one song with Miles Davis in 1967 (which is on *Miles In The Sky*), when the trumpeter was toying with the idea of adding a guitarist. Benson recorded mostly commercial albums of his own for Verve and A&M, where he was being groomed as Wes Montgomery's successor, but those record sales never approached that of Montgomery. He was at the height of his guitar playing during his CTI recordings of 1971–76, where Benson's distinctive tone, brilliant technique, versatility and bluesy style fit in perfectly next to Freddie Hubbard, Stanley Turrentine, Hubert Laws, the young Earl Klugh (whom he helped introduce), and Joe Farrell.

On *Breezin'*, his first album for Warner Brothers, Benson only took one vocal, but it ended up being a number-one hit: "This Masquerade." His trademark of singing in unison with his guitar, along with his warm voice on that selection, permanently changed his career, transforming him from a major jazz guitarist into a light R&B singer who also played occasional guitar. He had other hits with "On Broadway" and "Give Me The Night."

While George Benson teamed up in different projects with McCoy Tyner and the Count Basie band, most of his recordings (including a dull matchup with Al Jarreau in 2006 called *Givin' It Up*) are nearly as predictable as his live shows. One can certainly understand Benson's desire to be world-famous rather than a starving artist in the jazz world, but it has now been around 35 years since "This Masquerade" and he is still mostly just using his guitar as a tease. Even at 67, he has the potential to once again be one of the world's greatest guitarists, but George Benson apparently lacks the desire to upset the gravy train, even for a single album. One waits in vain for the entertaining but predictable performer to perform something that he did not play better 30 years ago.

**Recommended CDs:** *The New Boss Guitar Of George Benson* (Original Jazz Classics 461) teams Benson with the Jack McDuff band in 1964, when the guitarist was 21. George Benson's *It's Uptown* (Columbia/Legacy 66052) and *The George Benson Cookbook* (Columbia/Legacy 66054) are enthusiastic and frequently exciting sets of hard bop and soul jazz. *The Shape Of Things To Come* (A&M 6995) is the best of Benson's A&M albums, although it is far from the revolutionary statement one would expect from its title. The great Benson CTI albums are *Beyond The Blue Horizon* (Mosaic Contemporary 5010), *White Rabbit* (Columbia 40685), *Body Talk* (Columbia 45222), *Bad Benson* (Sony 724211), *Good King Bad* (Mosaic Contemporary 5003) and *In Concert: Carnegie Hall* (Columbia 44167). From that point on, only a few George Benson recordings are of strong interest for his guitar playing. Those include *Breezin'* (Warner Archives 76713); *Tenderly* (Warner Bros. 25907), which co-stars McCoy Tyner; *Big Boss*

*Band* (Warner Bros. 26295) with the Count Basie ghost orchestra; and the easy-listening *Guitar Man* (Concord 33099), which is pleasing if lacking in adventure. *Live* (Verve 84353) has a George Benson concert from 2000 that could easily have taken place in 2010 or 1980.

**Website:** www.georgebenson.com

## Gonzalo Bergara
*b. September 9, 1980, Buenos Aires, Argentina*

Although he did not start out with such a goal, Gonzalo Bergara has in recent years become a superior guitarist in the gypsy jazz movement, paying tribute to Django Reinhardt while moving the music ahead. Born in Buenos Aires, he remembers, "When I was 11, I was a huge fan of Slash from Guns N' Roses and I wanted to be like him. Along with my first guitar, my uncle gave me a tape of Oscar Alemán, but it wasn't until I saw Woody Allen's *Sweet And Lowdown* that I got really serious about jazz." Before that, he had a power trio when he was 16, playing Hendrix-style rock and blues. The following year, his trio was featured regularly on national television.

After discovering jazz and moving to the United States in 2000, he performed with Tim Hauser (of the Manhattan Transfer), Dan Hicks and the Hot Licks, and Howard Alden. During 2005–08, Bergara was a member of the John Jorgenson Quintet, touring the world extensively while playing a modern version of gypsy jazz. At the same time, he put together his own quartet in Los Angeles, playing locally and at the Sweet and Hot Music Festival. In 2010, his group featured his acoustic guitar, rhythm guitarist Jeffrey Radaich, Rob Hardt on clarinet and tenor, and bassist Brian Netzley; a later version featured the classical violinist Leah Zeger. Rather than just playing the usual swing tunes, the group also includes the guitarist's originals. Due to the instrumentation and their openness to bop and more modern styles, the Gonzalo Bergara Quartet sometimes recalls Django's mid-to-late-1940s groups.

**Recommended CDs:** Thus far Gonzolo Bergara just has one CD as a leader, the self-produced *Porteña Soledad* (available from his website), but more are upcoming, and he has great potential.

**Website:** www.gonzalobergara.com

## Peter Bernstein
*b. September 3, 1967, New York, NY*

A forward-looking bop-oriented guitarist, Peter Bernstein has been a consistent force in the jazz scene for the past 20 years. Bernstein was a student at the New School in New York when he was asked by Jim Hall to participate in an all-star concert at the 1990 JVC Jazz Festival, an event featuring several guitarists (including Pat Metheny and John Scofield) and released as a CD by Music Masters, *Live At Town Hall Vol. 2*. Soon after the concert, Bernstein became a regular member of Lou Donaldson's group, a gig that lasted throughout much of the 1990s and resulted in several recordings.

Since then, Bernstein has appeared on over 60 recordings, led quite a few of his own, and worked with Jimmy Cobb, Michael Hashim, Larry Goldings, Dr. Lonnie Smith, Melvin Rhyne, Jesse Davis, Geoff Keezer, Joshua Redman, Diana Krall, Nicholas Payton, Lee Konitz, Tom Harrell, Eric Alexander, Walt Weiskopf, Brian Lynch, Hendrik Meurkens, Kevin Mahogany, Grant Stewart, Harry Allen, Etta Jones, Alvin Queen, and David "Fathead" Newman. Peter Bernstein always sounds in fine form, keeping jazz's modern mainstream vital and swinging.

**Recommended CDs:** Since 1992, Peter Bernstein has led eight CDs: *Somethin's Burnin'* (Criss Cross 1079), *Signs Of Life* (Criss Cross 1095), *Brain Dance* (Criss Cross 1130), *Earth Tones* (Criss Cross 1151), *Heart's Content* (Criss Cross 1233), *Stranger In Paradise* (Tokuma 35324), *Monk* (Xanadu 500), and *Live At Smalls* (Smalls Live 004); the latter teams him with organist Larry Goldings and drummer Bill Stewart. Four of his CDs also feature pianist Brad Mehldau.

**Website:** www.peterbernsteinmusic.com

## Gene Bertoncini
*b. April 6, 1937, New York, NY*

Gene Bertoncini is best known for his lyrical, graceful and tastefully melodic playing on the nylon-stringed acoustic guitar. Bertoncini started playing guitar when he was nine, and seven years later he was working as a professional, performing on a children's television show. He was initially inspired to play jazz after hearing recordings and radio broadcasts by Benny Goodman. Later inspirations include Chuck Wayne, Johnny Smith, Tal Farlow and Barney Kessel. Wayne and Smith were among his teachers.

Bertoncini earned a degree in architecture from Notre Dame, although he also played guitar with their concert band and clarinet in Notre Dame's marching band. After serving in the Marines, he moved to Chicago, where he worked in local clubs and with Carmen McRae. Relocating to New York, Bertoncini worked with Mike Mainieri and through Mainieri became a member of a Buddy Rich combo that also featured Sam Most.

After Chuck Wayne played him Julian Bream's recording of Ravel's "Pavane," Bertoncini started seriously practicing classical guitar, and became one of those responsible for adding the instrument to jazz. A friend of João Gilberto, who used to borrow his guitar, Bertoncini learned bossa nova directly from Gilberto. He played bossa nova guitar on an Ahmad Jamal big band album (*Macanundo*) in 1963, became a studio musician, was in the big bands on *The Merv Griffin Show* and Johnny Carson's *Tonight Show*, appeared on many of Burt Bacharach's most famous recordings, and, during the next 20 years, worked with Benny Goodman, Wayne Shorter, Clark Terry, Hubert Laws, the Paul Winter Consort, Nancy Wilson, Paul Desmond, Tony Bennett, Lena Horne, Lalo Schifrin, Michel Legrand, and Charles McPherson.

Gene Bertoncini, who has had a long-time duo with bassist Michael Moore, played Sunday and Monday evenings at the Bistro La Madeleine in New York City for 18 years. He teaches at the Eastman School of Music and William Paterson University.

**Recommended CDs:** Gene Bertoncini's mostly unaccompanied solo recordings include *Acoustic Romance* (Concord 155); *Jobim: Someone To Light Up My Life* (Chiaroscuro 343), which includes two percussionists; the trio set *Gene Bertoncini: Live* (Chiaroscuro 354); *Body And Soul* (Orchard 4320); *Quiet Now* (Ambient 5); and *Concerti* (Ambient 007), which matches his acoustic guitar with a string quintet. Bertoncini has also recorded five duet albums with Michael Moore, three of which came out on CDs: *O Grande Amor* (Stash 258), *Strollin'* (Stash 272), and *Two In Time* (Chiaroscuro 308). In addition, he has recorded duet sets with guitarists Jack Wilkins (*Just The Two Of Us*—Chiaroscuro 362), Frank Vignola (*Meeting Of The Grooves*—Azica 72220), and Roni Ben-Hur (*Smile*—Motéma 18).

**LPs to Search For:** Bertoncini's first two duet albums with Michael Moore, *Bridges* (MPS) and *Close Ties* (Omnisound), have not yet appeared on CD.

**Website:** www.genebertoncini.com

## Skeeter Best
(Clifton Best)
b. November 20, 1914, Kinston, NC; d. May 27, 1985, New York, NY

Skeeter Best was both an excellent rhythm guitarist and a fine soloist, equally at home in swing and bop settings. Best started playing professionally in Philadelphia in 1935, working with Slim Marshall. He was with Erskine Hawkins for a few months in 1939 (appearing on two record dates) and was a member of Earl Hines' big band during part of 1941–42, recording four selections. Best served in the Navy during World War II. After his discharge, he worked with Lucky Millinder's orchestra before spending the 1950s playing in small groups. He toured Asia with Oscar Pettiford during part of 1951–52, worked with Nellie Lutcher, led his own trio, and made recordings with the Modern Jazz Sextet (featuring Dizzy Gillespie and Sonny Stitt), Etta Jones (*Don't Go To Strangers*), Mercer Ellington, Milt Hinton, Osie Johnson, Paul Quinichette, Jimmy Rushing, Sir Charles Thompson, Milt Buckner, Ellis Larkins, Ike Quebec, Lionel Hampton, Aretha Franklin, Mel Powell, Paul Quinichette, John Lewis, Howard McGhee, and in the late 1970s again with Earl Hines. Probably his best showcase was a trio date with tenor-saxophonist Lucky Thompson and bassist Oscar Pettiford that is quite exciting.

Skeeter Best spent his later years teaching in New York City before his death in 1985 at the age of 70.

**Recommended CDs:** Skeeter Best did not lead any record dates of his own. Lucky Thompson's *Tricotism* (GRP 135) has the trios with Oscar Pettiford. *Modern Jazz Sextet* (Verve 559834) finds the guitarist faring quite well in an all-star bebop group with Dizzy Gillespie, Sonny Stitt, John Lewis, Percy Heath and Charlie Persip. He is also in excellent form with Ray Charles (who doubles on alto) and Milt Jackson on an album called *Soul Brothers* and reissued as half of *Soul Brothers/Soul Meeting* (Rhino 81951).

## Ed Bickert
b. November 29, 1932, Hochfeld, Manitoba, Canada

Ed Bickert, one of Canada's best-known jazz guitarists, was always a very tasteful bop-based player. Bickert grew up in Vernon, British Columbia. His mother was an amateur pianist, and his father played violin. He often joined his parents to play at country dances in the 1940s. After moving to Toronto in 1952, he survived a period of struggle and became one of the top local musicians, evolving into a studio musician who played jazz on the side. Bickert was associated with Moe Koffman, the Phil Nimmons Nine and especially Rob McConnell. He was a member of Rob McConnell's Boss Brass throughout its entire existence.

Bickert became better known in the United States when he worked and recorded with the Paul Desmond Quartet during 1974–75, filling in the spot formerly occupied by Jim Hall (who recommended him to Desmond). Bickert also worked and recorded with Oscar Peterson (1980), Rosemary Clooney, Ken Peplowski, Ernestine Anderson, Ruby Braff and Benny Carter, in addition to recording some albums of his own for Concord and Sackville. His chordal style and relaxed solos earned him universal respect.

Ed Bickert, who made a comeback from a fall in the mid-1990s that temporarily damaged his arms, retired around the time that he turned 70.

**Recommended CDs:** *At The Garden Party* (Sackville 4005) matches Bickert with bassist Don Thompson and sometimes drummer Terry Clarke. The three Canadians often worked together through the years. *Mutual Street* (Jazz Alliance 10003) is a fun set of duets with valve trombonist Rob McConnell. Other worthy Bickert recordings include *I Wished On The Moon* (Concord 4284), *Third Floor Richard* (Concord 4380), *This Is New* (Concord 4414) with Lorne Lofsky, and *Out Of The Past* (Sackville 2065). He is also well featured on *The Paul Desmond Quartet Live* (A&M 543501) and *Pure Desmond* (CTI 5127882).

**LPs to Search For:** In 1975, Bickert had his first opportunity to lead his own record date, a trio outing titled *Ed Bickert* (PM 010). *At Toronto's Bourbon Street* (Concord 216) teams him with Scott Hamilton and Warren Vaché for one of his most heated sets. Also well overdue to be reissued are *Bye Bye Baby* (Concord 232), with pianist Dave McKenna, and *Dance To The Lady* (Sackville 4010).

## Jack Bland
*b. May 8, 1899, Sedalia, MI; d. August 1968, Van Nuys, CA*

A solid rhythm guitarist and banjoist, Jack Bland stuck to playing chords and was never considered a soloist, although he was a key part of the popular 1920s novelty group the Mound City Blue Blowers.

In 1923, Red McKenzie was a bellhop and a part-time singer in St. Louis who, with a comb and tissue paper, found his own musical voice. He used to jam for the fun of it with Larry Slavin, who played a more conventional kazoo. When they began teaming up with Bland, an up-and-coming banjoist, they gained the attention of some of the musicians from Gene Rodemich's orchestra. Rodemich took the trio to Chicago in early 1924, they recorded "Arkansas Blues" and "Blue Blues," and to everyone's surprise, the record was a big hit, selling a million copies.

The Mound City Blue Blowers moved to New York, added Eddie Lang on guitar, and recorded regularly for a year, also making records as Red McKenzie's Candy Kids. The unique group performed in London and, later in the decade, appeared in a few short films, including *The Opry House*. By then, Lang and Slavin had departed, Bland had switched to guitar, and the band also included Eddie Condon

on second guitar and Josh Billings playing rhythms on a suitcase.

Bland recorded with McKenzie as late as 1931, including sessions that had Coleman Hawkins, Jack Teagarden, Glenn Miller, Muggsy Spanier and Jimmy Dorsey in the lineup. In 1932, Bland appeared on three exciting record dates led by singer Billy Banks that included Henry Red Allen, Pee Wee Russell and, on the third session, Fats Waller and Eddie Condon. That year, he also led a similar band, Jack Bland and his Rhythmakers, for a session that included Allen, Russell, Condon and Tommy Dorsey, highlighted by hot versions of "Who Stole The Lock On The Hen House Door," "A Shine On Your Shoes" and "Someone Stole Gabriel's Horn."

Although he kept great company on the record dates, providing a solid rhythm, Jack Bland drifted into obscurity during the remainder of the 1930s. He appeared on an all-star record date led by drummer George Wettling in 1940, worked in the '40s at Jimmy Ryan's on 52nd Street, recorded as a sideman on a few dates for the Commodore label (including with Muggsy Spanier), played with Art Hodes during 1942–44, and led his own undocumented group during 1944–50. But in the 1950s, Bland stopped playing altogether, living in Los Angeles and working as a cab driver up until the time of his death in 1968.

**Recommended CDs:** Red McKenzie's *Vol. 1* (Sensation 29) and *Vol. 2* (Sensation 30) contain all of Jack Bland's recordings with the Mound City Blue Blowers, playing the straight man behind some very colorful (and at times crazy) music.

## Pascal Bokar
*(Pascal Bokar Thiam)*
*b. March 22, 1962, Paris, France*

An inventive guitarist, Pascal Bokar combines the African rhythms from his musical heritage with jazz to create his own fresh music.

Although born in France, he grew up in Segou, Mali, and Dakar, Senegal. "I was 12 years old when I started playing guitar in my middle school band in Dakar. My father, who loved jazz, played records all the time at the house (including the MJQ and Sonny Rollins), but my first jazz shock was when I heard guitarist Barney Kessel. I realized then that I needed to expand my musical vocabulary because I was listening to a lot of Jimi Hendrix and Muddy Waters and I had no idea how Barney Kessel was playing all of those beautiful phrases with just a guitar—no pedals or extra equipment. I subsequently discovered Wes Montgomery, Joe Pass, Kenny Burrell, Pat Martino, and George Benson in addition to the West African guitarists and kora masters Sekou Diabaté,

Franco and Soundioulou Cissokho, plus the music of Mali. I realized the link of the musical vocabulary and how close bebop was to traditional West African improvisational languages born out of the ngoni (ancestor of the banjo), kora (West African harp), and the balafon (ancestor of the xylophone)."

Bokar first played guitar in Dakar with a local band called Awkaba, accompanying West African stars from television shows. In 1980, he attended the National Conservatory of Nice, France, studying jazz and classical music. The following year, he was discovered by tenor-saxophonist Barney Wilen, and for a couple of years, they appeared at many European festivals. "Working with him made me realize that I could do this for a living and that I could contribute meaningfully." In 1983, Bokar applied to Berklee and moved to the United States. While at Berklee, Pascal played with the Back Bay Brass Orchestra and was briefly with Roy Haynes.

In 1984, the guitarist had the opportunity to work with Dizzy Gillespie. "I wasn't with Dizzy long, but he was very interested in African music and African rhythms and how they fit in bebop. We had great conversations about the need to re-introduce African rhythms and textures into American popular music and jazz. The development of my guitar sound (balafonics) is an extension of these conversations."

Bokar worked several nights a week with drummer Donald "Duck" Bailey and had a stint with Donald Byrd. He earned a master's from Cambridge College in 1998 and a doctoral degree from the University of San Francisco in 2006, teaching jazz and world music and directing the jazz band at the latter. Since 2005, he has operated the Savanna Jazz Club, a San Francisco venue that features jazz six nights a week.

Pascal Bokar, who balances his playing and occasional vocalizing with teaching and running the club, hopes in the future "to continue integrating West African rhythms and textures into all aspects of American music. Thank God for masters Randy Weston, Hugh Masekela and Abdullah Ibrahim, who keep the torch alive."

**Recommended CDs:** Pascal Bokar's *Beyond The Blue Sky* (Accurate 6000), from 1995, mixes together his originals with standards, and African rhythms with American jazz. 1996's *Yone Bi* (privately issued) has a jazz quartet plus two African percussionists. The recent *Savanna Jazz Club* (Savanna 3000) has ten bop and swing standards plus two originals transformed into a very percussive and infectious new music. Pascal Bokar deserves to have his musical concepts documented much more frequently.

**Website:** www.pascalbokarthiam.com

## Paul Bollenback
*b. June 6, 1959, Hinsdale, IL*

A fine straight-ahead and post-bop guitarist, Paul Bollenback brings understanding and high musicianship to every session on which he appears. "When I was about seven, my dad bought me a nylon string guitar. I liked the Beatles and Carlos Santana. I took some lessons and learned basic chords, folk songs and spirituals." The youth spent three years with his family living in New Delhi, India. After returning to the US, he remembers, "At 14 or 15, a friend introduced me to the Mahavishnu Orchestra and then to Miles Davis' *Big Fun*. That led me to other electric groups like Return to Forever and 11th House." Bollenback gained early experience playing rock gigs and, at 15, had a five-piece band that played every weekend, mixing together covers of Allman Brothers songs, blues and originals. "When I was 17, I met friends who listened to Monk, Trane and Miles. That year, when someone gave me the album *Best Of Coltrane* as a gift, that sealed the deal."

Living in Washington, DC, by 1975, he credits bassist Ed Howard, pianist Lawrence Wheatley and bassist Keter Betts as important musicians who taught him from the bandstand. "There were also many other players in the DC area that I learned from. It was a great guitar town, and I subbed a lot for Steve Abshire, Paul Wingo and Rick Whitehead." He attended the University of Miami and privately took lessons from Dr. Asher Zlotnik in Baltimore during 1987–95.

In 1987, Bollenback made his recording debut on Gary Thomas' *Seventh Quadrant*. In 1990, he began a 16-year association with organist Joey DeFrancesco, appearing on 14 of his CDs. "He became my main mentor, showing me many things and helping to put my name out there as a player and composer." A resident of New York City since 1997, Bollenback has also worked with Stanley Turrentine, Joe Locke, Gary Bartz, Tim Garland, Jeff "Tain" Watts, Sandip Burman, and singer Chris McNulty.

After leading his own sessions for Challenge, in 2005 he formed the Elefant Dreams label with Chris McNulty. In recent times, Bollenback has worked as an educator; played with Steve Gadd, Jim Snidero, Gary Thomas, Carol Sloane and Joey DeFrancesco; toured with McNulty; and led his own trio with bassist Johannes Weidenmuller and drummer Ari Hoenig.

**Recommended CDs:** Each of Paul Bollenback's five Challenge CDs is well worth hearing. These include *Original Visions* (Challenge 70022); *Double Gemini* (Challenge 70046), which has the guitarist transforming pop tunes into soul jazz; *Soul Grooves* (Challenge 70064), which does the same thing to R&B and soul songs; the excellent trio set *Dreams* (Challenge 70082); and *Double Vision* (Challenge 75030). On his own label, *Brightness Of Being* (Elefant Dreams 4548) has unlikely material ranging from pop to classical mixed in with Bollenback's originals, all of it played creatively. Tim Garland, Gary Thomas and Chris McNulty (who sings wordlessly on four numbers) make strong contributions. *Invocation* (Elefant Dreams 4550) features melodic and swinging treatments of a few jazz standards and newer songs with McNulty and Randy Brecker helping out.

**Website:** www.paulbollenback.com

## Luiz Bonfá
*b. October 17, 1922, Rio de Janeiro, Brazil; d. January 12, 2001, Rio de Janeiro, Brazil*

One of the originators of bossa nova, Luiz Bonfá's writing for the landmark film *Black Orpheus* gave him fame. Originally self-taught on guitar, Bonfá studied with classical guitarist Isaias Savio from the age of 12. Working locally, Bonfá gradually gained a strong national reputation, particularly in 1947, when he was featured on Rádio Nacional, a significant showcase for new talent. Bonfá's variety of musical experiences included working with the vocal group the Quitandinha Serenaders in the late 1940s, writing music for singer Dick Farney in the 1950s, and touring the US with singer Mary Martin. Bonfá collaborated with Antonio Carlos Jobim and Vinicius de Moraes in writing music for the play *Orfeu Da Conceição*, which eventually became the film *Black Orpheus*. Bonfá composed "Samba De Orfeu" and "Manhã De Carnaval"; the latter became well known in the United States when it was outfitted with English lyrics as "A Day In The Life Of A Fool."

Luiz Bonfá's guitar style predated João Gilberto and featured a beautiful tone, melodic improvising, impressive technique that sometimes resulted in fiery solos, and a more extroverted style than Gilberto's that still managed to be thoughtful. Bonfá moved to the United States in the early 1960s, made a notable appearance at a famous November 1962 bossa nova concert at Carnegie Hall, and worked with Stan Getz, Quincy Jones, Frank Sinatra and George Benson, among others. Bonfá returned to Brazil in 1975, where he continued working locally, making his last album in 1997 (*Almost In Love*) with singer Ithamara Koorax.

**Recommended CDs:** Luiz Bonfá recorded prolifically throughout his career. A strong sampling includes *Solo In Rio 1959* (Smithsonian Folkways 40483), *Amor: The Fabulous Guitar Of Luiz Bonfá* (Collectables 6160), *O Violão E O Samba* (Blue Note 42102), *Composer Of Black Orpheus Plays And Sings Bossa Nova* (Verve 1188402), *Jazz Samba Encore* (Verve 11172) with Stan Getz, *Le Roi De La Bossa Nova* (Sunnyside 3037), *Braziliana* (Verve 1126502), *The Brazilian Scene* (Verve 1126602), *Introspection* (RCA 72492), *Bonfá Burrows Brazil* (Orchard 386), *Non-Stop To Brazil* (Chesky 29), and *The Bonfá Magic* (Fantasy 9202).

## Jean-Paul Bourelly
*b. November 23, 1960, Chicago, IL*

An always-stimulating guitarist, Jean-Paul Bourelly has easily crossed over the boundary lines between post-bop jazz, fusion, rock and avant-garde music throughout his career. Four years after a brief period playing an acoustic guitar when he was nine, Bourelly worked at his uncle's gas station one summer, saved up his money, and bought an electric guitar, inspired by Jimi Hendrix. "That same year, there was a radio station that I stumbled upon very late at night before going to bed. They were playing a bootleg Charlie Parker record, and it was only drums and sax blazing. The bass, I believe, was there but not audible. This made the music sound so mysterious and expansive to me that I thought, 'Wow, human beings are capable of this?'"

Bourelly began his career playing at local clubs in Chicago. He learned from jam sessions run by Von Freeman, worked with the Haitian band Chicago Express, and studied for one year with Bunky Green at Chicago State University.

After moving to New York in 1979, Bourelly worked with such notables as Muhal Richard Abrams, Roy Haynes, McCoy Tyner, Elvin Jones (1985–87), Olu Dara's Okra Orchestra (1983–86), Pharoah Sanders, Archie Shepp, Steve Coleman, Cassandra Wilson (for whom he produced a few albums), Marc Ribot, David Torn and Elliott Sharp. Bourelly had a bit part in the movie *The Cotton Club* and was with Miles Davis in 1988, appearing on the *Amandla* recording. He began to record as a leader (starting with 1987's *Jungle Cowboy*) and led his group the BluWave Bandits during 1989–95. He was also part of the Black Rock Coalition, working with Vernon Reid in the Reid/Bourelly Project and with such rock musicians as Robin Trower, Jack Bruce and Buddy Miles.

Bourelly moved to Europe in 1994. He founded the JPGotMangos label, led the Vibe Music Quartet and Trio, headed the power trio 3kings (2006–08), and has recently formed Citizen X (with vocalist and poet Sadiq Bey) and Blues Bandits (with singer Dean Bowman). As much an avant-rock player as a jazz improviser, Jean-Paul Bourelly's music is impossible to categorize accurately.

"I don't use the word 'jazz' as a way of defining my style because it doesn't describe enough. I have elements of my Haitian roots, West, East and North African rhythms, blues, and a heavy rocky feeling mixed with abstract sounds. My career was defined during a time when the industry had to put you in a category, but that category was always changing for me. They called my music blackadelic, new wave, no wave, free form funk, avantfunk, nu-blues, nu-jazz, rock and other things. I always took this as a great compliment that the titles changed, meaning my music was expressing a constant change. A big part of my development came when I moved to Europe. This allowed me to get away from the commercial influences and have my music expand even more."

**Recommended CDs:** Jean-Paul Bourelly's development from being heavily influenced by Jimi Hendrix to evolving a more original voice of his own can be heard on *Jungle Cowboy* (Winter & Winter 919009), *Trippin'* (Enemy 127), *Saints & Sinners* (DIW 872), *Blackadelic Blu* (DIW 883), *Tribute To Jimi* (Koch 7848), *Prelude To Cacophony: Live* (Evidence 22167), *Rock The Cathartic Spirit: Vibe Music & Blues* (Koch 7849), *Vibe Music* (BMG 74321653052), *Boom Bop* (Jazz Magnet 2005) with guests Archie Shepp and Henry Threadgill, *Trance Atlantic* (Challenge 71023), the acoustic *News From A Darked Out Room* (Phonector 100103) and *Cut Motion* (JPGotMangos).

**Website:** www.bourelly.com

---

## Ned Boynton
*(Edward Boynton)*
b. August 18, 1961, New York, NY

Ned Boynton is based in the San Francisco Bay area and is best known as the leader of Café Americain, a gypsy-jazz group with an eclectic and modern repertoire. "When I was around nine years old, my mother started to take guitar lessons from a neighbor. When my mom wasn't practicing, I would try and play her guitar. At around that time, our local high school had some really talented musicians in the jazz program,

and the bands would come and play at the elementary schools and junior high schools. Seeing other kids actually playing the music I was listening to started me on my path." When he got a bit older, Boynton played in his high school big band and, ironically, was soon playing for the elementary and junior high schools in his community.

Boynton went to college in the Midwest and played jobs on the weekends, including with the Drake University Blues Band. He attended the Berklee summer program in 1986 and went to San Francisco State University. Settling in the Bay area, in 1993 Boynton started playing with both the Hot Club of San Francisco (playing rhythm guitar behind Paul Mehling's lead) and Los Pinkys. "The Hot Club of San Francisco opened up the Django Reinhardt resurgence in the States in the '90s. I did three CDs with them. Los Pinkys was a Tex-Mex outfit, and we would sometimes play polkas, cumbias, waltzes, schottisches, rock tunes, swing tunes, country and western, and post-punk folk for 18 hours a day." Boynton had a regular gig at Enrico's Sidewalk Cafe in North Beach from 1992 to 2007, first as a member of the Hot Club of San Francisco and then as a leader. He was also a featured artist at the Smithsonian Jazz Cafe and associate director of Jazzmasters Workshop, both during 1999–2007.

In recent times, Ned Boynton's main focus has been Café Americain. "Café Americain captures the improvisation and swing of gypsy jazz, but the repertoire is decidedly Americana, reflecting the diverse cultural melting pot of the US. We play everything from Italian favorites such as 'O Sole Mio' to an ABBA tune, 'Dancing Queen,' in the gypsy swing style, along with Django Reinhardt songs."

**Recommended CDs:** *Café Americain Social Club* (Boynton Productions) features Boynton along with Michael Zisman on mandolin, rhythm guitarist Jason Vanderford and bassist Simon Plantin, plus a few guest vocals by Kim Nalley. The guitarist also put out three CDs on his own Boynton Productions label during 2001–05: *The New Brass Ring*, *Ned Boynton Guitar* and *The North Beach Sound*. In addition, he can be heard on Jules Broussard's *With Strings Attached* (Darling & Kid 1210).

**Website:** www.nedboynton.org

---

## Sean Bray
b. February 3, 1966, Fort St. John, British Columbia, Canada

Sean Bray is an inventive straight-ahead guitarist from Canada who has played and recorded with many of the top Canadian musicians. He began playing the guitar when he was 11 after being inspired by

*The Buddy Holly Story.* "I was introduced to jazz harmony with the Doobie Brothers and then Steely Dan. That led me to checking out the sidemen on those records, like Larry Carlton and Wayne Shorter. Pat Metheny and Weather Report followed, and then the world of jazz opened up. My first professional gig, if making $25 plus a beer qualifies, was with a sax player and myself in a country lounge in Calgary owned by a Chinese fellow with a stutter. We flipped through the Real Book while getting glares from the patrons who wanted to hear country music. Needless to say, we didn't play there for long."

He had better luck at most of his gigs. Bray attended the music program at Mount Royal College in Calgary, Alberta (1985–86), and studied at the Manhattan School of Music a few years later. Since then, "I've been fortunate to be able to play and/or record with some great musicians. Some of those amazing musicians include saxophonists Pat LaBarbera, George Garzone, Bob Mintzer, Mike Murley, and Kirk MacDonald, vocalist and trombonist Big Miller, guitarist Matt 'Guitar' Murphy from the Blues Brothers, and pianist/bassist/vibraphonist Don Thompson, among others."

In recent times, Sean Bray has been leading his own group, the Peach Trio, which also includes bassist Mark Dunn and drummer Topher Stott. "It's a really fun band, original Americana/roots music played through jazz player sensibilities with lots of in-the-moment improvisation with no genre boundaries. For the future, I want to continue this lifelong journey I've embarked on with the guitar and hopefully keep making music into my 90s."

**Recommended CDs:** Sean Bray has led five CDs for the Counterpoint label: *Another Point Of View*, *Strategy*, *Tunes*, *Transcendence* and *This One's A Peach*. Of the latter CD, he says, "I overdub a bunch of electric and acoustic guitars and play mandolin on it as well. I think of it as rootsy/folky, but other people consider it jazz." His most recent recording is a roots rock album called *Travelling Songman*.

**Website:** www.seanbray.com

## Joshua Breakstone
*b. July 22, 1955, Elizabeth, NJ*

A superior hard-bop guitarist, Joshua Breakstone has carved out a place for himself in jazz's modern mainstream. He began playing guitar at 14, soon becoming serious and working locally. Although he played with a rock group (Moon Unit) while in high school, hearing Lee Morgan records was a key factor in turning him toward jazz. "My sister Jill had a friend named Rick Centalonza, who was playing

with Buddy Rich's band at the time. Through Rick, I first heard Charlie Parker and many others, and it was through Rick's example that I first came to understand what it is to really love music and be devoted to playing jazz."

Breakstone studied with Sal Salvador (1969–73), attended New College in Sarasota, Florida (1972–75), went to Berklee for one year (1973–74), and had his doctoral studies in creative arts education at New York University (1976–78). After finishing college, he made his recording debut on a record led by Canadian reedman Glen Hall. Breakstone played with Warne Marsh in the early 1980s and also worked early in his career with Vinnie Burke, Emily Remler, Dave Schnittner, Harry Leahey, Billy Hart and Barry Harris, making his recording debut in 1983.

On his four recordings for Contemporary, Breakstone used such sidemen as Jimmy Knepper, Pepper Adams, Tommy Flanagan and Kenny Barron. In 1988, he began touring Japan on a regular basis, and he recorded a few dates for the Japanese King label. Since then, Joshua Breakstone has recorded for a variety of labels, toured, taught, and continued playing the straight-ahead jazz that he loves.

"To me, playing jazz has always been melody, letting the melodies and ideas lead me to new places."

**Recommended CDs:** *Wonderful* (Sonora 222) features Barry Harris, Kenny Barron is the pianist on *Four Over Four Equals One* (Sonora 322), *Echoes* (Contemporary 14025) also features Pepper Adams, and *Evening Star* (Contemporary 14040) matches the guitarist with Jimmy Knepper and Tommy Flanagan. Otherwise, Breakstone is the main star on his CDs (many of which benefit from the presence of Kenny Barron), including *Self-Portrait In Swing* (Contemporary 14050), *Nine By Three* (Contemporary 14062), *Walk Don't Run* (Evidence 22058), *I Want To Hold Your Hand* (King 365), *Oh! Darling* (King 365), *Remembering Grant Green* (Evidence 22146), *Sittin' On The Thing With Ming* (Capri 74042), *Let's Call This Monk* (Double-Time 121), *This Just In* (Double-Time 149), *The Music Of Bud Powell* (Double-Time 172), a tribute to Wes Montgomery called *Tomorrow's Hours* (Capri 74054), *A Jamais* (Capri 74065), *Memoire* (Capri 74070) and *No One New* (Capri 74095).

**Website:** www.joshuabreakstone.com

## Lenny Breau
*b. August 5, 1941, Auburn, ME; d. August 12, 1984, Los Angeles, CA*

One of the finest guitarists of all time, Lenny Breau played jazz, country, flamenco, folk, classical and Indian music quite well by the time he was in his early twenties. While known during his lifetime, in the years since his tragic death, he has become an underground legend. Playing without a pick, Breau had the ability to play chords, single-note solos, and a bass line at the same time. And later in life, he mastered the seven-string guitar.

Breau's parents were professional country music performers. He began playing guitar when he was eight and at 12 was performing with his parents at country shows, sometimes being billed as Lone Pine, Jr. His first main influence was Chet Atkins. After moving with his parents to Winnipeg in Canada, Breau started listening to jazz, including Tal Farlow and Johnny Smith, and a little later Bill Evans, McCoy Tyner and John Coltrane. He worked as a studio musician on Canadian radio from the age of 15 (making his recording debut) and hosted his own radio program for a time. Breau continued playing with his parents' band until he was 18. By then, his playing was leaning more toward jazz than country. He formed his own jazz band and in 1962 moved to Toronto. Breau's group Three, with singer/actor Don Francks and bassist Eon Henstridge, was featured in a documentary, recorded at the Village Vanguard, and appeared on television. Breau also worked with a variety of other Canadian performers, including Peter Appleyard and Anne Murray. His sideman at times included bassist Don Thompson, drummer Terry Clarke and saxophonist Ron Park.

After meeting and hearing Breau, Chet Atkins wanted to sign him to RCA. Breau did not feel he was ready, but in 1968, he finally made his debut for RCA, resulting in *Guitar Sounds From Lenny Breau* and *The Velvet Touch*. However, neither album sold well. Breau suffered from a lack of self-confidence, he began to have difficulties with drugs and alcohol, and he did not record for another ten years. He did continue playing regularly but stayed in obscurity.

In 1978, Breau finally began to emerge. He co-led *Minors Aloud* with steel guitarist Buddy Emmons and recorded four other albums within the next year. In 1983, he moved to Los Angeles, appearing with Tal Farlow and playing regularly on Monday nights at the legendary Donte's jazz club. But on August 12, 1984, his body was found in a swimming pool; he had apparently been strangled, a murder that has never been solved.

Since his death, the legend of Lenny Breau has grown. Many previously unreleased recordings have been issued (particularly by the Guitarchives and Art of Life labels), and a documentary, *The Genius Of Lenny Breau*, sums up his musical legacy.

**Recommended CDs:** Nearly all of Lenny Breau's recordings, including sets that were not released until after his death, are currently available. *Boy Wonder* (Guitarchives 4) captures Lenny Breau when he was 15, while *Hallmark Sessions* (Art of Life 1007) was recorded when he was 20 in 1961. The latter includes jazz, country and flamenco numbers. *At The Purple Onion* (Art of Life 1009) features Three and their unusual show. *Guitar Sounds Of Lenny Breau* (Wounded Bird 4076) and *The Velvet Touch* (One Way 29315) are reissues of Breau's two RCA albums. The solo record *Five O'Clock Bells/Mo' Breau* (Genes 5006/12); *Lenny Breau Trio* (Genes 5018); *Cabin Fever* (Guitarchives 2); *Standard Brands* (One Way 290316), which is a set of duets with Chet Atkins; a duet concert with bassist Dave Young that is available as the two-CD set *Live At Bourbon Street* (Guitarchives 1); the two-CD *The Complete Living Room Tapes* (Art of Life 1004), which are solos and duets with clarinetist Brad Terry; *Jazz Live At Donte's* (String Jazz 1008); *Quietude* (Electric Muse 1001); *Mosaic* (Guitarchives 7); *Pickin' Cotton* (True North 272); *Chance Meetings* (Guitarchives 3) with Tal Farlow; *Last Sessions* (Genes 5024); and *Swingin' On A Seven-String* (Art of Life 1013) comprise quite a body of work. In addition, Breau recorded *Minors Aloud* (Art of Life 1014) with Buddy Emmons.

**LPs to Search For:** *Buddy And Lenny* (Flying Fish 088) with Emmons, *The Legendary Lenny Breau . . . Now!* (Sound Hole 10462) and *Legacy* (Relaxed Rabbit Records 427) have not yet been reissued on CD.

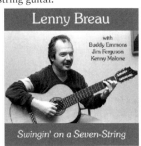

Lenny Breau
with
Buddy Emmons
Jim Ferguson
Kenny Malone

*Swingin' on a Seven-String*

## Zachary Breaux
b. June 26, 1960, Fort Arthur, TX; d. February 20, 1997, Miami Beach, FL

A fine guitarist whose playing was influenced by George Benson and Wes Montgomery and ranged from soul jazz to smooth, Zachary Breaux's premature passing cut short a potentially significant career.

Breaux started on guitar when he was nine. He studied music composition at North Texas State University. During 1984–90, he was a member of vibraphonist Roy Ayers' band, primarily playing R&B but some jazz. He also had opportunities to work with Stanley Turrentine, Jack McDuff, Lonnie Liston Smith and Dee Dee Bridgewater.

After leading two albums for the NYC label during 1992–94, Breaux was signed to Zebra Records, recording *Uptown Groove*. A big push was just starting that might have resulted in him becoming a major attraction at contemporary jazz festivals.

In 1988 while in Italy, Zachary Breaux had saved the life of a swimmer. But on February 20, 1997, while vacationing in Miami Beach, he tried unsuccessfully to save the life of another swimmer; both drowned.

**Recommended CDs:** Zachary Breaux's debut CD as a leader, *Groovin'* (NYC 6003), features him stretching out (mostly with a quartet) on a variety of originals, "Comin' Home Baby," and "Impressions." He shows that he could have been a major hard-bop guitarist if that had been his goal and if life had treated him better. *Laid Back* (NYC 6009) is more commercial although not without interest. *Uptown Groove* (Zebra 44002) is a mixed bag, with Breaux's Benson-inspired solos being more memorable than the funky material. "After 2:00 AM On The East Coast" is a purely acoustic number that has Breaux teaming up with fellow guitarist Ted Dunbar. But just a few months later, Zachary Breaux was gone.

## Terrence Brewer
b. August 3, 1975, Oklahoma City, OK

Terrence Brewer gained some long overdue attention in 2009 with the release of his Wes Montgomery tribute album *Movin' Wes*. Born in Oklahoma, Brewer grew up in California. He  started out playing saxophones, flute and clarinet when he was nine. "In high school, I found myself playing woodwind instruments at school during the day on jazz and classical music. But at night, my love for rock and roll (including Led Zeppelin, Jimi Hendrix, Pearl Jam and Guns N' Roses) led me to the guitar." In college, he was a woodwind major who still separated the guitar from jazz until one night. "I attended a jazz quintet performance with my sax professor. At the concert, I heard jazz guitar, live and in person, for the first time. My mind was blown. I had never known or heard the beauty, complexity, and range of the guitar. I changed my major to guitar studies and began the arduous task of applying years of knowledge on woodwinds to guitar."

Brewer, who considers his early guitar influences to be Joe Pass, Wes Montgomery and Grant Green, attended Los Medanos College in Pittsburg, California, during 1994–97, and after graduation studied with Charlie Hunter, Duck Baker and pianist Mark Levine. He gained important experience while still in college working with Pete Escovedo. A busy guitarist and educator Terrence Brewer, who formed his own Strong Brew label in 2004, played over 2000 shows in a seven-year period, mostly as a leader. He has also worked with Diana Krall, Gerald Albright, Anthony Brown, Dave Ellis and Calvin Keyes.

"Jazz, stylistically and harmonically, has such an endless amount to be learned that every day is a new adventure."

**Recommended CDs:** Terrence Brewer has thus far led five CDs, each for his Strong Brew label: *The Calling Volume One*, *The Calling Volume Two*, *QuintEssential*, *Groovin' Wes* (the most rewarding of the five) and *Citizen Rhythm*.

**Website:** www.terrencebrewer.com

## Bobby Broom
b. January 18, 1961, New York, NY

Bobby Broom is thus far best known for his periods playing with Sonny Rollins, although his solo career and work with the Deep Blue Organ Trio are becoming increasingly notable. Broom first heard  jazz on Charles Earland's *Black Talk* album and started playing guitar when he was 12. While attending the High School of Music and Art, he performed in a few off-Broadway productions and had jobs with Al Haig and Walter Bishop, Jr. Broom was invited to join Sonny Rollins' group when he was only 16 but had to say no in order to finish high school. However, he did play a Carnegie Hall concert with Rollins and Donald Byrd in 1977. Broom attended classes at Berklee during 1978–79 and at Long Island University.

In 1980, Broom had the opportunity to join Art Blakey's Jazz Messengers but in retrospect made a mistake by turning it down, instead joining Tom Browne's band. He also worked with Hugh Masakela and Dave Grusin, recording his first album as a leader in 1981, *Clean Sweep*. In 1982, Broom finally became a member of Sonny Rollins' group, playing, touring and recording with the great tenor for five years.

In the mid-1980s, Broom moved to Chicago where he has performed locally while also touring and spending time in New York. In 1987, Broom became a member of Kenny Burrell's short-lived Jazz Guitar Band and played a few gigs with Miles Davis. He also worked with Charles Earland, Stanley Turrentine,

**Andy Brown**

Kenny Garrett and Dr. John (1994–99), recording albums with all of the above (except Davis), plus Dave Valentin, Dizzy Gillespie, Sadao Watanabe, Ronnie Cuber, David Murray and Eric Alexander.

In 2005, after an 18-year "vacation," Broom rejoined Sonny Rollins, staying until the spring of 2010. He earned a master's from Northwestern University in 2005, taught at DePaul University during 2002–08, and is an active educator. Bobby Broom currently plays with the Deep Blue Organ Trio, which he formed in 1999 with organist Chris Foreman and drummer Greg Rockingham, keeping the legacy of soul jazz and hard-bop guitar very much alive.

**Recommended CDs:** Bobby Broom sounds consistently rewarding on *Clean Sweep* (GRP 5504), *No Hype Blues* (Criss Cross 1109), *Waitin' And Waitin'* (Criss Cross 1126), *Modern Man* (Delmark 530), *Stand!* (Premonition 90754), *Song And Dance* (Origin 82475), *The Way I Play: Live In Chicago* (Origin 82504), *Bobby Broom Plays For Monk* (Origin 82534) and *Upper West Side Story* (Origin 82617). The Deep Blue Organ Trio has thus far recorded *Deep Blue Bruise* (Delmark 556), *Goin' To Town— Live At The Green Mill* (Delmark 569), *Folk Music* (Origin 82489) and *Wonderful* (Origin 82595).

**LPs to Search For:** Bobby Broom's second album, *Livin' For The Beat* (GRP 8253), has not been reissued on CD yet.

**Website:** www.bobbybroom.com

## Andy Brown
b. March 18, 1975, New York, NY

A tasteful swing guitarist whose playing is fresh, Andrew Brown plays in several groups, including with his wife, singer Petra van Nuis. Brown had piano lessons and played saxophone in junior 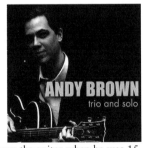 high before starting on the guitar when he was 15. "Both my dad and grandfather encouraged me, but I really got turned on by the two master jazz guitarists that were in Cincinnati where I was living. Kenny Poole and Cal Collins were two of the best jazz guitarists I've ever heard. Kenny Poole was probably my main inspiration in music. He was a font of knowledge when it came to jazz guitar recordings, players and tunes. We had a sort of master/apprentice relationship. I also came under the wing of Cal Collins. Whenever he would play, he would force me

to sit in. Scary as it was, it was so valuable to play with such a master."

By the time he was 17, Brown was playing blues gigs two or three times a week while still going to high school. He spent one year at Cincinnati's College Conservatory of Music and has been a professional ever since. Brown lived in New York for several years, moving to Chicago in 2003. Since then, Andrew Brown has worked with such artists as Harry Allen, Hod O'Brien, Kurt Elling, Ken Peplowski and Jon-Erik Kellso, recorded with Russ Phillips, played every week since 2006 at the Green Mill Jazz Club with singer Kimberly Gordan and organist Chris Foreman, been a member of jazz mandolinist Don Stiernberg's trio, performed unaccompanied solos, and worked in a duo and larger groups with Petra van Nuis.

"I think if you pursue your music honestly, then you can't help bringing something new to it. Between solo playing, trio playing, accompanying, learning tunes, deepening my command of melody, harmony and rhythm—that's plenty for me to play around in."

**Recommended CDs:** *Trio And Solo* (String Damper 2132) is Andrew Brown's debut as the sole leader and is an impressive effort on which he comes up with fresh melodic ideas on a variety of standards. *Far Away Places* (String Damper 2133) features him dueting with Petra van Nuis, and he also has a major supporting role on Russ Phillips' *One Morning In May* (Big Foot Jazz). The privately issued 2006 CD *Andy Brown & Andrew Lautenbach* teams the guitarist with saxophonist Lautenbach on a boppish date a little reminiscent of the Stan Getz–Jimmy Raney collaborations.

**Website:** www.andybrownguitar.com

## Jimmy Bruno
b. July 22, 1953, Philadelphia, PA

A hard-driving guitarist, Jimmy Bruno plays consistently exciting solos in straight-ahead settings. His father was a guitarist, and his mother was a singer. Bruno started on the guitar early, often practic- 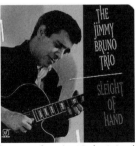 ing his guitar eight hours a day. At 19, he joined Buddy Rich's band. After that stint, Bruno worked with orchestras backing up Frank Sinatra, Doc Severinsen and Lena Horne and spent a long period as a session musician in Los Angeles. But he got bored despite the money and decided never again to play music that did not interest him. He moved back to Philadelphia in 1988, took a day job as a bartender, and played jazz in small clubs. After two years, he was a full-time musician. He signed with the Concord label in 1992 and has since recorded 13 albums as a leader.

In addition to his work as the leader of his trio, Bruno has performed with Joe Beck, Bobby Watson, Jack Wilkins, Tal Farlow, Howard Alden, Christian McBride, Kurt Elling and other major names. In 2007, he opened the Jimmy Bruno Guitar Institute, a successful online service for guitar students.

**Recommended CDs:** Jimmy Bruno's output of recordings has been consistently exciting. His CDs include *Sleight Of Hand* (Concord 4532), *Burnin'* (Concord 4612); *Like That* (Concord 4698); *Live At Birdland 1* (Concord 4768), which features Bobby Watson; *Live At Birdland 2* (Concord 4810) with Scott Hamilton; *Polarity* (Concord 4888), which he co-leads with Joe Beck; *Midnight Blue* (Concord 49890); the magnificent *Solo* (Mel Bay Records 9772); and *Maplewood Avenue* (Affiliated Artists 3415).

**Website:** www.jimmybruno.com

# John Bruschini
*b. June 15, 1953, Brooklyn, NY*

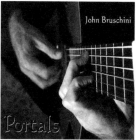

Not too many guitarists have fit comfortably into Cecil Taylor's music, but John Bruschini, who in his career has performed with a wide variety of challenging artists, excelled with Taylor, carving out his own niche in the music. "My father had played guitar and started me with lessons at age 12 with his guitar teacher, Al Cappi, who had worked with George Van Eps and Carl Kress. Early on, I studied with Billy Bauer, who provided me with a good foundation of theory and harmony." As a teenager, Bruschini played with blues bands, not only as a guitarist but also as a singer and harmonica player. In the late 1960s, he was attracted by fusion and inspired by the playing of John McLaughlin.

Switching to more adventurous music, among his key early associations starting in the mid-1970s were Makanda Ken McIntyre, Warren Smith, Wilber Morris and Craig Harris (touring Europe with his James Brown tribute band, Cold Sweat). Bruschini first joined Cecil Taylor in 1989, playing

and recording with several of his ensembles in the 1990s. In more recent times, he has worked with Dave Douglas, Mose Allison, Carlos Ward, Akira Tana, Butch Morris, Sonny Simmons, Myra Melford, David S. Ware, Antoine Roney, Guillermo Franco, and Dennis Mitcheltree, in duets with reed player Dale Kleps, and with his own trio.

"For me, music is the most spiritual experience I can be part of, the most honest and pure way to be. It's also a taskmaster that cannot be ignored for long without it taking a toll on you. It is truly a 'for better or worse' marriage. To me, music is a state of prayer when you're in harmony with it."

**Recommended CDs:** John Bruschini has thus far led two CDs: a creative fusion date with a quintet, *As You Were* (Cathexis 854545), and his atmospheric solo disc *Portals* (Abstract Logix 54551).

**Website:** www.johnbruschini.com

# Dennis Budimir
*b. June 20, 1938, Los Angeles, CA*

For just a little while, when he was with the Chico Hamilton Quintet during 1958–59, Dennis Budimir was on the brink of becoming a major name in jazz. He has survived and appeared on a countless number of studio recordings since, but he is still best known for his association with Hamilton.

Budimir began playing the guitar when he was 11. Within a couple of years, he was playing at dances and casuals. Among his childhood friends and associates were Eric Dolphy and Billy Higgins. In 1958, he toured with the Harry James Orchestra, primarily as a rhythm guitarist cast in the role of Freddie Green. Later in the year, he received an offer to join the popular Chico Hamilton Quintet, a group that Eric Dolphy had recently joined. While with Hamilton, Budimir's forward-looking style looked ahead to both Gabor Szabo and Ornette Coleman while being grounded in chordal improvisation. He played the diverse arrangements expertly and had a floating style that was adventurous for the time.

After the quintet broke up, Budimir resettled in Los Angeles and worked with Bud Shank and Peggy Lee. His jazz career was cut short when he was drafted, spending 1961–63 in the Army. After his discharge, he became a very busy studio musician in Los Angeles, appearing on thousands of recordings, including over 400 movie soundtracks. While he worked with Julie London, Bobby Troup and again with Shank, the price he paid for becoming a studio player was that he was largely forgotten in the jazz world. In the 1970s, he popped up on some Milt Jackson recordings and an occasional jazz date, but in general, he was lost to jazz after 1961. One wonders how his career might have been different had he settled in New York rather than Los Angeles in 1963.

**Recommended CDs:** Chico Hamilton's *Complete Studio Sessions 1958–1959* (Fresh Sound 522), a two-CD set, has all of Dennis Budimir's (and Eric Dolphy's) recordings with Hamilton and is full of intriguing and colorful performances.

**LPs to Search For:** *Alone Together* (Revelation 1) features Dennis Budimir playing overdubbed duets and also welcoming altoist Gary Foster to some selections. *Alone Together, A Second Coming* (Revelation 4) with bassist Gary Peacock, *Sprung Free* (Revelation 8) and *The Session With Albert* (Revelation 14), which features bassist Albert Stinson, are all quite scarce and would make a great box set.

## Hiram Bullock
*b. September 11, 1955, Osaka, Japan; d. July 25, 2008, New York, NY*

Hiram Bullock had the ability to play adventurous jazz, rock, fusion and music that fell in between. He was a flamboyant and colorful soloist who was well respected by his fellow musicians. Born to parents in the US military who were stationed overseas, Bullock grew up in Baltimore. He was originally a pianist, studying at the Peabody Conservatory of Music, and as a teenager was a saxophonist and a bassist. When he was 16, Bullock switched permanently to the guitar. He studied music at the University of Miami, where his fellow students included Pat Metheny and Jaco Pastorius. He played music in local clubs all throughout college, including with Phyllis Hyman's group. When Hyman brought her music to New York, he accompanied her.

Bullock quickly became a very busy session musician. Starting in the mid-1970s, he worked in a countless number of settings, including with the Brecker Brothers, the Gil Evans Orchestra, David Sanborn, Bob James, Miles Davis, Carla Bley, Spyro Gyra, Marcus Miller, Hank Crawford and Jaco Pastorius, plus Steely Dan, Billy Joel, James Brown, Paul Simon, Chaka Khan, Sting, Kenny Loggins, Barbra Streisand, Roberta Flack, James Taylor and many others. He probably gained his greatest fame beyond the jazz world as the barefoot guitarist on *Late Night With David Letterman*, from 1984 until

his passing. He also worked in the house band of *Saturday Night Live* and as the musical director of David Sanborn's *Night Music* show, and he acted in the role of a musician in the film *Under Siege*.

As a solo artist since 1983, Bullock recorded regularly and led his own bands, mixing together jazz, funk and rock. One of his groups was the 24th Street Band with keyboardist Clifford Carter, bassist Mark Egan and drummer Steve Jordan.

Hiram Bullock survived both drug problems and cancer but still died prematurely in 2006 at the age of 52.

**Recommended CDs:** Hiram Bullock's recordings are diverse, but each of these features a large dose of his intense and colorful guitar: *From All Sides* (Atlantic 81685), *Give It What U Got* (Atlantic 81790), *Way Kool* (Atlantic 82353), *World Of Collision* (Big World 2015), *Carrasco* (Fantasy 9672), *Late Night Talk* (Venus 35020), *Try Livin' It* (JVC Victor 61092), *Too Funky 2 Ignore* (BHM 1010) and *Plays The Music Of Jimi Hendrix* (BHM 10367).

## Teddy Bunn
*(Theodore Leroy Bunn)*
*b. 1909, Freeport, NY; d. July 20, 1978, Lancaster, CA*

During the first part of his career, Teddy Bunn was very active both in performances and on recordings, and he was one of the top acoustic guitarists of the 1930s. But despite playing regularly into the late 1960s, Bunn was in obscurity after 1941. Born to a musical family, Bunn first played professionally as an accompanist to a calypso singer. On September 16, 1929, he made his recording debut, appearing on two numbers with pianist-singer Walter "Fats" Pichon in a trio that also included trumpeter Henry "Red" Allen, and also guesting on four numbers with Duke Ellington's orchestra (including "The Duke Steps Out" and "Swanee Shuffle"). More typical of Bunn's career were two numbers from October 29 that he recorded with the Six Jolly Jesters, a group that matched Ellington and seven of his sidemen with Bunn, washboard and kazoo. The guitarist would appear on many spontaneous washboard/kazoo sessions during the next decade, many of which featured him as the most skilled soloist.

Bunn, whose bluish single-note lines were on the level of Eddie Lang although his chording was less sophisticated, was in demand from the start for small hot combos. He appeared on two numbers with James P. Johnson on November 18, 1929, including a rare outing on banjo during "You've Got To Be Modernistic." In 1930, Bunn can be heard on one of the two unique sessions that teamed together Jelly Roll Morton with the vaudevillian clarinetist Wilton

Crawley; on dates with singers Spencer Williams, Lizzie Miles and Victoria Spivey; and with both the Alabama Washboard Stompers and the Washboard Serenaders. The following year, he starred on some records with the Washboard Rhythm Kings.

But Bunn's most important association was with the Spirits of Rhythm. Comprised of Wilbur Daniels, Douglas Daniels and the great Leo Watson on vocals and tiples (small guitars similar to ukuleles), drummer-vocalist Virgil Scoggins and sometimes bassist Wilson Myers, the Spirits of Rhythm were a good-time skiffle-style group that swung hard. Bunn was its key solo star during 1933–41, appearing on all of the group's recordings, including dates in which they were fronted by singers Ella Logan and Red McKenzie.

Teddy Bunn also appeared on many hot jazz and blues sessions during 1937–41, including with the two classic New Orleans clarinetists Johnny Dodds and Jimmie Noone; singers Cow Cow Davenport, Bob Howard, Rosetta Crawford, Trixie Smith, Georgia White; and the team of Grant and Wilson. He was on the famous sessions organized by French jazz critic Hughes Panassie in 1938 that featured Sidney Bechet, trumpeter Tommy Ladnier and clarinetist Mezz Mezzrow (including "Really The Blues" and "Revolutionary Blues") and was part of some of the earliest recordings by the Blue Note label, including with the Port of Harlem Jazzmen and Port of Harlem Seven, trumpeter Frankie Newton, trombonist J.C. Higginbotham and Bechet (his hit recording of "Summertime"). Bunn also recorded with trumpeter Hot Lips Page (singing "Evil Man's Blues," which would become "Evil Gal Blues" when sung by Dinah Washington three years later), Lionel Hampton (a session in 1940 on electric guitar), and on four guitar solos (two with his vocals) during his only date as a leader, from March 28, 1940.

But after a final session with the Spirits of Rhythm in 1941, Bunn unaccountably stopped recording. He had carved out a place for himself apart from Charlie Christian and Django Reinhardt and had successfully switched to electric guitar, but relatively little was heard from him during the rest of his long career. Bunn settled in California, led the Waves of Rhythm in 1944, and worked with Edgar Hayes, Hadda Brooks, Jack McVea and, in 1959, Louis Jordan. He was involved in R&B and rock and roll revues until his declining health resulted in him being less active in the 1960s and retiring altogether in 1970. But it is a mystery why Teddy Bunn was not given his own record dates in the 1950s or opportunities to perform in swing settings in the '60s.

**Recommended CDs:** *Teddy Bunn* (RST 1509) contains Bunn's recordings with Spencer Williams, backing a few singers, playing with Mezz Mezzrow and Tommy

Ladnier, and his four performances from his lone solo session. *Spirits Of Rhythm* (Retrieval 79004) has all of the recordings by the popular group, which for a while caused a sensation on 52nd Street.

## Kenny Burrell
*b. July 31, 1931, Detroit, MI*

Among the most tasteful and melodic of guitarists, ironically Kenny Burrell was the first to popularize the "power trio" of guitar, bass and drums (which had been used by Jim Hall and Howard Roberts with Chico Hamilton in 1953) although, needless to say, his playing in that format in the 1950s was a bit different than that heard 15 years later in Cream and other rock groups. Burrell started playing guitar when he was 12, developing a Charlie Christian–inspired style that has been largely unchanged since the '50s. Burrell attended Wayne State University, and while still a college student in 1951, he made his recording debut with Dizzy Gillespie. He was an important part of the Detroit jazz scene of the early-to-mid-1950s, which served as a perfect training ground for his career.

After moving to New York in 1956, Burrell immediately became busy both on recordings and on live dates. In addition to studio work and leading many sessions of his own (which ranged from his pianoless trio to jam session–flavored sets), Burrell recorded as a sideman with most of the top jazz musicians of the 1950s and '60s. He can be heard on albums with Billie Holiday, Milt Jackson, John Coltrane (a project that they co-led), Stan Getz, Gil Evans, Sonny Rollins, Thad Jones, Tommy Flanagan, Hank Jones, Illinois Jacquet and Quincy Jones, among others. Burrell sounded at his best and most bluesy when teamed with Jimmy Smith, Stanley Turrentine and drummer Grady Tate.

Burrell moved to Los Angeles in 1972, where he became active as an educator. In 1978 at UCLA, he developed the first regular college course on Duke Ellington ever taught in the US ("Ellingtonia"). Although Ellington had called Burrell his favorite guitarist, unfortunately they never recorded together, although they did appear together once in a 1973 television special. In 1996, Burrell was appointed director of the Jazz Studies Program at UCLA. Since 2007, he has served as the Director of Jazz Studies at UCLA.

Other projects included touring with the Phillip

Morris Superband (1985–86), leading the Jazz Guitar Band (a quintet with three guitarists), making guest appearances, and taking an occasional vocal, often on his own lyrics. While Kenny Burrell's most rewarding recordings are generally from at least three decades ago (his playing in later years has tended to be laidback and mellow), he remains one of the most universally respected of all jazz guitarists.

**Recommended CDs:** Kenny Burrell has recorded prolifically and on a very steady basis since the mid-1950s. Some of his most significant recordings are *Introducing Kenny Burrell* (Blue Note 9107), *All Night Long* (Original Jazz Classics 427), *All Day Long* (Original Jazz Classics 456), *Blue Moods* (Prestige 9390), *Kenny Burrell* (Original Jazz Classics 019), *Two Guitars* (Original Jazz Classics 216) with Jimmy Raney, *Monday Stroll* (Savoy 246), *Blue Lights Vol. 1* (Blue Note 9183), *Blue Lights Vol. 2* (Blue Note 1597), *Kenny Burrell & John Coltrane* (Original Jazz Classics 300), *On View At The Five Spot Cafe* (Blue Note 46538) with Art Blakey, *Bluesy Burrell* (Original Jazz Classics 926) with Coleman Hawkins, *Blues Bash* (Verve 557453) with Jimmy Smith, *Soul Call* (Fantasy 8462), *Guitar Forms* (Universal 5098) with the Gil Evans Orchestra, *Ode To 52nd Street* (GRP 824), *Midnight Blue* (Blue Note 4123) with Stanley Turrentine, *Blues—The Common Ground* (Blue Note 89101), *For Charlie Christian And Benny Goodman* (Verve 831087), *God Bless The Child* (Columbia 40808), *Ellington Is Forever Vol. 1* (Fantasy 79005), *Ellington Is Forever Vol. 2* (Fantasy 79008), *Tin Tin Deo* (Concord 4045), *Moon And Sand* (Concord 4121), *Togethering* (Blue Note 46093) with Grover Washington, Jr., *Generation* (Blue Note 46756), *Pieces Of Blue And The Blues* (Blue Note 90260), *Guiding Spirit* (Contemporary 14058), *Sunup To Sundown* (Contemporary 14065), *Then Along Came Kenny* (Evidence 22160), *Live At The Blue Note* (Concord 4731), *Lucky So And So* (Concord 4951), *75th Birthday Bash Live* (Blue Note 74906), and *Be Yourself: Live At Dizzy's Club Coca-Cola* (Highnote 7208). Burrell is also in a featured role with Jimmy Smith on *Midnight Special* (Blue Note 6520) and *Back At The Chicken Shack* (Blue Note 7114).

## André Bush
*b. June 3, 1969, Sacramento, CA*

A versatile and adventurous if often introspective jazz guitarist, André Bush sounds at home in the jazz, pop and rock worlds. Bush received his first guitar when he was eight and began taking music seriously at 14. "I come from a very musically astute family that included many professional musicians and educators. So in addition to the rock music I was originally drawn

to, I was exposed to classical music and jazz. Pat Metheny was the first guitarist whose playing really had it all for me: the energy, tones and production values of the pop and rock music I loved, plus the intellectual/art music values of more creative forms. Other guitar heroes for me in high school were Mike Stern and John Scofield." Bush went to a performing arts high school in Fresno and, at 15, started playing at local clubs. After graduating, he attended Cal Arts during 1988–91, studying with Charlie Haden, James Newton and Larry Koonse. He earned a bachelor's in jazz performance and also studied privately with Tom Hynes, John Stowell and Joe Diorio.

After Cal Arts, Bush became part of the fertile San Francisco Bay area music scene of the 1990s. "Charlie Hunter, Will Bernard, Adam Levy, John Schott and a host of others were fusing hip-hop, jazz, R&B, electronica, etc., into a wild brew that was referred to as 'acid jazz' for a while. We were playing six to seven nights a week, and there was a club and audience scene to support that for a good five-year period." During the era, he often played in Dave Ellis' band. Other associations included Steve Smith (1995–2000), Dave Liebman and Jenna Mammina. With Mammina, Bush made three CDs and toured the country extensively, using pickup groups and appearing at some major jazz festivals.

André Bush also began playing with pianist Art Lande (a major inspiration) on an occasional basis since 2002. In addition, he worked with the pop group Essence in the 1990s, has toured with a variety of Filipino pop artists, and recorded on Nnenna Freelon's 2005 album *Blueprint Of A Lady*. "I got a little overwhelmed with all of the road stuff, so about four years ago, I decided that I needed a break. But now I'm feeling ready to be more active again and am considering a move to L.A., where I like a lot of the music that is going on."

**Recommended CDs:** André Bush's three CDs, *Darwin's Waiting Room* (X Dot 25 Productions 31), *Invisible City* (Quicksilver 8000), and *Start From Silence* (Odd Cultures 2005), which features Art Lande, emphasize originals, offbeat tone colors and thoughtful modern guitar solos.

**Website:** www.myspace.com/andrebush

## Billy Butler
*b. December 15, 1925, Philadelphia, PA; d. March 20, 1991, Teaneck, NJ*

Billy Butler was a fine guitarist able to stretch from rhythm and blues to soul jazz and hard bop. He had a distinctive sound and was always an asset on record dates and club appearances. Butler worked with the doo-wop group the Harlemaires in the late

1940s, with Doc Bagby's trio, and for a long period (1954–61) with Bill Doggett. During that time, he wrote "Honky Tonk," which became both a hit for Doggett and a durable standard. Butler led record dates for Prestige in the 1960s and appeared as a sideman on recordings with King Curtis, Dinah Washington, Panama Francis, Illinois Jacquet, Johnny Hodges, Jimmy Smith, Frank Foster, Eric Kloss, Sonny Stitt, Gene Ammons, Shirley Scott, Rahsaan Roland Kirk, Eddie "Lockjaw" Davis, Helen Humes, David "Fathead" Newman and Houston Person, plus many R&B stars.

Billy Butler worked in the pit bands for Broadway shows starting in the late 1960s, visited Europe in the 1970s and '80s, and kept busy up until shortly before his death in 1991.

**Recommended CDs:** *Legends Of Acid Jazz* (Prestige 24197), despite its title, is actually soul jazz. Butler's first (*This Is Billy Butler*) and fourth (*Night Life*) Prestige albums are reissued in full on this set, forming a definitive Butler release. Standards and basic originals are performed with a quintet also featuring either Houston Person or Jesse Powell on tenor. *Don't Be That Way* (Black & Blue 937) finds the guitarist in the 1970s playing swing standards in a trio with organist Wild Bill Davis.

## Charlie Byrd
*b. September 16, 1925, Suffolk, VA; d. November 30, 1999, Annapolis, MD*

Charlie Byrd was the first American jazz guitarist to perform Brazilian music widely, most notably the bossa nova. Equal parts Charlie Christian and Laurindo Almeida, Byrd was a well-rounded player who ranged from bop and bossas to classical music and swing. Byrd was first taught the acoustic guitar when he was ten by his father, who played guitar and mandolin. He worked with local groups in Virginia and Washington, DC, before being drafted. Byrd served in the Army during 1943–45 and had a unique opportunity to meet and play in France with his idol, Django Reinhardt, one of his influences. After his discharge, Byrd studied composition and jazz theory at the Harnett National Music School in New York, a period of time when he began to master the classical guitar. During that era, he also gigged in New York with Joe Marsala, Sol Yaged and Freddie Slack. Moving

back to Washington, DC, Byrd studied classical guitar extensively with Sophocles Papos (1950–54) and in Italy with Andrés Segovia.

In 1957, Charlie Byrd formed a trio with bassist Keter Betts, playing regularly at the Showboat in Washington, DC. He explored both bop and Brazilian sambas with the group, making several excellent recordings during 1957–61 that featured him on classical and occasionally electric guitar. He was also a key soloist during a short period with Woody Herman's orchestra in 1959.

Charlie Byrd went on a diplomatic tour of South America for the State Department in the spring of 1961, discovering bossa nova. Back in the US, he played Stan Getz some recordings by Antonio Carlos Jobim and João Gilberto, and they formed a brief musical partnership that resulted in the hit album *Jazz Samba*. They soon went their separate ways, particularly when Getz seemed to be taking all of the credit for the popularization of bossa nova. A few years later, Byrd successfully sued Getz and MGM Records for half of the album's royalties. *Jazz Samba* is still a big seller; its hit "Desafinado" was a major factor in launching the bossa nova craze.

Throughout the 1960s, Byrd recorded regularly, at first for Riverside and then for Columbia, usually performing concise versions of bossa nova and/or Brazilian songs. His brother, bassist Joe Byrd, was a member of his group from the 1960s on, with drummers Billy Reichenbach, Wayne Phillips and Chuck Redd spending long periods in the trio. In 1973, Byrd became a member of the Great Guitars alongside Herb Ellis and Barney Kessel, which gave him an opportunity to play bebop with two of his contemporaries. As it was, Byrd's Brazilian features often stole the show.

Other projects in his later years included four albums with Laurindo Almeida, two with the Annapolis Brass Quintet, a countless number of gigs at the King Of France Tavern in Annapolis (where he played regularly during 1973–99), and as much touring as he wanted. A popular figure in the jazz world, Charlie Byrd stayed active until his 1999 death from lung cancer, carving out his own fresh musical path.

**Recommended CDs:** *Jazz Recital* (Savoy 192), *Midnight Guitar* (Savoy 247); *Bamba-Samba Bossa Nova* (Collectables 0824); *The Guitar Artistry Of Charlie Byrd* (Concord 18694542); *Byrd's Word* (Original Jazz Classics 1054); *Byrd In The Wind* (Original Jazz Classics 1086); *Charlie Byrd At The Village Vanguard* (Original Jazz Classics 669); *Mr. Guitar* (Original Jazz Classics 998); *Bossa Nova Pelos Passaros* (Original Jazz Classics 107); *Byrd At The Gate* (Original Jazz Classics 262); *Brazilian Byrd* (Sony 724227); *Solo Flight* (Original Jazz Classics 1093); *Christmas Carols For Solo Guitar*

(Koch 9923); *Byrd By The Sea* (Fantasy 24757); *Blue Byrd* (Concord 4082); *Sugarloaf Suite* (Concord 4114); *Brazilville* (Concord 4173); *Charlie Byrd Christmas Album* (Concord 42004); *Isn't It Romantic* (Concord 4252); *Byrd And Brass* (Concord 4304); *It's A Wonderful World* (Concord 4374); *The Bossa Nova Years* (Concord 4468); *The Washington Guitar Quintet* (Concord 42014); *Aquarelle* (Concord 42016); *I've Got The World On A String* (Timeless 422), which has a few rare Byrd vocals; *Moments Like This* (Concord 4627); *Du Hot Club De Concord* (Concord 4674); *Au Courant* (Concord 4779); *My Inspiration: Music Of Brazil* (Concord 4850); *For Louis* (Concord 4879); with Stan Getz: *Jazz Samba* (Universal 5232142).

# Royce Campbell
b. June 7, 1952, Seymour, IN

Inspired by Wes Montgomery, Royce Campbell has recorded prolifically throughout his career, finding his own voice in straight-ahead jazz. "When I was nine, I saw Chuck Berry on TV and thought

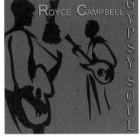

his guitar looked cool, so I told my mother that I wanted to play one." He was introduced to jazz by his uncle, Carroll DeCamp, an arranger-pianist who played with Wes Montgomery's group in Indianapolis in the 1950s. Campbell worked in blues-rock bands while a teenager, and by the time he was 16, he was a professional, playing shows where his expert sight-reading came in handy. When he was 21 in 1973, he toured with Marvin Gaye.

In 1975, Royce Campbell began a 19-year period working and touring with Henry Mancini. In addition to that association and extensive studio work, the guitarist worked with such singers as Mel Torme, Nancy Wilson, Mose Allison, Freddy Cole, Joe Williams, Cleo Laine, Sarah Vaughan, Rosemary Clooney and Vanessa Rubin. He has also worked with James Moody, Jack McDuff, Dave Brubeck, Eddie Daniels, Eddie Harris, Frank Morgan, Ken Peplowski, Gerry Mulligan, Houston Person, Fred Hersch and Phil Woods.

In addition to recording over two dozen CDs as a leader or co-leader, Royce Campbell has produced several CDs, including *Project G-5: A Tribute To Wes Montgomery*, *Six By Six*, and *Project G-5: A Tribute To Joe Pass*. Those ventures teamed him with such great guitarists as Herb Ellis, Tal Farlow, Jimmy

Raney, Cal Collins, Pat Martino, John Abercrombie, Bucky Pizzarelli, Dave Stryker, Larry Coryell, Charlie Byrd, Gene Bertoncini, Mundell Lowe and John Pisano.

"I've played just about every type of music there is, and jazz is by far the most demanding, and as a result the most rewarding."

**Recommended CDs:** Since 1983, Royce Campbell has led 30 albums, the majority of which were for his Moon Cycle label. A few of the most important releases are *Nighttime Daydreams* (Timeless 337), *Project G-5: A Tribute To Wes Montgomery* (Evidence 22001), *Make Me Rainbows* (Positive 78024), *A Tribute To Henry Mancini* (Episode 1001), *Pitapat* (Challenge 73126), *Project G-5: A Tribute To Joe Pass* (King/Japan), *Trioing* (Jardis 20244), *A Tribute To Charlie Byrd* (Jardis 20347), *Six By Six* (Moon Cycle Records 1975), *Plays For Lovers* (Moon Cycle 1995), *Gypsy Soul* (Moon Cycle 3064), *Elegy To A Friend* (Moon Cycle 1993), *Roses And Wine* (Philology 364), *The Art Of Chord Solo Guitar* (Moon Cycle 2001), *Solo Wes: A Solo Guitar Tribute To Wes Montgomery* (Moon Cycle Records 1929), and *Movie Songs Project* (Philology 428).

**Website:** www.roycecampbell.com

# Jim Campilongo
b. July 8, 1958, Burlingame, CA

Equally comfortable playing jazz or country music, Jim Campilongo has found his own voice somewhere in between. "Before I started playing, I was into improvisation, but I didn't really know what it

was or what is was called. I would just randomly buy records if there weren't many songs on them. I didn't care who the artist was, but if I saw that there were only two songs on a double album, I'd go for it. It might turn out to be something like John Coltrane *Live In Japan* or John McLaughlin's *Devotion* with Larry Young on organ. Finally, I found Roy Buchanan's first album, and I knew that I was going to be a guitar player."

At 17, Campilongo started working in clubs, first with a Doors-inspired band called Radio City and then with country and funk groups. He led the Ten Gallon Cats, a country/jazz group that made four colorful CDs. In 2002, he moved to New York, where he formed his Electric Trio, which has performed each Monday night at the Living Room since 2004. Jim Campilongo, who has appeared in a wide variety of settings and genres, has also been lead guitarist with the Little Willies, a band that features Norah Jones.

**Recommended CDs:** *Jim Campilongo & The 10 Gallon Cats* (Blue Hen 1), *Loose* (Blue Hen 2), *Table For One* (Blue Hen 3) and *Heavy* (Blue Hen 4) document his period leading the Ten Gallon Cats, mixing together country, blues and jazz. The music sometimes is close to Western swing but also points in more modern directions. *Table For One* is the most jazz-oriented of the releases. *Live At The Du Nord* (Ethic 4), *American Hips* (Blue Hen 8), *Heaven Is Creepy* (Blue Hen 28288), the unusual *Almost Christmas* (Blue Hen 1225) and the recent *Orange* (Blue Hen 50) trace Jim Campilongo's continued evolution. He has developed an increasingly individual style, performing mostly instrumental music that is sometimes rock-oriented but very difficult to classify.

**Website:** www.jimcampilongo.com

## Andre Caporaso
*b. March 4, 1952, Santa Maria, Italy*

Andre Caporaso is an adventurous guitarist who has been inspired by his time on the Chicago jazz scene and his work with Hal Russell. Born in Italy, Caporaso moved with his family to Caracas, Venezuela, when he was nine months old, and they moved to Chicago when he was three. "I got my first guitar in Germany at the age of 15, which is also when my whole musical world opened up. I started listening to everything. My friends in high school initially introduced me to jazz. We took many trips to Joe Segal's Jazz Showcase in Chicago to see greats like Dizzy Gillespie, Yusef Lateef, Kenny Burrell and Charles Mingus. Hearing John Coltrane's 'My Favorite Things' was a big moment in my musical awakening." Caporaso played gigs in coffee houses and the local Unitarian church, where he was allowed to organize jazz concerts.

The guitarist attended Elgin Community College (1969–71). He played with Paul Wertico, Gordon James, Jeff Czech and other local players. In 1979, he began a long-term association with Hal Russell's NRG Ensemble, performing Russell's personal avant-garde music and learning a great deal about improvising.

He also worked with drummer-composer Damon Short, was involved in the music department activities at Northern Illinois University, and became an important force on the Chicago jazz scene, playing three years at the Chicago New Music Festival. In 1984, he recorded his debut as a leader, *Collage.*

In 1987, Caporaso moved to Los Angeles, where he studied scoring, orchestration and electronics at UCLA and became an award-winning sound mixer and editor, working on many television shows and movies. As a jazz musician, he has led a variety of diverse recordings for his Blue Room label. "I am blessed to continue to play and record with many wonderful players who have been in my bands, including Mark Walker, Ken Haebich, Kurt McGettrick (RIP), Steve Marsh, Dean Taba, Kendall Kay, Randy Drake, Adam Cohen and Gordon James." Andre Caporaso recently wrote a three-movement suite for string quartet and also music for string quartet plus guitar, which will be recorded with the H.A.W.K. String Quartet in Chicago. "Although I love the music of the past, I feel my role is to look ahead and explore."

**Recommended CDs:** All of Andre Caporaso's recordings are available on his Blue Room label. These include *Pathways, Avenue 5, Rubber Space, While We Were Out,* and *Night In A Strange Land.*

**LPs to Search For:** The 1985 LP *Collage* (Blue Room 001) matches Caporaso with a saxophone quartet and a rhythm section, most of whom were members of Hal Russell's band.

**Website:** www.myspace.com/andrecaporasoband

## Steve Cardenas
*b. February 5, 1959, Kansas City, MO*

A versatile guitarist who is perhaps best known for his association with Paul Motian, Steve Cardenas has his own sound and flexible style. Cardenas discovered jazz through hearing Airto and Weather Report, soon exploring the earlier styles. "My first gigs were in Kansas City, mostly with guys already established on the scene, much older and gracious enough to include me on those jobs. By my first year out of high school, I was gigging and staying fairly busy. I couldn't imagine myself doing anything else. Music dominated my thoughts and world." He attended Johnson County Community College (1977–79) and the University of Missouri at Kansas City (1984–85) but mostly learned while on jobs. An important early association was with violinist-guitarist Claude Williams, playing in his swing quartet.

Since moving to New York in 1995, Steve Cardenas has performed with many major musicians. He started a long-term association with Paul Motian's Electric Bebop Band in 1997, an ensemble that has grown to become the Paul Motian Octet + 1. "Just playing with Paul has been nothing but amazing from the beginning. Much of what we do involves playing in and out of time." He has also worked with Joey Baron's Killer Joey, Charlie Haden's Liberation Music Orchestra, Ben Allison's groups, Paul McCandless, Mark Isham, Jeff Beal, Marc Johnson, John Patitucci, Jenny Scheinman, Madeleine Peyroux, Maria Muldaur, Steve Million, Norah Jones, and Marc Johnson's Sound of Summer Running Band. Cardenas spent some time in Los Angeles as a guest faculty member of the California Institute of the Arts, and he currently teaches at the New School in New York. He can be heard frequently in the New York area leading his trio.

**Recommended CDs:** In addition to recordings with Ben Allison, David Brandom, Chris Potter, Donny McCaslin, Charlie Haden, Arthur Kell, Alexis Cuadrado, Kate McGarry, Rebecca Martin, Mike Fahn, Joey Baron, Mark Isham, Tom Coster, the New York Guitar Trio, John Beasley, Jeff Beal, Paul Hanson and Paul McCandless, Steve Cardenas has led three CDs of his own: *Shebang* (Fresh Sound New Talent 079), *Panoramic* (Fresh Sound New Talent 171), and the one he is currently proudest of, *West Of Middle* (Sunnyside 1248), a trio outing with bassist Ben Allison and drummer Rudy Royston. He is also featured with Paul Motian's groups on *Plays Monk And Powell* (Winter & Winter 45), *Europe* (Winter & Winter 63), *Holiday For Strings* (Winter & Winter 69), and *Garden Of Eden* (ECM 1917).

**Website:** www.stevecardenasmusic.com

## Larry Carlton
b. March 2, 1948, Torrance, CA

A major studio guitarist who has long had a solo career, Larry Carlton can play very credible blues and hard bop but has often concentrated on pop-jazz/smooth during his own projects. Carlton first played guitar when he was six. He discovered jazz through Gerald Wilson's *Moment Of Truth* (which featured Joe Pass) along with recordings by Barney Kessel, Wes Montgomery, B.B. King and John Coltrane. Carlton began playing professionally in 1962 when he was 14. He made his recording debut as a leader in 1968, toured with the Fifth Dimension, and became a studio musician in 1970. In addition to his session work, he was a member of the Crusaders during 1971–76, developing his blues-oriented style.

Since then, Carlton has performed with a countless number of top artists from virtually every field, from Joni Mitchell to Sammy Davis, Jr., Michael Jackson to Dolly Parton. He had over 3,000 studio sessions on his resume by the early 1980s. About the time that he left the Crusaders, he recorded a series of solo albums for Warner Brothers that made him a popular attraction at contemporary jazz festivals.

In 1988, Carlton was shot in the throat by would-be robbers while sitting in his studio. Fortunately, with a great deal of therapy, he recovered within a year, resuming his career. Since then, Carlton has been a consistent musical force, usually heard with his own group but available to play with musicians whom he enjoys. Carlton was part of a Stanley Clarke all-star group in 1993, recorded a collaboration with Lee Ritenour in 1995, and was a member of Fourplay (where he succeeded Ritenour) during 1997–2010. Although he did not choose a career in creative jazz, Larry Carlton remains capable of playing brilliant music whenever he wants.

**Recommended CDs:** A sampling of Larry Carlton's recordings include *With A Little Help From My Friends* (Edsel 480), which was his debut; *Larry Carlton* (Warner Bros. 13446); *Strikes Twice* (Warner Bros. 13447); *Sleepwalk* (Warner Bros. 13448); *Eight Times Up* (Wounded Bird 3012); *Friends* (MCA 42214); *Alone/But Never Alone* (MCA 5689); *Discovery* (MCA 42003); *Last Nite* (MCA 18508), which is one of the few recordings where Carlton really stretches himself; *On Solid Ground* (GRP 106); *Kid Gloves* (GRP 9683); *Renegade Gentleman* (GRP 9723); *Larry & Lee* (GRP 9817); *Fingerprints* (Warner Bros. 47338); *Deep Into It* (Warner Bros. 48006); the blues-oriented *Sapphire Blue* (RCA 5767); *Greatest Hits Re-Recorded* (335 Records 0410607); *Live In Tokyo With Robben Ford* (335 Records 0410307); *Take Your Pick* (335 Records 1006) with Japanese guitarist Tak Matsumoto; and *Larry Carlton Plays The Sound Of Philadelphia* (335 Records 04054262).

**Website:** www.larrycarlton.com

## Danny Caron
b. November 2, 1955, Boston, MA

A fine jazz guitarist who is as well known for his work in blues, Danny Caron was a major asset to Charles Brown's groups for years. "At ten years old, I was playing accordion, which my mother was sure was going to catapult me to instant stardom. The

Beatles hit. The accordion was gone. The guitar was it from then on." A little later at summer camp, Caron learned about jazz from a counselor who was also a bassist, Marshall Smith. He gained experience while in high school in Silver Spring, Maryland, playing blues, soul and country rock in a group called Seneca. Caron graduated from Oberlin College in 1977 with a bachelor's degree in English (music was his minor) and worked in the Washington, DC, area in a trio, Threeplay. During 1978–79, Caron was in Los Angeles studying with Howard Roberts and the staff of the Guitar Institute of Technology (which included Joe Diorio, Ron Escheté, Tommy Tedesco, Jimmy Wyble and Howard Alden), attending workshops given by Joe Pass, Pat Martino, Lenny Breau, Larry Carlton, Pat Metheny and Lee Ritenour.

Danny Caron worked with Marcia Ball and toured the bayou country with Clifton Chenier during 1980–81. As a member of Charles Brown's band during 1986–99, he had opportunities to share the stage with Bonnie Raitt, Teddy Edwards, Clark Terry, Red Holloway, David "Fathead" Newman, Ruth Brown, Jimmy Scott, Linda Hopkins, Dan Hicks, Maria Muldaur, Dr. John, Lowell Fulsom, Gatemouth Brown, John Lee Hooker, Johnny Copeland, Ernie Andrews, Gerald Wilson and Nancy Wilson, among many others. Brown's music during this period included blues, swing standards, ballads and early R&B/jump tunes. Danny Caron fit right in and was an important part of Charles Brown's records during his comeback years. He also recorded with John Lee Hooker (*Don't Look Back*), John Hammond, Hadda Brooks, Houston Person and Maria Muldaur.

In more recent times, Caron has recorded with Van Morrison, Pamela Rose, Phil Berkowitz (a tribute to Louis Jordan), and Barbara Morrison, led two CDs for his own label, worked with Bettye La Vette, Robben Ford and Charles Musselwhite, and taught at the Jazzschool in Berkeley.

"My goal for the future is to continue learning how to play the guitar, keep recording my own music, and play with as many soulful people as I can find."

**Recommended CDs:** Both of Danny Caron's solo CDs, 2003's *Good Hands* and *How Sweet It Is* from 2009, have been put out by his own label (Danny Caron Music), showcasing him playing the same classy mixture of styles that were featured by Charles Brown.

**Website:** www.dannycaron.com

## Joe Carter
*b. February 13, 1955, Bridgeport, CT*

A tasteful and lyrical guitarist whose roots are in bebop, Joe Carter is a masterful interpreter of Brazilian jazz. He started taking guitar lessons when he was ten and heard Wes Montgomery records early in life. His older brother played guitar, as did two of his uncles, who had played with the bands of Guy Lombardo and Xavier Cugat. Carter earned a BA and a master's in jazz performance from New York University. He worked toward a PhD and studied privately with John Scofield, Sal Salvador, Lee Konitz and pianist Don Friedman.

In his career, he has worked with Lee Konitz, Junior Cook, Art Farmer, Bill Hardman, Cecil Payne, Hendrik Meurkens, Eddie Bert, Steve Kuhn, Mike Longo, and a variety of Brazilian jazz musicians, including bassist Nilson Matta. In 1981, Carter started the Empathy label to document his own music and those of artists whom he admires. After visiting Brazil in 1988 and hearing pianist Luiz Eça lead a quintet, he became very interested in Brazilian jazz. Carter, who generally leads his own small groups, has a thoughtful style and a cool quiet tone on the guitar that perfectly fits the music he interprets.

Joe Carter teaches at Sacred Heart University and Hartford Conservatory, both located in Connecticut. He also teaches privately in New York and has written four textbooks for guitar.

**Recommended CDs:** Joe Carter's recordings for his Empathy label include *Too Marvelous For Words*, *Chestnut*, *My Foolish Heart*, *Um Abraco No Rio*, *Samba Rio Trio*, *Two For Two*, *Samba Brasil*, and *Both Sides Of The Equator*.

**Website:** www.joecartermusic.com

## Al Casey
*b. September 15, 1915, Louisville, KY; d. September 11, 2005, New York, NY*

Al Casey gained his greatest fame by being a member of Fats Waller's Rhythm during 1934–42, but he actually had a very long career. An orphan living with uncles and aunts who performed in a spiritual group called the Southern Singers, Casey briefly took violin lessons but soon switched to ukulele. After moving to New York in 1930, he started playing guitar and, through an uncle, met Fats Waller in 1933 when he was in high school. He was still 18 when he joined Waller in 1934, and during the next eight years, he made over 200 records with the great pianist, often contributing short solos. Casey had occasional brief periods off. He was with Teddy Wilson's short-lived orchestra during 1939–40 and recorded with Billie Holiday, Frankie Newton and Chu Berry, but otherwise was a constant with Fats. Shortly after switching from acoustic to electric guitar, he had his best-known solo with Waller on "Buck Jumpin'" from 1941.

Considered one of the best of the Charlie

Christian–inspired guitarists of the early 1940s, Casey often led his own trio after leaving Waller, performing at the Downbeat Club on 52nd Street. Casey won *Esquire Magazine*'s polls as top guitarist in 1944 and 1945, and he appeared at their all-star concerts, which were recorded. He had stints with Coleman Hawkins, Art Tatum, and pianists Clarence Profit and Billy Kyle. After a period of struggle when his style of playing was considered out of date, Casey worked regularly during 1957–61 as a member of King Curtis' R&B band. He led his first record date (other than two numbers in 1945) in 1960.

In the 1970s, Casey often appeared with small swing bands, and he recorded with Helen Humes and Jay McShann. During 1981–2001, he was a member of the Harlem Blues and Jazz Band. Active until shortly before his death, Al Casey played in a style virtually unchanged from the early 1940s.

**Recommended CDs:** *Buck Jumpin'* (Original Jazz Classics 675) from 1960 has Al Casey featured with a quartet on acoustic guitar, performing standards (including three songs associated with Fats Waller) and basic originals. *Jumpin' With Al: The Definitive Black & Blue Sessions* (Black & Blue 873) from 1973 has Casey holding his own with the likes of Jay McShann, Arnett Cobb and Milt Buckner, playing hot swing. 1994's *A Tribute To "Fats"* features Casey at 79 still sounding in prime form in a quartet that includes 82-year-old pianist Red Richards.

**LPs to Search For:** *Al Casey Quartet* (Moodsville 12) is a long-scarce quartet set of standards from 1960 taken at a ballad pace. Casey was also featured on a few London sessions during 1981–85: *Six Swinging Strings* (JSP 1026), *Best Of Friends* (JSP 1051), *Genius Of The Jazz Guitar* (JSP 1062) and *Al Casey Remembers King Curtis* (JSP 1095).

## Oscar Castro-Neves
*b. May 15, 1940, Rio de Janeiro, Brazil*

When it comes to being part of the bossa nova and Brazilian jazz world, Oscar Castro-Neves has been there from the start. His ability to organize sessions and projects has sometimes overshadowed his guitar playing, but he is a brilliant musician and a tasteful singer. Born as one of triplets in a musical family, Castro-Neves started off playing the cavaquinho, a small Brazilian guitar. He also learned piano and classical guitar, performing with his three brothers (pianist Mario, bassist Iko and drummer Leo). When he was 16, he had a national hit in Brazil with his recording of "Chora Tua Tristeza." Among his early recordings were important sessions with Vinicius de Moraes, Dorival Caymmi and Quarteto em Cy. In 1962, Castro-Neves not only appeared at Carnegie

Hall at a historic bossa nova concert but also helped organize the date and accompanied many of the other musicians. After the event, he went on a tour with Dizzy Gillespie, Stan Getz, Lalo Schifrin and Laurindo Almeida that helped popularize bossa nova and Brazilian music in general.

Castro-Neves spent the next nine years back in Brazil working as an arranger, producer and guitarist. In 1971, he moved to Los Angeles, working with Sergio Mendes' Brazil 66 for the next decade as guitarist and music director and appearing on more than 15 albums with Mendes.

Since that time, he has been extremely busy, working with the greats of both Brazilian and American music, as a guitarist and arranger. In his career, Castro-Neves has worked with Antonio Carlos Jobim, Elis Regina, Flora Purim, Joe Henderson, Barbara Streisand, Stevie Wonder, Stan Getz, Eliane Elias, João Gilberto, Lee Ritenour, Airto Moreira, Toots Thielemans, Paul Winter, Diane Schuur, Herbie Hancock, Ella Fitzgerald and many others in addition to writing the scores for several films (including *Blame It On Rio*). He has also produced all-star concerts, including several at the Hollywood Bowl.

Although bossa nova would have existed without Oscar Castro-Neves, he has helped the music in a countless number of ways throughout his career.

**Recommended CDs:** As a solo artist, Oscar Castro-Neves has recorded several worthy albums, including *Big Band Bossa Nova* (Ubatuqui 302), *Brazilian Scandals* (JVC 3302), *Oscar* (Living Music 81516), *Maracuja* (GRP 3317), *More Than Yesterday* (JVC 2003), *Tropical Heart* (JVC 2026), *Playful Heart* (Mack Avenue 1011) and *All One* (Mack Avenue 1026).

**Website:** www.oscarcastroneves.com

## Philip Catherine
*b. October 27, 1942, London, England*

Whether it has been playing swing (and being called "Young Django" by Charles Mingus), coming up with a distinctive and intense style in fusion, or performing post-bop, Philip Catherine has long been a powerful force in several idioms.

Catherine was born to a Belgian father and an English mother during World War II. His grandfather played first violin with the London Symphony Orchestra. After the war ended, Catherine grew

up in Brussels. He took up the guitar as a teenager and became a professional at 17. He mostly played locally for the next decade, including working with organist Lou Bennett in 1961. It was not until 1970, when he recorded his debut album, *Stream*, that he began to get recognition outside of Belgium. Catherine spent much of 1971–72 playing fusion as part of the Jean-Luc Ponty Quintet.

After taking a 12-week course at Berklee and also studying with George Russell and Mick Goodrick, in 1973 Catherine formed his band Pork Pie. He also worked with the Paul Kuhn Orchestra. Other mid-1970s associations included Palle Mikkelborg, Karin Krog and Charles Mariano. Catherine recorded as a sideman for the Steeplechase label with Dexter Gordon (*Something Different*), the Kenny Drew Trio and Niels Pedersen (*Jay Walking* and *Double Bass*).

Catherine really rose to prominence in the United States when he and Larry Coryell formed an acoustic guitar duo in 1976, touring the world and recording *Twin House* and *Splendid*. However, he was actually more interested in playing electric guitar, which he returned to when recording with Charles Mingus in 1977 (*Three Or Four Shades Of Blues*), working with the Niels Pedersen Trio later in the decade, and heading his own trio.

He worked with Charlie Mariano on several projects, as well as Stéphane Grappelli, Michael Mantler and Benny Goodman (a two-week tour in 1980), and was in a colorful trio with violinist Didier Lockwood and guitarist Christian Escoudé in 1984. He recorded two great albums in a trio with Chet Baker and a bassist and spent much of 1985 touring Europe with Baker. In the early 1990s, Catherine recorded three albums with Tom Harrell (*I Remember You* and *Moods, Vol. I* and *Vol. II*) that are reminiscent of the Chet Baker dates.

Despite all of this, and work with Miroslav Vitous, Enrico Rava, Toots Thielemans, Sylvain Luc, the Brussels Jazz Orchestra and his own pianoless trio, Philip Catherine tends to be underrated in the United States. Many of his key recordings are difficult to find, and he has not toured the US that often, but in Europe they know what a special player he is.

**Recommended CDs:** These recordings give one a well-rounded picture of the eclectic and always stimulating Philip Catherine: *Transparence* (In-Akustik 8701), *September Sky* (September 5106), *Oscar* (Igloo 060), *I Remember You* (Criss Cross 1048), *Moods Vol. 1* (Criss Cross 1060), *Moods Vol. 2* (Criss Cross 1061), *Spanish Nights* (Enja 7023), *Live* (Dreyfus 36587), *Guitar Groove* (Dreyfus 36599), *Blue Prince* (Dreyfus 36614), *Summer Night* (Dreyfus 36637), *Meeting Colours* (Dreyfus 36675) with the Brussels Jazz Orchestra, *Guitars Two* (Dreyfus

46050) and *Concert In Capbreton* (Dreyfus 46050); with Chet Baker: *Chet's Choice* (Criss Cross 1016) and *Strollin'* (Enja 5005); with Stéphane Grappelli: *Young Django* (MPS 15510); with Dexter Gordon: *Something Different* (Steeplechase 1136); with Larry Coryell: *Twin House* (Act 92122).

**LPs to Search For:** Philip Catherine's earliest dates as a leader, *Stream* (Warner Bros. 46149), *September Man* (Warner Bros. 40562), *Guitars* (Warner Bros. 5019), *End Of August* (Warner Bros. 58 450), and *Nairam* (Warner Bros. 2850) remain difficult to find.

**Website:** www.philipcatherine.com

## Eugene Chadbourne
*b. January 4, 1954, Mt. Vernon, New York*

Due to his very eclectic musical tastes and crazy sense of humor, Eugene Chadbourne is often thought of as an eccentric. But as becomes obvious from exploring the vast range of his recordings and listening to him discuss his music, he knows exactly what he is doing. "I decided to get a guitar the day after the Beatles were on television. While I had not watched the actual show, I did notice that girls at school were very excited, and this was the first time anything made them excited other than boys fighting or sports, neither of which I was good at. I was 11 or 12 at the time."

Raised in Boulder, Colorado, Chadbourne was influenced early on by Jimi Hendrix's sound explorations. "I played in a garage band called Daytop Village. We played psychedelic parties at kids' houses. The average length of a song was about 45 minutes." As a teenager, he discovered jazz, seeing the Charles Lloyd Quartet and Bola Sete on television and buying a used copy of a Cal Tjader LP. "I love the way so many jazz artists—too many to name but of course Coltrane, Miles, Rahsaan—take the listener on such an exciting and ever-changing exploratory trip through their careers. That has been a big influence on my approach to making music."

During this era, Chadbourne also explored acoustic bottleneck blues and became interested in avant-garde jazz, including Derek Bailey. He studied to become a journalist but was persuaded to change his mind. "Anthony Braxton talked me into becoming a professional musician one night. Prior to him expressing great interest in my music, I really had no idea whether I was any good or not. Once I got his approval, I figured there must be something to what I am doing." After recording *Solo Acoustic Guitar* in 1975, the following year he became part of the New York downtown music scene, playing improvised music with John Zorn and Henry Kaiser and forming a duo with drummer Paul Lovens.

Since that time, Eugene Chadbourne has been

involved in a countless number of colorful and unusual projects. He combined country and Western music with free improvisation as early as 1977 and came up with new ways to play the banjo. He gained attention as the leader of Shockabilly in the early 1980s, performing a rather unique take on rockabilly. "After Shockabilly broke up in 1983, an important decision involved trying to freelance as much as possible, focusing on working as a wild card with already existing groups." At a Winnipeg folk festival, he performed with a Cajun band and a Russian folk group at the same time. He mixed together country and folk music and had collaborations with Fred Frith, Elliott Sharp, Charles Tyler, Frank Lowe, and Han Bennink. Chadbourne had a duo with former Frank Zappa drummer Jimmy Carl Black (called the Jack and Jim Show) that lasted two decades. In recent years, he has been part of the Aki Takase Fats Waller Project, which played at the Budapest and Istanbul jazz festivals in 2009.

"In 2008, I made a decision to make my repertoire consist primarily of my own original material, both songs with lyrics and instrumental pieces. Mainly I have been touring solo the last two years, hitting many places in the United States that I have not been to for many years. Anthony Braxton was a big musical influence in the beginning of my career, but more recently I decided he had initially led me down the wrong path with this concentration on big projects and being an incredible musical genius who is active constantly in so many areas. I realized that my specialty involves an intense focus on the simplest aspect of what I am doing, my songs. By paring down my activities in this nature, I can actually bring together more diverse elements of my musical expression and create something both complex and hopefully moving. Overall, my greatest inspirations, covering all manner of creative expression and personal philosophy, are Bugs Bunny and Boris Karloff."

**Recommended CDs:** Eugene Chadbourne has recorded many albums for his Parachute and House of Chadula labels since 1975. It all started with *Volume One Solo Acoustic Guitar* (House of Chadula 1975A), which originally was released on just 500 LPs. When asked what other recordings of his are his personal favorites, Chadbourne named *Volume Two: Solo Acoustic Guitar* (Rastacan 32), the avantgarde country record *There'll Be No Tears Tonight* (Fundamental 50062/House of Chadula 1980), *Vermin Of The Blues* (HOC 1986B), *Country Music In The World Of Islam* (HOC 1990B), *Think 69* (HOC 2008A) with Jimmy Carl Black, and *We Don't Have This Is The Home* (HOC 2009A). Among the many other Chadbourne CDs are such humorous titles (worthy of the Raymond Scott Quintette) as *Country Music Of Southeastern Australia* (Entropy 002), *New Directions In Appalachian Music, Insect And Western, Kitchen Concert: Torture In The '80s, Chad-Born Again, Locked In A Dutch Coffeeshop,* and *Sacred Insects Of Ancient Egypt.*

**Website:** www.eugenechadbourne.com

## Ed Cherry
*b. October 12, 1954, New Haven, CT*

Ed Cherry is a versatile and skilled guitarist who is still best known for his association with Dizzy Gillespie. He started playing the guitar when he was 12 or 13, receiving his first instrument as a Christmas present. "At that time in the mid-'60s, the guitar was seen on TV constantly. I was taken by how cool it looked and the sounds it made, from distorted acid rock and screaming clear-toned blues to the funky rhythmic 9th chords on anything James Brown was doing." He discovered jazz when his father played his records on weekends, including Thelonious Monk, Charlie Parker and Grant Green. Originally, Cherry played the popular soul music of the era at school dances in junior high school. He also was a clarinetist for a few years. Cherry attended Berklee briefly in 1972 before going on the road with an oldies group, the 5 Satins. He worked with Jimmy McGriff during 1974–75, moved to New York in 1978, and joined Dizzy Gillespie the same year.

Ed Cherry was associated with Gillespie for the next 14 years, playing with him in a pianoless quartet, on occasional big band projects, and finally with the United Nation Orchestra. The trumpeter's music during that era ranged from his bop classics to funk. Cherry was very significant to Gillespie both as a soloist and in his comping behind Dizzy's playing.

Since Gillespie's death, Cherry has led three albums of his own and worked with Paquito D'Rivera, John Patton, Henry Threadgill, Roy Hargrove's Crisol orchestra (1997–98), Hamiet Bluiett, Claudio Roditi, Sherman Irby, Reuben Wilson, Paula West and his own trio.

"I'm grateful to my parents for allowing me to express myself musically in the basement/garage with my friends, to have different types of music on in the house all the time, and especially my dad, who went to my first Jimi Hendrix concert with me. It is important to try to listen to as many types of music as you can and support live jazz. Don't just sit at home watching YouTube, for there is nothing like hearing this music live."

**Recommended CDs:** Although *First Take* (RTE 1009), *A Second Look* (RTE 1010) and the often-funky *The Spirits Speak* (Justin Time 155) are all fine efforts, Ed Cherry looks forward to recording with his own trio in the future. One of his best recordings with Dizzy Gillespie is *Musician, Composer, Raconteur* (Pablo 2620116).

**Website:** www.myspace.com/edcherrygroup

## Andrew Cheshire
*b. June 21, 1962, Queens, NY*

Andrew Cheshire learned how to play guitar his own way, which accounts for his original sound and voicings, and perhaps his ability to play both inside and outside. Cheshire first played piano, becoming interested in the guitar when he was eight.

ANDREW CHESHIRE

this is me

DON FRIEDMAN • RON McCLURE • MATT WILSON

He remembers having a paper route four years later in which one of his customers was drummer Mousey Alexander. "Sometimes Buddy Rich, a frequent visitor, would take the paper out of my hand and smack me in the head with it—always in an affectionate way of course." He started sitting in when he was 12. "They used to sneak me into bars on Long Island when I was 12, where I would be the guest blues guitarist, back in the early '70s. By the time I was 15, I had my own gigs."

Rather than attend music schools or college, Cheshire was self-taught and learned on the bandstand. He moved to Brooklyn when he was 17, started playing at jam sessions, and worked through the years with such notables as Joey Baron, Kenny Barron, Dewey Redman, Louis Hayes, Harold Mabern, Marvin "Smitty" Smith, Walter Perkins (1990–91), Ron McClure, Rich Perry, Don Friedman (1996–98), and in a trio with Dominic Duval and drummer Jay Rosen. Cheshire was in demand because he developed a fresh and personal style, whether playing chordal improvisations or freer music.

Andrew Cheshire, who founded his own Joule record label, also writes classical music, has built guitar amplifiers and is a poet and a painter. "For a long time, I didn't enjoy playing jazz. I always wanted to play music the way I wanted to play it, and I inadvertently sidestepped some important basics you should know if you're going to be playing jazz, like conforming to the established pre-existing vocabulary. But I slowly started finding things on my own and eventually got to the point where I could hear all of music in four or five distinct tonalities. When this began to happen, it was like a huge weight was being lifted from my shoulders. I knew that the building blocks—or what I like to call 'the source'—had my back. I was now free to express myself and actually look forward to whatever discoveries might be made on the spur of the moment."

**Recommended CDs:** Cheshire has led quite a few CDs of his own, all of which feature original playing and unpredictable moments: *This Is Me* (Joule 3557) with Don Friedman; *Another View* (Orchard 5266); *Water Street Revival* (Orchard 801184); *Relax, Keep The Tension* (CIMP 165); *Magic* (Joule 801643); the solo record *Guitar Noir* (Joule 05); *Faces* (Joule 06); *Morning Song* (Joule 07); *Pavane Pour Une Infante Difunte* (Joule 08); *Four Ages Of Bob* (Joule 09); *Silent Trees Falling* (Joule 11), on which Cheshire plays sitar; *Virtual String Quartet* (Joule 12), which features Cheshire's writing for MIDI performances that emulate a string quartet; and *Ballads* (Joule 13).

**Website:** www.andrewcheshire.com

## James Chirillo
*b. May 2, 1953, Waltham, MA*

James Chirillo is a superior swing guitarist who has appeared with many important groups in the New York area during the past 30 years. Growing up in Bellevue, Washington, Chirillo started on guitar at 12 and gained early experience playing in local funk groups. In his senior year of high school, he played with Heart during the period before the group caught on. He attended Bellevue Community College (1972–74) and North Texas State University (1975–78).

Chirillo worked with singer Marilyn Maye during 1978–79 and was a member of the US Military Academy Band at West Point during 1979–82. Since moving to New York in 1982, he has been a significant part of the mainstream jazz and swing scene. He studied with Tiny Grimes and Remo Palmieri and was a member of both the last Benny Goodman Orchestra (1985–86) and the Buck Clayton Big Band (1987–91). Among the greats whom he has performed with are Claude Williams, Bob Wilber, Benny Carter, Kenny Davern, Ken Peplowski, Warren Vaché, Loren Schoenberg, Wynton Marsalis and the Lincoln Center Orchestra, the Smithsonian Jazz Masterworks Orchestra, Eddie Durham, Eddie Barefield, Bob Haggart, Louie Bellson, Frank Wess, Roland Hanna, Joe Williams, and a few concerts with Ella Fitzgerald. Chirillo also recorded *Rush Hour* with Joe Lovano and Gunther Schuller. In

1995, he was awarded an NEA grant to write the "Homage Concerto For Clarinet And Jazz Orchestra" for Kenny Davern.

"My goal for the future is to establish, write for, and perform with a larger ensemble of my own. All I really try to do when playing or composing is to make the same 12 tones sound fresh every time they come my way. Really swinging ties me directly to all the great music and musicians of the past and puts me in a state of complete peace and joy."

**Recommended CDs:** James Chirillo has thus far only led one album, *Sultry Serenade* (Nagel Heyer 61), a well-rounded set that is highlighted by his duet with trumpeter-composer Johnny Carisi on "Counterpoise #2 For Electric Guitar And Trumpet." As a sideman, he has recorded with Joe Lovano, Kenny Davern, Marcus Roberts, Houston Person, Daryl Sherman, Joyce Breach, Claude Williams, David Lahm, Joe Temperley, Scott Robinson, Warren Vaché & the Scottish String Ensemble (*Don't Look Back*, for which he also contributed arrangements), Randy Reinhardt, the Loren Schoenberg Big Band, Keith Ingham, the Smithsonian Jazz Masterworks Orchestra, Joe Wilder, and Bobby Gordon.

## Charlie Christian
b. July 29, 1916, Dallas, TX; d. March 2, 1942, New York, NY

If one thinks of Eddie Lang as the Coleman Hawkins of the guitar in that he practically founded jazz guitar, and Django Reinhardt as Lester Young, a very viable and completely different stylist, then it would be logical to think of Charlie Christian as the Charlie Parker of the guitar. Not only was he the first major electric guitarist (although preceded slightly by George Barnes, Eddie Durham and Les Paul), but Christian also came up with most of the phrases used by jazz guitarists prior to the rise of fusion in the late 1960s. It might be a simplification to say that Christian merely transferred the ideas and phrasing of Lester Young to the guitar, but the tenor-saxophonist was certainly an influence, as were other horn players. And with just a few exceptions (Laurindo Almeida and Gabor Szabo among them), virtually every jazz guitarist until the rise of Larry Coryell and especially John McLaughlin a quarter century after Christian's death sounds like a loving relative.

Born in Dallas, Charlie Christian grew up in Oklahoma City. Part of a musical family that included a father and four brothers who were musicians, Christian had brief stints on trumpet and piano before settling on guitar when he was 12. He played in a family band, with Anna Mae Winburn, and, most notably, with Alphonso Trent. In 1937, he bought his first electric guitar, and now that he could be heard, he began to be noticed, including by Mary Lou Williams and Teddy Wilson.

In 1939, when he was working with Leslie Sheffield's band, Christian was heard by producer John Hammond, who, in August, arranged for him to come to Los Angeles and audition with Benny Goodman. Christian's flashy and out-of-date clothes at first repelled the guitarist, who stalled about auditioning the guitarist until Hammond insisted. Relenting, Goodman called out "Rose Room," and 45 minutes later he was still jamming the song with Christian.

Overnight, Charlie Christian became part of the new Benny Goodman Sextet, which also included Lionel Hampton. While he was occasionally used in Goodman's big band (having a superb feature on "Solo Flight"), most of his work was with the clarinetist's sextet and, after mid-1940 when the clarinetist reorganized, his septet with trumpeter Cootie Williams and tenor-saxophonist Georgie Auld. Christian's ability to come up with one riff-filled idea after another made him a favorite with Goodman and at jam sessions, including at Minton's Playhouse in 1941, where he sat in after hours with the house band (which included Thelonious Monk and drummer Kenny Clarke) and the many guests.

Other highlights of Christian's career included participation at John Hammond's 1939 From Spirituals to Swing concert at Carnegie Hall (playing with Goodman's sextet and with Count Basie in a small group with Lester Young and Buck Clayton), recording with the Metronome All-Stars, and soloing on many broadcast appearances with Goodman.

The parallels with bassist Jimmy Blanton are somewhat remarkable. Both Christian and Blanton revolutionized their instruments, they spent all of their most important years as a sideman with a famous bandleader, and they were never filmed despite the fame of Goodman and Ellington (who made many films in other periods). Sadly, they both had their lives cut short at a young age due to tuberculosis.

Charlie Christian became ill in June 1941 and spent his last eight months in a sanitarium. Although he rallied on several occasions, he passed away in 1942 when he was just 25. But he had made such a big impact during the 22 months that he was with Benny Goodman that the guitar can easily be divided into two time periods: Before and After Charlie Christian.

**Recommended CDs:** *The Genius Of The Electric Guitar* (Columbia Jazz Legacy 65564) is a definitive four-CD set that has all of the studio performances of Christian with Goodman including the alternate takes. Every one of the sextet/septet numbers are here (including "Rose Room," "Seven Come Eleven," and "Flying Home"), the occasional solos with Goodman's orchestra, Christian's appearance with the Metronome All-Stars, and the full version of a studio jam session. Much of this music is available elsewhere, but this box is the best way to acquire it. Christian's radio appearances with Goodman are scattered, but *Selected Broadcasts And Jam Sessions* (JSP 909), a three-CD set, has all of the best. Christian is heard not only with Goodman but also with Count Basie at the From Spirituals to Swing concert and with Monk and Clarke at Minton's Playhouse, where his lengthy solo on "Stompin' At The Savoy" finds him pointing toward the bebop era, a period that, tragically, he would not live to see.

## Corey Christiansen
*b. July 26, 1971, Logan, UT*

Corey Christiansen is a fine hard-bop/soul-jazz guitarist who is also a significant educator. "My father, Mike Christiansen, runs the guitar program at Utah State University and I have studied with him since I was five. We had a family band that mostly played bluegrass and folk music, playing gigs all around the valley I grew up in. My dad and I played the guitar, my brother played bass and my mom and sisters sang."

Christiansen earned a bachelor's degree at Utah State University in 1996 (his father was one of his teachers) and a master's degree at the University of South Florida in 1999. After teaching at South Florida for a year, during 2000–07, Christiansen was the main guitar clinician and senior editor for Mel Bay Publications. In that role, he conducted a countless number of clinics and performed around the world. In 2007, he became the director of curriculum for the Music School at Utah State University in addition to teaching part-time at Indiana University.

As a guitarist, Corey Christiansen has worked with Willie Akins, Vic Juris, Danny Gottlieb, Matt Jorgensen, Jimmy Bruno, James Moody and Christian McBride, and recorded as a leader for both Mel Bay and Origin. "I'd like to continue with serious education as well as performing and recording. I want to produce music that doesn't alienate an audience. I think this is possible by keeping swing and groove alive in the music."

**Recommended CDs:** *Awakening* (Mel Bay 20821) was a strong debut recording, while *Roll With It* (Origin 82513) is a bluesy set of originals performed in a quartet with tenor-saxophonist David Halliday, organist Pat Bianchi and drummer Matt Jorgensen, the same group that is featured on *Outlaw Tractor* (Origin 82562). Corey Christiansen is also featured in the quintet MB3 Trio with fellow guitarists Jimmy Bruno and Vic Juris on the exciting *Jazz Hits Vol. 1* (Mel Bay 10312).

**Website:** www.coreychristiansen.com

## Dave Cliff
*b. June 25, 1944, Hexham, Northumberland, United Kingdom*

An excellent swing and bop guitarist from England, David Cliff has also fit in well with Lennie Tristano's musicians. The son of a guitarist, Cliff began on the guitar when he was 13, first hearing jazz on BBC Radio. He gained some early experiences playing in skiffle groups. Cliff played in a trio with tenor-saxophonist Nigel Stanger and bassist Dave Murphy during 1966–67. He went to Leeds College of Music during 1967–70, where he earned a degree and had the opportunity to study with bassist Peter Ind. "What I learned at Leeds with Peter Ind and Bernie Cash has been invaluable: singing the great solos, slow practicing with a metronome, covering the basics, studying rhythm, self-awareness, and getting into Lester Young."

Cliff moved to London in 1971, becoming an important part of the local scene for decades. He toured several countries in Europe during 1976–77 with the Lee Konitz–Warme Marsh Quintet, played in the United Kingdom with Soprano Summit, and has often performed with visiting Americans, including Nina Simone, Spike Robinson, Herb Geller, Lanny Morgan, Harry Allen, Scott Hamilton, Lew Tabackin, Richie Cole, Ken Peplowski, Eddie "Lockjaw" Davis, Warren Vaché, Buddy Childers, Slide Hampton, Jack McDuff, Mundell Lowe, Bucky Pizzarelli, Phil DeGreg and Irene Reid. Naturally, most of Cliff's work has been with British musicians, including altoist Geoff Simkins, saxophonists Alison Neale and Jo Fooks, trumpeters Bruce Adams and Gary Kavanagh, Georgie Fame, keyboardist Mike Carr, and the late drummer Alan Ganley. In addition,

Dave Cliff teaches jazz guitar at London's Trinity College of Music, the Royal Welsh College of Music and Drama, and the Birmingham Conservatoire.

"What I love most about jazz is making it different every time."

**Recommended CDs:** Dave Cliff has recorded with Warne Marsh, Bob Wilber, Scott Hamilton and Warren Vaché. As a leader in the mid-1990s, he recorded *Sipping At Bells* (Spotlite 553) and *Play Tadd Dameron* (Spotlite 560), both with Geoff Simkins. On *When Lights Are Low* (Master Mix 18), he performs in a duo and quartet with Howard Alden.

**Website:** www.davecliff.com

## Nels Cline
*b. January 4, 1956, Los Angeles, CA*

A powerful and passionate improviser who has been heard in both free-form and fusion settings, Nels Cline is one of the few guitarists who could do a very creditable job taking John Coltrane's place in a revisit to his *Interstellar Space*. The twin brother of drummer/percussionist Alex Cline, he remembers, "I started messing about with guitar around the age of 11, inspired by surf music, psychedelic rock, blues and Indian classical music. I was a total primitive and did not really accomplish anything technically until years later. Around 1970 or '71, I was exposed to the music of John Coltrane, specifically the piece 'Africa,' which had my brother Alex and me moved and mystified. It was as though a door opened into another universe that no one had told us about."

Self-taught, Nels Cline and his brother played originals at their elementary school graduation and occasionally performed in public during their teenage years. In college, they had a group called Ring. "Even as I played more jazz-related music with a chamber jazz group called Quartet Music, we mostly put on our own gigs because the music was original and no one really knew us. In the '70s, we were really inspired by the 'loft jazz' scene in New York. Playing with people like woodwind master Vinny Golia was considered 'avant-garde,' so we just tried to make opportunities for ourselves. As such, sometimes that one gig per month took on such significance in one's mind that the playing was like that of wild beasts let out of a cage!"

Cline attended Occidental College during 1974–75 as a philosophy major and took some theory and orchestration classes from Santa Monica College. "I started working in a record store and, interestingly, it was at the store that I met a lot of musicians, many of whom I still play with to this day."

In the 1980s, Cline worked often with Charlie Haden, Julius Hemphill, Eric Von Essen, Vinny Golia, Bobby Bradford, Jeff Gauthier and Mark Isham. In the 1990s, he also worked with Mike Watt, Carla Bozulich, Leo Smith and Thurston Moore. In recent times, he has led the Nels Cline Singers (which, ironically, is an instrumental group), performed with Zeena Parkins, OrkestROVA, Celestial Septet (the Rova Saxophone plus the Nels Cline Singers), the Scott Amendola Band, the Jeff Gauthier Goatette, the Sons of Champignon (with Tim Berne and Jim Black), Jenny Scheinman, duos with Elliott Sharp and G.E. Stinson, and a sextet that perform the music of Andrew Hill. Since 2004, Nels Cline has had his biggest visibility as a member of the alternative rock group Wilco while still continuing with his own projects.

For the future, Nels Cline has typically ambitious goals. He would like to write for an electro-acoustic and micro-tonal ensemble, record an orchestrated "mood music" record of mostly standards, make nine albums of his trio the Singers with nine separate guitarists, record a seven-record vinyl set of duets with seven turntablists called *Remember The Turntable*, and study the lap steel guitar. "I am a mutt, a hybrid, an amalgam of acquired feelings and inspiration. I struggled for most of my life trying to reconcile what I felt were unresolvable dichotomies: electric versus acoustic, rock versus jazz, intimate versus monumental, etc. It was when I threw away those distinctions that I started to become happier in my life."

**Recommended CDs:** Nels Cline has recorded quite a few recordings since making his recording debut with Vinny Golia in 1979. As a leader, he has recorded for a large assortment of labels, many quite obscure. Some of his most important releases are *Angelica* (Enja 5063); *Silencer* (Enja 6098); *In-Store* (Father Yod 17); *Interstellar Space Revisited* (Atavistic 102), which is comprised of duets with percussionist Gregg Bendian that form a stunning John Coltrane tribute; *The Inkling* (Cryptogramophone 105); *Destroy All* (Atavistic 122); *The Entire Time* (Nine Winds 259), which is comprised of duets with Vinny Golia; a tribute to Andrew Hill called *New Monstery* (Cryptogramophone 130); *Draw Breath* (Cryptogramophone 133); and unaccompanied solos on *Coward* (Cryptogramophone 141). Nels Cline, Alex Cline, bassist Eric Von Essen and violinist Jeff Gauthier are featured as Quartet Music on *Summer Night* (Delos 4010) and several Nine Winds LPs. The Nels Cline Singers have thus far recorded *Instrumentals* (Cryptogramophone 113), *The Giant Pin* (Cryptogramophone 120), *Initiate* (Cryptogramophone 143) and *Ash And Tabula* (Atavistic 148).

**Website:** www.nelscline.com

## Joe Cohn
*b. December 28, 1956, Flushing, NY*

When it comes to swing-to-bop guitar playing performed with a cool tone and a quiet but driving style, Joe Cohn has long been one of the best. The son of Al Cohn and singer Marilyn Moore, he did not take up the guitar until he was 16. Despite the late start, Cohn developed fairly quickly, attending Berklee during 1975–78 and also playing occasional trumpet (giving it up in the 1990s) and bass. Cohn worked extensively with his father (1979–87), the Artie Shaw Orchestra (1982–88), Zoot Sims, Nick Brignola, Claude "Fiddler" Williams, Freddie Cole, Buddy DeFranco, Bob Mover, Warren Chiasson, Al Grey, Mose Allison, and Carmen Leggio. In addition, he occasionally performed with Mel Torme, Joe Williams, Dizzy Gillespie, Hank Jones, Freddie Hubbard, Clark Terry, Warne Marsh, Wynton Marsalis, Dave McKenna, Lee Konitz, Tommy Flanagan, James Moody, Eddie Daniels, Frank Wess and Daryl Sherman.

In recent times, Cohn has played regularly with the Jay Leonhart trio and the Grant Stewart quintet. He is perhaps best known for his work with Harry Allen, usually in a pianoless quartet. Joe Cohn, whose daughter Shaye is a classical pianist, keeps quite busy and is greatly in-demand on the East Coast for swinging sessions.

**Recommended CDs:** *Two Funky People* (Double Time 126) was a strong debut for Joe Cohn as a leader, teaming him with Doug Raney in 2000. *Restless* (Arbors 19329), with a quintet/sextet that includes altoist Dmitry Baevsky and sometimes Harry Allen, and the quartet date *Shared Contemplations* (Criss Cross 1309) are also quite enjoyable. As a sideman, Joe Cohn has recorded with Teddy Wilson, Buddy DeFranco, Al Cohn, Al Grey, Jesse Green, Nick Brignola, Duffy Jackson, Daryl Sherman, Claude Williams, Bob Dorough, Kenny Davern, Jay Leonhart, Ken Peplowski, Eddie Higgins, Grant Stewart, and Ray Kennedy, and on these CDs with Harry Allen: *I Won't Dance* (RCA 58126), *Hey Look Me Over* (Arbors 19333), *Hits By Brits* (Challenge 73258), *Music From Guys And Dolls* (Arbors 19354), and *Plays Music From South Pacific* (Arbors 19380).

**Website:** www.joecohn.com

## Cal Collins
*b. May 5, 1933, Medora, IN; d. August 27, 2001, Dillsborn, IN*

When he was in his forties, Cal Collins seemed to come out of nowhere to record regularly for the Concord label and be featured with all-star groups.

But within a decade, he had largely returned to obscurity, having made a permanent impression on the jazz world with his tasteful, melodic and lightly swinging playing.

Collins first played professionally as a mandolin player in bluegrass in the early 1950s. After serving in the Army, he settled in Cincinnati and worked as a jazz guitarist. Inspired by Charlie Christian, Irving Ashby, Oscar Moore and other swing players, Collins played regularly in the Cincinnati area for two decades before being discovered by Benny Goodman in 1976.

That was his big break. Collins, who was already 43, worked with Goodman for three years (including at Goodman's 40th anniversary Carnegie Hall concert) and recorded regularly as a leader and a sideman for the Concord label during 1978–81, being part of their small group swing movement along with Scott Hamilton and Warren Vaché. In addition to his own albums and dates with Hamilton and Vaché, Collins recorded with John Bunch, Marshall Royal, the Concord Super Band, Rosemary Clooney, Ross Tompkins, Al Cohn, and a Woody Herman small group during this busy time.

Moving back to Cincinnati in the early 1980s, Collins gradually receded from the national stage, although he continued playing and occasionally recording. In 1993, he was on the Masters of the Steel String Guitar tour with Doc Watson, Jerry Douglas and Cephas & Wiggins. He participated on some Wes Montgomery tribute CDs and made his last album as a leader in 1998. Cal Collins passed away in 2001 from liver failure at age 68, having made his mark on the jazz world.

**Recommended CDs:** *Interplay* (Concord 4137) teams Cal Collins in a quartet with Herb Ellis. Other worthy Collins albums include *Crack'd Rib* (Mopro 107), *Ohio Style* (Concord 4447) from 1991, and 1998's *S'Us Four* (U Curve 1064) with guitarist Kenny Poole.

**LPs to Search For:** Surprisingly, most of Cal Collins' recordings as a leader have not been reissued on CD. Concord has neglected many of the recordings that he made for them. The guitarist's first album as a leader, *Milestones* (Pausa 7159), was recorded in 1974, three years before his debut on Concord. Cut in Cincinnati, the trio set (with Kenny Poole on "epiphone guitar," which sounds like a bass) is very much in the Cal Collins style. Other albums long overdue to be reissued on CD include *Cincinnati To L.A.* (Concord 59), *In San Francisco* (Concord 71), *Blues On My Mind* (Concord 95) and his two LPs of unaccompanied guitar solos: *By Myself* (Concord 119) and *Cross Country* (Concord 166).

## John Collins
*b. September 20, 1912, Montgomery, AL; d. October 4, 2001, Los Angeles, CA*

John Collins spent the first part of his career with a whirlwind of activity, became Nat King Cole's last guitarist, and ended his life known as a tasteful if rarely documented guitarist who was also an educator. His quiet personality and gentle guitar style resulted in him being both widely respected and obscure. Born in Montgomery, Alabama, he grew up in Chicago. Both his grandmother and his mother were pianists, with his mother (Georgia Gorham) playing jazz quite well. Collins had his first gigs with her when he was 14. He developed quickly, and when he was 21 in 1933, he had the chance to play some jobs with Art Tatum. During the next 15 years, Collins worked with many of the major jazz names, including Fletcher Henderson, Billie Holiday, Roy Eldridge (1936–40), Lester Young (1941–43), Coleman Hawkins, Benny Carter, the Slam Stewart Trio, Dizzy Gillespie, Erroll Garner and Billy Taylor. Collins switched easily to the electric guitar in the late 1930s, and although based in swing, his complex harmonies and open-mindedness allowed him to fit perfectly in bop settings. He was on many record dates, particularly in the mid-1940s, and writer Leonard Feather, who produced sessions for Victor, utilized Collins often.

But because John Collins was rarely a leader, he was much better known to jazz musicians than to the general public. In 1951, when Irving Ashby left the Nat King Cole Trio, Collins took his place, staying until Cole's death in 1965. During this time, Cole quickly made the transition from a jazz pianist to a standup singer, and Collins was only featured on occasional trio numbers, usually being an anonymous part of the backup orchestra. One of Nat King Cole's few later jazz albums, *The After Midnight Sessions*, is Collins' best showcase with Cole, but even here he is just one of several soloists.

After Cole's death, John Collins worked on and off for Bobby Troup for five years, freelanced in the Los Angeles area, and became a music teacher. Recordings were rare, but, during a tour of Europe with bassist Jimmy Woode and drummer Alvin Queen, he had the opportunity to make his only recording as a leader, *The Incredible John Collins*. He lived to be 89, but John Collins' most important work in jazz was largely finished by the time he was 39.

**Recommended CDs:** Nat King Cole's *The After Midnight Sessions* (Capitol 9306) was one of the few opportunities with Cole on which Collins had a few solos.

**LPs to Search For:** *The Incredible John Collins* (Nilva 3412), which has Harry "Sweets" Edison on trumpet, has yet to return on CD.

## Eddie Condon
*(Albert Edwin Condon)*
*b. November 16, 1905, Goodland, IN; d. August 4, 1973, New York, NY*

During much of his lifetime (at least until the early 1960s), Eddie Condon was consistently the best-known guitarist in jazz. This was ironic since Condon did not solo and on some of his later recordings he is barely audible, but Condon was famous  in areas that had little to do with his playing. A propagandist for freewheeling Chicago jazz (essentially high-quality Dixieland), Condon had the knack for putting together all-star groups that overflowed with talent while managing to feature everyone. He was expert at setting tempos, coming up with spontaneous frameworks, and doing it all while being a wisecracking emcee.

Condon began his professional career as the banjoist with Hollis Peavey's Jazz Bandits in 1923. He was part of the Chicago jazz scene for the next six years, meeting and playing with the members of the Austin High School Gang, which included such longtime associates as Bud Freeman, Jimmy McPartland and Gene Krupa. In 1927, he co-led (along with Red McKenzie) and performed on a classic record date by the McKenzie–Condon Chicagoans. The four selections, featuring McPartland, Freeman, Joe Sullivan and Frankie Teschemacher, helped define Chicago jazz as opposed to New Orleans jazz (which was more ensemble oriented). Condon appeared on other hot jazz sessions of the period. In 1929, he moved to New York, gave up the banjo, and worked with Red Nichols' Five Pennies and Red McKenzie's Blue Blowers. Among his more notable record dates of the period were a session with Louis Armstrong in 1929 and one with Billy Banks' Rhythm Makers in 1932. Condon managed to ride out the worst years of the Depression without playing regularly in a big band. He co-led a combo with Joe Marsala during 1936–37.

In 1937, Eddie Condon began a seven-year period of performing nightly at Nick's in New York. He started leading record dates in 1938 for Commodore and became a major name. He utilized top Dixieland and swing musicians in racially mixed groups, and a great deal of exciting music resulted. Condon's legendary Town Hall concerts of 1944–45 were broadcast on a weekly basis. In 1945, he opened up his club, Condon's, which (at two different locations) lasted into the 1960s. Along the way, he wrote three colorful books, including his memoir *We Called It Music*, and he was a leader in keeping hot freewheeling jazz alive.

Despite drinking a lot and always seeming casual and frank, Condon was very skilled as a businessman and in fighting for the music he loved. Among the many musicians who had important associations with his groups were trumpeters/cornetists Wild Bill Davison, Max Kaminsky, Billy Butterfield, Bobby Hackett, Rex Stewart, and Hot Lips Page; trombonists Jack Teagarden, Lou McGarity, Cutty Cutshall, George Brunies, and Vic Dickenson; clarinetists Pee Wee Russell, Edmond Hall, Joe Marsala, Peanuts Hucko, and Bob Wilbur; Bud Freeman on tenor; baritonist Ernie Caceres; pianists Gene Schroeder, Joe Sullivan, Jess Stacy, Ralph Sutton and Art Hodes; drummers George Wettling, Dave Tough, Gene Krupa and Buzzy Drootin; several bassists, including Walter Page; and singer Lee Wiley.

Although Eddie Condon started to slow down during the second half of the 1960s, he stayed active up until the end, never amplifying his instrument or feeling compelled to solo.

**Recommended CDs:** While all of Eddie Condon's recordings are easily recommended to fans of hot jazz, none really showcase his guitar playing. But a good place to start in hearing his exciting music is *1927–1938* (Classics 742), *1938–1940* (Classics 759), *1942–1943* (Classics 772), *1944–1946* (Classics 1033), *1947–1950* (Classics 1177), any of his Columbia recordings of the 1950s, and the classic series of Town Hall radio broadcasts, which are available as *The Town Hall Concerts Vol. 1–11* (Jazzology 1101-1123), 23 CDs in all, released as ten double CDs and a final three-CD set.

## Bill Connors

*b. September 24, 1949, Los Angeles, CA*

Although he is to some extent the forgotten man of fusion, Bill Connors will always be best remembered for his playing on *Hymn Of The Seventh Galaxy* with Return to Forever. Connors began on the guitar when he was 14, originally playing rock and blues before he discovered jazz when he was 18. He moved to San Francisco in 1972, working with Mike Nock

and also having occasions to play with Art Lande and Steve Swallow. In 1973, Connors joined Return to Forever, playing next to his idol Chick Corea, Stanley Clarke and Steve Gadd (who was soon succeeded by Lenny White). His powerful guitar solos on *Hymn Of The Seventh Galaxy* became quite influential, setting a high standard for fusion guitar.

But after a year, Connors felt confined by the group despite the fame it was giving him. He left RTF, which, in retrospect, can only be seen as a very bad decision for his career. He worked with John

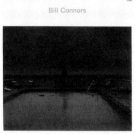

Bill Connors

Abercrombie and Jan Hammer and also recorded with Stanley Clarke before deciding that he would rather play acoustic guitar. Connors recorded three albums on acoustic guitar, which satisfied him artistically but resulted in his gradual slip into obscurity. He trained himself to become a classical guitarist, practicing for eight hours a day. During this era, he also recorded with Lee Konitz, Paul Bley and Jimmy Giuffre for the IAI label. Connors returned to the electric guitar later in the decade, but his moment in the spotlight had passed.

Connors recorded again in the mid-1980s but little else until a "comeback" CD in 2004. He appeared at a reunion concert with Return to Forever at the Hollywood Bowl in 2009, seeming a bit uncomfortable. Otherwise, he has mostly worked as a teacher. Bill Connors is still young enough to make another comeback, although it seems doubtful that he will make the impact that he could have made if he had stayed with RTF.

**Recommended CDs:** *Theme To The Guardian* (ECM 829387), *Of Mist And Melting* (ECM 1120) with Jan Garbarek, and the solo *Swimming With A Hole In My Body* (ECM 849078) are Connors' trio of acoustic guitar albums from the mid-1970s. *Step It* (Evidence 22080), *Double-Up* (Evidence 22081) and *Assembler* (Evidence 22095) feature Connors back on electric guitar. *Return* (Tone Center 4036) from 2004 has Bill Connors playing post-bop jazz rather than fusion and doing a fine job. But *Hymn Of The Seventh Galaxy* (Polydor 825336) with Return to Forever has his most memorable playing.

## Robert Conti

*b. November 21, 1945, Philadelphia, PA*

Although he has had several departures from his music career, Robert Conti is a consistently satisfying hard-bop guitarist. "The first recording to have a major impact on me was Toots Thielemans' 'Bluesette.' After that, I was introduced to Howard Roberts and Johnny Smith by Pat Martino, a close friend." Conti began performing when he was 14 and was on the road quite a bit during 1962–66 before settling in Jacksonville, Florida. In 1970, he left music and during the next six years had a very successful career in the securities industry. He is credited with advancing the concept of the financial supermarket.

Despite his successes in the business world, in 1976 he returned to playing jazz. Conti made his first recordings in 1979 (including *Solo Guitar*), starting a series on Trend and Discovery that included a 1981 album with Gerald Wilson (*Lomelin*). While continuing in jazz, he spent much of the 1980s back in the business world, including working with filmmaker Dino De Laurentiis in 1988, the year that he moved to Southern California. He was the resident jazz guitarist at the Irvine Marriott during 1988–98. In recent times, Conti has released 30 educational DVDs on jazz guitar.

Robert Conti, whose most recent CD is 2005's *To The Brink* on his Pinnacle label, says that his future goal is "to preserve and continue the rich legacy of the jazz art form, via exposure and education of younger players."

**Recommended CDs:** *Comin' On Strong* (Pinnacle 9902) with Pete Jolly and *To The Brink! Featuring Rocco Barbato* (Pinnacle 0501) feature Robert Conti in recent times playing at his peak.

**LPs to Search For:** Robert Conti's earlier recordings for Discovery and Trend, which include *Latin Love Affair*, *Solo Guitar*, *Robert Conti Jazz Quintet*, *Laura*, and *You Are The Sunshine Of My Life*, are scarce.

**Website:** www.robertconti.com

## Michael Coppola
b. April 9, 1956, Norwalk, CT

The master of the nine-string guitar, Michael Coppola improvises very well on his instrument, turning it into an orchestra without forgetting that he is playing a guitar. Coppola began playing a conventional guitar when he was 11, discovering jazz a few years later through the Mahavishnu Orchestra's *Inner Mounting Flame* album. He gained important experience playing in New Haven clubs with Charles McPherson and Eddie Buster when he was 18. Coppola studied with Sal Salvador during 1972–73, attended Boston Conservatory (1974–75), and later studied with Walter Bishop, Jr. He played guitar locally in a variety of groups and released his debut album, *Jet Blue*, in 1987, a set of unaccompanied solos.

In an attempt to play chordally like a piano, Coppola created the concept of an eight-string guitar, which he commissioned from James DeCava. Rather than adding a bass or treble string, his eight-string had more inner strings, resulting in tight voicings not heard on the guitar before. His 1997 recording *Virtuoso Too* demonstrates the instrument's potential.

In 1996, Coppola delved even further into the unknown, having James DeCava make him a nine-string guitar nicknamed "the Hydra." After a period of experimentation (including having the ninth string added as a lower bass note), by 2000 he settled on it being an upper-register string grouped between the fourth and fifth strings of a normal six-string guitar. He has recorded several albums on his nine-string and is thinking of titling an upcoming CD *Guitar And A Half*.

"I'd like to work on more Jelly Roll Morton pieces and come as close to solo piano on my guitar as humanly possible in one lifetime. My guitar playing is different than everyone else in your book, not because my instrument has nine strings, but because of the tuning of them and the technique I created to express myself on it. My chord voicings have been played by people such as Joe Beck, who had innovations of his own. However, most guitarists have lost improvisation skills in having the extra strings. I have the tight voicings available, while leaving the guitar tuned to the intervals I grew up with, thereby leaving all my notes in place. The extra strings provide the new colors in combination with the standard strings. They have taken me to new exciting places, which I had no clue were hidden therein."

**Recommended CDs:** Michael Coppola primarily plays standards on his recordings, but comes up with fresh ideas in addition to the unusual and very full sound. Thus far, he has recorded *Enter The Hydra* (String Jazz 1026), *Return Of The Hydra* (String Jazz 2021), *Guess Who I Saw Today!* (String Jazz 1039) with singer Rhonda Thomas and, for his Kalo label, *New Impressions*, *Monster Guitar*, and *On The Atkins Diet*.

**Website:** www.9string.com

## Larry Coryell
b. April 2, 1943, Galveston, TX

Larry Coryell has had a lengthy and wide-ranging career, but he will always be best known for being the first fusion guitarist, coming to jazz from a rock background and playing fusion before the music had its name. Coryell, who grew up in Washington State, began playing guitar when he was seven. He gained early experience as a teenager working in a group led by pianist Mike Mandel. Although he was familiar with Wes Montgomery, Tal Farlow, Barney Kessel and Johnny Smith, he was also open to the Beatles, Chuck Berry and the rock musicians of the mid-1960s during a period when jazz and rock were completely separate.

Taking time off from working on a journalism degree, Coryell went to New York in 1965 to see if he could make it in music. He worked with Killer Joe Piro and then gained attention in the jazz world when he joined Chico Hamilton's group as Gabor Szabo's successor. On Hamilton's 1966 album *The Dealer*, Coryell made his recording debut, playing in an electric blues/rock style on a jazz recording, probably the first time that that was done. He founded the legendary pioneering jazz-rock group the Free Spirits and then gained fame for his playing during 1967–68 with Gary Burton. Coryell was the first of a long string of guitarists to be featured in Burton's band and the most influential, combining a rockish sound with jazz improvisation.

Coryell recorded with Herbie Mann (*Memphis Underground*), toured with Jack Bruce, appeared on sessions with Charles Mingus, Billy Cobham and even the 5th Dimension, and recorded a very intriguing (if poorly reissued) body of work for the Vanguard label. He teamed up with saxophonist Steve Marcus in the groups Count's Jam Band in 1968 and Foreplay the following year; by 1973, the group had evolved into Coryell's Eleventh House (featuring Randy Brecker and Alphonse Mouzon). By that point in time, he had been overshadowed by John McLaughlin, and Eleventh House never enjoyed the success of the Mahavishnu Orchestra or the other major fusion bands.

In 1975, Coryell went in a completely different direction, switching to acoustic guitar and displaying his virtuosity with other guitarists. He worked and toured with Philip Catherine and has since also performed acoustically with John Scofield, Joe Beck and Steve Khan. In 1979 and again in the mid-1980s, he toured with an acoustic trio comprised of John McLaughlin and Paco de Lucía.

Since his fusion days, Larry Coryell's career has alternated between several different directions. He has continued his acoustic work on solo sets, in classical music projects, with Brazilian musicians and in further encounters with his fellow guitarists. He has occasionally returned to fusion, often in all-star settings. And Coryell has frequently played jazz standards in conventional hard-bop settings. Larry Coryell remains quite active today, while his sons Julian and Murali Coryell are developing into impressive up-and-coming guitarists.

**Recommended CDs:** *Lady Coryell* (Vanguard 6509); *Coryell* (Universe 21); *Spaces* (Vanguard 79345); *At The Village Gate* (Universe 22); *Fairyland* (Universe 180); *Offering* (Universe 2819); *Introducing The Eleventh House* (Vanguard 79342); *The Restful Mind* (Universe 33); *Planet End* (Vanguard 79367); *Aspects* (BMG 37352); *Twin House* (Wounded Bird 123) with Philip Catherine; *The Eleventh House At Montreux* (Vanguard 79410); *Back Together Again* (Wounded Bird 8220) with Alphonse Mouzon; *Splendid* (Wounded Bird 153) with Philip Catherine; *Return* (Universe 41); *Tributaries* (Novus 3072) with John Scofield and Joe Beck; *Quiet Day In Spring* (Steeplechase 31187); *Comin' Home* (Muse 5303); *Equipoise* (Muse 5319); *Together* (Concord 4289) with Emily Remler; *Token Du* (Muse 5350); *Shining Hour* (Muse 5360); *The Dragon Gate* (Shanachie 97005); *Twelve Frets To One Octave* (Shanachie 97015); *Sketches Of Coryell* (Shanachie 5024); *Spaces Revisited* (Shanachie 5033); *Cause And Effect* (Tone Center 40022); *Monk, Trane, Miles & Me* (High Note 7028); *Private Concert* (Acoustic Music 1159); *Coryells* (Chesky 192) with Julian Coryell; *New High* (High Note 7052); *Inner Urge* (High Note 7064); *Count's Jam Band Reunion* (Tone Center 4015); *Cedars Of Avalon* (High Note 7093); *The Power Trio: Live In Chicago* (High Note 7109); *Tricycles* (Favored Nations 7020); *Electric* (Chesky 308); *Laid Back & Blues* (Rhombus 7066); *Traffic* (Chesky 322); *Impressions: The New York Sessions* (Chesky 337); *Earthquake At The Avalon* (In-Akustik 9092); *Montgomery* (Patuxent); *Duality* (Random Act 1452427), which is a set of duets with pianist Kenny Drew, Jr.; with Chico Hamilton: *Dealer* (Impulse 547958); with Free Spirit: *Out Of Sight And Sound* (Sunbeam 5018); with Gary Burton: *Duster* (BMG 432125730), *Lofty Fake Anagram* (RCA 34489), *In Concert* (RCA 37365); with Herbie Mann: *Memphis Underground* (Atlantic 13435); with Sonny Rollins: *Don't Ask* (Original Jazz Classics 915); with Stéphane Grappelli: *Young Django* (Universal 5301).

**LPs to Search For:** *Barefoot Boy* (Flying Dutchman 10139), *The Eleventh House—Level One* (Arista 4052), *The Other Side Of Larry Coryell* (Vanguard 79360), *Basics* (Vanguard 79375), *The Lion And The Ram* (Arista 4108), *Two For The Road* (Arista 4156) with Steve Kahn, *European Impressions* (Arista 3005).

**Website:** www.larrycoryell.net

# Ray Crawford
b. February 7, 1924, Pittsburgh, PA; d. December 30, 1997,
Pittsburgh, PA

Ray Crawford is best remembered for his association with Jimmy Smith. Although he was a perfect comper and soloist in Smith's group, he was also a more versatile player than one might expect.

Crawford actually started out as a tenor-saxophonist and clarinetist, playing with the Fletcher Henderson Orchestra during 1941–43. But a bout with tuberculosis resulted in him having to give up playing horns. He worked hard at reinventing himself as a guitarist and, in 1949, started a six-year stint as the guitarist with the Ahmad Jamal Trio. In addition to his solos, Crawford hit his guitar percussively during some of the piano solos, creating rhythms and making his guitar sound like bongos; Herb Ellis adopted that sound with the Oscar Peterson Trio in the mid-1950s.

Crawford first joined Jimmy Smith in 1958 and was with the organist off and on into the 1980s. He was also featured on some of Gil Evans' recordings of 1959–60. As a leader on his first album, *Smooth Groove*, which was recorded in 1961 for Candid, he proved quite adept at hard bop. Unfortunately, the label soon went out of business, and the CD was not released until the 1980s. Crawford also led two little-known sets for Dobre in the mid-1970s.

Ray Crawford settled in Los Angeles in the 1960s, where he freelanced and appeared on recordings led by Curtis Amy, Charles Kynard, Lorez Alexandria, Sonny Criss, Lou Rawls and even Tom Waits, always being a dependable and soulful player.

**Recommended CDs:** *Smooth Groove* (Candid 79028) is a superior hard-bop session from 1961 that has Crawford leading a sextet also featuring trumpeter Johnny Coles, baritonist Cecil Payne and pianist Junior Mance. It is a shame that it went unreleased for a quarter of a century. As a sideman, Ray Crawford is an important part of such recordings as Ahmad Jamal's *Chamber Music Of The New Jazz* (GRP 268202) and *The Legendary Okeh And Epic Recordings* (Legacy 93580), Gil Evans' *Out Of The Cool* (GRP/Impulse 186), Curtis Amy's *Katanga* (Blue Note 4850), Sonny Criss' *Crisscraft* (32 Jazz 32049) and, from 1972, Jimmy Smith's *Bluesmith* (Lilith 120).

**LPs to Search For:** Ray Crawford's *It's About Time* (Dobre 1010) and *One Step At A Time* (Dobre 1021), both recorded with quartets featuring keyboardist Ronnell Bright, are quite scarce.

# Bill DeArango
b. September 20, 1921, Cleveland, OH; d. January 2, 2006,
Cleveland, OH

Arguably the most advanced and adventurous guitarist to arrive during the bebop era, Bill DeArango dropped out of the major-league jazz scene early on, living a long life out of the spotlight. He became a footnote in jazz history when he could have been recognized as an innovator. DeArango began his career in his native Cleveland playing Dixieland and swing. He attended Ohio State University and served in the Army during 1942–44. After moving to New York, his strikingly original style resulted in him becoming a member of the Ben Webster Quartet and getting the attention of the modernists. Dizzy Gillespie used him on a small group date in 1946 on which the guitarist's ideas are so advanced that during "Anthropology" and "A Night In Tunisia" he almost sounds as if he is playing his instrument backwards. DeArango also recorded during 1945–47 with Webster, Sarah Vaughan, Slam Stewart, Charlie Kennedy, Ike Quebec, Eddie "Lockjaw" Davis and Charlie Ventura. He led two sessions of his own and had a group that featured vibraphonist Terry Gibbs.

Then, in 1948, the 26-year-old DeArango moved permanently back to Cleveland, probably lengthening his life but insuring his obscurity. He ran a record store, taught, and played locally. In 1954, he visited New York and recorded a quartet date for EmArcy, but otherwise nothing was heard of him in jazz for decades.

During 1978–83, DeArango appeared on recordings by Barry Altschul, Kenny Werner and Jamey Haddad, showing that he was comfortable in modern jazz settings, revealing little of his bebop roots. In 1993, DeArango was captured on a surprising album, playing duets with tenor-saxophonist Joe Lovano and in a trio/quartet. Other than one original and three standards, the music is comprised of free improvisations, and Bill DeArango sounds quite at home. But then again, he was always ahead of his time.

It does make one wonder how the history of the jazz guitar would have been altered if Bill DeArango had chosen to stay in New York in 1948.

**Recommended CDs:** *Anything Went* (GM 3027), Bill DeArango's "comeback" album, is a surprise on all levels and is filled with stimulating music while having almost no connection to his playing of 1946.

**LPs to Search For:** *Bill DeArango* (Emarcy 26020)

has been out of print for many years. The guitarist's eight selections as a leader from 1946 (with groups that feature trumpeter Idrees Sulieman, Ben Webster and Tony Scott) remain scarce.

## Angelo Debarre
*b. August 19, 1962, St. Denis, France*

One of the top gypsy-jazz guitarists to be discovered in the 1980s, Angelo Debarre has been an important force in the European movement ever since. Debarre began playing guitar when he was eight and learned to play Django Reinhardt–style swing as part of the gypsy community. In 1984, he formed his first regular group and within a year was discovered, becoming a regular at jazz festivals throughout Europe. He recorded his debut, the Gypsy Guitars, for the Hot Club label during that period.

Angelo Debarre's interest in the gypsy music of Eastern Europe and his abilities as a composer have widened his repertoire way beyond re-creations of swing standards. His playing has added to both the legacy and the momentum of the gypsy-jazz movement.

**Recommended CDs:** Angelo Debarre has recorded for several European labels, with the Hot Club CDs being the most readily available. He is featured on *Gypsy Guitars* (Hot Club 56), *Caprice* (Hot Club 116), *Romano Baschepen* (Al Sur 248), *Portrait Of Angelo Debarre* (Hot Club 127), *Come Into My Swing* (Le Chant du Monde 1249), *Memoires: Memories Of Django* (Le Chant du Monde 1230), *Entre Amis* (Le Chant du Monde 1288), *Swing Recontre* (Le Chant du Monde 1293), *Entre Ciel Et Terre* (Le Chant du Monde 1435), *Live At Djangofest Northwest* (Gypsy Jazz), *Trio Tout À Cordes* (Le Chant du Monde 1622), and *Gipsy Unity* (Le Chant du Monde 1772).

## Graham Dechter
*b. July 23, 1986, Los Angeles, CA*

Graham Dechter's career has gotten off to a good start with his debut recording, *Right On Time*. Born into a musical family (his father Brad Dechter is a fine soprano-saxophonist), he began taking violin lessons when he was five. While attending the Idyllwild Arts Academy, the teenager discovered jazz and switched to the guitar. He studied jazz with bassist Marshall Hawkins and privately with guitarist Jim Fox. After graduating high school, Dechter attended the Jazz Studies program at Eastman for a year. Back in Los Angeles, he joined the Clayton-Hamilton Jazz Orchestra when he was 19, a big band that he still performs with.

Dechter, who has developed a bop-oriented style, has played with a long list of names, including touring with Michael Bublé and having brief associations with Regina Carter, Bill Charlap, Kurt Elling, Jon Faddis, Roberta Gambarini, Benny Golson, Wycliffe Gordon, Benny Green, Roy Hargrove, Wynton Marsalis, James Moody and Phil Woods, among others. He has also recorded with baritonist Adam Schroeder. Whether Graham Dechter will develop into a major voice on the guitar in the future is not known, but he is already a fine bop soloist.

**Recommended CDs:** Dechter's debut as a leader, *Right On Time* (Capri 74096), is an excellent straight-ahead quartet outing. The guitarist is also featured on Adam Schroeder's *A Handful Of Stars* (Capri 74103) and organist Atsuko Hashimoto's *Until The Sun Comes Up* (Capri 74107).

**Website:** www.grahamdechter.com

## Phil deGruy
*b. July 18, 1955, New Orleans, LA*

A brilliant virtuoso, Phil deGruy is very highly rated by other guitarists but less known to the general public. DeGruy is the master of the guitarp, a 17-string guitar that combines a seven-string guitar with ten short strings that are pitched and tuned in the upper register of a harp. Growing up in New Orleans, deGruy heard plenty of music. "I remember being between two corners hearing two bands playing jazz simultaneously. This was my first time experiencing polytones. I was forbidden to play my older brother's guitar when I was 11. Naturally, I disobeyed and started sneaking it and was intrigued. Eventually, my brother gave me his guitar." He played in a band when he was in seventh grade, took jazz guitar lessons from Hank Mackie, and had his first professional jazz gig with saxophonist Gregg Mazel at Tipitina's. deGruy studied with Lenny Breau starting in 1976 and later with Ted Greene. "When Lenny Breau introduced me to Chet Atkins and had me play for him on my 25th birthday, it was certainly one of the high points in my career.

"I started on a conventional 6-string guitar, switched to a 7-string guitar with a high A string after studying with Lenny and, in 1983, commissioned a 17-string harp guitar (the guitarp), which has seven strings on the fretboard and ten tunable harp strings down near my right hand, which are accessible for continuing arpeggios into a higher register or for playing melodies against chords. The first two guitarps were built for me by Jimmy Foster in New Orleans. Presently, I play a guitarp made by Ralph Novak using his fanned-fret system."

Phil deGruy has spent much of his career playing in New Orleans and occasionally on the West Coast. Recently he been playing solo gigs and also in the three-guitar band Twangorama. "My goals in music are freedom, letting go, and speaking in tongues without a religious mess."

**Recommended CDs:** Although Phil deGruy has not recorded often enough, each of his CDs are special. *Innuendo Out The Other* (NYC 6013), *Hello Dali* (Otter Print) and *Just Duet* (Heard Instinct) not only have humorous album and (in the latter two cases) label titles, but they also feature deGruy in a wide variety of styles and on an eclectic repertoire but with an emphasis on improvising. While the first two CDs are solo affairs, *Just Duet* has deGruy dueting with Larry Coryell, Steve Masakowski, Hank Mackie, Mike Stern, Charlie Hunter, Reeves Gabrels and Tronzo.

**Website:** www.guitarp.com

## Cary DeNigris
b. July 28, 1955, Albany, NY

Best known for his longtime association with Chico Hamilton, Cary DeNigris is a superior post-bop and fusion guitarist with a versatile style. DeNigris started on guitar when he was fifteen. "My second guitar teacher, a man named Peter Menella, was a big fan of guitarists Johnny Smith and Tal Farlow. He gave me a lot of their early recordings and I went from there. I began doing gigs in high school around 1971, playing all of the Friday night dances and also at Elks Clubs. Then I landed a gig in the mid-'70s with a gospel group called the Downings and moved to Nashville for two years. I ended up in NYC in 1981, playing a stint with organist Jack McDuff."

DeNigris, who had attended Berklee in 1974, worked with saxophonist Eric Person starting in 1983, played free funk as a member of Ronald Shannon Jackson's Decoding Society (1985–88), and joined Chico Hamilton in 1988, working with the drummer for 20 years. During the past two years, he has toured and recorded with drummer Drori Mondlak and saxophonist Karolina Strassmayer.

"In the future, I want to continue composing, studying classical guitar, and record duo projects with vocalist Brenna Bavis and drummer Drori Mondlak. I'm very grateful to be able to make music

my life's work and to have the opportunity to challenge myself and grow on a daily basis."

**Recommended CDs:** *Between The Lines* (One Peace 1) is a superior trio set with bassist Paul Ramsey and Drori Mondlak. Of the many sets that he has recorded with Chico Hamilton, DeNigris has a particularly prominent role on *Euphoria* (Swallow 7), *Arroyo* (Soul Note 121241), *Trio* (Soul Note 121246) with Hamilton and Person in a bassless trio, *My Panamanian Friend* (Soul Note 121265), *Timely* (All Points Jazz 3001), *Juniflip* (Joyous Shout 1), *Believe* (Joyous Shout 2), *6th Avenue Shout* (Joyous Shout 3), *Heritage* (Joyous Shout 4) and *Trio! Live @ Artpark* (Joyous Shout 11). He has also recorded with Ronald Shannon Jackson, including *When Colors Play* (Knitting Factory Works 3027), and with Eric Person, Errol Parker, and Drori Mondlak.

## Bob DeVos
b. February 2, 1946, Paterson, NJ

Bob DeVos is a veteran bop and soul-jazz guitarist who has uplifted many sessions through the years. He started on the guitar when he was 12 so he could join a friend's band, which he became part of within weeks of getting his first instrument. "I would listen and play along to my older brother's R&B records, learning every guitar solo I could find. I wanted to play like B.B. King and Chuck Berry. I learned the guitar solo to 'Honky Tonk'; years later, I got to play it with Bill Doggett at a George Wein concert." DeVos took lessons from jazz guitarist Joe Cinderella, but it was in high school, when he heard some Jimmy Smith records that featured Kenny Burrell, Stanley Turrentine and Grady Tate, that he became interested in jazz. "Shortly afterward, I heard Wes Montgomery on recordings, particularly *Incredible Jazz Guitar*, and was hooked on jazz forever."

DeVos played with an R&B band in high school that went on the road after he graduated. He also toured with Frankie Valli and the Four Seasons but was much more interested in playing jazz in the long term, taking lessons from Harry Leahy and Dennis Sandole. In 1969, he landed a job with organist Trudy Pitts' group, succeeding Pat Martino. "That began my first tenure of years of on-the-bandstand training, playing four to five sets per night, six nights a week with a matinee on Sundays. It was exactly what I needed."

Other important jobs included working with Richard "Groove" Holmes for most of 1979 (including a month in which Sonny Stitt joined the group), Gerry Niewood's Timepiece (1978–82), the Teo Macero Nonet (1981–82), Charles Earland (1984–86), Jimmy McGriff/Hank Crawford (1988–93), Charles

Earland's final band (1995–99), which also featured Eric Alexander, and the Ron McClure Quartet with Jed Levy (since 2001). He has also had opportunities to play with Harry Allen, Freddy Cole, Junior Cook, Joey DeFrancesco, Kenny Drew, Jr., Etta Jones, Hendrik Meurkens, David "Fathead" Newman, Greg Osby, Houston Person, Irene Reid, Dr. Lonnie Smith, Stanley Turrentine, Bill Warfield's New York Jazz Repertory Orchestra, and duo guitars with Dave Stryker. "I've played and recorded with many of the great musicians I listened to early on when I was learning jazz." DeVos teaches privately and as a member of the music faculty at Lehigh University in Bethlehem, Pennsylvania.

Since the late 1990s when Charles Earland produced his first record on Savant, Bob DeVos has frequently been heard as a leader. His current trio includes organist Dan Kostelnik and drummer Steve Johns. "In the future, I would like to write, arrange and record with a nine- or ten-piece ensemble, something like the instrumentation on 'Birth of the Cool.'"

**Recommended CDs:** As a sideman, Bob DeVos has appeared on over 100 recordings, including with Richard "Groove" Holmes, Teo Macero, Charles Earland, Irene Reid, Ron McClure, Bill Warfield and Hendrik Meurkens. As a leader, he has continued being heard with organ combos. His four CDs, *Breaking The Ice* (Savant 2017), *DeVos' Groove Guitar* (Blues Leaf 9822), *Shifting Sands* (Savant 2077) and *Playing For Keeps* (Savant 2088), the latter two utilizing his working trio plus Eric Alexander, are all excellent and groove with spirit.

**Website:** www.bobdevosjazzguitar.com

# Al Di Meola
b. July 22, 1954, Jersey City, NJ

One of the greatest and most influential of all fusion guitarists, Al Di Meola's interest in both world music and the acoustic guitar have resulted in him growing far beyond the guitar "gunslinger" of his youth. Di Meola grew up in Bergenfeld, New Jersey. He began playing guitar as a child and was already technically skilled as a young teenager, practicing the guitar eight to ten hours per day. While he originally listened to Tal Farlow and Kenny Burrell, Larry Coryell became his early musical role model. He attended Berklee during 1971–74. A tape of him playing with keyboardist Barry Miles was heard by Chick Corea, who needed a replacement for the departed Bill Connors in Return to Forever in early 1974. He picked Di Meola, who was just 19.

Starting his career on top, playing with RTF at Carnegie Hall, Di Meola quickly became well known in the jazz and music world. During his two and a half years with Chick Corea, Stanley Clarke and Lenny White, Di Meola was on three albums and set the standard for fusion guitar. While he was criticized for playing too many notes (few guitarists could approach his speed) and for not showing enough feeling in his solos during the period, Di Meola's playing was actually quite phenomenal and was listened to closely by both fusion and rock guitarists. At about the time that Return to Forever was set to break up in 1976, Di Meola signed with Columbia, and recorded seven albums of his own, including *Land Of The Midnight Sun*, *Elegant Gypsy*, *Casino* and *Splendido Hotel*. On these and his other recordings, Di Meola showed his mastery not only of fusion but also of other idioms influenced by Latin and world music, such as flamenco and Mediterranean music.

In 1980, Di Meola switched to acoustic guitar to play with John McLaughlin and Paco de Lucía in a remarkable guitar trio. Their recordings (*Friday Night In San Francisco* and *Passion, Grace & Fire*) are full of brilliance and special moments. In addition to touring and recording with his World Sinfonia Band, Di Meola (who focused mostly on the acoustic guitar in the 1990s) has been involved in other projects. In 1996, he had a trio with violinist Jean-Luc Ponty and bassist Stanley Clarke called the Rite of Swings. He has worked with artists from other fields (Luciano Pavarotti, Paul Simon, classical guitarist Manuel Barrueco, Carlos Santana, Stevie Wonder and Frank Zappa), matched ideas with keyboardist Jan Hammer, explored the tango music of Astor Piazzolla, and occasionally been featured with all-star groups, including the 2008 reunion of Return to Forever.

In recent times, Al Di Meola has been leading the New World Sinfonia, playing music that is both dazzling and beyond classification.

**Recommended CDs:** *Land Of The Midnight Sun* (Columbia 34074), *Elegant Gypsy* (Columbia 34461), *Casino* (Columbia/Legacy 47482), *Splendido Hotel* (Columbia 46117), *Friday Night In San Francisco* (Sony 64410), *Electric Rendezvous* (Columbia 37654), *Tour De Force: Live* (Columbia 38373), *Passion, Grace And Fire* (Sony 9657), *Scenario* (Columbia 38944), *Cielo E Terra* (EMI 46146), *Soaring Through A Dream* (Manhattan 46337), *Tirami Su* (EMI 19059), *Kiss My Axe* (Mesa/Bluemoon

79751), *World Sinfonia* (Mesa/Bluemoon 79750), *Heart Of The Immigrants* (Wounded Bird 9052), *Orange And Blue* (Mesa/Bluemoon 79197), *Di Meola Plays Piazzolla* (Atlantic 92744), *Rite Of Strings* (Capitol 34167), *The Infinite Desire* (Telarc 83433), *Winter Nights* (Telarc 83458), *The Grande Passion: World Sinfonia* (Telarc 83481), *Flesh On Flesh* (Telarc 83543), *Vocal Rendezvous* (PPV 78600), *Consequence Of Chaos* (Telarc 83649), *He And Carmen* (In-Akustik 8793), *Diabolic Inventions And Seduction For Solo Guitar* (In-Akustik 9080), *Cosmopolitan Life* (SPV 25652), *Live In London* (Di Meola), *Pursuit Of Radical Rhapsody* (Telarc 8358); with Return to Forever: *Where Have I Known You Before* (Polydor 825206), *No Mystery* (Polydor 827149), *Romantic Warrior* (Columbia 46109), *Returns* (Eagle 20149).

**Website:** www.aldimeola.com

## Joe Diorio
b. August 6, 1936, Waterbury, CT

A major jazz guitarist who could outswing most other players, Joe Diorio's prominence as an educator has resulted in him often being overlooked as a jazz soloist. While he started out learning guitar and playing gigs in Connecticut, it was when he moved to Chicago in the early 1960s that Diorio began to be noticed. Inspired by Wes Montgomery and Jim Hall, Diorio co-starred on Eddie Harris' popular *Exodus To Jazz* album. He also appeared on other records with Harris and with Sonny Stitt, working constantly during those years. Diorio stayed in Chicago until moving to Miami in 1972, where he played post-bop and avant-garde jazz with Ira Sullivan, including a regular Friday night engagement at a Unitarian church. He also collaborated with the up-and-coming Jaco Pastorius. And along the way, he had opportunities to work with Stan Getz, Pat Metheny, Horace Silver and Freddie Hubbard, particularly after moving to Los Angeles.

Diorio, who recorded his first album as a leader in 1975 (*Solo Guitar*), became one of the founders of the Guitar Institute of Technology in 1977. The school, which is in Hollywood, has become very important in training young guitarists in a variety of idioms. Diorio was one of its most influential instructors during 1977–97. He also spent a period

teaching at USC and published several instructional books and videos. Among his recordings are collaborations with such fellow guitarists as Robben Ford, Mick Goodrick and David Becker.

In April 2005, Joe Diorio suffered a stroke. Living back in Connecticut, he has worked hard to recover ever since.

**Recommended CDs:** Joe Diorio has been very consistent in his recordings, and there are many gems to discover on *Solo Guitar* (Art of Life 1020); *Bonita* (Art of Life 1023); *Minor Elegance* (In-Akustik 1735) with Robben Ford; *Joe Diorio Trio: Live* (Mel Bay 09872); *We Will Meet Again* (Ram 4501); *Double Take* (Ram 4502) with bassist Riccardo Del Fra; *Rare Birds* (Ram 4505) with Mick Goodrick; *The Breeze And I* (Ram 4508), which has duets with Ira Sullivan; *More Than Friends* (Ram 4514); *Narayani* (Ram 4519); the solo *To Jobim With Love* (Ram 4529); *I Remember You: A Tribute To Wes Montgomery* (Ram 4523); *Stateside* (Diorio); *20th Century Impressions* (Diorio); *It's About Time* (Diorio); and *The Color Of Sound* (Acoustic Music 319 1262) with David Becker.

**LPs to Search For:** *Straight Ahead To The Light* (Spitball 5).

## Diz Disley
(William Disley)
b. May 27, 1931, Winnipeg, Manitoba, Canada; d. March 22, 2010, Hampstead, England

Diz Disley is best known for his association with Stéphane Grappelli. His guitar playing helped the violinist build upon his earlier successes with Django Reinhardt. Born in Canada, Disley lived in England from the age of four. He started out playing banjo, taking up the guitar at 14 after discovering Django's music. He studied art at Leeds College of Art (becoming a cartoonist and an illustrator), and also played banjo in the college band, the Vernon Street Ramblers. After college, he worked with the Yorkshire Jazz Band (1949–50). Disley served in the Army during 1950–53, moved to London, and played with Mick Mulligan and George Melly. He formed his Soho String Quartet in 1958, one of the first Django Reinhardt–inspired groups of the era.

Disley worked steadily during the trad-jazz craze in England and then took a detour in the late 1960s. He became an attraction on the folk club scene, where he was known as a comedian, appearing at many folk festivals during the next decade. He was also a cartoonist for Melody Maker.

In 1973, Disley persuaded Stéphane Grappelli to appear at the Cambridge Folk Festival with a string group that he organized. Up to that time,

Grappelli had resisted putting together Django-nostalgia bands, but Disley convinced him that he could play the music he loved in that format without merely recreating the past. They were a great success, and Grappelli and Disley worked together on and off for a decade, traveling the world four times.

A colorful figure, in later years Disley worked with Biréli Lagrène, ran a nightclub in Spain, and played swing guitar whenever the opportunity arose.

**Recommended CDs:** Diz Disley's late 1950s group is featured on four numbers on *Best Of British Jazz From The BBC Jazz Club* (Upbeat 122), while *At The White Bear* (Jazzology 212) and *Zing Went The Strings* (Waterfront 031) feature Disley in his post-Grappelli years. Some of his better recordings with Grappelli include *Live In London* (Black Lion 760139), *Live At Corby Festival Hall 1975* (Storyville 8345), and *Shades Of Django* (Verve 825955).

## Christy Doran
*b. June 21, 1949, Dublin, Ireland*

Christy Doran is an adventurous guitarist who has been inspired by avant-garde musicians and Jimi Hendrix. Born in Ireland, Doran grew up in Lucerne, Switzerland. His dad was a singer of Irish ballads. "My father had a few jazz records (such as the Jazz Messengers). I used to play them at double speed. At 13, I started to take lessons in classical guitar. As a teenager, I was playing dance gigs with Italian immigrants in Switzerland." He attended the Swiss Jazz School Berne, the Conservatory of Lucerne and the Conservatory of Berne in the early 1970s.

Doran helped found the band OM in the 1972, recording with the group for ECM and performing at the Montreux Jazz Festival. OM (which also included saxophonist Urs Leimgruber, bassist Bobby Burri and drummer Fredy Studer) lasted until 1982. Doran worked with Red Twist & Tuned Arrow (which included Studer and bassist Stefan Wittwer) during 1985–87, played duets with trombonist Ray Anderson (1988–95) and has led Christy Doran's New Bag since 1997. Along the way, he has also worked with Marty Ehrlich, Robert Dick, Carla Bley, Albert Mangelsdorff, Louis Sclavis, Marilyn Mazur, Herb Robertson, Bobby Previte, Charlie Mariano, Manfred Schoof, Irene Schweizer, Lauren Newton, Tim Berne, Hank Roberts, Joe McPhee and Jamaaladeen Tacuma, among others. He has also been involved in groups celebrating the music of Jimi Hendrix and performed at solo guitar concerts.

In addition to his worldwide touring, Christy Doran teaches at the Musikhochschule of Lucerne.

"Jazz means so much to me because it is one of the most complete musical art forms, including composition, improvisation, groove, feeling, individuality, interaction with other musicians, and a lot more. It is the music where I can express myself best and feel the greatest freedom. Of course, I have an open-minded idea of what 'jazz' is."

**Recommended CDs:** *Phoenix* (Hat Art 6074) has Doran performing duets with several artists, including Ray Anderson, Marty Ehrlich and Hank Roberts. He is heard solo on *What A Band* (Hat Art 6105). Other intriguing sets include *Music For 2 Basses, Electric Guitar and Drums* (ECM 1436), *Corporate Art* (JMT 849 155), *Play The Music Of Jimi Hendrix* (Intuition 2134), *Confusing The Spirits* (Cue 001), *Black Box* (Double Moon 71022), *Heaven Is Back In The Streets* (Double Moon 71031), *Perspectives* (Between the Lines 71204), *Jimi* (Double Moon 71048), *La Fourmi* (Creative Works 1044), *Red Twist & Tuned Arrow* (ECM 1342), *Now's The Time* (Between the Lines 71214), and *The Competence Of The Irregular* (Between the Lines 72119). Christy Doran also can be heard with OM on *Retrospective* (ECM 857 452).

**Website:** www.christydoran.ch

## Ted Dunbar
*b. January 17, 1937, Port Arthur, TX; d. May 29, 1998, New Brunswick, NJ*

A highly rated teacher, Ted Dunbar was a versatile guitarist who kept his own musical personality no matter what the setting. He first became interested in playing music after seeing a Duke Ellington performance when he was seven. Within a few years, he was showing skill on both guitar and trumpet. He played in groups as a teenager and throughout college. Dunbar studied pharmacy at Texas Southern University and became a pharmacist, a day job he would keep on and off into the 1970s. After applying for a job in Indianapolis and discovering Wes Montgomery, he moved with his family to the city and worked as a pharmacist while studying with Montgomery and Dave Baker.

Dunbar moved to New York in 1966, where he became in-demand for jobs with jazz groups and big bands. During the next decade, he made important records with McCoy Tyner, Gil Evans, and Tony Williams' Lifetime (playing briefly as John McLaughlin's successor), also working with Sonny Rollins, Ron Carter, Billy Harper, Roy Haynes and Billy Taylor.

Ted Dunbar became an educator, first at Jazzmobile and in 1972 at Rutgers University. His many students included Kevin Eubanks, Rodney Jones and Peter Bernstein. He also wrote four guitar instructional books that became influential. He stayed active as an educator and a guitarist up until the end, when his life was cut short by a stroke.

**Recommended CDs:** Most of Ted Dunbar's albums as a leader have not been reissued, although *Gentle Time Alone* (Steeplechase 31298), a 1992 quintet set, is available. As a sideman, he recorded with Gloria Coleman (1965), David "Fathead" Newman, Lou Donaldson, Reuben Wilson, Johnny Hammond Smith, Gene Ammons, Curtis Fuller, Charles McPherson, Frank Foster, Frank Wess, Albert "Tootie" Heath, Kenny Barron, Sam Rivers, Richard Davis, Charles Mingus (1978), the Xanadu All Stars, Earl Coleman, Mickey Tucker, Michael Urbaniak, Susannah McCorkle, Billy Taylor, Joe Williams, Kenny Burrell, J.J. Johnson, Hamiet Bluiett, and Randy Weston. Three of his most significant sessions as a sideman are McCoy Tyner's *Asante* (Blue Note 93384), Tony Williams' *Ego* (Verve 314 559 512) and especially Gil Evans' *Svengali* (Koch 8518).

**LPs to Search For:** A quintet date with Tommy Flanagan, *Opening Remarks* (Xanadu 155); a quintet outing with Kenny Barron and Steve Nelson, *Secundum Artem* (Xanadu 181); and Ted Dunbar's set of unaccompanied solos, *Jazz Guitarist* (Xanadu 196), have yet to be reissued on CD.

## Cornell Dupree

b. December 19, 1942, Fort Worth, TX; d. May 8, 2011, Fort Worth TX

While Cornell Dupree spent much of his life playing R&B and soul music with studio groups, every once in a while he recorded a jazz date that showed his expertise in bluesy settings. Self-taught as a guitarist, Dupree became a working musician while still a teenager. He started off playing in Fort Worth, moved to New York, and was a member of King Curtis' band, sometimes appearing opposite Jimi Hendrix. Influenced by blues, R&B and country guitarists, he became an influential force himself when he started recording regularly on sessions for the Atlantic label in the late 1960s and during a long period with Aretha Franklin (1967–76). Among Dupree's countless number of recordings are albums with Aretha Franklin, King Curtis, Brook Benton, Donny Hathaway, Joe Cocker, James Brown, Ray Charles, Paul Simon, and Esther Phillips. He was a member of the mid-1970s band Stuff (with keyboardist Richard Tee) and its successor, the Gadd Gang. Dupree also led occasional albums of his own starting in 1974.

Among his jazz sessions were dates with Rahsaan Roland Kirk, Elvin Jones, Herbie Mann, Jimmy Smith, David "Fathead" Newman, Sonny Stitt, Lou Donaldson, Buddy Rich, Archie Shepp (*Attica Blues*), Stanley Turrentine (*Cherry*), Grover Washington, Jr., Hank Crawford, Carla Bley (*Dinner Music*) and even Miles Davis (*Get Up With It*). Around 2000, he led Cornell Dupree and his Bayou Buddies and, in 2006, played with Les McCann in a group called the Soul Survivors.

Cornell Dupree was on literally thousands of sessions over a 45-year period. In 2011, he died from the effects of emphysema while waiting for a lung transplant.

**Recommended CDs:** Most of Cornell Dupree's recordings as a leader are R&B-ish but with some jazz selections, including *Teasin'* (Warner Bros. 13457), *Shadow Dancing* (Unidisc 4102), *Coast To Coast* (Antilles 842717), *Can't Get Through* (Amazing 1025), *Child's Play* (Amazing 1034), *Uncle Funky* (Kokopell 1316), and *Unstuffed* (PMEC 58846). *Bop 'N' Blues* (Kokopelli 1302) from 1994 is his strongest jazz album, utilizing Bobby Watson, Terell Stafford and Ronnie Cuber on a variety of bop standards and blues. Dupree sounds fine in what was for him an unusual setting.

## Eddie Duran

b. September 6, 1925, San Francisco, CA

Eddie Duran has been a significant guitarist since the 1950s, being a treasure of the San Francisco jazz scene. Duran first had piano lessons from his sister when he was quite young. "My older sister played piano while my older brother played guitar and later bass. I started messing around on his guitar when I was six. My older brothers and I entered amateur shows and won when I was eight and he was nine. When I was 15, I accompanied my sister, who sang in a Mexican nightclub. When I was

22, my brothers and I formed a group patterned after the Nat King Cole Trio. Manny Duran played piano and sang while Carlos played bass."

Duran says that he knew that he was going to be a professional guitarist by the time he was seven. He never attended music school and did not need to, practicing constantly and learning on the bandstand. He was inspired early on by Django Reinhardt, George Van Eps and Charlie Christian. When asked to mention some of his most memorable associations, he named Charlie Parker (two weeks in 1953), Johnny Hodges, Chet Baker (1952 and 1983), Cal Tjader, Vince Guaraldi, Bobby Troup, Julie London, Earl Hines, Peggy Lee, Helen Humes, Stan Getz (1965), Barbra Streisand, Teddy Wilson, Jon Hendricks, Paul Desmond, Red Norvo, Benny Goodman (1976–80), Toots Thielemans, George Shearing, the Louie Bellson Big Band, Tania Maria and Tom Harrell. But in reality, he has played with pretty much every significant jazz musician who has passed through San Francisco since the early 1950s.

Eddie Duran had slowed down by the early 1980s, and he was a widower. Meeting and marrying saxophonist Madeleine (Mad) Duran in 1984 gave his career a renaissance. They have performed together in a variety of settings, including duos, and the guitarist has remained quite active up until the present time. "I consider playing jazz with its musical freedom to be akin to having outer body experiences; the music is spiritual."

**Recommended CDs:** Eddie Duran is featured playing unaccompanied solos on *Eddie Rides Again*, with Mad Duran on a trio of duet albums (*Brazilian Passion*, *Samba Cocktail* and *That Bossa Nova Thing*) that are tributes to Stan Getz and João Gilberto, on a date split between straight-ahead and Latin jazz (*From Here To The Moon*) and with a pianoless quartet titled *Simply Mad*. Each of the sets is on the Mad Eddie label (available through his website), and Mad Duran is well featured on all of the CDs except *Eddie Rides Again*.

**LPs to Search For:** Eddie Duran's earlier albums as a leader, 1957's *Jazz Guitarist* (Fantasy 3247), *Let There Be Love* (Concord 036) with Dee Bell and Stan Getz, *Ginza* (Concord 94), and *One By One* (Concord 271), are thus far languishing in Concord's vaults.

## Eddie Durham

b. August 19, 1906, San Marcos, TX; d. March 6, 1987, New York, NY

Eddie Durham had many talents. He was a fine section trombonist who could take a decent solo, a skilled big band arranger-composer, and one of the very

first electric guitarists. While George Barnes beat him into the recording studios by 15 days to record on electric guitar with Big Bill Broonzy, Durham's playing on dates with the Kansas City Five and Six in 1938 predated Charlie Christian by a year.

Along with six siblings, he started out playing music with the Durham Brothers Band. As a trombonist who doubled on guitar, he worked in Kansas City with Walter Page's Blue Devils and Bennie Moten (1929–33). After moving to New York, Durham wrote arrangements for the Willie Bryant big band. While a member of Jimmie Lunceford's orchestra during 1935–37, he took an occasional guitar solo including on "Bird Of Paradise," "Avalon," "Hittin' The Bottle," and "He Ain't Got Rhythm." During a year spent with Count Basie (1937–38), Durham contributed such significant originals as "Swinging The Blues," "Topsy," "Jumpin' At The Woodside," "Sent For You Yesterday," and "John's Idea." He also wrote "I Don't Want To Set The World On Fire," a hit for Andy Kirk.

In 1938 with the Kansas City Five (March 18) and the Kansas City Six (September 8), Durham played electric guitar while Freddie Green (Basie's regular guitarist) strummed on acoustic. Durham took a few solos, taking his place next to Buck Clayton and (on the second date) Lester Young. His solos may seem basic today, but they found him holding his own with horn players, a real rarity for guitarists of the pre–Charlie Christian era.

But strangely enough, Durham never went further as a guitarist. He worked primarily as an arranger for years, writing for such bands as Artie Shaw, Glenn Miller (the arrangement for "In The Mood") and Harry James. He led a big band of his own briefly in 1940, was the musical director for the International Sweethearts of Rhythm (1941–43), and hardly played guitar or trombone again until the late 1960s. While he did work in his later years with Buddy Tate, the Countsmen, and the Harlem Blues and Jazz Band, by then no one thought of Eddie Durham as the leading jazz electric guitarist. But for a brief moment in history, he was.

**Recommended CDs:** *The "Kansas City" Sessions* (Commodore 402) has the Kansas City Five and Six sessions from 1938 plus an unrelated Kansas City Six date from 1944. Eddie Durham led one four-song session in 1940, but that has not been reissued. Durham is well showcased on 1981's *Blue Bone* (JSP 1030), which features him on both trombone and guitar.

**LPs to Search For:** *Eddie Durham* (RCA 5029) from 1973–74 has a generous sampling of Durham's guitar.

## David Eastlee
*b. December 14, 1955, Rochester, MN*

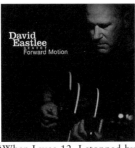

An excellent bop-based guitarist, David Eastlee also writes originals that would have fit perfectly in the repertoire of late-1940s bebop combos. Eastlee lived in Kasson, Minnesota, until his family moved to Seattle in 1963. "When I was 12, I stopped by my friend's house on the way home from baseball practice. He had just gotten a Sears Silvertone guitar and amp. I watched and listened for a while, got him to teach me a couple songs, and left with an old acoustic that he had in the closet."

Originally, Eastlee was attracted to the blues and rock music of the 1960s. His interest in jazz was gradual, evolving from blues to fusion and finally straight-ahead jazz. He played at church and school dances, parties, restaurants, bars, lounges and clubs. "Those were the years you would have a gig for weeks or months." He played with a rock group called The at festivals. At 18, Eastlee spent a month on the road in Alaska. He also worked in bands with Hendrix-inspired guitarist Randy Hansen. Strictly an ear player up to this point, a turning point occurred when he met guitarist Don Mock. "He is a great player and was into Brian Auger, Alvin Lee, John McLaughlin, early George Benson and jazz guys. He opened me up to the realm of chords, scales and diatonic harmony, and introduced me to the repertoire of jazz."

In 1977, Eastlee visited Los Angeles to study music, learning from Ron Escheté, Joe Diorio, Pat Martino, Howard Roberts and his friend Howard Alden. "Howard and I hung out in Hollywood, jamming and playing gigs. He had just started playing guitar after spending his last five years playing banjo in a Dixie style at Disneyland and other places. He already knew hundreds of tunes."

After more time back in Seattle playing fusion with Jeff Simmons, in 1980 Eastlee moved permanently to Los Angeles. He has since dedicated himself to bop and hard bop, writing songs and gigging locally. His recording debut, *Left Coast Blues*, teamed him with some veteran jazz greats. He led a group with Sam Most on flute and tenor, trumpeter Jack Coan, bassist Harvey Newmark and drummer Nick Martinis for a couple of years and recently has headed a quartet featuring tenor-saxophonist Doug Webb. "Doug and I both love Trane, Sonny Rollins, Joe Henderson and Hank Mobley, so it is a great hard-bop band. I am essentially a blues-based bebop player that is moving into the '60s a bit more stylistically. Other people are starting to perform my compositions and write lyrics for them, which is a lot of fun to hear."

**Recommended CDs:** Dave Eastlee's first recording, *Left Coast Blues* (Bop-O-Phonic 001), features him with six different quartets, including with veteran pianists Gerald Wiggins, Frank Strazzeri, Pete Jolly (his last session) and Page Cavanaugh, plus bassist Eugene Wright and drummers Nick Martinis and Larance Marable. *Forward Motion* (Bop-O-Phonic 002) and the two-CD set *Live At Mr. B's* (Bop-O-Phonic 003) have Eastlee, Sam Most, Jack Coan, Harvey Newmark and Martinis mostly playing the guitarist's catchy originals.

**Website:** www.davideastlee.com

## Bruce Eisenbeil
*b. August 21, 1963, Chicago, IL*

One of the most vital of the avant-garde jazz guitarists around today, Bruce Eisenbeil's music has sometimes been called revolutionary, although he is quite familiar with the jazz tradition. Born in Chicago, he grew up in Plainfield, New Jersey. "That was a multiethnic area where I heard music from all over the world. It seemed like there was a guitar in everybody's house. Some of my friends had older brothers and sisters who played pop hits on guitar and a couple of my cousins played too. These friends and relatives started showing me chords when I was four years old."

Eisenbeil's father was an amateur trumpeter, his mother played piano, and an aunt was a piano instructor. His parents were supportive of his desire to play guitar. "On my tenth birthday, I got an acoustic guitar and took lessons for about six months. By the time I was 13, I was playing guitar six to eight hours a day." He started playing at parties and dances when he was 15, and at bars he often jammed rock and blues tunes for up to 15 minutes apiece. At 17, he worked at clubs and parties with older musicians in addition to playing with his high school jazz ensemble. Eisenbeil studied advanced mathematics, physics (general relativity and quantum mechanics), organic chemistry, computer languages, electrical engineering, acoustics, art history, philosophy and psychology at the New Jersey Institute of Technology with plans to become an engineer. "I've worked as an electrical technician, draftsman, auto mechanic, welder, painter, farmhand and in construction." But he changed course and instead enrolled at the Musicians Institute, graduating with honors in 1985. "While there, I learned a lot from Joe Pass, Howard Roberts, Joe Diorio, Ron Escheté, Jeff Berlin, Frank Gambale, Scott Henderson and Don Mock. One time at Musicians Institute, I was playing a Joe Henderson tune called 'Inner Urge' real fast. The room was packed with guitarists and several instructors. Out of the corner of my eye, I saw Howard Roberts come in the room and, wouldn't you know, he walked right up to me. He stood right over me, staring at my hands. 'Oh man,' I thought, 'Fingers don't fail me now.' After we finished the song, he complimented me in front of everybody. Howard Roberts cured me forever of stage fright!"

While in Los Angeles, Eisenbeil shared an apartment with Tim Buckley, with whom he played some jobs. "The biggest turning point in my career came about in 1987. I stopped listening to guitarists. Previously, I realized I had an uncanny ability to be a musical chameleon. I could play and sound just like Pat Metheny, John Scofield, Mike Stern or Bill Frisell. Other instrumentalists seemed to like that, and I got work playing those roles. But at some point, I said to myself, 'Why would you want to play like somebody else? After all, I'll never be them. It's hard enough just to be myself.' So since that time, my quest has been to be myself."

That year Eisenbeil moved to Philadelphia, where he studied regularly with Dennis Sandole. He worked with saxophonist Jimmy Stewart, Rob Brown, Ian Ash and Wilbo Wright. When he moved to New York in 1995, his first job was with Rashied Ali, which served as his entry into the modern jazz scene. Playing with Andrew Cyrille and Leon Dorsey at the Knitting Factory led to him working with Cecil Taylor and later Milford Graves. Other associations during the past decade include David Murray, Evan Parker, David Fox, Ellery Eskelin, Steve Swell, David Taylor, Karl Berger, Perry Robinson, Michael Manring, William Parker, Kent Carter, Lisle Ellis, Badal Roy, Nasheet Waits, Jay Rosen, William Hooker, Lou Grassi and many others. Eisenbeil currently leads Totem with bassist Tom Blancarte and drummer Andrew Drury.

"I think it's important to do new things. The best music is an original expression of one's self. After a while, I realized how much material is not being explored by guitarists. What interests me most is making music that is emotionally eloquent at any energy level, whether it's lyrical or aggressive playing. I enjoy developing colorful harmonies from multiple-octave

scales and discovering the rich hidden emotions. The average guitar has almost four octaves to deal with. I have a lot of stuff to do. And in addition, I have at least ten guitar books I'd like to finish writing and publish."

**Recommended CDs:** "I'm proud of having a diverse discography that demonstrates many unusual ideas with unusual instrumentations." *Nine Wings* (CIMP 144) has Bruce Eisenbeil, Rob Brown and Lou Grassi playing free improvisations in 1997. *Mural* (CIMP 194) features his Crosscurrent Trio with bassist Jason Brunka and drummer Ryan Sawyer. Other stimulating, complex and colorful recordings include *Opium* (CIMP 241); *Particle Data Group* (Cadence 1139); *Keep The Meter Running* (Nine Winds 0246); *Carnival Skin* (Nemu 003); *Inner Constellation Vol. 1* (Nemu 007); *Ashes* (Freedom Jazz); *Solar Force* (ESP 4046), which was the debut of Totem; and *Shadow Machine* (Pogus 21051), which teams the guitarist with analog synthesist Tom Hamilton for some otherworldly sounds.

**Website:** www.eisenbeil.com

## Herb Ellis
### (Mitchell Herb Ellis)
b. August 4, 1921, Farmersville, TX; d. March 28, 2010, Los Angeles, CA

The perfect guitarist for the Oscar Peterson Trio of the 1950s, Herb Ellis was a boppish player with a Texas twang in his sound. During an interview from June 19, 1995, he remembered, "I was raised on a farm and heard music on the radio. I especially remember hearing the Light Crust Doughboys; they always had a good guitarist. I played harmonica when I was three, and my folks bought me a banjo when I was six. My older brother had a guitar, but he tuned it incorrectly. I wanted to be better than him, so I got a book, tuned it properly and showed him how to play it. That's when I started getting interested in playing guitar."

Ellis played locally, went to North Texas State University as a music major (switching to bass since they did not have a guitar program) and, in 1941, dropped out to tour for six months with a group from the University of Kansas. He also spent some time in Kansas City before playing with Glen Gray's Casa Loma Orchestra during 1943–45. While with Jimmy Dorsey's band (1945–47), Ellis had occasional opportunities to solo, including on his record of "J.D.'s Jump." In 1947, the guitarist, along with pianist Lou Carter and bassist Johnny Frigo, left Dorsey's orchestra to form the Soft Winds, a group based a little on Nat King Cole's trio. Although they helped to popularize "Detour Ahead" and "I Love

You, I Love You, Now Get Out" (both composed by Frigo), the Soft Winds only made four obscure studio recordings (not counting some radio transcriptions unearthed decades later). They lasted until 1952.

The following year, Oscar Peterson picked Ellis to be Barney Kessel's successor in his trio with bassist Ray Brown. "That was quite a challenge, following Oscar's solos. Oscar always gave more than 100 percent, so it was up to me and Ray Brown to always be at our best." The Peterson-Ellis-Brown trio performed and recorded prolifically during 1953–58, both as a separate unit and on Jazz at the Philharmonic tours, also accompanying such artists as Louis Armstrong, Ella Fitzgerald, Ben Webster, Roy Eldridge, Dizzy Gillespie and Stan Getz on records. The trio, which had complex routines worked out by Ellis and Brown, was often quite astounding.

After Ellis tired of the road, he left the group. Peterson, in a tribute to Ellis, decided to replace him not with another guitarist but with drummer Ed Thigpen. Ellis spent part of 1959–60 with Ella Fitzgerald, had gigs and recordings with the Dukes of Dixieland and Charlie Byrd, and mostly worked in Los Angeles as a studio musician. In the 1970s, he became more active in the jazz world again, recording with Joe Pass for Concord, making albums of his own (many of which were pretty laidback), and sounding at his most inspired when touring with Byrd and Kessel as the Great Guitars. He had occasional reunions with Oscar Peterson and, during 1990–92, performed with Peterson, Ray Brown and drummer Bobby Durham at the Blue Note a few weeks each year. Herb Ellis remained active until the early part of the 21st century, when he had to retire due to Alzheimer's.

"I never tried to change my style once I had it. I formed it out of Charlie Christian, Lester Young and Charlie Parker. This is my advice to younger players: Find your niche. Always try to get better, but stay who you are."

**Recommended CDs:** Herb Ellis told me that his personal favorite recordings were *Nothing But The Blues* (a quintet set with Roy Eldridge and Stan Getz) and a reunion with Oscar Peterson called *Hello Herbie*. Many of his recordings are rewarding, particularly the earlier ones, which tend to be more energetic than the later Concord releases. His discography includes *Ellis In Wonderland* (Verve 593002), *Nothing But The Blues* (Verve 9173), *Herb Ellis Meets Jimmy Giuffre* (Polygram 559826), *Thank You Charlie Christian* (Verve 2754), *Midnight Roll* (Wounded Bird 7034), *Guitar/Guitar* (Wounded Bird 9130) with Charlie Byrd, *Together* (Koch 7805) with Stuff Smith, *Jazz/Concord* (Concord 4001) with Joe Pass, *Seven Come Eleven* (Concord 1015), *Two For The*

*Road* (Original Jazz Classics 726) with Joe Pass, *Soft Shoe* (Concord 4003), *After You've Gone* (Concord 4006), *Rhythm Willie* (Concord 4010), *Hot Tracks* (Concord 4012), *Herb* (Musical Heritage Society 512686), *Windflower* (Concord 4056) with Remo Palmieri, *Soft & Mellow* (Concord 4077), *Doggin' Around* (Concord 4372), *Roll Call* (Justice 1001), *Texas Swings* (Justice 1002), *An Evening With Herb Ellis* (Jazz Focus 19), and *Burnin'* (Acoustic Music 1164); with the Soft Winds: *Then And Now 1946–1996*; with Oscar Peterson: *At Zardi's* (Pablo 20118), *At The Stratford Shakespearean Festival* (Verve 2574), *Hello Herbie* (Universal 9664), and *Live At The Blue Note* (Telarc 83304); with the Great Guitars: *Great Guitars* (Concord 6004), *Great Guitars II* (Concord 4023), *Straight Tracks* (Concord 4421), *Great Guitars At The Winery* (Concord 4131), and *Great Guitars At Charlie's Georgetown* (Concord 4209).

## Danny Embrey
*b. August 27, 1952, Kansas City, MO*

Best known for his long time association with Karrin Allyson, Danny Embrey has long been a major guitarist in the Kansas City area. Embrey started out on the drums, but then "the Beatles appeared, and I switched from drums to the guitar." He gained experience playing at veteran's hospitals and battle of the bands contests. Always interested in playing straight-ahead jazz, his most important musical training was studying harmony for three years with a piano teacher, John Elliott. "A week out of high school, I went on the road with a variety band and knew this was it; I would be a guitarist."

He worked with organist Greg Meise and with local musicians in Kansas City. Embrey toured with Sergio Mendes (1980–87) and worked in Los Angeles with Clare Fischer's Latin group (1982–87) and with such notables as Gary Foster, Shelly Manne, Monty Budwig, Alan Broadbent, Bobby Shew, Leroy Vinnegar, Steve Houghton, Gene Harris, Bob Brookmeyer, Bob Sheppard, Sam Most and Annie Ross.

After leaving Mendes, Embrey spent two years living in Seattle, where he became a guitar instructor at Western Washington University. Back in Kansas City, Embrey started working with Karrin Allyson in the early 1990s and played with her extensively during 1997–2005, touring regularly and becoming a major part of her group. He also recorded two albums with Interstring and has recorded as a sideman with Clare Fischer, Ashley Alexander, Steve Houghton, Frank Mantooth, Mike Metheny, Angela Hagenbach, the Kansas City Boulevard Big Band, and several local performers along the way.

"Playing in different formats and 'locking in' with various players is what makes me tick."

**Recommended CDs:** Except for a privately issued CD that has since sold out (*Dues Blues*), Danny Embrey has not recorded yet as a leader. He is well featured with Interstring, a quartet also including Rod Fleeman on acoustic guitar, bassist Bob Bowman and drummer Todd Strait. They have released *Odahoda* (Igmod 49801) and the privately issued *Winter Song.* Embrey can also be heard with Karrin Allyson on *I Didn't Know About You* (Concord 4543), *Sweet Home Cookin'* (Concord 4593), *Azure-Te* (Concord 4641), *Collage* (Concord 4709), *Daydream* (Concord 4773), *From Paris To Rio* (Concord 4865) and *In Blue* (Concord Jazz 2106).

**Website:** www.dannyembrey.com

---

## James Emery
*b. December 21, 1951, Youngstown, OH*

A founding member of the String Trio of New York, James Emery is very active both with the group and in his own solo career. "I began playing organ at age six but stopped when I was eight. After that, I wanted to play clarinet, oboe or alto-saxophone, but my parents refused to go along. When I asked for a guitar at age 12, they acquiesced. While in high school, I was a teacher at Bill DeArango's music store. During a break, he showed me the changes to 'Cherokee' and had me play the changes while he soloed. Though I grew up in a musical household, hearing a lot of music all the time, I had never heard anything like that and it was inspirational."

While a teenager, Emery played in a rock band at dances. After his graduation, he attended Cleveland State University and worked in local clubs and bars around Cleveland, often playing blues. He moved to New York in 1974 and became part of the very viable loft scene. "The most important creative dynamic was to be yourself and to bring out your own sound and ideas, not to reference historical eras and players."

In 1975, Emery made his recording debut with Leroy Jenkins. Through working with Jenkins, the guitarist met such performers as Anthony Braxton, Muhal Richard Abrams, Wadada Leo Smith, Henry Threadgill, and the Human Arts Ensemble (which included Lester Bowie and George Lewis), all of whom he would work with.

"Being a founding member of the String Trio of New York in 1977 has probably been the most important turning point of my career. We're still actively performing and recording after 32 years of playing all over the world and recording 18 CDs. I don't know of another group of our genre which has not only performed extensively internationally but has performed in over 40 states here in America. We're still together because the music is still growing and going into new places." The innovative avant-garde group has featured Emery and bassist John Lindberg from the start, while its violinists have included Billy Bang, Regina Carter, Diane Monroe, Charles Burnham and most recently Rob Thomas.

In addition, James Emery has had long associations with Anthony Braxton (1978–92), Henry Threadgill (1994–99), Joe Lovano (1997–2003), Steve Reich (performing Reich's *Electric Counterpoint*), Sam Rivers, Dave Holland, the late Ed Blackwell, Muhal Richard Abrams, John Zorn and Leo Smith, along with many others in the who's who of modern jazz. A well-respected composer, he received a Guggenheim Fellowship for composition in 1995. Recently, Emery completed his second large-scale work for the String Trio of New York, "First Light," and has written over 100 compositions for jazz ensembles, solo guitar, chamber groups and orchestras and symphony orchestras. James Emery also leads his own trio, quartet, sextet and septet in addition to performing occasional solo concerts.

"Over the past 15 years, I have been attempting to open in a new way both in music and in life. In musical expressions, this means that I am trying to get out of the way and let the music flow where it will."

**Recommended CDs:** As a leader, James Emery is well featured on *Artlife* (Lumina 007), which is comprised of solos and duets with Leroy Jenkins; the solo *Exo Eso* (FMP 59); *Turbulence* (Knitting Factory Works 106); *Standing On A Whale Fishing For Minnows* (Enja 9312); *Spectral Domains* (Enja 9344); *Luminous Cycles* (Between the Lines 15); *Fourth World* (Between the Lines 1990), which co-stars Joe Lovano; and *Transformations* (Challenge 10197). The latter is dominated by Emery's eight-part "Music For Three Improvisers And Orchestra," which also features Tony Coe and Franz Koglmann. Of the many releases by the String Trio of New York, Emery says that his favorites are *Area Code 212* (Black Saint 120048), *Octagon* (Black Saint 120131), *Faze Phour 20th Anniversary Retrospective* (Black Saint 120168), *Gut Reaction* (Omnitone 2202), and *The River Of Orion: 30 Years Of Running* (Black Saint 120178).

**Website:** www.james-emery.com

## Eddie Erickson
*b. April 4, 1948, San Francisco, CA*

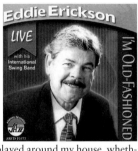

A witty jokester on stage and an excellent jazz singer, Eddie Erickson is also a talented if underrated guitarist and banjoist who enjoys playing swing and trad jazz.

"When I was young, there was always music being played around my house, whether on the radio, records, or from my dad. He played 'closet guitar,' never professionally, but he loved it. I got my first instrument at age seven, a ukulele." While Erickson has also played cornet (on which he worked at Disney World) and trombone, most important was his concentration on banjo when he was 13. "I learned by listening to Kenny Ball, Louis Armstrong, Eddie Peabody, George Van Eps and everybody I could."

Erickson earned an AA degree in business but never attended music school. "I think every situation I have been in musically has been a learning experience, from my first job at 15 for Me 'N Ed's Pizza Parlor to now. I especially enjoyed working with Jake Stock in a group called the Abalone Stompers. In the late '80s, I teamed up with Jackie Coon as the Jack 'n' Ed Show. I learned so much from Jake and Jackie, and from Rick Fay, who got me started in the jazz party circuit."

Erickson was a member of the Banjo Kings, led the Riverboat Rascals (1978–83) on a Disneyland steamboat, and co-led "Fast Eddie and Big Mama Sue" for years with singer–washboard player Sue Kroninger. In 2002, he began playing with B.E.D., a group also featuring singer Rebecca Kilgore, trombonist Dan Barrett and bassist Joel Forbes, which has recently been renamed the Rebecca Kilgore Quartet. The band has been a perfect forum for Eddie Erickson's ad-libbing, singing, and guitar and banjo playing. "It is the most rewarding group I've been in so far and also the most demanding. I feel I have to push myself more because I'm the rhythm player. In general, I think the beauty of jazz is the 'moment,' and that's how I try to live. Jackie Coon, when asked 'How do you play those great phrases?' replied, 'Don't think.'"

**Recommended CDs:** *On Easy Street* (Arbors 19111) puts the spotlight on Eddie Erickson with assistance from Rick Fay, Jackie Coon and Johnny Varro. *I'm Old-Fashioned* (Arbors 19373) is a concert performance from Germany with trombonist Bill Allred

and clarinetist Antti Sarpila. Erickson has also recorded with Jackie Conn, Dottie Dodgion, John Lithgow, Harry Allen and John Sheridan. Most notable are his recordings with B.E.D. and Rebecca Kilgore, including *Get Ready For Bed* (Blue Swing 001), *Bedlam* (Blue Swing 003), *Watch Out* (Blue Swing 005), *Bed Four + 1* (Blue Swing 008) and *Yes Indeed* (Blue Swing 011).

**Website:** www.eddieerickson.com

## Ron Escheté
*b. August 19, 1948, Houma, LA*

A widely respected guitarist and educator, Ron Escheté has long been based in Southern California. Escheté was born 50 miles southwest of New Orleans. "I grew up in the beautiful bayou country of southern Louisiana with loving and supportive parents and an extended family of hard-working French Cajun relatives of all ages. We didn't know we were poor; we had everything we needed. I grew up with rhythms of daily life and music from blues to Bach all around. I am deeply connected to these roots and have developed into a musician who prefers a life of discipline over dedication to the limelight."

Escheté sang in vocal choirs all through school. He played rock-and-roll piano with friends when he was 12 and two years later got his first guitar, purchased partly by earning money mowing lawns. He discovered jazz when he heard a Howard Roberts record playing in a music store. While in high school, Escheté had a band that played country and rock music at dance parties in Houma. After graduating from high school in 1966, he played in Florida at a club called the Wind Jammer and worked at his first jazz gig in New Orleans in the fall at the Jamaican Village. While he had a day job for a year, at night he played guitar in strip clubs on Bourbon Street. Escheté attended Loyola University during 1967–69, majoring in classical guitar and minoring in flute. He also continued playing on Bourbon Street at night, at the Roosevelt Hotel Blue Room and at shows for Kay Starr, Jimmy Rogers and Frankie Laine. While at Loyola, Escheté played at a collegiate competition on New Orleans, where he impressed Mundell Lowe.

The guitarist left Loyola in his senior year (1969) to play with Buddy Greco. The following year, he settled in Los Angeles. While he credits Wes Montgomery, Joe Pass and George Van Eps as the main influences on his playing, Escheté's background in blues and knowledge of country and Western swing can also be heard in his playing at times.

Among Escheté's more significant associations have been Dave Pike (1974–81), Gene Harris (1975–96), Hampton Hawes (1976–77), Ray Brown and Milt Jackson (1978–82), Bob Brookmeyer, Harry

"Sweets" Edison, Frank Rosolino, Warne Marsh, Jerome Richardson, Buddy Collette, Gary Foster, Pete Christlieb, Dewey Erney and Mort Weiss. In his career, he has recorded 18 albums under his own name.

As an educator, Escheté was one of the first instructors at the Guitar Institute of Technology, being involved with the school during 1976–98. He currently teaches at California State University at Fullerton and at Long Beach. Escheté, who has mastered the seven-string guitar, has a regular trio with six-string electric bassist Todd Johnson and drummer Kendall Kay. He is also rehearsing a septet for which he has written 45 charts.

"I have an insatiable appetite for harmonic improvisation, which is about developing independent fingers. With notes simultaneously played in chord progressions, individual notes are always being held at the same time that other notes are still moving. All of the notes are playing the melody, the accompaniment, and, with seven-string, the bass line all at the same time as moving lines inside beautiful four-part harmony while keeping the time going within the chosen rhythm. Music is humbling. The more you know, the more you are humbled."

**Recommended CDs:** Ron Escheté has recorded with Ernestine Anderson, Ray Brown, Judy Chamberlain, the Clayton Brothers, Joey DeFrancesco, Dewey Erney, Gene Harris, Luther Hughes, Milt Jackson, Warne Marsh, Jack McDuff, Dave Pike, Don Rader, Charlie Shoemake, Mary Stallings, and Mort Weiss, among others. Of his own CDs, easily recommended are *Christmas Impressions* (Bainbridge 6267); *Stump Jumper* (Quicksilver 4012); *Mo' Strings Attached* (Jazz Alliance 10020); the unaccompanied set *A Closer Look* (Concord 4607); *Rain Or Shine* (Concord 4665); *Soft Winds* (Concord 4757); *Live At Rocco* (Orchard 7964); *No Place To Hide* (SMS 1), which consists of duets with clarinetist Mort Weiss; and *In The Middle* (Rev Jazz 2264).

**LPs to Search For:** Two of Escheté's first albums as a leader, *To Let You Know I Care* (Muse 5186) and *Line Up* (Muse 5246), are scarce.

**Website:** www.roneschete.com

# John Etheridge
b. January 12, 1948, London, England

In his career, John Etheridge has played a remarkably wide variety of music, excelling in each genre. He began playing guitar when he was 12. "My dad was a jazz pianist and Charlie Christian fan, and my best friend at school had a father who was a jazz guitarist and introduced me to Django Reinhardt's music, which blew my mind. I was about 14 at the time, and these influences were primary. Later, I was caught up in the British blues boom, Eric Clapton and Jimi Hendrix particularly. Clapton was the first guy to get a singing tone from the electric guitar through the use of overdrive. Everybody else copied him as fast as they could."

In 1963, he had his first gigs, playing at school before film showings in sets frequently ranging from the Beatles to Django Reinhardt. He also gained experience playing in blues/jazz groups. Although he went to college, Etheridge never had a music lesson. "My first gig as a professional was in 1970 in a sleazy London nightclub, playing six hours a night continuously. It was great experience."

Etheridge made his recording debut playing progressive rock with violinist Darryl Way in 1972. He really made his mark on music during 1975–78 when he was with Soft Machine, arguably the top European fusion band of the era. During 1976–81, he also played regularly with Stéphane Grappelli, so he frequently went from fusion to swing and back. Since then, Etheridge has worked in many settings, including with classical violinist Nigel Kennedy (1990–2000), with Andy Summers of the Police (1994–97), and with classical guitarist John Williams (since 1999), including duo concerts.

During the past couple of years, John Etheridge has been alternating between his main musical interests, touring with John Williams, playing solo guitar at concerts in the United Kingdom, composing music for television, playing duos with violinist Chris Garrick, touring Europe with the Soft Machine Legacy, and working with his group Sweet Chorus, a band dedicated to Stéphane Grappelli.

"I am by temperament an improviser, and it is this element of jazz that attracts me rather than specific jazz styles. Some of the best music I have ever made has been with musicians I have hardly spoken to, let alone rehearsed with. To maintain perspective and balance in professional music is a high wire act, and I have fallen down often. My advice to young musicians would be to remember that music is fostered, not undermined, by strong human relationships."

**Recommended CDs:** Of John Etheridge's own recordings, *Sweet Chorus* (Dyad 001) and *Chasing Shadows* (Dyad 023) feature his Stéphane Grappelli–inspired group, while he is heard leading a trio on *In House* (Dyad 025). Other dates include *Ash* (Jazz Print 102); *I Didn't Know* (Dyad 024); *Live In Leeds* (Jazzprint 122), which is the music of Frank Zappa played with the Zappatistas; *Stitched Up* (New Note 111); and *Break Even* (Dekkor 027). He is also featured in duets with Vic Juris on *Bohemia* (Jazzpoint 1023) and Andy Summers on *Invisible Threads* (In-Akustik 9024).

**LPs to Search For:** John Etheridge is featured with Soft Machine on *Softs* (Harves 4056), *Rubber Riff* (Voice-Print 190) and his favorite from that era, *Alive & Well Recorded In Paris* (Harves 4083). He is also in fine form with Stéphane Grappelli on *Live At Carnegie Hall* (Doctor Jazz 1001) and *At The Winery* (Concord 139).

**Website:** www.johnetheridge.com

## Bus Etri
*(Anthony Etri)*
b. 1917, New York, NY; d. August 21, 1941, Culver City, CA

A long-forgotten name, Bus Etri was one of jazz's first electric guitarists and one of the very few guitarists to be featured regularly soloing with a swing-era orchestra. The cousin of Tony Mottola and the brother of saxophonist Ben Etri, Bus Etri began his musical career with the Hudson-DeLange Orchestra in 1935. He stayed with the band when it became the Will Hudson Orchestra and was featured on such recordings as "Bugle Call Rag," "Stardust" and "Hangover In Hong Kong." In 1938, Etri joined the Charlie Barnet Orchestra. Switching to electric guitar, he took occasional short solos (typically a chorus) on such recordings as "Tappin' At The Tappa," "A Lover's Lullaby," "Wanderin' Blues," "Flying Home," "The Reverie Of A Moax," "Nowhere," and "Harlem Speaks." He also arranged a few numbers, including "Haunted Night," which has a vocal by Lena Horne.

Bus Etri might have become a significant guitarist in jazz history, but he died in a car accident (along with singer-trumpeter Harold Hundling) while coming home from a party in 1941 when he was just 24.

**Recommended CDs:** Some Bus Etri solos can be found on Charlie Barnet's *Clap Hands, Here Comes Charlie* (Bluebird 6273) and *The Transcription Performances 1941* (Hep 53). A comprehensive reissue of Etri's solos (he only recorded with Will Hudson and Barnet) has never been compiled.

**LPs to Search For:** *Hudson-DeLange 1936–39* (Bandstand 7105) has three Bus Etri solos from his period with Will Hudson's orchestra.

## Kevin Eubanks
b. November 15, 1957, Philadelphia, PA

One of the most widely seen guitarists in the world due to his 18-year stint as Jay Leno's sidekick and musical director on the *Tonight Show*, Kevin Eubanks has thus far had his artistic career stunted by the association, although there is still time to regain his former stature.

The nephew of the great pianist Ray Bryant, son of gospel and classical pianist-organist Vera Eubanks, brother of trombonist Robin Eubanks and Duane Eubanks, and cousin of pianist Charles Eubanks and the late bassist David Eubanks, it would not be an exaggeration to say that Kevin Eubanks came from a talented musical family. He originally studied violin, trumpet and piano before settling on guitar. After attending Berklee, Eubanks moved to New York. He worked with the Art Blakey Big Band during 1980–81 and had stints with Roy Haynes, Slide Hampton and Sam Rivers. In 1983, he formed his own group and made his recording debut as a leader. Eubanks followed his *Elektra/Musician* album (reissued by Wounded Bird) with seven diverse CDs for GRP, which sometimes included R&B, funk and freer explorations, and four more consistent efforts for Blue Note, coming across as an open-minded post-bop guitarist. He also worked and recorded with Dave Holland's sextet in 1989.

In 1992, Eubanks joined the Tonight Show Band. When its bandleader, Branford Marsalis, departed, he took his place, staying until the end of May 2010. The job (which seemed to mostly involve laughing at Leno's jokes and playing occasional background music) kept the guitarist in Los Angeles. Although he occasionally played locally and recorded for his own Insoul Music label (emphasizing his acoustic guitar), it greatly reduced his prominence on the jazz scene.

It will be very interesting to see what Kevin Eubanks does in his post–Jay Leno period, which began with his 2010 recording, *Zen Food*.

**Recommended CDs:** *Guitarist* (Wounded Bird 213), *Sundance* (GRP 9506), *Opening Night* (GRP 9520), *Face To Face* (GRP 9539), *The Heat Of Heat* (GRP 9552), *Shadow Prophets* (GRP 9565), *The Searcher* (GRP 9580) and *Promise Of Tomorrow* (GRP 9604) are a mixed bag, ranging from substantial music to throwaway tunes. Most of Kevin Eubanks' best work thus far can be found on his four Blue Note projects: *Turning Point* (Blue Note 98170), *Spiritalk* (Blue Note 89286), *Live At Bradley's* (Blue Note 30133) and *Spiritalk 2* (Blue Note 30132). His Insoul albums (*Live, Shrine, Angel, Slow Freight, Genesis* and *Soweto Sun*), which are mostly acoustic, relaxed and subtle, are generally worth the search. The fairly recent *Zen Food* (Mack Avenue 1054) shows that his improvising chops did not go stale during the long Leno years.

**Website:** www.kevineubanks.com

## Tal Farlow
*(Talmage Farlow)*
b. June 7, 1921, Greensboro, NC; d. July 25, 1998, Sea Bright, NJ

Tal Farlow, one of the top jazz guitarists of the 1950s, had a simple goal in life. He wanted to have an easy lifestyle, preferably as a sign painter, while playing jazz for the fun of it. After gaining fame in the '50s, he surprised many in the jazz world by avoiding further fame and achieving exactly what he wanted.

Farlow, who had huge hands for a guitarist, had a light touch and the ability to play very fast lines while sounding and looking relaxed. He was already 20 before he started playing guitar but was a professional within a year. Inspired and influenced by Charlie Christian and Lester Young, Farlow's horn-like lines eventually put him at the top of his field. He had stints with pianist Dardanelle (1947), vibraphonist Marjorie Hyams, and Buddy DeFranco (1949) before joining Red Norvo (1949–53). The vibes-guitar-bass trio (with at first Charles Mingus and later Red Mitchell on bass) was a perfect format for Farlow, who was able to play the rapid unisons with ease and say a lot during short solos. After being a member of Artie Shaw's Gramercy Five for six months during 1953–54, he had the first of several reunions with Norvo and then led his own brilliant trio, which for a time featured pianist Eddie Costa and bassist Vinnie Burke. Farlow recorded regularly as a leader for Verve during the 1950s.

In 1959, it stopped, at least for a time. Tal Farlow settled with his new wife in Sea Bright, New Jersey, worked as a sign painter, and confined his playing to local gigs. During 1960–75, he only led one record date. While he appeared on an album by altoist Sonny Criss and worked a bit in the late 1960s with the Newport All-Stars, otherwise the question "Whatever happened to Tal Farlow?" was fitting.

During 1976–84, Farlow returned to jazz on his own terms, making some recordings, touring when he wanted, and showing that he was still in his prime even if some of the earlier fire was gone. During his final 14 years before his death at age 77 from cancer, Farlow's public appearances were infrequent but almost always a major event. The wonderful film *Talmage Farlow* by Lorenzo DeStefano, which is available on DVD, gives viewers a definitive profile of the guitarist. Despite his desire to avoid the limelight, Tal Farlow ranks as one of the true greats, a powerful if soft-spoken guitarist who showed that in straight-ahead jazz, the guitar could be as vital as the tenor-saxophone.

**Recommended CDs:** Some of the performances by the Red Norvo Trio with Farlow are on *1950–1951* (Classics 1422) and the nearly impossible-to-find *Volume Two: The Norvo-Mingus-Farlow Trio* (Vintage Jazz Classics 1008). Tal Farlow's first session as a leader, which resulted in a Blue Note ten-inch LP, has been reissued as part of *Howard McGhee Volume 2/Tal Farlow Quartet* (Blue Note 95748). The most logical way to acquire Tal Farlow's brilliant recordings for Verve is to get the seven-CD set *The Complete Verve Tal Farlow Sessions* (Mosaic 7-224). Unfortunately, this box is a limited-edition set that is out of print. Some of the individual albums are available as single CDs. *Autumn In New York* (Verve 2591) is a relaxed date with pianist Gerry Wiggins, bassist Ray Brown and drummer Chico Hamilton. Both *Tal* (Universal 5111) and *The Swinging Guitar Of Tal Farlow* (Verve 314 559 515) have the classic Farlow-Costa-Burke trio of 1956. *This Is Tal Farlow* (Universal 5274) features a slightly later group that also includes Costa. *The Complete 1956 Private Recordings* (Definitive 11263) reissues a pair of Xanadu LPs of live sessions by the Farlow-Costa-Burke trio that were not flawlessly recorded but are nevertheless quite exciting. *The Return Of Tal Farlow: 1969* (Original Jazz Classics 356) temporarily broke the silence from the guitarist and finds him still in excellent form with a quartet. Of Farlow's later recordings, *A Sign Of The Times* (Concord 4026), a live reunion with Norvo for *On Stage* (Concord 4143), *Chromatic Palette* (Concord 4154), and *Cookin' On All Burners* (Concord 4204) all have their moments, with *Cookin'* being the most highly recommended of Tal Farlow's Concord recordings.

**LPs to Search For:** Those collectors who have not been unable to find the Mosaic box set should search for *The Tal Farlow Album* (Verve 2584), which has Farlow with a quartet that, on a few songs, includes rhythm guitarist Barry Galbraith. *The Interpretations Of Tal Farlow* (Verve 8138) has Farlow playing fresh versions of ten standards with a quartet that also features pianist Claude Williamson. *A Recital By Tal Farlow* (Verve 8123) is a tightly arranged West Coast cool jazz date with three horn players. After becoming semi-retired, Farlow returned briefly in 1959 to record enough music for two albums. *The Guitar Artistry Of Tal Farlow* (Verve 6143) finds the guitarist teamed with such players as pianist Dick Hyman and either Frank Wess or Bobby Jaspar on tenor. *Tal Farlow Plays The Music Of Harold Arlen* (Verve 6144) includes additional quartet numbers with Wess plus three songs with a septet. *Tal Farlow 78* (Concord 57) and *The Legendary Tal Farlow* (Concord 266), the latter featuring Sam Most on tenor and flute, are long overdue to be reissued on CD.

## Mordy Ferber
*b. August 26, 1958, Israel*

Long before the current crop of talented Israeli musicians relocated to the US, Mordy Ferber was leading the way, holding his own with Americans and playing adventurous jazz. Ferber was originally a singer as a child, leading a trio that performed at school events when he was nine. He began classical guitar lessons when he was 12. Ferber was mostly interested in rock music initially, touring Israel in a rock band while going to school during the day. But at 17, he heard a Django Reinhardt record on the radio. "That had a tremendous effect on me. He had great technique (using only two fingers), humor, and lots of soul in his playing. I sat for hours every day transcribing his music and solos. I soon did the same thing with other jazz guitar greats like Charlie Christian, Joe Pass, Wes Montgomery and Jim Hall. This became my school of music."

After three years serving in the Israeli Army (including playing with the military band), Ferber became one of Israel's top musicians, working in the studios, making records, accompanying singers (including Arik Einstein) and appearing regularly on radio and television shows. But jazz is what he wanted to play, so he moved to the United States and studied at Berklee during 1982–87. After graduating, he stayed in the Boston area for a few years before moving to New York in 1990.

Since then, Ferber has performed with Michael Brecker, Jack DeJohnette, Eddie Gomez, Bob Mintzer, Dave Liebman, Miroslav Vitous, Jeff Berlin, Bob Moses, Richie Beirach, Richard Bona, Larry Coryell, George Garzone and many others. He has also written quite a few television and film scores and has been teaching jazz for the past 26 years.

"Jazz is the highest art form I know, and I love everything about it. Those few moments of pure improvisation are so fresh, so rewarding, that I'm addicted to it."

**Recommended CDs:** *All The Way To Sendai* (Enja 79643), *Mr. X* (Half Note 4205) and *Being There* (CBS Europe) feature Mordy Ferber holding his own with the likes of Bob Mintzer, Miroslav Vitous, Jack DeJohnette, Dave Liebman, George Garzone and Michael Brecker. 2011's *Reflection* (Abstract Logix) has colorful Ferber originals and fine interplay with keyboardist Greg Goebel.

**Website:** www.mordyferber.com

## Boulou Ferré
*b. April 24, 1951, Paris, France*

Boulou Ferré Quartet
*Relax and Enjoy*
SteepleChase

Long before the Rosenberg Trio gave a great deal of momentum to the gypsy-jazz movement, there were musical gypsies in Europe who were keeping alive the legacy of Django Reinhardt. Boulou Ferré and his younger brother Elios were among the most talented of the guitarists who emerged in the late 1960s, and both brothers are still active today.

Their father, Matelo Ferret, and especially their uncle, Pierre "Baro" Ferret, both had opportunities to play in the Quintet of the Hot Club of France with Django Reinhardt as rhythm guitarists. Boulou (who, along with his brother, later changed his last name to Ferré) was always interested in bebop in addition to Django. By the time he was seven, he was working on transferring Charlie Parker solos to his guitar. He played his first concert when he was just eight, had his recording debut at ten, and made his first album as a leader at 12.

In 1963, Ferré started studying classical music at the Conservatoire National de Paris. In 1964, when he was 13, he had an opportunity to play with John Coltrane during the first half of the saxophonist's concert at the Antibes Jazz Festival. When he was in his twenties, Boulou worked with American greats when they toured France, including Dexter Gordon, T-Bone Walker, Warne Marsh, Philly Jo Jones, Chet Baker and a stint with Dizzy Gillespie. He also played with Stéphane Grappelli and composed music for films and television.

In 1978, Boulou Ferré and his brother formed a guitar duo that continues to this day. While emphasizing acoustic guitars, they also utilize electric guitars at times in a group that is sometimes as large as a quintet. The careers of the Ferré brothers have been intertwined ever since 1978, with Boulou usually getting the lion's share of the attention, although the siblings are equally talented soloists. And because they utilize modern rhythms, they have succeeded in modernizing the gypsy-jazz tradition.

**Recommended CDs:** Boulou Ferré is heard at the beginning of his career on *Bluesette—13 Year Old Jazz Sensation From France* (Universal 3016). With his brother Elios (usually as the Ferré Brothers but sometimes under Boulou's name), he has recorded *Pour Django* (Steeplechase 31120), *Gypsy Dreams* (Steeplechase 31140), *Trinity* (Steeplechase 31171),

*Relax And Enjoy* (Steeplechase 31210), *Nuages* (Steeplechase 31222), *Confirmation* (Steeplechase 31243), *Guitar Legacy* (Steeplechase 37009), *New York, N.Y.* (Steeplechase 31404), *Intersection* (La Lichère 306), *Parisian Passion* (Bee Jazz), *Shades Of A Dream* (Bee Jazz), *The Rainbow Of Life* (Bee Jazz), *Live At Djangofest Northwest* (DFM), *Live In Montpellier* (Le Chant du Monde 2741512) and *Brothers To Brothers* (Nocturne 4511). Boulou Ferré has also recorded with Gunter Hampel, with Steve Lacy (*Dreams*), and in a guitar trio with Christian Escoudé and Babik Reinhardt on *Three Of A Kind* (JMS 038).

**LPs to Search For:** Some of Boulou Ferré's earliest recordings are difficult to find, including *Boulou & Les Paris All Stars* (Barclay 4211) and *Jazz/Left Bank* (Barclay 4234).

**Website:** www.boulou-elios-ferre.com

## Elios Ferré
*b. December 18, 1956, Paris, France*

Elios Ferré has had a parallel career with that of his older brother, Boulou Ferré, although he displays his own personality on the guitar. Like his brother, Ferré started quite young. He was playing guitar when he was six and gave his first concert at 13. He studied with his father and attended the Conservatoire National de Paris. Ferré became very interested in the flamenco guitar as a teenager and, by the late 1960s, was also being influenced by Jimi Hendrix. But he never lost sight of his roots in Django Reinhardt's music and always said that Django was his favorite guitarist.

Elios Ferré recorded his first album in 1970, spent some time playing with Larry Coryell and, like Boulou, wrote music for movies and television. In 1978, the brothers formed a duo, and that has been their main musical activity ever since. While Elios often plays rhythm while Boulou plays lead, Elios is also a skilled soloist. Together, they create a great deal of excitement, keeping the Django Reinhardt legacy alive while bringing the music into modern times.

**Recommended CDs:** Elios Ferré can be heard on many CDs with his brother Boulou, and those are listed under the previous entry. Oddly enough, Elios Ferré has apparently not led any sessions of his own.

**Website:** www.boulou-elios-ferre.com

## Garrison Fewell
*(Alexander Garrison Fewell)*
*b. October 14, 1953, Charlottesville, VA*

A versatile guitarist based in New England, Garrison Fewell excels both in guitar duos and in adventurous post-bop explorations. Raised in Philadelphia, when he was ten, he was given a Spanish guitar by his father for Christmas. "My father had all of Benny Goodman's records, and that's where I first heard Charlie Christian. I didn't think about playing jazz at that time because I was into Delta blues guitarists like Mississippi John Hurt, Fred McDowell and Gary Davis. At 18, I left the US with my acoustic guitar for a tour of the Middle East, headed towards India. I ended up as a disk jockey in Kabul, Afghanistan, spinning mostly rock and blues records. Oddly enough, there were a few Coltrane LPs there too, including *A Love Supreme*. When I came back in 1973, I went to Berklee, and when I heard Lester Young in an ear training class, that's when I wanted to play jazz."

He first performed in public in 1967, playing solo and with another guitarist at several clubs, including the Main Point. After he enrolled in Berklee, Fewell had an incident that convinced him of his future course. "Living on food stamps, trying to pay my rent, I took a jazz fake book to a restaurant in Harvard Square and just read tunes out of it all night. I got $25 and a meal, spent the food stamps on beer, and knew that I wanted to be a professional musician!" Fewell played regularly in the Boston area and graduated from Berklee in 1977 with a bachelor's degree in performance. He also had valuable lessons with Lenny Breau, Pat Martino and Tal Farlow. "I met Tal while I was a student at Berklee, shook his hand, and immediately realized why I could never play like Tal: his hand was twice the size of mine!"

After graduating from Berklee, Fewell became a professor at the school and has often taught since then. As a performer, in 1986 he formed a quartet with pianist Frank Carlberg, bassist Ben Street and drummer George Schuller that lasted for four years. Other important associations have included Fred Hersch, Cecil McBee and Matt Wilson (they had a quartet during 1992–93); a duo tour of Europe in 1996 with Tal Farlow; playing in Benny Golson's quintet (2001); tours of Italy with Billy Harper and Cecil Bridgewater (2002–04); Lazlo Gardony; Don Friedman; Steve LaSpina; Cameron Brown; Jeff Williams; Khan Jamal; Roy Campbell; and various projects with John Tchicai. "I had already changed directions and was playing improvised music. With John Tchicai, the power of deep listening was added, for it could enable me to know what to play, not through intellect but through instinct. I learned not to hesitate and to move with the first idea, turning even a missed note into an opportunity."

Fewell has spent time living, teaching and performing overseas, living in Paris for a time. In recent times, Fewell has worked and recorded with the Variable Density Sound Orchestra, with Eric Hofbauer (freely improvised guitar duos), with John Tchicai, with a trio including saxophonist Charles Kohlhase, and in Europe with the Global Music Foundation.

"There was a time I almost regretted that I chose the guitar as my primary instrument because of some difficult years I had to go through, when I leaned away from blues and fell into jazz. My tastes in music changed, and my capabilities needed to expand. But now I have accepted the individual musical qualities I once thought were shortcomings as the very things that make me unique."

**Recommended CDs:** *A Blue Deeper Than The Blue* (Accurate 4700) from 1992 teams Fewell with Fred Hersch, Cecil McBee and Matt Wilson, easily holding his own with his better-known sidemen. *Are You Afraid Of The Dark?* (Accurate 4701), with Laszlo Gardony in Hersch's place, displays both the influence of Pat Martino and Fewell's travels to the Middle East in the music. *Reflection Of A Clear Moon* (Accurate 4702) is a set of explorative duets with Gardony taken from a Hungarian radio broadcast. *Birdland Sessions* (Koch 8575) with Jim McNeely, Steve LaSpina and Jeff Williams has some of Fewell's most memorable originals. *City Of Dreams* (Splasc(h) 820) is a fine outing in a quintet that includes saxophonist Tino Tracanna and pianist George Cables; equally rewarding is the quartet date *Red Door Number 11* (Splasc(h) 857). *The Lady Of Khartoum* (Creative Nation Music 10) features Fewell at his most adventurous, playing guitar duets with Eric Hofbauer. Close to Garrison Fewell's heart is the dynamic avant-garde music of his *Variable Density Sound Orchestra* (Creative Nation Music 014), a sextet/septet that is expanded to a tentet on the identically titled *Variable Density Sound Orchestra* (Sound Particle 47). He is also a major part of the trio with John Tchicai (the leader) and Charles Kohlhase on *Good Night Songs* (Boxholder 050/051).

**Website:** www.garrisonfewell.com

## Andy Fite
b. Feb 13, 1958, San Diego, CA

The only guitarist in this book who also calls himself a comic, Andy Fite has had a wide-ranging career. He grew up in Pittsburgh. "I turned six the same week the Beatles came the US and played the Ed Sullivan show. 'I Want To Hold Your Hand' was the song that really woke me up to music." After a few years of piano lessons, he switched to guitar when he was 11 but did not take it seriously until he was 14. Two years later, he discovered jazz, being particularly impressed by Joe Pass on *Sounds Of Synanon*, Charlie Parker and Lennie Tristano. Fite played rock as a teenager, but by the time he attended the University of Pittsburgh (1976–80), jazz was his main interest. He played some gigs with the jazz department head Nathan Davis and local musicians, and his guitar teacher was Joe Negri. An early highlight was playing a concert with Kenny Clarke in 1978, and he also worked at a lot of weddings, often on bass. "I learned a lot of songs during those years. Because there were so many singers around, I considered it a basic musical skill to learn every song in every key."

After moving to New York in 1984, Fite had ten years of lessons from Connie Crothers. "She really showed me how to be myself, to be in the moment, and to be open to the flow of inspiration." Fite had a duo with Liz Gorrill (1988–90) that recorded two CDs. The increasingly adventurous guitarist also worked with pianist/trombonist Ulf Johansson, Richard Tabnik, Carol Tristano, Roger Mancuso, Bob Casanova, Dori Levine, Carol Liebowitz, Harry Schulz, Sean Smith, Rich Califano and John McCutcheon. Most of those musicians were associated with New Artists Records and the music and concepts of Lennie Tristano's students.

Fite moved permanently to Sweden in 1994, becoming a music theory teacher, writing over 400 songs, and often working with bassist Ulf Akerhielm, singing in addition to playing guitar. In 2001, he toured Estonia and Sweden with Connie Crothers and Richard Tabnik. Fite has recorded prolifically for his Other Street Music label since that time, and he has dreams of working in comedy. He occasionally visits New York, leading a trio called the Andy Fite Funtet that plays humorous originals and unusual transformations of standards.

**Recommended CDs:** *Everybody Get Happy* (New Artists 1014) is a set of spirited duets by Andy Fite and bassist Red Mitchell. *Whirlwind* (New Artists 1022) features Fite on unaccompanied solos. His two duet albums with Liz Gorrill are *Phantasmagoria* (New Artists 1004) and *Cosmic Comedy* (New Artists 1012). He has also led over 35 CDs for the Other Street Music label, including *If You're Gonna Do What You're Gonna Do*, *Live In Moscow*, *Jazz Conversations With Bach*, *Jazz Comic Philosopher*, *Life's A Bitch (And I'm Her Guy)*, *Other People's Problems* and *Time For My Therapy*. In recent times, Fite has been recording and releasing one CD per month. In addition, Andy Fite recorded in his earlier period on New Artists with Richard Tabnik, Bob Casanova, Carol Liebowitz (*Time On My Hands*), Harry Schulz, Linda Satin and Charle Krachy.

**Website:** www.andyfite.se

## David "Fuze" Fiuczynski
*b. March 5, 1964, Newark, NJ*

A powerful soloist who effortlessly crosses over several musical genres, David Fiuczynski has often said that he does not want to be known only as a jazz guitarist. Fiuczynski lived in New Jersey until he was eight, relocating with his family to Germany until he was 19. After a brief stint on piano when he was seven, he switched to guitar, saying half-jokingly that he stuck to playing music because "my mother forced me." His first musical jobs were playing with fusion bands in Moenchengladbach, Germany. Fuze attended the New England Conservatory (1985–89 and 2006–08), earning a master's. He credits Billy Hart with taking him under his wing when he moved to New York in 1989.

Fuze considers some of the musical high points of his career to be leading the Screaming Headless Torsos since 1991, making his first recording in 1994 with John Medeski, working with George Russell's Living Time Orchestra, being part of the Hasidic New Wave (1997–2004) and working with Jack DeJohnette since 2008. "Playing with Western and Moroccan musicians at the World's Fair in Seville, Spain, in 1992 was important because it gave me ideas about mixing microtonal music, Eastern melodic concepts and black beats."

In addition to touring with the Screaming Headless Torsos, Fuze (who is a professor at Berklee) plays Arabic funk/jazz with KiF and funk-rock, rap and punk with Black Cherry Acid Lab. Among his other associations through the years have been George Russell, Hiromi, Cindy Blackman, Muhal Richard Abrams, the Mandala Octet, Jack Walrath, Me'shell Ndegeocello, Branford Marsalis, Don Pullen, Kenny Kirkland, Mark Shim, Geri Allen, Ronald Shannon Jackson, and Five Guitars Play Mingus. David Fiuczynski's intense playing and musically wide-open style make him in demand for complex and genre-crossing music.

**Recommended CDs:** *Lunar Crash* (Video Arts 1315) put Fuze on the map, and *Screaming Headless Torsos* (Video Arts 1316) gives one a strong sampling of the guitarist's passion and eclecticism. Since then, most of his recordings have been for his own Fuzelicious Morsels (FM) label, including *JazzPunk* (FM 8898), which ranges from Pat Metheny and Chick Corea to John Philip Sousa; *Amandala* (FM 8899); *Headless Torsos: Live* (FM 8990); *KiF* (FM 8903); and *KiF Express* (FM 8908).

**Website:** www.torsos.com

## Rod Fleeman
*(Rodney Fleeman)*
*b. April 27, 1953, Kansas City, MO*

While Rod Fleeman gained some attention for his playing in a fusion band in the 1970s, during the past 15 years, he has earned a strong reputation as an accompanist to singers and for his mainstream guitar solos on both acoustic and electric guitars. Fleeman began playing the guitar at 11. Originally, his goal was to be in a rock band. But in high school, he made the stage band as a freshman, and that turned him toward jazz. "George Alter, my band director, turned my life around as did John Elliott, everyone's jazz theory guru in Kansas City." Fleeman attended the University of Utah during 1971–72, played his first jazz gigs with organist Greg Meise in Kansas City in 1972–73 (six nights a week at a club called the Wildhawker), and finished college at the University of Miami (1974–76).

Fleeman played during 1978–81 with the fusion group Dry Jack, making two albums for Inner City. He worked steadily in Kansas City for the next decade. But it was not until the early 1990s that he began to gain a national reputation. "Meeting Karrin Allyson and starting a great musical relationship with her was a turning point for me." Fleeman has worked with her since 1992, has often played with Ken Peplowski during the past decade, and has toured with Diane Schuur since 2005.

"My future goal is to record something under my own name and get my original music out. I have been blessed to do what I love to do and still earn a living at it. Over the course of time, I've fallen in love with so many of the great standards. Playing the songs is like visiting an old friend. That may be one of the reasons I love working with the best vocalists."

**Recommended CDs:** Rod Fleeman is on nine Karrin Allyson CDs, including *Collage* (Concord 4709), *From Paris To Rio* (Concord 4865) and *Imagina* (Concord 30428). He has also recorded with Angela Hagenbach, Mike Metheny, Laura Caviana, Diane Schuur, and on two albums (*Odahoda* and *Winter Song*) with Interstring, a quartet comprised of Allyson's backup group with Danny Embrey on electric guitar.

**Website:** www.myspace.com/quotlightningrod quotfleeman

## Chris Flory
*b. November 13, 1953, New York, NY*

An excellent swing and mainstream-based guitarist who ranks with Howard Alden in his generation, Chris Flory helped pave the way for other young guitarists to play creatively in earlier idioms. Flory began playing guitar at ten or eleven. The first jazz records he heard were Charles Lloyd's *Forest Flower* and a Pharoah Sanders/Leon Thomas album. Seeing B.B. King and Jimi Hendrix perform in 1968 and Rahsaan Roland Kirk at the 1969 Newport Jazz Festival made strong impressions. "By age 15, I was friends with Scott Hamilton, who introduced me to many great blues players as well as some of the canon of more mainstream jazz. When I was 17 and first living on my own in NYC, my girlfriend and I had a job taking care of Gil Evans' kids. I had the run of his record collection, and I taped many LPs, including Miles, Bird, Lester Young and Nat Cole."

Flory's first gigs were with rock bands when he was 13. He left home at 16, had two jazz guitar lessons with Tiny Grimes in 1971, and started seriously playing jazz at 20. He attended Hobart College during 1972–73 but mostly learned on the bandstand. Flory played with Scott Hamilton's groups on and off during 1975–93, performed for a month at Michael's Pub with Hank Jones and Milt Hinton, and played with such older giants as Roy Eldridge, Jo Jones, and Buddy Tate. Flory was a member of the Benny Goodman Sextet during 1977–83 and performed at Goodman's final big band concert in 1986. He also worked with Bob Wilber (1977–81), Ruby Braff, Illinois Jacquet, Maxine Sullivan, Judy Carmichael (with whom he toured China in 1992), Duke Robillard and Harry Allen.

"B.G.'s death in 1986 and the demise of Scott Hamilton's working quintet showed me that I had to work harder to establish a career as a leader and not just a sideman. My first Concord CDs and subsequent tours in Spain and the UK through the 1990s helped me grow as a musician." Chris Flory's gradual evolution continues to this day.

**Recommended CDs:** As a leader, Chris Flory is in fine form on *For All We Know* (Concord 4403), *City Life* (Concord 4589), *Word On The Street* (Double-Time 119), *Blues In My Heart* (Stony Plain 1288), the joyful *For You* (Arbors 19357) and on the swinging *Chris Flory Quintet Featuring Scott Hamilton* (Arbors 19440). As a sideman, Flory has recorded with Hamilton, Rosemary Clooney, Maxine Sullivan, Buck Clayton's Swing Band, Flip Phillips, Ruby Braff, Duke Robillard and Bob Wilber.

**Website:** www.chrisfloryjazz.com

## Robben Ford
*b. December 16, 1951, Ukiah, CA*

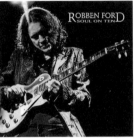

One could be excused if one thought that there were two Robben Fords. He has had overlapping careers as a fusion/pop jazz guitarist and as a bluesman. While his singing and songwriting are not that memorable, his guitar playing is always excellent and often inspired. His father, Charles Ford, was a country singer and guitarist while his mother, Kathryn, played piano and sang. Robben Ford played the saxophone from the age of ten until he was in his mid-twenties. However, when he was 13, he taught himself the guitar, inspired by Michael Bloomfield and Elvin Bishop. He discovered both rock (often going to the Fillmore West) and jazz as a teenager.

After high school, Ford came together with his brothers, drummer Patrick and harmonica player Mark, to form the Charles Ford Blues Band, named after their father. The group recorded for Arhoolie, and Ford had an opportunity to tour with Charlie Musselwhite. Some of his best work from this period was a year spent with Jimmy Witherspoon (1972–73).

Discovered by Tom Scott, Ford worked with the L.A. Express and toured with Joni Mitchell for two years. He also worked with George Harrison for two months. In 1977 when he recorded *The Inside Story*, he used a group of musicians who would soon join him as the Yellowjackets. After this period (1977–83), Ford worked for six months with Miles Davis in 1986.

After working as a studio musician and having a stint with David Sanborn (1990), in 1992, Ford returned to his roots, forming the Blue Line with bassist Roscoe Beck and drummer Tom Brechtlein. Although the group broke up eight years later, Robben Ford has continued playing (and occasionally singing) blues-oriented music up to the present time while being a diverse guitarist capable of playing rock and fusion.

**Recommended CDs:** *Anthology: The Early Years* (Rhino 76760), *Discovering The Blues* (Rhino 72727), *Schizophonic* (Rhino 71624), *The Inside Story* (WEA 25054), *Talk To Your Daughter* (Warner Bros. 25647), *Robben Ford & The Blue Line* (Stretch 1102), *Mystic Mile* (Stretch 1107), *Handful Of Blues* (Blue Thumb 7004), *Tiger Walk* (Blue Thumb 7011) and *Soul On Ten* (Concord 31528) are Robben Ford's most rewarding recordings.

**Website:** www.robbenford.com

## Bruce Forman
b. May 14, 1956, Springfield, MA

A bop-oriented guitarist with a fiery and creative style, Bruce Forman can liven up any jam session. After several years of classical piano lessons, Forman switched to the guitar when he was 13. He heard jazz through a high school friend, bassist Ratso Harris, whose father plays trumpet. He was most impressed by Charlie Parker. "I never knew music could be so free, exhilarating and spirited—melodic and rhythmically complex while still rooted in the blues. It still amazes me."

Forman moved with his family to San Francisco in 1971 and became an important part of the San Francisco jazz scene after high school. He skipped college to work with many of the local greats, including Smith Dobson, Eddie Marshall, Vince Lateano, Eddie Duran and Al Plank in addition to Bobby Hutcherson, Joe Henderson, Woody Shaw, Freddie Hubbard, Ray Brown and George Cables. For years, Forman was a regular at the Monterey Jazz Festival, and during 1978–82, he toured and recorded with Richie Cole, an association that gave him national exposure.

Since that time, Forman has continued playing with many of the straight-ahead jazz greats, published a novel (*Trust Me*) about a fictional guitarist's life in jazz, written several guitar instructional books, and been an enthusiastic and insightful educator. He is the founder and executive director of JazzMasters Workshop ("which mirrors my philosophy that playing and mentoring are the true future of our music, not some institutionalized approach to the idiom") and moved to Southern California to be on staff at USC in their Studio/Jazz Guitar Department.

Forman has composed a libretto for a one-man show called *The Red Guitar*, in which he discusses how the music picked him and the effect of jazz on his life. In addition to leading a trio, he has founded and plays regularly with a boppish Western swing band called Cow Bop, which he calls "more fun and swingin' than is legal and definitely too hick for the room."

**Recommended CDs:** *There Are Times* (Concord 4332), with Bobby Hutcherson and George Cables in a quintet, is a fine effort from 1990. *Pardon Me* (Concord 4368) features the guitarist on an adventurous quartet date with pianist Billy Childs. *Still Of The Night* (Kamei 7000) is a trio outing, while *Forman On The Job* (Kamei 7004) has him in an all-star group that on various selections includes Joe Henderson, steel drummer Andy Narell and pianist Marc Levine. After a few years off records, *Dedication* (Blu Jazz 5008), recorded in 1999 but not released until 2003, shows that Bruce Forman had not lost his fire. Most recently, he recorded the boppish *Formanism* (B4M 102) with his trio. With the unique Cow Bop, he recorded *Swingin' Out West* (Blujazz 3318) and *Route 66* (Blujazz 3362). The current version of the spirited and witty band, in addition to Forman, includes vocalist Pinto Pammy, Phil Salazar on fiddle, bassist Alex King and drummer Jake Reed.

**LPs to Search For:** Bruce Forman's first seven albums as a leader, *Coast To Coast* (Choice 1026), *River Journey* (Muse 5251), *20/20* (Muse 5273), *In Transit* (Muse 5299), *The Bash* (Muse 5315), *Full Circle* (Concord 251) and *Dynamics* (Concord 279)—the latter a set of guitar-piano duets with George Cables—have yet to be reissued despite their consistently high quality.

**Website:** www.bruceforman.com

## Mimi Fox
b. August 24, 1956, Queens, NY

A powerful guitarist based in San Francisco, Mimi Fox has continued to grow rapidly as an improviser during the past few years. She started playing drums when she was nine. "Like most kids from my time period, I was into the Monkees when I was ten, and that got me interested in playing guitar. I kept on badgering my mother for a guitar until she finally got me one." She grew up hearing jazz, including her father's Dixieland records. Fox played drums in her junior high and high school band but was also interested in playing guitar. "My first steady gig was when I was 17, playing at a cocktail lounge at a Chinese restaurant in Stamford, Connecticut. Every time I would try to play something pretty, they would get the blender going." She left high school to go on the road with pop bands in the 1970s.

A turning point in her musical life occurred after she moved to Northern California in 1979, saw Bruce Forman play, and started studying with him. "I devoted six to eight hours a day to practicing guitar and to jazz." She also studied with Joe Pass, who was a major inspiration, and considers Charlie Byrd to be one of her mentors.

Mimi Fox recorded her first album as a leader in 1987, and by the time she cut her second one in 1995, she was a passionate guitarist who came up with fresh interpretations of standards in addition to writing colorful originals. Since then, she has worked with Joey DeFrancesco, Branford Marsalis, David Sanchez, Houston Person, Dr. Lonnie Smith, and other major names. She has performed at many festivals in the US, Asia, the Caribbean, Australia, Canada and Europe, usually with her own group. She is also an educator who has released *Mimi Fox's Jazz Performances* as educational videos, and she has written scores for documentary films and dance projects.

"If it hadn't been for Bruce Forman, I'd be wealthy today, because if I hadn't gotten excited about his playing and jazz, I probably would have been a very successful pop artist. But once bitten by the jazz bug, I didn't care about rock or pop music much anymore." To see her in action, her DVD *Live At The Palladium* from Favored Nations is a good place to start.

**Recommended CDs:** *Turtle Logic* (Monarch 1008), *Kicks* (Sugo 1020), the unaccompanied *Standards* (Origin 82389), *Two For The Road* (Origin 82411) with singer Greta Matassa, *She's The Woman* (Favored Nations 7010), *Perpetually Hip* (Favored Nations 7050).

**LPs to Search For:** *Against The Grain* (Catero 023) was Mimi Fox's debut recording.

**Website:** www.mimifoxjazzguitar.com

## Bill Frisell
*b. March 18, 1951, Baltimore, MD*

One of the most unique guitarists in jazz and improvised music, Bill Frisell started out as a fiery avant-gardist, but during the past decade, he has been a mostly mellow guitarist strongly influenced by his interest in Nashville's music. Innovative in the range of sounds that he creates, Frisell usually makes the presence of a bass unnecessary even though he plays a six-string (as opposed to a seven- or eight-string) guitar.

Frisell grew up in Denver. He began playing clarinet when he was nine, performing with a marching and concert band (the Gold Sash Band) for eight years, also playing tenor in school bands. At 11, he started on guitar, inspired by blues and rock guitarists. Three years later after getting his first electric guitar, Frisell put together his first band. He took guitar lessons from Dale Bruning starting in 1969. By then, he had become interested in the music of Wes Montgomery and Jim Hall without losing his interest in Jimi Hendrix. At the University of Northern Colorado, he was a music major on clarinet while also playing tenor and guitar in the school big band. In 1971, Frisell decided to concentrate exclusively on guitar. He studied with Johnny Smith, attended Berklee for one semester, and studied for eight weeks with Jim Hall. After a period back in Denver working as a teacher and playing locally, he attended Berklee during 1975–77. Frisell spent a year in Belgium, playing in a band and making his recording debut on Mauve Traffic. He also toured England with the Mike Gibbs Orchestra, and recorded on Eberhard Weber's Fluid Rustle.

Moving back to New York in 1979, Frisell's career really got underway. During the next decade, he worked with Paul Motian's Trio (which also included Joe Lovano), toured Europe as a duo with Eberhard Weber, recorded albums for ECM (including with Weber and Jan Garbarek) and Nonesuch, played with John Zorn, toured with Julius Hemphill, performed at a duet concert with Jim Hall (one of his idols), and formed his first band, a classic unit with bassist Kermit Driscoll, drummer Joey Baron and cellist Hank Roberts. During this period, Frisell (one of the stars of New York's downtown jazz scene) would frequently change styles, moods and sounds every few minutes in concert, jumping between free improvisations, Jim Hall–style modern jazz, country, swing, heavy metal, R&B, and noise. His playing was unlike anyone else's and was very unpredictable.

In 1989, Frisell moved to Seattle. In addition to his own projects, he has since worked with Motian, Jim Hall, Don Byron, Charlie Haden, David Sanborn, and Tim Berne, among many others. His 1992 album, *Have A Little Faith*, has tributes to Bob Dylan, Sonny Rollins, Stephen Foster, Charles Ives, Madonna, Muddy Waters, Aaron Copland and John Philip Sousa, displaying both Frisell's wide musical interests and his sense of humor. In the mid-1990s, he formed a new band, a quartet comprised of trombonist Curtis Fowlkes, trumpeter Ron Miles, violinist Eyvind Kang and his own guitar—no piano, bass or drums. He also composed music for three silent Buster Keaton films.

In 1997, Bill Frisell recorded *Nashville*, which teamed him with country musicians and became the turning point of his career. Instead of having the Nashville sound as one of a variety of elements in his music, it has since dominated many of his recordings and performances, which now tend to be laidback (even lazy sounding), folk-oriented modern Americana. Even when playing with veteran jazz musicians or exploring world music, Frisell's style is unhurried and a bit introspective.

**Recommended CDs:** There is no shortage of Bill Frisell recordings, all of which have their moments of interest: *In Line* (ECM 837019), *Rambler* (ECM 825234), *Smash & Scatteration* (Rykodisc 10006) with Vernon Reid, *Lookout For Hope* (ECM 833495), *Before We Were Born* (Nonesuch 60843), *Is That You?* (Nonesuch 60956), *Where In The World?* (Nonesuch 61181), *Live* (Hannibal 1517), *Have A Little Faith* (Nonesuch 79301), *This Land* (Nonesuch 79316), *Go West: Music For The Films Of Buster Keaton* (Nonesuch 79350), *High Sign/ One Week* (Nonesuch 79351), *Bill Frisell Quartet* (Nonesuch 79401), *Nashville* (Nonesuch 79415), *Gone, Just Like A Train* (Nonesuch 79479), *Songs We Know* (Nonesuch 79468), *Good Dog, Happy Man* (Nonesuch 79536), *Ghost Town* (Nonesuch 79583), *Blues Dream* (Nonesuch 79615), *With Dave Holland And Elvin Jones* (Nonesuch 79624), *The Willies* (Nonesuch 79652), *The Intercontinentals* (Nonesuch 79610), *Richter 858* (Songlines 1551), *East/West* (Nonesuch 79863), *Bill Frisell, Ron Carter, Paul Motian* (Nonesuch 79897), *History, Mystery* (Nonesuch 435964), *Beautiful Dreamers* (Savoy 17799), *Sign Of Life* (Savoy 17818), his John Lennon tribute set *All We Are Saying* (Savoy 17836), and *Floratone II* (Savoy 17855).

In demand since the early 1980s, Frisell has also recorded with Eberhard Weber, Arild Anderson, Jan Garbarek, Bob Moses, Tim Berne, Jim Pepper, John Zorn, Leni Stern, Lyle Mays, Billy Hart, Wayne Horvitz, Chet Baker, Gunter Hampel, Herb Robertson, Marc Johnson, Paul Bley, Hank Roberts, Bobby Previte, Henry Kaiser, Julius Hemphill, Joe Lovano, John Scofield, Don Byron, Lee Konitz, Jerry Granelli, Ginger Baker, Gary Peacock, Mick Goodrick, Robben Ford, Kenny Wheeler, Nguyen Le, Joey Baron, Ron Miles, Mike Stern, Michael Brecker, Dave Douglas, Lizz Wright, David Binney, Jack DeJohnette, Jenny Scheinman, Tony Malaby, Tim Ries, and McCoy Tyner. He has also recorded at least 16 CDs with Paul Motian.

**Website:** www.billfrisell.com

# Slim Gaillard
*(Bulee Gaillard)*
*b. January 1, 1916, Santa Clara, Cuba; d. February 26, 1991, London, England*

A fine musician who was one of the first guitarists

to be influenced by Charlie Christian, Slim Gaillard was most famous for his jive talk, often-bizarre vocals, and crazy sense of humor. Gaillard's early life was purposely shrouded in mystery by the entertainer. His father was a steward on a cruise liner and once accidentally left Slim behind for a time on the island of Crete. Raised in Detroit, Gaillard claimed to have worked as a boxer, a mortician, and an importer of bootleg rum. He did have a vaudeville act in which he played guitar and tap danced at the same time, and he also learned blues and boogie-woogie piano. After moving to New York in 1936, Gaillard formed a quartet with bassist Slam Stewart, called Slim and Slam, that had a giant novelty hit with "Flat Foot Floogie (With The Floy Floy)." Basing most of his repertoire on the blues and the chord changes used on "Flying Home" and "I Got Rhythm," Gaillard also recorded such nutty numbers as "Chicken Rhythm," "Buck Dance Rhythm," "Laughin' In Rhythm," "Tutti Frutti," "Matzoh Balls," "Boot-Ta-La-Za," "Sploghm" and "African Jive." Slim and Slam were quite popular until they were both drafted in 1943.

After being discharged in 1945, Gaillard formed an even crazier group with bassist Bam Brown in which Slim's lingo became more and more esoteric while Bam's singing was merely demented. They worked regularly in  Los Angeles for a few years. In addition to the comic monologues and patter (which utilized such "words" as "o-voutie," "o-rooney" and "vout"), Gaillard usually took a credible solo on guitar that fell between swing and bebop, and between serious Charlie Christian–inspired jazz and satire. Gaillard used Charlie Parker and Dizzy Gillespie as sidemen for one session. Among the tunes in his repertoire were "Cement Mixer (Putti Putti)," "Dunkin' Bagel," "Laguna," "Ya Ha Ha," "Ding Dong Oreenee," "Penicillin Boogie," "Minuet In Vout," "Popity Pop," "Oxydol Highball," "When Banana Skins Are Falling," "Avocado Seed Soup Symphony" and the four-part "Opera In Vout."

The fun lasted until the early 1950s. By that time, Gaillard was in New York, recording such numbers as "Babalu," "Yo Yo Yo," "Potato Chips," "Mishugana Mambo," "Serenade To A Poodle" and the modestly titled "Genius." Off records after 1953 other than a 1958 album, Gaillard appeared in two films (1954's *Go, Man, Go* and *Too Late Blues* in

1961), ran a motel in San Diego and, starting in the late 1960s, worked as an actor on television. In 1982, Dizzy Gillespie convinced him to return to performing, and Gaillard recorded a final album that showed that while he had not declined, he had not evolved much since the mid-1940s. Slim Gaillard spent his last years living in England, where he was celebrated as a living legend.

**Recommended CDs:** *The Complete Recordings 1938–1942* (Affinity 1034-3) is a three-CD set that is comprised of all of the Slim and Slam recordings, with Gaillard making the transition from acoustic to electric guitar. *1945* (Classics 864), *The Absolute Voutest* (Hep 28), *In Birdland 1951* (Hep 21) and *Laughing In Rhythm* (Verve 314 521 651) cover the 1945–53 period, including the studio sides and some of the more hilarious radio broadcasts. *Anytime, Anyplace, Anywhere* (Hep 2020) is Slim Gaillard's last act. While one can pretend that one is listening to these recordings to hear Gaillard's guitar solos, the zany vocals always steal the show.

## Barry Galbraith
*b. December 18, 1919, Pittsburgh, PA; d. January 13, 1983, Bennington, VT*

Barry Galbraith spent his career as a busy studio musician and a sideman on a wide variety of jazz sessions. While much of the time he played rhythm guitar or was buried in the background, he could effectively solo in nearly any jazz style and was a fine swing-to-bop musician.

As early as 1941, Galbraith was a staff guitarist at radio station WJAS in Pittsburgh. He enjoyed brief associations with Art Tatum, Red Norvo, Hal McIntyre and Teddy Powell before having two stints with the Claude Thornhill Orchestra (1941–42 and 1946–49), which sandwiched a period spent in the Army. After leaving Thornhill, Galbraith settled in New York and had a very busy 20 years in the studios, only emerging to tour with Stan Kenton in 1953. Among the hundreds of jazz sessions he was on were dates headed by George Russell, Gil Evans, Neal Hefti, Benny Goodman, Art Farmer, Ruby Braff, Clifford Brown, Charlie Shavers, Clark Terry, Don Elliott, Eddie Bert, Jimmy Cleveland, Jack Teagarden, Hal McKusick, Woody Herman, Sam Most, Phil Woods, Illinois Jacquet, Coleman Hawkins, Hank Jones, John Lewis, Joe Puma, Milt Hinton, Ella Fitzgerald, Helen Merrill, Jackie Paris, Dinah Washington, Lee Wiley, Billie Holiday, Eddie Jefferson, Sheila Jordan, Joe Williams and Johnny Hartman. The list is endless, and the style did not matter, for Galbraith fit comfortably into every setting.

Barry Galbraith became an educator in the 1960s, and after surgery in 1970 for calcium deposits, he concentrated much more on teaching, publishing the Barry Galbraith Guitar Study Series in 1982, a year before his death.

**Recommended CDs:** With all of his activity, Barry Galbraith only led one album of his own. *Guitar And The Wind* (Universal 9103), which is currently just available in Japan, features the guitarist with a rhythm section, four trombones, three reeds, and Bobby Jaspar on tenor and flute. Some of Galbraith's more significant recordings as a sideman are George Russell's *Jazz Workshop* (Bluebird 6467) and *Jazz In The Space Age* (GRP 18262), Coleman Hawkins' *Desafinado* (Impulse 227), *Portrait Of Sheila Jordan* (Blue Note 89002) and Hal McKusick's *The Complete Barry Galbraith, Milt Hinton & Osie Johnson Recordings* (Lone Hill 10176).

## Eric Gale
*b. September 20, 1938, Brooklyn, NY; d. May 25, 1994, Baja, CA*

For 30 years, Eric Gale seemed to be everywhere. The quintessential sideman and studio guitar player, Gale could always be relied upon to play a bluish solo and to add soul to any session. Gale started on the bass when he was 12 and also had stints on tenor, trombone and tuba before settling on guitar. He majored in chemistry at Niagara University, but soon after he left college, he was very busy as a musician. Gale's soulful style made him a natural part of R&B and soul groups, but he was also a fine jazz improviser. In his career, he appeared on over 500 sessions, including working with the Drifters, Jackie Wilson, the Flamingos, Aretha Franklin, Diana Ross, Paul Simon, Lena Horne, Joe Cocker, Billy Joel, King Curtis, Jimmy Smith, David "Fathead" Newman, Illinois Jacquet, Clark Terry, Bobby Timmons, Nina Simone, Gary Burton, Mongo Santamaria, Herbie Mann and Quincy Jones. Gale recorded regularly for producer Creed Taylor, including in the late 1960s for Verve and A&M and in the 1970s for CTI and Kudu, on dates led by John Hammond Smith, George Benson, Bob James, Lalo Schifrin, Grover Washington Jr., Esther Phillips, Freddie Hubbard, Stanley Turrentine, Idris Muhammad and Hank Crawford.

During the second half of the 1970s, Gale often played with Cornell Dupree, Richard Tee and Steve Gadd as the jazz/funk group Stuff. Later sessions included dates with Sadao Watanabe, Dave Grusin and Al Jarreau. Eric Gale passed away from lung cancer in 1994 when he was just 55.

**Recommended CDs:** *Forecast* (originally for Kudu and last released as King 2216); *Multiplication* (Sony

9544); *Touch Of Silk* (Columbia 5058), which has a great version of Charlie Parker's "Au Privave" with Arthur Blythe; *Blue Horizon* (Discover 71008); *Let's Stay Together* (Artful Balance 7215); and *Utopia: Last Recording* (BMG 7025) all have their moments. But the Eric Gale jazz CD to get is *In A Jazz Tradition* (Emarcy 836369), an often-fiery set of bebop and soul jazz that teams Gale with Houston Person, Dr. Lonnie Smith and Grady Tate.

## Frank Gambale

*b. December 22, 1958, Canberra, A.C.T., Australia*

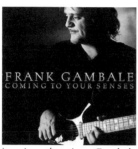

A major fusion guitarist who also sounds quite comfortable in postbop settings, Frank Gambale realized a lifelong dream when he became a member of Chick Corea's Elektric Band, although he has continued evolving since that time. Gambale started playing guitar in his native Australia when he was seven. "I played blues, country and pop for about ten years. Then I heard an early Steely Dan album, and I thought it was the hippest thing I'd ever heard. I started frequenting my local import record shop. I didn't have a lot of money to buy records, so I would agonize over which ones to buy. The record store owner knew that and decided that he would loan me any album, and if I liked it, I could buy it. He introduced me to Chick Corea, Jean-Luc Ponty, Brecker Brothers, George Duke, Coltrane, Joe Farrell's CTI recordings—so much stuff. I was hooked."

Chick Corea soon became his favorite. "When I was 17, I was so into Chick Corea that I gave up guitar for two years and dove headlong into piano. I bought an upright piano and a Fender Rhodes. I learned everything by ear. At my peak, I was playing some of Chick's solo pieces from the *Piano Improvisation* albums from the early '70s. However, my brother Nunzio encouraged me to play guitar again. He was a bass player and we had always played together. I'm very glad he did. Otherwise, I could never have played with Chick. The last thing he needs is another piano player!"

In September 1982, Gambale moved to Los Angeles and attended the Guitar Institute of Technology. After graduating, he taught at the Guitar Institute for four years. Gambale toured with Jean-Luc Ponty during the summer of 1986 and worked with Jeff Berlin's group as the successor to Scott Henderson.

Gambale recorded *Pump It* with Berlin at Mad Hatter Studios, which by coincidence was Chick Corea's studio. "I was in awe of the place. I sat at Chick's pianos and looked at original artwork from many of my favorite albums on the walls. As I was packing up my gear into my car on the last day of recording, a woman came out from Chick's offices. I approached her and said, 'If there is ever an opportunity to play with Chick, please let me know,' handing her my card. She read it and said 'Hey, my husband has played with you and he says you play great.' She was Evelyn Brechtlein, the wife of drummer Tom Brechtlein and Chick's manager's personal assistant. Six months later I got a call to audition, which landed me the Elektric Band gig for the next six years and changed my life forever."

Frank Gambale's association with Chick Corea's Elektric Band, which included five albums, made him well known, playing alongside Corea, John Patitucci, Dave Weckl and Eric Marienthal during a countless number of concerts. After that period ended, Gambale worked with Steve Smith's Vital Information for 12 years, recording seven albums. As a leader, Gambale began recording albums for the Legato label in 1986, signing with JVC in 1990, and having commercial success (particularly in Japan) with *Thunder From Down Under*. He has since recorded for several labels, including his own Wombat Records, which he formed in 1998, and he has reissued many of his earlier dates.

In addition to his tours as a leader, a reunion with the Elektric Band in 2002, and his many recordings, Gambale has been an important educator. He developed the influential sweep picking technique, outlined in his book *Speed Picking*, which he wrote while still attending school.

In 2011, Gambale was part of Return to Forever IV, an all-star quintet with Chick Corea, Stanley Clarke, Jean-Luc Ponty and Lenny White. They performed at over 100 concerts during a worldwide tour, recorded a double-CD and made a DVD. In 2012, Gambale teamed up with singer Boca in a new band, recording *Goldmine*.

For the future, Frank Gambale says, "I have a burning desire to make vocal music. I am writing a lot of songs, which will be recorded soon with my wife Boca singing. She is a huge talent."

**Recommended CDs:** All of Frank Gambale's recordings as a leader are currently available: *Brave New Guitar* (Wombat 7001), *A Present For The Future* (Wombat 7002), *Frank Gambale Live* (Wombat 7003), *Thunder From Down Under* (JVC 3321), *Note Worker* (Samson 29919), *The Great Explorers* (Samson 29918), *Passages* (Samson 29920), *Thinking*

*Out Loud* (Samson 29921), *Coming To Your Senses* (Favored Nations 2001), *Resident Alien—Live Bootlegs* (Wombat 7011), *Absolutely: Live In Poland* (Wombat 7013), *Raison D'Être* (Wombat 7014), *Natural High* (Wombat 7015), *Natural Selection* (Wombat 8219), *Goldmine* (Wombat 8220); with Chick Corea's Elektric Band: *Lightyears* (GRP 9546), *Eye Of The Beholder* (GRP 9564), *Inside Out* (GRP 9601), *Beneath The Mask* (GRP 9649), *To The Stars* (Stretch 9043); with Vital Information: *Come On In* (Tone Center 4034); with Steve Smith: *Show Me What You Can Do* (Tone Center 40012), *The Light Beyond* (Tone Center 40102); with Return to Forever IV: the two-CD, one-DVD set *The Mothership Returns* (Eagle 202572).

**Website:** www.frankgambale.com

## Oliver Gannon
*b. March 23, 1943, Dublin, Ireland*

A cool-toned player who swings hard but quietly, Oliver Gannon has been one of Canada's top jazz guitarists for decades. Gannon did not start playing guitar until he was 18, four years after his family moved to Winnipeg. "Knowing nothing about jazz or guitar players, I asked a musician for a listening suggestion. Based on his answer, I luckily ended up with a copy of Barney Kessel's *The Poll Winners*, a record that I love and recommend to this day. I never knew that a guitar could sound like that, and I soon wore out the grooves of the first side of the record."

His first gigs were playing in Winnipeg with a quartet led by his father pianist Joe Gannon. "I had been playing three gigs a week and studying engineering at the same time. One morning, the blackboard was filled with 'The Second Law of Thermodynamics.' In one of the great moments of my life, I asked myself, 'Do I want to spend my life doing this stuff or would I rather have fun playing gigs?' I left engineering that morning and decided to go to Berklee." He earned his degree in 1969.

After Berklee, Gannon worked with a big band at the Cave in Vancouver. A month with Buddy Rich was followed by an association with Ian McDougall's sextet, which continues to this day, and plenty of studio work. "My longest musical association was with tenor-saxophonist Fraser MacPherson. I joined his trio in 1976, we did a lot of traveling, and we

made about 12 records over the next 15 years." Highlights included three tours of the Soviet Union (1978, '82 and '84).

Since that time, Oliver Gannon has handled much of the musical production for his brother Peter Gannon's company, PG Music, including their "Band-in-a-Box" musical accompaniment program. He also leads his own quartet in Vancouver.

**Recommended CDs:** As a leader, Oliver Gannon is heard in top form on three CDs released by Cellar Live: *Live At The Cellar*, *That's What* and *Too Much Guitar* (which he co-leads with guitarist Bill Coon).

**Website:** www.olivergannon.com

## Paulinho Garcia
*(Paulo Garcia)*
*b. August 16, 1948, Belo Horizonte, Brazil*

A talented performer from Brazil, Paulinho Garcia plays and sings a repertoire that ranges from jazz to folk music. Garcia first heard jazz through Chet Baker's records. He sang on a kids' radio program when he was nine. After a stint on drums, Garcia was a professional bassist in Brazil. Although he started playing guitar when he was 16, Garcia did not perform in public on guitar until 1979 when he moved to Chicago. By then, he had earned a degree in physics, led the band Os Agitadores, worked as a studio musician, and recorded two albums in Brazil.

"When I came to the USA, people found out that I could play guitar and sing, and that was the end of my bass years and the beginning of a new me. I listened to many guitarists but was never really influenced by anyone. I think that is because I used my guitar to learn my own songs for singing and ended up creating my own style."

Garcia recorded two albums with his group Made in Brazil. In the 1990s, he led and toured all over the world with Jazzmineiro. In 2001, he started teaming up with tenor-saxophonist Greg Fishman as Two for Brazil, a duo that recalls João Gilberto and Stan Getz, if Gilberto and Getz had worked as a duo. When they added Polish singer Grazyna Auguscik to the group during 2001–02, it was renamed Three for Brazil. Paulinho Garcia's music is always a delight.

**Recommended CDs:** *Jazzmineiro* (Southport 26), *Solo* (Southport 49), *Two For Brazil Plays The Standards* (Jazzmin), *Two For Brazil Plays Two For Noel* (Jazzmin), *Three For Brazil's Homage* (Pony 1609), *Two For Brazil's Take Five* (Jazzmin 3375), and *Two For Brazil Goes To The Movies* (Jazzmin).

**Website:** www.paulinhogarcia.com and www.twoforbrazil.com

# Hank Garland
*(Walter Garland)*
*b. November 11, 1930, Cowpens, SC; d. December 27, 2004, Orange Park, FL*

Hank Garland was a greatly in-demand country guitarist in the 1950s who was just starting to make a strong impression in the jazz world when a tragic car accident ended his career when he was just 30. Born and raised in South Carolina, he was originally inspired by the playing of Maybelle Carter (of the Carter family) on the record "Wildwood Flower." Garland began playing guitar at six, and at 15, was performing country music in Shorty Painter's band. At 16, he made his recording debut with the Arkansas Cotton Pickers before spending two years playing with Cowboy Copas. In 1949, Garland recorded an instrumental, "Sugarfoot Rag," and later in the year made a second recording of the song, this time with lyrics and under Red Foley's name; the latter version became a major hit.

While Garland worked almost exclusively in the studios of Nashville and in the country music world for much of the 1950s (including touring with Eddy Arnold), he listened regularly to Django Reinhardt's recordings and took lessons from Barry Galbraith. Along the way, he appeared on records by the Everly Brothers, Don Gibson, Patti Page, Jim Reeves, Webb Pierce, Patsy Cline, Brenda Lee, Charlie Rich, Jerry Lee Lewis and Elvis Presley, but whenever he had a chance, he worked nights at local jazz clubs.

In 1960, Hank Garland recorded *Jazz Winds From A New Direction*, a jazz album with the young vibraphonist Gary Burton (who was making his recording debut), bassist Joe Benjamin and drummer Joe Morello. A slightly earlier set (*Subtle Swing*, which was later reissued as *The Unforgettable Guitar Of Hank Garland*) and the slightly later *Velvet Guitar* feature Garland turning often-unlikely material into jazz. It seemed clear that his musical future would be in jazz.

On September 8, 1961, tragedy struck. After an argument with his wife, Garland was speeding and crashed his station wagon. He spent weeks in a coma, and although he partly recovered, the brain damage he suffered made it impossible for him to play guitar for quite some time. He never regained his fluency and lost his prominence. Ironically, two years later, his wife died in a car accident. Hank Garland was never a professional guitarist again, although in 1975, he made a rare appearance at a show, managing to play "Sugarfoot Rag" one last time.

**Recommended CDs:** *Move! The Guitar Artistry Of Hank Garland* (Sundazed 178) is a two-CD set that collects together Garland's three jazz-oriented albums: *Velvet Guitar*, *The Unforgettable Guitar Of Hank Garland* and the legendary *Jazz Winds From A New Direction*. *Hank Garland And His Sugar Footers* (Bear Family 15551) is a single CD that has 20 of Garland's solo recordings from the late 1940s/early '50s. While his vocals on the latter are just so-so, his guitar playing was already top-notch. Both versions of "Sugarfoot Rag" are included.

# Arv Garrison
*(Arvin Garrison)*
*b. August 17, 1922, Toledo, OH; d. July 30, 1960, Toledo, OH*

Arv Garrison is chiefly remembered today for briefly being in the right place at the right time, in Los Angeles in 1946, where he recorded with Charlie Parker. Influenced by Django Reinhardt, Charlie Christian and to a lesser extent Les Paul, Arv Garrison spent much of his life and career in Toledo, Ohio. He began on the ukulele when he was nine and was playing guitar professionally within three years. In 1941, when he was 18, he was leading his own group in Albany, New York. He worked with a variety of groups, led a trio and married bassist Vivien Garry. They performed as the Vivien Garry Trio for years, although unfortunately they only had one confirmed record date (as a quartet), in 1945.

In 1946, Arv Garrison was in Los Angeles, recording with Dizzy Gillespie and Charlie Parker on "Diggin' Diz" and on Parker's session of March 28 that resulted in "Yardbird Suite," "Ornithology" and "Night In Tunisia." He had the unique opportunity to play alongside Parker, Miles Davis, Dodo Marmarosa, Lucky Thompson, and Roy Porter. Also that year, Garrison recorded "Five Guitars In Flight" with Earle Spencer's orchestra as part of a "guitar choir" also including Barney Kessel, Irving Ashby, Tony Rizzi, Gene Sargent and Spencer's usual rhythm guitarist Walt Ellefson.

But otherwise, Garrison was in the wrong place throughout his career, playing in obscurity in the Midwest with his wife, respected locally but out of the spotlight. He died in 1960 when he suffered an epileptic seizure while swimming.

**Recommended CDs:** Arv Garrison's recordings with Charlie Parker can be found on Parker's *Vol. 2 1945–1946* (Blue Moon 1008).

**LPs to Search For:** The Vivien Garry date was last available on an Onyx LP, *Central Avenue Breakdown Vol. 1* (Onyx 202).

## Danny Gatton

b. September 4, 1945, Washington, DC; d. October 4, 1994, Newburg, MD

A virtuoso guitarist who could play nearly any style of music, Danny Gatton was concentrating more on jazz during the last few years before his early death. Gatton, whose father had been a rhythm guitarist, began playing guitar when he was nine. Les Paul and Charlie Christian were early influences. He was in his first band, the Lancers, by the time he was 12. He played jazz with the Offbeats during 1960–64 and spent time in Nashville, where he worked briefly as a session musician. After a period of working day jobs and playing at bars at night, in the 1970s he gained some attention for his work with Liz Meyer & Friends and with other groups in the Washington, DC area. Gatton recorded *American Music* in 1975 and the intriguing *Redneck Jazz* in 1978, performing jazz on the latter with a band that included steel guitarist Buddy Emmons. He later led a group called the Redneck Jazz Explosion.

However, Gatton's reputation was made in country music (he toured with Roger Miller) and rockabilly, where he was considered one of the top guitarists. He was nicknamed "the Telemaster" and was sometimes dubbed the world's greatest unknown guitarist. His recordings ranged from rockabilly to rock, bluegrass to blues, and he always seemed on the verge of making it big, although that never happened. In 1992, Gatton switched gears, recording a straight-ahead set (*New York Stories*) for Blue Note. Some setbacks resulted in him returning to session work, but in 1994, he worked with organist Joey DeFrancesco on *Relentless*. Due to mostly unknown personal problems, later that year Danny Gatton committed suicide, leaving behind no explanation. He was just 49.

**Recommended CDs:** Danny Gatton's recordings are generally quite eclectic and most have at least a few examples of swinging jazz. *Hot Rod Guitar: The Danny Gatton Anthology* (Rhino 75691); *American Music* (NRG 3422); *Redneck Jazz* (NRG 2916); *Redneck Jazz Explosion* (Ichiban 4223); *Unfinished Business* (NRG 2479); *88 Elmira Street* (Elektra 61032); *Portraits* (Big Mo 2030); *Untouchable* (NRG 1242); *New York Stories* (Blue Note 98959), which teams Gatton with Bobby Watson, Roy

Hargrove and Joshua Redman; *Relentless* (Big Mo 2023) with Joey DeFrancesco; and *In Concert* (Big Mo 2028) are the most jazz-oriented, and all display his brilliant guitar playing.

## Grant Geissman

b. April 13, 1953, Berkeley, CA

Grant Geissman's career has evolved through several phases, from being a pop/crossover jazz artist to one now mostly playing straight-ahead jazz. Geissman grew up in San Jose, California. As a teenager, he played in rock groups (becoming a big fan of the Beatles) but also occasional jazz bands. He studied with Jerry Hahn when he was a high school senior. Geissman attended De Anza Junior College and played in its jazz band. In 1973, he moved to Southern California, where he went to Cal State Fullerton for a semester before transferring to Cal State Northridge. While at Northridge, the young guitarist became part of the studio scene and worked with both the Gerald Wilson Orchestra and the Louie Bellson Big Band, recording several times with the latter. He also played with Tony Rizzo's Five Guitars Play Charlie Christian.

Geissman became a member of Chuck Mangione's group in November 1976, staying for over four years. It is his guitar that is prominently heard on Mangione's big hit "Feels So Good." In 1978, Geissman recorded his first album as a leader, the boppish *Good Stuff* for Concord. In 1981, he left Mangione to work more as a studio musician and as a leader. His solo career found him playing and recording pop/jazz in addition to sessions with smooth performers (Keiko Matsui and David Benoit), with singers (Cheryl Bentyne, Lorraine Feather and Diane Schuur) and in pop settings (Quincy Jones, Ringo Starr). He also had occasional reunions with Mangione and has been very active writing and playing for television.

It was in 2006 that Geissman finally returned to jazz, recording *Say That*. He has since led a quintet, performed with big bands (including Gordon Goodwin's Big Phat Band), and continued to show that he is a fine jazz improviser.

Apart from his music, Grant Geissman is considered an expert on *Mad Magazine* and EC Comics, having written three books and contributed to many others about *Mad* and comics in general.

**Recommended CDs:** In his career, Grant Geissman has recorded many light and pleasant enough pop/jazz sets, including *Snapshots* (TBA 224), *All My Tomorrows* (TBA 241), *Take Another Look* (Mesa/Bluemoon 79152), *Flying Colors* (Blue Moon 79165), *Reruns* (Blue Moon 79172), *Time Will Tell* (Mesa/Bluemoon 79178), *Rustic Technology* (Mesa/Bluemoon 79189), *Business As Usual* (Positive 77783) and *In With The Out Crowd* (Higher Octave 46228). However, his best jazz recordings are his most recent ones: *Say That* (Futurism 1953), *Cool Man Cool* (Futurism 2054) and *Bop! Bang! Boom!* (Futurism 2055).

**LPs to Search For:** Geissman's debut, *Good Stuff* (Concord 62), has not yet been reissued, nor have his crossover sets *Drinkin' From The Money River* (TBA 217) and *Put Away Childish Things* (Pausa 7150).

**Website:** www.grantgeissman.com

## Egberto Gismonti
*b. December 5, 1947, Carmo, Rio De Janeiro, Brazil*

Best known to the American and European public through his ECM recordings, Egberto Gismonti is a notable Brazilian guitarist and pianist. Gismonti's grandfather and uncle were bandleaders. He started on the piano at five (beginning 15 years of classical training), added the flute and clarinet, and became masterful on the acoustic guitar as a teenager. He sought to transfer his piano playing to the guitar and in time utilized three custom-made instruments, with 10, 12 and 14 strings on his guitars. Gismonti attended the Nova Friburgo Music Conservatory. He turned down a scholarship to study classical music in Vienna, instead deciding to work in popular music.

In 1968, Gismonti wrote a composition, "O Sonho," that was presented at an International Song Festival and ended up being recorded by 18 different artists. He spent part of 1968–70 in France as the orchestrator and conductor for French singer Marie Laforêt. Back in Brazil, Gismonti (who recorded his first album in 1969) settled near Rio. He wrote soundtracks, played locally, and recorded regularly, including for EMI/Odeon. In 1974, Gismonti met Manfred Eicher, the founder of ECM. His first ECM set, cut in 1977, was a set of duets with percussionist-singer Naná Vasconcelos, *Danças Das Cabeças*. The music, which could be considered Brazilian folk music, put Gismonti on the international map. Other albums followed. In 1981, he toured and recorded with Magico, a trio with Jan Garbarek and Charlie Haden.

Gismonti, whose melodic and sometimes haunting music is equally influenced by his Brazilian heritage and his love for classical music (including Ravel), often emphasizes space, which fits in well on ECM. Yet surprisingly, he considers both Django Reinhardt and Jimi Hendrix to have been early influences on his guitar style.

**Recommended CDs:** Egberto Gismonti's ECM recordings (mostly from 1976–85) are the most readily available of his CDs. *Dança Das Cabeças* (ECM 1089) is a duet set with Naná Vasconcelos, *Sol Do Meio Dia* (ECM 1116) also includes Jan Garbarek, Collin Walcott and Ralph Towner, and *Solo* (ECM 1136) features him on eight-string guitar plus piano and bells. *Magico* (ECM 1151) and *Folksongs* (ECM 1170) showcase Gismonti's trio with Charlie Haden and Garbarek. Other rewarding Gismonti recordings include *Sanfona* (ECM 829391), *Duas Vozes* (ECM 1279), *Dança Dos Escravos* (ECM 1387), *Música De Sobrevivência* (ECM 1509), *Zig Zag* (ECM 529349), *Meeting Point* (ECM 533681), *Estreia* (Universal 314 521 980), *Antologia* (EMI 592357), *Retratos* (EMI 325866551), and *Saudações* (ECM 2082/83).

## Mick Goodrick
*(Michael Goodrick)*
*b. June 9, 1945, Sharon, PA*

A superior post-bop guitarist, Mick Goodrick always made a strong impression, although ultimately much of his career has been as an educator. Inspired by Elvis Presley, he took up the guitar when he was 11. A few years later, the album *Sonny Rollins And The Contemporary Leaders* (which features Barney Kessel) led him toward jazz. Goodrick began playing professionally at 15, performing with an organ trio at a restaurant. He attended a Stan Kenton Band Camp when he was 16, studied at Berklee during 1963–67, and remembers the importance of a trio gig with pianist Alan Broadbent and bassist Rick Laird. "We played five 40-minute sets a night, six nights a week, for nine months in 1969."

Goodrick was already teaching at Berklee when he joined Gary Burton's band in 1972, spending four years touring and recording with the vibraphonist. After 1976, he went back to being an educator in the New England area. His guitar was heard with a few versions of Charlie Haden's Liberation Music Orchestra (1982–96), in a prominent role with Jack DeJohnette's Special Edition (1987–90), and with Steve Swallow's quintet (1996–99). There were other highlights, including a duo concert with Pat Metheny at the 2005 Montreal Jazz Festival and a duo engagement with Wolfgang Muthspiel at New York's Jazz Standard in 2008.

Still, Mick Goodrick's most significant contributions to jazz will probably be his work as an influential teacher at Berklee and author of guitar books.

**Recommended CDs:** With his openness toward free playing and sound textures, Mick Goodrick would seem to have been a natural candidate for leading albums for ECM, but surprisingly, there has only been one. 1978's *In Pas(s)ing* (ECM 847327) is a fine effort with John Surman, Eddie Gomez and Jack DeJohnette. *Biorhythms* (CMP 46) from 1990 has Goodrick playing what can be called sparse funk in a chance-taking trio with Harvie S. and drummer Gary Chaffee. *Rare Birds* (Ram 4505) is a unique set for Goodrick, playing tunes (including some standards) with fellow guitarist Joe Diorio. *Sunscreams* (Ram 4507) is an originals project that co-stars tenor-saxophonist Jerry Bergonzi, while 1995's *In The Same Breath* (CMP 71) has Goodrick interacting with David Liebman and Wolfgang Muthspiel. Mick Goodrick is long overdue to record as a leader again.

## Jimmy Gourley
b. June 9, 1926, St. Louis, MO; d. December 7, 2008, Villeneuve-Saint-Georges, France

Many jazz experts, when asked to name Jimmy Gourley's nationality, would say French. Gourley lived in France so long that it has often been forgotten that he was an American expatriate. Gourley's father founded the Monarch Conservatory of Music in Hammond, Indiana. Gourley began playing guitar as a youth, and one of his high school friends was Lee Konitz. He worked with a few dance bands in the South before spending 1944–46 in the Navy. After his discharge, one of his first jobs was playing with Jay Burkhart's group in Chicago, succeeding Jimmy Raney, who was one of his early influences. He also worked with Anita O'Day, Jackie & Roy, Sonny Stitt and Gene Ammons.

In 1951, Gourley moved to France, settling in Paris, where he worked steadily as part of the French jazz community during the next half-century, except for a period during 1956–57 when he was back in the US. In addition to playing with Henri Renaud, Bobby Jaspar, Martial Solal, Barney Wilen, Richard Galliano, Stéphane Grappelli, Lou Bennett, Kenny Clarke, and Eddy Louiss, and working in the house bands of several clubs (including the Blue Note), he had opportunities to record with many visiting Americans. Those included Clifford Brown, Gigi Gryce, Lester Young, Zoot Sims, Lee Konitz, Bob Brookmeyer, Roy Haynes, Bud Powell, Stan Getz and Lucky Thompson.

Gourley, the father of guitarist-singer Sean Gourley,

visited the United States only on rare occasions, and it was not until 1986 that he had an opportunity to record in the US. Although largely forgotten in his native land, Jimmy Gourley was considered legendary in France, where his hard-bop guitar solos always swung and never disappointed.

**Recommended CDs:** Jimmy Gourley led his first full album in 1972 and, although hard to find, most of his sessions have been reissued by the Elabeth label. Those include *And The Paris Heavyweights* (Elabeth 621030), which has Gourley with René Urtreger, Eddy Louiss and Kenny Clarke; *The Jazz Trio* (Elabeth 621018); *Our Delight* (Elabeth 621021); *Repetition* (Elabeth 621026); and *Double Action* (Elabeth 621032), which features Barney Wilen on tenor. *Graffiti* (Promophone 14) is a 1970s set with pianist Henri Texler, while *No More* (Musica 3034) teams Gourley with Stan Getz (who used the pseudonym of Dju Berry) in 1981. *The Left Bank Of New York* (Uptown 2732), Gourley's only American album, is his most widely available set and has trio and quintet performances from 1986. Of Jimmy Grouley's many sideman recordings, *Clifford Brown Sextet In Paris* (Original Jazz Classics 358), *Lee Konitz/Bob Brookmeyer In Paris* (Vogue 68359), Stéphane Grappelli's *Satin Doll* (Vanguard 8182), and Eddy Louiss' *Jazz In Paris: Bohemia After Dark* (Verve 13140) are all quite rewarding.

## Freddie Green
b. March 31, 1911, Charleston, SC; d. March 1, 1987, Las Vegas, NV

Freddie Green was a very reliable rhythm guitarist who stuck to the acoustic guitar throughout his career and did not take any solos after 1939. He was considered the heartbeat of the Count Basie Orchestra, where his playing was often felt more than heard. He also wrote one jazz standard, "Corner Pocket," which, as a vocalese number, became known as "Until I Met You."

Green started out playing banjo when he was 12, switching to guitar by the late 1920s. He worked in South Carolina with a group called the Nighthawks, toured with the Jenkins Orphanage Band, and left the latter group when they reached New York. Green spent the early years of the Depression working as an upholsterer while playing dance band gigs at night.

In late 1936, Green was discovered by producer

John Hammond, who thought that his unselfish rhythmic playing would be a better fit for the up-and-coming Count Basie Orchestra than its guitarist-violinist Claude Williams. On January 25, 1937, Green made his recording debut on a Teddy Wilson date that featured Billie Holiday, Benny Goodman and such Basie sidemen as Lester Young, Buck Clayton, bassist Walter Page and drummer Jo Jones. By March, Green was a member of the Basie big band, and he never really left. While he took brief and rare solos on "On The Sentimental Side" with Billie Holiday and "Dinah" during a freelance session with clarinetist Pee Wee Russell in 1938, there were very few other exceptions in his entire career. Green was happy to be part of the "Million Dollar Rhythm Section" with Basie, Page and Jones, swinging the Basie band in a light but firm manner.

When Basie broke up his big band in late 1949, Freddie Green was temporarily out of a job. For a few months, Basie led a small group without Green, but one night, the guitarist simply set up his instrument on stage and joined the band without being asked; Basie was happy to have him back. Freddie Green was not only an integral part of the new Count Basie big band in 1952, but he was still there when Basie passed away in 1984, remaining with the orchestra (under the leadership of Thad Jones and Frank Foster) until his own death in March 1987, 50 years after he originally joined Basie. There was no better big band rhythm guitarist.

**Recommended CDs:** Nearly every Count Basie CD (other than a few jam sessions) has Freddie Green playing quietly in the background. He led an album in 1955 (*Mr. Rhythm*) that was reissued along with an Al Cohn record that included Green as *Natural Rhythm* (Bluebird 6465). Typically, Green does not take a single solo, not even on a song called "Freddie's Time." He also co-led an album with Herb Ellis in 1975, *Rhythm Willie* (Concord 4010); all of the guitar solos are by Ellis.

## Grant Green

b. June 6, 1931, St. Louis, MO; d. January 31, 1979, New York, NY

One of the top guitarists to emerge during the 1960s, Grant Green was on the level of Wes Montgomery and George Benson, although both overshadowed him. He learned the guitar as a child from his father, who also played guitar. Green was a professional when he was 13, playing with a gospel group, but it would take him a bit of time before he emerged in the jazz world. He worked locally with both jazz and R&B groups for a decade. It was not until 1959, when he was already 28, that Green first recorded, making an album with Jimmy Forrest in St. Louis. When he was discovered by Lou Donaldson and toured with him, he moved to New York and was signed by Blue Note.

By then, Green had developed his own style, influenced by both Charlie Christian and Charlie Parker. He rarely ever played chords or accompanied others, sticking almost exclusively to single-note lines just like a saxophonist, and could be considered more of a horn player than a member of the rhythm section. Alfred Lion of Blue Note recognized Green's talent and versatility, and used him as Blue Note's house guitarist during 1961–65. Green recorded with organ groups, as the leader of a quartet with pianist Sonny Clark, and as a sideman in settings ranging from bebop to Latin jazz (including the classic *The Latin Bit*), spirituals to soul jazz and post-bop. Whether teamed with McCoy Tyner or Baby Face Willette, Stanley Turrentine or Joe Henderson, he uplifted every session.

Green's golden period ended by early 1966 when he left Blue Note. He was a heroin addict and took time off during the next couple of years to reassess his life and career. When he emerged in 1969 (returning to Blue Note, which was now a very different label), his tone was familiar, but he primarily played funky solos on an R&B repertoire. Perhaps he felt that it was necessary in order to be noticed, but he largely stuck to that course during his final decade, playing quite well at times, although much of the material was clearly beneath him. To his disappointment, he did not become a major commercial success.

Grant Green was hospitalized in 1978 and passed away the following year. While there is divided opinion on the merits of his work from the 1970s, his recordings from the first half of the 1960s make him one of the immortals.

**Recommended CDs:** *First Session* (Blue Note 275482), *Grant's First Stand* (Blue Note 21959), *Green Street* (Blue Note 6492), *Grantstand* (Blue Note 5917232), *Standards* (Blue Note 21284), the two-CD set *The Complete Quartets With Sonny Clark* (Blue Note 57194), *Sunday Morning* (Blue Note 6517), *Born To Be Blue* (Blue Note 84432), *The Latin Beat* (Blue Note 6489), *Goin' West* (Blue Note 90843), *Feelin' The Spirit* (Blue Note 4132), *Am I Blue* (Blue Note 4139), *The Matador* (Blue Note 4971882), *Blues For Lou* (Blue Note 21438), *Solid* (Blue Note 33580), *Talkin' About* (Blue Note 4183), *Street Of Dreams* (Blue Note 9579), *Idle Moments* (Blue Note 4154), and *I Want To Hold Your Hand* (Blue Note 4202) are from the prime Blue Note period of Grant Green. The two transitional albums, *His Majesty King Funk* (Verve 9197) and 1967's *Iron City* (32 Jazz 32048), which was Green's only album as a leader during 1966–68, are also worthwhile. The merits of Green's later work, which includes *Carryin' On* (Blue Note 31247), *Green Is Beautiful* (Blue Note 28265), *Alive* (Blue Note 89793), *Shades Of Green* (Blue Note 4413), *Live At Club Mozambique* (Blue Note 63522), *Visions* (Blue Note 84373), *The Final Comedown* (Blue Note 9522), *Live At The Lighthouse* (Blue Note 4933812) and *The Main Attraction* (Epic/Legacy 86145), are more debatable. But if one comes to that music with lower expectations and a healthy love of funky jazz, there are enjoyable moments. Green is also well featured as a sideman with Jimmy Forrest (*All The Gin Is Gone*—Delmark 404) and during his classic Blue Note period with Herbie Hancock, Hank Mobley, Jack McDuff, Lou Donaldson, Baby Face Willette, Stanley Turrentine, Horace Parlan, Ike Quebec, Don Wilkerson, Jimmy Smith, Dodo Greene, Harold Vick, Bobby Hutcherson, Lee Morgan, Larry Young, Donald Byrd, and Booker Ervin.

## Sonny Greenwich
### (Herbert Lawrence "Sonny" Greenidge)
b. January 1, 1936, Hamilton, Ontario, Canada

One of Canada's top jazz guitarists, Sonny Greenwich is sometimes classified as an avant-garde player. In reality, he is simply an adventurous improviser who can fit comfortably into many genres. His father and uncle were both guitarists and tap dancers, and his father also played piano. "I started playing guitar when my father brought one home from Germany after the war. I was introduced to Ellington, Basie, Roy Eldridge, Bud Powell, Art Tatum, Charlie Parker and others at a young age. I am completely self-taught and apparently even have an original way of using the guitar pick, using mostly upstrokes. I also do not use the little finger in my solo playing and so get a thicker sound from the higher notes using the fourth finger."

Due to a printing mistake, he took the name Greenwich early in his career. "One day, a passing car full of musicians drove by and noticed me sitting on my front porch playing Charlie Parker licks. They backed up and asked if I could do a dance gig with them, and that is where it started." Greenwich had his first gigs playing R&B for dances in a band in which everyone was actually a jazz player. After more engagements playing at R&B clubs in Toronto, he was picked by Al Haig to work with him at a Toronto jazz club. After Haig left town, Greenwich

played with other jazz musicians, soon forming his own band. Among the visiting Americans who came by to hear him were Lee Morgan, Horace Silver, Wayne Shorter and Charles Lloyd.

In 1965, Greenwich played at the Village Vanguard with Charles Lloyd. He was a member of the John Handy Quintet from December 1966 to March 1967, appearing at Carnegie Hall at John Hammond's From Spirituals to Swing concert. During this period, he recorded with Hank Mobley (*Third Season*). All set to record as a leader for the Milestone label, Greenwich had difficulties with his green card and had to return to Canada.

While Greenwich mostly played in Toronto, moving to Montreal in 1974, he had occasional visits to the US. In 1968 he led a quartet at the Village Vanguard that included pianist Teddy Saunders, Jimmy Garrison and Jack DeJohnette. When the Miles Davis Quintet (with Wayne Shorter, Chick Corea, Dave Holland and Tony Williams) played in Toronto in December 1969, Greenwich temporarily made the group a sextet. That year, he had his recording debut as a leader on *The Old Man And The Child* (CBC). After Wayne Shorter went out on his own in 1971, Greenwich was briefly a member of his short-lived group, the New York Art Quartet (with Ron Carter and Joe Chambers).

Otherwise, Greenwich has primarily led his own bands up to the present time. He has become more involved in composition, leading medium-sized ensembles for special projects, and working with Kenny Wheeler, Jane Bunnett and pianist Marilyn Lerner. In the mid-1990s, he recorded a collaboration with his son guitarist Sonny Greenwich Jr. (who plays with the funk-rock group Bootsauce).

Sonny Greenwich has long said that he is more influenced by saxophonists (particularly Sonny Rollins and John Coltrane) and pianists (Bill Evans) than by other guitarists. "I have always tried to get a saxophone kind of sound from my linear playing and a piano type sound from my chordal approach. I play a wide range, from ballads to very fiery, very free pieces. It's like having the storm and the calm that comes after; the one thing helps the other express itself."

**Recommended CDs:** Sonny Greenwich has recorded often, mostly for Canadian labels. Among his many rewarding recordings are 1970's *The Old Man And The Child* (Sackville 2003); *Sun Song* (CBC 39); *Days Gone By* (Sackville 2052) with Ed Bickert; *Evol-ution* (PM 016); *Bird Of Paradise* (Justin Time 22); *Live At Sweet Basil* (Justin Time 26); *Standard Idioms* (Kleo 1), which features his nonet in 1993; *Outside In* (Justin Time 69) in a duo with Paul Bley; *Hymn To The Earth* (Kleo 2); *Welcome: Mother Earth* (Justin Time 80); *Spirit In The Air* (Kleo 3); *Kenny And Sonny Live At The Montreal Bistro*

(Justin Time 114) with Kenny Wheeler; *Fragments Of A Memory* (Cornerstone 116); *Special Angel* (CBC 3006) with Marilyn Lerner; *Essence* (Kleo 6); and *Portraits* (Kleo 7).

**Website:** www.kleo-records.com

## Tiny Grimes
### (Lloyd Grimes)
b. July 7, 1916, Newport News, VA; d. March 4, 1989, New York, NY

After the passing of Charlie Christian, Tiny Grimes was one of the first electric guitarists to emerge who sounded a bit like Christian, partly filling the gap, although he did not evolve all that much after his fast start. Grimes began his musical career as a drummer and pianist, playing gigs in Washington, DC and New York. In 1938, he switched to the four-string electric tenor guitar, an instrument that he played throughout his career. Grimes was a member of the Cats and a Fiddle during 1939–41 and then gained some fame for his work with the Art Tatum Trio of 1943–44. Although there was no way that the guitarist could compete with the remarkable pianist, he added fire and a bit of recklessness to the trio, giving Tatum an opportunity to interact with a very brave sideman.

Tiny Grimes' most famous recording date was in 1944, when he headed a quintet that featured the young Charlie Parker. Grimes took vocals on two numbers, including "Romance Without Finance (Is A Nuisance)," but it was Parker's playing on "Red Cross" and "Tiny's Tempo" that gained the most attention. After playing in small swing combos and recording with Buck Clayton, Ike Quebec, Cozy Cole, Don Byas, and Leonard Feather, in 1947 Grimes organized an R&B-oriented band called Tiny "Mac" Grimes and His Rocking Highlanders. The group, which lasted six years and sometimes dressed in kilts, featured the passionate tenor of Red Prysock (Benny Golson and John Hardee also had stints with the band) and at times vocals from Screamin' Jay Hawkins.

Grimes' swing style was unchanged during that period and in the years that followed. He led a trio of swinging records during 1958–59, made it through the 1960s, worked with Earl Hines in 1972, and visited Europe on a regular basis in the 1970s. Along the way, he recorded with Coleman Hawkins, Illinois Jacquet, Roy Eldridge, Johnny Hodges, Ray Nance, Arnett Cobb and Billie Holiday. Tiny Grimes stayed active until near the end.

**Recommended CDs:** The second half of Art Tatum's *1940–44* (Classics 800) and the first half of *1944* (Classics 825) have the classic Tatum trio recordings with Grimes and bassist Slam Stewart; most of the other performances are dazzling piano solos. Tiny Grimes' *1944–1949* (Classics 5048) features the guitarist's session with Charlie Parker, his 1946 date for Blue Note, and the first recordings of his Rocking Highlanders. *1949–1951* (Classics 5106) and *1951–1954* (Classics 5146) complete the reissuance of the Highlander recordings. Jumping around chronologically, *Tiny Grimes And His Rocking Highlanders Volume 1* (Collectables 5304) and *Volume 2* (Collectables 5317) have a strong sampling of the work of this colorful group, although all of *Volume 1* is covered in the Classics series. *Volume 2* is of particular interest because 10 of its 14 performances were previously unissued. *Blues Groove* (Original Jazz Classics 817), which has sometimes been reissued under Coleman Hawkins' name (the tenor takes a long and stirring solo on "Marchin' Along"), is a blues and standards date. Grimes is teamed with trombonist J.C. Higginbotham and tenor-saxophonist Eddie "Lockjaw" Davis on *Callin' The Blues* (Original Jazz Classics 191). While those two sets have their stirring and riotous moments, *Tiny In Swingville* (Original Jazz Classics 1796) is Grimes' best showcase from the 1958–59 period, with performances of "Annie Laurie," "Frankie And Johnnie," "Ain't Misbehavin'" and three originals with a quintet also featuring Jerome Richardson on reeds and pianist Ray Bryant. Later in life, Grimes led several excellent albums for the French Black & Blue label, including *Some Groovy Fours* (Black and Blue 874), which features the guitarist still in prime form in 1974.

**LPs to Search For:** *Profoundly Blue* (Muse 5012) from 1973 is a particularly strong Tiny Grimes release, with definitive versions of "Tiny's Exercise" and "Profoundly Blue." Tenor-saxophonist Houston Person co-stars. Very obscure is a 1962 album with organ called *Big Time Guitar* (United Artists 6232). Most of Grimes' later work, including *Chasin' With Milt* (Black & Blue 33017) and *Food For Thought* (Black & Blue 33030), deserves to be reissued.

## Marty Grosz
b. February 28, 1930, Berlin, Germany

A singer inspired by Fats Waller and a sharp and sometimes hilarious wit, Marty Grosz is also a superior chordal acoustic guitarist who is influenced by Carl Kress, Dick McDonough and Bernard Addison. He keeps the

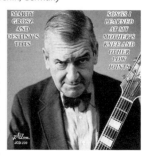

mid-1930s guitar tradition alive and is one of the very few jazz guitarists around who plays without an amp.

The son of artist George Grosz, he was born in Germany but lived in New York by the time he was three. Grosz began playing ukulele when he was eight, taking up the acoustic guitar at 13. Even by then (1943), the electric guitar was becoming dominant, but Grosz was never worried about following trends.

He went to Columbia University for a year, spent time in the military after being drafted, and went to the University of Chicago for six months. He soon dropped out to play jazz. After a few years in New York (including making his recording debut in 1950), Grosz settled in Chicago in 1954. During his 20 years in the Midwest, he played guitar and banjo in a large assortment of Dixieland, swing and trad bands, performing with Art Hodes, Albert Nicholas, clarinetist Frank Chace and many others. He also took occasional good-humored vocals. Despite all of this activity, he was mostly in obscurity until he joined Soprano Summit in 1975 and moved back to New York.

Grosz was with Soprano Summit (1975–79), Dick Wellstood's Friends of Jazz, the New York Jazz Repertory Orchestra, and the Classic Jazz Quartet. But he has mostly headed a series of hot and freewheeling combos that perform superior swing obscurities and some Dixieland standards with heated yet clean ensembles, superior melodic solos, and plenty of rhythm and joy. Among the names of his groups have been the Orphan Newsboys, Destiny's Tots, Paswonky Serenaders, the Sugar Daddies, the Imps, and the Hot Puppies. Marty Grosz has been a regular at classic jazz parties and festivals for quite a few years and should be regarded as a national treasure. While only a few of his monologues have thus far been captured on record (his live shows should be filmed), Marty Grosz's humor is as timeless (and as rare) as his guitar playing and vocals.

"I want to continue exploring the guitar and trying out some of the forgotten songs that I like. The stuff they produce at Juilliard, the Berklee School, etc., bores me. Jazzmen used to be part of the underground, anti-establishment. Now they're on their way to becoming teachers, jingle writers and movie score technicians. There's a world of difference between what the academics produce and the sort of music that my heroes laid down."

**Recommended CDs:** Although Marty Grosz seemed to emerge in the jazz world in the 1970s, *Hooray For Bix* (Good Time Jazz 10065) from 1957 features him sounding quite recognizable, playing and occasionally singing songs with his Honoris Causa Jazz Band that were associated with Bix Beiderbecke. Grosz has recorded frequently during the past 30 years. All of his recordings are rewarding, and these include *Swing It* (Jazzology 180), *Extra* (Jazzology 190), *Unsaturated Fats* (Stomp Off 1214), *Songs Of Love And Other Matters* (Jazzology 210), *Marty Grosz And The Keepers Of The Flame* (Stomp Off 1158), *Marty Grosz And Destiny's Tots* (Jazzology 220), *Songs I Learned At My Mother's Knee And Other Low Joints* (Jazzology 220), *Keep A Song In Your Soul* (Jazzology 250), *On Revival Day* (Jazzology 260), *Rhythm For Sale* (Jazzology 280), *Thanks* (Jazzology 310), *Ring Dem Bells* (Nagel-Heyer 022), *Left To His Own Devices* (Jazzology 330), *Just For Fun* (Nagel Heyer 039), *Rhythm Is Our Business* (Sackville 2060), *Chasin' The Spots* (Jump 1228), *Marty Grosz And His Hot Combination* (Arbors 19319), *Acoustic Heat: Jazz Guitar Duets* (Sackville 2071) with Mike Peters, *Hot Winds: The Classic Sessions* (Arbors 19379) and *The James P. Johnson Songbook* (Arbors 19427). In his career, Marty Grosz has also recorded with Albert Nicholas, Soprano Summit, Dick Hyman, Dick Meldonian, Maxine Sullivan, the Classic Jazz Quartet, Randy Sandke, Ed Pocler, Peter Ecklund, Bob Greene, Tom Saunders, Rick Fay, Bobby Gordon, the New York All Stars, Connie Jones, Dick Sudhalter, Scott Robinson, Bob Schulz, Ralph Sutton, Jeff Healey and Ruby Braff, but get his highly enjoyable CDs as a leader first.

**LPs to Search For:** *I Hope Gabriel Likes My Music* (Aviva 6004) features Grosz with a quartet in 1981.

**Website:** www.martygrosz.com (a worthwhile fan site)

## Fred Guy
b. May 23, 1899, Burkesville, GA; d. November 22, 1971, Chicago, IL

Throughout his career, Duke Ellington rarely had any real purpose for guitarists in his music. While he was quoted as calling Kenny Burrell his favorite guitarist, he never recorded with him. When Django Reinhardt toured with the Ellington Orchestra in 1946, Duke wrote no special music to feature Django and just had him play with the rhythm section. A fine quartet album with Joe Pass (*Duke's Big 4*) and *Side By Side* with Johnny Hodges and Les Spann were two of his very few combo dates with a guitarist. And once Fred Guy switched from banjo to guitar, he became a nearly invisible member of the Ellington Orchestra.

Fred Guy grew up in New York and worked for a time with Joseph C. Smith's dance orchestra. In the spring of 1924, when Elmer Snowden left the Washingtonians and Ellington became their leader, Guy joined the band as a banjoist. Although he never really soloed, Guy can be heard prominently on many of Ellington's records of the late 1920s, adding a strong rhythm and drive to the ensembles.

One assumes that Guy played the same way on

guitar. But when he switched to guitar, gradually at first and then permanently by 1934, he seemed to disappear. Although he was present on virtually all of the orchestra records until he left after 24 years in January 1949, Fred Guy was mostly inaudible, possibly kept on for old time's sake. When Guy (who never switched to electric guitar) left the band, Ellington never again felt the need to add a rhythm guitarist. Fred Guy retired from playing, moved to Chicago, and managed a ballroom for over 20 years. He committed suicide in 1971.

**Recommended CDs:** Fred Guy never led his own sessions and was exclusively heard in the world of Duke Ellington. He can be heard (mostly on banjo) in the ensembles of the Ellington Orchestra on *Early Ellington* (Bluebird 6852), *Jungle Nights In Harlem* (Bluebird 2499), *Jubilee Stomp* (Bluebird 66038), *Complete Brunswick And Vocalion Recordings* (Decca/GRP 3-640), and *The Okeh Ellington* (Columbia 461770).

## Jerry Hahn
*b. September 21, 1940, Alma, NE*

Jerry Hahn made a strong impact during the second half of the 1960s with his work with John Handy and Gary Burton. Hahn, who was raised in Kansas, first played a lap steel guitar owned by his stepfather when he was seven. He became a professional guitarist when he was 11, performing daily with the Bobby Wiley Rhythmaires on television in Wichita. Hahn was involved with Western swing dance gigs as a teenager. He remembers, "I first heard jazz backstage at a Grand Ole Opry show by steel guitarist Buddy Emmons." He attended Wichita State University during part of 1959 but was too busy as a musician to stick to college.

In 1962, Hahn moved to San Francisco, joining the John Handy Quintet in 1964. Alongside Handy, violinist Michael White, bassist Don Thompson and drummer Terry Clarke, Hahn was part of Handy's famous recorded performance at the 1965 Monterey Jazz Festival. In 1967, he began a year with the Gary Burton Quartet (which also included Steve Swallow and Roy Haynes), where, as the successor to Larry Coryell, his open-minded playing helped pave the way for fusion; he is featured on *Country Roads*, *Good Vibes* and *Throb*. In 1970, he founded the Jerry Hahn Brotherhood, recording for Columbia

and performing early fusion. The following year, he played on Paul Simon's first solo album.

In 1972, his career changed. Jerry Hahn moved back to Wichita, where he became a member of the Wichita State University faculty, establishing their jazz guitar degree program. He was at WSU for 15 years before moving to Portland in 1987, where he became a member of the Bennie Wallace Quartet. In 1992, Hahn moved to Denver, where he taught at the Colorado Institute of Art for a year and toured with Ginger Baker. In 1995, he began a nine-year period on the faculty of Portland State University, returning to Wichita in 2004, where he has stayed active as both an educator and guitarist. In recent times, Hahn has often worked with his fellow student Grant Geissman.

But all of this activity as an educator has resulted in Jerry Hahn having a lower profile than in the late 1960s and making few recordings. However, he is still enthusiastic about playing music. "I have tried to be open and absorb and assimilate all kinds of music, including every era of jazz, blues, country and contemporary classical."

**Recommended CDs:** *Jerry Hahn And His Quintet* (Arhoolie 9011), *Time Changes* (Enja 9007), *Hahn Solo* (Migration 101), *Jazz Hymns* (Migration 102), *Hahn Songs* (self-released); with John Handy: *Live At The Monterey Jazz Festival* (Koch 7820); with Gary Burton: *Country Roads And Other Places* (Koch 7854), *Good Vibes* (Koch 8515), *Throb* (Atlantic 1531).

**LPs to Search For:** *The Jerry Hahn Brotherhood* (Columbia 1044) and one of Hahn's finest albums, 1975's *Moses* (Fantasy 9426), have yet to be reissued on CD.

**Website:** www.jerryhahn.com

## Jim Hall
*b. December 4, 1930, Buffalo, NY*

A quiet yet endlessly creative guitarist, Jim Hall's harmonically advanced style and unhurried approach have made him an increasingly influential force through the years. It is a measure of his impact that Bill Frisell, John Scofield and Pat Metheny all cite him as a creative inspiration yet none of those guitarists really sound like Hall.

After attending the Cleveland Institute of Music and studying classical guitar with Vicente Gomez,

Hall was a member of four of the most intriguing and rewarding groups of the 1955–65 period. He was the original guitarist with the Chico Hamilton Quintet (1955–56), one of the premier chamber jazz groups. Hall was a member of the Jimmy Giuffre Three during 1956–59, usually interacting with Giuffre's reeds and a bassist, but for a time in 1958, he was the entire rhythm section behind Giuffre and valve trombonist Bob Brookmeyer. After working with Ella Fitzgerald during 1960–61 (including appearing on her famous *Ella In Berlin* album) and occasionally playing duos with Lee Konitz, Hall was with the Sonny Rollins Quartet (1961–62), recording *The Bridge* and inspiring the tenor-saxophonist, who had just come out of retirement. When Hall left Rollins, he co-led a very underrated but rewarding quartet with Art Farmer during 1962–64. In addition, he recorded with Paul Desmond in a quartet fairly regularly during 1959–65 and was on important sessions by Teddy Charles, Bill Perkins (Grand Encounter), Hampton Hawes, Bob Brookmeyer, John Lewis, Mark Murphy, Bill Evans (the classic duet albums *Undercurrent* and *Intermodulation*), Sonny Stitt (*Stitt Plays Bird*) and even the Dukes Of Dixieland. It was quite a decade for the guitarist.

While Jim Hall was initially associated with cool jazz and then with hard bop, he always had his own approach along with a distinctive sound. A master of subtlety, he has consistently come up with fresh ideas, used space brilliantly, and made every note count. Hall has been heard mostly as a leader ever since the group with Farmer broke up, usually in a trio or duo. He has been involved in one stimulating project after another up to the present time, whether it is performing classic duets with Ron Carter, recording with George Shearing or Michel Petrucciani, interacting with guitarists from later generations, or performing his quiet brand of explorative chamber jazz with his own group. At 80, Jim Hall is still inspiring younger guitarists.

**Recommended CDs:** *Jazz Guitar* (Capitol 46851), *Where Would I Be* (Original Jazz Classics 649), *Alone Together* (Original Jazz Classics 467) with Ron Carter, *It's Nice To Be With You* (Verve 843035), *Concierto* (Columbia/Legacy 65132), *Commitment* (Universal 5247), *Live!* (Universal 9225), *Big Blues* (Columbia 45220), *Live At The North Sea Jazz Festival* (Challenge 70063) with Bob Brookmeyer, *Concierto De Aranjuez* (Evidence 22004), *Circles* (Concord 4161), *Live At Village West* (Concord 4245), *Jim Hall's 3* (Concord 4298), *These Rooms* (Denon 3000), *All Across The City* (Concord 4384), *Live At Town Hall Vol. 1* (Music Masters 65050), *Live At Town Hall Vol. 2* (Music Masters 65066), *Subsequently* (Music Masters 65078), *Youkali* (CTI 67226), *Something Special* (Music Masters 65105),

*Dedications & Inspirations* (Telarc 83365), *Dialogues* (Telarc 83369), *Panorama* (Telarc 83408), *Textures* (Telarc 83402), *By Arrangement* (Telarc 83436), *Jim Hall & Pat Metheny* (Telarc 83442), *Jazzpar Quartet + 4* (Storyville 4230), *Grand Slam* (Telarc 83485), *Jim Hall & Basses* (Telarc 83506), *Magic Meeting* (Artistshare 0002), *Free Association* (Artistshare 30) with Geoff Keezer, *Duologues* (CAM Jazz 5009) with pianist Enrico Pieranunzi, *Hemispheres* (Artistshare 79) with Bill Frisell, *Conversations* (Artistshare 83) with drummer Joey Baron; with Chico Hamilton: *The Chico Hamilton Trio* (Fresh Sound 471); with Bill Perkins: *Grand Encounter* (Pacific Jazz 46859), with Jimmy Giuffre: *Jimmy Giuffre 3* (Atlantic 90981), *Western Suite* (WEA 25160); with Paul Desmond: *The Complete RCA Victor Recordings* (RCA 68687); with Sonny Rollins: *The Bridge* (BMG 38076); with Art Farmer: *Live At The Half Note* (Atlantic 90666); with Bill Evans: *Undercurrent* (Blue Note 90583), *Intermodulation* (Verve 833771); with George Shearing: *First Edition* (Concord 4177).

**LPs to Search For:** *Good Friday Blues* (Pacific Jazz 10).

**Website:** www.jimhallmusic.com

## Mary Halvorson
b. October 16, 1980, Boston, MA

One of the more impressive guitarists of her generation, Mary Halvorson is a fierce improviser whose avant-garde explorations point toward the future. She grew up in Boston and started playing guitar when she was 12. After studying jazz at Wesleyan University and the New School, Halvorson became part of the New York jazz scene in 2002. She first gained attention as a member of the Anthony Braxton Quartet. Since then, Halvorson has played with a large assortment of forward-looking improvisers, including Trevor Dunn's Trio-Convulsant, Joe Morris, Nels Cline, John Tchicai, Elliott Sharp, Andrea Parkins, Marc Ribot, Tony Malaby, Jason Moran, the avant-rock group People, Tim Berne, Taylor Ho Bynum, Myra Melford, Nicole Mitchell, and Curtis Hasselbring.

Mary Halvorson's trio recording *Dragon's Head* from 2008 gained her strong attention among jazz critics. She also leads a quintet and co-leads a chamber music duo with violist Jessica Pavone in which they both sing.

**Recommended CDs:** *Dragon's Head* (Firehouse 12 401007) teams the guitarist with bassist John Hebert and drummer Ches Smith in 2009. Halvorson duets with violist Jessica Pavone on *On & Off* (Skirl 007) and *Thin Air* (Thirsty Ear 357188) and interacts with drummer Weasel Walter on *Opulence* (UgExplode 026). She is also well featured on *Calling All*

*Portraits* (Skycap 30121492), *Crackleknob* (Hatology 662), Anthony Braxton's *Live At The Royal Festival Hall 2004* (Leo 449), *Saturn Sings* (Firehouse 12 401013), *Departure Of Reason* (Thirsty Ear 57200), and *Bending Bridges* (Firehouse 12 401015).

**Website:** www.maryhalvorson.com

## Steve Hancoff
*b. February 13, 1948, Baltimore, MD*

In his career, Steve Hancoff has played the guitar as if it were an orchestra, transferring vintage American jazz, blues and ragtime (often from piano arrangements) to his instrument.

Hancoff started off on trumpet and trombone. "When I was 13 years old, I attended a concert by the Weavers. I fell in love. The next day, I went out and got myself a beat-up old Harmony classic for $25. I wanted to be a folk singer. I taught myself by playing along with LPs. When there was more than one instrument on the record, I tried to make my playing sound like the multiple instruments I heard. That is what gave rise to my style."

Within six months of starting on the guitar, the 13-year-old Hancoff was performing at two folk clubs in Baltimore: Le Flambeau and the Blue Dog. He learned from watching other performers, and he listened regularly to the rural blues fingerstyle players, including Rev. Gary Davis, Mississippi John Hurt, Brownie McGhee, Big Bill Broonzy, Lightnin' Hopkins and the still-active Dave Van Ronk. Later on, he became interested in Django Reinhardt, Lonnie Johnson, and Eddie Lang, plus more modern jazz, early country, and Mike Seeger and the New Lost City Ramblers.

Hancoff graduated from St. Johns College in Annapolis, Maryland, in 1970. "Because I fingerpicked, accompanying songs with syncopated rhythmic patterns, a lot of uninformed people told me that my playing sounded like 'ragtime.' So, in order to find out about ragtime, I picked up a book of Scott Joplin piano pieces and Joshua Rifkin's first Joplin recording and started to do note-for-note guitar transcriptions." Twenty-three at the time, Hancoff was among the very first to play Joplin on the guitar, not realizing how unique that was. In 1974, when he attended the first annual Scott Joplin Ragtime Festival in Sedalia, Missouri, he entered and won the competition. The ragtime world took notice, and he recorded two albums of rags for the Dirty Shame

label, including *Classic Ragtime Guitar*. "Starting in 1974, Trebor Tichenor, the maven of American ragtime, Max Morath, Turk Murphy and Dick Hyman all took the trouble to teach and encourage me." He also did a concert with Eubie Blake.

In 1983, after meeting historian and producer Al Rose, Hancoff was invited to New Orleans, where he was introduced to veteran musicians and learned firsthand about the music. In 1992, he was designated by the USIA and later the US State Department as an Artistic Ambassador. During the next 14 years, he gave concerts and taught music classes in around 60 countries, often being teamed with banjoist Bud Wachter.

Steve Hancoff has written several series of guitar arrangements that have been published. He is currently transcribing, arranging and recording the six Suites for Solo Cello by Bach for acoustic guitar. "My desire for future concerts is to play folk and blues songs, ragtime, New Orleans jazz pieces, swing, improvisations and Bach, including telling the stories of the life and times of the seminal creators of our music."

**Recommended CDs:** *Steel String Guitar* (Out of Time 920) and *New Orleans Guitar Solos* (Out of Time 925) mostly have pieces from the 1920s plus a few rags. *Duke Ellington For Solo Guitar* (Discipline 9914) and *The Single Petal Of A Rose: Duke Ellington For Solo Guitar, Vol. 2* (Out of Time 950) are full of surprising choices, covering Ellington's entire career.

**LPs to Search For:** *Classic Ragtime Guitar* (Dirty Shame 4553) is an important album that has yet to be reissued.

**Website:** www.stevehancoff.com

## Fareed Haque
*b. January 1, 1963, Chicago, IL*

East meets West in the multicultural jazz of Fareed Haque. Born to a Pakistani father and a Chilean mother, the pattern was set from the start in Haque's life. Although partly raised in Chicago, he traveled extensively with his parents while growing up, spending time in Spain, France, Iran, Pakistan and Chile.

The many cultures that he experienced and the music that he heard became part of Haque's guitar playing. He studied jazz at North Texas State

University and classical music at Northwestern University in Chicago. Haque picked up important experience and exposure while playing with Paquito D'Rivera during the second half of the 1980s. He also worked with Tito Puente, Toots Thielemans, Von Freeman, Joe Henderson, Lester Bowie, Joe Zawinul, Brad Goode, Edward Peterson, Joey Calderazzo, Bob Belden, Ramsey Lewis, Renee Rosnes, Dianne Reeves, the Ethnic Heritage Ensemble, Dave Holland, Cassandra Wilson, Kurt Elling, Arturo Sandoval, and Medeski, Martin & Wood.

Fareed Haque, who has recorded as a leader regularly since 1988, was a member of George Brooks' group Summit (which included Zakir Hussein and Steve Smith), co-founded the ethnic fusion group Garaj Mahal (which became popular in jam-band circles) in 2001, and also leads the Fareed Haque Group. A master on both acoustic and electric guitars, Fareed Haque has also performed all of the major guitar concertos with symphony orchestras, teaches at Northern Illinois University, and in 2004 premiered his Lahara Double Concerto for Sitar/Guitar and Tabla.

**Recommended CDs:** Fareed Haque's recordings range from fusion and pop elements to post-bop jazz and strong influences from various countries, with many of his musical interests being combined on the same set. His recordings as a leader are *Voices Rising* (Pangaea 42158); *Manresa* (IRS 13021); *Sacred Addiction* (Blue Note 89662); *Opaque* (Blue Note 29270); *Déjà Vu* (Blue Note 52419), which is a jazz interpretation of a Crosby, Stills, Nash & Young album; *Cosmic Hug* (Magnatude 2307); and *Flat Planet* (Owl 133). Garaj Mahal has recorded *Live Vols. 1–3* (Harmonized 006-008), *Mondo Garaj* (Harmonized 010), *Blueberry Cave* (Harmonized 023), *Woot* (Owl 125), and *More Mr. Nice Guy* (Owl 135).

**Website:** www.fareed.com

## Bill Harris

b. April 14, 1925, Nashville, NC; d. December 6, 1988, Washington, DC

A local legend in Washington, DC, Bill Harris (no relation to the trombonist of the same name) had an unusual career. The son of a preacher, he was very familiar with religious music while growing up, although he particularly loved the playing of Oscar Moore with the King Cole Trio. After serving in the Army during part of World War II, Harris studied guitar at the Columbia School of Music, becoming adept at both jazz and classical music. However, he then became the guitarist for the Clovers, spending quite a few years playing and touring with the R&B vocal group.

Along the way he recorded *Solo Guitar* in 1956,

which is arguably the first important full-length solo jazz guitar album. Harris also recorded two other albums in the 1960s, a period when he settled down in Washington, DC. An influential teacher at the Howard University School of Music, during his last 15 years Bill Harris operated a restaurant/nightclub called Pigfoot.

**Recommended CDs:** Bill Harris, one of the first guitarists to be equally comfortable playing jazz and classical music, recorded surprisingly little throughout his career. The best introduction to his music is *The Fabulous Bill Harris* (V.S.O.P. 66), which was recorded live at a variety of venues during 1957–86. Harris not only plays guitar but also sings a bit and directs the Howard University Ensemble on two movements of his suite dedicated to Wes Montgomery. Also of strong interest is Harris' *Definitive Black & Blue Sessions: Down In The Alley* (Black & Blue 938).

**LPs to Search For:** Bill Harris' other recordings, *Solo Guitar* (Emarcy 36097), *Great Guitar Sounds* (Wing 16220), *Caught In The Act* (Jazz Guitar 100), and *Bill Harris Rhythm* (Black & Blue 33062), all deserve to be reissued.

## Jerome Harris

b. April 5, 1953, Flushing, NY

Jerome Harris, an adventurous improviser, has gained great respect as a guitarist, an electric bassist, and an occasional acoustic bass guitarist. He moved with his family to Brooklyn when he was one. "I liked hearing music as long as I could remember, and I enjoyed singing in school. My kindergarten teacher played piano in our classroom, and I found that fascinating. After briefly dabbling with accordion lessons, I wanted to play an instrument to accompany singing. I pestered my parents for a guitar. They bought me a department store–grade acoustic guitar as a Christmas present when I was around ten years old." He heard his parents' jazz vocal recordings along with the pop music of the day. "I found myself drawn to the instrumental solos and interludes (improvised and written) in many pop recordings of the time. The progressive rock/blues/pop/R&B of the 1960s, with its prominent use of improvised soloing, served as a type of proto-jazz in my listening diet."

Harris played with R&B/funk bands while in high school. He earned a degree in psychology and social relations at Harvard (1969–73) and a master's in jazz guitar at the New England Conservatory of Music (1973–77), where he studied with George Russell. Harris played with the local jazz-funk group Ghetto Mysticism in the mid-1970s. "During my spring semester of my junior year at Harvard, I realized that I didn't want to become an academic social psychologist. I decided to pursue my love of music and somehow turn that into a career."

In 1978, Jerome Harris joined Sonny Rollins' band on bass guitar, staying for three years. He was back with the great tenor on bass guitar during 1984–87, becoming Rollins' guitarist during 1988–94. Other key associations include Oliver Lake & Jump Up (1980–86), Amina Claudine Meyers (three stints during 1983–97), Ned Rothenberg, Bobby Previte, Ray Anderson, Bob Stewart, Jack DeJohnette, Paul Motian, David Krakauer, Bill Frisell, Don Byron, Julius Hemphill, Bob Moses, Sam Newsome, Marvin Sewell, Jamie Baum, Jay Hoggard, Fred Wesley and Christian Muthspiel.

"For the future, I want to work on doing more composing (I've been giving that short shrift), intensified practicing and studying, and doing more work as a bandleader."

**Recommended CDs:** Jerome Harris has appeared on many recordings during the past 35 years, starting with the New England Conservatory Ragtime Ensemble's LP *The Road From Rags To Jazz* (Golden Crest 31042), on which he played banjo and guitar. Concentrating on his more significant guitar records, Harris is a strong asset on Bob Stewart's *Goin' Home* (JMT 834 427), Sonny Rollins' *Falling In Love With Jazz* (Milestone 9179) and *Here's To The People* (Milestone 9194), Bobby Previte's *Slay The Suitors* (Avant 036) and *Dangerous Rip* (Enja 9324), Ray Anderson's *Don't Mow Your Lawn* (Enja 8070) and Jack DeJohnette's *Oneness* (ECM 1637). On his own albums, Harris has primarily played bass, including on *In Passing* (Muse 5386), *Hidden In Plain View* (New World 80472) and *Rendezvous* (Stereophile 1).

**LPs to Search For:** Ironically, the only Jerome Harris album to feature him on guitar was his debut, *Algorithms* (Minor Music 1011), which has yet to be reissued on CD. Harris is also heard on Ran Blake's typically dramatic *Rapport* (Arista Novus 3006).

**Website:** www.jeromeharris.com

"My guitar teacher Dave Gould played in the style of Django Reinhardt. I also listened to guitarists like Jeff Beck who were crossing over into jazz along with Al Di Meola and John McLaughlin. I remember hearing Miles playing 'It Ain't Necessarily So' when I was in high school, and it was an epiphany." While attending high school in Sarasota, Florida, Hart played shows with Frankie Laine, Steve Allen, Phyllis Diller, Red Skelton and Tennessee Ernie Ford. He attended the University of Miami (1979–83) and considers his first important jazz gig to be working with Duffy Jackson's group in 1980.

Hart moved to New York after graduating in 1983. Among his most important associations since then have been working with Jack McDuff (1986–2000), Terumasa Hino, Chris Potter, Larry Goldings, Brian Blade and Shunzo Ono. He has also performed with Jimmy Smith, Lou Donaldson, James Moody, the Maria Schneider Orchestra, Bob Belden, Steve Davis, Diane Hubka, Melody Breyer-Grell and Ralph Lalama, among others.

"These days, I do some gigs in NY with my trio and play in about ten other bands in the vicinity. I have a steady Sunday in Manhattan at the Café Loup that has been going on for over five years, with saxophonist Bob Kindred and bassist Steve LaSpina. I have also been touring Japan and Europe with vocalist Hilary Kole during the past year. Improvising for me is the pinnacle of musical expression. I love that I can start a song or solo and I really don't know what will happen. The music unfolds as the sounds hit the air. And there is such joy when it really swings."

**Recommended CDs:** All of John Hart's CDs as a leader, which include 1988's *One Down* (Blue Note 93476), *Trust* (Blue Note/Somethin' Else 95206), *High Drama* (Concord 4688), *Bridges* (Concord 4746), and *Scenes From A Song* (Hep 2080), are well worth acquiring. His two best most rewarding overall are his most recent recordings: *Indivisible* (Hep 2088) and *Standards: Green And Blue* (Hep 2090).

## John Hart
*b. June 15, 1961, Ft. Belvoir, VA*

John Hart is a valuable modern mainstream guitarist who has uplifted a countless number of sessions with his swing and creative ideas. He received his first guitar as a Christmas present when he was 12.

## Ken Hatfield
*b. November 18, 1952, Portsmouth, VA*

Ken Hatfield is a multitalented musician whose music is difficult to classify. Although he has played fine electric guitar, his emphasis in recent years has been on the acoustic guitar. While he also plays dobro

*Ken Hatfield Trio*

and mandolin, some of his most significant work has been as a composer, not only of jazz originals but also of chamber pieces for several different types of jazz and classical ensembles, choral works, ballet scores, and music for documentary films and television. He has also written a song cycle using poems by Langston Hughes for the lyrics.

Ken Hatfield wanted to play guitar when he was four but had to wait until he was eight before his parents finally gave in and bought him one. "Music is what I've always wanted to do with my life—then, now, and in the future." He grew up listening to R&B, bluegrass, blues and rock, although from the start, he was attracted to the groups that featured improvised solos. "The result was that everyone told me I was a jazz musician, because I didn't play what was on the records they all knew. So I began to check out this mysterious music called jazz and found that I liked it." At the time, Norfolk, Virginia, had many bars with live music for the naval personnel that were stationed nearby, and Virginia Beach had many hotels and clubs for tourists. At 14, Hatfield was playing in cover bands in both towns, often seven nights a week. He attended the Berklee College of Music during 1971–74 (joining the faculty when he was 19) and by then considered Ralph Towner and Wes Montgomery to be his main guitar influences. In 1993, he received a bachelor of arts from the State University of New York.

After Berklee, Hatfield lived in Baltimore before ultimately settling in New York. He picked up important experience working with Charlie Byrd during 1973–76 (and later in 1997–99), Jack McDuff and Chico Hamilton. Asked to name a few of the high points of his career since then, he answered, "Being recommended by Jeff Mironov and Bob Cranshaw for studio work, composing the ballet scores for works by choreographer Judith Jamison, playing with the great Dom Salvador, and learning more about Brazilian music. The two major turning points for me have been switching my focus to the nylon string guitar as my primary instrument and making composition the driving force of my music and the prism through which I view its creation."

**Recommended CDs:** *Music For Guitar And Bass* (Arthur Circle Music 9708) features originals performed as duets with bassist Hans Glawischnig. *Explorations For Solo Guitar* (Arthur Circle Music 9802) is highlighted by the six-part "New York Suite For Guitar." *Dyad* (Arthur Circle Music 3482) displays Hatfield's interest in Brazilian music and has spots for singer Maucha Adnet and percussionist Duduka Da Fonseca. *Phoenix Rising* (Arthur Circle Music 9512) has Hatfield's trio with Glawischnig and Da Fonseca joined on some selections by pianist Dom Salvador, tenor-saxophonist Billy Drews and

trumpeter Claudio Roditi. *The Surrealist Table* (Arthur Circle Music 162), which Hatfield considers his best recording as a guitarist so far, features him with his trio (Glawischnig and drummer Jeff Hirschfield), while *String Theory* (Arthur Circle Music 7502), a set of guitar solos with a little bit of overdubbing, has Hatfield performing originals (including the 12-part "Snowhill Variations") that fall between folk and classical music although with improvising. *To Be Continued* (M Pub 002) is a particularly strong effort that showcases Hatfield (who contributed the arrangements) with a versatile quintet that includes Jim Clouse on soprano and tenor performing eight colorful originals by Bill McCormick.

**Website:** www.kenhatfield.com

## Gilad Hekselman
*b. February 3, 1983, Kfar Saba, Israel*

A promising young guitarist, Gilad Hekselman has made a strong impression ever since his 2006 recording debut. Hekselman took three years of classical piano lessons before switching to guitar when he was nine. "I initially wanted to play the drums, but my neighbor couldn't stand the noise. I started out playing rock music. Slowly I got into some progressive rock and then fusion. Later on when I attended Thelma Yellin School, I majored in jazz performance, and it was there that I was exposed to more traditional jazz."

When he was twelve, Hekselman started a two-year stint playing regularly with the band on a weekly children's television show. He graduated from the Thelma Yellin School of Arts when he was 18. For a few years, he played jazz gigs with other Israeli musicians, including Uzi Finerman, Doron Tirosh and Shay Zeiman.

In 2004, Gilad Hekselman moved to New York, where for the next four years he attended the New School University. In 2005, he won the Gibson Montreux International Guitar Competition, which resulted in him gaining some important recognition. He has worked with Marcus Gilmore, Ari Hoenig, Mark Turner, Joe Martin, Chris Potter, John Scofield, Gretchen Parlato and Aaron Parks. Hekselman has also had associations individually with the 3 Cohens. "Avishai Cohen joined my trio for a very memorable concert in Israel. I studied with Yuval and eventually started playing with him. And I have had a strong musical relationship with Anat since I moved to New York.

"When I'm playing the guitar, I'm able to express myself in ways that words don't normally allow, and connect with people on a deeper level. Through improvisation, I have learned a lot not only about myself, but also about human nature and the world around me."

**Recommended CDs:** Gilad Hekselman has thus far led three CDs: *SpiritLife* (Smalls 15), *Worlds Unspoken* (Late Set 29632) and *Hearts Wide Open* (Le Chant Du Monde), each of which feature him in top form with small groups. He is also well featured on Ari Hoenig's *Burt's Playground* (Dreyfus 36919) and Anat Cohen's *Notes From The Village* (Anzic 400117).

**Website:** www.giladhekselman.com

## Scott Henderson
b. August 26, 1954, West Palm Beach, FL

During the 1980s and '90s, when fusion was thought of by many as burnt-out or just a predecessor to commercial "smooth" music, Scott Henderson performed consistently ferocious fusion guitar, helping to keep the idiom alive. Henderson's background was in rock and electric blues. He grew up in South Florida, played in a variety of rock and R&B bands, and listened closely to Jimi Hendrix, Jeff Beck and Buddy Guy. After graduating from Florida Atlantic University, Henderson moved to Los Angeles in 1980 to attend the Guitar Institute of Technology. After studying with Joe Diorio and graduating, he became a teacher at GIT. Noticed early on, he worked with Jeff Berlin, Jean-Luc Ponty, the original version of Chick Corea's Elektric Band (1985) and Joe Zawinul's Syndicate (1987–89).

In 1984, Henderson and bassist Gary Willis formed Tribal Tech, a group that not only stayed together during the guitarist's stints with Corea and Zawinul but is still active on a part-time basis. Henderson recorded a string of explosive albums, switching a bit in 1994 to electric blues/rock fusion with the release of *Dog Party*. He has also led his own trio with bassist John Humphrey and drummer Alan Hertz and has recorded with bassist Victor Wooten and drummer Steve Smith as "Vital Tech Tones."

Scott Henderson serves as consistent proof that there is still plenty of life to be found in fusion guitar.

**Recommended CDs:** With Tribal Tech, Henderson has recorded *Nomad* (Relativity 1028), *Dr. Hee* (Relativity 1029), *Spears* (Relativity 1030), *Tribal Tech* (Relativity 1049), *Illicit* (Mesa/Bluemoon 79180), *Face First* (Mesa/Bluemoon 79190), *Reality Check* (Mesa/Bluemoon 92549), *Thick* (Tone Center 03659) and *Rocket Science* (Tone Center 03669). As a leader, he has cut *Dog Party* (Mesa/Bluemoon 79073), *Tore Down House* (Mesa/Bluemoon 92722), *Well To The Bone* (Tone Center 2045), and *Scott Henderson Live* (Tone Center 4037).

**Website:** www.scotthenderson.net

## Al Hendrickson
*(Alton Hendrickson)*
b. May 10, 1920, Eastland, TX; d. July 19, 2007, Coos Bay, OR

An extremely busy studio guitarist for over 25 years, Al Hendrickson's playing was heard by virtually everyone, although few outside of the music industry knew his name. Al Hendrickson grew up in Los Angeles, and during 1940–41 (when he was just 20), he was a member of the Artie Shaw Orchestra. His electric guitar is prominent on Shaw's eight Gramercy Five recordings, including "Summit Ridge Drive," "Cross Your Heart" and "My Blue Heaven." After serving in the Coast Guard during World War II, he became a major part of the Los Angeles studio scene. Hendrickson worked briefly with the orchestras of Benny Goodman (including taking the lead vocal on a hit recording of "Slow Boat To China"), Freddie Slack, Boyd Raeburn, Ray Noble, Billy May, Neal Hefti and Woody Herman but mostly stayed in L.A., where he recorded constantly if often anonymously.

Among Al Hendrickson's countless number of associations were Billie Holiday, Ella Fitzgerald, Mel Torme, Peggy Lee, Bing Crosby, Dinah Washington, Nat King Cole, Frank Sinatra, Louis Armstrong, Ray Charles, Nelson Riddle, Quincy Jones, Lalo Schifrin and (along with four other guitarists) Guitars Inc., not to mention the Weavers, Elvis Presley, and the Monkees. He also recorded with bebop pianist Dodo Marmarosa, Mildred Bailey, Stan Hasselgard, Barney Kessel, Anita O'Day, and Dave Pell and, in the 1970s, was a member of the Juggernaut. All in all, it is estimated that he was on more than 15,000 recording dates and the soundtracks of over 5,000 movies. He also found time to write quite a few guitar instruction books.

Al Hendrickson, who retired in the late 1980s, was a superior rhythm guitarist who was also a fine soloist. But he never led a record date of his own and was known by very few beyond those in the music industry.

**Recommended CDs:** Al Hendrickson's recordings with Artie Shaw's Gramercy Five are on *The Complete Gramercy Five Sessions* (Bluebird 7637).

## Steve Herberman
b. September 10, 1966, Bethesda, MD

Steve Herberman started off with piano lessons when he was six and played the trombone in grade school. "When I was 11 years old, my parents went on a trip to Hawaii and brought me back a ukulele as a souvenir. It came with a little aluminum pick, and I couldn't put the thing down. I tuned the ukulele like the top four strings of a guitar and started learning chords from a beginning guitar book, also picking out melodies by ear. I begged my parents for a 'real' guitar, and luckily a few months later they got me one and got me started with a teacher."

Herberman played in a rock band as a teenager and got hooked on jazz when he heard Jean-Luc Ponty's *Enigmatic Ocean* album on the radio. That brought him to Return to Forever and soon Wes Montgomery and Thelonious Monk. He went to Berklee during 1984–88 and had his first jazz gigs with local musicians. Herberman has since resettled in the Baltimore/Washington, DC area, playing primarily on the East Coast. Among his most significant musical associations were Keter Betts (with whom he often played in 2004), John Pisano, Larry Willis, Buster Williams, Gary Bartz, Jim Snidero, Chuck Redd and Ali Ryerson.

Steve Herberman has taught at Towson University in Baltimore since 1999 and also teaches in online video master classes. He adopted the seven-string guitar in 1993. "Working through all of George Van Eps' incredible books gave me the tools to approach the instrument like it was a string trio or quartet. I enjoy creating arrangements on the spot, and hopefully they will be on the level of good composed arrangements."

**Recommended CDs:** Thus far, Steve Herberman has recorded three CDs as a leader: *Thoughtlines* (String Jazz 1031); *Action Reaction* (Reach 7120), which is comprised entirely of his originals; and *Ideals* (Reach 9280). The latter is programmed as if it were a club date.

**Website:** www.reachmusicjazz.com

## Jim Hershman
*b. July 16, 1961, Sacramento, CA*

Jim Hershman started playing guitar when he was 12. His mother had begun guitar lessons and, since there was a guitar around the house, she taught him three chords; that was the beginning. "My junior high school had a very good music program. I joined the jazz stage band even though I didn't know the first thing about jazz. It was okay because the piano player was very good and the guitar amp was small." He improved quickly and in high school often played in trios with accordionists, including Elaine Lord and Joe Nardone.

Hershman moved to Southern California in 1982, where he attended Cal State Northridge and earned a degree in political science. For 13 years, he was part of the jazz scene in Los Angeles, working with the Matt Catingub Big Band (succeeding Howard Alden) and becoming a longtime member of the

Clayton-Hamilton Jazz Orchestra. "That was amazing. I was with them for 10 years, and every gig and rehearsal was a learning experience."

In 1995, Hershman moved to New York to study jazz and classical guitar at the Manhattan School of Music. While in school, he formed the Other Quartet, a group that recorded *13 Pieces*. He has since worked with Lee Konitz, Steve Swallow and Jon Hendricks in jazz while also performing with the Los Angeles Philharmonic (debuting John Adams' piece *El Niño* in 2003), the San Francisco Ballet and the Los Angeles Opera. Jim Hershman does a lot of theater work in New York and has a steady Monday night engagement with his trio. "I love the feeling of not knowing what will happen next musically. When listening to the other players on stage becomes the primary goal, music takes on a life of its own."

**Recommended CDs:** The fine straight-ahead guitarist has led three CDs to date: *Small Talk* (Laughing Buddha Productions); *342* (Sea Breeze 3055), which has Lee Konitz on half of the selections; and *Partners In Crime* (Azica 72231) with Bill Cunliffe on organ. The Other Quartet's *13 Pieces* (Knitting Factory Works 262) from 1999 features Jim Hershman on adventurous music with trumpeter Russ Johnson, saxophonist Ohad Talmor and drummer Michael Sarin.

**Website:** www.jimhershman.com

## Allan Holdsworth
*b. August 6, 1946, Bradford, Yorkshire, England*

An innovative guitarist who puts many other guitarists in the rock and fusion worlds in awe of his technique, wide range of sounds and ideas, Allan Holdsworth also gives one the impression that, given his choice, he would have been a Coltrane-inspired jazz saxophonist.

Holdsworth actually played saxophone first and was taught music by his father, an amateur pianist. It was not until he was 17 that Holdsworth started on the guitar, but he developed quickly and was soon playing with local groups. Skilled in fusion, rock and jazz, he moved to London, worked with the rock group Tempest during 1972–73, and became a member of the legendary British fusion band Soft Machine in December 1973. He stayed until March 1975, when he joined a later version of the Tony Williams Lifetime, which gave him exposure in the

United States. Holdsworth soon moved on to play with rock group Gong in addition to guesting on recordings by Jean-Luc Ponty, Gordon Beck, Jack Bruce, and UK (with Bill Bruford).

While Holdsworth's guitar playing greatly impresses others in the rock world, he is a restless improviser at heart. In 1978, he formed his own group, IOU, which originally had bassist Paul Carmichael and drummer Gary Husband. The guitarist moved to Los Angeles and continued with new lineups in IOU through the mid-1980s. His solo career since then has emphasized instrumental music and occasional collaborations with jazz players, including Alan Pasqua, Billy Childs, Vinnie Colaiuta, Dave Carpenter, Stanley Clarke, Billy Cobham, Michael Brecker and Randy Brecker, sometimes in all-star groups. He has even recorded jazz standards on rare occasions, including on the *None Too Soon* CD with pianist Gordon Beck. In the mid-1980s, Holdsworth was one of the first guitarists to use a Synthaxe, a type of guitar synthesizer that has a breath controller. He has since designed several of his own guitars, including baritone and piccolo guitars, not wanting to settle for just having a conventional sound.

Allan Holdsworth has continued producing a steady output of impressive recordings up to the present time, never playing it safe.

**Recommended CDs:** Of Allan Holdsworth's many recordings, the most rewarding from the jazz and fusion standpoints are *The Things You See* (JMS 48), *I.O.U.* (Restless 72563), *Metal Fatigue* (Restless 72562), *Atavachron* (Restless 72561), *Sand* (Restless 72593), *With A Heart In My Song* (JMS 44), *Secrets* (Restless 72573), *Hard Hat Area* (Restless 72716), *None Too Soon* (Restless 72928), *I.O.U. Band Live* (Cleopatra 9970), *The Sixteen Men Of Tain* (JMS 187132), *Flat Tire: Music For A Nonexistent Movie* (Megazoidal 2100), *All Night Wrong* (Favored Nations 2330), and *Blues For Tony* (Moon June 29). He is also featured with the Tony Williams Lifetime on *Believe It* (Sony 512898).

**Website:** www.therealallanholdsworth.com

## Sol Hoopii
*(Solomon Ho'opi'i Ka'ai'ai)*
b. 1902, Honolulu, HI; d. November 16, 1953, Seattle, WA

Sol Hoopii is considered the top Hawaiian steel guitarist of the 1920s and '30s. His playing influenced steel guitarists in Western swing and country, and a good portion of his recordings were jazz-oriented.

The youngest of 21 children, Hoopii played Hawaiian steel guitar, ukulele and guitar as a teenager in Hawaii, working with Johnny Noble's orchestra.

A legend is that he stowed away along with some of his brothers on an ocean liner in 1919 that was heading to San Francisco. But most likely, he performed regularly on ocean liners before settling in San Francisco in 1922. He eventually moved to Los Angeles, where he formed a trio and began working as a leader. Hoopii made his recording debut in 1925 and became quite popular, performing in a group comprised of saxophone, guitar, ukulele and his steel guitar. Hoopii's mixture of traditional Hawaiian music with classic jazz and blues was innovative, alternating Hawaiian songs with such standards as "Singin' The Blues," "Farewell Blues," "I Ain't Got Nobody," "Feelin' No Pain," and of course, "Song Of The Islands." He recorded over 200 selections in his career.

Sol Hoopii stayed busy for a decade, working in clubs and occasionally having small parts and feature numbers in Hollywood films. He switched to the electric lap steel guitar in 1935, and two of his best-known numbers were "Hula Girls" and "Ten Tiny Toes." In 1938, he became involved in religion, performing religious music and joining the crusade of evangelist Aimee Semple McPherson. Sol Hoopii stayed active, recording as late as 1951, two years before his early death at the age of 51 from diabetes.

**Recommended CDs:** *Sol Hoopii In Hollywood* (Grass Skirt Records) has his early trio recordings. *Sol Hoopii And His Novelty Quartette* (Origin) dates from 1933–34 and includes his last recordings on acoustic steel guitar.

## Toninho Horta
*(Antonio Mauricio Horta de Melo)*
b. December 2, 1948, Minas Gerais, Brazil

One of Brazil's top jazz-inspired guitarists, Toninho Horta has been influenced both by his Brazilian heritage and by his love for jazz. Born to a musical family, Horta began playing the guitar when he was  ten. He met Milton Nascimento when he was 14, and they not only became lifelong friends but often worked together through the years. As a teenager, Horta played at dances with local groups and wrote compositions. He entered two songs at the International Folk Song Festival 1967, making a strong impression. Horta worked with Nascimento, Elis Regina, Antonio Carlos Jobim, the Tribe (which included Joyce and Naná Vasconcelos), Gal Costa, Nana Caymmi, João Bosco and others. He became quite busy throughout the 1970s in Brazil as a guitarist, composer and arranger.

Horta began to be recognized outside of Brazil when he recorded his debut as a leader, *Land Of Birds*. Moving to the United States, he attended Juilliard and was discovered by the American jazz world. Horta worked with Wayne Shorter, Gary Peacock, Pat Metheny, the Manhattan Transfer, Sergio Mendes, the Gil Evans Orchestra, and George Duke. He also appeared in concert with Bobby McFerrin, Toots Thielemans, Philip Catherine, Herbie Hancock and Keith Jarrett.

Equally skilled on electric guitar and nylon string guitar (in addition to being a warm vocalist), Toninho Horta appeared on over 200 recordings in the 1980s and '90s alone, both in the US and Brazil. He also released six albums as a leader in the 1980s and nine more in the following decade, appealing to listeners in both the American jazz and Brazilian music worlds.

**Recommended CDs:** *Terras Dos Passaros* (EMI-Odeon 422855), which translates to *Land Of The Birds*; *Toninho Horta* (EMI 793865); *Diamond Land* (Verve Forecast 835 183), which has Wayne Shorter as a guest; *Moonstone* (Verve Forecast 839734); *Toninho Horta And Flávio Venturini* (Dubas 0630199872); *Once I Loved* (Verve 513 561), which is a standards-oriented set in a trio with Gary Peacock and Billy Higgins; the unaccompanied *Durango Kid* (Big World 2012); *Foot On The Road* (Polygram 523844); *Durango Kid 2* (Big World 2014); *Serenade* (Truspace 9705); a Jobim tribute called *From Ton To Tom* (Discmedi 89230); *Com O Pe No Forro* (Minas 3504); *Duets* (Adventure Music 1020); *Toninho In Vienna* (PAO 10400); and *To Jobim With Love* (Resonance 2004) form a strong overview of Toninho Horta's recording career.

**Website:** www.toninhohorta.art.br

# Charlie Hunter
b. May 23, 1967, Providence, RI

The master of the eight-string guitar (although in recent times he has removed one string), Charlie Hunter's control of his instrument is so thorough that he can sound like a guitarist, bassist and organist at

the same time. When he plays duets with a drummer, it sounds like a quartet. Although he has at times been marketed as a revolutionary or as part of the jam-band scene, in reality Hunter is a bop-based guitarist with an open mind toward funk and R&B.

He was born in Rhode Island and raised in Berkeley. Hunter's mother repaired guitars for a living, so he grew up around guitars, taking lessons from Joe Satriani. His early influences were Joe Pass and Tuck Andress. At 18, Hunter spent some time in Paris, performing as a one-man band on the streets. Back in the San Francisco Bay area, he played a seven-string guitar and organ in a political rap group and freelanced with jazz and R&B bands. Signed to Blue Note, in 1993 he recorded his debut using a seven-string guitar. Two years later when he made his second CD, he was playing a specially designed eight-string guitar that made him sound unlike any other guitarist.

In addition to leading his trio, which originally had Dave Ellis on saxophones and drummer Jay Lane (no need for any bassist or keyboardist), Hunter also co-founded the fusion band Garage A Trois, worked with Bobby Previte (Groundtruther, a trio with several different musicians), and was part of T.J. Kirk in the mid-1990s. The latter group exclusively played songs associated with Thelonious Monk, James Brown and Rahsaan Roland Kirk. Other projects included an instrumental remake of Bob Marley's *Natty Dread* album, using vibraphonist Stefon Harris in his group Pound for Pound in 1998, and a trio in 2007 with keyboardist Erik Deutsch and drummer Simon Lott.

Charlie Hunter's popularity, versatility and consistently creative playing have allowed him to play both major rock festivals and jazz clubs. His most recent group is a quintet with three horns, drums and the always stimulating guitarist.

**Recommended CDs:** *Charlie Hunter Trio* (Mammoth 980066), *Bing, Bing, Bing!* (Blue Note 31809), *Ready . . . Set . . . Shango* (Blue Note 37101), *Natty Dread* (Blue Note 52420), *Return Of The Candyman* (Blue Note 23108), *Duo* (Blue Note 99187) with drummer Leon Parker, *Solo Eight-String Guitar* (Contra Punto), *Charlie Hunter* (Blue Note 25450), *Songs From The Analog Playground* (Blue Note 33550), *Right Now Move* (Ropeadope 93137), *Come In Red Dog, This Is Tango Leader* (Ropeadope 93188), *Friends Seen And Unseen* (Ropeadope 51539), *Latitude* (Thirsty Ear 57150), *Longitude* (Thirsty Ear 57160), *Earth Tones* (Green Streets 704), *Copperopolis* (Ropeadope 060), *Innovation* (BHM 1017), *Mistico* (Fantasy 30265), *Altitude* (Thirsty Ear 357181), *Baboon Strength* (Spire Artists Media), *Gentlemen, I Neglected To Inform You You Will Not Be Getting Paid* (Spire Artists Media), and *Public Domain* (Spire Artists Media), which is a set of unaccompanied solos on songs copyrighted before 1925.

Website: www.charliehunter.com

## Ron Jackson
b. July 27, 1964, Manila, Philippines

A fine hard-bop-based guitarist, Ron Jackson's music also includes the influences of R&B, soul jazz and the musical heritage of the Philippines, where he was born when his father was stationed in the military. Jackson grew up near Boston. He began on the guitar when he was nine because he liked the electric guitar on Elvis Presley recordings. He was self-taught. "I was first involved with rock music, playing with a local band in the Boston area when I was 15. At the same time, I started composing music and getting into jazz introduced by my friends in high school. I always thought that music would be a tough field to be in, but I loved it so much that I stuck with it and persevered. I didn't want to do anything else. You need to be really dedicated, versatile and resourceful."

Jackson attended Berklee during 1982–85. He spent 1985–87 living in Paris, where he played electric bass exclusively, including with pianist Bobby Few and saxophonists Hal Singer and Leo Wright. In 1987, he returned to the United States, switching back to guitar. Since then he has worked with James Spaulding, Jimmy McGriff, Rufus Reid, Cecil Brooks III, Melvin Rhyne, Ralph Peterson, Craig Handy, Benny Golson, Randy Weston, Oliver Lake, Dee Dee Bridgewater, Dewey Redman, Lonnie Smith, Gary Bartz and others. He also has written and recorded with a variety of pop artists, is an educator, sometimes works in the pit orchestras of Broadway shows, and leads his own groups. Recently Ron Jackson has been recording for his Roni label.

Recommended CDs: All of Ron Jackson's seven CDs as a leader are enjoyable and easily recommended to fans of Melvin Sparks (one of his mentors), Grant Green, and George Benson's earlier work. His first two recordings as a leader, *A Guitar Thing* (Muse 5456), which also features pianist Benny Green, and *Thinking Of You* (Muse 5515), will be difficult to find since that label is long obsolete. *Song For Luis* (Mastermix 115) is a fine set of duets with bassist Rufus Reid, while *Concrete Jungle* (Airmen) is a set co-led by bassist Nicki Parrott. Ron Jackson's most recent recordings are each on his Roni Music label: *The Dream I Had*, *Flubby Dubby*, and *Burning Gums*.

Website: www.ronjacksonmusic.com

## Rolf Jardemark
b. November 23, 1960, Gothenburg, Sweden

A top guitarist from Sweden, Rolf Jardemark is a versatile player with a long series of recordings for the Imogena label. Jardemark started on guitar when he was 12. "I bought my first guitar from a friend for one dollar! I had no teacher. I started with a blues record and a chord book." Inspired by Barney Kessel, Larry Carlton and Pat Metheny, Jardemark also learned about jazz from Peter Almqvist when they both worked at a guitar store. Jardemark went to music college when he was 16, studying classical guitar but playing jazz at night. While in college, he performed in a guitar duo with Per Hovensjö; they made a recording in 1978. Jardemark eventually graduated from Gothenburg University in 1985 with a fine arts degree, but there was never any doubt in his mind that he would be a professional guitarist.

Jardemark has played with the Swedish artists Margaretha Evmark and Erik Gullbransson since the mid-1980s, toured Scandinavia with pianist-singer Michael Ruff in 1987, worked with the Bohuslän Big Band since 1990, and had his own group since 1989. He has also played on over 60 television shows in Sweden and worked with Nils Landgren, David Wilczewski, Lars Danielsson, Al Harewood, Bob Mintzer, Lew Soloff and Rune Gustafsson.

Rolf Jardemark teaches electric guitar, plans a duo record with the Estonian guitarist Jaak Sooaar, and recently released a CD with vocalist-bassist Margaretha Evmark. "To be a jazz musician is like being a scientist. You can always progress and explore and learn more."

Recommended CDs: Rolf Jardemark's evolution and consistency are very much in evidence on *Soft Landing* (Liphone 3095), *Jungle Crunch* (Imogena 027), *Guitarland* (Imogena 044), *Further Adventures In Guitarland* (Imogena 067), *Toco* (Guitarland Records 001), *Rosewood* (Imogena 114), *Get Out Of Town* (Imogena 157), and *Sunset In Guitarland* (Zink Music 012).

Website: www.rolfjardemark.com

## Chris Jentsch
b. May 3, 1959, Philadelphia, PA

An explorative guitarist with his own sound, Chris Jentsch is actually becoming best known as a composer. "I started playing rudimentary drums in a garage rock band. I was drawn to the guitar, frequently borrowing my guitarist's instrument between rehearsals until I eventually acquired my own when I was 17." After playing rock covers at parties and touring with a top forty band, he discovered jazz when he became a staff member of a college radio station. "I also played tuxedo society music and weddings in the Washington, DC area, featuring improvised medleys of standards and show tunes with hand signals from the leader for key changes."

Jentsch attended Gettysburg College in 1981 and later studied at Berklee, the New England Conservatory, the Eastman School of Music, and the University of Miami School of Music, where he earned a doctor of musical arts degree. He moved to New York in 1999, starting both a small unit and a large group that year. He has since received a number of composition grants to bolster his large ensemble activities. Jentsch has recorded both of his groups and is gradually becoming a bigger name, both for his adventurous guitar solos and for his innovative writing. For the future, his goals include writing an entirely new repertoire, forming a medium-size group to go with his two other bands, possibly writing an opera, and releasing the Jentsch Underground Series, around a dozen unreleased recordings that he has made since 1990.

"As an eclectic conglomerate of styles, my music sounds the way it does because of the worldwide explosion of communications technology, allowing access to music from around the world."

**Recommended CDs:** Chris Jentsch's first CD, *Media Event* (Blue Schist 001), puts the focus on his guitar playing in a trio on both originals and standards. *Miami Suite* (Blue Schist 002) with the University of Miami Concert Jazz Band, *Brooklyn Suite* (Fleur De Son 57987), and *Cycles Suite* (Fleur De Son 57994) form a trilogy of large band works. *Fractured Pop*, a quartet outing, is forthcoming.

**Website:** www.chrisjentsch.com

## Art Johnson
*(Norman Arthur Johnson)*
*b. October 18, 1945, San Diego, CA*

A very versatile guitarist with a sound of his own, Art Johnson is a superior jazz improviser who in his career has played in many different idioms. Johnson seriously took up the guitar when he was 17 and seriously ill. "I was recovering from a major leg operation. A friend dropped off a cheap arch-top guitar at my house. I was confined to bed for six months, and that is when I really became interested in the guitar. The perpendicular strings and frets of the fingerboard intrigued me. I began by drawing geometric figures on paper and then experimented with the sound of them on the guitar. I was lucky enough to start on the guitar before the Beatles arrived. In San Diego in the mid

and late sixties, there were over 150 nightspots with live music. By the time I was 20 years old, my chops were good enough to be working six nights a week year after year until I left for Los Angeles in 1968." In addition, he took up the violin (recording two CDs on fiddle), mandolin, electric bass and drums.

After high school, Johnson had brief periods attending Mesa College and SDSU but soon dropped out. In 1989, when he returned to San Diego, he became a professor at both campuses.

"I met Wes Montgomery when I was 20 years old. He was kind enough to spend an entire break between sets talking to me and giving me advice about approaching the instrument. I still remember clearly his smile and encouragement after I stumbled around on his L-5 for a few minutes. Barney Kessel was like a second father to me, and he produced my solo CD *Solo Jazz Guitar* in 2002. We hung out a lot during the last ten years of his life. Jim Hall and Django Reinhardt have had the hugest influences on my playing over the years, but I never tried to copy anyone."

Shortly after moving to Los Angeles, Johnson recorded as a leader for the Philips label, he became a very busy studio musician and worked on quite a few film scores and with many artists, including Willie Bobo, Paul Horn, John Klemmer, Tim Weisberg, Shelly Manne (1969–71), Mark O'Connor and Ray Pizzi. He also played in many settings beyond jazz, including with the eccentric country group Gas, Food & Lodging, Pat Boone, Tim Buckley, Judee Sill, O.C. Smith, Randy Crawford and Lena Horne. "Accompanying Luciano Pavarotti on classical guitar was a real thrill."

After 22 years in Los Angeles and a period in San Diego, in 2003 Art Johnson moved to France. Recently, he has recorded two CDs and written his autobiography *Memoirs Of A Sideman*.

**Recommended CDs:** As a leader, Art Johnson has recorded a variety of intriguing and rewarding CDs. *Heart Bound* (Cafe 729) is a fusion record with keyboardist Dwayne Smith. The duet album *Time Remembered* (ITI 30214), which features pianist Joanne Grauer, was dedicated to Bill Evans. Also of strong interest are a quartet CD from 1998 with his San Diego quartet, *Textures* (WLW 3789); *Contact* (Fidelio Audio 001) with bassist Frédéric Alarie; and a pair of other CDs with Dwayne Smith: *Jazz Live* (Rhythm Cafe) and *Bar Talk* (DP Records Monaco). "The album that means the most to me is *Solo Jazz Guitar* (DP Records Monaco), which Barney Kessel produced."

**Website:** www.art-johnson.com

## Eric Johnson
*b. September 14, 1954, Pittsburgh, PA*

A bluesy soulful guitarist, Eric Johnson helps keep classic soul jazz alive. He got his first guitar when he was 13. "My earliest gigs were of the R&B dance band nature. In those days, people really supported the bands and would rather dance to a live band instead of the jukebox. If you couldn't keep them dancing, you didn't get gigs!" Johnson credits George Benson, Lou Donaldson and pianist-vocalist and nightclub owner Walt Harper with making strong impacts on his life and career.

Johnson began his career in Pittsburgh in the late 1960s, playing in the R&B/jazz funk circuit. After graduating from high school and on Benson's recommendation, he joined Jack McDuff in 1972 and went out on the road. "We went coast to coast by car, pulling a trailer full of equipment and luggage. It was a great learning experience and a dream come true." In 1978 after Johnson moved to New York, he traveled the world with Jimmy Owens. Along the way, he also worked with Leon Spencer Jr., Lou Donaldson, Stanley Turrentine, Hank Crawford, Ramsey Lewis, George Coleman, Willis Jackson and Shirley Scott.

After recording his first CD as a leader, *Bumpin' In L.A.*, the guitarist moved to Los Angeles in 1993. During his three years on the West Coast, he led a trio and also played with Lorez Alexandria and Buddy Collette. He spent 1996–2000 back in Pittsburgh, working locally with Walt Harper and Harold Betters and recording his second album, *Makin' Whoopie*.

In 2000, Eric Johnson relocated to New York, working with Dr. Lonnie Smith, Lou Donaldson, organist Akiko Tsuruga, Radam Schwartz, and his own trio with organist Nathan Lucas and drummer Matt Baronello. Recently, he returned to Pittsburgh, where he leads the Fabalous A-Team, a group with bassist Bob Insko and drummer Mike Finch.

"In my opinion, the African American jazz guitarist is being ignored. Not one of us has a group that is headlining nightclubs or festivals. George Benson does not count because he is a pop star. All of the rest of us are sidemen or ignored. But I am doing my best to keep on playing my favorite style, bluesy funky jazz."

**Recommended CDs:** Each of Eric Johnson's fine CDs, *Bumpin' In L.A.* (Clarion Jazz 89301), *Makin' Whoopee* (Bluejay 5002), and *Supahighway* (Clarion Jazz 80808), feature his distinctive voice in the soul-jazz tradition.

**Website:** www.fabalousej.com

## Henry Johnson
*b. January 28, 1954, Chicago, IL*

A fine straight-ahead guitarist with a soulful sound who is a bluesy, swinging and an appealing singer, Henry Johnson has been a valuable player on many sessions through the years. He began on the guitar when he was 13. His grandfather used to play guitar in the church, so an instrument was available. "I heard jazz around the house growing up because my parents were Joe Williams and Count Basie fans, but I felt that it was their music, not mine. My band teacher at the time, Paul Meacham, took us to see the University of Illinois Jazz Band when they came to Memphis, and that was my first jazz concert live. Seeing that big band closed the deal for me and hooked me on jazz forever." Seeing Wes Montgomery in 1967 was also an important event.

When he was 14, Johnson had his first gigs with a group called the Soul Diplomats. Around that time, he also had the opportunity to play with Isaac Hayes. He attended Indiana University in 1973. "Jack McDuff was my first road gig, and with him I realized how important it was to be an apprentice with jazz masters, because people like him helped to create the music that we love." Johnson also worked with Sonny Stitt (1975), Ramsey Lewis (for whom he wrote "Romance Me," which became a radio hit), Joe Williams (1986), Freddie Hubbard (1992), Hank Crawford, Stanley Turrentine, Jimmy Smith and Nancy Wilson (2003). "For the last two years, I have been concentrating on teaching jazz guitar to young students and trying to inspire them to be the next generation of jazz musicians while also being on the faculty of Roosevelt University in Chicago, Illinois.

"When I was playing with Jack McDuff, I was trying to play all the bebop licks, so I was listening to a lot of Charlie Parker. One night, I played a solo, and nobody clapped. So after the set, Jack took me aside and said, 'Listen, playing bebop is all right, but if you don't play the blues with it, then nobody is going to feel it. You don't have no jazz without the blues. You aren't the first guitar player coming through here that has had to learn this—George Benson had to learn the same thing.' That's how I ended up finding my own personal voice. It's a hybrid of many, many things, but I think the basis of it is bebop and blues."

**Lonnie Johnson**

**Recommended CDs:** Henry Johnson's first five CDs, *You're The One* (MCA 5754) from 1986, *Future Excursions* (MCA 42089), *Never Too Much* (MCA 6329), *New Beginnings* (Heads Up 3019) and *Missing You* (Heads Up 3029), all feature his fine playing (inspired by George Benson and Wes Montgomery) on funky and often commercial material. Those recordings consistently give one the impression that he is capable of much more. But 2000's *Evening At Sea* (Chiaroscuro 367) was a breakthrough, an excellent live date that features Johnson stretching out in a quartet also featuring pianist Kenny Drew, Jr. *Organic* (A 440 Music 4028), with his soul-jazz organ trio and guest Nancy Wilson, is Henry Johnson's strongest recording to date.

**Website:** www.henryjohnsonjazz.com

# Lonnie Johnson
*b. February 8, 1899, New Orleans, LA; d. June 16, 1970, Toronto, Canada*

Of the many blues guitarist-singers who were active in the 1920s and '30s, Lonnie Johnson was the one who crossed over into the jazz world most frequently and effortlessly. He ranks with Eddie Lang as the top jazz guitarist of the 1920s even though he only played jazz on a part-time basis. Even later in his career, Johnson was occasionally heard with Dixieland groups, although he was ultimately best known as a blues singer-guitarist.

Johnson heard plenty of early jazz in his native New Orleans, learning both guitar and violin. He worked in London during 1917–19, returning home in 1919 to discover that most of his family had perished in the flu epidemic. Johnson worked on riverboats with Fate Marable and, in 1921, moved to St. Louis. While there, he worked in a steel foundry by day and played guitar, violin and piano in local clubs at night, including with Charles Creath.

In 1925, Lonnie Johnson won a talent contest sponsored by the Okeh label. That launched his recording career, and he was a constant on records for most of the next 44 years. His own recordings as a leader (which numbered over 130 selections during 1925–32 alone) were often blues and ballads, but there were also quite a few jazz-oriented instrumentals performed for variety, most notably including "6/88 Glide." Johnson's guest appearances on jazz records during 1926–29 are pretty phenomenal. He recorded with Louis Armstrong's Hot Five ("I'm Not Rough," "Savoy Blues" and trading off with Armstrong's scatting on "Hotter Than That"), Duke Ellington ("Hot And Bothered" and "The Mooche"), McKinney's Cotton Pickers, the Chocolate Dandies, Victoria Spivey, Clara Smith, Clarence Williams, and Blind Willie Dunn's Gin Bottle Four (a group that teamed Johnson with Eddie Lang, King Oliver and Hoagy Carmichael). In addition, Johnson recorded ten intriguing guitar duets with Lang (billed as "Blind Willie Dunn") on which he mostly played bluesy single-note lines that blended in perfectly with Lang's sophisticated chords.

Johnson toured with Bessie Smith in 1929. He spent part of the 1930s playing in Cincinnati with singer Putney Dandridge but otherwise spent the decade based in Chicago. Johnson kept on recording and performing throughout the Depression, usually solo or with small groups, including dates in the late 1930s with veteran clarinetists Johnny Dodds and Jimmie Noone. In 1939, he switched to the electric guitar without altering his laidback style. In 1948, he had a surprise hit with the R&B ballad "Tomorrow Night."

Johnson toured England in 1952, but by the mid-1950s, he was largely forgotten, working as a janitor at a hotel. Fortunately, he was rediscovered in 1959 by writer-disc jockey Chris Albertson, who recorded him, resulting in a comeback that was fueled by the folk music movement and the younger fans' interest in the early blues survivors. Johnson worked and recorded throughout the 1960s, made a pair of duet albums with banjoist Elmer Snowden (*Blues And Ballads* and *Blues, Ballads And Jumpin' Jazz*), had reunions with both Victoria Spivey and Duke Ellington, visited Europe, and occasionally played in jazz settings.

Lonnie Johnson moved to Toronto in 1965. His career ended in 1969 when he was hit by a car; he passed away a year later at the age of 71.

**Recommended CDs:** All of Lonnie Johnson's recordings as a leader during 1925–32 (including the duets with Lang) are on *Vols. 1–7* (Document 5063–5069). While the majority are solo blues performances, there are also quite a few that are fine examples of early jazz. In addition to his guitar work, *Vol. 1* has some rare examples of Johnson playing banjo, violin and harmonium. *Steppin' On The Blues* (Columbia 46221) is a good sampler of the early days, while *He's A Jelly Roll Baker* (Bluebird 66064) is a fine overview of the 1937–47 period, which is much more fully covered in Lonnie Johnson's *Vols. 1–3* (Document 6024–6026). *Tomorrow Night* (King 1083) and *Me And My Crazy Self* (Charly 266) have most of his recordings of 1947–52. Johnson's "comeback" years are documented on *Blues And Ballads* (Bluesville 531), *Blues, Ballads And Jumpin' Jazz* (Bluesville 570), *Losing Game* (Bluesville 543), *Another Night To Cry* (Bluesville 550), the often-Dixielandish *Stompin' At The Penny* (Columbia/Legacy 57829), *The Unsung Blues Legend* (Blues Magnet 1001), and 1967's *The Complete Folkways Recordings* (Smithsonian Folkways 40067).

## Wayne Johnson
*b. November 11, 1951, Spokane, WA*

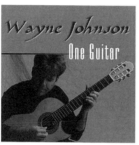

A superior guitarist, Wayne Johnson has often been heard behind the scenes, but his solo recordings are also quite rewarding. "I was eight years old and watching Elvis Presley on the *Ed Sullivan Show*. I told my dad, 'That's what I want to do!' He got me a guitar and it all started." At first he learned standards before switching to rock. At ten, Johnson won the Northwest Guitar Championship in the junior division, and the following year won in both the junior and senior divisions. Johnson was in bands all throughout school, being inspired originally by the music of the Beatles, Led Zeppelin, Cream and Jimi Hendrix. "My parents were so supportive. It still blows me away to this day that they trusted me (and the band members) to leave after school on Fridays, drive to Portland, Seattle or Missoula, Montana, with these older players, play gigs, and return on Sunday to get my homework done." In 11th and 12th grade, Johnson played guitar in his high school jazz band. He attended Spokane Falls Community College during 1971–72 before starting at Berklee (1973–74).

"My first important musical association was with Gary Burton. He was a judge at a high school jazz band three-day competition that took place in Seattle. Our high school won first place and I was awarded 'jazz soloist of the festival.' Gary presented the award to me and later in a conversation mentioned that I should go to Berklee after high school. That experience pretty much set my path. One day in my second year at Berklee, I got a call from Gary Burton, whom I was taking improv lessons from. He asked if I could sub for Steve Swallow (his bassist) in a few days, playing a workshop at the school. Gary said, 'You do play bass don't you,' as if every guitar player naturally played bass and also as if it were no

big effort to fill Steve's shoes. I studied the few tunes we were to play and actually played Steve's bass on the gig as I didn't have one."

After college, in 1977 Johnson formed a trio with bassist Jimmy Johnson and drummer Bill Berg that lasted for 20 years. His current group often uses bassist Dave Curtis and drummer Duncan Moore. Also in 1977, he became a longtime member of the Manhattan Transfer's band. Other important associations include Rickie Lee Jones, Natalie Cole, and currently Bette Midler. He also does guitar clinics for Taylor Guitars. In recent times, Wayne Johnson has played acoustic guitar, performed solo concerts, and been a record producer and an occasional guitar instructor.

"There is nothing like playing in a group where everyone is so in tune that it feels like one. If you fall, you all go down. When you rise, everyone is there with you."

**Recommended CDs:** *Grasshopper* (MoJazz 530377), *Spirit Of The Dancer* (Zebra 42228), *Keeping The Dream Alive* (MoJazz 7005), *Kindred Spirits* (GTS 531604), *Apache* (Nefer 23142) with guitarist Jeff Richman, and *One Guitar* (Solid Air 2040), which is a set of acoustic guitar solos.

**LPs to Search For:** *Arrowhead* (Inner City 1098), *Everybody's Painting Pictures* (Zebra 5003).

**Website:** waynejohnsononline.com

## Randy Johnston
*(Randolph Barksdale Johnston, Jr.)*
*b. December 5, 1956, Detroit, MI*

A top-notch straight-ahead guitarist who invigorates the hard-bop/soul-jazz tradition, Randy Johnston always swings. As with many guitarists of his generation, he took up the guitar (at the age of seven) after seeing the Beatles on *The Ed Sullivan Show*. "I was introduced to the idea of jazz through the extended soloing of rock players in the late '60s and early '70s (Hendrix, Allman Bros., etc.) then Mahavishnu and late-period Coltrane. But my real introduction to jazz was from hearing Charlie Parker's music on an album called *The Smithsonian Collection Of Jazz*." The first jazz guitarist that he listened to closely was Kenny Burrell, and another influence was Grant Green.

Johnston played gigs as a teenager around Richmond, Virginia (where he and his family moved when he was 13), mostly at high school dances, coffee houses and parties. He attended the music school at the University of Miami. After moving to New York in 1981, Johnston's first important musical association was playing with Warne Marsh during 1982–84. Since then he has worked with Lee Konitz,

Houston Person, Joey DeFrancesco, Irene Reid, Etta Jones, and since 1997 with both Lou Donaldson and Dr. Lonnie Smith.

Johnston made his first album as a leader (*Walk On*) for Muse in 1991. He has also recorded for J Curve and most often for High Note, both as a leader and as a sideman, including with Houston Person, Lou Donaldson, Jack McDuff, Etta Jones, Eddie Marshall, John DeFrancesco and Dr. Lonnie Smith. In addition to touring the US, Europe and Japan with his own trio, Randy Johnston has taught at NYU, SUNY Purchase and the University of Hartford; played with guitarist Danny Kalb (formerly with the Blues Project); and recently formed a blues/rock/jazz band with younger musicians.

**Recommended CDs:** Randy Johnston has recorded prolifically since 1991. *Walk On* (Muse 5432), *Jubilation* (Muse 5495) and *In-A-Chord* (Muse 5512) are all scarce since Muse is long defunct, but his other CDs, *Somewhere In The Night* (High Note 7007), *Riding The Curve* (J Curve 1072), *Homage* (J Curve 7010), *Detour Ahead* (High Note 7027), *Hit & Run* (High Note 7098), *Is It You* (High Note 7122), *People Music* (Random Act 4501568159), and his DVD *Live At The Smithsonian* (Mel Bay 21188), are all readily available.

**Website:** www.randyjohnston.net

## Stanley Jordan
b. July 31, 1959, Chicago, IL

The master of tapping, Stanley Jordan always has the potential to play the most amazing music. His ability to play the guitar one-handed means that he can sound like two guitarists (or a very talented keyboardist) and that he can play two guitars at once (or play guitar and one-handed piano) whenever the spirit moves him. He can play bebop with the best, but his recording career has been a bit erratic, shifting between styles with some efforts being clearly poppish.

Jordan played piano from the age of six, but after hearing Jimi Hendrix's music, he switched to guitar when he was 11. Soon he had discovered jazz and was working hard on mastering tapping. While tapping had been used to a limited degree as early as the 1920s (Jack Bland) and been utilized by Eddie Van Halen in rock, no one had mastered it to the degree

of Jordan. He attended Princeton (earning a BA in digital music composition), gigged locally, and had early opportunities to play with Dizzy Gillespie and Benny Carter when he was still an unknown.

Jordan made his recording debut in 1982 with *Touch Sensitive*, recorded for his own Tangent label. However, few listeners heard it, and he worked as a street musician in New York and Philadelphia, continuing to grow as a soloist. By the time he recorded *Magic Touch* in 1985 for Blue Note, Jordan was ready. He was immediately considered a sensation, and he should have been, for he made most other guitarists sound one-handed in comparison.

Jordan had a lower profile in the 1990s, recording on an occasional basis but with varying quality. In recent times, he has been attending Arizona State University, working toward a master's in music therapy. He still gigs regularly and is often heard with a band, and he is in excellent form interacting with other jazz greats on *Friends*, but there is nothing like hearing Stanley Jordan playing an uptempo blues unaccompanied.

**Recommended CDs:** The most rewarding (and often remarkable) recordings by the tapping master are *Magic Touch* (Blue Note 46092); *Standards Vol. One* (Blue Note 46333); *Live In New York* (Blue Note 97810); *Cornucopia* (Blue Note 92356), whose first half makes up for its tedious second half; the mostly satisfying *Stolen Moments* (Blue Note 97159); *State Of Nature* (Mack Avenue 31040) and *Friends* (Mack Avenue 1062). Do yourself a favor and skip *Flying Home* (EMI 48682), *Bolero* (BMG 46924), and *Dreams Of Peace* (Edel 63).

**LPs to Search For:** *Touch Sensitive* (Tangent 1001) is Stanley Jordan's long-elusive debut recording.

## Steve Jordan
b. January 5, 1919, New York, NY; d. September 13, 1993, Alexandria, VA

Steve Jordan, who always regarded himself as a rhythm section guitar player, was the last of the original acoustic rhythm guitarists. He did not take any solos until his later years, when he reluctantly took a few with combos. He spent his life happily making other soloists and ensembles sound very good.

Jordan considered his main influences to be Allan

Reuss (with whom he took lessons) and Reuss' earlier teacher, George Van Eps. He began his career with the Will Bradley Orchestra (1939–41), worked with Artie Shaw for four months during 1941–42, and was briefly with Teddy Powell before being drafted into the Navy. After World War II, Jordan worked with the orchestras of Bob Chester, Freddie Slack, Glen Gray, Stan Kenton (1947), Jimmy Dorsey and Boyd Raeburn.

The rhythm guitar disappeared from modern jazz along with most big bands, so Jordan became a studio musician for NBC. He was often employed for mainstream swing dates in the 1950s, appearing on sessions led by Gene Krupa, Mel Powell, Vic Dickenson, Sir Charles Thompson, Buck Clayton and Ruby Braff. Jordan worked occasionally with Benny Goodman during 1953–57, and in later years was the rhythm guitarist on records headed by Wild Bill Davison, Clancy Hayes, Buddy Tate and Ed Polcer. Although he spent a period outside of music in the early 1960s, working as a tailor, he had a regular gig with Tommy Gwaltney at Blues Alley in Washington, DC, during 1965–72. He also appeared at classic jazz and swing festivals.

Jordan, who turned down the opportunity to be Freddie Green's successor with the Count Basie Orchestra (he felt that he was too old to go out on the road), recorded his only album as a leader in 1972 for Fat Cat Jazz. Shortly before his death in 1993, he wrote his colorful memoirs, *Rhythm Man*.

**Recommended CDs:** Steve Jordan's lone album as a leader is *Here Comes Mister Jordan* (Audiophile 114).

# John Jorgenson
b. July 6, 1956, Madison, WI

What do Elton John and Django Reinhardt have in common? John Jorgenson. One of the pioneers of the gypsy-jazz movement in the US, he has had an overlapping dual career. Jorgenson began on the piano when he was five, took up the clarinet at eight, picked up the ukulele at ten, and got his first guitar when he was 12. His father was a music educator at the University of Redlands who started the jazz orchestra residence program that brought Stan Kenton and Don Ellis to Redlands. In addition to seeing those orchestras, Jorgenson remembers enjoying the big bands that appeared at Disneyland, including those of Count Basie, Woody Herman, Buddy Rich, Maynard Ferguson and Cab Calloway.

Jorgenson always had wide musical taste. "My first paying gig was playing the bassoon at a church performance of *The Messiah* at Christmastime. My first rock gig was a youth dance at our church on bass with my band, Aftermath." He earned a college degree in woodwind performance from the University of Redlands in 1978 and was on his way to mastering guitar, mandolin, bass, dobro, pedal steel guitar, bassoon, clarinet and various saxophones. His versatility, both in the instruments he played and in his musical interests, has kept Jorgenson busy ever since.

He was a member of the Desert Rose Band (1986–90), the Hellecasters (1990–2000) and Elton John's band (1995–2000). Along the way, Jorgenson has played with the Byrds, Bob Dylan, Johnny Cash, Willie Nelson, Bonnie Raitt, Bob Seger, Earl Scruggs, Barbra Streisand, Luciano Pavarotti, Sting, and Billy Joel, in addition to Benny Goodman and Louis Bellson.

While finding some fame and lots of work in the country and rock music worlds, John Jorgenson's main significance to jazz has been his strong interest in the music of Django Reinhardt. In 1988, he recorded *After You've Gone*, a CD of 1930s swing that also featured David Grisman and Darol Anger. He has performed Django's music for two feature films, *Gattaca* and *Head In The Clouds*. In the latter film, Jorgenson actually portrayed Reinhardt briefly on camera. In 2003, he formed his own swing-oriented quintet, and his 2004 CD *Franco-American Swing* was influential in the US.

"Headlining the Django Reinhardt Memorial Jazz Festival in France was definitely a high point for me, as was performing at the Montreal Jazz Festival multiple times. Sitting in with Les Paul in NYC was a lot of fun and a great honor too. For gypsy jazz, the most recent John Jorgenson Quintet CD, *One Stolen Night*, is very representative of my playing, and the orchestral *Istiqbal Gathering* showcases my composing for a larger ensemble as well as playing. I have studied and performed in many different styles over the years and love to learn the particular elements that make a style unique."

**Recommended CDs:** *After You've Gone* (Curb 77278) was John Jorgenson's first swing recording, and it still sounds brilliant. *Franco-American Swing* (JJ 7009) mostly features his colorful originals in the gypsy swing style. *One Stolen Night* (J2 37015) and *Istiqbal Gathering* (J2K 7016), the latter with the Nashville Orchestra, showcase Jorgenson's playing and writing in recent times.

**Website:** www.johnjorgenson.com

# Vic Juris
(Victor Edward Jurusz)
b. September 26, 1953, Jersey City, NJ

Vic Juris first started playing guitar when he was nine. "My dad had some Chess label recordings of Chuck Berry, also Duane Eddy and Tony Mottola. Several kids in my neighborhood played guitar in established garage bands that copied what the Ventures and Chuck Berry were playing." Juris was introduced to jazz in his lessons with Ed Berg, which led him to listen to Django Reinhardt, Johnny Smith and Barney Kessel. He also studied piano.

After graduating from high school in 1971, he decided to skip college and instead play jazz in New York. "On Pat Martino's recommendation, I joined the Don Patterson Organ Trio with Billy James on drums. I also played fusion music with pianist Barry Miles and saxophonist Eric Kloss." Juris made his recording debut with Kloss.

From that point on, he has amassed an endless number of credits playing with the greats of jazz, including Dizzy Gillespie, Phil Woods, Jimmy Smith, Sarah Vaughan, Chico Hamilton, Dave Liebman (since 1991), Mel Torme, Eddie Jefferson, Nancy Wilson, Gary Peacock, Jeremy Steig, James Moody, Charles Mariano, Lee Konitz, and Richie Cole, appearing on most of Cole's best recordings. A hard-driving but flexible bop-based player who can also play very adventurous music, Juris has teamed up on an occasional basis with other guitarists, including mid-1980s tours with Biréli Lagrène, Larry Coryell, John Abercrombie and Russell Malone. He was the musical director of the Charles Mingus Guitar Quintet, has led 20 albums of his own and has appeared on over 150 recordings as a sideman.

"I would like to tour with my trio with bassist Jay Anderson and drummer Adam Nussbaum a lot more in the future. To me, playing jazz is such a rewarding spiritual experience; it is so uplifting."

**Recommended CDs:** Vic Juris named *Omega Is The Alpha* (Steeplechase 31696) and *Blue Horizon* (Zoho 200409) as his finest recordings. *Night Tripper* (Steeplechase 31353), *Pastels* (Steeplechase 31384), *Music Of Alec Wilder* (Double Time 118), *Moonscape* (Steeplechase 31402), *Remembering Eric Dolphy* (Steeplechase 31453), *Songbook* (Steeplechase 31483), *Songbook 2* (Steeplechase 31516), *While My Guitar Gently Weeps* (Steeplechase 31553), *A Second Look* (May Bay 9782), *Journey* (Jardis 20145), and *Bohemia* (Jazz Point 1023) feature the guitarist playing a wide range of music, from John Scofield–style post-bop to standards and the superior set of Alec Wilder tunes. He is also in stimulating form on *Biréli Lagrène Ensemble Live* (Jazzpoint 1015) from 1985.

**LPs to Search For:** Vic Juris' early fusion albums, *Roadsong* (Muse 5150), *Horizon Drive* (Muse 5206), and *Bleecker Street* (Muse 5265), have not yet been reissued on CD.

**Website:** www.vicjurisjazz.com

## Henry Kaiser
*b. September 19, 1952, Oakland, CA*

Henry Kaiser, a masterful and colorful free improviser, has stretched far beyond jazz in many of his explorations. His guitar playing is difficult to classify as anything but "free." Kaiser did not take up the guitar until he was 19, in 1972. He drew his early inspiration from such unusual sources as Derek Bailey, country blues, music from Asia, Hawaiian music, 20th-century classical, and the guitarists in Captain Beefheart's Magic Band.

Kaiser has worked with Fred Frith since 1979, collaborated with the Rova Saxophone Quartet, and co-founded the Metalanguage label in 1978 with Larry Ochs of Rova. Kaiser has kept very busy since then, working on projects with artists from a wide variety of genres. In jazz, he has collaborated with such notables as Herbie Hancock, Elliott Sharp, Bill Laswell, Steve Lacy, John Abercrombie, Sonny Sharrock, John Zorn, David Torn, Bill Frisell, Joey Baron, Eugene Chadbourne, Evan Parker, John Medeski, John Tchicai, George Lewis, Kazumi Watanabe, Peter Brotzmann, and Cecil Taylor. In addition, he has led groups of his own and performed unaccompanied solos. Kaiser, who has appeared on over 140 recordings, has not only played throughout the US, Europe and Japan, but also visited Madagascar in 1991, recording six albums with local musicians. Kaiser has also been prolific as a composer and producer, scoring the weekly television series *Secrets & Mysteries*. He has produced a lengthy guitar instructional video, *Eclectic Electric: Exploring New Horizons Of Guitar And Improvisation*.

In his other career, Kaiser worked as a senior instructor in underwater scientific research at Berkeley for 15 years. He visited Antarctica for the first time in 2001, working as a research diver. His underwater camerawork has been featured in films.

Probably Henry Kaiser's most accessible jazz project has been his collaborations with trumpeter Wadada Leo Smith for *Yo Miles!*, a tribute to Miles Davis' electric fusion of the 1970s.

**Recommended CDs:** *Lemon Fish Tweezer: Solo Guitar Improvisations, 1973–1991* (Cuneiform Rune 45), *Invite The Spirit: 1983* (Tzadik 7622), *Marrying For Money* (Minor Music 1010), *Re-Marrying For Money* (SST 222), *Those Who Know History*

Are Doomed To Repeat It (SST 198), *Heart's De-sire* (Reckless 19), *Hope You Like Our New Direction* (Reckless 21), *The Five Heavenly Truths* (FOT 03193), *Eternity Blue* (Shanachie 6016), *Acoustics* (Victo 025), *Yo Miles!* (Shanachie 5046), *Yo Miles!: Sky Garden* (Cuneiform 20191), *Yo Miles!: Upriver* (Cuneiform 201/202), *Invite The Spirit: 2006* (Tzadik 7617), *Plane Crash* (UgExplode 30).

**LPs to Search For:** *Ice Death* (Parachute 005), *Outside Pleasure* (Metalanguage 111), *Protocol* (Metalanguage 102), *With Friends Like These* (Metalanguage 107), *Aloha* (Metalanguage 109), *Who Needs Enemies* (Metalanguage 123), *It's A Wonderful Life* (Metalanguage 124).

## Ryo Kawasaki
b. February 25, 1947, Tokyo, Japan

Ryo Kawasaki is best known as a major fusion guitarist—one with his own passionate sound and intense style—but he is also masterful on acoustic guitar, and a scientist at heart. Kawasaki had violin lessons for two years starting when he was five, played ukulele when he was ten, and got his first guitar at 15. "I was into audio and electronics, building my own radio, amp, speakers and turntables as a child. I needed to test the audio equipment I built, so I collected many different kinds of music and had some singles by Nat King Cole and Les Paul & Mary Ford. The first serious jazz LP I bought was *West Coast Blues* by Harold Land with Wes Montgomery."

In high school, Kawasaki was part of his school's jazz club and played his first gigs at cabarets, accompanying singers. He originally planned to become a science or physics college professor, and he earned a degree in quantum mechanics from Tokyo's Nippon University in 1969. "But I was already a professional guitarist by my late teens, taking numerous calls for gigs and studio sessions, so I abandoned that ambition." He made his recording debut as a leader and became both a sound engineer and a studio musician.

Wanting to play more creative music, in 1973 Kawasaki moved to New York. Within a few months he joined the Gil Evans Orchestra, participating on Evans' recorded tribute to Jimi Hendrix. "Gil was very kind to become a sponsor for me to obtain permanent residency in the US." Playing regularly with Evans' band at the Village Vanguard gave Kawasaki

important exposure in the United States and allowed him to become established. During 1973–78, the guitarist was especially busy. "I was the guitarist for the Gil Evans Orchestra, Chico Hamilton's band, Elvin Jones' Time Machine and many other groups, such as the New York local fusion band Tarika Blue as well as my own group. Finally, I settled with Elvin's band, since his group toured for almost ten months a year." In 1976, Kawasaki became the first Japanese jazz artist to sign with a major American label when he recorded *Juice* for RCA. He also worked with Dave Liebman and Joanne Brackeen.

Since the late 1970s, Ryo Kawasaki has primarily been a leader (including his jazz-rock group, the Golden Dragon) and used electronic rhythm sections on his recordings. He invented his own guitar synthesizer in 1979, performing at solo shows during the next few years. He has been active in other areas of music, including inventing his own music software programs for computers, forming his Satellites label, and producing popular techno dance singles (mostly during 1986–90). During 1988–93, he was the producer and director of two Japanese national weekly music radio programs. In 1991, Kawasaki returned to playing jazz more actively, including recording an acoustic solo guitar album (*Here, There And Everywhere*). In recent times, he has played duets with bassist Yoshio "Chin" Suzuki and had a trio with bassist Toivo Unt and drummer Brian Melvin, an organ trio with Tonu Naissoo, a trio with Estonian singer Jaanika Ventsel, and another trio with Syrian bassist Omar Harb and Lebanese drummer Fouad Afra.

Ryo Kawasaki remains a wide-ranging artist with equal interests in performing and the technological aspects of music. "While I love playing guitar, jazz and composing, I also love computer programming, software/web application, designing developments and sound/audio engineering."

**Recommended CDs:** Ryo Kawasaki recorded prolifically as a leader during 1976–2002, although more infrequently during the past decade. *Juice* (BMG 37366) was his American debut from 1976. *Ring Toss* (YZSO 10008); *Mirror Of My Mind* (One Voice 1004); *Little Tree* (One Voice 5); *Live* (One Voice 7); *Here, There And Everywhere* (One Voice 1001); *My Reverie* (One Voice 1005), which features the guitarist playing the music of Bill Evans, Debussy, Ravel and Gershwin; *Love Within The Universe* (One Voice 1009); *Sweet Life* (Satellites 1017); *Cosmic Rhythm* (Satellites 1030); *Reval* (Satellites 1010); *E: Relaxing Guitar Solo* (Video Arts 1042) and *Late Night Willie* (YZSO 10004) give listeners a well-rounded portrait of the guitarist. His most recent recordings are *Tribute To Keith Jarrett, Live*

*In Beirut 2011*, and a set of unaccompanied guitar solos, *Spain*. Each are available through his website.

**Website:** www.ryokawasaki.com

## Pat Kelley
*b. March 12, 1952, Tulsa, OK*

A studio guitarist and a longtime educator at USC, Pat Kelley is also a fine jazz guitarist, as can be heard on his recent *Reset* CD. "My dad had Les Paul and Chet Atkins records, which I heard early in life. My father was an amateur guitarist and he used to play with a few of his friends at home on weekends." Kelley played ukulele at four, switching to guitar at five. He had his first band while in sixth grade, performing at county fairs, and was in a variety of groups throughout his school years. Kelley studied music composition at the University of Tulsa, moving out to California after graduating. "I had gone to a Howard Roberts guitar seminar in Hollywood right after high school. I knew that I would move to Nashville, New York or L.A. I was fortunate because, after moving to Los Angeles, I seemed to meet all of the right people." Within a week of arriving in L.A., he auditioned successfully for Ronnie Laws' band, performing with Laws at Carnegie Hall three weeks later and then beginning a longtime association with Hubert Laws.

A versatile musician who also plays dobro, mandolin, banjo, bass and drums, Kelley became a studio musician, worked with several television bands, and was a member of George Benson's group for five years. "Playing with George Benson, an idol of mine, was always a thrill. We all know that when he wants, he can burn us all!"

Other associations have included David Benoit, Rick Braun, Jeff Lorber, Richard Elliot, Dave Koz, Eric Marienthal, Al Jarreau, Keiko Matsui, B.B. King, and most recently, Natalie Cole. "In general, people hire me when they are doing jazz but also want someone who can play some crossover, rock and R&B too." He has taught at USC's Thornton School of Music for the past 15 years. "I've always been a teacher. I had some guitar students when I was still in sixth and seventh grade, teaching in music stores. I tell students, to get really good, you have to really love playing."

Pat Kelley's most recent recording, *Reset*, is boppish. On that CD, he performs in an organ trio with Joe Bagg, in a different pianoless trio, and as an unaccompanied soloist, also taking two vocals along the way. "I grew up wanting to play straight-ahead jazz. So after my first few recordings, in the early 1990s I made a commitment to return to that type of playing, developing more of a jazz guitar sound rather than

an overdrive sound—not as fusion-oriented. I look forward to performing solo more often in the future and conducting more clinics."

**Recommended CDs:** In his nine releases as a leader, *Views Of The Future* (Nova 8704), *I'll Stand Up* (Nova 8915), *High Heels* (Denon 73764), *The Road Home* (Positive 7018), *Good News* (ID Net 0004), *Moonlight Dance* (Award 80006), *3 Guitars Live At The Jazz Bakery* with John Stowell and Frank Potenza, *In The Moment*, and most recently *Reset* (the latter three CDs for his Artsong label), Pat Kelley has evolved from playing fusion and crossover to more of a straight-ahead direction.

**Website:** www.patkelley.com

## Barney Kessel
*b. October 17, 1923, Muskogee, OK, May 6, 2004, San Diego, CA*

Although many guitarists were strongly influenced by Charlie Christian in the 1940s and '50s, Barney Kessel was the first to develop his own significant voice out of the Christian style. Like Christian, Kessel was from Oklahoma. Other than three months of lessons, Kessel was self-taught on guitar. He gained early experience playing with local swing groups. After moving to Los Angeles in 1942, he worked with the Chico Marx Big Band (1942–43), which was a group organized by Ben Pollack. Discovered by Norman Granz, Kessel was featured in the Lester Young short film *Jammin' The Blues* in 1944. He worked with the orchestras of Charlie Barnet (1944–45) and Artie Shaw, also playing with Shaw's Gramercy Five.

After the Shaw period, Kessel became a studio musician in Los Angeles while also playing bop-oriented jazz at night. He recorded with Charlie Parker in 1947, toured with Jazz at the Philharmonic, and during 1952–53 was a member of the Oscar Peterson Trio. While he left Peterson after a year to stick close to the studios, Kessel recorded his most significant recordings in the 1950s, leading a string of very rewarding albums for Contemporary. While he remained a boppish soloist, the settings ranged from swing to West Coast jazz. An additional series of recordings teamed him with Ray Brown and Shelly Manne as the Poll Winners, since they often won the *Downbeat* and *Metronome* polls of the era. Kessel also recorded with Art Tatum and Sonny Rollins.

Kessel remained prominent on the scene during the next few decades. He appeared on many pop recordings including with the Monkees and the Beach Boys, often creating well-known solos anonymously. He toured with George Wein's Newport All-Stars in 1968 and teamed up with Stéphane Grappelli on several occasions during 1969–70. While his later recordings as a leader generally lack the excitement and enthusiasm of his earlier dates, Barney Kessel still sounded at his most fiery when performing with Herb Ellis and Charlie Byrd as the Great Guitars during 1974–82.

A major stroke put an end to Barney Kessel's career in 1992, 12 years before his death.

**Recommended CDs:** *Vol. 1: Easy Like* (Original Jazz Classics 153), *Vol. 2: Kessel Plays Standards* (Original Jazz Classics 238): *Vol. 3: To Swing Or Not To Swing* (Original Jazz Classics 317), *Music To Listen To Barney Kessel By* (Original Jazz Classics 746), *Let's Cook* (Original Jazz Classics 1010), *Kessel Plays Carmen* (Original Jazz Classics 269), *Some Like It Hot* (Original Jazz Classics 168), *Swinging Party At Contemporary* (Original Jazz Classics 1066), and *Workin' Out* (Original Jazz Classics 970), all recorded during 1953–61, are the most essential Barney Kessel records. His work with Ray Brown and Shelly Manne is available as *The Poll Winners* (Original Jazz Classics 156), *The Poll Winners Ride Again* (Original Jazz Classics 607), *Poll Winners Three* (Original Jazz Classics 692), *The Poll Winners: Exploring The Scene* (Original Jazz Classics 969) and *The Poll Winners: Straight Ahead* (Original Jazz Classics 409), with the first four CDs dating from 1957–60 and the *Straight Ahead* CD being a reunion date from 1975. The best of Kessel's later albums— which include *Autumn Leaves* (Black Lion 760112), *Limehouse Blues* (Black Lion 760158), *Feeling Free* (Original Jazz Classics 1043), *Yesterday* (Black Lion 760183), *Two Way Conversation* (Emarcy 814885), *Just Friends* (Sonet 685), *Barney Kessel & Friends* (Concord 6009), *Soaring* (Concord 6033), *Poor Butterfly* (Concord 4034), *Live At Sometime* (Storyville 4157), *Jellybeans* (Concord 4164), *Solo* (Concord 4221), *Spontaneous Combustion* (Contemporary 14033) and *Red Hot And Blues* (Contemporary 14044)—is *Limehouse Blues*, since it co-features Stéphane Grappelli. Also of strong interest are the recordings of the Great Guitars: *Great Guitars* (Concord 6004), *Great Guitars II* (Concord 4023), *Straight Tracks* (Concord 4421), *Great Guitars At The Winery* (Concord 4131), and *Great Guitars At Charlie's Georgetown* (Concord 4209).

## Steve Khan
*(Steven Harris Cahn)*
*b. April 28, 1947, Los Angeles, CA*

A brilliant guitarist who initially became known for his playing in fusion but is quite well-rounded, many of Steve Khan's projects fit more into the unclassifiable area of post-bop. The son of lyricist Sammy Cahn, he studied piano for seven years starting when he was five, and also played drums with the instrumental surf group the Chantays. "Jazz was always around in my home, as my father loved to hear recordings of any and all versions of his songs. I recall Bob Spickard, Chantays' guitarist, introducing me to the Jazz Crusaders' *Tough Talk* and Wes Montgomery's *Boss Guitar*. But it was years later, when I purchased Wes Montgomery's *Movin' Wes* and heard 'Caravan,' that I knew I would never be a drummer on the level of a Grady Tate."

At 17, he switched to guitar and was soon playing gigs in the Los Angeles area. "Through an unexpected set of circumstances and my working with the R&B group the Friends of Distinction, I ended up playing and recording with keyboardist Phil Moore, Jr. That led me to playing on Wilton Felder's solo LP, *Bullitt*. I couldn't believe that I was doing something with one of the Jazz Crusaders, one of my heroes."

Khan graduated from UCLA in 1969 with a BA in composition and theory. "My father tried to guide me away from the possible existential pain of artistic mediocrity and toward a life as a lawyer. But of course, I didn't and wouldn't listen to that." After having played with vibraphonist David Friedman and bassist John Miller while on a gig with Tim Buckley, Khan was invited to come to New York during the summer of 1969, playing for a few weeks at the Music Inn. He soon moved there permanently.

A member of the Brecker Brothers by 1971, Khan performed acoustic duets with Larry Coryell during 1974–75. "Bob James and Bobby Colomby, who signed me to Columbia Records in 1977, gave me the opportunity when no one else seemed to see or hear something in me. On my first recordings as a leader, *Tightrope*, *The Blue Man* and *Arrows*, I was trying to single-handedly keep alive the sound of the original Brecker Brothers Band.

"It is interesting to note that, at one point in time in the 1970s, in or near the Chelsea area of Manhattan, the following guitarists (all friends) lived within a few blocks of one another: John McLaughlin, Ralph Towner, John Abercrombie, Bill Connors, John Scofield, and me. I would run into those guys on the street or in the markets."

Since that time, Khan recorded a solo guitar set highlighted by a lengthy Thelonious Monk medley

(*Evidence*); founded and played with Eyewitness (a quartet with electric bassist Anthony Jackson, drummer Steve Jordan and percussionist Manolo Badrena) during 1981–85; toured with Joe Zawinul's Weather Update in 1986; worked with a variety of trios, including Ron Carter and Al Foster, during 1991–92; and was with Dave Samuels' Caribbean Jazz Project during 1999–2002. Steve Khan has appeared as a guest on many dates, with everyone from Miles Davis to Steps Ahead, Gil Evans to Freddie Hubbard, in addition to leading his own bands.

**Recommended CDs:** *The Collection* (Sony 57907) is a compilation drawn from Steve Khan's three Columbia albums. *Evidence* (Novus 3074) has Khan as the only performer. While some of the songs utilize his overdubbed guitars ("In A Silent Way" has eight), a nine-song, 18-1/2 minute Thelonious Monk medley is purely solo. *Eyewitness* (Antilles 48821) and *Casa Loco* (Antilles 48822) are by Eyewitness in the early 1980s. *Local Colour* (Denon 81757) is a popular duet set by Khan and pianist Rob Mounsey; they came back together a decade later for *You Are Here* (Siam 50004). *Public Access* (GRP 9599) is a 1989 reunion of Eyewitness with Dave Weckl in Jordan's place. *Let's Call This* (Bluemoon 79168) and most of *Headline* (Bluemoon 79179) find Khan playing primarily straight-ahead jazz in a trio with Ron Carter and Al Foster. *Crossings* (Polygram 523269), which features Michael Brecker, was dedicated to the recently deceased Sammy Cahn. *Got My Mental* (Escapade 36992) matches Khan with John Patitucci and Jack DeJohnette, playing challenging post-bop jazz. *The Green Field* (Tone Center 4004) from 2005 has the same group plus percussionist Manolo Badrena stretching out on standards and originals. 2007's *Borrowed Time* (Escapade 37172) finds Khan welcoming Bob Mintzer and Randy Brecker to the group on some numbers, while *The Suitcase* (Escapade 37222), a two-CD set, consists of previously unreleased performances by Steve Khan, Anthony Jackson and Dennis Chambers from 1994. *Parting Shot* (Tone Center 4070) is his first Latin jazz recording.

**Website:** www.stevekhan.com

# Mark Kleinhaut
*b. April 6, 1957, New York, NY*

Mark Kleinhaut plays hard-bop and post-bop jazz with his own sound and conception. "My older sister had a little folk guitar she bought with S&H Green Stamps. I absconded with it when I was nine, screwed a Radio Shack clip microphone to its top, and plugged it into our home stereo—my first electric guitar! Around 12, I started playing one-chord jams with my friends." Kleinhaut primarily played

rock as a teenager. "But when I heard the likes of Mahavishnu, Return to Forever and Weather Report, it changed everything for me. The virtuosity, extended compositions and interaction of the musicians was overwhelming—pure magic to behold. I couldn't imagine anything beyond this. Inevitably, I learned that all of these magicians had a common link: Miles Davis. I then worked backwards from Miles' electric groups to Trane and Bird, branching out to everyone and everything jazz."

While attending Rutgers, Kleinhaut was inspired by his teacher Ted Dunbar. "He showed me how the guitar was unique among all musical instruments, like a slide rule that could map out the melodies laid atop harmonic structures with horizontal and vertical axis. He imparted that it wasn't about the notes, rather that it was the 'touch' upon the instrument that would make the guitar speak." Kleinhaut also took master classes from Jim Hall and Pat Martino. After graduating from Rutgers in 1979, he took an unusual career path and became a banker while continuing to play guitar in clubs in Burlington, Vermont. "We played the usual standards and then, when we thought nobody was paying attention, we would play some completely free stuff. It was amazing. Apparently, a restaurant crowd can or will tolerate just about anything as long as it's not too loud."

Kleinhaut lived in the Portland, Maine area during the 1990s up to 2006. He eventually gave up his banking career, becoming a faculty member of the University of Southern Maine. He often performed with the Orion Ensemble, a quintet with alto flugelhornist Scott Reeves and pianist Scott Oakley that emphasized original compositions, and he also led his own trio with which he recorded for the Invisible Music label. As president of the Maine Jazz Alliance for three years, Kleinhaut brought in many major players to Southern Maine and worked on introducing kids to jazz. As a member of a local house band, he had opportunities to work with Greg Abate, Jerry Bergonzi and Alex Foster.

Mark Kleinhaut moved with his wife Erika to Cleveland in 2006. Since his move, he has had opportunities to play with the Cleveland Orchestra whenever they need a guitarist, and has maintained a higher visibility on the jazz scene while continuing to go his own way.

**Recommended CDs:** *Amphra* (Invisible Music 2005), *Secrets Of Three* (Invisible Music 2021), *Chasing Tales* (Invisible Music 2024) with guest Tiger Okoshi, *Balance Of Light* (Invisible Music 2031) with Bobby Watson, and *Holding The Center* (Invisible 2035) put the spotlight on Mark Kleinhaut's playing, his compositions and his regularly working trio.

**Website:** www.markkleinhaut.com

## Earl Klugh
*b. September 16, 1954, Detroit, MI*

His music has been called pop/jazz, crossover, fusion and smooth. But in reality, Earl Klugh is a melodic acoustic guitarist with a pretty tone. He has often said that he does not consider himself a jazz player and that his main influence is Chet Atkins. Klugh began studying piano when he was three, switching to guitar when he was ten. He started his career early, making an appearance on a Yusef Lateef album when he was just 15. At 17 in 1971, his playing on George Benson's *White Rabbit* album put him on the map. Klugh toured with Benson in 1973 and, in what must have been a classic case of miscasting, was briefly in Return to Forever in 1974, following Bill Connors and preceding Al Di Meola. No recordings resulted from this stint, making one wonder what it sounded like.

Klugh found his niche with his series of recordings from the mid-1970s through the 1980s. He generally stuck close to the poppish melodies that he interpreted, showing taste but not much adventure in his playing. While his collaborations with Bob James included such popular albums as *One On One*, *Two Of A Kind* and, more recently, *Cool*, his finest recordings were generally his unaccompanied sets (such as *Solo Guitar*) or trio outings in which he played superior standards.

Having found his own sound and style early on, Earl Klugh has remained consistent throughout his career, retaining his popularity, performing regularly at jazz festivals, and playing predictable but often pleasing music.

**Recommended CDs:** The guitarist has led many CDs in his career, including *Earl Klugh* (EMI 46553), *Living Inside Your Love* (Blue Note 48385), *Finger Paintings* (Blue Note 48386), *Magic In Your Eyes* (Blue Note 48389), *Heart String* (Blue Note 23546), *Dream Come True* (EMI 48388), *Crazy For You* (EMI 48357), *Low Ride* (Capitol 46007), *Wishful Thinking* (Mosaic Contemporary 5008), *Soda Fountain Shuffle* (Warner Bros. 25262), *Nightsongs* (Mosaic Contemporary 5007), *Life Stories* (Warner Bros. 25478), *Whispers And Promises* (Warner Bros. 25902), *Midnight In San Juan* (Warner Bros. 26293), *Sounds And Visions Vol. 2* (Warner Bros. 45158), *Move* (Warner Bros. 45596), *Sudden Burst Of Energy* (Warner Bros. 45884), *The Journey* (Warner

Bros. 46471), *Peculiar Situation* (BMG 37567), and *The Spice Of Life* (Koch 4500). The ones to acquire for those who enjoy quiet background guitar playing melodic versions of standards are *Late Night Guitar* (Blue Note 98573), *Solo Guitar* (Warner Bros. 26018), *The Earl Klugh Trio Vol. 1* (Warner Bros. 26750) and *Naked Guitar* (Koch 9949).

**Website:** www.earlklugh.com

## Dave Koonse
*b. August 26, 1937, St. Joseph, MO*

A lyrical guitarist who has played on many sessions in the Los Angeles area, Dave Koonse has been a reliable player for quite a few decades. Koonse's father played guitar, steel guitar and piano although not professionally. "We always had all kinds of music instruments around. When I was four, my father bought me a Martin four-string guitar and taught me a few chords so I could accompany him. I also sang and accompanied myself on the radio and in church." He was inspired not only by his father but also by Western swing guitarist Jack Rivers.

After moving with his family to Los Angeles in 1951, Koonse became familiar with jazz and began playing at clubs while in high school with his friend bassist Putter Smith. He also worked in a trio with guitarist Dennis Budimir and bassist Chuck Berghofer. "It was a great time for me to learn the fundamentals and also an opportunity to play with a lot of seasoned musicians." He studied with Howard Roberts when he was 15. "I became aware of players like Jimmy Wyble, Barney Kessel, Tal Farlow, Jimmy Raney, Johnny Smith and George Van Eps. I listened to them at every opportunity."

Koonse attended Los Angeles City College during 1955–56, earning his degree at Cal State L.A. a decade later. He worked with the Harry James Orchestra during 1957–60. "We played six months out of the year in Las Vegas at the Flamingo Hotel and the rest of the year on the road, traveling on a bus. Joe Pass was playing downtown at the Fremont Hotel. Joe and I would play every night after we got off our gigs."

He also worked with the Chico Hamilton Quintet in 1960 and Red Norvo in 1965, and he was a member of the George Shearing Quintet during 1967–70. Otherwise, Dave Koonse has primarily played in the Los Angeles area, both at nightclubs and in the studios. Among his favorite projects were recording with his son Larry Koonse, working with the Phil Norman Tentet in recent times, and playing with the late Stacy Rowles, Roger Neumann, Gary Foster, Richard Simon and Putter Smith. For the future, he says, "I'd like to do a vocal CD. I've sung all my life, and when I play, I always think of the words. I would also love to do another CD with my son Larry."

**Recommended CDs:** Surprisingly, Dave Koonse has never led his own record date, although he was co-leader with his son on the 1978 LPs *Father And Son Jazz Guitars* (Dobre 1035) and *Son Of Jazz Guitar* (Dobre 1048). Years later, they teamed up for the 1997 CD *Dialogues Of The Heart* (Jazz Compass 1005). Koonse has also recorded with Gary Foster, Madeline Vergari, Dick Cary, Phil Norman, Betty O'Hara and George Shearing.

## Larry Koonse
b. July 11, 1961, San Diego, CA

Larry Koonse is a versatile guitarist who often plays harmonically adventurous solos. While connected to the bebop tradition, he has also performed in very modern settings, always sounding comfortable and relaxed. The son of Dave Koonse, he started studying guitar at seven. "My father had taken me to see Andrés Segovia and that was it for me. Dad was always playing the music of Bill Evans, Miles Davis, Stan Getz, etc., so the sound was in my ear. There was an amazing jazz program at Eagle Rock High School (a six-year school) under the direction of John Rinaldo. Once I connected with other kids my age that were doing the same thing, I really got the desire to dig in." While he was still in high school, he played in a quartet with bassist Herbie Lewis and Billy Higgins, and when he was 15, he made his recording debut on an album co-led by Dave Koonse, already sounding impressive. He attended USC and, in 1984, was the university's first recipient of a bachelor's of music in jazz studies.

After graduation, Koonse began a six-year period touring as a member of the John Dankworth Quartet, accompanying Cleo Laine. Some of his favorite musical associations since that time include playing with Warne Marsh in duo and quartet formats in 1987, Karrin Allyson, the John Patitucci Trio of 2007–08 (with Brian Blade), a trio with Tom Warrington and Joe LaBarbera, Billy Childs' Jazz Chamber Sextet, and (since 1994) the L.A. Jazz Quartet. Koonse has toured and in many cases recorded with Mel Torme, Bob Brookmeyer, David Friesen, Luciana Souza, Natalie Cole, Lee Konitz, Alan Broadbent,

Ray Brown, Toots Thielemans and Charlie Haden, plus an unusual trio with Tierney Sutton and Hubert Laws. In addition, Larry Koonse has been a faculty member at the California Institute of the Arts since 1990. He is the co-founder of the Jazz Compass label along with Clay Jenkins, Tom Warrington and Joe LaBarbera.

"Jazz is about finding a new journey each time. There are always surprises and you never stop learning and growing."

**Recommended CDs:** Larry Koonse has recorded extensively since the mid-1980s. His albums as a leader and co-leader include *Three Play* (Nine Winds 0133), *Storybook* (Jazz Compass 1013) with Darek Oles, and a tribute to the music of Jimmy Wyble, *What's In The Box* (Jazz Compass 1016). He also teamed up with his father in 2003 for *Dialogues Of The Heart* (Jazz Compass 1005). With the L.A. Jazz Quartet, Koonse has recorded *Astarte* (GOWI 13), *Look To The East* (Naxos Jazz 86009), *Family Song* (Not Two 705) and *Conversation Piece* (Naxos Jazz 86045). In addition, Koonse has recorded as a sideman with a long list of artists, including Cleo Laine, Bob Sheppard, Clay Jenkins, Mel Torme, Bill Perkins, Steve Houghton, Terry Trotter, David Sills, Ray Brown, Warne Marsh, Andy Martin, Tom Warrington, Terry Gibbs, Bob Brookmeyer, Bob Florence's Limited Edition, the Phil Norman Tentet, Jack Nimitz, Charlie Haden, Cheryl Bentyne, Billy Childs, David Friesen, Brian Swartz, Diane Hubka, Bobby Shew, Mike Fahn, Ron Kalina, Robin McKelle, Paul Gormley, Luciana Souza, Angela Hagenbach and Calabria Foti.

**LPs to Search For:** Larry and Dave Koonse recorded together on *Father And Son Jazz Guitars* (Dobre 1035) and *Son Of Jazz Guitar* (Dobre 1048) in 1977.

## Wayne Krantz
b. July 26, 1956, Corvallis, OR

Throughout his career, Wayne Krantz's playing has drawn equally from both jazz and rock. While one could call him a leading fusion player, he does not fall simply into one style. After first hearing the Beatles when he was 14, Krantz took up the guitar. He played in rock and country groups before discovering some jazz recordings in his father's record collection, particularly enjoying the playing of Barney Kessel.

Krantz's first significant musical jobs were playing with the D Sharp Group in Boston (a band that included Bill Frisell) and touring with Carla Bley. Early on, he formed a longtime musical relationship with Leni Stern, with whom he recorded the acoustic album *Separate Cages* in 1996. Krantz started recording as a leader in 1991 and became known as a major fusion guitarist who often performed at the 55 Bar in New York. While his first important trio included bassist Lincoln Goines and drummer Zach Danziger, later in the 1990s he put together his long-term trio with electric bassist Tim Lefebvre and drummer Keith Carlock.

Mostly heard as a leader during the past 15 years, Wayne Krantz has also worked with Michael Brecker, Billy Cobham, Steely Dan and Chris Potter, sounding very individual in every setting.

**Recommended CDs:** *Signals* (Enja 79642), *Long To Be Loose* (Enja 7099), *2 Drink Minimum* (Enja 9043), *Separate Cages* (Alchemy 1007), *Greenwich Mean, Your Basic Live, Your Basic Live '06* (the latter three CDs are privately issued and made available from the guitarist's website), *Krantz Carlock Lefebvre* (Abstract Logix 18) and *Howie 61* (Abstract Logix 2012). Krantz has also been a sideman on recordings led by his wife, singer Gabriela Anders, as well as by David Binney, Leni Stern, Victor Bailey, Michael Formanek, Harvie Swartz, Jasper van't Hof, Jay Anderson, Nguyen Le, Chris Potter, and Michael Leonhart.

**Website:** www.waynekrantz.com

## Jonathan Kreisberg
*b. June 10, 1972, New York, NY*

A virtuoso on the guitar, Jonathan Kreisberg has the ability to play both straight-ahead jazz and fusion with equal credibility. He grew up in Florida and picked up the guitar at ten. "I started playing guitar after hearing Eddie Van Halen's 'Eruption.'" Although he loved listening to jazz, Kreisberg did not see a place for the guitar in jazz at the time and instead played with a rock band while studying classical music, performing Bach recitals. In high school, when he started hearing the recordings of Pat Martino, Pat Metheny, Allan Holdsworth, Jim Hall and John Scofield, he had a revelation. "It all started making sense, and I feel like I found my direction in combining a passion for the jazz tradition with my other experiences and influences." He developed so quickly that he gained some early recognition in print from *Downbeat* and *Guitar Player* while still in high school.

Kreisberg attended the New World School of the Arts and the University of Miami (1991–94). He spent a few years gaining experience with local groups ranging from the New World Symphony to the rock group Third Wish and his own jazz trio. Kreisberg made his recording debut in 1995. In 1997,

he moved to New York. "My first important gigs were leading my own bands. It wasn't until later that I had important gigs as a sideman. I was pretty focused on my own idea of music." He has worked with Lee Konitz, Lenny White, bassist Jeff Andrews, Greg Tardy, Joel Frahm, Joe Locke, Jane Monheit, Ari Hoenig and Dr. Lonnie Smith. Kreisberg has led several groups of his own including trios with drummer Mark Ferber and either organist Gary Versace or bassist Matt Penham, appearing in Europe and Japan. He performs with his trio each Wednesday night at La Lanterna in Greenwich Village.

"Hopefully, someday my music will send a message to Bird, Monk and Miles, saying, 'We are so thankful, inspired, and in awe. Respectfully, we'll try and learn from your ideas, take it our own way, and maybe you'll get a kick out of it, wherever you are.'"

**Recommended CDs:** *Jonathan Kreisberg Trio* (Batboy 2); *Trioing* (a set of standards that was privately released); *Nine Stories Wide* (Criss Cross 1244); *New For New* (Criss Cross 1266); *Unearth* (Mel Bay 9812), which features Kreisberg's originals; *The South Of Everywhere* (Mel Bay 10452); the ballad album *Night Songs* (Criss Cross 1310) and *Shadowless* (Abstract Logix 21); with Dr. Lonnie Smith: *Spiral* (Palmetto 2142).

**Website:** www.jonathankreisberg.com

## Carl Kress
*b. October 20, 1907, Newark, NJ; d. June 10, 1965, Reno, NV*

A guitarist with very advanced chord voicings who loved to play guitar duets, Carl Kress spent most of his career in the studios, but his occasional contributions to jazz were always notable. Kress spent the early part of his career in Eddie Lang's shadow. His first instrument was piano before he learned banjo. By the time he joined Paul Whiteman's orchestra in 1926, he was a guitarist, with banjo just being a rare double. Kress was not with Whiteman long, for he was soon busy recording with a countless number of largely anonymous studio orchestras, often when Lang was not available. Among his more notable early recordings were sessions with Red Nichols (mostly during 1927–29), Miff Mole, Boyd Senter, the Cotton Pickers, the All-Star Orchestra, and the Dorsey Brothers (1928–30 and 1932). Kress crossed paths on a few occasions with Bix Beiderbecke and Frankie Trumbauer, being part of their Chicago Loopers session and, in 1928, recording "Mississippi Mud" and "San" (the latter under Whiteman's name). In the 1930s, he emerged for sessions with the Boswell Sisters, Hoagy Carmichael (1934), Adrian Rollini,

Frankie Trumbauer (1936) and Toots Mondello (1939). But most of the time, Kress was well buried in large ensembles.

However, some of the other exceptions were rather stunning. In 1932, Kress recorded a pair of brilliant guitar duets with Eddie Lang ("Pickin' My Way" and "Feeling My Way") on which his chords interacted perfectly with Lang's single-note lines. In 1934 and 1937, Kress cut four guitar duets with Dick McDonough ("Danzon," "Stage Fright," "Chicken A La Swing," and "Heat Wave") that are tightly arranged but also let the individual personalities of the two guitarists shine through. An additional duet from a radio show, "I've Got A Feeling You're Fooling," has also been released. During 1938–39, Kress recorded five sophisticated unaccompanied guitar solos ("Peg Leg Shuffle, "Helena," "Love Song," "Sutton Mutton" and the three movements of "Afterthoughts"). And in 1941, he performed ten guitar duets with Tony Mottola that were released as radio transcriptions.

Taken as a whole, Carl Kress' solos and duets form quite a legacy, although they have only been influential on relatively few guitarists, such as Bucky Pizzarelli, John Pizzarelli and Marty Grosz, and were eventually overshadowed by Charlie Christian and Django Reinhardt. With the premature deaths of Eddie Lang and Dick McDonough, Kress should have had much of the field to himself in the 1930s, but he remained little known to the general public, mostly working in the studios. He was a co-owner of the Onyx Club on 52nd Street in the mid-1930s, played some Dixieland dates in the mid-1940s with Muggsy Spanier, Pee Wee Russell and Bobby Hackett, and produced a few records for the Capitol label. There was also a 1958 album of unaccompanied solos for the Music Minus One label.

During 1961–65, Kress had a higher profile than he had during the past 30 years, teaming up with George Barnes as a guitar duo. They appeared at a recorded Town Hall concert and came out with a few albums together, including one in which tenor-saxophonist Bud Freeman made the group a trio on a few selections. Carl Kress, whose unique style was unchanged from the 1930s, died of a heart attack during a tour in 1965 at the age of 57.

**Recommended CDs:** *Pioneers Of Jazz Guitar* (Challenge 79015) contains a dozen small-group features for Eddie Lang during 1927–28, the two remarkable Kress-Lang duets, the four Kress-McDonough studio duets, and all of Carl Kress' solos of 1938–39. Much more difficult to find will be *Two Guitars And A Horn* (Jass 636), which has many delightful Kress-Barnes duets from 1962 plus the selections with Bud Freeman.

**LPs to Search For:** *Fun On The Frets* (Yazoo 1061) has the ten intriguing Kress-Mottola duets of 1941. In addition to repeating two of Kress' 1939 solos and "Danzon," it contains the 1936 radio duet of Kress and McDonough on "I've Got A Feeling You're Fooling" plus a George Van Eps studio session from 1949.

## Julian Lage
*b. December 25, 1987, Santa Rosa, CA*

Julian Lage started his career fast as a child prodigy and has been consistently impressive ever since. He began on the guitar when he was five, first performed in public at six, and two years later, played with Carlos Santana. He was the subject of a 1997 documentary, *Jules At Eight*, which was nominated for an Academy Award. Lage made his recording debut as a duo with David Grisman on *Dawg Duos* in 1999 when he was 11. The following year, he recorded "In A Sentimental Mood" with Grisman and Martin Taylor. He also worked while still very young with Pat Metheny, Kenny Werner and Toots Thielemans, and he became a member of the teaching staff at the Stanford Jazz Workshop when he was 15.

Lage was classically trained at the San Francisco Conservatory of Music and has studied at Sonoma State University, the Ali Akbar College of Music, and Berklee. He recorded two albums with Gary Burton during 2004–05, and worked with Herbie Hancock, Christian McBride, Nnenna Freelon, Béla Fleck, Gretchen Parlato, Mark O'Connor's Hot Swing Trio, and Taylor Eigsti. In 2009, he recorded his debut album as a leader, *Sounding Point*.

Julian Lage, who is still just 25 at the time of this writing, has unlimited potential.

**Recommended CDs:** *Sounding Point* (Emarcy 1266602), on which he displays the influence of Pat Metheny and Jim Hall in spots, and *Gladwell* (Emarcy 602527656601). He is also prominent on Gary Burton's *Generations* (Concord 2217) and *Next Generation* (Concord 2277) and on Taylor Eigsti's *Lucky To Be Me* (Concord 2299) and *Let It Come To You* (Concord 30330).

**Website:** www.julianlage.com

## Biréli Lagrène
*b. September 4, 1966, Soufflenheim, France*

When Biréli Lagrène emerged as a 13-year-old guitar virtuoso on his recording debut, *Routes To Django*, in 1980, it was a remarkable event. Somehow, the young teenager was able to sound exactly like Django Reinhardt, not by merely re-creating his recorded solos but by living each note, mastering the style and sound and improvising just like Django. He has since lived up to his enormous potential.

Lagrène was born to a gypsy family that included a father who played violin and guitar and a grandfather who was a guitarist. Lagrène began playing the guitar when he was four. By the time he was eight, he was playing credible versions of Django Reinhardt's repertoire. After his recording debut, Lagrène continued in the Reinhardt style for a few more years, meeting and playing with Stéphane Grappelli. In the mid-1980s, he began to search and develop his own voice. He switched to electric guitar, explored fusion, recorded with Jaco Pastorius, performed with Al Di Meola and Larry Coryell, and largely hid the Django influence for a time. Lagrène also explored jazz standards of the hard-bop era, documented originals, and showed that he was a top-notch modern jazz player.

As he progressed through his thirties, Lagrène returned to the gypsy-jazz style on a regular basis, both emulating Reinhardt closely at tribute concerts and displaying his own voice in the style, feeling free to stretch himself beyond swing whenever it seemed right. In 2002, he formed the Gipsy Project. At the 2006 Montreal Jazz Festival, he performed a stunning set in a trio with organist Joey DeFrancesco.

It seems clear that no matter what musical path Biréli Lagrène may choose on a given night, he is one of the most gifted guitarists in the world.

**Recommended CDs:** *Routes To Django* (Jazz Point 1003) is as wondrous now as it was in 1980. Also in the vintage style from early in his career are *Biréli Swing '81* (Jazz Point 1009), *15* (Antilles 848 814), and *A Tribute To Django Reinhardt* (Jazz Point 1061). Lagrène's middle period, in which he ventured into both fusion and modern jazz, can be heard on *Live With Vic Juris* (In-Akustik 865), *Stuttgart Aria* (Jazz Point 1019), *Lagrène And Guests* (In-Akustik 8610) with Larry Coryell and Miroslav Vitous, *Inferno* (Blue Note 48016), *Foreign Affairs* (Blue Note 90967), *Acoustic Moments* (Blue Note 95263), *Standards* (Blue Note 80251), *Live In Marciac* (Dreyfus 36567), *My Favorite Django* (Dreyfus 36574), and *Blue Eyes* (Dreyfus 36591). His more recent work, mostly updated swing except for the modernistic *Electric Side*, are best represented by *Gypsy Project* (Dreyfus 36626), *Move* (Dreyfus 36668), *Djangology* (FDM 36696), *Solo: To Bi Or Not To Bi* (FDM 36697), *Just The Way You Are* (Dreyfus 36908), *Electric Side* (Dreyfus 36922) and *Gipsi Trio* (Dreyfus 36927).

## Nappy Lamare
*(Joseph Hilton Lamare)*
*b. June 14, 1905, New Orleans, LA; d. May 8, 1988, Newhall, CA*

A regular with the Bob Crosby Orchestra and the Crosby Bob Cats, Nappy Lamare was an underrated soloist, a fine rhythm guitarist and a humorous novelty singer. Born and raised in New Orleans, he was given the lifelong nickname of "Nappy" by his childhood friend tenor-saxophonist Eddie Miller due to his curly hair. Lamare first became interested in jazz when he heard Louis Armstrong playing in a New Orleans marching band. After an unsuccessful period on the trumpet, at 13 he switched to banjo and developed so quickly that within a month he was playing with the Midnight Serenaders. As a teenager, Lamare worked with Sharkey Bonano, Monk Hazel and Johnny Wiggs. He toured with Johnny Bayersdorffer's band for a few months in California in 1925 and also briefly visited Chicago and New York. Back home, as a member of the New Orleans Owls, he made his recording debut in 1927. When work became scarce in 1930 (by then he was mostly heard on guitar), Lamare moved to New York, recording with Red Nichols and joining the Ben Pollack Orchestra. Lamare's vocalizing (heard on Pollack's recording of "Two Tickets To Georgia") and wit made him a popular attraction with the band.

After Pollack broke up the orchestra in late 1934, Bob Crosby became its new leader. Although a swing orchestra, the Bob Crosby Orchestra also featured some Dixieland tunes, and its small group the Bob-cats performed some of the best New Orleans jazz of the era. Lamare was with Crosby during 1935–42, appearing on virtually all of the big band and combo recordings and in seven films with the orchestra. While he was rarely heard taking a guitar solo, his good-humored vocals were a major contrast to the straight singing of Crosby. He also recorded in 1935 with Red McKenzie's Mound City Blue Blowers, taking eight vocals.

**Eddie Lang**

When Crosby broke up his orchestra, Lamare moved to California, recording regularly for the Capitol label, including with Eddie Miller and Wingy Manone. He led the Louisiana Levee Loungers, which included some Crosby alumni and made a few records. With saxophonists Doc Rando and Noni Bernardi in 1947, Lamare bought the Club 47 nightclub, which lasted for five years.

Although Lamare was with Jimmy Dorsey during part of 1948, he mostly played Dixieland during the remainder of his life. In the late 1940s, he led Nappy Lamare's Straw Hat Strutters, which played in local clubs, appeared in the film *Hollywood Rhythm*, and was featured on a weekly TV variety show called *Dixie Showboat*. In the 1950s, Lamare led the Riverboat Dandies and had occasional reunions with Bob Crosby. Due to an injury on his pinky later in the decade, he switched to the electric bass for a few years until his finger recovered and he resumed playing guitar and banjo.

Nappy Lamare spent his later years appearing at Disneyland, touring with the World's Greatest Jazz Band, playing at jazz festivals, and participating in Bob Crosby reunions. During his final day, he sang and played banjo with a local band, passing away that evening in his sleep at the age of 82.

**Recommended CDs:** *South Rampart Street Parade* (GRP/Decca 615) has a strong cross section of the best recordings by the Bob Crosby Orchestra, all with Nappy Lamare in the personnel.

**LPs to Search For:** One of Nappy Lamare's very few albums as a leader, *Hilton "Nappy" Lamare And His Rendezvous Ballroom Orchestra* (Fairmont 105), has some hot Dixieland from 1947.

## Eddie Lang
*(Salvatore Massaro)*
*b. October 25, 1902, Philadelphia, PA; d. March 26, 1933, New York, NY*

Although he was not the first jazz guitarist (Nick Lucas was one of those who preceded him), it would not be an exaggeration to say that the jazz guitar largely began with Eddie Lang. It was due to both the rapidly improving recording quality in the 1920s (particularly the change from acoustic to electric recording during 1925–26) and the rise in prominence of Lang that the guitar gradually replaced the banjo.

While the change was inevitable, Lang's influence is not to be underestimated. He was not only jazz's first virtuoso guitarist and a fine soloist but also a master at accompanying both singers and ensembles, resulting in him being greatly in demand for recordings, studio and radio work, and live performances throughout his brief life.

Eddie Lang actually began his career as a violinist. A childhood friend of Joe Venuti, he started on violin at seven and studied it for 11 years, appearing in public as a violinist as early as 1917 and working the following year with Chuck Granese's Trio. However, by 1920 he had switched to banjo, playing with Charlie Kerr (1920–23), Bert Estlow, Vic D'Ipplito and Billy Lustig's Scranton Sirens, the latter a territory band that also included Tommy and Jimmy Dorsey. By 1924, he was doubling on guitar, permanently switching the following year. Lang was a member of Red McKenzie's popular Mound City Blue Blowers during 1924–25, which led to him being discovered and becoming a very busy freelance guitarist.

The violin-guitar team of Joe Venuti and Eddie Lang ("Venuti and Lang") was utilized by many record labels and bands. They made important appearances on records with Roger Wolfe Kahn (1926–27) and Jean Goldkette, and were members of the Paul Whiteman Orchestra during 1929–30, appearing briefly in the Whiteman film *The King Of Jazz*. Venuti and Lang, who often uplifted commercial performances with a feature chorus, were also part of Adrian Rollini's unrecorded all-star band in 1927 and appeared with many other short-term groups in quite a few settings. Most notably, Venuti and Lang recorded as a duet and with Venuti's Blue Four. Lang, who made many records accompanying singers, was also on dates with Frankie Trumbauer's Orchestra (including "Singin' The Blues" with Bix Beiderbecke), Louis Armstrong ("Knockin' A Jug"), Hoagy Carmichael, Jack Pettis, Annette Hanshaw, Clarence Williams, Red Nichols, and Bessie Smith. He recorded historic interracial guitar duets with Lonnie Johnson, using the pseudonym of "Blind Willie Dunn." On those sessions (which were mostly comprised of blues), Lang generally played chords behind Johnson's single-note lines. However, on a pair of classic guitar duets with Carl Kress from 1932 ("Pickin' My Way" and "Feelin' My Way"), he primarily played lead and bass lines with Kress providing the chords. During an era when guitar solos were rare, Lang also recorded 20 selections as a leader during 1927–29, many of which showcased his guitar being accompanied by a pianist.

The onset of the Depression did not slow down Eddie Lang's activities. Along with such admirers as Carl Kress, Dick McDonough and George Van Eps, he was the top freelance guitarist in the studios.

In 1932, Lang became Bing Crosby's regular accompanist, and his future looked very bright, for Crosby was just about ready to become internationally famous. But tragically, the guitarist's life was cut short in 1933 due to complications resulting from a botched tonsillectomy. Eddie Lang was just 30. How he would have dealt with the swing era, the electric guitar and bebop will never be known, but his legacy as the start of it all is secure.

**Recommended CDs:** The remarkable but limited-edition eight-CD set *The Classic Columbia & Okeh Joe Venuti & Eddie Lang Sessions* (Mosaic 8-213) has the great bulk of Lang's most significant recordings. The single-disc *Eddie Lang/Carl Kress/Dick McDonough* (Retrieval 79015) has all of Lang's dates as a leader other than six titles with larger bands. Included are mostly numbers where he is either heard on unaccompanied solos or playing duets with a supportive pianist (Arthur Schutt, Frank Signorelli or Rube Bloom). Such gems as "Eddie's Twister," "Perfect," "Add A Little Wiggle" and "There'll Be Some Changes Made" are included, as are Lang's two classic guitar duets with Carl Kress. All of that music is also on the Mosaic box, although the Retrieval CD also has the four Carl Kress–Dick McDonough duets from 1934 and 1937, and Kress' six solo recordings of 1938–39.

**Website:** www.eddielang.com (a very informative fan site)

## Jon Larsen
*b. January 7, 1959, Jar, Norway*

A fine guitarist, Jon Larsen is also very important as the founder and producer of recordings for his Hot Club label, which has been the pacesetter in documenting the gypsy-jazz movement. "I had some friends with guitars and paid them from my stamp collection to be allowed to play on their instruments. At 13, I inherited an old acoustic steel string guitar and could finally play as much as I wanted. My parents were terrified." He was originally self-taught, starting by learning from rock and soul records. "Then I met some guys who played blues and traditional jazz. We jammed day in and day out." A friend showed him some flamenco guitar, and another friend who was studying classical guitar showed him what he knew. "One late evening, I heard Django Reinhardt on the radio. It was 'Tears' (the 1947 version) and it went directly to my heart. That music combined all of my earlier influences, and I made up my mind there and then to figure out how it was possible to get the guitar to sound like Django. I was 14."

Larsen had his first gig with his own string trio Clo-Z (two guitars and a bass) when he was 17, playing a classical guitar. "Since then, I've had an average of 100 concerts every year, with too many ups and downs to count. Some of it has been horrible stuff, such as fellow musicians' ODs, hospitalizations, arrests, and fighting, but also heaven on earth, with the best guitar music you can imagine. And since I started recording in 1982, I have produced more than 350 records, which means that I have spent about half of my time in the recording studio, working with such musicians as Chet Baker, Stéphane Grappelli, Warne Marsh, the Zappa alumni, and all the great guitar players, from Biréli Lagrène and Jimmy Rosenberg to Babik Reinhardt and Philip Catherine."

As early as 1975, Larsen was playing with guitarist Per Frydenlund and bassist Svein Aarbostad. In 1980, they formed the Hot Club de Norvège (a quartet with violin), which has been Larsen's main group ever since. "The Django-inspired music was not even allowed into the jazz clubs thirty years ago. We played in the streets. Every night, when the weather allowed it, we met at the main drag and jammed. It was wonderful. One day, a locally famous pop singer-songwriter (Lillebjørn Nilsen) stopped and invited us to the studio. We joined him, and the song became a radio hit. Voilà, overnight we got indoors gigs and were even allowed to play in jazz clubs. Today, we are one of the few bands who attract a full house in jazz clubs all over the country."

Jon Larsen—who is also a highly respected painter—in addition to Hot Club, runs Zonic Entertainment, a new label for music influenced by Frank Zappa (another of his interests). While a bit modest about his own guitar playing, he is particularly proud of the music that he has produced for his labels. "My talent has been to discover things that were already there, to choose quality, and to contribute as a team player to many good projects. Each time I play together with Stochelo Rosenberg or Biréli Lagrène, I think to myself that I should have spent more time practicing the guitar instead of so much time working on the record productions. But then I realize that, nevertheless, here I am in the midst of this splendid music, and who else would have produced all of the records?"

**Recommended CDs:** *Swing In Paris* (Hot Club 34), *Super Strings* (Hot Club 69), *Guitaresque* (Hot Club 81), *Vertavo Live In Concert* (Hot Club 84), *The Swinging Guitar Of Jon Larsen* (Hot Club 88), *Vertavo* (Hot Club 96), *Hot Shot* (Hot Club 102), *Larsen And Loutchek* (Hot Club 124), *Best Of Hot Club De Norvège* (Hot Club 139), *White Night Stories* (Hot Club 150), *The Next Step* (Hot Club 137), *Angelo Is Back In Town* (Hot Club 140), *White Night Live* (Hot Club 155), *Stranger In Town* (Hot Club 171), *Hot Cats* (Hot Club 181), *Short Stories From Catalonia* (Hot Club 196), *Strange News From*

*Mars* (Zonic 2001), and *Portrait Of Jon Larsen* (Hot Club 224). He also appears on quite a few Jimmy Rosenberg records.

**Website:** www.hotclub.no/jon

## Nguyen Le
*(Le Hong Nguyen)*
*b. January 14, 1959, Paris, France*

One of the most inventive guitarists of the past 20 years, Nguyen Le has always had his own sound and style, whether playing music that could be called fusion, folk-jazz, world, or post-bop jazz. He has been involved in a countless number of often-overlapping projects since the mid-1980s, carving out his own niche.

Born in France to Vietnamese parents, Nguyen Le started playing drums at 15. "The guitar player in my band left his instrument in my bedroom where we were rehearsing. The first note I played on his electric guitar, I felt that I had discovered my voice and that I could make the instrument sing." He first heard jazz one day when his sister brought home a record of Return to Forever. "I was astonished by this complex, mysterious and beautiful music. From there, I got into Mahavishnu, Miles Davis and Coltrane."

Self-taught on guitar (he also played fretless bass), Le studied visual arts and philosophy in college. He never really planned to become a professional guitarist, but as he became more adept at jazz, he had more and more gigs and less time for his college studies. In 1983, Le met pianist Mario Canonge from Martinique. They formed Ultramarine, a pioneering multiethnic band based on their roots and jazz knowledge. Another important association that continues to this day took place in the United States in 1985, when Le met and played with pianist Art Lande, who is on Le's recording debut as a leader, *Miracles*. Among his most important associations since then have been Peter Erskine, Vince Mendoza ("a deep influence on my compositions and always a supreme thrill to work with"), trumpeter Paolo Frescu and Vietnamese singer Huong Thanh.

The list of Le's other associations (which include such notables as Johnny Griffin, Carla Bley, Randy Brecker, Toots Thielemans, Gil Evans, Dee Dee Bridgewater, Miroslav Vitous, Dewey Redman, Kenny Wheeler, John Taylor, Paul McCandless, Terri Lynne Carrington, Maria Schneider, John McLaughlin, Michel Petrucciani, Enrico Rava, Ray Anderson, Dave Douglas and Uri Caine) is quite endless, not even counting the O.N.J. (French National Jazz Orchestra), the Metropole Orchestra, or being a regular guest with the NDR Orchestra.

Nguyen Le gained a lot of attention for his 1996 recording *Tales From Viet-Nam*. "It was my first recording to really integrate where I come from (my own roots) and where I want to go. Each career high point is a deep learning experience because of the way it transforms your identity. This integration happened in my writing, but also in my playing, because that's when I started to really 'ethnicize' my guitar." Other key recordings include 1998's *Maghreb & Friends*, which found him exploring African music with Algerian drummer Karim Ziad, and his most popular recording, *Purple: Celebrating Jimi Hendrix*.

Among Nguyen Le's recent groups are a guitar-bass-drums trio; the Jimi Hendrix Project; his band Purple; Dragonfly, which he co-leads with Huong Thanh; a quartet with Art Lande, Paul McCandless, and Jamey Haddad; and a trio with Peter Erskine. When asked what his future goals are, he simply replies, "Creating the unheard."

**Recommended CDs:** It is fair to say that there is no shortage of Nguyen Le recordings currently available. His recordings as a leader include *Miracles* (Universal 983 881), *Zanzibar* (Universal 983 882), *Million Waves* (ACT 92210, *Tales From Viet-Nam* (ACT 9225), *3 Trios* (ACT 9245), *Maghreb & Friends* (ACT 9261), *Bakida* (ACT 9275), *Purple* (ACT 9410), *Walking On The Tiger's Tail* (ACT 9432), *Homescape* (ACT 9444), *Saiyuki* (ACT 9483), *Songs Of Freedom* (ACT 9506) and the two-CD sampler *Signature Edition* (ACT 6004), which has highlights from Nguyen Le's 15 years on the ACT label. In addition, he recorded three CDs with Ultramarine and is on sessions with Ray Charles (*Strong Love Affair*), Michel Portal, Paolo Frescu, Eric Vloeimans, Uri Caine, Vince Mendoza, Peter Erskine and Huong Thanh.

**Website:** www.nguyen-le.com

## Bob Leary
*b. August 28, 1953, Brockton, MA*

A fine swing-based rhythm guitarist and soloist, Bob Leary also plays banjo and ukulele, takes occasional vocals, and has been heard in many Dixieland-oriented settings through the years. "I've always played. I have no recollections of not playing." He started lessons when he was four and first heard jazz through his father's Dixieland records, including albums by Phil Napoleon, Eddie Condon and Dick Hyman. Leary had his last guitar lessons at 11 and just played for fun until he attended college (UNC at Chapel Hill in North Carolina), where he jammed with a student Dixieland band. After graduating, he moved to Cape Cod, where "I played every bar, clambake, Elks, VFW and Lions Club in any number of different combinations, solo to big band."

In 1986, Leary moved to Florida, where he began playing at Disney World. That led to work all over Orlando, including 14 years working at Rosie O'Grady's, often with Bill Allred. "I first got into traveling with a band called the Black Dogs, all Orlando guys, which was the first (for my money) Dixieland band to put a true New Orleans street beat to trad tunes. The beat and the band caught on like wildfire. Mat Domber started Arbors records with all Orlando guys. I made four of the first five Arbors CDs and have done one or two a year ever since." Leary also has worked extensively with Allan Vaché, has been part of the Bob Crosby Bobcats and Big Band for nearly 20 years, plays with local society bands, and performs at occasional jazz festivals and cruises, often with the great stride pianist Jeff Barnhart or the Midiri Brothers.

"What do I love about playing jazz? The rhythm section. When we in the back row are right, and I'm pleased to say I've never worked with better ones than I've got right now in Barnhart's band and the Midiris—it's better than a hot corned beef and swiss."

**Recommended CDs:** Among the finer recordings that Bob Leary has been on as a sideman (he has yet to lead his own CD) are Allan Vaché's *Florida Jazz All-Stars* (Nagel Heyer 32); *Revisited!* (Nagel Heyer 44), which has a pianoless and drumless quartet led by Vaché; pianist John Sheridan's *Easy As It Gets* (Arbors 19309); and *If Bix Played Gershwin* (Arbors 19283), an intriguing project co-led by Dick Hyman and cornetist Tom Pletcher.

**Website:** www.bobleary.com

## Peter Leitch
b. August 19, 1944, Ottawa, Ontario, Canada

A major fixture in the New York straight-ahead jazz scene for nearly 30 years, Peter Leitch has helped to keep the legacy of bebop guitar alive. When he was a teenager, his parents gave him a guitar for his birthday. He had a few lessons but was largely self-taught. Through friends, Leitch was introduced to jazz. "I was very fortunate in that at that time, Montreal was on the circuit, so we had all the major players coming through town. I played at many Montreal nightclubs, although not necessarily great jazz. I played for dancing and floor shows including

accompanying hypnotists, dog acts, comedians and strippers." He also did some studio work and toured with R&B bands.

Leitch made his recording debut in the early 1970s with pianist Sadik Hakim. He was based in Toronto during 1977–81 (working with such players as Milt Jackson, Kenny Wheeler and Red Norvo), traveled and recorded with the Al Grey–Jimmy Forrest group during 1979–80, and toured the Soviet Union with tenor-saxophonist Fraser MacPherson.

In 1982, Leitch moved permanently to New York. Since then, in addition to leading his own groups, he has worked with quite a few major players, including Kirk Lightsey, John Hicks, Jaki Byard's Apollo Stompers, Gary Bartz, Bobby Watson, Ray Drummond and Smitty Smith. He has also recorded with Oscar Peterson, Woody Shaw, Jaki Byard, Dominique Eade, Pete Yellin and Jeri Brown, plus many sessions of his own.

An insightful jazz journalist, a skilled photographer and an educator, Peter Leitch has always kept busy. "I've been doing a regular Sunday night gig at Walker's in Manhattan with a different duo partner every week, working with some great bassists and saxophonists: Ray Drummond, Sean Smith, Harvie S, Dwayne Burno, Charles Davis, Jed Levy, etc. I've also been working with filmmaker Pamela Timmins, composing and recording original guitar music soundtracks."

**Recommended CDs:** All of Peter Leitch's recordings are excellent, for he always stays true to himself. His sessions as a leader include *On A Misty Night* (Criss Cross 1026), *Exhilaration* (Reservoir 118) with baritonist Pepper Adams, *Red Zone* (Reservoir 103), *Mean What You Say* (Concord 4417), *Portraits And Dedications* (Criss Cross 1039) with altoist Bobby Watson, *Trio/Quartet '91* (Concord 4480), *From Another Perspective* (Concord 4535), *A Special Rapport* (Reservoir 129), *Duality* (Reservoir 134) with John Hicks, *Colours And Dimensions* (Reservoir 140), *Up Front* (Reservoir 149), *Blues On The Corner* (Reservoir 160), *Autobiography* (Reservoir 179) and the unaccompanied solo guitar program *Self Portrait* (Jazz House 7003). Also well worth acquiring is *The Montreal Concert* (DSM 3037), a set of duets from 2003 with Gary Bartz.

**LPs to Search For:** Peter Leitch's first two albums as a leader, *Jump Street* (Jazz House 7001) and *Sometime In Another Life* (Jazz House 7002), are from 1981–82 and find him already playing in a recognizable style.

**Website:** www.peterleitch.com

## Adam Levy
*b. November 27, 1966, Encino, CA*

Adam Levy has had a productive and varied career, which is reflected in his eclectic and original style. His grandfather George Wyle was a pianist-arranger who was the musical director for several television variety series, including the Andy Williams and Flip Wilson shows. "Spending a lot of time with him as a kid, at his house and at TV studios, was one of the big things that inspired me to take up music. He made me wonder if music may be the fountain of youth. He was 50 years older than me, but he always had so much joy and vitality in life and in music. There were always guitars around our family. Two of my uncles played folk guitar and my cousin played rock and roll. My mom saw that I was interested and told me that she had taken some guitar classes. She still had her nylon string folk guitar, gathering dust in the closet. I dusted it off and played the couple of chords I knew. It felt so natural in my hands that I just couldn't put it down."

Levy played with a community big band as a teenager, performing Count Basie–style charts at local festivals and parties. After high school he attended the Dick Grove School of Music and often played duo gigs with jazz singers. He was inspired by lessons with Ted Greene and Jimmy Wyble, the playing of Bill Frisell, and the songwriting of Leni Stern.

In 1990, Levy moved to San Francisco, where he played jazz, worked in the studios, and appeared on many sessions. He played and recorded with Tracy Chapman during 1994–95 (including her album *New Beginning*). Levy worked with Joey Barron's quartet Killer Joey (1998–99) next to Steve Cardenas and bassist Tony Scherr. "Besides the prestige of playing in Joey's group, in terms of power and prowess, it was the best band I've ever been part of."

After moving to New York, Levy was a member of Norah Jones' group during 2000–07. "I played with Norah on her first gig in New York City, and we played lots of gigs together in town before anything big happened for her career-wise. Then I got to be part of her first album, *Come Away With Me*, and the next two albums that followed—three albums, three DVDs and three world tours in all. I've moved on, but I'll always be grateful for that time together, from brunch gigs at a café in Greenwich Village to worldwide success at the highest level." He has also worked with Rosanne Cash, Lisa Loeb and Chris Difford (of the band Squeeze) and recorded with Amos Lee.

Since then, Adam Levy has been playing jazz guitar while also working on writing songs and singing. "I wouldn't consider many of my songs 'jazz,' but my background in jazz affects how I perform the songs live with my trio, the Mint Imperials."

**Recommended CDs:** *Buttermilk Channel* (Lost Wax 101), while featuring seven of his originals, is a jazz trio date with organist Larry Goldings and drummer Kenny Wollesen that Adam Levy calls the album that he is proudest of. *Get Your Glow On* (Lost Wax 301) has his versions of an eclectic variety of pop tunes, while *Loose Rhymes: Live On Ludlow Street* (Lost Wax 601), *Washing Day* (Lost Wax 701) and *Nice Place To Visit* (Lost Wax 901) put the focus on Levy's singing and songwriting, although he does take some jazz guitar solos. *Nice Place To Visit* (Lost Wax 801) brings him back to jazz on a quartet set with violinist Jenny Scheinman.

**Website:** www.adamlevy.com

## Rudy Linka
*b. May 29, 1960, Prague, Czech Republic*

Inspired by Jim Hall and John Abercrombie, Rudy Linka has developed his own modern mainstream style. Born and raised in Czechoslovakia, Linka started on the violin when he was six, switching to guitar at 14, inspired originally by the Beatles. He studied classical guitar at the Prague Conservatory during 1975–79, a period when he became interested in jazz. First Linka heard Miles Davis' *Jack Johnson* and then explored a greatest-hits album that featured some of Davis' earlier recordings. He played covers of Carlos Santana and Billy Cobham songs in a college band.

In 1980, Linka left Czechoslovakia for Sweden, where he became a citizen, studied composition at the Stockholm Music Institute (1981–84), and worked with Red Mitchell. In 1985, he moved to the United States, where he studied at Berklee (1985–86), the New School (1986–88), and privately with John Scofield, Jim Hall and John Abercrombie. Linka, who has recorded for Punc, Arta, Timeless, Enja, Acoustic Music, Midlantic, SMD, Tap Shoe, Universal and Sony/BMG, enjoys working with other guitarists and has recorded with Abercrombie and Scofield. In recent times, Rudy Linka has performed with his trio in Europe, had a duo project with pianist Bob Stenson, and founded the Bohemia Jazz Fest in the Czech Republic.

"I think you can hear in my music that I was born

in the Czech Republic but have lived in the US for the last 26 years." Jazz is definitely Rudy Linka's main language.

**Recommended CDs:** *News From Home* (Arta 26-2511), *Mostly Standards* (Arta 38), *Live It Up* (Timeless 407), *Czech It Out* (Enja 90012), *Always Double Czech* (Enja 9301), *Every Moment* (Acoustic Music 31912502) with John Abercrombie, *Simple Pleasures* (Midlantic 105), *Lucky Southern* (SMD 303) with Scofield and Abercrombie, *Emotions In Motion* (Tap Shoe), *Just Between Us* (Universal 013313), *Songs* (Sony/BMG).

## Jeff Linsky
*b. April 12, 1952, Whittier, CA*

A melodic guitarist who loves playing Brazilian and Latin jazz, Jeff Linsky has a highly appealing sound and superior technique. His father was an amateur drummer who loved Gene Krupa. Linsky started playing the guitar when he was ten. As a teenager, he often went to the Lighthouse in Hermosa Beach. "As a kid, I used to stand outside of the club and watch the performances through the open top half of their Dutch door, which faced the sidewalk. I was too young to go inside, but where I stood was only twenty feet from the stage. I remember a particularly inspiring performance by saxophonist Sonny Stitt as being the first time that I felt some understanding of what was going on harmonically. Sonny played an unaccompanied version of 'Misty,' and that one solo performance changed my whole view of music."

Linsky played surf music with friends in instrumental bands. He performed at his first church dance when he was 11, the same year that he saw his first Segovia concert. At 17, he was part of a national tour with pop/rock groups, playing before large audiences. He also played with the Gene Leis Trio and with singer Ann Richards. Linsky, who had important guitar lessons with Joe Pass and Spanish guitarist Vicente Gomez, became interested in both the sound of the classical guitar and improvisation. He lived in Hawaii during 1972–88, mostly playing solo guitar gigs in the US and in Europe. In 1988, he moved to the San Francisco Bay area and began to get a higher profile, appearing at jazz festivals including Monterey, leading his own groups, and recording for labels including Concord. These days, he often tours with a duo that also includes percussionist Michael Spiro.

"I've played some wonderful concert venues throughout the US, Europe and Asia. Yet I have to admit, I still enjoy the 'romantic getaway' gigs, like my New Year's Eve concerts in Chiang Mai,

my recording sessions in Brazil, or the month we spent not long ago in an overwater bungalow at the St. Regis Bora Bora. Although I have played jazz festivals, recorded for jazz record labels, and even been on the cover of *Just Jazz Guitar Magazine*, I don't necessarily consider myself a jazz musician. I play with a classical guitar technique and have a repertoire that includes many styles of music from around the world. But when I said this to a classroom of students at a workshop where I was teaching in Helsinki, Jim Hall (who was also teaching at the festival) yelled from the back of the room, 'You are a jazz musician!'"

**Recommended CDs:** Jeff Linsky, who really is a jazz musician, is heard at his best on *Up Late* (Concord 4363), *Simpatico* (GSP 7001), *Rendezvous* (GSP 2230), *Solo* (GSP 5000), *Angel's Serenade* (Concord 4611), *California* (Concord 4708) and *Passport To The Heart* (Concord 4764). But although he has recorded privately and for the digital market, his last solo CD as of this writing is from 1997.

**Website:** www.jefflinsky.com

## Chuck Loeb
*(Charles Samuel Loeb)*
*b. December 7, 1955, Suffern, NY*

In Chuck Loeb's career, he has often been associated with crossover and pop/jazz, although he is quite capable of playing his guitar very credibly in nearly any style. He began on guitar at 11 and was largely self-taught until he started studying jazz when he was 16. "I had a neighbor who was a musician that gave me *Smoking At The Half Note* by Wes Montgomery, and around the same time, I heard *Inner Mounting Flame* by John McLaughlin and the Mahavishnu Orchestra." He started out playing with a local soul/R&B group called the Sinclairs when he was 13. Early jazz gigs included playing rhythm guitar for guitarist Ritchie Hart and working with saxophonist Gary Keller.

After attending Berklee during 1974–76, Loeb moved to New York, worked with Chico Hamilton, Ray Barretto and Hubert Laws, and gained attention for his playing with Stan Getz during 1979–81. Loeb, who was a member of Steps Ahead during 1984–86, also worked along the way with such notables as Freddie Hubbard, Gary Burton, Jaco Pastorius, Eddie Daniels, Bob James, Gato Barbieri, Pat Martino, John Abercrombie and John Scofield. He started working on jingles and soundtracks in the 1980s, became a record producer, and gradually switched his focus to more commercial music while being quite capable of playing creative jazz. Loeb began recording as a leader in 1989 (making 17 CDs thus far), and more than ten of his songs have topped the charts. In addition to leading his own groups, he was part of Petite Blonde (with saxophonist Bill Evans) and the Fantasy Band, co-leads Metro, and in 2010 became a member of Fourplay.

Married to singer Carmen Cuesta, Chuck Loeb says, "Music is a never-ending challenge and it is universal in its appeal. I have traveled to India, Africa, Europe, Japan, Indonesia and America in the last year, and the music works in all of those places flawlessly. I want to continue doing my best to create music that touches people."

**Recommended CDs:** *Magic Fingers* (DMP 472), *Life Colors* (DMP 475), *Balance* (DMP 484), *Mediterranean* (DMP 494), *Simple Things* (DMP 504), *The Music Inside* (Shanachie 5022), *The Moon, The Stars And The Setting Sun* (Shanachie 5038), *Listen* (Shanachie 5057), *In A Heartbeat* (Shanachie 5078), *All There Is* (Shanachie 5090), *eBop* (Shanachie 5103), *When I'm With You* (Shanachie 5123), *Presence* (Heads Up 3117), *#1 Smooth Jazz Radio Hits* (Shanachie 5169) and *Between 2 Worlds* (Heads Up 3151) all emphasize easy-listening music with strong melodies and light but soulful playing. Ironically, Chuck Loeb's lone straight-ahead jazz album under his own name, *My Shining Hour* (Pony Canyon 30035), was made for the Japanese market.

**Website:** www.chuckloeb.com

## Bruce Lofgren
*b. September 29, 1942, Seattle, WA*

Bruce Lofgren Jazz Orchestra

THE BLUES and Other Passions

A longtime fixture in the Los Angeles area, Bruce Lofgren leads a big band and is often heard with his own combos. At 12 or 13, Lofgren heard a family friend who was a rock guitarist, Dan Olason, and he immediately wanted one. "In the following weeks, I worked for my uncle, digging a trench for a water line to his house, in order to earn enough money to buy my first guitar, a blue and white arch-top Silvertone from Sears. My first teacher was Don Alexander, a retired pro who introduced me to jazz, though at the time I was mostly interested in rock and blues." Within a year, he had formed a garage band, the Vegas, that played local dance gigs. He also played in his high school stage band and was amazed by the playing he heard on a Tal Farlow record and by seeing Barney Kessel play in a club.

Lofgren attended the University of Washington as an English major. As a sophomore, he landed a job working with an organ trio at St. Michael's Alley in Seattle, a gig that lasted two years. He also played with a seven-piece dance band, the Pacific Northwest Territory Band, for whom he wrote over 50 arrangements. "During this time, I was teaching guitar, studying privately and freelancing, and playing casuals and shows at places like the Marine Room at the Olympic Hotel in downtown Seattle, where I met Jonah Jones and Cozy Cole."

In 1970, Lofgren moved to Los Angeles. He worked with a traveling show (Brother Love) for a year, which was followed by a period with Ray Anthony's band, mostly in Las Vegas. Lofgren played electric bass with the group for a few weeks before becoming Anthony's guitarist. In 1972, he moved back to Los Angeles, where he has played and written for the studios and for such notables as Bobby Darin, Airto Moreira & Flora Purim (1973), Buddy Rich (1975), Doc Severinsen's Tonight Show Orchestra (1981–85) and a variety of pop groups. He arranged the music for Keith Emerson's guest appearance at a Led Zeppelin reunion concert, which led to an association that continues today. Lofgren also worked with Tony Rizzi's Five Guitars Plus Four (1976–87), playing harmonized Charlie Christian solos.

Bruce Lofgren formed his big band in 1972, and the orchestra has continued on a part-time basis ever since, including a two-year weekly gig at the One for L.A. club (1984–86). Lofgren also worked regularly with a small group during the first three years of a five-year Monday night residency at the Typhoon Restaurant in Santa Monica (1997–2002), bringing in his big band for the final two years. His music for his orchestra falls effectively between jazz and rock and reflects his eclectic musical tastes, as does his playing.

**Recommended CDs:** 1993's *Sky Sailor* (White Wolf 4000), a sextet date, was Bruce Lofgren's recording debut as a leader. On *Heart Of The Night* (Sea Breeze 2070), Lofgren mixes together the big band tradition and funky jazz in his writing for his 17-piece orchestra. Also from his orchestra, *The Blues And Other Passions* (Sea Breeze 2103) and *Red Shift* (Sea Breeze 2126) are at times rockish but swing hard, even when utilizing tricky time signatures. *Eventide* (Sea Breeze 3075) showcases Lofgren as a guitarist with a trio/quartet. "From the standpoint of playing, my most recent recording, *The Bruce Lofgren Jazz Trio* (Sea Breeze 3087), with bassist Mike Flick and drummer Ron Wagner, is my best."

**Website:** www.brucelofgren.com

## Lorne Lofsky

b. May 10, 1954, Toronto, Canada

A tasteful cool-toned guitarist, Lorne Lofsky is in the tradition of Ed Bickert, Jimmy Raney and early Jim Hall. One could never tell from his jazz recordings that he started out playing rock and roll with garage bands and at high school dances. However, after hearing Miles Davis' *Kind Of Blue*, Lofsky completely changed his musical direction. He studied music at York University in the mid-1970s, worked regularly in Toronto, and was heard regularly at such clubs as George's Spaghetti House and Bourbon Street. In addition to playing with such Canadians as saxophonist Jerry Toth and trombonist Butch Watanabe, he had the opportunity to work with visiting Americans, including Chet Baker, Pepper Adams, Carl Fontana and Bob Brookmeyer.

After meeting Oscar Peterson in 1980, Lofsky recorded for Pablo (*It Could Happen To You*) with Peterson as his producer. Lofsky worked and toured with Peterson in addition to playing with Pat LaBarbera, Kirk Macdonald, Dizzy Gillespie, Rob McConnell's Boss Brass, Tal Farlow, Johnny Hartman, Rosemary Clooney, Ruby Braff, and Clark Terry, and in a quartet with Ed Bickert that resulted in two recordings.

During 1994–96, Lorne Lofsky was a member of the Oscar Peterson Quartet, touring and making three albums. In the years since, the guitarist has had a lower profile, teaching at York University and the University of Toronto. While his style has become more influenced by Bill Evans, he is still recognizable as the tasteful guitarist who impressed Oscar Peterson years ago.

**Recommended CDs:** *All Of You* (Jazz Inspiration 31081), *Bill, Please* (Jazz Inspiration 49307), *What Is This Thing?* (Romhog); with Ed Bickert: *This Is New* (Concord 4414); with Joey DeFrancesco: *One Take, Vol. 1* (Alma 148282).

**LPs to Search For:** *It Could Happen To You* (Pablo 2312122), *The Quartet Of Lorne Lofsky & Ed Bickert And Friends* (Unisson 1002).

**Website:** www.lornelofsky.com

## Lionel Loueke

b. April 27, 1973, Cotonou, Benin

The quality that is immediately apparent about Lionel Loueke's playing is that he has a tone of his own, sounding unlike anyone else. While his style is influenced by both post-bop jazz and African music, his tone by itself makes it obvious that he is a very individual guitarist. In addition, he makes clicking sounds with his mouth, occasionally sings along with his playing, and creates percussive sounds on his guitar that add to the power and joy of his music. Born and raised in Benin in West Africa, Loueke played percussion as a child but began on guitar much later. "I started on guitar because my older brother was playing it at that time; I was 17. I got introduced to jazz by listening to such guitarists as Wes Montgomery, Joe Pass, Kenny Burrell and George Benson."

Loueke attended the National Institute of Art in the Ivory Coast, the American School of Music in Paris (1994–98), Berklee (1999–2001) and the Thelonious Monk Institute (2001–03). Fortunately, all of that education did not result in the guitarist losing any of his individuality, and instead it inspired him to fuse what he learned about jazz with his African heritage. At the Monk Institute, Loueke's teachers included Herbie Hancock, Wayne Shorter and Terence Blanchard, all of whom have played significant roles in his career.

Loueke gained a great deal of attention for his playing with the groups of Blanchard (2003–07) and Hancock (starting in 2004), sometimes appearing in the latter band alongside Shorter. He signed with the Blue Note label (featuring Hancock and Shorter as guests on his debut CD, *Karibu*) and has appeared on recordings by Blanchard (*Flow* and *Bounce*), Hancock (*River: The Joni Letters* and *Possibilities*), trumpeter Avishai Cohen, Gretchen Parlato, Angelique Kidjo, Francisco Mela, Kendrick Scott, Charlie Haden and Alison Wedding. Lionel Loueke also co-leads the trio Gilfema, which features bassist Massimo Biolcati and drummer Ferenc Nemeth.

"For the future, I hope to continue learning from different musicians and want to help young musicians from Africa by opening a music school."

**Recommended CDs:** Lionel Loueke's debut recording as a leader is the privately issued *Incantation*. *Virgin Forest* (Object 104) and *In A Trance* (Tokuma 32094) trace his rapid development, while *Gilfema* (ObliqSound 504) and *Gilfema + 2* (ObliqSound 512), the latter with clarinetist Anat Cohen and bass clarinetist John Ellis as important guests, display the uniqueness of Loueke's trio. *Karibu* (Blue Note

12791), *Mwaliko* (Blue Note 88508) and *Heritage* (Blue Note) gave Lionel Loueke well deserved fame in the jazz world.

**Website:** www.lionelloueke.com

## Mundell Lowe
*(James Mundell Lowe)*
b. April 21, 1922, Laurel, MS

A consistently swinging and harmonically rich guitarist, Mundell Lowe, as of this writing, has had one of the longest careers in jazz among active guitarists. "My sister and father were my guitar teachers. I started when I was eight." Lowe left home when he was 13, worked in Nashville, and became part of the local scene in New Orleans, playing at clubs on Bourbon Street. He was with Jan Savitt's orchestra in 1942 before serving in the military during World War II. Producer John Hammond introduced him to drummer-bandleader Ray McKinley. After his discharge, Lowe worked with McKinley's big band during 1945–47, an important training ground in which he developed his style.

Moving to New York, Lowe played at Café Society and other jazz clubs for a few years, quite frequently with Mary Lou Williams, Red Norvo and Ellis Larkins. He became a staff musician at NBC in 1950 and, during the next 15 years, worked on radio and television, including being part of Dave Garroway's *Today Show* studio band and the *Kate Smith Hour*. However, he never stopped playing jazz. Lowe was with the Sauter-Finegan Orchestra during 1952–53 and played with Benny Goodman, Billie Holiday, Lester Young, Charlie Parker, Charles Mingus, Bill Evans and many of the who's who of 1950s and '60s jazz. He led record dates of his own for several labels.

In 1965, Lowe moved to California, where for a time he seemed to be working more as a film and television composer (teaching film composition during 1979–85) than he was as a guitarist. During this period, he did record with Sarah Vaughan (*After Hours*) and Carmen McRae, work with Benny Carter, and perform regularly at the Monterey Jazz Festival. In the 1980s, he decided to go back to emphasizing playing guitar. Lowe worked and recorded with the Andre Previn Trio and Tete Montoliu, was a member of the mid-1990s version of the Great Guitars, and continued documenting his own projects. At 90, he remains in excellent playing form, married to singer Betty Bennett, and still has a goal for the future. "I want to finish a symphony that I have been working on for a while."

**Recommended CDs:** There is no shortage of Mundell Lowe CDs, not even taking into consideration his countless number of sessions as a sideman. From the 1950s are *Mundell Lowe Quartet* (Original Jazz Classics 1773), *Guitar Moods* (Original Jazz Classics 1957), *A Grand Night For Swinging* (Original Jazz Classics 1940), *Blues For A Stripper/Satan In High Heels* (Fresh Sound 1626) and a particularly inventive version of *Porgy And Bess* (RCA 74321364052). Starting with 1972's *California Girl* (Famous Door 7116) and continuing with *Souvenirs* (Jazz Alliance 10011), *Mundell's Mood* (Nagel Heyer 65) with Hendrik Meurkens on harmonica, and 2000's *This One's For Charlie* (Azica 72213), which teams Lowe with guitarist Lloyd Wells, Mundell Lowe can be heard in undiminished form, playing the brand of straight-ahead jazz that he loves.

**Website:** www.mundelllowe.com

## Romero Lubambo
b. July 20, 1955, Rio de Janeiro, Brazil

The favorite Brazilian guitarist of many jazz musicians, Romero Lubambo is masterful both as an accompanist to singers and as a soloist. "I started on guitar when I was 13 years old be-cause of an uncle of mine. Since I was born, I heard him playing guitar in our house. He was our neighbor and was always visiting, and he was crazy about jazz. I played classical piano for two years before stopping, but on guitar I never stopped, even for one week. My family loved jazz, and we grew up listening to American jazz, Brazilian, and classical music. Since we did not have schools or teachers for jazz music, I had to learn by myself with LPs and anything I could get hold of. I had to create my own technique since nobody was there to tell me what to do."

Lubambo first played professionally when he was 14 with another uncle who had a band. He studied classical guitar at the Villa-Lobos School of Music during 1972–77, and in college earned a degree in mechanical engineering, graduating in 1980. But when he graduated, he decided to pursue a career as a musician. "My father said to me, 'No problem, just try to be the best and you will have no problems.' That was the key to my happiness as a musician."

In 1985, he moved to the United States, working at first with Astrud Gilberto. In 1986, Lubambo began a longtime association with Herbie Mann that lasted until the flutist's death in 2002. "I consider him my American father, my mentor for life." With fellow Brazilians drummer-percussionist Duduka Da Fonseca and bassist Nilson Matta, Lubambo has toured the world and recorded often as Trio da Paz. Among his other key associations have been Leny Andrade, keyboardist Weber Drummond, Hermeto Pascoal, Pat Metheny, Michael Brecker, Diana Krall, Wynton Marsalis, Jane Monheit, Ivan Lins, Flora Purim & Airto, Paquito D'Rivera, Larry Coryell, Gato Barbieri, James Carter, Claudia Acuña, Jason Miles, Regina Carter, and Dave Douglas.

In recent times, Romero Lubambo has been working as a guitarist-arranger for Dianne Reeves (he and Russell Malone often provide her only accompaniment), with Trio da Paz, Luciana Souza, and playing solo guitar concerts.

**Recommended CDs:** *Face To Face* (GSP 5003), *Shades Of Rio* (Chesky 85), *2* (GSP 5004), *Lubambo* (Avant 23), *Brazilian Routes* (Rob 051), *Rio de Janeiro Underground* (JVC Victor 2), *Softly* (Max Jazz 603); with Herbie Mann: *Caminho De Casa* (Chesky 40); with Trio da Paz: *Brasil From The Inside* (Concord 4524), *Black Orpheus* (Kokopelli 1299); *Partido Out* (Malandro 71005), *Cafe* (Malandro 71019), *Somewhere* (Blue Toucan 5), *Live At JazzBaltica* (Max Jazz 140701); with Lee Konitz: *Brazilian Rhapsody* (Musicmasters 65151); with Luciana Souza: *The New Bossa Nova* (Verve 9848539).

**Website:** www.romerolubambo.com

## Sylvain Luc
*b. 1965, Bayonne, France*

Not too many guitarists can hold their own on duets with Biréli Lagrène and Philip Catherine, but Sylvain Luc is in their league. He started playing guitar when he was four, added violin, and studied cello for ten years at the Bayonne Conservatory since no guitar courses were available. His two older brothers, accordionist Gérard Luc and drummer Serge Luc, were early inspirations. Luc not only played with them in public while still a child but also made his recording debut with his brothers on *Elgarrekin* when he was just nine.

At 15, Luc led the Bulle Quintet, a jazz group that lasted a few years, toured and appeared at festivals. In 1988, when he was 23, Luc moved to Paris, where he played bass with the Richard Galliano trio,

worked as an arranger, composer and accompanist to a variety of pop artists (including Al Jarreau), and played guitar with trumpeter Eric Le Lann.

Luc's career has not slowed down since. Among the many top musicians with whom he has performed and made a strong impression are Wynton Marsalis, Michel Legrand, Elvin Jones, Dee Dee Bridgewater, Andy Sheppard, Victor Bailey, Larry Coryell, Al Di Meola, Didier Lockwood, John McLaughlin, Billy Cobham, and many French and European musicians. He led his first album in 1993, and his 2000 duet set with Biréli Lagrène was a big seller; they had a reunion for 2009's *Summertime*. Luc has led the Trio Sud Band (which includes drummer André Ceccarelli and bassist Jean-Marc Jafet) since 2000. During 2006–07, he toured France and Europe with an all-star group that included Jacky Terrasson and, in 2008, was in the String Quartet band with Didier Lockwood, Victor Bailey and Billy Cobham. In 2009, Luc not only performed duo guitar concerts with Biréli Lagrène and Philip Catherine but also played in Nomad's Land with Didier Lockwood and had a trio with Richard Bona and Steve Gadd.

Sylvain Luc, who considers his influences to include Keith Jarrett, Egberto Gismonti, John Scofield, Pat Metheny and Joe Pass, has his own original sound and the ability to sound like himself in settings ranging from advanced swing to post-bop jazz. He deserves to be much better known in the United States.

**Recommended CDs:** Many of Sylvain Luc's most important recordings are available through the Dreyfus label, including *Duet* (Dreyfus 36604) with Biréli Lagrène; *Sud* (Dreyfus 36612); *Trio Sud* (Dreyfus 36632); *Solo Ambre* (Dreyfus 36650), a set of unaccompanied acoustic guitar solos; *Joko* (Dreyfus 36692); *Young And Fine* (Dreyfus 36917); *Summertime* (Dreyfus 36932) also with Lagrène; and *Standards* (Dreyfus 36942).

**Website:** www.sylvainluc.fr

## Nick Lucas
*(Dominic Nicholas Anthony Lucanese)*
*b. August 22, 1897, Newark, NJ; d. July, 28, 1982, Newark, NJ*

Although best known throughout his life as singer, Nick Lucas was the first to record unaccompanied jazz guitar solos, predating everyone in jazz and blues. His list of accomplishments is remarkable. Nick Lucas sang and played guitar as a youth, in time adding banjo, mandolin and ukulele. When he was ten, he and his brother Frank played on trains (as opposed to playing with trains) as a mandolin-accordion duet for money. When Frank left home to become active in vaudeville, Nick Lucas played banjorine (a combination banjo-mandolin) in a group because the guitar was considered too soft. By 1915, he was often heard on tenor banjo in cafes and restaurants, although guitar was his main love.

After graduating high school, Lucas formed the Kentucky Five (which included pianist Ted Fio Rito) to play in vaudeville. Lucas first recorded on test cylinders in 1912. He made his official recording debut in 1921 with the Vernon County Club Orchestra. The following year, he and his brother Frank recorded as the Lucas Novelty Quintet and the Lucas Ukulele Trio. In 1922, three years before the emergence of Eddie Lang and during an era when banjos were dominant and guitarists very rarely heard on records, he recorded "Pickin' The Guitar" and "Teasing The Frets" as solo displays. Lucas remade both of the pieces in 1923 and 1932, making one wish that all six of the performances were available on the same CD instead of being scarce.

Lucas played guitar with the Don Parker Trio (with whom he recorded) and worked with Sam Lanin, becoming a studio musician. A major victory for the guitar took place when Lucas talked Lanin into letting him switch from banjo to guitar, showing that it could be heard on records, becoming possibly the first rhythm guitarist to record.

As early as 1924, Lucas was endorsing guitars for the Gibson Company. He was the first musician to have a custom guitar made in his name, 1925's Gibson Nick Lucas Special, and his endorsement of the guitar pick (the first ever) helped lead to the pick becoming established. In the early 1930s, the first guitar pick named after an individual had Nick Lucas' name on it. And while he did not invent the guitar strap, he was among the first to use one.

Despite all of this, Nick Lucas' nationwide fame in the 1920s was due to his singing. He was featured on the radio in 1924 when he was with the Russo-Fiorito Orchestra (they appeared at the Edgewater Beach Hotel in Chicago for two years) and was billed as "The Singing Troubadour." His intimate style of crooning predated Bing Crosby by a few years. Lucas' high-pitched voice, which is now an acquired taste, sounds much more dated than Crosby's friendly baritone. Nevertheless, he had a steady string of big hits during 1925–32, including "Tip-Toe Through The Tulips," "I'm Looking Over A Four Leaf Clover," "Yes, We Have No Bananas," "Bye Bye Blackbird," "The Song Is Ended," "In A Little Spanish Town," "I'm Sitting On Top Of The World," "Side By Side," "Somebody Stole My Gal," "I'll Get By," "My Best Girl," "Painting The Clouds

With Sunshine" and "Brown Eyes, Why Are You Blue?" On many of his records, Lucas accompanied himself on guitar, although one regrets that there were relatively few solos.

Lucas set attendance records when he appeared in London in 1926. He appeared on Broadway in *Sweetheart Time* and *Show Girl* and was in the early talkies *Gold Diggers Of Broadway* (introducing "Tip-Toe Through The Tulips," which eventually sold eight million copies) and *The Show Of Shows*. However, he made the biggest mistake of his career in the early 1930s. Warner Brothers wanted to sign him to a seven-year movie contract but Lucas turned it down because he was making $3,000 a week in vaudeville. Dick Powell got the contract instead, and by 1933, vaudeville was dead.

But Nick Lucas was never out of work. A masterful entertainer, he was a fixture in Hollywood clubs during the 1930s, appeared in some movie shorts, and was a regular on the radio. He worked in Las Vegas in the 1950s, made many appearances on the Ed Sullivan show and other variety programs, and recorded some movie soundtracks, including 1974's *The Great Gatsby*. His high-pitched style of singing was copied in later years by Tiny Tim (as was "Tip-Toe Through The Tulips").

Nick Lucas' recordings reportedly sold 84 million copies in his lifetime. He stayed active until 1981, one year before his death.

**Recommended CDs:** *The Crooning Troubadour* (ASV/Living Era 5329) has some of Nick Lucas' most significant early recordings, including a version of "Pickin' The Guitar." One of the early versions of "Teasing The Frets" is included on *Pioneers Of The Jazz Guitar* (Yazoo 1057).

**Website:** www.nicklucas.com (a very valuable source for information)

## Lawrence Lucie
*b. December 18, 1907, Emporia, VA; d. August 14, 2009, New York, NY*

When Lawrence Lucie passed away in 2009, he was one of the last living links to jazz of the 1930s and the last person alive who had recorded with Jelly Roll Morton, played at the Cotton Club with Duke Ellington, or been on the famous "Body And Soul" session with Coleman Hawkins. Lucie's career as a rhythm guitarist lasted over 75 years.

He started off on banjo, mandolin and violin, playing as a child (starting when he was eight) with his family at dances. In 1927, Lucie moved to New York, where he was originally going to study medicine but soon chose music. He studied banjo at the

Brooklyn Conservatory of Music, but by the time he started playing professionally, he had switched to guitar, which he studied at the Paramount Music Studios. Lucie substituted for Freddy Guy for a few nights with Duke Ellington's orchestra in 1931, even taking a guitar solo on a radio broadcast that got him some attention. He gained a strong reputation playing with Benny Carter's big band during 1932–34. Lucie kept busy during the swing era, working with Fletcher Henderson (1934), the Mills Blue Rhythm Band (1934–36), Lucky Millinder, Henderson again (1936–39), Coleman Hawkins (1940) and the Louis Armstrong big band (1940–44). Strictly a rhythm guitarist, Lucie did not solo, including on records with Spike Hughes, Putney Dandridge, Teddy Wilson, Billie Holiday, Jelly Roll Morton, Big Joe Turner and Henry "Red" Allen.

After serving in the Army, the end of the big band era found him playing more with combos and doing quite a bit of session work, including in R&B settings. Lucie led a swing quartet, the Lucienaires, but mostly worked in the studios other than a tour with Cozy Cole in the late 1950s. In the 1970s, Lucie formed his own label, Toy Records, so he could record with his wife, bassist Nora Lee King, and document his own easy-listening originals. He took a few rare solos on those records. Lucie worked in the 1970s with the Harlem Jazz and Blues Band and the New York Jazz Repertory Company and also played concerts with Panama Francis' Savoy Sultans in the 1980s and '90s.

Lawrence Lucie taught jazz guitar, classical guitar and African-American studies at the Borough of Manhattan Community College for over 30 years, until he was 96 in 2004. He stayed active as a guitarist, playing solo guitar on Sunday nights at Arturo's in Greenwich Village until he was 99, two years before his death.

**Recommended CDs:** Although Lawrence Lucie is on recordings by the likes of Louis Armstrong, Benny Carter, Fletcher Henderson, Sidney Bechet, Roy Eldridge, Chu Berry, Hot Lips Page, Billie Holiday, Jelly Roll Morton, Henry "Red" Allen and Ben Webster, he is always heard in a background role. It was only late in his career that he began to take solos.

**LPs to Search For:** Lawrence Lucie's own LPs on his Toy label, including *Cool And Warm Guitar* (Toy 1001), *Sophisticated Lady/After Sundown* (Toy 1003), *Mixed Emotions* (Toy 1006) and *It Was Good . . . It Is Good* (Toy 1007), tend to be disappointing easy-listening sets with no real adventure or unpredictability. Best of the lot is *This Is It . . . The Innovator* (Toy 1005), which has six Lucie originals plus two songs by Jelly Roll Morton played by

a quintet that includes Lucie's wife, Susan Lenore King, on bass.

## Doug MacDonald
*b. September 10, 1953, Philadelphia, PA*

A fine bop-based guitarist based in Southern California and inspired by Johnny Smith, Howard Roberts and Wes Montgomery, Doug MacDonald has also developed into a skilled arranger. "I was about 13 years old when I first picked up the guitar. I also started the trombone in the school band, but the guitar won." He originally listened to blues, gradually switching to jazz. Growing up in Honolulu, MacDonald played a wide variety of gigs—everything from playing at a strip club called the Hubba Hubba to working with the Gabe Baltazar Quartet. In 1984, after living for a year in Las Vegas, he moved to Los Angeles, quickly making a strong reputation for himself as a versatile straight-ahead guitarist.

He has been in great demand ever since, including the period when he lived in New York. Among his many musical associations have been Hank Jones, Bob Cooper, Ray Brown, Herb Ellis, Snooky Young, Stan Getz, Sarah Vaughan, Buddy Rich, Jack Sheldon and Bill Holman.

In addition to having his own combos and appearing often as a sideman (gigging an average of five nights a week), Doug MacDonald has led and written for his 13-piece band the Jazz Coalition (formed in 2001), which was augmented by strings on his most recent recording, *Fourth Stream.*

"The most important thing for an artist is perseverance. Stick to it. That is the one sure way of moving forward."

**Recommended CDs:** 1990's *The Doug MacDonald Quartet* (Cexton 5678) helped put the guitarist on the map. It was followed by the equally rewarding *The Doug MacDonald Trio* (Cexton 5680). *Warm Valley* (Resurgent 111) was MacDonald's debut as an arranger, as he supplied the charts for his nonet. *Organizing* (Resurgent 116) features the guitarist in a quartet with tenorman Plas Johnson and Art Hillary on organ. *Blue Capers* (Sea Breeze 3046) has MacDonald leading a small group that features Hillary on piano. He leads his Brass/Winds Coalition on *Turn* (Sea Breeze 3061). *Gentle Rain* (Sea

**Russell Malone**

Breeze 3084) is a relaxed standards date with small groups; MacDonald takes the title cut unaccompanied. *Beautiful Friendship* (Blu Jazz 3360) is in a similar vein with a quartet. But the project closest to Doug MacDonald's heart is *Fourth Stream* (Blu Jazz 3375), which has him leading, arranging and playing with a greatly expanded (30 pieces with strings) version of his renamed Jazz Coalition. As usual, the music is cool-toned West Coast jazz, swinging hard but often quietly.

**Website:** www.dougmacdonald.net

### Russell Malone
*b. November 8, 1963, Albany, GA*

One of the top straight-ahead jazz guitarists of the past 20 years, Russell Malone seems to know every standard ever written. His wide knowledge of jazz and guitar history is reflected in his solos, even on his originals. Malone was originally interested in blues and country music, but he turned toward jazz when he was 12 after seeing George Benson play with Benny Goodman on television. He was self-taught and worked locally in Georgia until he joined Jimmy Smith (1988–90). Malone began to get noticed when he was with Harry Connick Jr.'s big band (1991–94), appearing on three Connick CDs. He also guested with such artists as Mulgrew Miller, Kenny Barron, Branford Marsalis, Wynton Marsalis, Eddie "Cleanhead" Vinson and Jack McDuff. Malone recorded his debut as a leader in 1992.

As the guitarist with the Diana Krall Trio during 1995–99, Malone was a major asset to the group, challenging Krall with his strong solos and gaining a lot of visibility and acclaim. Since that time, he has led his own quartet, worked with Roy Hargrove (the Crisol big band), Bill Frisell (touring as a duo), Ron Carter (in the Golden Striker Trio with Mulgrew Miller), Dianne Reeves (as her backup along with Romero Lubambo) and Sonny Rollins. Malone's wise smile, sly wit and creative solos are a major asset to every setting.

While his own groups are excellent and every recording he has made is easily recommended, Russell Malone is at his absolute best on the rare occasions that he is teamed in a duo with pianist Benny Green.

**Recommended CDs:** *Russell Malone* (Sony 52825), *Black Butterfly* (Sony 53912), *Wholly Cats* (Venus 35069), *Sweet Georgia Peach* (Impulse 282), *Look Who's Here* (Verve 543543), *Heartstrings* (Verve 549 786), *Playground* (Maxjazz 601), *Live At Jazz Standard Vol. One* (Maxjazz 602), *Live At Jazz Standard Vol. Two* (Maxjazz 604), *Triple Play* (Maxjazz 607); with Diana Krall: *All For You* (Impulse 182), *Love Scenes* (Impulse 233), *When I Look In Your Eyes* (GRP 304), *The Look Of Love* (Verve 549846); with Benny Green: *These Are Soulful Days* (Blue Note 99527) and *Naturally* (Telarc 83498) are trio sets with bassist Christian McBride, while *Jazz At The Bistro* (Telarc 83560) and *Bluebird* (Telarc 83604) are duo outings.

### Ahmad Mansour
*b. June 7, 1960, Tehran, Iran*

A major post-bop guitarist from Iran, Ahmad Mansour has always had his own sound. He began playing guitar when he was 14. "For me, it was a natural progression from pop to rock, prog rock to fusion and finally jazz." After graduating high school, he attended Berklee during 1981–84, playing in local clubs in Boston.

Mansour worked with pianist Laszlo Gardony regularly in a quartet during 1983–85. Since moving to New York in 1987, he has freelanced, played in a quintet with saxophonist Donny McCaslin and pianist Marc Copland, and had several groups. His trio with electric bassist Stomu Takeishi and drummer Ted Poor, which was formed in 2005, has been the perfect outlet for his adventurous guitar solos, which have become more extroverted and freer with time.

"What I love most about jazz is being 'out on a limb,' and despite a strong tradition, it allows for any outside influence to be used."

**Recommended CDs:** *Episode* (Timeless 341), *Oxiana* (Timeless 344), *Penumbra* (Timeless 404), *Tumbleweed* (Gorgone 595), *Creatures* (Gorgone 1295), *Apples And Oranges* (Resonant 72), *Nightlight* (Resonant 11), *Short Cuts* (Open Sky 8902), *Public Domain* (ESC 37032), *Free Speech* (ESC 37202).

**Website:** www.ahmadmansour.com

## Pat Martino
*(Pat Azzara)*
*b. August 25, 1944, South Philadelphia, PA*

One of the most creative guitarists to emerge during the second half of the 1960s, Pat Martino was a masterful post-bop soloist before an aneurysm, surgery, and amnesia interrupted his career and his life. He has made an inspiring comeback ever since, recapturing and building on his musical legacy.

Martino first learned about jazz through his father, Carmen "Mickey" Azzara, who had studied guitar with Eddie Lang and sang locally. He took his son out to see the jazz giants of the time. Martino, who was particularly inspired by Johnny Smith and Wes Montgomery, started playing guitar at 12 and left school in tenth grade to become a professional musician in 1961 when he was 16. While he started out playing with rock-and-roll bands, he made his early reputation with soul-jazz organ groups, including those led by Charles Earland, tenor-saxophonist Willis Jackson, Jack McDuff and Don Patterson. He also worked with Sonny Stitt, Gene Ammons, Bobby Hutcherson, Eric Kloss and organists Jimmy Smith, Richard "Groove" Holmes, Trudy Pitts, Gene Ludwig, and Jimmy McGriff. Martino, who recorded as a leader for the first time in 1964, was open to the influences of avant-garde, rock and world music. After working with John Handy in 1966, he led his own groups during the next dozen years. Although less publicized than the top fusion guitarists, Martino became influential, playing very original solos no matter what the context, whether it was hard bop, free jazz, fusion, introspective music, or all of the above. In the mid-1970s, he led the fusion group Joyous Lake.

After having suffered from headaches and seizures for several years, in 1980 he had brain surgery to correct a potentially terminal aneurysm. Although that problem was solved, Martino was stricken with amnesia, which, among other things, left him with no memory of playing guitar. It took him four years before he began playing again in public, having retaught himself the guitar partly by listening to his own records. By 1987, Martino was recording again, and soon he regained his earlier prominence. He took a few years off due to his ill parents, but from 1994 on, he has resumed being a regular part of the jazz scene, continuing to evolve as a guitarist and an improviser.

A half-century after his debut and 30 years after he forgot all about playing music, Pat Martino is still one of the top jazz guitarists around.

**Recommended CDs:** Pat Martino has played in many different jazz-oriented styles throughout his career, always finding something fresh to say while doing justice to the music. His recordings include *El Hombre* (Original Jazz Classics 195); *Strings!* (Original Jazz Classics 223); *East* (Original Jazz Classics 248); *Baiyina* (Original Jazz Classics 355); *Desperado* (Original Jazz Classics 397); *Footprints* (Savoy 17252); *Consciousness/Live* (32 Jazz 32050); *We'll Be Together Again* (Savoy 17226); *First Light* (Savoy 17282), which combines together *Starbright* and *Joyous Lake*; *Comin' And Going* (32 Jazz 32143), which has *Exit* and his 1984 comeback album *The Return*; *The Maker* (Evidence 22121); *Mission Accomplished* (32 Jazz 32151), which combines together *Night Wings* and *Interchange*; *All Sides Now* (Blue Note 37627); *Stone Blue* (Blue Note 53082); *Live At Yoshi's* (Blue Note 99749); *Think Tank* (Blue Note 42722); *Remember: A Tribute To Wes Montgomery* (Blue Note 11227); *Undeniable: Live At Blues Alley* (High Note 7231); and *Alone Together* (High Note 7242), which is a set of duets with fellow guitarist Bobby Rose. Martino also recorded prolifically as a sideman (especially in the 1960s) with Willis Jackson, Don Patterson, Jack McDuff, Eric Kloss, Trudy Pitts, Richard "Groove" Holmes, John Handy, and Charles McPherson.

**Website:** www.patmartino.com

## Steve Masakowski
*b. September 2, 1954, New Orleans, LA*

Steve Masakowski is a skilled modern jazz guitarist born and based in New Orleans. "I owned a guitar in my pre-teen years and took some lessons from a teacher who ultimately said that I was wasting her time and my parents' money. When I was about 15, I started playing electric bass and joined a rock band called Truth, which was loosely based on Cream." Although he became interested in jazz guitar by the time he was 17, Masakowski actually worked many of his early paying gigs on bass.

He attended Berklee during 1974–76, meeting Emily Remler. They moved to New Orleans and for a time had a group called Fourplay consisting of their two guitars, bass and drums. In 1978, Masakowski invented an early guitar synthesizer called the key-tar. He has also designed seven-string guitars.

Masakowski, who considers his four main early influences on the guitar to be Joe Pass, Wes Montgomery, Pat Martino, and Lenny Breau, long ago developed his own flexible style, being equally comfortable in post-bop jazz, straight-ahead, and funk. Among his most important associations have been being a member of the Astral Project since 1987, having a regular duet gig with Ellis Marsalis for three years, touring with Dianne Reeves (1993–96), and recently leading Nova NOLA, which includes his son and daughter. In addition, he has played with Rick Margitza, Mose Allison, Red Tyler, Johnny Adams, Woody Shaw, Carl Fontana, Dave Liebman, Jimmy Smith, Sam Rivers, Bobby McFerrin, Nicholas Payton and Bennie Wallace.

Steve Masakowski is particularly proud that Danny Barker willed him his guitar. "In the future, I hope to make a solo guitar record and continue to grow musically and spiritually."

**Recommended CDs:** *Friends* (Nebula 5010) from 1991 also features tenor-saxophonist Rick Margitza. *Mars* (Nebula 5004) is named after a short-lived group. *What It Was* (Blue Note 80591) is a fairly laidback set of originals. *Direct AXEcess* (Blue Note 31108) includes tributes to Wes Montgomery, Emily Remler and Danny Barker, while *For Joe* (Compass 4289) is dedicated to Joe Pass. Masakowski has also recorded as a sideman with Astral Project, Red Tyler, Tony Dagradi, David Torkanowsky, Rick Margitza, Mose Allison, Johnny Adams and Johnny Vidacovich.

**LPs to Search For:** In 1983, Steve Masakowski led his first album. The date featured Dave Liebman, was simply called *Masakowski/Liebman*, and came out as an LP on the guitarist's short-lived Prescriptions label.

**Website:** www.stevemasakowski.com

## Carmen Mastren
(Carmen Mastandrea)
b. October 6, 1913, Cohoes, NY; d. March 31, 1981, Valley Stream, NY

A fine rhythm guitarist whose chordal work on acoustic guitar was always impressive, Carmen Mastren's main significance to jazz is in his early work. Mastren started out on banjo and violin. He played in a family band, becoming a professional in 1931 and soon switching to guitar. After moving to New York in 1934, he worked in a group with Wingy Manone and Joe Marsala, recording "Swinging That Famous Door" and "Farewell Blues" in a quartet with Marsala and Roy Eldridge. He was an important part of the rhythm section of the Tommy

Dorsey Orchestra during 1936–40 and occasionally contributed arrangements. Mastren's most famous recordings took place in 1940 when he was on two recording dates of the Sidney Bechet–Muggsy Spanier Big Four, a pianoless and drumless quartet in which he is quite prominent. After a second stint with Joe Marsala (1940–41) and the beginning of his career as a studio musician (working with Raymond Scott), Mastren served in the Army, becoming part of Glenn Miller's Army Air Force Band.

In his career, Carmen Mastren had opportunities to appear on records with the likes of Billie Holiday, Mildred Bailey, Muggsy Spanier, Red McKenzie, Jack Teagarden, Louis Armstrong, Bud Freeman, Benny Carter and Johnny Hartman. But after his discharge from the military, he primarily spent the remainder of his musical life as a studio musician, and jazz dates were rare. Mastren was the musical director for Morton Downey and a member of the staff of NBC during 1953–70. In the 1970s, he emerged now and then to play jazz with Dick Hyman and the New York Jazz Repertory Company.

**Recommended CDs:** Sidney Bechet's *1940* (Classics 619) has the eight selections recorded by Bechet, Spanier, Wellman Braud and Mastren, which show how strong a rhythm guitarist and occasional soloist Carmen Mastren could be.

**LPs to Search For:** Ironically, the only album that Carmen Mastren ever led, *Banjorama* (Mercury 20304), is a commercial Dixieland date in which he only plays banjo.

## Pete McCann
b. August 10, 1966, Eau Claire, WI

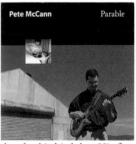

Although he occasionally leads groups of his own, Pete McCann is best known as a very valuable sideman who works in the New York area. McCann started playing guitar when he was eight, receiving one from his mother for his birthday. His first gig was playing New Year's Eve when he was 16 in a duo with a bassist. McCann went to the University of North Texas (1985–89). "When I moved to New York in 1994, I hooked up with a band called East Down Septet. We recorded two CDs, which were my first recordings in New York as a sideman. Since that time, playing with Kenny Wheeler, Dave Liebman and Lee Konitz have been high points for sure. A turning point in my career was my first CD as a leader: *Parable*, which was released in 1998."

Since leaving the East Down Septet in 1997, McCann has worked with Bobby Previte, Lindsey Horner, Tom Varner, Dave Pietro, Jim Cifelli, the Mahavishnu Project, the Other Quartet, Pete Mills, Dave Willis, Patti Austin, Alison Wedding, JD Walter, the Lee Konitz Nonet, Chris Terry, the New York Nonet, Kenny Garrett, Gary Thomas, Greg Osby, Brian Blade, the Maria Schneider Orchestra, Curtis Stigers, George Schuller and Melissa Stylianou. His versatile playing has allowed him to feel comfortable in settings ranging from bop to fusion and the avant-garde.

For the future, Pete McCann is interested in touring with his own group, although the odds are very good that he will continue being in demand for sideman gigs. "When I first heard jazz, I wanted to find out everything I could about the music. This quest has no ending for me. Every day is a new search into what I can do as a guitarist."

**Recommended CDs:** In addition to appearing on over 40 CDs as a sideman, Pete McCann has led several excellent CDs of his own: *Most Folks* (Omnitone 15213), *Parable* (Palmetto 2041), *You Remind Me Of Someone* (Palmetto 2066) and his recent *Extra Mile* (19/8 1010).

**Website:** www.petemccann.com

## Dick McDonough
*b. July 30, 1904, New York, NY; d. May 25, 1938, New York, NY*

One of the finest guitarists to emerge from the 1920s, Dick McDonough worked prolifically in the studios, often being the second choice after Eddie Lang. Whether he was poised for stardom in the long run  or doomed to slip into obscurity never became clear, because he did not survive to see the period where the rise of the electric guitar might have made his style obsolete.

McDonough was originally a banjoist and he had a natural ability, developing his style independently of Lang. While studying at Georgetown University, he began doubling on the guitar. By 1926, McDonough had become a top session musician, recording with Cliff Edwards (Ukulele Ike), Russ Gorman, Frank Signorelli and Don Voorhees early

on. While primarily a banjoist at first, he had largely switched to guitar by 1927, just playing banjo on an occasional basis after that time. During the next 11 years, McDonough appeared on a countless number of recordings with groups ranging from hot jazz combos to anonymous studio orchestras plus sessions accompanying vocalists of various styles. In his large discography are dates with the Charleston Chasers, the Alabama Red Peppers, Rube Bloom, Red McKenzie, Gene Gifford, Glenn Miller (two early sessions in 1937), Ben Selvin, Fred Rich, the New Orleans Blackbirds, Miff Mole's Molers, Jack Pettis, the Red Heads, Red Nichols' Five Pennies (including the hit version of "Ida, Sweet As Apple Cider"), the Whoopee Makers, Irving Mills' Hotsy Totsy Gang, Steve Washington, Frankie Trumbauer, Adrian Rollini, Ethel Waters (including the original version of "Stormy Weather"), the Sunshine Boys, Ramona, Smith Ballew, Baby Rose Marie, Mildred Bailey and Chick Bullock. He was a regular on recordings with the Boswell Sisters (1931–36), the Dorsey Brothers Orchestra (during 1932–34, before they became a working unit) and Annette Hanshaw (1929–33). McDonough also recorded with Benny Goodman (including his own instrumental "Dr. Heckle And Mr. Jibe"), Adelaide Hall (when her pianist was Art Tatum), Billie Holiday (her first two recordings plus her debut as a leader), Red Norvo's two chamber jazz dates (most notably "In A Mist" and "Dance Of The Octopus"), and a 1933 session with Joe Venuti shortly after Eddie Lang's death.

Equally skilled at playing single-note solos and in a chordal style but usually heard in an accompanying role, McDonough remained greatly in demand throughout the Depression years. While he led his own radio dance band during 1936–37, he takes surprisingly few solos on the 46 selections that they recorded. Best among McDonough's recordings of his own playing are two songs from 1937 ("Honeysuckle Rose" and "Blues") with a quintet also featuring Fats Waller, Tommy Dorsey, Bunny Berigan and drummer George Wettling that was billed as "A Jam Session At Victor," and four guitar duets with Carl Kress from 1934 and 1937. On "Danzon," "Stage Fright," "Chicken A La Swing" and "Heat Wave," McDonough (usually playing single-note lines) and Kress make for a perfectly compatible team on the complex arrangements.

Dick McDonough would later become an important influence on Marty Grosz and Bucky Pizzarelli. But unfortunately, he was an alcoholic, and his health declined during 1937–38. McDonough collapsed while working in the NBC studios, passing away on May 25, 1938, from pneumonia when he was just 33.

John McLaughlin

**Recommended CDs:** Dick McDonough's recordings are scattered among many 1920s and '30s collections. His radio band of 1936–37 is showcased on *Dick McDonough And His Orchestra Vol. 1* (Swing Time 2001) and *Vol. 2* (Swing Time 2002), while the McDonough-Kress duets are on *Eddie Lang/ Carl Kress/Dick McDonough* (Retrieval 79015). For the "Jam Session At Victor" selections, search under all-star collections headed by Bunny Berigan and Fats Waller.

## John McLaughlin
*b. January 4, 1942, Doncaster, Yorkshire, England*

One of the greatest guitarists of all time, John McLaughlin was one of the few who changed the way that the guitar is played in jazz, opening it up to an endless number of possibilities. Not only was he one of the fastest guitar slingers ever, but he also brought the power, passion and sound of rock into jazz and has been a restless improviser ever since.

"I'd studied piano for three years when a guitar was brought into the house by one of my brothers when I was 11. I fell in love with the guitar then and there." He discovered jazz through the recordings of Django Reinhardt and, a little later, Miles Davis. McLaughlin first played in a band at school when he was 15, and the following year he went on the road for the first time. He moved to London in the early 1960s and worked with a variety of British groups, including those led by Alexis Korner, Georgie Fame, Brian Auger, the Graham Bond Quartet and Gordon Beck. Rare recordings from the mid-1960s find him sounding comfortable playing straight-ahead jazz. He was also a session musician.

1969 was the turning point in his career. McLaughlin recorded his first album as a leader, *Extrapolation*, was discovered by Tony Williams, and was invited to come to the United States and join Williams' new band, Lifetime. Miles Davis was also very impressed and used McLaughlin on *In A Silent Way*, *Bitches Brew*, *On The Corner*, *Big Fun* and *A Tribute To Jack Johnson*. Although never a regular member of Davis' group, he sat in with his band several times, including on one night when the music was recorded and later became part of *Live-Evil* and *The Cellar Door Sessions*. As a member

of Tony Williams' Lifetime, a trio also including organist Larry Young, McLaughlin took remarkable solos that, despite the poor recording quality of the band's records, were innovative. Larry Coryell may have preceded him as the first fusion guitarist, but McLaughlin had the greatest impact and proved to be a stunning player. Finally, nearly 30 years after his death, no longer would jazz guitarists look first to Charlie Christian for their ideas.

Lifetime did not last long, and in 1970, Miles Davis suggested to McLaughlin that it was time for him to form his own group. McLaughlin considers that the first step toward him forming the Mahavishnu Orchestra. But even this early, he showed much more versatility than one might have expected. McLaughlin's *My Goal's Beyond* album features him on acoustic guitar, blending jazz with Indian classical music on "Peace One" and "Peace Two," and playing melodic versions of jazz tunes (including "Goodbye Pork Pie Hat") on the other selections. Shortly before that recording, McLaughlin was introduced to the Indian religious figure Sri Chinmoy, and he took the name of Mahavishnu.

The Mahavishnu Orchestra was formed in 1971, and although the original version only lasted two years, it is still widely remembered. Consisting of McLaughlin, violinist Jerry Goodman, keyboardist Jan Hammer, electric bassist Rick Laird and drummer Billy Cobham, it was the ultimate power fusion band. Thought of as a rock group by many at the time due to its volume and intensity, it played complex originals (often in unusual time signatures) and featured high-powered improvising. But after three albums, the group split apart due to personality conflicts.

The guitarist soon came back with a second version of the Mahavishnu Orchestra (with violinist Jean-Luc Ponty, keyboardist-singer Gayle Moran, bassist Ralphe Armstrong, and drummer Narada Michael Walden, plus occasional strings and a horn section) that was less successful than the original group. There would be a third version of the Mahavishnu Orchestra in the 1980s with saxophonist Bill Evans that was the least memorable of the three. McLaughlin's next move after the breakup of the second Mahavishnu Orchestra was very surprising. He switched to acoustic guitar and explored virtuosic Indian music with his new group Shakti. He had previously recorded a spiritual album with Carlos Santana in 1973 (*Love, Devotion, Surrender*) that included part of John Coltrane's "A Love Supreme" along with Eastern-flavored pieces. Shakti consisted of violinist L. Shankar, Zakir Hussain on tabla, and musicians on ghatam and mridangam in addition to McLaughlin. The group recorded three albums during 1975–77, introducing many fusion and jazz listeners to Indian music.

In the decades since, McLaughlin has proven that he plays brilliantly in every setting, whether electric or acoustic. The Trio of Doom in 1979 (with Jaco Pastorius and Tony Williams) only had one live performance, although they cut a few songs in the studio. That same year, he had more success teaming up for acoustic music with Paco de Lucía and Larry Coryell; they have had several reunions (with Al Di Meola in Coryell's place) since then. The One Truth Band features a mixture of styles with violinists L. Shankar and keyboardist Stu Goldberg in a quintet. McLaughlin had an acoustic trio with bassist Kai Eckhardt and percussionist Trilok Gurtu. And the guitarist was quite effective during his spots in the 1986 Dexter Gordon movie *Round Midnight*, playing as if it were 1959.

During the past 20 years, McLaughlin has kept busy. His *The Heart Of Things* CD matched him with saxophonist Gary Thomas and pianist Otmaro Ruíz. His 1993 *Time Remembered: John McLaughlin Plays Bill Evans* gave him a chance to play acoustic jazz with an emphasis on ballads. He has had reunions of Shakti under the name Remember Shakti. The guitarist had a trio with organist Joey DeFrancesco and either Dennis Chambers or Elvin Jones on drums that was a bit reminiscent of Tony Williams' Lifetime. In 2007, he put together the still-active fusion band the 4th Dimension, which includes keyboardist Gary Husband, bassist Hadrian Feraud and drummer Mark Mondesir; it is often inspired by John Coltrane's "A Love Supreme" but features original music. And in 2009, McLaughlin toured with Chick Corea in an all-star quintet called the Five Peace Band, which also featured altoist Kenny Garrett, bassist Christian McBride and drummer Vinnie Colaiuta.

"Music is itself a marvelous power for peace in the world, and I am privileged and honored to be a musician. Since it is a power, responsibility comes with the power. My life has been, and is today, dedicated to music. This is the only way I know how to discharge this responsibility correctly."

**Recommended CDs:** John McLaughlin names as his personal favorite recordings among the vast number that he has made *Inner Mounting Flame* and *Visions Of The Emerald Beyond* with the Mahavishnu Orchestra, the Bill Evans tribute *Time Remembered*, the classical album *Thieves And Poets*, *Floating Point*, and the 4th Dimension's *To The One*. But in reality, every John McLaughlin recording is of strong interest: *Extrapolation* (Universal 9195), *My Goal's Beyond* (Knitting Factory Works 3010), *Devotion*

(Varese 061133), *Inner Mounting Flame* (Sony 65523), *Birds Of Fire* (Sony 66081), *Love Devotion Surrender* (Sony 723831) with Carlos Santana, *Between Nothingness And Eternity* (Columbia 32766), *Lost Trident Sessions* (Sony 5046942), *Apocalypse* (Sony 724167), *Visions Of The Emerald Beyond* (Sony 4679042), *Inner Worlds* (Sony 4769052), *Shakti With John McLaughlin* (Sony 467905), *Handful Of Beauty* (Sony 494448), *Natural Elements* (Sony 489773), *Electric Guitarist* (Sony 4670932), *Electric Dreams* (Columbia 48892), *Friday Night In San Francisco* (Sony 4512) with Al Di Meola and Paco de Lucía, *Belo Horizonte* (WEA 57001), *Passion, Grace And Fire* (CBS 9657), *Mahavishnu* (Wounded Bird 5190), *Music Spoken Here* (Wounded Bird 3723), *Adventures In Radioland* (Polygram 519397), *Live At The Royal Festival Hall* (Winter & Winter 919035), *Qué Alegría* (Verve 837280), *Time Remembered* (Verve 519861), *Tokyo Live* (Verve 521870), *After The Rain* (Verve 314 527 4674), *The Promise* (Verve 529828), *The Heart Of Things* (Verve 539153), *The Heart Of Things: Live In Paris* (Verve 543536), *Remember Shakti: The Believer* (Verve 549044), *Thieves And Poets* (Verve 113702), *Industrial Zen* (C&B Media 706602), *Floating Point* (Abstract Logix 11), *Five Peace Band Live* (Concord 31397), *To The One* (Abstract Logix 027); with Miles Davis: *In A Silent Way* (Sony 10088), *Bitches Brew* (Sony 10089/90), *Tribute To Jack Johnson* (Sony 5153); with Tony Williams: *Emergency* (Universal 5382573), *Turn It Over* (Universal 9192); with Wayne Shorter: *Super Nova* (EMI 9239).

**Website:** www.johnmclaughlin.com

## Paul Mehling
*b. February 18, 1958, Denver, CO*

Leader of the Hot Club of San Francisco, Paul Mehling has long been one of the most important American gypsy-jazz guitarists. He started on guitar when he was six. "I saw the Beatles on the *Ed Sullivan Show* and decided then and there that I wanted to make girls scream. I begged my folks for a guitar though I didn't have the discipline to follow the boring lessons they gave me at the music store. My father was a record collector who listened only to jazz, swing and blues pre-1946. My mother would often play this one Django Reinhardt record. I loved that record and went back to it many many times in my early life."

Mehling, who also learned banjo, mandolin and bass, played with his school band and orchestra, and performed rock at local club gigs during his high school years in Pleasanton, California. However, he preferred to play acoustic guitar. He was particularly impressed by Dan Hicks & the Hot Licks and their combination of rock and hot club swing. After high school, he worked with Jake Stock's Abalone Stompers once a week for the next 15 years. "They were all 60-, 70-, and 80-year-olds while I wasn't even old enough to drink. I learned a ton of tunes and musicianship from those cats. I still love to play New Orleans–style music." He also gigged with the Magnolia Jazz Band and led the Hot Club of Friends.

Mehling played violin for a time, performing with the Santa Cruz Symphony for a season. "The experience of studying the instrument was invaluable in learning to play gypsy guitar. It's true that many gypsies learn violin first and then adapt all of that to the guitar. Many guitar players miss out on this part of the technique."

While visiting Europe in 1981, he saw a Belgium gypsy-jazz band Waso, which inspired him to return two years later and play guitar and violin with gypsies. During 1985–90, Mehling was a member of Dan Hicks' Acoustic Warriors. In 1990, he moved to San Francisco and started the Hot Club of San Francisco, a group that has grown in power and significance through the years. "When our ace violinist Evan Price came into the Hot Club in 1999, it was like we were long-lost brothers."

The Hot Club of San Francisco has thus far released 11 CDs and become a San Francisco institution. In 2000, they became the first American band to play at the Festival de Jazz Django Reinhardt in Samois-sur-Seine. "I've always tried to run the HCSF as a synergistic experiment, bringing out the best in each of us to achieve something unique that none of us could do without the other. The Hot Club of SF is trying to preserve the memory and music of Django Reinhardt while at the same time demonstrating to people that jazz can be accessible and enjoyable."

**Recommended CDs:** At the time that they recorded *The Hot Club Of San Francisco* (Clarity 1006) in 1993, the group was a quartet (no violin yet) but was already stretching the idiom. Maria Muldaur, Dan Hicks and Barbara Dane are featured on two songs apiece. *Live* (Hot Club 2702), *Claire De Lune* (Hot Club 2703) and *The Lady In Red* (Clarity 2019) joyfully trace the group's evolution through the 1990s. *Veronica* (Panda 211) and *Be That Way* (Panda 217) are sets of Mehling's originals, while *Swing This* (Panda 219) has gypsy versions of more modern jazz tunes. *Postcards From Gypsyland* (Lost Wax 502) has some magical interplay by Mehling and Price on lots of unlikely material, as does *Yerba Buena Bounce* (Reference 109), which even converts the Beatles' "I'm Happy Just To Dance With You" into gypsy jazz. *Bohemian Maestro* (Azica 72241)

ranges from originals and obscure Django compositions to Jelly Roll Morton's "The Pearls" (which has Mehling on banjo) and pieces from Debussy and Villa-Lobos, while *Hot Club Yule* (Azica 72242) is one of the most swinging of all Xmas albums. *Live At Yoshi's San Francisco* (Azica 72249) is their most recent recording.

**Website:** www.hcsf.com

## Pat Metheny
*b. August 12, 1954, Lee's Summit, MO*

One of the most significant and distinctive guitarists of the past 40 years, Pat Metheny's airy tone is immediately recognizable within two notes. The music that he has created with the Pat Metheny Group and on his many side projects has been continually intriguing, forming a very impressive body of work.

During a March 29, 1995, interview, he spoke about his beginnings. "I started playing guitar when I was eight or nine. My initial attraction to it was because of the Beatles. The odd thing about my taste is that I was into rock and roll for about two weeks, heard Miles Davis, and that completely changed my direction. By the time I was 12, I was into bebop, Miles, Coltrane, Sonny Rollins, Wes and Kenny Burrell. I completely missed Jimi Hendrix like he never happened. Wes Montgomery was a very strong influence on me when I was quite young, the first couple of years that I played. Today, I could still do one of the best Wes Montgomery imitations if I wanted, and right now I hear a lot of guys sounding like Wes. But that's not the point of it all. We are supposed to sound like ourselves, not copy our idols."

Metheny's older brother Mike Metheny was originally a classical trumpeter who Pat persuaded to play jazz. After graduating high school, the guitarist attended the University of Miami in 1972 and, at 18, became the school's youngest instructor. While in Miami, he met Jaco Pastorius, who became his best friend. Metheny went to Berklee briefly and also became that school's youngest teacher. In 1974, both he and Jaco Pastorius arrived in New York. "He would call up all of the great musicians and say, 'Hello, I'm Jaco, and I'm the best bass player you've ever heard.' He called up Keith Jarrett, Tony Williams, everybody. They all thought he was nuts until they heard him play. One of the people he called was Paul Bley, who responded by telling him to come over. Jaco told Paul that he wanted to bring me too, we did some gigs with Paul, and also made a weird record, one that we didn't know was being made. Jaco sounded great, but I wasn't quite there yet."

By the following year, Metheny was ready. He was featured with Gary Burton's group during 1974–77, at first next to Mick Goodrick but eventually as the only guitarist. "Gary was always one of my favorite musicians. He uses the guitar as a frontline instrument. At the time, except for John Handy, there were hardly any other gigs for guitar players except with trios." In 1975, Metheny met pianist-keyboardist Lyle Mays at a college jazz festival in Wichita, Kansas. "Lyle was representing North Texas State. Within about 15 seconds, I knew that I wanted to talk to him. He was doing so many of the same kind of things that I wanted to do. About three weeks later I booked us a gig, and it was felt like we'd always been playing together."

Metheny made his first record as a leader in 1975, *Bright Size Life*. By the time he left Burton in 1977, he was ready to form his own band, and the result was the Pat Metheny Group. Lyle Mays was in the original version, and he is still in the unit over 30 years later. "We felt that it was time to move beyond bebop, explore much more advanced music. We wanted to provide a different outlook on what jazz could be, come up with something new rather than just repeating the past. Our only agenda was to play what we like. I was shocked by how popular the group became."

In 1978, the Pat Metheny Group featured Mays (who has co-written many songs with Metheny through the years), bassist Mark Egan and drummer Dan Gottlieb. The Group's recordings for ECM, Geffen, Warner Brothers and Nonesuch have been largely beyond any simple classification. While certainly falling into jazz, the music was always open to other influences, including the use of space à la New Age, rock, classical, folk, Brazilian, world music, and electronics, and yet it sounded unlike any other music being created. By the time the band recorded *American Garage* in 1980, they were one of the most popular in jazz yet; like Dave Brubeck a quarter-century ago, they became commercially successful while simply playing the music they loved.

Steve Rodby succeeded Mark Egan with the band in 1982, Paul Wertico was its drummer during 1983–2001, and Antonio Sanchez has been the drummer for most of a decade. Trumpeter Cuong Vu, bassist Richard Bono (mostly heard on vocals), Mark Ledford (vocals and trumpet), harmonica player Grégoire Maret and guest percussionist Naná Vasconcelos also spent time with the unit. While playing,

recording and touring with the Pat Metheny Group, Metheny has played not just the standard guitar but was also one of the first to fully explore the guitar synthesizer in addition to the twelve-string electric guitar, the 42-string Pikasso guitar, an acoustic sitar guitar and a baritone guitar.

Through the years, Metheny has also had many additional projects that have found him performing and recording with such notables as Dewey Redman, Michael Brecker, Jim Hall, Dave Holland, Charlie Haden, Roy Haynes, Derek Bailey, Chick Corea, Sonny Rollins, John Scofield, Jack DeJohnette, Joshua Redman, Abbey Lincoln, Herbie Hancock, Brad Mehldau and a remarkable set with Ornette Coleman (*Song X*). 2010's *Orchestrion* was a very unusual project in which his guitar triggered the playing of several acoustic instruments, giving him an opportunity to "play an orchestra." One of his most recent projects has been leading the Unity Band, a quartet with Chris Potter, bassist Ben Williams and drummer Antonio Sanchez.

"For a time, I was sorry that I played guitar rather than trumpet, tenor, piano, bass or drums. The guitar did not seem to fit into the jazz world, and to an extent it was uncharted territory. Only since the 1970s have there been a sizable number of guitarists who were harmonically and rhythmically advanced enough to hang with the best horn players; there were just a few before that. But now in the post-Coltrane era, there are many great guitarists and endless possibilities for the instrument."

**Recommended CDs:** *Bright Size Life* (ECM 9027), *Water Colors* (ECM 9028), *Pat Metheny Group* (ECM 9029), *New Chautauqua* (ECM 1182702), *80/81* (ECM 9032/3), *American Garage* (ECM 1162402), *As Falls Wichita, So Falls Wichita Falls* (ECM 9034), *Offramp* (ECM 9035), *Travels* (ECM 9036/7), *First Circle* (ECM 9047), *Song X* (Nonesuch 79007) with Ornette Coleman, *Still Life (Talking)* (Nonesuch 79948), *Letter From Home* (Nonesuch 79940), *Question And Answer* (Nonesuch 511494), *Secret Story* (Geffen 24468), *I Can See Your House From Here* (Blue Note 27765) with John Scofield, *The Road To You* (Nonesuch 79941), *We Live Here* (Nonesuch 79955), *Quartet* (Nonesuch 79956), *The Sign Of 4* (Knitting Factory Works 197) with Derek Bailey, *Imaginary Day* (Warner Bros. 46791), *A Map Of The World* (Warner Bros. 47366), *Trio 99/00* (Warner Bros. 47632), *Trio Live* (Warner Bros. 47907), *Speaking Of Now* (Warner Bros. 48025), *One Quiet Night* (Warner Bros. 48473), *The Way Up* (Nonesuch 79876), *Metheny Mehldau* (Nonesuch 79964), *Metheny Mehldau Quartet* (Nonesuch 79995), *Day Trip* (Nonesuch 76828), *Orchestrion* (Nonesuch 516668), *What's It All About* (Nonesuch

528173), *Unity Band* (Nonesuch 531257); with Jaco Pastorius: *Jaco* (Improvising Artists 123846); with Gary Burton: *Dreams So Real* (ECM 1161702), *Passengers* (ECM 835016).

**Website:** www.patmetheny.com

## Paul Meyers
*b. June 28, 1956, New York, NY*

Paul Meyers grew up around music. His father was a studio trombonist, his mother a classical singer-pianist, and brother John Meyers became a drummer. He studied piano and violin before starting to take classical guitar lessons in the late 1960s. Meyers discovered jazz as a teenager, playing locally. He studied at the State University of New York at Postdam, the Eastman School of Music, and the New England Conservatory, where he graduated in 1979. That year, he was part of Gunther Schuller's New England Ragtime Ensemble.

After moving to New York in 1980, Meyers led his own groups, made his first recordings and, in 1986, earned a master's degree from the Manhattan School of Music. Meyers, who worked for a time in a quintet with Red Rodney, started teaching guitar at William Paterson University in 1988 and, since 1993, New Jersey City University.

Meyers has worked with many jazz all-stars during the past three decades, including Gary Burton, Kenny Barron, Ron Carter, Clare Fischer, Sonny Fortune, Annie Ross, Wynton Marsalis, Rufus Reid, Kenny Werner, Geri Allen, Eliane Elias, Frank Wess, David Sanchez, Brazilian percussionist Cafe, the Woody Herman Orchestra, Santi Debriano and the New York Jazz Guitar Ensemble. He has been a regular member of Jon Hendricks' band since 1993, was with Andy Bey during 1997–2008, and has also been active playing Brazilian jazz, including with Terra Brasil and as co-leader of Brasil & Company, which also features singer Vera Mara. His own bands have included the Latin jazz trio Euforia and the eclectic Trio Concertant.

In every setting, Paul Meyers displays his own sound and consistently comes up with fresh ideas.

**Recommended CDs:** On his own PM label, Paul Meyers has released a trio of unaccompanied guitar sets: 1997's *Blues For The Millennium*, 2004's *Dusk To Dawn* and 2011's *Welcome Home*. He has also made available two of his earliest recordings, *Trio Concertant* and *Blues For Henry Miller*, plus *Brasil & Co.* *Euforia* (Mapleshade 5732) has Meyers in a Brazilian jazz trio playing complex post-bop tunes. *Spirit And Samba: From J.J. To Jobim* (Mapleshade 9832) teams him in duets with bassist Santi Debriano. *World*

*On A String* (Miles High 8608) is a fine all-around showcase for his acoustic guitar, while *Paul Meyers Quintet Featuring Frank Wess* (Miles High 8609) has the guitarist's take on standards. As a sideman, Paul Meyers has appeared on many recordings, including ones with Linda Ciofalo, the New York Jazz Guitar Ensemble, the Lincoln Center Jazz Orchestra, Ann Hampton Callaway, Don Byron (*Bug Music*), Ken Peplowski, Andy Bey, Richard Stolzman, Sue Maskaleris, Susannah McCorkle, Andy Bey, Michelle Samuels, and Beat Kaestli.

**Website:** www.paulmeyers.info

## Jane Miller
*b. January 6, 1957, Fitchburg, MA*

Jane Miller is a fine post-bop guitarist, a very individual composer, and a longtime educator at Berklee. She got her first guitar when she was 11, inspired by watching Laura Weber on the PBS television series *Folk Guitar*. "I started gigging in my teens doing the folk circuit around New England. I tried the singer-songwriter gig on for size, playing at clubs and coffeehouses and bars. The problem with that was that I didn't actually want to be a singer and, as for songwriting, I wanted to compose and arrange instrumentals for a small jazz group, as opposed to writing songs. Once I sorted that all out, I put a group together and steered toward different sorts of gigs."

Miller did not hear much jazz until she attended Berklee (1975–76). While she retained her ties to folk music, she explored the recordings of jazz singers and guitarists, developing her own style. In the early 1980s, she worked at WCUC-FM in Worcester, Massachusetts, including hosting a jazz show. One year, Miller booked Emily Remler for a local concert series. "Emily and I became fast friends. She even let me sit in on the gig, which was pretty generous. I learned so much from her in a short time. Thankfully, we fit a lot of friendship and mentoring into the next couple of years."

In 1991, Jane Miller started playing duo gigs with saxophonist Cercie Miller. Soon, David Clark joined on bass to form a trio that still performs today. "That has been a great opportunity for me to challenge myself with new roles beyond the standard trio or quartet format." She also works with pianist Tim Ray, plays duets with harmonica player Chet Williamson, and has performed and recorded with singer-songwriter Sonia. In addition, Jane Miller has been a member of the faculty of the Guitar Department at Berklee since 1994 and writes regularly for *Acoustic Guitar Magazine* and *Premier Guitar*.

**Recommended CDs:** Jane Miller has led three CDs so far: *Postcard* (Pink Bubble 9801), *Secret Pockets* (Pink Bubble 9802) and *The Other Room* (Pink Bubble 9803). She is currently planning a solo guitar recording.

**Website:** www.janemillergroup.com

## John Mills, Jr.
*b. October 19, 1910, Piqua, OH; d. January 23, 1936, Bellefontaine, OH*

The oldest of the Mills Brothers, John Mills, Jr., was arguably the most important member of the group in its early days. In addition to singing bass notes, he was the band's only instrumentalist, accompanying the four brothers on acoustic guitar, which made it possible for the group to be billed as Four Boys and a Guitar.

The Mills Brothers, which consisted of Herbert, Harry, and Donald Mills in addition to John, were the sons of John Mills, Sr., who owned a barbershop and founded a barbershop quartet, the Four Kings of Harmony. The four brothers at first performed around Piqua, Ohio, as a conventional a cappella quartet, with Harry Mills sometimes playing kazoo. During one performance, Harry forgot his kazoo and spontaneously tried to imitate the instrument by cupping his hand over his mouth, surprising everyone by sounding like a trumpet. Soon each of the Mills Brothers was imitating horns with remarkable effectiveness, sounding like two trumpets, a trombone, and a tuba when all they actually had was John's acoustic guitar. They became a hit in vaudeville, began broadcasting regularly from a Cincinnati radio station in the late 1920s, and became a sensation in New York in 1931. They recorded regularly, appeared in films and toured Europe.

It was during the first European tour that John Mills, Jr., contracted pneumonia. After a few months, it looked as if he would recover, so the family returned to England. But this time, he had a relapse and died at the age of 25. When the Mills Brothers recovered from the shock and regrouped, John Mills, Sr., was singing in his son's place with Bernard Addison on guitar.

**Recommended CDs:** *Chronological, Vol. 1* (JSP 301), *Vol. 2* (JSP 302), *Vol. 3* (JSP 303) and *Vol. 4* (JSP 304) have all of the Mills Brothers recordings with John Mills, Jr., who is just on the first four selections of *Vol. 4*. The first two CDs are particularly recommended, not only for the unique singing of the Brothers but also for John's superior accompaniment of the group and his many short solos.

## Dom Minasi
*b. March 6, 1943, Queens, NY*

An adventurous guitarist whose roots are in the 1970s but who has continued to grow quite a bit since then, Dom Minasi gives one the impression that due to his steady development, his best

work is still in the near future. "I saw Roy Rogers playing the guitar in a movie in 1947. I wanted to play then, but my father waited until I was seven years old, so I got my first guitar in 1950." In high school, Minasi was part of his school's swing band. One of his teachers played him Johnny Smith's "Moonlight In Vermont." "I later saw that Johnny was playing at Birdland. I begged my father to take me. When I saw Johnny play, I knew that's what I wanted to do the rest of my life."

He gained experience as a teenager playing at church dances and accompanying rock-and-roll singers, becoming a professional musician when he was 18. An educator from an early age, by the time he was 20 he had more than 100 students. He considers his first important gig to have taken place in 1967 when Chris White hired him to play at a function that included pianist Roland Hanna.

In 1973, Minasi's trio came to the attention of the Blue Note label. But after recording two records, it was obvious that Blue Note was declining rapidly. He left the label and freelanced, often playing with pianist Dennis Moorman and in a quartet with organist Dr. Lonnie Smith. Minasi went back to school when he was 48 and earned a BS in composition from CUNY at Lehman College. He kept very busy playing off-Broadway shows, writing over 250 compositions, teaching in the New York public school system, writing several music books, conducting workshops for kids, and reinventing his playing.

One can say that Dom Minasi really began his playing career in 1993 when he was 50. He became the principal composer for the Manhattan Improvisational Chamber Ensemble and was involved in many projects as a leader and sideman. Since 2000, he has had a trio with bassist Ken Filiano and drummer Jackson Krall. Minasi sometimes plays in duos with pianist Michael Jefry Stevens, saxophonist Blaise Siwula, pianist Borah Bergman and Minasi's wife, vocalist Carol Mennie. He heads DDT + 2, which also includes Mennie, Filiano, cellist Tomas Ulrich and drummer John Bollinger, has an organ quartet with Bollinger, altoist Mark Whitecage, and organist Koehler, and has worked and recorded with fellow guitarist Jon Hemmersam in a quartet. In addition, he and Carol Mennie founded CDM (Can Do More) Records, which they continue to run.

"Jazz has become the essence of everything I do. Within the music is all I can hope for, dream and accomplish."

**Recommended CDs:** While Dom Minasi's two Blue Note albums have long ago disappeared, *Finishing Touches* (CIMP 96) from 1999 is his earliest significant recording. With bassist Michael Bocchicchio and drummer Jay Rosen, three standards are reinvented and some of the guitarist's originals are introduced in inventive fashion. *Takin' The Duke Out* (CDM 1001) features Minasi, Filiano and Krall coming up with very fresh, surprising and somewhat controversial versions of six songs made famous by Duke Ellington. *Goin' Out Again* (CDM 1002), with the same trio, offers "outside" versions of standards and originals. *Time Will Tell* (CDM 1003) features DDT + 2 and is a bit more mellow and melodic although still quite inventive. *Quick Response* (CDM 1005) deconstructs three standards and some of Minasi's originals with Mark Whitecage often co-starring. *The Vampire's Revenge* (CDM 1006), a double-CD set, features Minasi, Filiano and Krall along with 22 other musicians in various combinations interpreting the leader's intriguing through-composed originals. The recent *Dissonance Makes The Heart Grow Fonder* (Konnex 5235) has Minasi leading a very different string quartet also including violinist Jason Kao Hwang, cellist Tomas Ulrich and Ken Filiano. The music falls between avant-garde jazz and twenty-first-century classical music. Dom Minasi is also featured on *The Jon Hemmersam/ Dom Minasi Quartet* (CDM 1008) and Carol Mennie's *I'm Not A Sometime Thing* (CDM 1004).

**Website:** www.domminasi.com

## Chieli Minucci
*b. April 17, 1958, New York, NY*

The co-founder (along with the late percussionist George Jinda) of Special EFX, Chieli Minucci has been very busy ever since, performing his own personal blend of world music and jazz. Minucci had piano lessons for three years starting

when he was five. His father, Ulpio Minucci, was a songwriter who wrote tunes recorded by Bing Crosby and Nat King Cole. "I grew up in a house of melody. As a kid, I thought my father tried to discourage me from music, when in fact he was encouraging me to study other subjects, to enhance my abilities as a musician. I learned that the more we are exposed to, the broader our musical palette. I was about eight when I got my first guitar. I took a course at the YMCA once, when I had a $30 acoustic guitar, and saw some kid with an electric with four pickups. It changed my life, seeing that. I had to play that guitar!" Minucci took lessons for three years with guitarist Jack Hotop (who had worked with Joe Mooney in the late 1940s), learning standards. "At that point in time, I couldn't quite improvise over those chords to save my life. I'd write out my solos and try to fool my teacher."

When he was 13, Minucci started a group with his friends called Taurus. They were booked on cruise ships as teenagers, also playing at dances, parties and restaurants. "By the time I was 18, I'd played literally hundreds of shows and had developed quite an appetite for music and travel, as well as some other less prestigious activities." He was a classical guitar major at Ithaca College for one year (1977), and although he switched his major to English, he continued taking music classes. Minucci played with the fusion group Gumbo, wrote many pop vocal songs, performed with Lou Reed, and worked with Eartha Kitt for two years.

While playing in a pop/rock group led by singer Fran Eckhart in 1982, he met Hungarian percussionist George Jinda. "The relationship with the late George Jinda in Special EFX has since been the real root of my career and influenced my writing style for contemporary jazz ensembles. At first, this collaboration had no artistic censorship whatsoever, and it resulted in many, many opportunities to write and arrange in an eclectic way, which certainly has set the stage for what I do now." Minucci and Jinda formed the group Special Delivery, which recorded an album for the Dutch label Keytone called *Special EFX*. GRP distributed the album in the United States, and that was the start, resulting in the group changing its name. Special EFX became very popular on the so-called "contemporary jazz" circuit but stood apart from other groups in its openness to music from other cultures.

Special EFX, which was originally a duo although it expanded to become a full group, lasted until 1995, resulting in 13 albums. The breakup, due to artistic differences, was friendly, and Jinda recorded an album under the Special EFX name without Chieli. However, a massive stroke in 1997 forced George Jinda into retirement, and he passed away in 2001.

THE 342 GREAT JAZZ GUITARISTS

Chieli, who had recorded a few solo albums while still with the group, has since revived Special EFX (they recently recorded a 25th-anniversary set), has worked with pop, R&B, and pop/jazz artists, and has been busy as both a producer and a writer for soundtracks and television (including for the soap opera *Guiding Light*). In addition to his work with Special EFX, he plays in a trio with pianist Lao Tizer and violinist Karen Briggs called Tizer.

**Recommended CDs:** Chieli Minucci's solo CDs, which usually have music similar in style to that found on the Special EFX releases, are *Jewels* (Samson 29928), *Renaissance* (Samson 29929), *It's Gonna Be Good* (Samson 29927), *Sweet On You* (Shanachie 5066), *Night Grooves* (Shanachie 5096), *Got It Goin' On* (Shanachie 5124), *Sweet Surrender* (Shanachie 5145) and *East Of The Sun* (Watchfire). He is also well featured with Special EFX on all of their CDs: *Special EFX* (GRP 9505), *Modern Manners* (GRP 9521), *Slice Of Life* (GRP 9534), *Mystique* (GRP 9543), *Double Feature* (GRP 9559), *Confidential* (GRP 9581), *Just Like Magic* (GRP 9609), *Peace Of The World* (GRP 9640), *Global Village* (GRP 9670), *Play* (JVC 2017), *Catwalk* (JVC 2038), *Body Language* (Samson 29902), *Masterpiece* (Shanachie 5054), *Butterfly* (Shanachie 5083), *Party* (Shanachie 5107) and *Without You* (ChieliMusic).

**Website:** www.chielimusic.com

## Roman Miroshnichenko
*b. June 4, 1977, Dneprodzerzhinsk, Ukraine*

A major jazz guitarist from the Ukraine, Roman Miroshnichenko was introduced to jazz early on through his father, Maxim Miroshnichenko, a saxophonist and arranger. He began on the drums when he was 11, switching to guitar when he was 14. "Jazz music was played in our home all the time, although I started learning guitar from listening to blues and rock. But after two years of practice, I started to become more interested in richer sounds and harmonies. That was my first step towards the world of jazz improvisation." During 1994–99, he was a member of his father's big band, gaining experience playing a variety of styles. Trained as an engineer at the Dnepropetrovsk University in Ukraine, after graduating in 2000, he enrolled in the Moscow State University of Culture, studying jazz guitar.

In 2003, Miroshnichenko formed his own group, the RMProject, which has toured throughout Europe and appeared regularly at jazz festivals. He has also performed with Saskia Laroo, Milcho Leviev, Richie Cole, the Cuban group Sexto Sentido, Al Di Meola (whom he considers one of his main influences), percussionist Frank Colon, João Donato, Igor Butman

and Alexey Zubov. In the fall of 2009, he went on an extensive tour of Russia with fellow guitarist Hernan Romero as a duo. "During the past two years, I was on tour a lot. I visited and performed in about 50 cities in Russia and Europe. From 2007 to the end of 2009, I have produced three albums, and taken part as a guest on ten others." In addition, Miroshnichenko has written soundtracks for Russian films, acted in several television series and one movie, and recorded as a guest with Russian pop stars.

"I like to play the music that brings me joy. I don't play standards but new music. I'm happy that I can be myself and play what I wish and be real. I breathe, eat and sleep this music. It is a passion of my heart."

**Recommended CDs:** Thus far Roman Miroshnichenko has led three albums for his own label, *GuitaRomania*, *The Infinity* and *Temptation And Quasipsychedelic*, in addition to releasing the DVD *Live In Jazz Town*.

**Website:** www.romanmiroshnichenko.com

## Amanda Monaco
*b. October 27, 1973, New Haven, CT*

Amanda Monaco is a fine modern jazz guitarist with lots of potential. "My entire family is very musical (they break into song spontaneously every time we get together), and because of all the fun stories I heard from my dad who played guitar, it inspired me to play the guitar. I started playing two days after my 12th birthday." She worked with a 1950s cover band, the Dimensions, for two years during high school and also played French horn in high school and college. Monaco attended the Educational College of the Arts during her last two years of high school, playing alongside such fellow students as saxophonists Jimmy Greene and Wayne Escoffery and pianist Noah Baerman. She went to Rutgers (1991–93), graduated from William Paterson College in 1996, and received her master's degree from City College in 2008.

Amanda Monaco, an excellent post-bop guitarist, freelances in the New York area in addition to leading a quartet with altoist and baritonist Michael Attias and a quintet called Playdate with Baerman and Escoffery. She is a resident musician at Congregation B'nai Jeshurun, for which she is working on a suite of music.

**Recommended CDs:** So far, Amanda Monaco has led four CDs: *Amanda Monaco 4* (Genevieve), *Intention* (Innova 667), *I Think I'll Keep You* (Lateset 72279) with Michael Attias, and *The Pirkei Avot Project Volume One* (Genevieve Records). She is also prominent on Noah Baerman's *Playdate* (Posi-tone 8055).

**Website:** www.amandamonaco.com

## Ben Monder
*b. May 24, 1962, New York, NY*

A very busy guitarist in the New York modern jazz scene who has appeared on over 100 CDs as a sideman, Ben Monder is versatile but also has his own distinctive sound. He played violin for two years before switching to guitar at 11, teaching himself the fundamentals. He was introduced to jazz through a music teacher at school and played at parties as a teenager. Monder attended the Westchester Conservatory of Music, the University of Miami and Queens College during 1979–84. His first important musical job was with Jack McDuff for six months during 1986–87. "It made me realize how much I had to learn and crushed whatever budding ego I may have had at the time. Every gig since has been a breeze by comparison."

There have been a countless number of gigs and recordings during the past 15 years, including with Patrick Zimmerli, the Maria Schneider Jazz Orchestra, the Paul Motian Electric Bebop Band, Marc Johnson, Lee Konitz, George Garzone, Tim Berne, Kenny Wheeler, Toots Thielemans, David Binney, Dave Liebman, Tim Reis, Jon Gordon, Charles Pillow, Dan Willis, Chris Cheek, Michael Leonhart, Drew Gress, Bill McHenry, Guillermo Klein, Frank Kimbrough, Donny McCaslin, John Hollenbeck, Miguel Zenon, Josh Roseman, Jerome Sabbagh, Rebecca Martin, Kendra Shank, Julie Hardy, Pete Robbins, and a regular duo project with singer Theo Bleckmann. Monder also served on the faculty of the New England Conservatory from 2002 to 2005.

"I like the idea of spontaneous composition, and the feeling that there is no limit to one's imagination. My music is a result of everything I've listened to and experienced over a lifetime. I guess it is kind of a mixture of a lot of things, most notably jazz, classical, and rock. I'm really just trying to organize sounds in ways I find interesting and exciting."

**Recommended CDs:** Each of Ben Monder's recordings as a leader is a fine example of adventurous postbop explorations with small groups: *Flux* (Songlines 1509), *Dust* (Arabesque 131), *Excavation* (Arabesque 148), *Oceana* (Sunnyside 1146) and *Bloom* (Sunnyside 1247). The guitarist also collaborated with Theo Bleckmann on *No Boat* (Songlines 1516) and *At Night* (Songlines 1561).

**Website:** www.benmonder.com

## Wes Montgomery
*(John Leslie Montgomery)*
*b. March 6, 1923, Indianapolis, IN; d. June 15, 1968, Indianapolis, IN*

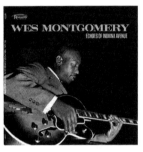

One of the greatest of all guitarists, Wes Montgomery extended the legacy of Charlie Christian, added his own mastery of octaves, and ended up being a huge influence on many of the guitarists who followed. He was born in Indianapolis in 1923 (although some sources say 1925). His brothers were vibraphonist and pianist Buddy Montgomery (1930–2009) and Monk Montgomery (1921–1982), who by the early 1950s had become the first significant electric bassist.

Wes Montgomery did not start playing guitar until he was already 19 in 1942. He heard the recording of "Solo Flight" that showcased Charlie Christian with Benny Goodman's band and soon began to teach himself guitar; he never had a guitar lesson. So neighbors would not complain about the volume when he practiced, Montgomery began to use his thumb instead of a pick, achieving a softer sound. His first musical job was playing Christian solos with a local band.

Montgomery's career had a false start. He toured with Lionel Hampton's orchestra during 1948–50. Although mostly utilized as a rhythm guitarist, he can be heard taking short solos on some of the radio broadcasts, including a version of "Hot House." But missing his family and (as was usual with Hampton's sidemen) being underpaid, Montgomery left the band in January 1950 and returned to Indianapolis. During the next six years to support his family (which included seven children), he worked a day job as a welder for a radio parts manufacturer and frequently played at two clubs each night, getting very little sleep, perhaps four hours a night. A clean liver and a devoted family man, Montgomery's lack of sleep for years probably weakened his heart in the long run.

By 1957, Buddy and Monk Montgomery were having success with their group the Mastersounds. Wes occasionally played with them, and also made his first post-Hampton recordings (other than recording "Love For Sale" in 1955 with his brothers in a quintet led by drummer Robert Johnson) in December 1957. He made a few other recordings with his brothers in 1958, but the following year was the beginning of his breakthrough. Cannonball Adderley heard Montgomery playing in an Indianapolis club, was amazed, and told producer Orrin Keepnews of Riverside Records about him. By that time, he had developed his technique, which found him able to play octaves during uptempo solos effortlessly. The octave sound became his trademark at all tempos, although he never used it to excess.

Later in 1959, Montgomery made his debut for Riverside, leading a trio with organist Mel Rhyne. The guitarist's second Riverside album, *The Incredible Jazz Guitar Of Wes Montgomery*, lived up to its title, introduced two of his best compositions ("Four On Six" and "West Coast Blues") and made him very well known in the jazz world. At 37, Montgomery was an overnight discovery. In 1961 and 1962, he topped the *Downbeat* polls as the best guitarist. Other than a few months in 1961 when he was part of the John Coltrane Sextet (which also included Eric Dolphy), Montgomery had his own group. With the demise of the Mastersounds and the acclaim given the guitarist, Buddy and Monk Montgomery sometimes were sidemen with their brother.

During 1959–63 for Riverside, Montgomery recorded many of his finest recordings, mostly in freewheeling settings that allowed him to stretch out. Included were dates with Milt Jackson and Cannonball Adderley. One exception to the small group format was the ironically titled *Fusion*, which was his first recording with a string ensemble.

In early 1964, the Riverside label went bankrupt. Montgomery signed with Verve Records, which at the time was headed by producer Creed Taylor. During his two years with Verve, Montgomery saw his popularity rise as he recorded orchestral dates utilizing arrangements by Don Sebesky. His 1965 version of "Goin' Out Of My Head" became a pop hit, and his recordings became more concise with less improvising and more of an emphasis on the melodies. However, during this period he also recorded two exciting albums with organist Jimmy Smith, and he utilized the Wynton Kelly Trio for some of his most inspired quartet playing, the classic *Smokin' At The Half Note*.

After having struggled for so many years to take care of his family, commercial success was finally his. In 1967, Montgomery went with Creed Taylor to the A&M label, and now his recordings were much more pop-oriented. His album *A Day In The Life* not only had a hit with the title tune but was also the best selling jazz album of the year. Most of the selections that he recorded during 1967–68 found him stating the melody with octaves, taking a very brief solo while backed by strings and woodwinds, and finishing the piece, clocking in at around three minutes. Montgomery's recordings became a stable of AM radio, introducing many listeners to the flavor of jazz. While decades later some would claim

that these recordings were the direct ancestor of so-called "smooth jazz," in reality they were simply easy-listening jazzy pop records.

In live performances, Wes Montgomery's playing remained largely the same as it had been during his Riverside years, taking inventive and lengthy solos on standards, blues and ballads. He was well aware that many in the jazz world were upset by the direction of his recordings, and he called his A&M records "popular music," saying that they really were not jazz.

Just when he was getting to the point of being prosperous, Wes Montgomery died of a heart attack at the age of 45. Chances are that if he had lived, the guitarist would have followed Creed Taylor to the CTI label (possibly instead of George Benson), and he would have found more of a balance between the music that he loved to play and that which attracted millions of listeners. How he would have handled fusion and later jazz developments will never be known, but in his short life, he proved to be one of the most important jazz guitarists in history.

**Recommended CDs:** Virtually all of Wes Montgomery's recordings from 1957 on are easily available. *Echoes Of Indiana Avenue* (Resonance) is a recently discovered set of great value that features Montgomery playing in Indianapolis clubs shortly before he was discovered. Montgomery's studio sessions of 1957–58 are available as *Fingerpickin'* (Blue Note 37987) and *Far Wes* (Blue Note 94475). A 12-CD set *The Complete Riverside Recordings* (Riverside 4408) has all of his recordings of 1959–63 and is a must for listeners who really love his music. For those who prefer individual sets, *The Wes Montgomery Trio* (Original Jazz Classics 034), *The Incredible Jazz Guitar Of Wes Montgomery* (Original Jazz Classics 036), *Movin' Along* (Original Jazz Classics 089), *So Much Guitar!* (Original Jazz Classics 233), *Bags Meets Wes* (Original Jazz Classics 234), *Full House* (Original Jazz Classics 106), and *Portrait Of Wes* (Original Jazz Classics 144) are all great examples of his playing. *Movin': The Complete Verve Recordings* (Hip-O Select) reissues all of Montgomery's 1964–65 for Verve on an attractive box set. The best music from this period is also available individually as *Smokin' At The Half Note* (Verve 393 402), which has him in peak form with the Wynton Kelly Trio; *Bumpin'* (Verve 821 985); *The Dynamic Duo: Jimmy and Wes* (Universal 9358); and *The Further Adventures Of Jimmy Smith and Wes Montgomery* (Universal 9359). His other Verve recordings, *Movin' Wes* (Verve 810 045), *Willow Weep For Me* (Verve 589 486), *Goin' Out Of My Head* (Verve 825 676), *Tequila* (Polygram 547 769), and *California Dreaming* (Verve 827 842), all have their interesting moments along with some more commercial tracks.

As for Montgomery's A&M recordings, *A Day In The Life* (A&M 9422), *Down Here On The Ground* (A&M 6994) and the posthumously released *Road Song* (A&M 75021-0822) are all pleasant and harmless enough. If only Wes Montgomery had lived longer so he could have enjoyed his success. Also of strong interest is Jon Hendricks' *A Good Git-Together* (EMI 69812), which teams Montgomery in 1960 with the singer plus Cannonball and Nat Adderley.

**LPs to Search For:** A single obscure Wes Montgomery selection, "Love For Sale" from 1955, was last on the sampler *Almost Forgotten* (Columbia 38509).

## Oscar Moore
b. December 25, 1912, Austin, TX; d. October 8, 1981, Las Vegas, NV

Although his name is largely forgotten by the general public, Oscar Moore's playing has been heard by virtually everyone, for he played guitar on Nat King Cole's recordings of "The Christmas Song" and "Route 66." Oscar Moore has been listed as having been born in both 1912 and 1916, always on Christmas. He grew up in Los Angeles and played professionally with his brother, guitarist Johnny Moore, in a variety of settings in the 1930s. Joining Nat Cole in 1937, Moore was an integral part of the group's piano-guitar-bass sound. The trio with Cole and bassist Wesley Prince (later Johnny Miller) was hugely influential on such bandleaders as Art Tatum, Page Cavanaugh, Oscar Peterson and Ahmad Jamal, all of whom had piano-guitar-bass trios for a time. Moore took solos on nearly every Cole record up to 1947 and sometimes joined in on the group vocals. While influenced a little by Charlie Christian, he had his own warm sound and developed a melodic yet harmonically advanced style.

During those years, Oscar Moore also recorded with Lionel Hampton (as part of the Cole Trio), Art Tatum, Lester Young and the Capitol Jazzmen. When Moore left Cole in 1947, he worked with his brother Johnny Moore's Three Blazers alongside pianist-singer Charles Brown, appearing on their records. But the group declined in popularity after Brown went out on his own. Although he recorded two albums as a leader in 1954, Moore slipped away into obscurity. Other than a Nat King Cole tribute album from 1965, little was heard from Moore in the music world during his final 20 years. He worked outside of music, including bricklaying and running a gas station, a strange ending for a friendly guitarist who always sounded good.

**Recommended CDs:** *Oscar Moore* (V.S.O.P. 22) and *Oscar Moore* (V.S.O.P. 34) are both from 1954 and feature Moore in a quartet/quintet with pianist Carl Perkins, bassist Joe Comfort and drummer George Jenkins; bongoist Mike Pacheco is also on V.S.O.P. 34. Both are nice easy-listening swing albums. *Oscar Moore & Friends* (Fresh Sound 202) combines together two complete albums. The first half is a very rare 1957 session in which Moore is featured as a sideman with singer Inez Jones, who was working in San Francisco at the time. The other date is the 1965 Nat King Cole tribute (originally titled *We'll Remember You Nat*) in which Moore, pianist Gerald Wiggins and bassist Joe Comfort revive songs from the Cole Trio, including some obscurities. But the best way to hear Oscar Moore is on his many sessions with Nat King Cole, particularly the Capitol sets from 1943–47.

## Joe Morris
b. September 13, 1955, New Haven, CT

A major avant-garde jazz guitarist, Joe Morris has been a true original since near the start of his career. He played trumpet for two years but switched to guitar when he was 14. "I first became interested in  playing the guitar when I saw the Beatles on the Ed Sullivan Show. I saved money by working at school, borrowed 50 dollars from my brother, and bought a guitar and an amp. Then I practiced eight hours a day for 15 years." He began by playing rock, influenced by Jimi Hendrix; he then evolved to the blues and, at 17, switched to jazz. "I took a half-dozen lessons from Tony Lombardozzi, who had studied with Sal Salvador. He taught me how to play scales and the beginnings of how to play changes. Then, I heard John McLaughlin. I copied him for a year until, during a long practice session, it dawned on me that I liked him because he was original and played his own way. Since then, I've tried to do the same. Soon after that event, I opened my ears to Ornette Coleman, Cecil Taylor, the AACM and everything else."

Otherwise self-taught, Joe Morris (who also plays bass) considers his first important gig to be when he performed solo in Boston in April 1977. Among his earliest writing projects was composing music for a trio of guitar, trombone and drums. In 1981, he performed solo in Amsterdam and Paris and formed his own Riti record label. Since then, he has worked with Lowell Davidson (1982–90), bassist Sebastian Steinberg, Dewey Redman, Butch Morris, Andrew Cyrille, Billy Bang, Joe McPhee,

Peter Kowald, William Parker, Thurman Barker, Mat Maneri, Joe Maneri, Matthew Shipp, Ken Vandermark, Barre Phillips, David S. Ware, Anthony Braxton, Rob Brown, Raphe Malik, Ivo Perelman, Borah Bergman, Karen Borca, Eugene Chadbourne, Hamid Drake and many others. Morris has also led his own groups, including ones called Sweatshop and Racket Club. He has taught at the New England Conservatory of Music since 2000.

"My goal as a guitar player has always been to speak with my own voice and to expand the range of expression on guitar. I have made it a point to never repeat myself. Every one of my recordings has something different from the others. It's always about adding things to what was there. To me, the most challenging things in all of music are to find new ways to make melody and to find another way to swing."

**Recommended CDs:** There are many worthy Joe Morris CDs available. These include *Sweatshop* (Riti 1), *Flip & Spike* (Riti 2), *Symbolic Gesture* (Soul Note 121204), *Racket Club* (About Time 010), *Illuminate* (Leo Lab 008), *Like Rays* (Knitting Factory Works 224), *Invisible Weave* (No More), *Elsewhere* (Homestead 5233), *You Be Me* (Soul Note 121304), *Antennae* (AUM Fidelity 4), *Deep Telling* (Okka 12027), *A Cloud Of Black Birds* (AUM Fidelity 9), *Underthru* (Omnitone 11904), *Many Rings* (Knitting Factory Works 243), *At The Old Office* (Knitting Factory Works 272), *Soul Search* (AUM Fidelity 14), *Singularity* (AUM Fidelity 18), *No Vertigo* (Leo 226), *Age Of Everything* (Riti 4), *Beautiful Existence* (Clean Feed 050), *Fur* (Skycap 30121152), *Rebus* (Clean Feed 083), *High Definition* (Hatology 670), *MVP LSD* (Riti 10), *Elektrik Toboggan* (Victo 116), *Colorfield* (ESP 4056), *Today On Earth* (AUM Fidelity 58), *Camera* (ESP 4063), and *Elm City Duets* (Clean Feed 130).

**LPs to Search For:** Joe Morris' first two albums on his RITI label, *Wraparound* and *Human Rites*, have long been out of print.

**Website:** www.joe-morris.com

## Tony Mottola
b. April 18, 1918, Kearny, NJ; d. August 9, 2004, Denville, NJ

A very talented guitarist who was influenced by Carl Kress, Dick McDonough and Eddie Lang, Tony Mottola primarily worked as a studio guitarist during his long career. Mottola originally wanted to play the saxophone, but since he was only nine, he was considered too young to take the bus by himself to his teacher's home. As compensation, his father offered to give him guitar lessons at home. Mottola developed quickly and, in high school, had a group with fellow guitarist Al Caiola that was modeled after

the Quintet of the Hot Club of France. He worked as a teenager on radio station WAAT and, in the late 1930s, played with George Hall's orchestra alongside pianist Johnny Guarnieri.

Due to his musicianship and versatility, in 1941 Mottola was hired by CBS to become a member of their radio orchestra. While he recorded jazz now and then, Mottola was primarily a studio musician and arranger for the remainder of his life. He worked on radio and television with Raymond Scott, Frank Sinatra, Perry Como (arranging for his 1950s television show), *The Sid Caesar Comedy Hour*, *Sing Along With Mitch* and the Tonight Show Band (1958–72). Mottola wrote the score for several television shows and films, with his work for the CBS suspense series *Danger* in the 1950s gaining the most recognition. A Johnny Mathis recording in which Mottola and Caiola served as the backup (*Open Fire, Warm Guitars*) brought him to the attention of producer Enoch Light. Mottola recorded over 30 albums for Light's Command and Project 3 labels, often on acoustic guitar, performing pretty and melodic music that appealed to a large middle-of-the-road audience. Mottola ended his career as Frank Sinatra's regular guitarist during 1980–88.

From the jazz standpoint, Mottola's most significant work was a set of ten guitar duets with Carl Kress recorded as radio transcriptions in 1941 and six selections from 1946 in a quartet that also features Johnny Guarnieri. But considering his great talent, it is a shame that Tony Mottola recorded so little jazz in his career.

**LP to Search For:** *Fun On The Frets* (Yazoo 1061) has the Tony Mottola–Carl Kress guitar duets along with other titles by Carl Kress and George Van Eps.

## Matt Munisteri
b. April 28, 1964, New Haven, CT

A valuable part of the East Coast trad-jazz scene, Matt Munisteri has been very interested and quite skilled in a wide variety of musical styles throughout his career. Munisteri, who grew up in Brooklyn, started on banjo when he was nine and added guitar the following year. "I remember hearing a Louis Armstrong birthday broadcast on WKCR when I was 12. I first started learning about jazz chord progressions and swing in my early teens from Russ Barenberg, and by listening to and learning a lot of Western swing. George Benson's 'Clockwise' and Danny Gatton's 'Rock Candy' amazed me around 16. Later, a teacher in high school gave me a couple of Wes Montgomery records, including the live with Johnny Griffin sides, which thoroughly blew my mind." Munisteri was largely self-taught on guitar, although two lessons that he took from Tal Farlow when he was 22 made a strong impression. His interests from an early age ranged from country and ragtime guitar to American popular song, blues and several styles of jazz.

Munisteri played banjo on the streets and at coffee houses while in junior high school and had some rock and jazz gigs on guitar in high school. "The New York City bluegrass scene of the 1970s included many uncategorical musicians who were accomplished, open-minded, irreverent, smart, funny and creative. Among the musicians I would see and hear on a regular basis were Andy Statman, Russ Barenberg, Matt Glaser, Kenny Kosek, Richard Leiberson and Richard 'Citizen Kafka' Shulberg." Also making a strong impact were Randy Newman (whose music inspired Munisteri to write lyrics and sing), James "Blood" Ulmer, Vernon Reid, and, by the mid-1990s, Eddie Lang.

He graduated from Brown University, majoring in religious studies. After enduring a day job for a few years, Munisteri worked with the Flying Neutrinos (1995–1999) as a guitarist and songwriter. Other important associations since then include Steven Bernstein's Millennial Territory Orchestra, Jon-Erik Kellso, Catherine Russell, Mark O'Connor's Hot Swing, Vince Giordano's Nighthawks, Andy Stein, Jenny Scheinman, Holly Cole, Madeline Peyroux, Evan Christopher, Frank Vignola, Howard Alden and his own band, Brock Mumford, which is named after Buddy Bolden's guitar player.

"In the future, I hope to record a solo acoustic guitar record and a record with my as-yet-unnamed Italo-Caribbean string band. I also want to continue my quest to have the rhythmic surety of Oscar Peterson or Earl Scruggs and the elastic play and soulfulness of Ben Webster or Lester Young."

**Recommended CDs:** With Brock Munford, Matt Munisteri is heard in colorful form on *Love Story* (Old Cow 0001), *Still Running 'Round In The Wilderness—The Lost Music Of Willard Robison* (Old Cow 0002), and *Hell Among The Hedgehogs* (Old Cow 0003). He is also an important and spirited part of such CDs as Jon-Erik Kellso's *Blue Roof Blues* (Arbors 19346), Steven Bernstein's Millennial Territory Orchestra's *We Are MTO* (Mowo 540001), Barbara Rosene's *Everything's Made For Love* (Stomp Off 1393) and Catherine Russell's *Inside This Heart Of Fire* (World Village 46809).

**Website:** www.mattmunisteri.com

## Michael Musillami
b. July 28, 1953, Sacramento, CA

Founder of the Playscape label, Michael Musillami has been a major post-bop guitarist since the 1980s. Musillami began taking guitar lessons when he was

nine in 1962. "In middle school and high school, I was in a rock band playing music by the Rolling Stones, the Yardbirds, Jefferson Airplane, and Hendrix. This all came about with my ability to play the blues." He went to college for two years as an anthropology major. "Reality set in, and I decided that music was my true quest. I was 21 and had been a shoeshine boy, haberdasher, bricklayer, cement mason and college student. I was better at guitar than I was at any of the above." He dropped out of school and took lessons from Joe Diorio.

After moving to the East Coast, Musillami picked up important experience playing the chitlin' circuit with organist Bobby Buster during 1981–83. Other significant associations included the reformation of the Teddy Charles Tentet (1981–82), Richard "Groove" Holmes, Junior Cook, Dewey Redman, Curtis Fuller, Bill Barron (1986–1989), Thomas Chapin (1983–1998), Joe Fonda, and Mario Pavone. In 2000, Musillami started the Playscape label in order to document his own projects and those of musicians he admires. In 2002, he formed his current group, the Michael Musillami Trio, with Peter Madsen and George Schuller. In addition, he is the director of Jazz Studies at the Hotchkiss School in Lakeville, Connecticut.

"I have tried and will continue to try to bend the rules in jazz harmony, melody and rhythm. Predictability is no friend to creative music."

**Recommended CDs:** Michael Musillami has led over 15 CDs thus far. A strong sampling of his work as the head of a trio and of other size groups is heard on *Glass Art* (Playscape 120192), *Pivot* (Playscape 121001), *Part Pitbull* (Playscape 122001), *Beijing* (Playscape 121802), *Those Times* (Playscape 12603), *Spirits* (Playscape 20104), *Dachau* (Playscape 20505), *The Treatment* (Playscape 50607), *From Seeds* (Playscape 20109), *Old Tea* (Playscape Recordings 91009) and *Mettie* (Playscape).

**Website:** www.michaelmusillami.com

## King Benny Nawahi
*(Benjamin Keakahiawa Nawahi)*
b. July 3, 1899, Honolulu, HI; d. January 29, 1985, Long Beach, CA

King Benny Nawahi was considered, along with Sol Hoopii, the top Hawaiian steel guitar player of the 1920s and '30s. Like Hoopii, he played both traditional Hawaiian songs and

jazz, often combining the two. One of 12 children, Nawahi was self-taught on the acoustic slack key guitar. He was a professional musician by the time he was 15. Nawahi, who expertly played guitar, mandolin and ukulele in addition to steel guitar, worked with his brother Joe's group, the Hawaiian Novelty Five, starting in 1919. They performed on an ocean liner that sailed between Honolulu and San Francisco, and they toured in vaudeville.

After he began his solo career, Nawahi worked as a singer and ukulele virtuoso in addition to playing steel guitar. Starting in 1928, he recorded for a variety of labels under such group names as the Red Devils, Q.R.S. Boys, Slim Smith, the Hawaiian Beach Combers, the Georgia Jumpers and Four Hawaiian Guitars. He settled in Los Angeles in the early 1930s, leading King Nawahi and the International Cowboys, a group that included a young Roy Rogers.

In 1935, Nawahi suddenly became blind, and there was never any explanation for his affliction. Despite that, he continued performing in local restaurants and clubs, often recording with his brother in the Nawahi Trio. A long distance swimmer, in 1946 Nawahi became the only blind man to swim from San Pedro to Catalina Island, a 22-hour journey. He remained musically active for decades, and his career did not end until he suffered a stroke in the late 1970s.

**Recommended CDs:** *King Bennie Nawahi: Hawaiian String Virtuoso* (Yazoo 2055) has 23 selections that give listeners a definitive look at his brilliance in the 1920s and '30s.

## Bern Nix
*b. September 21, 1947, Toledo, OH*

Guitarist with Ornette Coleman's Prime Time for a dozen years, Bern Nix has long had a highly original and adventurous style. "At the age of 11, I commenced studying guitar with a private teacher who  said I had no future in music. Fortunately, one of my hometown musical influences was John Justus, a local guitar instructor who taught me the fundamentals of jazz improvisation in addition to introducing me to the recordings of Wes Montgomery and Barney Kessel. And hearing Charlie Christian also had a profound impact." His earliest gigs were with local blues, funk and R&B groups. Nix attended Berklee,

graduating in 1975, the same year that he joined Ornette Coleman.

Prime Time often consisted of Coleman's alto, two electric guitars (with Nix playing alongside Charles Ellerbee), two electric bassists and two drummers. The music, which Coleman termed "harmolodic," emphasized group soloing with Ornette the first among equals. Often quite dense and loud, Prime Time gave Nix an opportunity to master Coleman's music and to make a major contribution to the group's sound. "During that watershed period, I discovered that jazz was about more than the musical negotiation of standard chord sequences."

Since leaving Prime Time in 1987, Nix has primarily led his own trio in addition to working on projects with John Zorn, Marc Ribot, Elliott Sharp, Jemeel Moondoc and Ronald Shannon Jackson. He also wrote a film score for the documentary *A James Lord Portrait*.

"Jazz is a genre that embodies all the complexity, contradiction, and need for spontaneous yet disciplined self-expression inherent in human nature. This is why I enjoy the pleasant agony of trying to have a career in music. My future goal is to hopefully cultivate my own musical postage stamp of Earth."

**Recommended CDs:** Bent Nix's two albums as a leader, *Alarms & Excursions* (New World 80437) and *Low Barometer* (Tompkins Square), display his original conception to playing jazz guitar along with his command of harmolodics. He is also featured with Ornette Coleman's Prime Time on *Dancing In Your Head* (Universal 5175), *Body Meta* (Verve 531916), *Of Human Feelings* (Antilles 20002), *In All Languages* (Polygram 531915) and *Virgin Beauty* (Epic 7709).

**Website:** www.myspace.com/bernnix

## Oz Noy
*b. April 24, 1972, Tel Aviv, Israel*

Oz Noy, an up-and-coming player with quite a bit of experience and a strong sense of humor, is equally skilled at fusion and post-bop jazz. Although he originally wanted to be a drummer,  when he was ten he went with a friend to a guitar lesson and was hooked from then on. He was in a pop/rock band when he was 12 and soon became a professional who was skilled at playing jazz, blues, pop and rock. "When the Pat Metheny Group came to play in Israel in the '80s (when *Still Life Talking* came out), that changed my life. I saw the Pat Metheny Group, Pat playing with a jazz trio, and him conducting a master class. After that, I was not the same anymore. It was the most profound three days of my life. I was also affected by hearing the first Chick Corea Elektric Band record with Scott Henderson and listening to Allan Holdsworth for the first time."

At 16, Noy was already an increasingly significant musical voice in Israel. He became a top studio guitarist. When he was 24 in 1996, he moved to New York. Since then, in addition to working with many pop singers and playing on commercials and soundtracks, he has worked with Richard Bona, Chris Botti, Mike Clark, Jeff "Tain" Watts and, most importantly, his own groups, where his open-minded style results in consistently unpredictable music.

"If you are looking to develop your own voice as a musician, there are a lot of limitations if you just think of yourself as playing in a particular style. I think the best idea is to learn the styles that you like as deeply as you can and then forget about it; let go and do what you feel is right for you."

**Recommended CDs:** Each of Oz Noy's five recordings as a leader are full of creative use of tonal distortions, surprising ideas and wit: *Ha!* (Magnitude 2308), *Live* (Magnitude 2310), *Fuzzy* (Magnitude 2314), *Schizophrenic* (Magnitude 2317), and *Twisted Blues Vol. 1* (Abstract Logix 32).

**Website:** www.oznoy.com

## Jordan Officer
*b. November 29, 1976, Montreal, Quebec, Canada*

Jordan Officer, a fine swing and blues guitarist, is best known for his association with Susie Arioli, although at this writing he is in the process of releasing his long overdue solo debut recording. Officer started out on violin and drums before switching to guitar at 14. "There was a lot of music at home growing up, and my mother brought us to see live groups as much as possible, so I was in contact with all kinds of music very young. Since there was a guitar at home, I decided that I should learn how to play. And very quickly, guitar just took over."

He mostly played in blues bands during his formative years, including Sunday nights at the L'Exterieur. Officer met Susie Arioli during a jam session in 1997, and a bond quickly formed. "Susie and I quickly

started playing together and much of her repertoire was jazz—many songs that had been sung by Billie Holiday, for instance. And there was something in that music that I had been wanting for a while. I discovered Lester Young and Charlie Christian along with Thelonious Monk and Charlie Parker. The jazz from the swing era was a perfect bridge from the blues because the blues was still a very important part of that music, and the language and approach was still similar, but at the same time it was sophisticated, more and more complex, and I liked that."

Susie Arioli, who plays snare drums while singing, and Jordan Officer formed a trio that also included a bassist. After a year of playing in small bars locally, the group had its big break when it had an opportunity to open for Ray Charles at the 1998 Montreal Jazz Festival as a substitute for an ailing Charles Brown. "It was a very big step. Playing that show gave us an audience, media coverage, and most importantly showed us that our music worked even better in a concert setting, where we were able to use silences and dynamics much more effectively than in bars."

The group has flourished ever since, recording and performing regularly. Jordan Officer, whose Charlie Christian–inspired guitar style fits perfectly in the band, also plays electric guitar and mandolin on Neapolitan songs with operatic tenor Nils Brown and occasionally works with blues performer Steve Barry. His forthcoming solo debut CD features his original material.

**Recommended CDs:** Jordan Officer's debut as a leader, *Jordan Officer* (Spectra 678 142) was released in 2011. Otherwise, his best playing is with Susie Arioli on their albums *It's Wonderful* (Justin Time 8493); *Pennies From Heaven* (Justin Time 181); *That's For Me* (Justin Time 195); the unusual *Learn To Smile Again* (Justin Time 214), which is a successful tribute to country singer Roger Miller; and *Night Lights* (Spectra 7806). Each set is a delight and features plenty of fine guitar.

**Website:** www.jordanofficer.com

## Mary Osborne
*(Mary Orsborn)*
*b. July 17, 1921, Minot, MD; d. March 4, 1992, Bakersfield, CA*

Mary Osborne was one of the best bop guitarists to emerge in the 1940s. She began playing music quite early. Both of her parents were guitarists, and Mary started on ukulele when she was four. When she was ten, she played banjo in her father's string band. At 15, she alternated between playing acoustic guitar, violin and bass in a trio in addition to singing and dancing. In 1938, Osborne heard Charlie Christian play in North Dakota with Alphonso Trent's band.

The next day, she went out and bought an electric guitar. In the 1940s, she worked with several second-level big bands, including those of Buddy Rogers, Dick Stabile, Terry Shand, Joe Venuti and Russ Morgan. By the mid-1940s, she had made the transition from swing to bop and was in strong demand for record dates.

Osborne recorded 16 numbers under her own name during 1945–52 (they have yet to be reissued) and did quite well on record dates with Mary Lou Williams (in an all-female group), the Beryl Booker Trio, Coleman Hawkins, Mercer Ellington, Stuff Smith and Wynonie Harris. She assumed the role of jazz's only significant female guitarist during the era with dignity, holding her own with any other guitarist. Osborne was featured on Jack Sterling's daily radio show on CBS during 1952–63 as part of the Elliot Lawrence Quintet, worked in the studios, and appeared on several jazz television specials, including accompanying Billie Holiday in 1958.

In the 1960s, Mary Osborne mostly worked behind the scenes and, after moving to Bakersfield with her husband trumpeter Ralph Scaffidi in 1968, she was in semi-retirement, operating the Mary Osborne Guitar Company, which manufactured amplifiers and public address systems. From the late 1970s until her 1992 death, she occasionally appeared at classic jazz festivals, always serving as an inspiration to younger female guitarists.

**Recommended CDs:** Other than her earliest sessions, *A Memorial* (Stash 550) has all of Mary Osborne's recordings as a leader. Unfortunately, the CD will be difficult to find. Her 1959 set for the Warwick label features her leading a quintet with Tommy Flanagan and Jo Jones, while six numbers from 1981 have her playing with a pianoless trio that also includes bassist Steve LaSpina and drummer Charlie Persip.

**LPs to Search For:** Mary Osborne has a featured role in 1977 on Marian McPartland's *Now's The Time* (Halcyon 115), performing with an all-female group that includes saxophonist Vi Redd, bassist Lynn Milano and drummer Dottie Dodgion.

## Remo Palmieri

b. March 29, 1923, New York, NY; d. February 2, 2002, Bronx, NY

Remo Palmieri could have been a contender. One of the leading jazz electric guitarists of the mid-1940s and a swing-based player who sounded credible playing bebop, Palmieri chose a much more secure life as a studio guitarist, largely dropping out of the jazz world after 1945. Originally, he planned to become an artist and began playing guitar just so he could pay for his studies. However by the time he was 19 in 1942, Palmieri was on his way to the top. He

was influenced by Charlie Christian and was in the early stages of developing his own voice. Palmieri was a member of the Nat Jaffe Trio, and during 1943–45, he worked with Coleman Hawkins, Red Norvo, Barney Bigard, Billie Holiday, Teddy Wilson, Cozy Cole, the Phil Moore Four and Dizzy Gillespie. Palmieri recorded with Gillespie and Charlie Parker in 1945 (including "Groovin' High" and "Dizzy Atmosphere") and that year won a "new star" award from *Esquire* magazine.

And then just as quickly, he dropped out of the big leagues. Palmieri (who changed his name to Palmier in 1952) joined the staff of CBS and worked for 27 years (1945–72) with *Arthur Godfrey Time*. By the mid-1950s he could have been a perfect candidate for a "Whatever Happened To?" article. It was not until 1972 that he started occasionally playing jazz clubs in New York again. In 1977, Palmeri played duets with Herb Ellis at the Concord Jazz Festival. He recorded on Ellis' *Windflower* album and, in 1979, led his only record. He also played with Benny Goodman and Dick Hyman in the 1970s, toured and recorded with an all-star group called Swing Reunion in 1985, and occasionally performed at festivals in the 1990s.

Still, one wishes that there had been much more from Remo Palmieri, who lived until 2002.

**Recommended CDs:** *Remo Palmier* (Concord 4076) was the guitarist's only album as a leader. Rather than playing bebop standards, he performed both modern jazz tunes (including "Dolphin Dance") and relaxed melodic pieces with a quartet, showing that he still had a lot to offer 30 years after his creative prime. *Windflower* (Concord 4056), from 1976, was issued under Herb Ellis' name but has Palmieri getting as much solo space as the leader. The two-guitar quartet session is more cooperative than competitive, but some sparks fly on the straight-ahead performance.

## Joe Pass
*(Joseph Passalacqua)*
b. January 13, 1929, New Brunswick, NJ; d. May 23, 1994, Los Angeles, CA

Joe Pass was the ultimate bebop guitarist, a superb player whose solo concerts found him playing uptempo unaccompanied versions of "Cherokee," "How High The Moon" and Charlie Parker

tunes without a moment of hesitation. His technique was conventional (with no tapping) but was at such a high level that he could play melody, harmony and bass lines simultaneously at blazing tempos.

Pass started playing guitar when he was nine and developed quickly. He worked with Tony Pastor's orchestra while still in high school and was with the Charlie Barnet big band in 1947 before serving in the military. But the 1950s were a lost decade for him as he struggled with drug addiction, even serving some time in prison. In 1961, when he was already in his thirties, he was a complete unknown in the jazz world. But that would soon change.

By 1962, Pass, who spent two and a half years at Synanon, was finally clean. He made his recording debut on *Sounds Of Synanon*. Pass worked regularly on the West Coast during the 1960s, recording for Pacific Jazz and World Pacific, including sessions with the Gerald Wilson Orchestra, Les McCann, Bud Shank, Clare Fischer, Bill Perkins and Groove Holmes. He recorded some dates of his own, including two classics (*Catch Me* and *For Django*), worked in television orchestras, gigged with Louie Bellson, Sarah Vaughan and Joe Williams, and was in the George Shearing Quintet during 1965–67, also working with Benny Goodman in 1973.

All of that was a warmup for what was to come. Producer Norman Granz was so impressed by Pass' solo playing that he recorded him extensively for the Pablo label, starting with the 1973 solo masterpiece *Virtuoso* and running through 1992. Pass' many unaccompanied solo recordings and concerts made him famous, but he was also heard with all-star groups that included Duke Ellington, Oscar Peterson, Benny Carter, J.J. Johnson, Ella Fitzgerald (they recorded six vocal-guitar duet albums), Sarah Vaughan, Milt Jackson, Dizzy Gillespie and Count Basie.

Joe Pass, who passed away from liver cancer at the age of 65, was also featured with trios and quartets, but it was the solo albums that resulted in him being rated as one of the greatest jazz guitarists of all time.

**Recommended CDs:** Most of Joe Pass' pre-Pablo sessions as a leader are difficult to find. Other than *Joy Spring* (Blue Note 35222) and a limited-edition Mosaic box set of his Pacific Jazz recordings that is now out-of-print, his key early sessions are only available as Japanese imports or on tiny labels, including *Sounds Of Synanon* (Toshiba EMI 6382), *Catch Me* (Toshiba EMI 6383) and *For Django* (Beat Goes On 430). But there is no shortage of his Pablo recordings. *Guitar Virtuoso* (Pablo 4423) is an excellent four-CD sampler of his output. Completists will want *Virtuoso* (Pablo 2310-708), *Virtuoso #2* (Pablo 2310-788), *Virtuoso #3* (Original Jazz Classics 684), *Virtuoso #4* (Pablo 2640-102), *At The Montreux Jazz Festival 1975* (Original Jazz Classics

934), *Montreux '77* (Original Jazz Classics 382), *I Remember Charlie Parker* (Original Jazz Classics 602), *Blues Dues* (Original Jazz Classics 934), *University Of Akron Concert* (Pablo 2308-249), *Blues For Fred* (Pablo 2310-931), *Virtuoso Live* (Pablo 2310-948), *Songs For Ellen* (Pablo 2310-955) and *Unforgettable* (Pablo 2310-964), all of which are sets of unaccompanied solos with *Virtuoso #4* being a double-CD. His group sides as a leader include *Portraits Of Duke Ellington* (Pablo 2310-716), *Quadrant* (Original Jazz Classics 498), *Tede Bem* (Original Jazz Classics 685), *Chops* (Original Jazz Classics 786), *Checkmate* (Original Jazz Classics 975), *Ira, George And Joe* (Original Jazz Classics 828), *We'll Be Together Again* (Original Jazz Classics 909), *Whitestone* (Pablo 2310-912), *One For My Baby* (Pablo 2310-936), *Summer Night* (Pablo 2310-939), *Appassionato* (Pablo 2310-946), *Duets* (Pablo 2310-959), *Joe Pass Quartet Live At Yoshi's* (Pablo 2310-951), *Nuages*, and *Live At Yoshi's Vol. 2* (Pablo 2310-961). His post-Pablo recordings include *Six String Santa* (Laserlight 15 470), *Finally* (Verve 314 512 603), *My Song* (Telarc 83326), and the offbeat but successful *Roy Clark And Joe Pass Play Hank Williams* (Buster Ann Music). Of Pass' many sideman dates during the Pablo years, not to be missed are Ella Fitzgerald's *Take Love Easy* (Pablo 2310-702), Duke Ellington's *Duke's Big Four* (Pablo 2310-703), Dizzy Gillespie's *Dizzy's Big 4* (Pablo 9447), and Oscar Peterson's *À La Salle Pleyel* (Pablo 2625-705).

**LPs to Search For:** *Live At Dante's* (Pablo 2620-114), *Northsea Nights* (Pablo 2308-221), *All Too Soon* (Pablo 2312-117) and *Eximious* (Pablo 2310-877).

## Lino Patruno
*(Michele "Lino" Patruno)*
b. October 27, 1935, Crotone, Italy

In many ways, Lino Patruno is the Eddie Condon of Italy, a rhythm guitarist whose main significance to music is his promotion of freewheeling pre-swing jazz. "I started as a self-made man, playing piano when I was 15 or 16 years old. At 18, I started again with the guitar and banjo. Friends played me jazz records, and I remember hearing Johnny Dodds' 'Perdido Street Blues' and hitting the roof." Patruno played his first gig at a jazz festival in 1956 and led the Riverside Jazz Band in the 1950s and '60s but worked as a designer during the day, not becoming a full-time musician and performer until 1964.

While he is proudest of an LP that he recorded with Albert Nicholas in 1966, Patruno has consistently worked with the who's who of traditional jazz, setting up their tours of Italy and sometimes recording with the artists. Among the musicians whom he has worked with are Joe Venuti, Bill Coleman, Wild Bill Davison, Wingy Manone, Bud Freeman, Jimmy McPartland, Dick Cary, Teddy Wilson, Billy Butterfield, Eddie Miller, Kenny Davern, Ralph Sutton, Yank Lawson, Dick Wellstood, Bob Haggart, Bob Wilber, Barney Bigard, Peanuts Hucko, Vince Giordano, Tom Pletcher, Jon-Erik Kellso, Dick Sudhalter, Dan Barrett, and Rebecca Kilgore; that is just a partial list.

In his productive career, Lino Patruno has been an actor, the producer of television shows, and a cabaret performer. He led the Milan College Jazz Society in the '70s, has often headed all-star groups of Europeans and Americans, wrote the script and produced the soundtrack to the movie *Bix*, and has had several jazz television series in Italy, including *Lino Patruno Remembers*. In addition to being involved in promoting classic jazz in many ways, he has also been a fine acoustic guitarist in the tradition of Carl Kress and Dick McDonough.

"My main activities in the last two years are History of Jazz lessons at the Casa del Jazz in Roma and managing the Roman Classic Jazz Festival each year. Unfortunately, many of today's festivals feature music that is around jazz instead of having real jazz. Often, real jazz is forgotten. My goal is always to promote jazz by every means and to expand classic jazz."

**Recommended CDs:** Lino Patruno has recorded many albums through the years. Some of his most rewarding ones are *Joe Venuti In Milan* (Ricordi 64484), *Lino Patruno And His Friends* (Ricordi 365932 74321), *Lino & His American Friends* (Carosello 300 556-2), *Remembering Bix* (Carosello 300-666), *Big Four/Jazz For Two* (Lino Patruno Jazz Show 01) with trumpeter Oscar Klein, *Bix: An Interpretation Of A Legend* (RCA 74766), *Hello Satch!* (Platinum 044), *Echoes Of Harlem* (Hitland 14), *Jammin' For Condon* (Jazzology 400), *Lino Patruno & His Blue Four* (Platinum 066), *Presents A Tribute To Bix Beiderbecke* (Jazzology 343), *Celebrating 50 Years In Jazz* (Jazz Me Blues 01), and *It Had To Be You* (Jazzology 369). His *Stringing The Blues* (Jazzology 329) CD teams him with fellow guitarists Bucky Pizzarelli, Frank Vignola, Howard Alden, Al Viola, Marty Grosz and Michele Ariondante.

**Website:** www.linopatruno.it

## Roy Patterson
*b. March 20, 1954, Nova Scotia, Canada*

A tasteful and quietly inventive guitarist, Roy Patterson has been making rewarding music in Canada for over 35 years. "I caught the tail end of the 1960s and was inspired by the whole 'British Invasion,' so was initially drawn to blues and blues-based rock music. I started a band when I was 16 that played gigs at local fire halls and community centers. Our first gig was in an asylum for the mentally ill. I think we knew three or four songs: 'Pipeline,' 'Wipeout,' 'House of the Rising Sun' and maybe one other one. We just repeated each song until it was time to finish. The audience loved it, and it felt great. I was hooked and never really wanted to do anything since then except play music."

In the 1970s, Patterson worked with a wide variety of ensembles, including commercial groups, country bands, and groups for bar mitzvahs. After moving to Toronto in 1978, he attended York University (1979–84) as a music major and later did graduate work at McGill University. By the time he finished at York, Patterson was a strong enough jazz guitarist that he could concentrate on the music he loved. In addition to being a freelance musician in Toronto, he led his own groups, including a quartet during 1991–2000. "We did some touring, released some CDs, and had some critical success. It was like having a musical family where each member can grow and learn to trust on a musical level." Patterson's quartet won first prize at the Montreal Jazz Festival in 1996. He has also worked as an educator and played with such musicians as Don Thompson, Doug Riley, Phil Dwyer, Barry Elmes, Bob Mover, Mike Murley and Bernie Senensky.

"Recently I have cut back on my teaching and am writing for a new project called RPG (Roy Patterson Group). It will be different than my past work in that the band will have electric bass, organ, drums and guitar, so the textural possibilities are very expansive. As I wind down my teaching, I am also finishing a book on guitar harmony that is based on a decade of articles that I wrote for a magazine called *Just Jazz Guitar*."

**Recommended CDs:** Each of Roy Patterson's CDs are rewarding, and they often feature his original compositions for his combos: *The Release* (Unity 113), *Arcadian Suite* (Unity 138), *The Coming Of Angels* (Unity 149), *Inland Passages* (Justin Time 20930), *On A Cloud* (Unity 172) and *Atlantic Blues* (Toronto Jazz Composers Collective 001).

**Website:** www.roypatterson.com

## Les Paul
*(Lester Polsfuss)*
*b. June 9, 1915, Waukesha, WI; d. August 13, 2009, White Plains, NY*

Les Paul's accomplishments as a guitarist, inventor, designer of guitars, and master of multitrack recording are vast. His musical roots were always in country and swing, but his guitar playing crossed over into rock, pop and bop, and he was thoroughly appreciated by guitarists from all genres (including many much younger rock players) for his development of the Les Paul guitar, his playing and his constant good humor.

Paul began on the harmonica when he was eight and also played banjo briefly. He was completely self-taught on the guitar, with his only music lessons being a few on the piano. An inquisitive genius from an early age, Paul developed quickly on the guitar. He invented a neck-worn harmonica holder so he could play the harmonica and the guitar at the same time. When he was 17, he played country and hillbilly music with Rube Tronson's Cowboys. A local performer, Sunny Joe Wolverton, gave Paul the stage name of Rhubarb Red when the 17-year-old dropped out to play with his radio band in St. Louis on KMOX. By 1934, he was based in Chicago, playing hillbilly music on the radio as Rhubarb Red and jazz as Les Paul. His first recordings were in 1936 as Rhubarb Red and as an accompanist to blues singer Georgia White. Even that early, he was one of the first American guitarists to be influenced by Django Reinhardt.

Dissatisfied with the acoustic guitar, Paul was already experimenting with his instrument by the mid-1930s. During an interview from October 26, 1991, he remembered: "I was playing in a barbecue place, and people said they could hear my singing and harmonica playing but couldn't hear my guitar. I took a phonograph needle, stole my dad's radio, and jammed the needle into my guitar, which amplified my guitar out of the radio. However, the sound was pretty barbaric. I took a telephone apart, attached half of it to the microphone and the other half to the strings of the guitar. There was a problem of feedback because the strings vibrated. I put towels and cotton in the guitar, trying to stop the vibrations. Finally, I got a piece of a railroad track, strung a string across it, and that worked better." While electric guitars first became available in 1937, Paul was still not happy with its sound. In 1940, he created "The Log," a piece of four-by-four lumber with a pickup that he made look like a guitar by attaching the body of an Epiphone hollow-body guitar. That was the basis for his future solid-body guitars. It took him a few years to interest the Gibson Guitar Corporation in his design, but by 1946, he was endorsing the Gibson Les Paul model.

Paul led a jazz trio, moved to New York in 1938, and became a featured player with Fred Waring's Pennsylvanians for the next three years, performing regularly on the radio. "Every night when I finished with Fred Waring, I'd go up to Harlem and play with Art Tatum, Roy Eldridge, Lester Young or Coleman Hawkins, sometimes Count Basie and John Kirby. When Charlie Christian came to New York, we would go up to Harlem and jam. I was always being caught by the union and scolded for jamming. They asked why I was doing that when I had such a good job, and I said that the music that the black musicians were playing was what was really happening."

In 1943, Les Paul moved to Hollywood where he formed a new trio. At the very first Jazz at the Philharmonic concert in 1944, he was a last-second substitute for Oscar Moore. The highlight of the concert was a humorous tradeoff between Paul and Nat King Cole. "When the concert came out as a recording, I couldn't use my name because I was signed with Decca, so I was listed as being Paul Leslie. One of the critics said, 'That Paul Leslie can outplay Les Paul about ten times over.'"

Later in 1944 and into 1945, Paul worked a bit with Bing Crosby. His trio was featured on Crosby's show, and they recorded a few numbers together, including a hit version of "It's Been A Long Long Time." Crosby encouraged the guitarist to build his own studio, which he did. After a great deal of experimenting with overdubbing, Paul recorded a version of "Lover" that had him playing eight electric guitars and using different effects. The recording became a hit for Capitol. But a serious car accident almost ended his career and put the guitarist on the sidelines for over a year.

As he began to make a comeback, he was dating a country singer named Colleen Summers. "When I met her, I had only heard her singing country songs on a radio show. I was already recording multiple guitars and having some hits. I had made around 22 sides but now I was looking to use a singer. I had thought of Doris Day, Rosemary Clooney and Kay Starr and had settled on Doris Day. My father and brother had a tavern and one night the guitarist and singer never showed up, so I filled in and I asked her to join me. It worked out very well and

I said to my dad, 'I've found the girl that I've been looking for.'" He renamed her Mary Ford, they were married in 1949, and the team of Les Paul and Mary Ford recorded a series of hits between 1950 and '55, including "How High The Moon," "The World Is Waiting For The Sunrise," "Tiger Rag," "In The Good Old Summertime," "Bye Bye Blues," and "Vaya Con Dios." Using extensive overdubbing, delay effects and multitrack recording, Paul not only made recordings that were revolutionary, but the results were fun records that featured multiple guitars and voices. During an era when the hits tended to be dated novelties, the recordings of Les Paul and Mary Ford were a welcome relief. And while the records may not have always been technically jazz, they were influenced by Paul's background in jazz.

For a time they were so popular that *The Les Paul Show* was a fifteen-minute radio program in 1950 and there was a regular five-minute show on television during 1954–55. With the rise of rock and roll, the hits stopped after 1955. Les Paul and Mary Ford remained a popular attraction for the rest of the decade. Marital problems resulted in them getting divorced in 1964, and a few years later Paul retired from live performing. He came back in the mid-1970s to record a pair of delightful sets with Chet Atkins, made a guest appearance on Al Di Meola's 1980 CD *Splendido Hotel*, and in 1984 began playing every Monday night at Fat Tuesday's in New York, switching to the Iridium in 1996. "My doctor suggested that I go back to playing because it is good for my arthritis. I can only use two fingers on my left hand, which is always stiff, so it has taught me to do more with less. It is good therapy for me." Paul's weekly gig gave him opportunities to have many guitarists who were inspired by him (including Jeff Beck and quite a few rock musicians) sit in with their idol.

Les Paul, whose shows were full of swing tunes, cornball humor and joyful spirits, stayed active until his death in 2009 at the age of 94.

**Recommended CDs:** *The Trio's Complete Decca Recordings Plus, 1938–47* (MCA/Decca 11708), *Les Paul Trio* (Laserlight 15 741), the definitive four-CD *The Legend & The Legacy* (Capitol 97654), *16 Most Requested Songs* (Columbia/Legacy 64993); with Jazz at the Philharmonic: *The Beginning* (Charly 41); with Chet Atkins: *Chester & Lester* (RCA 76379).

# Mike Peters

b. January 6, 1954, Queens, NY

Due to his work behind the scenes as a researcher on early jazz guitarists, producer of Django Reinhardt and Joe Venuti–Eddie Lang box sets for Mosaic, and curator of an Eddie Lang website, it is easy to overlook Mike Peters' excellent guitar playing. However, he has also been successful at keeping 1920s and '30s guitar alive through his own performances and recordings.

Peters began playing guitar when he was ten after hearing recordings by the Ventures and the Beatles. "At 16, I was a waiter in a catering hall and was fascinated with the club date band. It included guitarist Joe Sinacore, who in the 1950s was accompanist for Frankie Laine and Patti Page. I struck up a conversation with him every time he played gigs at the catering hall. I rambled on about George Harrison, Eric Clapton, and Jimi Hendrix, and he countered with Eddie Lang, Django Reinhardt, and Charlie Christian. He won!" Peters soon took guitar lessons from Sinacore. "At the end of each lesson, he would grab an acoustic guitar off the wall and play unaccompanied just for me. It took my breath away, and it drove me to quit my job, lock myself in my parent's basement for a couple of years, and teach myself how to play jazz guitar by studying the recordings of Django, Hawkins, Venuti/Lang, Armstrong and Carter."

Peters often went to Eddie Condon's and Jimmy Ryan's in Manhattan and had some opportunities to sit in, getting to know Marty Grosz and Wayne Wright, both of whom encouraged him. In 1974, he not only enjoyed seeing the Ruby Braff–George Barnes Quartet and Soprano Summit but also met Joe Venuti. Peters, who also plays banjo and mandolin (and has dabbled with the cornet, clarinet and violin), was a member of Venuti's group during 1974–78, even sitting in Eddie Lang's spot on such violin-guitar duets as "Doin' Things" and "Wild Cat."

He led Jazz A Cordes, a Quintet of Hot Club–type group that included Carmen Mastren, during 1977–80 including two years at the West End Cafe. He also headed Mike Peters String Fever (1981–82), Django's Music (1982–84), and the classic jazz ten-piece group Mike Peters New Yorkers (1999–2000). In addition, Peters has worked with Bob Wilber (particularly in the 1980s), the Louisiana Repertory Jazz Ensemble (2000–05) and in acoustic guitar duos with Marty Grosz.

Beyond playing music, Mike Peters has done extensive research on Django Reinhardt (including working closely with Charles Delauney), Eddie Lang and Joe Venuti, produced the two box sets for Mosaic, worked at Sirius Satellite Radio as a broadcast producer and director (1999–2008), and recently built a website dedicated to Eddie Lang (www.eddielang.com). However, he deserves more recognition for his own guitar playing.

**Recommended CDs:** Mike Peters is featured on acoustic guitar duets with Marty Grosz on *Acoustic Heat*

(Sackville 2071) and with Bob Wilber on *Live At The Vineyard* (Challenge 70018).

## John Pisano
b. February 6, 1931, New York, NY

John Pisano, one of the most modest of all guitarists, loves to play in the background and accompany other guitar players. However, he is also a fine soloist who, while based in swing and bop, can hold his own in more adventurous styles. His father was an amateur guitarist, and an uncle played banjo. Pisano took piano lessons when he was ten, switching to guitar three years later. Early on, he liked Charlie Christian and George Van Eps and became a big Django Reinhardt fan, even seeing Reinhardt play with Duke Ellington at Carnegie Hall in 1946. Pisano played occasional local gigs before serving in the Air Force during 1952–56. He worked with the Air Force band and with a small combo called the Crew Chiefs that was in one of the Bob Hope USO shows in Greenland and appeared on *The Steve Allen Show*.

Shortly after his discharge, Pisano became a member of the Chico Hamilton Quintet (1956–58) as Jim Hall's successor. After leaving Hamilton, Pisano became a studio musician in Los Angeles. Among his most significant projects through the years were recording two albums of duets with Billy Bean (*Makin' It* and *Take Your Pick*) and playing with the Joe Pass Quartet in the early 1960s (including recording the *For Django* album), Peggy Lee throughout the 1960s, Benny Goodman, and Herb Alpert's Tijuana Brass during 1965–69. He also worked with Frank Rosolino, Buddy Collette, Bud Shank, Red Norvo, Page Cavanaugh and other Los Angeles–based musicians.

Pisano worked and recorded with Joe Pass during several periods, touring with Pass during 1989–94. In addition to his work with his wife, singer Jeanne Pisano, as a group called the Flying Pisanos, he has become famous for hosting the weekly "John Pisano Guitar Nights" at several different Southern California jazz clubs. Each show has a different featured guitarist, giving Pisano an opportunity to play with the who's who of jazz guitar (just as Marian McPartland welcomes pianists to her Piano Jazz radio programs) while cheering on his guests.

**Recommended CDs:** *Makin' It Again* (String Jazz 1003) and *West Coast Sessions* (String Jazz 1006) feature John Pisano with Billy Bean. A rare gathering of the Chico Hamilton Quintet in later years is featured on *Reunion* (Soul Note 121191). *Among Friends* (Pablo 2310-956) and *Conversation Pieces* (Pablo 2310-963) date from the 1990s and have guest appearances from many guitarists. That concept is fully realized on the two-CD *John Pisano's Guitar Night* (Mel Bay 10412), which has Pisano

happily playing a supportive role behind a dozen different guitarists. Pisano is featured with Jeanne Pisano on *The Flying Pisanos* (FP 01), *Ensemble* (FP Music 02) and *Lazy Afternoon* (FP Music 03). Among his many recordings with Joe Pass are the classic *For Django* (Pacific Jazz 85), *Ira, George and Joe* (Pablo 2312-133), *Whitestone* (Pablo 2310-912), *Summer Nights* (Pablo 2310-939), *Appassionato* (Pablo 2310-946), *Joe Pass Quartet Live At Yoshi's* (Pablo 2310-951), *Duets* (Pablo 2310-959) and *Nuages* (Pablo 2310-961).

**Website:** www.johnpisano.com

## Bucky Pizzarelli
*(John Pizzarelli, Sr.)*
b. January 9, 1926, Paterson, NJ

The epitome of tasteful jazz guitar, Bucky Pizzarelli is a melodic swing soloist, a skilled rhythm guitarist, and a masterful accompanist. His uncle Bobby Domenick played guitar with accordionist Joe Mooney, whose music Pizzarelli loved. Mostly self-taught, he began his career in 1944 when he joined the Vaughn Monroe Orchestra. After serving in the military, Pizzarelli rejoined Monroe during 1946–51. While the music was not jazz, playing with the dance orchestra was perfect training for the guitarist, who was involved in his lifelong quest to learn the chords to every song.

In 1952, Pizzarelli became a member of the staff of NBC, staying until 1964 when he switched to ABC. He became part of a core of musicians who recorded on a daily basis in all kinds of settings, from commercials to pop singers, from rock and roll dates and television orchestras (starting with *The Kate Smith Show* in 1953 and including *The Tonight Show* when it was based in New York) to occasional jazz sessions. He also worked with the Three Suns during 1956–57 under the name of Johnny Buck.

Pizzarelli always found some time to play jazz. He was with Benny Goodman on several occasions starting in the mid-1950s and was in his last bands in the mid-1980s. After two decades of anonymously uplifting sessions, starting in the 1970s he became more prominent in the jazz world. By then, he was playing the seven-string guitar, which he learned from George Van Eps. Pizzarelli worked with Joe Venuti, Stéphane Grappelli, Zoot Sims, and Bud Freeman, had a duo with George Barnes, and was featured in Manhattan Swing, a trio with pianist John Bunch and bassist Jay Leonhart. In addition to appearing on a countless number of albums as a sideman, he has also led albums of his own and paid tribute to the music and styles of Carl Kress and Dick McDonough.

One of his records, *Green Guitar Blues*, included playing from his daughter Mary, who is a classical guitarist. Since then, his sons, John Pizzarelli and bassist Martin Pizzarelli, have often appeared with him (and vice versa) and he has also played with his daughter-in-law, singer Jessica Molaskey. At 84, Bucky Pizzarelli has remained quite active up to the present time.

**Recommended CDs:** *Guitar Quintet* (Audiophile 238) has Pizzarelli and his guitar group playing Bill Challis' arrangements of Bix Beiderbecke songs plus classic pieces by Carl Kress and Dick McDonough. *Solos & Duets* (Jazz Classics 5007) features Pizzarelli as a soloist on seven-string guitar and in duets with his son John from 1981 and 1986. Other worthy Bucky Pizzarelli sets, some with John Pizzarelli on second guitar, include *Nirvana* (Delta 17163), *Live At The Vineyard Theatre* (Challenge 70025), *Contrasts* (Arbors 19209), *April Kisses* (Arbors 19227), *One Morning In May* (Arbors 19254), *Swing Live* (Chesky 223), *Manhattan Swing: A Visit With The Duke* (Arbors 19226), *Moonglow* (Hyena 9339) with Frank Vignola, *5 For Freddie* (Arbors 19344), *Generations* (Arbors 19345), *So Hard To Forget* (Arbors 19370), *Diggin' Up Bones* (Arbors 19394), *Challis In Wonderland* (Arbors 19435) and *Family Fugue* (Arbors 19436); with Stéphane Grappelli: *Duet* (Black & Blue 916).

**LPs to Search For:** *Green Guitar Blues* (Monmouth/Evergreen 7047), *Buck & Bud* (Flying Dutchman 1378) with Bud Freeman, *Nightwings* (Flying Dutchman 1120) with Joe Venuti.

## John Pizzarelli
b. April 6, 1960, Paterson, NJ

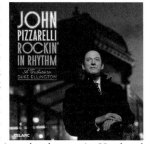

One of the most popular performers in jazz today, John Pizzarelli is a very fluent guitar soloist on the seven-string and a charming singer who often scats in unison with his solos. The son of Bucky Pizzarelli, he began playing guitar when he was six. He played with a variety of garage bands while learning his instrument, but his main lessons were with his father. "I grew up listening to and hanging out with Zoot Sims, Joe Venuti, Joe Pass, Slam Stewart and other jazz greats who would come over to our house in Jersey when they were in town. Nat King Cole's music is the reason I do what I do. I also played trumpet through college until I realized it was hard!" He attended the University of Tampa and William Paterson College during 1978–81. "Most important, I went to the school of Bucky Pizzarelli during 1980–1990; it was truly the learning experience for me. I got to hear and perform with Benny Goodman, Ray Brown, Slam Stewart, Zoot Sims, Joe Pass, Bob Haggart, Marshall Royal and the like at jazz parties and concerts."

While influenced by his father, John Pizzarelli developed his own swing style, which is distinctive and more high-powered. He began singing in the early 1980s, starting with a popular version of "I Like Jersey Best." His 1990 CD *My Blue Heaven* was a motivation for him to start his own group. With his younger brother bassist Martin Pizzarelli and pianist Ray Kennedy, he became a popular attraction in the 1990s. In addition to his work with his group (which, with the addition of a drummer, is now a quartet), Pizzarelli opened for Frank Sinatra in a series of concerts in 1993, worked with George Shearing and Rosemary Clooney, had the lead in the 1997 Broadway production of *Dream*, which was a tribute to Johnny Mercer, and has appeared with the Clayton-Hamilton Jazz Orchestra. In recent times, he and his wife, Broadway and cabaret star Jessica Molaskey, have been co-hosting the nationally syndicated radio program *Radio Deluxe With John Pizzarelli*. When asked his future musical goals, Pizzarelli replied, "A small group CD with string quartet à la Sinatra's *Close To You* and a CD of songs from the past 30 years."

**Recommended CDs:** John Pizzarelli has been very consistent with his recordings, and all are enjoyable. His pair of sets from the 1980s, *I'm Hip—Please Don't Tell My Father* (P-Vine 2332) and *Hit That Jive Jack* (P-Vine 233), will be difficult to find, but the others are all readily available: *My Blue Heaven* (Chesky 38), *All Of Me* (Novus 673129), *Naturally* (Novus 01241), *New Standards* (Novus 63172), *Dear Mr. Cole* (Novus 63182), *After Hours* (Novus 63191), *Let's Share Christmas* (RCA 66986), *Our Love Is Here To Stay* (RCA 67501), *Meets The Beatles* (RCA 61432), *P.S. Mr. Cole* (RCA 63563), *Kisses In The Rain* (Telarc 83491), *Let There Be Love* (Telarc 83518), *The Rare Delight Of You* (Telarc 83546) with George Shearing, the double CD *Live At Birdland* (Telarc 83577), *Bossa Nova* (Telarc 83591), *Knowing You* (Telarc 83615), *Dear Mr. Sinatra* (Telarc 83638), *With A Song In My Heart* (Telarc 83676), the excellent Duke Ellington tribute album

*Rockin' In Rhythm* (Telarc 31921) and the pop-oriented *Double Exposure* (Telarc 33221). He has also recorded as a guest on several pop albums and with such notables as Rosemary Clooney, Ruby Braff, Johnny Frigo, Harry Allen and Buddy DeFranco.

**Website:** www.johnpizzarelli.com

## Jimmy Ponder
*b. May 10, 1946, Pittsburgh, PA*

A superior soul-jazz guitarist with a bluesy style, Jimmy Ponder is an asset to any session on which he appears. He began on the guitar when he was 11, had his first gig shortly after, and was playing regularly in Philadelphia  nightclubs by the time he was 13. Completely self-taught, he was offered a job with Charles Earland in 1963 but waited until he graduated from high school. He toured and recorded with Earland's group during 1965–68.

Influenced by Wes Montgomery and Kenny Burrell but having his own soulful sound, Ponder has been in demand for decades. He worked with Lou Donaldson, Houston Person, Donald Byrd, Stanley Turrentine, Dizzy Gillespie, the Thad Jones/Mel Lewis Orchestra, Hank Crawford, Jack McDuff, Sonny Stitt, Jimmy McGriff, Willis Jackson, Andrew Hill, and many others through the years.

Jimmy Ponder, who has led many albums of his own, has a style that is largely unchanged from the late 1960s and is still fresh and timeless.

**Recommended CDs:** *Steel City Soul* (32 Jazz 32075) has some of the highlights from Jimmy Ponder's long out-of-print Muse CDs, which include *Mean Streets: No Bridges* (Muse 5324), *Jump* (Muse 5347), *Come On Down* (Muse 5375), *To Reach A Dream* (Muse 5394), *Soul Eyes* (Muse 5514) and *Something To Ponder* (Muse 5567). A solo set, *Live At The Other Side* (Explore 26), features Ponder at a club date that actually predates his Muse recordings. Fortunately, his work for High Note is readily available, including *James Street* (High Note 7017), *Guitar Christmas* (High Note 7034), *Ain't Misbehavin'* (High Note 7041), *Alone* (High Note 7069), *Thumbs Up* (High Note 7080), *What's New* (High Note 7100), *Somebody's Child* (High Note 7165) and his 2010 release *Steel City Blues* (Savoy).

**LPs to Search For:** Among the early Jimmy Ponder LPs

are *While My Guitar Gently Weeps* (Cadet 50048), *Illusions* (ABC 9313), *White Room* (ABC 9327) and *So Many Stars* (Milestone 9132).

## Frank Potenza
*b. February 10, 1950, Providence, RI*

Frank Potenza, the protégé of Joe Pass, has long been important in Southern California as both a guitarist and an educator. After a period playing his sister's acoustic guitar, at 12 Potenza was inspired by his  cousin Jimmy Galiardi to play R&B on electric guitar. "Jimmy played and sang in rock and roll shows and nightclubs. He had a slick haircut, drove a Cadillac convertible, smoked Lucky Strikes, and could blow the most perfect smoke rings ever. To me, he was the epitome of cool. He knew the guitar parts to all the great R&B songs and started showing me Duane Eddy and Bill Doggett tunes. He got a kick out of how fast I could soak it all up." Potenza was exposed to jazz through his father's record collection, but at first he played rock and roll, until he heard George Benson. At that point, he was turned toward Wes Montgomery, Pat Martino and jazz in general. Potenza went to Berklee straight after high school, graduating four years later. He later earned a master's from Cal State L.A.

"I had the good fortune to meet Joe Pass in Boston in 1974 during his solo engagement at the Jazz Workshop in Boston when I took my father to see him play. I had my first lesson with him the very next day, and that was the beginning of my 20-year friendship with him. It was a great blessing to be able to spend as much time as I got to spend with Joe."

Potenza worked in a variety of bands in New England, including with Diamond Centofanti, a local legend who played nearly every instrument. In 1981, the guitarist moved to Los Angeles, where, during 1981–86, he was an adjunct instructor on the Commercial Music Faculty at Long Beach City College. "The director, Dr. George Shaw, brought in a series of guest artists to play with the student big band that he directed. These guests commonly asked for a professional rhythm section to play for them, and I was fortunate to get the chance to play with Dizzy Gillespie, Bill Watrous, Wilton Felder, Ronnie Laws, Joe Pass, and others." Potenza toured with Ronnie Laws for a year and, during 1996–2000, was a member of the Gene Harris Quartet. "Gene inspired me with his soulful, heartfelt playing and his amazing ability to rise above the health problems he was having. Some nights he would have to be helped to the stage and even to the piano bench, but Gene would summon up his energy, and in no time he was swinging and jubilant, leading the quartet with a vitality that could only be attributed to the healing power of music itself."

These days, Frank Potenza is the chair of the studio/jazz guitar faculty at USC and leads an organ trio. "I have a strong commitment to education and have invested a great deal of my time and energy to insure that the next generation of jazz guitarists keeps the music alive, relevant, and moving forward."

**Recommended CDs:** Frank Potenza's first four albums, cut for the TBA label during 1986–90, will be difficult to locate: *Sand Dance* (TBA 206), *Soft And Warm* (TBA 222), *When We're Alone* (TBA 235) and *Express Delivery* (TBA 249). Fortunately, his other four sets as a leader, which are superior, are much more readily available. *In My Dreams* (Azica 72212) is a set of duets with bassist Bob Magnusson, *Three Guitars At The Jazz Bakery* (Art Song Music 2002) teams Potenza with John Stowell and Pat Kelley, *First Takes* (Azica 2233) has him matching wits in brilliant duets with pianist Shelly Berg, and *Old, New, Borrowed And Blue* (Capri 74093) features his organ trio/quartet.

**Website:** www.frankpotenza.com

---

## Baden Powell
*(Baden Powell de Aquino)*
*b. August 6, 1937, Rio de Janeiro, Brazil; d. September 26, 2000, Rio de Janeiro, Brazil*

Arguably the definitive Brazilian bossa nova guitarist, Baden Powell was influential during his prime years, mixing together jazz harmonies with classical technique. His father was a violinist who often had famous entertainers over to the house to play music, so Powell grew up around music. He had guitar lessons for five years starting when he was eight. Quickly becoming a guitar virtuoso, he won many talent contests as a youth and was a professional by the time he was 15. After high school, he worked on Radio Nacional, often touring Brazil with the station's singers. In 1955, Powell was a member of Ed Lincoln's trio, playing jazz. It was during this period that he decided to exclusively play acoustic guitar. Always a songwriter, he had success in 1959 with "Samba Triste," a song that would be recorded by Stan Getz and Charlie Byrd on their *Jazz Samba* album. In 1962, he began writing with lyricist Vinicius de Moraes, which resulted in many popular songs in

Brazil, "Berimbau" being perhaps the best known.

Powell continued to advance as a guitarist and, while most associated with bossa nova, he could also play Latin jazz, traditional Brazilian music and what was called "Afro-Sambas." Powell began recording albums as a leader in 1959; his *Tristeza On Guitar* from 1966 is considered one of his best. He recorded with Herbie Mann in 1962, performed in Paris, played regularly in Brazil and worked in Elis Regina's television show *O Fino Da Bossa*. In 1966, Powell worked in the United States with Stan Getz. The following year, he was featured at the Berlin Jazz Festival with Jim Hall and Barney Kessel. In 1968, Powell moved to France, where he lived for over 20 years.

While he remained active, he had a lower profile in the 1970s and '80s, partly due to erratic health. In the 1990s, Baden Powell moved back to Brazil and made a comeback, often playing quiet solo guitar, before his death in 2000 at the age of 63.

**Recommended CDs:** Four of Baden Powell's MPS LPs have been reissued as the two-CD set *Tristeza/ Poema/Canto/Images On Guitar* (MPS 9824376). A sampling of Powell's many recordings should include *Solitude On Guitar* (Sony 464344), *Canta Vinicius De Moraes E Paolo Cesar Pinheiro* (Sunnyside 3038), *The Frankfurt Opera Concert 1975* (Crown 8548), *Seresta Brasileira* (Milestone 9212), *At The Rio Jazz Club* (Polygram 8471112), *Live In Hamburg* (Acoustic Music 31910372), *Live In Montreux* (Fremeaux & Associes 410), and *Baden Live À Bruxelles* (Sunnyside 1148).

---

## Jeanfrançois Prins
*b. February 18, 1967, Uccle, Brussels, Belgium*

A versatile jazz guitarist from Belgium, Jeanfrançois Prins has had a wide-ranging career. Prins did not begin playing guitar until he was almost 18, although he came from a musical family. One grandfather owned a record store, was a classically trained pianist and produced Django Reinhardt's Brussels recordings in 1942. Jeanfrançois' parents also worked in record stores. "Six months after starting to play, I convinced my parents that I needed an electric guitar. From then on, I pretty much started playing gigs in clubs in Belgium. The first real band I put together was around the time I was 19. I had heard and met Toots Thielemans many times by then. One day, after one of his concerts, his bassist Michel Hatzigeorgiou told him that he should hear me play. That was when he took me under his wing and became my musical godfather. Toots is not just the harmonica genius we all know. His guitar playing is fantastic and very original. One of my first international gigs was when my quartet was hired to play with Bud

Shank. Toots came and sat in with us, and the music was wonderful."

The guitarist says that he was inspired by the music of Chet Baker (whom Prins knew), Miles Davis, Lee Konitz and Kenny Werner. Although he earned a degree as a sound engineer, upon his graduation Prins enrolled in the jazz department of the Royal Conservatory of Music in Brussels (1988–92). In 1991, he met his future wife, singer Judy Neimack, and they have performed together regularly since then, living in both Berlin and New York.

In addition, Prins has worked with a large assortment of musicians, including Lee Konitz (particularly during 1993–2004), Fred Hersch, Billy Hart, Kenny Wheeler, Kirk Lightsey, Gary Bartz, Randy Brecker, Mal Waldron, Stephen Scott, trumpeter Richard Rousselet (in a Belgian All Stars tribute to Miles Davis), drummer Bruno Castellucci, the Berlin Jazz Orchestra (since 2000), soprano-saxophonist Meike Goosmann, Lew Tabackin, Gary Foster, Jiggs Whigham, Tim Hagans, Jim McNeely, Walter Norris, Jay Clayton and Janice Borla. He also works as a record producer, an educator, and as the musical director and guitarist for Judy Niemack's groups.

"For the future, I want to tour more extensively with my bands, particularly my New York Trio with Cameron Brown and Victor Lewis, my Colliding Universes sextet (a trio plus 2 tenors and 1 fluegelhorn), All Strings Attached (my trio and a classical string quartet), and a quartet that I co-lead with saxophonist Andy Middleton."

**Recommended CDs:** Jeanfrançois Prins has thus far led six CDs of his own: *N.Y. Stories* (GAM Jam 911), *Beauty And The Prince* (GAM 916) with Judy Niemack and Fred Hersch as guests; *Live* (GAM 915) which teams Prins' trio with Lee Konitz; *All Around Town* (TCB 99402), which showcases his trio on a musical portrait of New York City; *Light* (GAM 918) and *El Gaucho* (Challenge 73337).

**Website:** www.jfprins.com

## Joe Puma
b. August 13, 1927, New York, NY; d. May 31, 2000, New York, NY

An excellent cool-toned guitarist who appeared on many jazz dates, Joe Puma tended to have a low profile, but his fellow musicians knew how valuable he was. Puma's family had

several relatives who played guitar, including his father and two brothers, but he was self-taught. After serving in the Army, his first major job was with vibraphonist Joe Roland's group during 1949–50. The 1950s were a busy period for Puma. He worked with Les Elgart, Sammy Kaye, Louie Bellson, Lee Konitz and the final version of Artie Shaw's Gramercy Five. Puma appeared on many record dates during this era, including sessions led by Joe Roland, Louie Bellson, Artie Shaw, Eddie Bert, Herbie Mann, Mat Mathews, and Paul Quinichette, among others. He accompanied Morgana King for two years and had a strong reputation for his work with singers, including Chris Connor, Billie Holiday, Carmen McRae, Peggy Lee, Mark Murphy, Helen Merrill and Carol Sloane. In the 1960s, he worked with Bobby Hackett and Gary Burton, and had a highly rated two-guitar group with Chuck Wayne during 1972–77.

Joe Puma stayed active as both a guitarist and a teacher until his death in 2000, never gaining much fame but always being widely respected by his contemporaries and the younger guitarists who followed him.

**Recommended CDs:** Joe Puma's only 1950s session as a leader to be reissued on CD thus far is *Wild Kitten* (Dawn 109), which finds him in a quartet with the accordionist Mat Mathews. The Joe Puma–Chuck Wayne duo is featured on *Interactions* (Choice 1004). *Shining Hour* (Reservoir 102) from 1984 is an especially enjoyable set, showcasing Puma engaging in interplay with pianist Hod O'Brien and bassist Red Mitchell in a drumless trio. Joe Puma's final recording, 1999's *It's A Blue World* (Euphoria 175), shows that he was creative and swinging up until the end, this time with a pianoless trio.

**LPs to Search For:** Joe Puma's debut as a leader, *East Coast Jazz Series, Vol. 3* (Bethlehem 1012), has him leading a quintet with rhythm guitarist Barry Galbraith and vibraphonist Don Elliott in 1954. *Joe Puma Jazz Trio And Quartet* (Jubilee 1070) teams him with Bill Evans and vibraphonist Eddie Costa in 1957. Most intriguing is 1961's *Like Tweet* (Columbia 1618). Producer Eddie Hall notated birdcalls that Dick Hyman wrote out and used as the basis for arrangements that put Puma in the lead with an orchestra.

## Tony Purrone
b. October 18, 1954, Bridgeport, CT

A fine straight-ahead guitarist, Tony Purrone is best known for his long-time association with the Heath Brothers. Purrone had his first guitar lesson in 1964. His favorite group of the late 1960s was Blood, Sweat & Tears until his mother bought him a Duke Ellington record, which drew him into jazz. He was more interested in listening to horn players than current guitarists, although Johnny Smith, Tal Farlow, Jim Hall and Jimmy Raney from earlier eras were among his early influences.

Purrone began playing gigs at 14, mostly casuals. Although he was still in high school, at 15 he joined the University of Bridgeport Jazz Ensemble. At 18, he was a member of Bobby Buster's R&B group and the following year had opportunities to play with Don Elliott and Gerry Mulligan. Purrone attended the University of Bridgeport and New York University, earning a degree in music performance.

In 1978, Purrone joined the Heath Brothers, starting an association that lasted for 21 years and resulted in him being featured on records with the group, Jimmy Heath and as a leader. He had periods where he dropped out of music for health reasons and out of frustration at being under-recognized, but he has remained at his musical prime. Along the way, Purrone has performed with Dizzy Gillespie, the Count Basie Orchestra, Freddie Hubbard, Paquito D'Rivera, Pepper Adams, Randy Brecker, Dave Liebman, Kenny Garrett and Grover Washington, Jr. Tony Purrone's current trio includes bassist Preston Murphy and drummer Thierry Arpino.

**Recommended CDs:** All of Tony Purrone's recordings as a leader, the majority of which feature him with a pianoless trio, are worth acquiring: 1993's *Electric Poetry* (B & W 28), *Set 'Em Up* (Steeplechase 31389), *In The Heath Zone* (Steeplechase 31410), *Six-String Delight* (Steeplechase 31438), *Temperament* (Steeplechase 31475), *The Tonester* (Steeplechase 31495), *Rascality* (Steeplechase 31514), *Guitarisk* (Steeplechase 31550), *Incubation* (Steeplechase 31591) and *Live At The Red Door* (Vision); the latter is also available as a DVD. Purrone has also recorded with the Heath Brothers, Jimmy Heath (*You've Changed* and *You Or Me*, both for Steeplechase), Lenny White and Ed Thigpen (*Mr. Taste*).

**Website:** www.tonypurrone.com

## Snoozer Quinn
### (Edward Quinn)
b. 1907, Pike County, MS; d. April 21, 1949, New Orleans, LA

Snoozer Quinn is an obscure guitarist whose abilities would have been lost to history altogether if it were not for cornetist Johnny Wiggs. A guitarist from an early age, Quinn grew up in Bogalusa, Louisiana. Becoming a professional musician as a young teenager, he gained experience playing with Paul English's Traveling Shows, Mart Britt's Sylvan Beach Orchestra, and with Peck Kelly as a member of Peck's Bad Boys. He mostly worked in Texas and Louisiana

during this time. When Paul Whiteman heard Quinn playing backstage at the St. Charles Theatre in New Orleans in October 1928, he hired him for his band. The guitarist was with Whiteman for seven months, playing with the band during the same period as Bix Beiderbecke and Frankie Trumbauer. But although he allegedly made some private recordings with Bix and Tram, they were never issued and are long lost. Quinn did record with the Whiteman Orchestra (but is inaudible), with singer Bee Palmer (two titles not released until the 1980s), and in 1931 with country singer Jimmie Davis, but these give little reason to include him in this book. He also worked as an accompanist to Bing Crosby in the early 1930s, where he gained the nickname of "Snoozer," but no recordings resulted from that association. He soon moved permanently to New Orleans.

In 1948, Snoozer Quinn was sick with tuberculosis, dying in a sanitarium. Johnny Wiggs, who had a home recording machine, convinced Quinn to record some guitar solos and he also joined him on cornet for a few duets. Those recordings, recorded six months before Quinn's death and released on a Fat Cat Jazz LP decades later, show that Snoozer Quinn was a superior early swing guitarist who deserves to be remembered.

**LP to Search For:** *The Legendary Snoozer Quinn* (Fat Cat Jazz 104).

## Adam Rafferty
b. January 26, 1969, New York, NY

A fixture in the New York jazz scene for the past two decades, Adam Rafferty was born and raised in Harlem. He started studying fingerstyle blues guitar with Woody Mann when he was just six. When he was 12, he joined a rock band, but he really began to take the guitar more seriously when he started studying classical guitar four years later. "When I met my classical teacher Dennis Cinelli, I started getting referred for gigs, and it was a more responsible role to play than just being a student. He was an important teacher for me." Rafferty attended State University of New York in Purchase, gigged regularly while at college, and began studying jazz and counterpoint with Mike Longo, which continued on and off through 2005.

In 1991, Rafferty worked with organist Jimmy "Preacher" Robbins and with the Tippy Larkin

Quintet. Since then, he has played with Lou Donaldson, Frank Wess, Benny Golson, the Dizzy Gillespie Alumni All Star Big Band, the Mike Longo Big Band, Dr. Lonnie Smith, Alvin Queen and Bennie Wallace. He has also toured with guitarist Tommy Emmanuel, including concerts in Finland and Thailand.

Adam Rafferty is active as an educator, conducting workshops, writing two books, and making an instructional DVD. In recent times he has been working at playing fingerstyle solo guitar. His future goal is "to keep finding the sweet spot where musical invention, guitar, jazz, harmony, counterpoint, and groove all intersect. I truly love playing music that people can relate to, and I'd like to tastefully push the envelope of guitar sophistication without 'losing' the listener. Rhythm and groove are medicine for the soul and can elevate people to a place that perhaps they themselves cannot access. If the people are groovin', I am happy."

**Recommended CDs:** *First Impressions* (Consolidated Artists 905) has Adam Rafferty teamed with the Mike Longo Trio, and Longo is in the rhythm section on *Blood, Sweat & Bebop* (Consolidated Artists 937). Rafferty moves beyond bop on *Kush* (Consolidated Artists 955); *Three Souls* (Consolidated Artists 974), which features his originals; and, on his Crescent Ridge label, the unaccompanied solos of *Gratitude*, *Chameleon*, *A Christmas Guitar Celebration*, and *I Remember Michael*; the latter is certainly the first-ever solo jazz guitar tribute to Michael Jackson.

**Website:** www.adamrafferty.com

# Doug Raney
b. August 29, 1956, New York, NY

Doug Raney grew up and started his career in the shadow of his father, Jimmy Raney. But while influenced by his dad, Raney has long proven to be a major guitarist himself. He began on the guitar when he was 14, at first playing rock and blues. But by the time he was 17, he was listening to his father's records, taking lessons with Barry Galbraith, and turning completely toward straight-ahead jazz. The following year, he worked with pianist Al Haig. Raney, who made records with his father and sometimes played duos with him, went on a European concert tour with Jimmy and permanently settled in

Denmark. He worked in Europe with Johnny Griffin and Dexter Gordon and began a long association with Steeplechase Records, cutting many rewarding sets for the label.

Raney has worked with Chet Baker (including three memorable records in a trio with Baker and Niels Pedersen), Bernt Rosengren, Kenny Drew, Clifford Jordan, Horace Parlan, Kenny Barron, Joey DeFrancesco and Duke Jordan, in addition to his own groups. Spending most of his life in Scandinavia has resulted in Doug Raney being overlooked by American jazz fans, but he is a guitarist well worth discovering. He has been less active, particularly on recordings, since 2000, but his *Japanese Marshmallow* CD is of recent vintage.

**Recommended CDs:** *Introducing Doug Raney* (Steeplechase 31082), *Cuttin' Loose* (Steeplechase 31105), *Meeting The Tenors* (Criss Cross 1006), *Listen* (Steeplechase 31144), *I'll Close My Eyes* (Steeplechase 31166), *Blue And White* (Steeplechase 31191), *Lazy Bird* (Steeplechase 31200), *Guitar Guitar Guitar* (Steeplechase 31212), *Something's Up* (Steeplechase 31235), *The Doug Raney Quintet* (Steeplechase 31249), *Blues On A Par* (Steeplechase 31341), *Raney '96* (Steeplechase 31397), *Back In New York* (Steeplechase 31409), *The Backbeat* (Steeplechase 31456), *You Go To My Head* (Steeplechase 31474), and *Blues, Ballads, Bebop and a Blue Girl* (Marshmallow 128) comprise a solid body of work. In addition, Doug Raney recorded two quartet albums with his father, *Stolen Moments* (Steeplechase 31118) and *Raney '81* (Criss Cross 1001), and the Raneys recorded a pair of duo sets, *Duets* (Steeplechase 31134) and *Nardis* (Steeplechase 31184). Not to be missed are the three exquisite albums by the Chet Baker–Doug Raney–Niels Pedersen Trio: *Touch Of Your Lips* (Steeplechase 31122), *This Is Always* (Steeplechase 31168) and *Someday My Prince Will Come* (Steeplechase 31180).

# Jimmy Raney
b. August 20, 1927, Louisville, KY; d. May 10, 1995, Louisville, KY

In the 1950s when he was at the peak of his influence, Jimmy Raney could be thought of the Stan Getz of the guitar. His tone was cool and attractive, and he played at a quiet volume. But also like Getz, there was a great deal of inner heat brewing just beneath the surface. Raney managed

to play in a relaxed manner, even at the most raging tempos, while making it all sound easy.

Raney moved to Chicago as a teenager and played with the Jerry Wald Orchestra in 1944 when he was 17. After working with local groups, he was with Woody Herman's Second Herd for nine months in 1948. Raney's talent was soon noticed, and he recorded with Al Haig, Buddy DeFranco and Terry Gibbs, working with Artie Shaw's short-lived bop big band in 1949.

It was his association with Stan Getz during 1951–52 that made him well known and influential in the jazz world. Raney's rapid yet seemingly effortless unison lines with Getz and the way that they both blended together and challenged each other made this a very notable if relatively brief musical partnership. Raney also did well as Tal Farlow's successor in both the Red Norvo Trio (1953–54) and Artie Shaw's Gramercy Five (1954). While Raney spent much of 1954–60 working in supper clubs with pianist Jimmy Lyon, his own recordings as a leader were excellent, and he was heard with many top jazz artists, including Bob Brookmeyer, Bobby Jaspar, Urbie Green, Gigi Gryce, Zoot Sims and Al Cohn. A second and less eventful matchup with Getz during 1962–63 was followed by the guitarist returning to Louisville in 1967 and obscurity as he fought to overcome alcoholism.

Raney made no jazz records in the studios during 1966–73. But in 1975, he had a full comeback, recording often for the Xanadu label in the same style that he had developed by the early 1950s. He also recorded notable sets for Criss Cross and sometimes teamed up with his son Doug Raney, who played in a complementary style.

Jimmy Raney, who never declined on records, was less active during his final decade, passing away from heart failure in 1995.

**Recommended CDs:** *Together* (Xanadu 1228), *Visits Paris* (Vogue 40935), *A* (Original Jazz Classics 1706), *Visits Paris* (Dawn 115), *Visits Paris, Vol. 2* (BMG 43480), *Complete Recordings 1954–1956* (Fresh Sound 423), *Two Jims And Zoot* (Mobile Fidelity 833) with Jim Hall and Zoot Sims, *The Influence* (Prevue 23), *Solo* (Prevue 8), *Live In Tokyo 1976* (Prevue 14), *Stolen Moments* (Steeplechase 31118), *Duets* (Steeplechase 31134), *Here's That Raney Day* (Black & Blue 756), *Raney '81* (Criss Cross 1001), *The Master* (Criss Cross 1009), *Nardis* (Steeplechase 31184), *Wisteria* (Criss Cross 1019), *But Beautiful* (Criss Cross 1065); with Stan Getz: *The Complete Studio Sessions: Stan Getz & Jimmy Raney* (Definitive 11257), *Jazz At Storyville Vol. 1–2* (Roulette 94507).

**LPs to Search For:** *Too Marvelous For Words* (Biograph 12060); *Featuring Bob Brookmeyer* (ABC Paramount 129); 1957's *Strings And Swings* (Muse 5004), which features Raney's five-part "Suite For Guitar Quintet."

## Ernest Ranglin
*b. June 19, 1932, Manchester, Jamaica*

A major force in both ska and early reggae music, Ernest Ranglin has performed jazz on a fairly regular basis throughout his career. A child prodigy, Ranglin had two uncles who played guitar. Inspired by their music, he practiced on one of their instruments. When one of the uncles could not make it for a recording session, Ranglin played quite credibly in their place; he was just six years old.

Ranglin was a professional while a young teenager. When he was 15, he was in Val Bennett's band, also performing in later years with Eric Deans, Count Boysie and other groups in Jamaica and in the Bahamas. Ranglin, who made his recording debut in 1958, joined Cluett Johnson's Clue J and his Blues Blasters. Their instrumentals, particularly "Shuffling Bug," are considered the earliest examples of ska. Ranglin's "scratching" guitar sound became an influential force in both ska and its successor, reggae. He appeared on a long series of important record dates that were very influential in Jamaica, including sets with Jimmy Cliff, Prince Buster, the Skatalites, Bab Brooks and Bob Marley, often with the young Monty Alexander as the pianist. In 1964, he played guitar on one of the first Jamaican recordings to become a hit internationally, Millie Small's "My Boy Lollipop."

It was also in 1964 that Ernest Ranglin began to gain a reputation for his jazz playing. He was the house guitarist at Ronnie Scott's in London for nine months. He started to record his own jazz albums and was a sideman on a Sonny Stitt record in 1966 while still a major studio musician and arranger in Jamaica. Ranglin moved to Florida in the late 1970s and worked and recorded with Monty Alexander, with whom Ranglin had worked in the early 1960s.

While continuing his work in reggae, Ernest Ranglin has frequently played and recorded jazz during the past 40 years, displaying his own sound and exciting improvising style.

**Recommended CDs:** *Now's The Time: The Legendary MPS Sessions* (Motor 5599122), *Ultimate Ranglin Roots* (Tropic 15), *Memories Of Barber Mack* (Polygram 524339), *Gotcha!* (Telarc 83533), and *Surfin'* (Telarc 83632) are some of Ernest Ranglin's more jazz-oriented releases. He is also featured with Monty Alexander on *Jamento* (Original Jazz Classics 904) and *Yard Movement* (Polygram 524 232).

**LPs to Search For:** *Monty Strikes Again* (MPS 99437) with Monty Alexander.

## Django Reinhardt
*(Jean Baptiste Reinhardt)*
b. January 23, 1910, Liberchies, Belgium; d. May 16, 1953,
Fontainebleau, France

He was arguably jazz's greatest guitarist ever, a hero for gypsy families of the past 75 years, the first truly major European jazz musician, and a guitarist whose influence and legacy continues to grow through the gypsy jazz movement. Despite being physically handicapped, functionally illiterate, often unreliable, and short-lived, Django Reinhardt is a magical name whose musical legacy is remarkable.

Although best known for his work with violinist Stéphane Grappelli in the Quintet of the Hot Club of France during 1933–39, Reinhardt's career can be divided into three, with the Grappelli days only being the first of three significant periods.

He was born as part of a family of Romani gypsies. Early on he was given the nickname of Django (which in Romani means "I awake"). His family had a few amateur musicians, and Reinhardt started on the violin before switching to banjo, sometimes doubling on guitar. He made his first recordings as a banjoist in 1928, playing the French dance music of the time. One night, disaster struck in his caravan when he accidentally knocked over a candle, causing his wife's artificial flowers to catch on fire. He was severely burned on his left hand and right leg. While doctors debated whether to amputate his leg, a couple of Reinhardt's friends snuck him out of the hospital. He recuperated at home and within a year was walking again. However, he would never be able to use the fourth and fifth fingers of his left hand (his chording hand) again. Over a two-year period, Django relearned how to play his instruments, coming up with new ways to state chords. During his recovery, he heard American jazz for the first time on the Louis Armstrong record "Dallas Blues." He decided to pursue jazz and stick exclusively to the guitar.

Once he had recovered, Reinhardt developed quickly as a jazz improviser even though, outside of Eddie Lang, there were few musical role models on his instrument. He met Stéphane Grappelli in 1931 (they were soon playing together at jam sessions), and continued performing and occasionally recording as a sideman. In 1934, the Hot Club of France invited Reinhardt and Grappelli to form a jazz string group. Consisting of the pair plus two rhythm guitarists (originally Django's brother Joseph Reinhardt and Roger Chaput) and bassist Louis Vola, the group became a sensation and began recording regularly. Reinhardt, who combined the influences of Armstrong and Eddie Lang with his gypsy heritage and his vivid musical imagination, amazed listeners.

During the next five years, the Quintet of the Hot Club of France made Django Reinhardt and Stéphane Grappelli famous in Europe and gained attention in the American jazz world. Never before in jazz had an acoustic guitarist showed such virtuosity and been featured so extensively. While Eddie Lang spent most of his career accompanying others, Django was a star. His solos were on the level of the top trumpeters and saxophonists, and when visiting Americans such as Coleman Hawkins, Benny Carter and Rex Stewart were in Europe, they went out of their way to record with the guitarist. It is a pity that Django and Louis Armstrong (who met and jammed together) never had the opportunity to share a recording date.

This period in Reinhardt's life, which found him introducing such songs as "Nuages," "Minor Swing," "Daphne," and "Djangology," came to an end with the outbreak of World War II. The Quintet of the Hot Club of France was in the United Kingdom on tour when Django impulsively decided to return to Paris; Grappelli opted to spend the war years in England. Reinhardt put together a new quintet, which often had Hubert Rostaing on clarinet instead of the violin. Despite the Nazi occupation, Reinhardt recorded often during 1940–43. He was one of the first guitarists to lead a big band (at least at recording sessions), he continued to evolve as a musician, and somehow, he managed to survive. His celebrity status could have hurt him, but the Nazis mostly tolerated his presence as a symbol of France and he escaped the fate of many other gypsies through his street smarts and pure luck.

Nothing was heard of Django Reinhardt outside of the occupied countries until the liberation of France in 1944. It was big news that he was alive and well. Reinhardt began the final period of his career performing all over Europe, usually having a clarinetist in his quintet, and enjoying the first of several reunions with Grappelli in 1946. But he had two new barriers to conquer: the electric guitar and bebop.

In 1946, Reinhardt switched to electric guitar, and over the next few years, he developed his own tone and style on the instrument. Some of his longtime fans were not happy with that development, feeling that his unique personality was a bit lost on the instrument. But Django developed into a major electric guitarist pretty quickly, and his unique sound was not lost, just altered a bit.

In that same year, Reinhardt made his only visit to the United States, touring as a guest with the Duke Ellington Orchestra. Unfortunately, Ellington did not write any special music for the guitarist, and Django was only featured with Duke's rhythm section for a few songs each night, including at a pair of Carnegie Hall concerts. Reinhardt, who used to drive Grappelli a bit crazy in the 1930s by spontaneously disappearing to hang out with friends or play pool, was unhappy that he was not treated as a visiting celebrity in the United States (where many did not know who he was) and he became less reliable as the tour progressed, showing up late to some concerts. The tour was a disappointment, and Django never visited the US again.

Before joining Ellington, Reinhardt had become interested in the music of Charlie Parker and Dizzy Gillespie. Rather than adopt some of their songs into his repertoire, he modernized both his playing and his writing, performing boppish originals. While some of his songs during 1947 were a bit rhythmically awkward, he eventually mastered the music, and by 1949, he was one of the finest bop guitarists in the world, but ironically, few knew about that. That year, he had some marathon recording dates with Grappelli (their last together). Django was less active during 1950–53 but on a few occasions reappeared and played his electric guitar with young French modernists. The guitarist sounds remarkable on the recordings and radio broadcasts that survive, showing that he was playing bop at least on the level of Tal Farlow and Barney Kessel. He had found himself in the new style.

Negotiations were underway for Django Reinhardt to return to the United States as part of Norman Granz's Jazz at the Philharmonic, but he died suddenly from a stroke in 1953 when he was only 43. The Django Reinhardt story would normally have ended there, but his music has had a very surprising afterlife. While Reinhardt had influenced Les Paul and Charlie Byrd, his legacy seemed to be much less than that of Charlie Christian, whose ideas were played constantly by most guitarists of the 1940s, '50s and early '60s. A few guitarists continued playing in Django's style during this period, but they were very much underground. Joseph Reinhardt emerged occasionally but was not noticed by many. Stéphane Grappelli mostly played with standard piano groups. But in 1973, the violinist was persuaded by Diz Disley to lead a string group, and he so enjoyed the experience that he soon was playing all over the world. That could be considered the beginning of the gypsy-jazz movement, the first time in many years that Django Reinhardt's music became widely visible beyond the gypsy world.

By 1980, Jon Larsen had established the Hot Club

de Norvège, and two years later, he began to document the music. Django Reinhardt festivals popped up in Europe and proliferated as the music made a comeback. More and more young guitarists sought to play Reinhardt's music (particularly from his first period) and tried to find their own voice in the music, including Biréli Lagrène. When the Rosenberg Trio became a sensation in 1989 and were followed by Jimmy Rosenberg, the lid came off. Since that time, dozens of "Hot Club" groups have emerged, including some in the United States, and the influence and legacy of Django Reinhardt have again become a major force in jazz more than a half-century after his death.

**Recommended CDs:** There are quite a few Django Reinhardt reissues currently available. For those who really want to dig into his music, the five box sets from the British JSP label are the ones to get and contain virtually all of his recordings: the five-CD *Musette To Maestro 1928–1937: The Early Work Of A Guitar Genius* (JSP 59066), the four-CD *Paris And London: 1937–1948* (JSP 904), the five-CD *Django On The Radio* (JSP 953), the four-CD *Django In Rome 1949–1950* (JSP 919), and the five-CD *Postwar Recordings 1944–1953* (JSP 955). For those doubting that Reinhardt was as brilliant a guitarist after World War II as he had been in the 1930s, the latter three box sets offer plenty of proof as to his continuing brilliance. More general collectors may want to begin with *First Recordings* (Original Jazz Classics 1895), *The Best Of Django Reinhardt* (Blue Note 37138), *The Swing Sessions, Vol. 1* (Frog 50) and/or *Djangology 49* (Bluebird 9988), but since they will eventually become addicted, they should probably just save time and invest in the JSP boxes!

---

## Joseph "Nin Nin" Reinhardt
*b. March 1, 1912, Paris, France; d. February 7, 1982, Paris, France*

There was not much chance that Joseph Reinhardt would ever get out of the shadow of his older brother Django Reinhardt, having a similar fate as Frank Sinatra, Jr. However, the younger Reinhardt was actually an excellent guitar soloist who, if his last name were different, probably would have had a more viable career.

Due to Django's phenomenal playing, Joseph Reinhardt spent many years accompanying his sibling, defining the role of a rhythm guitar. The Reinhardt's musical relationship began in the 1920s, and during 1934–37, Joseph was a member of the Quintet of the Hot Club of France, unselfishly playing behind Django and Stéphane Grappelli. After leaving the Quintet in 1937, he worked with Aimé Barelli's big band and Alex Combelle and recorded with Combelle, Hubert

Rostaing and Gus Viseur. His occasional solos were very credible. In 1947, he switched to electric guitar, playing briefly with Stéphane Grappelli.

After Django's death in 1953, Joseph Reinhardt did not play guitar for a year, returning to the scene in 1955. In the late 1950s, he led his own quintet and recorded two albums. In the 1960s, he was frequently heard with a quartet comprised of his electric guitar, two acoustic rhythm guitarists and a bassist. By then, Reinhardt's playing could be considered an extension of his brother's late 1940s work, sounding boppish and forward-looking.

Joseph Reinhardt was less active in the 1970s, although he visited England and recorded with Diz Disley. He passed away in 1982 at the age of 69, 29 years after his brother.

**Recommended CDs:** *Joue . . . Django* (Label Quest) features Joseph Reinhardt in the late 1950s in a similar group to the Quintet of the Hot Club of France except that he is the main soloist. *Live In Paris* (Hot Club 66) features Reinhardt with his 1966 quartet as virtually the only soloist, performing four of his originals, six standards and two Django tunes. His consistently inventive and highly expressive playing is a revelation.

**LPs to Search For:** Joseph Reinhardt also recorded eight songs as a leader in 1943 for Decca and on little-known albums in 1959–60: *Joue Pour Django* (Discophiles Français 25114) and *Hommage À Django Reinhardt* (JLE 192).

## Emily Remler

*b. September 18, 1957, New York, NY; d. May 4, 1990, Sydney, Australia*

During her brief life, Emily Remler was an inspiration to younger female musicians. Her early death has resulted in her being thought of as a legend although, in reality, she was still searching for her own sound when she passed away. Her great potential was never really fulfilled. She began playing the guitar when she was ten and was originally a rock guitarist. But while attending Berklee (1974–76), Remler immersed herself in straight-ahead jazz, becoming influenced by Wes Montgomery and Herb Ellis. After leaving Berklee, she spent a period based in New Orleans, performing with local bands (including FourPlay and Little Queenie and the Percolators) at clubs.

In 1981, Remler made her recording debut as a leader for the Concord label, the company where she recorded six of her seven albums. In addition to leading her own jazz groups, she played in the Los Angeles version of the Sophisticated Ladies show (1981–82); worked with Astrud Gilberto, Rosemary Clooney, Ray Brown, Susannah McCorkle

and Richie Cole (with whom she appeared at the Monterey Jazz Festival); and appeared on Broadway, in blues bands, and in all-star settings. Married to Monty Alexander during 1981–84, she was later involved with Larry Coryell; they recorded an album of guitar duets (*Together*). Her last recording project, a collaboration with David Benoit, found her exploring pop/jazz and sounding a bit more individual than she did on her usual hard-bop sessions.

But tragically, Emily Remler became a heroin addict, and in 1990, while touring Australia, she died of heart failure. She was just 32.

**Recommended CDs:** Emily Remler is heard as a fine bop and hard-bop guitarist on *Firefly* (Concord 4162), *Take Two* (Concord 4195), *Transitions* (Concord 4236), *Catwalk* (Concord 4265), *Together* (Concord 4289) with Larry Coryell, and *East To Wes* (Concord 4356). On *This Is Me* (Justice 0501), she sounds credible exploring pop/jazz with David Benoit. Remler also recorded with Ray Brown, John Colianni, Rosemary Clooney, Richie Cole, Susannah McCorkle and Benoit (*Waiting For Spring*).

## Allan Reuss

*b. June 15, 1915, New York, NY; d. June 4, 1988, Los Angeles, CA*

Greatly admired by Steve Jordan and Freddie Green, Allan Reuss was considered by some to be the finest rhythm guitarist of the swing era. His steady rhythm, with its accents on two and four, drove the Benny Goodman Orchestra of 1935–38. Unlike Jordan and Green, Reuss occasionally soloed and quite well.

Reuss started out on banjo. After just one lesson, the 12 year old earned 12 dollars during his first gig, which took place on 12/12/1927. He switched to guitar after taking lessons from George Van Eps, his main influence. Van Eps, who worked with the Benny Goodman Orchestra in 1934, recommended to Goodman that Reuss take his place. The 19 year old fit in very well, and over time, the clarinetist really came to appreciate his contributions to the band.

After leaving Goodman, Reuss was a busy freelancer during 1938–39, recording with Teddy Wilson, Billie Holiday, Les Brown, Paul Whiteman, Glenn Miller, Lionel Hampton and Bunny Berigan. He was a member of the Jack Teagarden Orchestra during 1939–40 and had stints with the big bands of Ted Weems (1940–41), Jimmy Dorsey (1941–42), Goodman (1943) and Harry James (1943–44) in addition to working for NBC during 1942–43. He was rated so high that in 1944 he won a *Downbeat* poll as best guitarist despite mostly being a rhythm guitarist.

In 1945, Reuss moved to Los Angeles, where he became a studio musician. During 1945–46, he appeared on several significant record dates, including dates with Coleman Hawkins/Howard McGhee, Benny Carter/Arnold Ross, and Corky Corcoran. After 1946, he was on jazz dates less frequently, although he was part of occasional reunions with Benny Goodman and Dixieland gigs with Red Nichols. Much more often, Reuss was in an anonymous role, adding his classy brand of rhythm guitar to records by the likes of Frank Sinatra, Ricky Nelson, Glen Campbell, Pat Boone and a variety of 1950s rock-and-rollers plus movie soundtracks.

In his career, Allan Reuss took a few worthy solos, including "If I Could Be With You" and "Rosetta" with Benny Goodman, "Pickin' For Patsy" with Jack Teagarden, and short spots on records with Arnold Ross and Corky Corcoran. He went into semi-retirement after the 1960s.

**Recommended CDs:** *The Birth Of Swing* (Bluebird 61038) with Benny Goodman.

## Alvino Rey
*(Alvin McBurney)*
*b. July 1, 1907 (also sometimes listed as 1908 and 1911), Oakland, CA; d. March 2, 2004, Salt Lake City, UT*

While not exclusively a jazz player, Alvino Rey has a special place in jazz history. He was the only important American guitarist to lead a big band during the swing era. Rey was a skilled pedal steel guitarist in addition to playing guitar. He grew up in Cleveland and began playing music as a young teenager when he was given a banjo for his birthday. He was interested in amplifying his banjo as early as the mid-1920s and, in 1935, developed a prototype pickup for the Gibson Guitar Corporation that was used in the first electric guitars. Rey played with Ev Jones in 1927, switching to guitar when he joined Phil Spitalny's orchestra, taking lessons from Roy Smeck and becoming friends with Eddie Lang. He changed his name to Alvino Rey in 1929 because Latin music was popular at the time. Rey worked with a variety of dance bands for a few years before becoming a featured performer with Horace Heidt's Music Knights during 1932–38. While with Heidt, he switched his focus to steel guitar and also married Luise King, one of the King Sisters.

In 1938, Alvino Rey started his own orchestra, featuring the King Sisters and his innovative and unique steel guitar playing, which often utilized otherworldly sounds. Working regularly on the radio,

Rey had a successful band from the start and had a big hit in 1942 with "Deep In The Heart Of Texas." That year, he became interested in greatly expanding his orchestra's jazz content, and such musicians as tenors Al Cohn and Zoot Sims, trumpeter Neal Hefti, trombonist Ray Coniff and arranger Billy May became part of his organization. Other musicians who worked with Rey during the 1940s included arrangers Johnny Mandel, Nelson Riddle and George Handy, drummer Dave Tough, and altoist Herbie Steward.

The Musicians' Union recording strike of 1943 led to one of Rey's best bands going undocumented, and that, coupled with the war, resulted in him breaking up his orchestra. After working as a mechanic with Lockheed, in 1944 Rey joined the Navy, where he led a service band. After his discharge, he re-formed his orchestra with 15 horns (including six trumpets and four trombones), an ensemble that lasted until 1950 and had a hit with Slim Gaillard's "Cement Mixer." In the 1950s, he occasionally led combos that showcased his steel guitar.

Alvino Rey became the musical director for the King Sisters (performing on their television shows in the 1960s) and played his steel guitar on popular exotica records by Esquivel, George Cates, Jack Costanzo, and the Surfmen. He continued leading occasional bands, including at Disneyland up until the late 1980s. Rey retired with his wife to Salt Lake City a few years later but continued playing in local clubs until 1994.

**Recommended CDs:** *Classic Rey* (Collectors' Choice 702427) has 24 selections from the early 1940s, ranging from features for the Four King Sisters to excellent instrumentals that show off Alvino Rey's steel guitar and his sidemen.

**LPs to Search For:** *Alvino Rey And His Orchestra—1946* (Hindsight 121) is a jazz-oriented set of radio transcriptions by Rey's postwar big band.

## John Reynolds
*b. May 28, 1953, Palo Alto, CA*

John Reynolds has long kept the legacy of classic jazz guitar alive, being able to emulate Eddie Lang and Django Reinhardt while developing his own style, which falls somewhere in between. "I started on the banjo, and that same year, 1964, my brother Ralf got a guitar. I messed around with it when he wasn't looking. Around the house, there were records from the Good Time Jazz label, including by Lu Watters, Turk Murphy and the Firehouse Five. Later on, I discovered jazz of the 1920s. My influences on guitar, banjo and ukulele became Eddie Lang, Django Reinhardt, Harry Reser, Eddie Peabody and Nick Lucas."

Reynolds played in pickup bands throughout junior high and high school, while Ralf developed into a colorful and very skilled washboard player. An art major at Long Beach State, Reynolds had his first major musical job playing at Disneyland during 1974–79. During that period, he also took lessons from studio guitarist George Smith. He was with a trio called Mood Indigo in the 1980s that later evolved into the popular Palm Spring Yacht Club. In addition to his expertise on guitar, banjo and vintage string instruments, Reynolds sings in a relaxed high voice a little reminiscent of Cliff Edwards and Hoagy Carmichael and is a skilled whistler.

During the past 30 years, Reynolds has often teamed up with Ralf Reynolds, playing hot classic jazz as the Rhythm Rascals and the Reynolds Brothers. The grandsons of actress Zasu Pitts, they have released many of their recordings on their Zasu label. "I think it's really cool if you can entertain somebody, you make a connection, and they really get it."

**Recommended CDs:** Whether known as the Reynolds Brothers or the Rhythm Rascals, the music that the siblings have made for their Zasu label is fun, heated and infectious. *Futuristic Jungleism* (Zasu 2) has the Rhythm Rascals as a sextet with the hot clarinets of Jim Snyder and Jim Buchmann, highlighted by a dazzling version of "High Society." *Reynolds Brothers Rhythm Rascals* (Zasu 3) not only has the two clarinetists but also finds John Reynolds leading a three-piece guitar section. *Blue Drag* (Zasu 4) retains the guitars and has four horn players, including cornetist Scott Black and Dan Levinson on C-melody sax. *Reynolds Brothers* (Zasu 5) drops the extra guitars while featuring three horns, including Levinson and clarinetist Allan Vaché. *Reynolds Brothers Rhythm Rascals* (Zasu 6) features the band as a sextet with cornetist Corey Gemme, while the current *A Rhythm Rascal Cocktail* (Zasu 7) features the group as a quartet with cornetist Marc Caparone and bassist-singer Katie Cavera. In every case, the music is vintage 1920s/'30s jazz with a large number of concise but heated guitar solos from John Reynolds.

**Website:** www.reynoldsbrothers.net

## Marc Ribot
*b. May 21, 1954, Newark, NJ*

An avant-garde guitarist who is never shy to take chances, Marc Ribot's career has always stretched far beyond jazz. Ribot began on guitar when he was 11, playing trumpet for a little while in junior high school. While studying with Haitian classical guitarist-composer Frantz Casseus, he played in a variety of garage rock bands. Ribot studied at the University of Maine at Augusta and moved to New York in 1978, working with the punk group Realtones, Jack McDuff, Wilson Pickett, Carla Thomas, Chuck Berry and, during 1984–89, John Lurie's Lounge Lizards. Even at that early stage, he was a very versatile guitarist with wide musical interests who was active in the New York downtown scene.

Ribot has continued becoming more eclectic as time passes. In addition to his extensive work in R&B, soul, and just plain noise music (with everyone from Allen Ginsberg to Elvis Costello and Tom Waits), he has recorded in the jazz world with John Zorn, McCoy Tyner, the Jazz Passengers, Wadada Leo Smith, Jamaaladeen Tacuma, Medeski, Martin & Wood, and James Carter. His own bands have included Rootless Cosmopolitans, Shrek and Los Cubanos Postizos. Ribot has been a part of the Radical New Jewish Culture Festival. He has also performed on some film soundtracks, written a few scores himself, and been showcased on a guitar concerto with a symphony orchestra. Most recently, Ribot has been working with the Albert Ayler tribute band Spiritual Unity and his avant-rock group Ceramic Dog.

It is fair to say that Marc Ribot did not take the guitar questionnaire too seriously. Here are a few of his responses to my questions:

Who have been some of your main inspirations in life and music?

"Everything Iggy Pop ever said or played."

When did you know that you were going to try to be a professional guitarist?

"When I got your email."

What are your future musical goals?

"Make lots of money and retire to Vegas."

**Recommended CDs:** Rock, free jazz, noise and clarinetist Don Byron are featured on *Rootless Cosmopolitans* (Antilles 510 091). *Requiem For What's His Name* (Les Disques du Crespuscule 969), *Shrek* (Avant 33), the fascinating unaccompanied guitar album *Don't Blame Me* (DIW 902), *The Prosthetic Cubans* (Atlantic 83116), *Muy Divertido* (Atlantic 83293), *Saints* (Atlantic 83461), *Spiritual Unity* (Pi 15), *Exercises In Futility* (Tzadik 8046) and *Party Intellectuals* (Pi 27) give listeners a well-rounded portrait of the adventurous and thoroughly unpredictable guitarist.

**Website:** www.marcribot.com

## Lee Ritenour
*b. January 11, 1952, Hollywood, CA*

Lee Ritenour is a major studio musician who became a popular attraction on the "contemporary" jazz/smooth circuit. When he plays jazz, he tends to emulate Wes Montgomery. Otherwise, he is "Captain Fingers," a technically skilled pop/jazz guitarist who has retained his popularity for decades by playing melodic music that many in the jazz world consider lightweight and merely pleasant.

Ritenour developed quickly after taking up the guitar, and at 16, he made his recording debut with the Mamas & the Papas. He accompanied Lena Horne and Tony Bennett two years later and became an extremely busy studio guitarist. Ritenour toured with Sergio Mendes' Brasil '77 in 1973, played on a weekly basis at the Baked Potato in Los Angeles for five years (Ernie Watts, Dave Grusin and Patrice Rushen were also in the band), and launched his solo career in 1975 with his debut recording as a leader, *First Course*. While some of his early dates were fusion-oriented, his output became increasingly poppish and oriented toward the smooth audience as the 1980s progressed. In 1985 with *Harlequin*, which was recorded with Dave Grusin, Ritenour began a long association with GRP and also displayed his interest in Brazilian music. He had a change of pace with his late 1980s album *Stolen Moments*, which was a jazz set strongly influenced by Wes Montgomery. Ritenour also paid tribute directly to Montgomery on 1992's *Wes Bound*. In 1991, he became a founding member of Fourplay, a pop/jazz quartet with Bob James, bassist Nathan East and drummer Harvey Mason, touring and recording with the group for six years.

Lee Ritenour has stayed busy since that time with constant recording and touring. He has appeared on over 3,000 sessions in his career and led more than 40 albums. His most recent recording, *String Theory*, is one of his most interesting, for it teams him with guitarists from a wide variety of genres, including John Scofield, Pat Martino and Mike Stern.

**Recommended CDs:** Fans of the pop/jazz guitarist will want to acquire *First Course* (Epic 46114), *Captain Fingers* (Epic 34426), *Lee Ritenour And His Gentle Thoughts* (JVC 61033), *Sugar Loaf Express* (JVC 2008), *The Captain's Journey* (Warner Bros. 75367), *Friendship* (JVC 2009), *Rio* (GRP 9524), *Feel The Night* (Discovery 71010), *Rit* (Discovery 71013), *Rit 2* (Discovery 71017), *On The Line* (GRP 9525), *Banded Together* (Discovery 71018), *Harlequin* (GRP 9522), *Earth Run* (GRP 9538), *Portrait* (GRP 9553), *Festival* (GRP 9570), *Color Rit* (GRP 9594), *Larry & Lee* (GRP 9817) with Larry Carlton, *Alive In L.A.* (GRP 9882), *A Twist Of Jobim* (I.E. Music 314 533 893), *This Is Love* (I.E. Music 314 557 290), *A Twist Of Marley* (GRP 1003), *Rit's House* (GRP 01197), *A Twist Of Motown* (GRP 115-02), *Overtime* (Peak 8531), *World Of Brazil* (GRP 4926), *Smoke N' Mirrors* (Peak 30018), *Amparo* (Decca 1192) and *Lee Ritenour's 6 String Theory* (Concord 31911) along with the three Fourplay CDs *Fourplay* (Warner Bros. 26656), *Between The Sheets*

(Warner Bros. 45340) and *Elixir* (Warner Bros. 293). Listeners who specialize in jazz guitar will be most interested in *Stolen Moments* (GRP 9615) and *Wes Bound* (GRP 9697).

**Website:** www.leeritenour.com

## Tony Rizzi
*(Trefori Rizzi)*
*b. April 16, 1923, Los Angeles, CA; d. June 2, 1992, Huntington Beach, CA*

Tony Rizzi loved the sound of multiple guitars. While he spent much of his career as a studio guitarist, in the early 1970s he achieved his lifelong goal of having a guitar group play the solos of Charlie Christian. Rizzi, who originally played violin, did not start on guitar until he was 19. He grew up in Los Angeles, served in the Army during 1943–46, played with Alvy West and Boyd Raeburn, and in 1947, joined Les Brown's orchestra. After three years with Brown, he became a member of the NBC staff orchestra. In addition to working on television shows such as those hosted by Dinah Shore and Danny Kaye, he stayed very busy in the studios, playing guitar, mandolin, banjo, ukulele, sitar, six-string bass and bouzouki. Rizzi recorded with everyone from Louis Armstrong to Elvis Presley, Anita O'Day to Frank Zappa, often in an anonymous role.

Rizzi was featured on record with Alvy West in 1947 (including "Tony's Guitar"), made jazz records with Paul Smith and the Dave Pell Octet in the 1950s, and was a sideman on recordings led by Ted Nash, Dick Nash and Herbie Mann in the 1960s. In 1947 with Earle Spencer's orchestra, he was part of a guitar choir on "Five Guitars In Flight" along with Arv Garrison, Barney Kessel, Irving Ashby and Gene Sargent. Twenty-five years later, he formed the Wire Choir, a five-guitar band that played the solos of Charlie Christian. Their harmonized parts, a bit reminiscent of Supersax (a saxophone section that performed Charlie Parker solos), are documented on a classic album from 1975, with Rizzi joined by Jimmy Wyble, Grant Geissman, Mike Rosati and Tim May. The Wire Choir played gigs in the Los Angeles area for over a decade and was regarded by Tony Rizzi as the most important musical project of his life.

**Recommended CDs:** Tony Rizzi used the "Wire Choir" concept on several albums, including *Rhythm Pacific* (Outstanding 106), which has the guitarists (Rizzi, Grant Geissman, Bruce Lofgren, Michael Rosati and Tim May) playing train songs, and the pop-oriented *Surfin' Pacific* (Outstanding 127), which has Rizzi, Rosati, Lofren, Ronald Cook and Steve Carnelli. Strangely enough, the most significant recording, *Tony Rizzi And His Five Guitars Plus Four Play Charlie Christian* (Milagro 1000), has thus far only been issued on CD in Japan (Norma 5654). Rizzi took many short solos on the Dave Pell Octet's recordings in the 1950s. Two excellent CDs are *The Dave Pell Octet Plays Irving Berlin* (Fresh Sound 503) and *Plays Rodgers & Hart* (Fresh Sound 60505).

## Howard Roberts

*b. October 2, 1929, Phoenix, AZ; d. June 28, 1992, Seattle, WA*

Although much of his career was spent as a studio guitarist, Howard Roberts could play jazz on the level of a Barney Kessel or a Tal Farlow. He was an influential jazz guitarist and educator, but first he had to be coaxed out of the studios. Roberts started playing guitar when he was eight. As a teenager, he had gigs in Phoenix. When he was 20, he moved to Los Angeles, gradually finding his place in the jazz world. In 1956, he worked with Bobby Troup, recorded for Verve, and started getting very busy in the studios. Roberts played on a countless number of television and movie soundtracks, accompanied top names, and was greatly in demand for the next 15 years. He emerged to play jazz on a few of his own recordings and enjoyed gigging in Los Angeles–area jazz clubs (such as Donte's). Along the way, he recorded with Bobby Troup, Frank Morgan, Pete Jolly, Joe Morello, June Christy, Chico Hamilton, Julie London, Pete Rugolo, Peggy Lee, Gerry Mulligan and Hank Jones. But his day job was lending his talents to recording commercial music.

In the late 1960s, Howard Roberts shifted the emphasis for the remainder of his life from working in the studios to being an educator. He was a co-founder of the Guitar Institute of Technology, wrote guitar books, and had a monthly column for *Guitar Player* in addition to playing jazz whenever he wanted, inspiring many young jazz guitarists.

**Recommended CDs:** Howard Roberts led two record dates during the second half of the 1950s for Verve. One of the sets, *Mr. Roberts Plays Guitar* (Fresh Sound 478), features him in several settings, including with strings, with reeds, and teamed with vibraphonist Red Norvo. In the mid-1960s, Howard Roberts led a series of records for Capitol in which the playing time was brief (usually under three minutes) and the music was geared toward potential radio airplay. However, Roberts plays quite well on these sessions, and most of the music is jazz-oriented. The Euphoria label has reissued eight of these albums, two to a CD. Best are *Something's Cookin'/Goodies* (Euphoria 184) and *Color Him Funky/H.R. Is A Dirty Guitar Player* (Euphoria 190).

*Whatever's Fair/All Time Great Instrumental Hits* (Euphoria 185) and *Jaunty-Jolly/Guilty!!* (Euphoria 186) are also worth picking up. *The Magic Band Live At Donte's* (V.S.O.P. 94) and *The Magic Band II* (V.S.O.P. 2102) are privately recorded live sessions by Roberts finding him jamming happily with his talented friends. V.S.O.P. 94 is drawn from dates in the 1960s and '70s, while *The Magic Band II* is from 1968. However, the guitarist's best recording since the 1950s was his last jazz album, *The Real Howard Roberts* (Concord 4053). Recorded in 1977, Roberts is showcased in a quartet with pianist Russ Tompkins, bassist Ray Brown and drummer Jimmie Smith, stretching out on standards with such enthusiasm and creativity that one wishes he had recorded many more albums like this one.

**LPs to Search For:** *Good Pickin's* (Verve POCJ 2755) from 1959 features Roberts in a cool but swinging quintet with tenor-saxophonist Bill Holman, pianist Pete Jolly, bassist Red Mitchell and drummer Stan Levey.

## Duke Robillard

*(Michael John Robillard)*
*b. October 4, 1948, Woonsocket, RI*

Duke Robillard is a superior blues, early R&B and swing guitarist. He always sounds credible no matter what the setting, and he returns to playing jazz from other projects on a regular basis. Robillard grew up playing jazz and blues in Rhode Island, with one of his early associates being tenor-saxophonist Scott Hamilton. He had his own band in high school. In 1967, Robillard formed Roomful of Blues, staying as its leader until he left in 1979. He led the group during the period when it became a major name and helped revitalize the blues/swing scene.

After leaving Roomful of Blues, Robillard (who is also a personable singer) played rockabilly with Robert Gordon, was a member of the Legendary Blues Band, and during much of the 1980s, led Duke Robillard & The Pleasure Kings. He also had a solo career in which he often played jazz, including a 1986 recording with Scott Hamilton. In 1990, he joined the Fabulous Thunderbirds while continuing his own solo projects.

In 1993, Robillard signed with the Stony Plain label, an association that continues up to this writing. Among his many albums since then (most but not all for Stony Plain) are two collaborations with Herb Ellis, a tribute to T-Bone Walker, teaming up with Jay Geils and Gerry Beaudoin as the New Guitar Summit (on which the three guitarists perform enthusiastic renditions of swing standards), a matchup with fellow blues guitarist Ronnie Earl, sessions focusing on jump blues and early R&B, and a tribute to Les Paul

& Mary Ford. Robillard has also played as a sideman on sets by Jimmy Witherspoon, Jay McShann, Ruth Brown and Bob Dylan along with many top blues artists. For some of his projects, he records for his own Blue Duchess label, recently producing Mickey Freeman's CD.

Throughout his career, Duke Robillard has gone his own way, frequently crossing over stylistic boundaries to play the music he loves.

**Recommended CDs:** *Duke Robillard & The Pleasure Kings* (Rounder 3079), *Too Hot To Handle* (Rounder 3082), *Rockin' Blues* (Rounder 11548), *You Got Me* (Rounder 3100), *Swing* (Rounder 3103) with Scott Hamilton and Chris Flory, *After Hours Swing Session* (Rounder 3114), *Temptation* (Virgin 36952), *Turn It Around* (Rounder 3116), *Duke's Blues* (Stony Plain 1195), *Dangerous Place* (Virgin 42857), *Stretchin' Out* (Stony Plain 1250), *New Blues For Modern Man* (Shanachie 9017), *Conversations In Swing Guitar* (Stony Plain 1260) with Herb Ellis, *Explorer* (Stony Plain 1265), *Retrospective: New Guitar Summit* (Q&W Music 1002) with Jay Geils and Gerry Beaudoin, *Living With The Blues* (Stony Plain 1277), *More Conversations In Swing Guitar* (Stony Plain 1292) with Herb Ellis, *Exalted Lover* (Stony Plain 1293), *Blue Mood: The Songs Of T-Bone Walker* (Stony Plain 1300), *New Guitar Summit* (Stony Plain 1301) with Jay Geils and Gerry Beaudoin, *Guitar Groove-A-Rama* (Stony Plain 1316), *A Swingin' Session With Duke Robillard* (Stony Plain 1331), *Stomp! The Blues Tonight* (Stony Plain 1342), *Passport To The Blues* (Stony Plain 1349), *Tales From The Tiki Lounge* (Blue Duchess), *Low Down And Tore Up* (Stony Plain 1357), *Wobble Walkin'* (Blue Duchess); with Roomful of Blues: *The First Album* (32 Jazz 32003); with Jimmy Witherspoon: *Spoon's Blues* (Stony Plain 1211); with Jay McShann: *Hootie's Jumpin Blues* (Stony Plain 1237), *Still Jumpin' The Blues* (Stony Plain 1254); with Ronnie Earl: *The Duke Meets The Earl* (Stony Plain 1303); with Scott Hamilton: *Across The Tracks* (Concord 30388).

**Website:** www.dukerobillard.com

## Adam Rogers
*b. 1966, New York, NY*

A superior, versatile and brilliant modern guitarist, Adam Rogers has been greatly in demand ever since he arrived on the scene. Early on, he studied guitar with Barry Galbraith, Howard Collins and John Scofield. Rogers studied classical guitar for five years including attending the Mannes Conservatory of Music for four. Since then, his resume has been remarkable.

As the co-leader of Lost Tribe for 11 years, Rogers played alongside saxophonist David Binney and guitarist David Gilmore on a regular basis. Rogers was a member of Michael Brecker's band for five years. He has also worked and often recorded with such notables as Cassandra Wilson, Regina Carter, John Zorn, Randy Brecker, the Brecker Brothers, the Mingus Big Band, Terence Blanchard, the Gil Evans Orchestra, John Patitucci, Ravi Coltrane, saxophonist Bill Evans, Lizz Wright, Jacky Terrasson, Kenny Barron, George Russell, Brian Blade, Eliane Elias, Larry Coryell, Chris Potter, Jack McDuff, Alex Sipiagin, Uri Caine, Grace Kelly, Kenny Werner, James Carter, and Ronald Shannon Jackson, in addition to Norah Jones, Walter Becker, Paul Simon, Laurie Anderson and performers from other genres. Thus far, Rogers has appeared on over 200 CDs, including many soundtracks, and was even the featured soloist with the Dresden Symphony Orchestra in the summer of 1999.

**Recommended CDs:** On its three CDs, *Lost Tribe* (Windham Hill Jazz 10143), *Soulfish* (Windham Hill Jazz 10327), and *Many Lifetimes* (Arabesque 133), Lost Tribe displayed its ability to somehow segue smoothly through high-powered fusion, avant-rock, rap/hip-hop, and avant-garde jazz. Of his solo CDs, Rogers uses the same rhythm section (pianist Edward Simon, bassist Scott Colley and drummer Clarence Penn) on *Art Of The Invisible* (Criss Cross 1223), *Allegory* (Criss Cross 1242) and *Apparitions* (Criss Cross 1263), with saxophonist Chris Potter also being on the latter two. *Time And The Infinite* (Criss Cross 1286) has Rogers with Colley and drummer Bill Stewart, while *Sight* (Criss Cross 1313) has bassist John Patitucci and Clarence Penn. Whether introducing his unpredictable originals or reshaping standards on *Time And The Infinite*, Adam Rogers never plays the predictable.

**Website:** www.adamrogersmusic.com

## Jimmy Rosenberg
*b. April 10, 1980, Helmond, The Netherlands*

Of all of the guitarists to emerge in what would be called the gypsy-jazz movement, Jimmy Rosenberg was the youngest and the one with the greatest potential. A cousin of Stochelo Rosenberg, he played violin as a child. When he was seven, he switched to guitar, and it was obvious very quickly

that he had a phenomenal talent. By the time he was nine, he was leading a trio named the Gipsy Kids. They appeared in the British television documentary called *Django Legacy*. Two years later, Rosenberg performed at the Django Reinhardt Festival in France, and at a concert in Amsterdam, he played a duet with Stéphane Grappelli. The following year the Gipsy Kids made their first recording, *Safari*. Rosenberg was still just 12.

When he was 13, Rosenberg played festivals, recorded *Swinging With Jimmy Rosenberg* and appeared at concerts with Biréli Lagrène, Angelo Debarre, Philip Catherine and Stochelo Rosenberg in addition to the Gipsy Kids. In 1995, the Gipsy Kids (which included rhythm guitarist Johnny Rosenberg and bassist Rinus Steinbach) toured the US, and performed in Oslo and at the Django festival in Paris. The following year, after being threatened with a lawsuit by the Gypsy Kings, the group's name was changed to Sinti.

In 1997 when he was 17, Rosenberg began his solo career. He toured constantly and recorded regularly, and his fame continued to grow. In 1998, he had opportunities to play with Les Paul, George Benson and Frank Vignola, and in 2000, he was one of the stars at the first US Django Reinhardt Festival. Rosenberg appeared on quite a few records, worked with the Hot Club de Norvège, Jon Larsen and even Willie Nelson, and continued being one of the major attractions at Django Reinhardt tribute concerts.

Unfortunately, drug problems have plagued his life during the past decade, as can be seen in the Dutch film *The Father, The Son And The Talent* and the documentary *Jon & Jimmy*; the latter is about the ups and downs in his musical relationship with Jon Larsen. After drugs began seriously affecting his health and behavior, his performance schedule became quite erratic. In 2007, he had a brief comeback, but Jimmy Rosenberg has not performed in public since 2008.

Jon Larsen says this about him: "Jimmy Rosenberg is one of the greatest talents in the jazz guitar world, ever, and one of the greatest tragedies. His guitaristical skills were shocking. He could play rings around everybody else and had ears like nobody I have ever heard. We worked together for 12 fantastic years before his final collapse in 2004, and we were like brothers, touring for months on end and making nine studio recordings together. During those years, I heard some of the most fantastic music ever played on guitar. Today, Jimmy is in a closed mental institution, and we must keep our fingers crossed that he can come back to a normal life some time in the future. I miss him beyond description."

Still just 32 at this writing, Jimmy Rosenberg should have many productive years ahead of him if he can conquer his personal problems.

**Recommended CDs:** The Gipsy Kids' *Safari* (Dino 1311), *Swinging With Jimmy Rosenberg* (Hot Club 153), *Sinti* (Columbia 67327), *Hot Shots* (Hot Club 102), *The One And Only Jimmy Rosenberg* (Hot Club 117), *Gypsy Swing* (Refined 1001), *Ola & Jimmy* (Hot Club 130), *Hot Club De Suede* (Hot Club 144), *Django's Tiger* (Hot Club 146), *Trio* (Hot Club 170), *Rose Room* (Hot Club 180).

## Stochelo Rosenberg
*b. February 19, 1968, The Netherlands*

The gypsy-jazz movement gained a great deal of momentum when Stochelo Rosenberg and the Rosenberg Trio made their debut recording in 1989. "I started to play suddenly at the age of ten. Before that, I had no particular interest in the instrument, although there were guitars at home, and many guitarists—and players of other instruments—in the family. As I am a Sinti gypsy, music was always around all places where my family lived. The greatest Sinti musician was Django Reinhardt. As a child, I either heard my father and uncles play, or we had a Django record on, all the time."

While ten was considered a late age to start playing guitar in a gypsy family, Rosenberg practiced constantly, and his abilities quickly became apparent. "I was lucky enough as a child to have fantastic role models in the persons of my father Mimer Rosenberg and my uncle Wasso Grunholz, both great guitarists and passionate teachers. Also in my family, Fapy Lafertin was literally my idol as a youth, and he was the most reputed lead guitarist in this style during the '70s and '80s. It was music school every day at home."

Although Stochelo Rosenberg had several possible opportunities to record as a teenager, his parents kept him protected from the music world during the early years while he developed his style and technique. Rosenberg played with family members at gatherings, forming the Rosenberg Trio with his cousins rhythm guitarist Nous'che Rosenberg and bassist Nonnie Rosenberg.

1989 was the breakthrough year for Rosenberg, his trio, and gypsy jazz in general. At that year's Django Reinhardt Festival in Samois, Rosenberg performed for the first time outside of the gypsy community, creating such a major stir that it led to his first recording, *Seresta*. From that point on, Stochelo Rosenberg and his trio were in great demand for concerts, dates all over Europe, and recordings. Soon there were scores of similar "Hot Club" groups all over the world.

When Stéphane Grappelli heard the Rosenberg Trio in the early 1990s, he immediately asked them to become his band. They recorded two albums together and did some touring in addition to playing at Grappelli's 85th birthday celebration at Carnegie Hall. "Can you imagine something more incredible for us? We're the biggest Django fans around and his alter-ego, his partner in the years of pure genius, adopts our band at once and takes us with him all around the globe."

In addition to keeping the legacy of Django Reinhardt alive, Rosenberg has composed new songs and has never been content merely to copy Django. Twenty-one years after their initial triumph, the Rosenberg Trio is still in great demand. "We've been on the road for more than 20 years now and always try to do our best, from the most obscure little stage to some of the most prestigious venues in the world, staying true to ourselves and keeping our musical direction."

**Recommended CDs:** *Seresta* (Hot Club 59) started it all in 1989. Since then, the Rosenberg Trio has recorded *Gipsy Summer* (Universal 531 144); *Live At The North Sea Jazz Festival '92* (Universal 519 446); *Impressions* (Universal 531 145), which utilizes a greatly expanded group; *Caravan* (Universal 523 030) with guest Stéphane Grappelli; *Gipsy Swing* (Universal 527 806); *Noches Calientes* (Universal 557 022); *Sueños Gitanos* (Universal 549 580) with guest Toots Thielemans; *Live In Samois* (Universal 981 156); *Louis Van Dijk & The Rosenberg Trio* (Pink 2004001); *Live 1992–2005* (Brilliant Jazz 8151); *Roots* (Iris 3001 970); *Tribute To Stéphane Grappelli* (FM Jazz 93 691) with violinist Tim Kliphuis; and 2010's *Djangologists* (Enja), which also features Biréli Lagrène and includes a DVD documentary.

**Website:** www.therosenbergtrio.com

and learned banjo, mandolin, dobro and bass. He earned a bachelor's degree from the New England Conservatory of Music and a master's degree at Cal Arts in Valencia (1995), learning from such musicians as Jimmy Giuffre, Charlie Haden, Mick Goodrick, George Russell, Bob Moses, Cecil McBee, Ran Blake and Wadada Leo Smith.

After getting his master's, Rosenn began playing on a weekly basis at the Gypsy Cafe in Westwood with trombonist Alan Ferber, bassist Todd Sickafoose, drummer Mark Ferber and others. He worked with Us & Them (which also included Alan and Mark Ferber, keyboardist Joe Bagg and saxophonist David Sills) during 1997–2000 and currently plays with Option 3 (a trio with Mark Ferber and organist Bagg), Joe-Less Shoe (which features saxophonist Matt Otto and drummer Jason Harnell), and Sigmund Fudge.

Chosen by the State Department to participate in the Jazz Ambassador program, Rosenn and pianist Art Hirahara performed as a duo during a two-month tour of the Middle East and Asia. Jamie Rosenn teaches at the Musician's Institute, the L.A. Music Academy and Saddleback College. He also is a core member of the Los Angeles Jazz Collective and helps to organize their festivals and recording projects.

"I'm fascinated by the conversational nature of group improvisation and how input from the various members of the rhythm section and listening audience alike can influence a soloist and vice-versa. The collective experience of searching for the unknown and making something out of nothing is an aspect of jazz that I find thrilling."

**Recommended CDs:** Option 3's *Points Subtracted* (Jazz Collective) and Joe-Less Shoe's self-titled debut thus far offer the best examples of Jamie Rosenn's playing.

**Website:** www.jamierosenn.com

## Jamie Rosenn
*b. July 10, 1970, Gallup, NM*

An important member of Los Angeles' under-publicized post-bop jazz scene, Jamie Rosenn can always be relied upon to play the unexpected. He grew up in Wellesley, Massachusetts. "I was about 12 years old. John Lennon had recently been killed, and me and my friends were crazy about the Beatles. We wanted to start a band, and since my mom had a guitar sitting in the closet, I decided to play guitar. I loved the concept of improvisation." He played in a jazz ensemble at a music school when he was 15 and at high school dances with his rock band Auditory Nerve. Rosenn also played alto sax for a period

## Kurt Rosenwinkel
*b. October 28, 1970, Philadelphia, PA*

One of the most inventive jazz guitarists of the past 20 years, Kurt Rosenwinkel is one of the leading guitarists on the current scene. "I had a band with my best friend Gordon Townsend for seven years, since we were nine years old. I originally was playing piano while he was on drums. I would write songs, we'd practice every day, and we put on concerts for the people who lived on our block. The first time I played guitar, I was 12, a friend was taking guitar lessons, and I picked it up at his house and played along to the Beatles' *Sgt. Pepper* record." Rosenwinkel first heard jazz through a jazz sampler album that his mother brought home when he was 15. In high school, he listened to jazz on WRTI every night before going to bed. He played guitar at parties and also worked on piano in restaurants and learned to play bass and drums. "I knew when I was eight that I would be a musician. I decided to focus on guitar instead of piano when I was 18."

Rosenwinkel attended Berklee during 1988–91. In 1991, he dropped out of school, joined Gary Burton's band (recording *Six Pack*) for two years, moved to New York, and became part of Paul Motian's Electric Bebop Band for a decade (1991–2001). Being with Burton resulted in him being discovered by the jazz world and working steadily. In 1993, Rosenwinkel formed his quartet. "Being a part of the New York scene based around Smalls jazz club in the '90s with hundreds of amazing musicians was a great experience. Playing every Tuesday night at Smalls for years gave me a chance to develop my music with Mark Turner, Jeff Ballard and Ben Street."

Kurt Rosenwinkel has also worked with Human Feel, Seamus Blake, Joe Henderson (1998–99), the Brian Blade Fellowship, Brad Mehldau, and from the world of hip hop, Q-Tip (2001–present). During the last few years, he has taught and been the head of the guitar department at the Jazz Institute Berlin.

"There are many albums I already know that I must make. I would also like to eventually write something for an orchestra and to continue improving as a guitarist, pianist and drummer."

**Recommended CDs:** *East Coast Love Affair* (Fresh Sound 16), *Intuit* (Criss Cross 1160), *Enemies Of Energy* (Verve 314 543 042), *The Next Step* (Verve 314 549 162), *Heartcore* (Verve 73202), *Deep Song* (Verve 392802), *The Remedy* (Wommusic 0001), *Reflections* (Wommusic 0002), and *Our Secret World* (Wommusic 0003). The guitarist has also recorded with Human Feel, the Metta Quintet, Gary Burton, Seamus Blake, Mark Turner, Paul Motian, Larry Goldings, Chris Cheek, Myron Walden, Chris Potter, George Colligan, Tim Hagans, Jill Seifers, Danilo Perez, Matthias Lupri, Brian Blade, Rebecca Martin, Barney McAll, Phil Grenadier, Joshua Redman (*Momentum*), Aaron Goldberg, Miles Donahue, and Jason Lindner.

**Website:** www.kurtrosenwinkel.com

## Avi Rothbard
*b. May 21, 1967, Kibbutz Gan Shmuel, Israel*

A fine straight-ahead guitarist, Avi Rothbard emerged from Israel to become an important part of the New York jazz scene. Rothbard, who played mandolin when he was ten, began playing guitar at an after-school music program when he was 14. "I got introduced to jazz from LPs I collected from several Kibbutz members and volunteers from abroad. Later on, my aunt gave me her jazz collection, which was a mind opener. I discovered records by Joe Pass, Lee Morgan, Wes Montgomery, John Coltrane, Bird and Monk." He played guitar in his high school band and had his first professional job when he was 16 at a Tel Aviv pub, the Slick.

After serving in the Israeli military, Rothbard attended the Rubin Academy during 1989–91 and also taught guitar. He played in Boris Garner's band, Eight Till Late, which led to his first recording and an appearance

Avi Rothbard
Jared Gold
Joe Strasser
*Going Somewhere*

at the 1990 Red Sea Jazz Festival. He spent a year living in the United States (1991–92), returning to Israel to become a teacher. After a few years of playing gigs in Tel Aviv and Jerusalem (on both guitar and electric bass), including gigs with Avishai Cohen and Arnie Lawrence, Rothbard moved back to the United States in 1995, attending Berklee for four years and graduating in 1999. Since that time, he has taught at the annual Berklee Guitar Sessions and privately, earning his master's degree from the City College of New York in 2009.

As a guitarist, Avi Rothbard has played with such musicians as Richie Cole, Jeremy Pelt, Ben Riley, Ted Rosenthal, Carolyn Leonhart, Jay Leonhart, Warren Vaché, Ray Drummond and Uri Caine. In recent times he has been the co-leader of the Uptown Quartet with tenor-saxophonist Wayne Escoffery, led his own trio, and performed unaccompanied guitar solos.

"I am currently working on a new solo guitar album. My goals are to keep recording, performing, teaching, writing music and completing my first instructional guitar book. Music is a universal language and it is through jazz that people with very different backgrounds can really have a conversation."

**Recommended CDs:** *Going Somewhere* (Midlantic 106) features Avi Rothbard in a trio with organist Jared Gold and drummer Joe Strasser, while *Twin Song* (Midatlantic 2005) has the same group plus Wayne Escoffery. Both CDs are excellent examples of modern soul jazz, with *Twin Song* being comprised entirely of the guitarist's originals.

**Website:** www.rothbardmusic.com

# Issi Rozen

b. April 20, 1967, Haifa, Israel

Issi Rozen, one of several excellent Israeli jazz guitarists to emerge during the past 20 years, mixes aspects of Middle Eastern music into his playing. He grew up in Tel Aviv and started playing guitar when he was ten. After serving in the Israeli military, in 1991 he moved to Boston to attend Berklee.

After completing his education at Berklee, Issi Rozen became a fixture in the Boston jazz scene. In 1998, he made his recording debut as a leader with *Red Sea* and he has since formed his own record label, New Step Music. His use of space in his unhurried style is a bit reminiscent of Pat Metheny and Jim Hall, although he also considers Joe Pass to have been an important influence.

**Recommended CDs:** *Red Sea* (Brownstone 9805), *Homeland Blues* (Brownstone 20001), *Dark Beauty* (New Step Music 3101).

# Art Ryerson

b. May 22, 1913, Columbus, OH; d. October 27, 2004, Brookfield, CT

A superior guitarist who was a fine swing stylist, Art Ryerson spent most of his career in the studios. At 13, his parents bought a banjo for him, during half a series of 50 banjo lessons, from a door-to-door salesman. At 16, he sat in with a band that needed a guitarist, so he quickly learned the guitar. Inspired by Eddie Lang and Carl Kress, Ryerson worked with local groups around Columbus, Ohio. In the early 1930s, he moved to Cincinnati, where he joined the house band (the Rhythm Jesters) at radio station WLW. By 1935, he was living in New York, appearing in jazz clubs and at Nick's Tavern in Greenwich Village. In addition to radio work (which included the Saturday Night Swing Club), Ryerson appeared on some very early television shows in the late 1930s. By then, he had followed George Van Eps' example and was doubling on the seven-string guitar along with banjo, mandolin and ukulele.

In 1939, Ryerson started a two-year stint as the guitarist with the Paul Whiteman Orchestra. During this time, he wrote the arrangements for the small groups taken out of the orchestra, including Whiteman's Swinging Strings, Bouncing Brass and Sax Soctette. He utilized up to four guitarists with the Swinging Strings, while the Sax Soctette arrangements had three guitarists: Ryerson, Tony Gottuso and Dave Barbour. Switching to electric guitar during 1941–43, he was a member of the Raymond Scott Orchestra, which appeared regularly on the radio, taking a prominent role on Scott's theme "Pretty Little Petticoat." Ryerson served in the Army during World War II, leading a service band that played for the US troops in England, Belgium and France.

After his discharge, Ryerson resettled in New York, where he was a major studio guitarist for decades. His credits on radio, television and studio work are endless, including the original *Tonight Show* with Jerry Lester, *The Hit Parade* with Raymond Scott, *The Jack Benny Show*, Jackie Gleason, Steve Allen, Ed Sullivan and Johnny Carson. As a sideman, he recorded not only with Frank Sinatra and Tony Bennett but also with Red Norvo, Fats Waller, Ella Fitzgerald, Ruby Braff, Ellis Larkins, Erroll Garner, Lionel Hampton, Artie Shaw, Mildred Bailey, Hot Lips Page, Mel Torme, Sarah Vaughan, Louis Armstrong (including the original version of "What A Wonderful World"), Bobby Hackett and Anita O'Day. With Peggy Lee and Frankie Laine, he utilized multiple guitars. Ryerson was on dates with both Charlie Parker (*Bird With Strings*) and Elvis Presley (his early Decca recordings). Some of the guitar solos on Bill Haley's mid-1950s recordings are by an uncredited Ryerson.

Art Ryerson, who was active in the Musicians' Union, visited the Soviet Union in 1975 on a State Department tour that celebrated Louis Armstrong. He retired in the late 1970s, although he did an occasional gig after that. His daughter, flute player Ali Ryerson, remembers: "His last concert was in 1991 in duo with me in Columbus, Ohio, where he was born. It was during that visit that he was inducted into the Columbus Senior Hall of Fame. I always thought of him as the consummate rhythm guitarist. He came up during the swing era and leaned in that direction. He was a very thoughtful player with a more orchestral than single-note solo approach. He used to transcribe and play Chopin etudes (that I remember well, practicing for hours in the living room) and was a fine arranger who composed several beautiful pieces."

**Recommended CDs:** Unfortunately, Art Ryerson never led a record date of his own. Eight selections that he performed and arranged for Paul Whiteman's Swinging Strings are on the collection *Guitar Rarities, Vol. 2* (IAJRC 1018). He also appears with Paul Whiteman's Swing Wing and Bouncing Brass on *Hooray For Spinach* (Hep 1082), often contributing the arrangements along with some guitar solos. Ryerson is featured in a trio with pianist Ellis Larkins and bassist Beverly Peer during lengthy medleys on Larkins' *Manhattan At Midnight* (Lone Hill Jazz 10175) from 1956. A very good session of guitar duets with George Barnes from the mid-1970s that were made for Concord has never been released.

## Terje Rypdal
b. August 23, 1947, Oslo, Norway

Of all of the guitarists associated with the ECM label, Terje Rypdal's airy yet often rockish tone, thoughtful solos, and unclassifiable music most fits the ECM sound. While he never considered himself a traditional jazz player, his improvisations and constant desire to take chances are full of the spirit of jazz. His father was the leader of an orchestra and a composer. Rypdal originally studied classical piano and trumpet before teaching himself guitar when he was 13. At 15, he formed the Vanguards, a band that had a string of regional pop hits. Most influenced by rock and Jimi Hendrix, he was also inspired by Jeff Beck, Eric Clapton and Steve Winwood in his early days. At the same time, he was very interested in contemporary classical music, which he studied, and the great jazz guitarists.

Rypdal studied at Oslo University, where one of his teachers was George Russell. In the late 1960s, he worked and recorded with Russell, first played with Jan Garbarek (a longtime associate), and was in a Lester Bowie group at the Baden-Baden Free Jazz Meeting in 1969. In 1970, he made his first album for ECM. Forty years later, he is still with the label. His recordings range from spacey sound explorations and rockish outings to works with orchestras and post-bop jazz. Rypdal is also an important composer who has written five symphonies, two operas, and a concerto for bassist Barre Phillips.

Terje Rypdal, who first formed his group Odyssey in 1972 (using the name for many of his later bands), is a very original guitarist whose music continues to occupy its own category.

**Recommended CDs:** *Bleak House* (Polydor 547 885), *Terje Rypdal* (ECM 1016), *What Comes After* (ECM 1031), *Whatever I Seem To Be Far Away* (ECM 1045), *Odyssey* (ECM 1067/8), *After The Rain* (ECM 1083), *Waves* (ECM 1110), *Rypdal/Vitous/DeJohnette* (ECM 1125), *Descendre* (ECM 1144), *To Be Continued* (ECM 1192), *Eos* (ECM 1263), *Chaser* (ECM 1303), *Blue* (ECM 1346), *The Singles Collection* (ECM 1383), *Undisonus* (ECM 1389), *Q.E.D.* (ECM 1474), *If Mountains Could Sing* (ECM 1554), *Skywards* (ECM 1608), *Double*

*Concerto/5th Symphony* (ECM 1567), *Lux Aeterna* (ECM 1818), *Vossabrygg* (ECM 1984), *Crime Scene* (ECM 2041); with George Russell: *The Essence Of* (Soul Note 121044), *Electronic Sonata For Souls Loved By Nature* (Soul Note 121034); with Jan Garbarek: *Esoteric Circle* (Freedom 41031), *Afric Pepperbird* (ECM 1007).

## Sal Salvador
*(Silvio Smiraglia)*
b. December 21, 1925, Monson, MA; d. September 22, 1999, Stamford, CT

Best known for his work in the 1950s, Sal Salvador had a swinging style, an appealing tone, and impressive technique. Salvador, who was self-taught, originally played hillbilly music until he heard a record of Charlie Christian. Switching immediately to jazz, he began his career as a teenager in Massachusetts, where his musical associates included Phil Woods and Joe Morello. He moved to New York in 1949, worked with Terry Gibbs and Eddie Bert, and became a staff musician at the Columbia label. During 1952–53, Salvador toured with Stan Kenton's orchestra (1952–53), where he was showcased on "Invention For Guitar And Trumpet" and "Frivolous Sal."

Salvador led his own groups for the next dozen years (sidemen included Phil Woods and Eddie Costa), co-led a combo with Joe Morello, and during 1958–65 had a part-time big band that he called Colors in Sound. By the early 1960s, Salvador was mostly teaching (he became the head of the guitar department at the University of Bridgeport in 1970) and writing guitar instructional books. In 1978, he made a comeback on records and had a higher profile during his last 20 years, leading an adventurous quintet (Crystal Image) while keeping his roots in creative straight-ahead jazz.

**Recommended CDs:** *Sal Salvador Quintet/Kenton Presents Jazz: Sal Salvador* (Blue Note 96548) has all of the music from two Salvador albums dating from 1953–54. The performances are concise (only two of the 18 songs are over 3 1/2 minutes), but Salvador is in top form with three different combos, playing cool-toned bop. Hard to find but reissued on CD are his 1956 album *Shades Of Sal Salvador* (Toshiba EMI 62021) and a big band record, *Colors In Sound* (Dauntless 6002), in which his trumpet section includes Maynard Ferguson, Ernie Royal and Doc Severinsen. Because Salvador's later recordings were made for now-defunct labels (Stash, Bee Hive and Jazz Mania), they are pretty scarce. The two Jazz Manias, *The Way Of The Wind* (Jazz

Mania 6014) and *Lorinda's Kitchen* (Jazz Mania 6017), were issued on CD and are worth a search, while a collaboration with fellow guitarist Mundell Lowe, *Second Time Around* (Westside 2006), is quite worthwhile. "Invention For Guitar And Trumpet" is on Stan Kenton's *New Concepts Of Artistry In Rhythm* (Capitol 386).

**LPs to Search For:** Among Sal Salvador's more obscure albums are *Frivolous Sal* (Bethlehem 59), *Tribute To The Greats* (Bethlehem 74), and many of the recordings from his comeback years. *Starfingers* (Bee Hive 7002) teams Salvador in 1978 with Eddie Bert and Nick Brignola, *Juicy Lucy* (Bee Hive 7009) is a trio set with Billy Taylor, and *Parallelogram* (GP 5016) has Salvador exploring post-bop. His three Stash albums, *In Your Own Sweet Way* (Stash 224), *World's Greatest Jazz Standards* (Stash 234) and especially *Plays Gerry Mulligan* (Stash 251) show that Sal Salvador still had a lot to offer in the 1980s.

## Gray Sargent
b. June 10, 1953, Attleboro, MA

A tasteful swing-based guitarist, Gray Sargent had a strong reputation in the Boston area before joining Tony Bennett in 1997. Sargent studied at Berklee and has been in great demand since the mid-1970s. Among his associations were Illinois Jacquet, Ruby Braff, George Wein's Newport All-Stars, Scott Hamilton and Dave McKenna. He made appearances on some Concord recordings in the 1980s and '90s that gave him more of a national reputation.

But it was joining Tony Bennett and touring the world with the singer during the past 15 years that has given Gray Sargent his greatest fame. His tasteful, subtle and lightly swinging style perfectly fit the singer's music.

**Recommended CDs:** *Shades Of Gray* (Concord 4571) from 1993 is Gray Sargent's only recording as a leader, a relaxed quartet date that includes Dave McKenna. He has also recorded with McKenna (*No More Ouzo For Puzo*), the Newport Jazz Festival All-Stars, Lou Colombo, the Concord Jazz All-Stars, Donna Byrne, Billy Novick, Ruby Braff, Dave Whitney, Herb Pomeroy, Ralph Sharon, Dick Johnson, and of course Tony Bennett. *Concord Duo Series, Vol. 2* (Concord 4552), which teams Sargent with McKenna in 1993, may very well be his finest recording.

## Dorado Schmitt
b. May 29, 1957, St.-Avold, Lorraine, France

Dorado Schmitt has long been one of the giants of gypsy jazz. He was born into a gypsy family that was quite musical. His father taught him guitar when he was seven, and he also learned violin. In 1978, Schmitt formed the Dorado Trio, which had rhythm guitarist Hono Winterstein and bassist Gino Reinhardt. He began recording as a leader in 1981 and had opportunities to play at festivals with Philip Catherine and Oscar Peterson. Schmitt was featured in a movie (*Latcho Drom*) about gypsies, for which he wrote the soundtrack. His best-known originals are "Bossa Dorado" and "Tchavolo Swing."

Schmitt was involved in a car accident in 1988 that put him in a coma for 11 days and resulted in many broken bones. After two years of rehabilitation, he fully recovered and resumed playing with the trio. The group lasted until Gino Reinhardt's death in 1997. Schmitt took time off before putting together a new band in 1999. Since then, he has often utilized his son, guitarist Samson Schmitt, in his group. Schmitt had a gypsy trio with fellow guitarists Christian Escoudé and Babik Reinhardt, worked with Angelo Debarre and the Ferré Brothers, and has played with Paquito D'Rivera, James Carter, Biréli Lagrène and a Django Reinhardt tribute band put together by Brian Torff (featuring accordionist Marcel Loeffler), with which he toured the US in 2009. Dorado Schmitt has also been part of the annual Django Week each year at Birdland since 2001.

Throughout his career, Dorado Schmitt manages to pay tribute to Django Reinhardt while displaying his own witty and hard-swinging musical personality.

**Recommended CDs:** *Gipsy Reunion* (Djazz 515), *Parisienne* (Djazz 523), *Latcho Drom* (Son/Virgin 1776), *Djieske* of Samson Schmitt (EMD 0201), *Rendez-vous* (Harmonia Mundi 1294), *Dorado Sings* (EMD 0501), *Family* (Dreyfus 369442).

**LPs to Search For:** *Hommage À La Romenes* (Leico 7707), *Notre Histoire* (Blue Flame 8593).

**Website:** www.dorado.schmitt.free.fr

## Reg Schwager
(Reginald Schwager)
b. May 7, 1962, Leiden, The Netherlands

For the past 30 years, Reg Schwager has been one of the top jazz guitarists in Canada, playing in the modern mainstream while being versatile. Born in the Netherlands, at three he moved with his family to New Zealand, where he studied violin. Three years later, the Schwager family settled in Canada. He took lessons on flute and piano and at first was self-taught on ukulele and guitar, playing folk and blues songs. "At age 12, I found a good teacher (Ben Rinaldo) who showed me that it was possible to play jazz on guitar. My earliest gigs were with my sister Jeannette when I was 15 and she was 12. We played at the local folk festival and at coffeehouses and restaurants. My first inspirations on guitar were Herb Ellis and Joe Pass." Schwager, who also played alto sax in his high school stage band, picked up experience playing guitar with a trio and a big band. After high school, he moved to Toronto in 1979, played with Phil Nimmons and Peter Appleyard, and met many of the musicians on the Toronto jazz scene. He has not stopped since.

Schwager has since worked with Ralph Bowen, Renee Rosnes, Herbie Spanier, Pat LaBarbera, George Shearing (on and off during 1996–2006), Diana Krall, Rob McConnell, Don Thompson, his sister Jeannette Lambert and her husband drummer Michel Lambert, Hermeto Pascoal, the Dave McMurdo Jazz Orchestra (for whom he has also written arrangements) and such avant-gardists as Misha Mengelberg and Han Bennink.

In recent times, Reg Schwager has been writing for a nonet project with Don Thompson, playing with singer Emilie-Claire Barlow and trombonist Darren Sigesmund, and freelancing in the Toronto area. For the future, he says, "I want to keep playing but also develop and document my writing, including a collection of songs with lyrics. And I want to try to bring the various parts of my musical experience—including straight-ahead, free playing and more compositional ideas—together more."

**Recommended CDs:** *Resonance* (Justin Time 13) from 1985 is an excellent trio session with bassist Dave Piltch and drummer Michel Lambert. *Live At Mezzetta* (Sackville 2057) is a fine duo date with bassist Don Thompson from 2002. Most of Schwager's other albums as a leader have been for his own Rant label, including *Never Swim Alone* (Rant 9101), *Know Your Zones* (Rant 9108), *Border Town* (Rant 9274) and the recent *Duets*. As a sideman, he can be heard with saxophonist George Benson, the Dave McMurdo Jazz Orchestra, Junior Mance, Gary Burton, Mel Torme, George Shearing, Bob Barnard, Bob Mover, and many talented Canadian artists (in addition to Don Thompson, Emilie-Claire Barlow, Darren Sigesmund and Jeannette Lambert), including Trudy Desmond, Lenny Solomon, George Evans, Sophie Millman, Phil Nimmons, Richard Underhill, Mike Murley, P.J. Perry, Barry Elmes, Dave Young, Peter Appleyard, and Oliver Jones.

## Thornel Schwartz
*b. May 29, 1927, Philadelphia, PA; d. December 30, 1977, Philadelphia, PA*

Thornel Schwartz was a member of the original Jimmy Smith trio, and nearly every recording he made was with an organist. A superior comper who inspired organists with his boppish chords, Schwartz was also a fine soloist. He studied at the Landis School of Music and worked early on with Earnest Deaton, Chris Powell and Don Gardner. After playing with Freddie Cole (1952–55), Schwartz joined Smith's trio, having met the organist when they both worked with Gardner. He was with Jimmy Smith during his early successes, when Smith hit New York and changed the way that the organ was played in jazz.

After having made history with Smith, Schwartz worked with Johnny "Hammond" Smith, Larry Young (1960–62), Jimmy McGriff (1964–66), back with Johnny Smith, a second tour with Jimmy Smith, Reuben Wilson, Jimmy McGriff again, Richard "Groove" Holmes and Milt Buckner (1972).

Although overshadowed by Grant Green, Kenny Burrell and the other guitarists of the 1960s, Thornel Schwartz (who passed away when he was just 50 in 1977) helped pave the way for soul-jazz guitarists.

**Recommended CDs:** Thornel Schwartz was a valuable sideman on many records starting with Jimmy Smith's *A New Sound, A New Star Vols. 1 & 2* (Blue Note 1512 and 1552), and *At Club Baby Grand Vols. 1 & 2* (Blue Note 92785 and 92787). Among his other significant recordings were Johnny "Hammond" Smith's *That Good Feelin'* (Prestige 24164); Larry Young's *Testifyin'* (Original Jazz Classics 1793), *Young Blues* (Original Jazz Classics 1831) and *Groove Street* (Original Jazz Classics 1853); Jimmy Forrest's *Forrest Fire* (Original Jazz Classics 1992); and Jimmy McGriff's *The Worm* (Blue Note 38699).

**LPs to Search For:** Thornel Schwartz one album as a leader, 1962's *Soul Cookin'* (Argo 704), which also features Larry Young (under the pseudonym of Lawrence Olds), has not been reissued yet.

## John Scofield
*b. December 26, 1951, Dayton, OH*

One of the major guitarists of the past 35 years, John Scofield has had his own distinctive sound since near the beginning of his career. Even when he plays a fairly standard bop solo, he sounds unique due to his rockish tone. Scofield's technical mastery of the guitar and consistently creative playing have allowed him to sound quite comfortable in post-bop groups, with funky ensembles, in fusion groups, on soul-jazz outings, and in jam-band settings.

He remembers first playing guitar when he was 11. "My mother said, 'You like music, why don't you try guitar?' We rented an acoustic. After a week, it was too hard, so I asked to play drums, but my parents said no way. My dad bought me a Django record when I was 12, and I loved it, but I got into the blues first. At about 14, I started studying with a local jazz guitarist at a music store in Wilton, Connecticut, Alan Deane, and he really turned me on to jazz." As a teenager, Scofield often took the train to New York to see top jazz artists at the Village Vanguard (including Thelonious Monk, Bill Evans, Rahsaan Roland Kirk, Freddie Hubbard, Gary Burton and Ornette Coleman), the Guitar (Jim Hall and Kenny Burrell), Cafe Au Go Go or the Fillmore East (Cream, Sly Stone and Jimi Hendrix).

Scofield played in a local rock band in junior high school and performed at high school dances and youth clubs. "But every weekend, I was playing at bars in NYC, starting when I was 16; I had a phony draft card." He attended Berklee during 1970–73. In 1972, he met Gary Burton (jamming with him on a weekly basis) and also met Steve Swallow. In the fall of 1974, he had his first important gig, being recommended by Alan Dawson to play with Gerry Mulligan at the Jazz Workshop in Boston. Scofield made his recording debut with Mulligan at a Carnegie Hall concert that also featured Chet Baker. After meeting Billy Cobham and joining his band in January 1975, the guitarist moved to New York.

Scofield worked with Cobham in what soon became the Billy Cobham–George Duke Band for two years, was featured with the Brecker Brothers, and spent 1977 as a member of the Gary Burton Quartet. That same year, he made his first records as a leader and also recorded with Charles Mingus. Although primarily heard as a leader from that point on, Scofield has also worked with Dave Leibman (1979–81), Miles Davis (1982–85), Joe Lovano (off and on from 1989), Bass Desires, Joe Henderson, Eddie Harris (a collaboration in 1996), Herbie Hancock's New Standards Band, and Jack DeJohnette and Larry Goldings in Trio Beyond (2007). "I got to play and record with many of my idols, including Mingus, Mulligan, Miles, Chet, Jay McShann, Joe Henderson, Herbie,

Chick, Roy Haynes and Elvin Jones. I'm so lucky."

Scofield's own groups have included a trio with bassist Steve Swallow and drummer Alan Nussbaum (1979–84), his Blue Matter band with Dennis Chambers (1986–89), and the Uberjam band (2000–04). Starting in 1998, he has occasionally toured with Medeski, Martin & Wood (especially during 2006–07). In recent times, Sco has played New Orleans gospel, soul and jazz with singer-keyboardist Jon Cleary in the Piety Street Band.

John Scofield, who has recorded over 30 albums as a leader, including collaborations with Pat Metheny, Bill Frisell, Brad Mehldau, Joe Lovano, Charlie Haden, Eddie Harris, Medeski, Martin & Wood and Jim Hall, is a faculty member in the jazz department of New York University. He remains a vital and influential force on the jazz scene.

**Recommended CDs:** *Live* (Enja 3013), *First* (Venus 79027), *John Scofield Quartet* (Storyville 5002), *Rough House* (Enja 79657), *Who's Who* (Novus 30712), *Bar Talk* (Novus 34512), *Shinola* (Enja 4004), *Out Like A Light* (Enja 4038), *Electric Outlet* (Gramavision 79404), *Still Warm* (Enja 79401), *Blue Matter* (Gramavision 79403), *Loud Jazz* (Gramavision 79402), *Pick Hits Live* (Gramavision 79405), *Flat Out* (Gramavision 79400), *Time On My Hands* (Blue Note 92894), *Meant To Be* (Blue Note 95479), *Grace Under Pressure* (Blue Note 98167) with Bill Frisell, *What We Do* (Blue Note 99586), *Hand Jive* (Blue Note 27327) with Eddie Harris, *I Can See Your House From Here* (Blue Note 27765), *Groove Elation* (Blue Note 32801), *Quiet* (Verve 533185), *A Go Go* (Verve 539979), *Bump* (Verve 543430), *Works For Me* (Verve 549281), *Uberjam* (Verve 589356), *ScoLoHoFo—Oh!* (Blue Note 42081), *Up All Night* (Verve 065596), *EnRoute* (Verve 169902), *That's What I Say* (Verve 436002), *This Meets That* (Emarcy 1734085), *Piety Street* (Emarcy 1265602), *A Moment's Peace* (Emarcy 15590); with Miles Davis: *Star People* (Sony 9765), *Decoy* (Sony 9766), *You're Under Arrest* (Sony 1237); with Trio Beyond: *Saudades* (ECM 6421); with the Metropole Orchestra: *54* (Emarcy 1459902). John Scofield's significance and influence can be measured by the fact that he has also recorded as a featured sideman with an enormous number of major artists, including John Abercrombie, George Adams/Don Pullen, Mose Allison, Franco Ambrosetti, Ray Anderson, Teodross Avery, Chet Baker, Richie Beirach, Bob Belden, Paul Bley, Gary Burton, Terri Lyne Carrington, Dennis Chambers, Billy Cobham, Larry Coryell, Joey DeFrancesco, Jack DeJohnette, Ray Drummond, John Ellis, Peter Erskine, David Friesen, Hal Galper, Mike Gibbs, Mack Goldsbury, Bill Goodwin, Jon Gordon,

George Gruntz, Jim Hall, Herbie Hancock, Tom Harrell, Jimmy Haslip, Roy Haynes, Joe Henderson, Terumasa Hino, Ron Holloway, Robert Irving III, Marc Johnson, Lee Konitz, Niels Lan Doky, Dave Liebman, Albert Mangelsdorff, Ron McClure, Jim McNeely, Jay McShann, Vince Mendoza, Charles Mingus, Bob Moses, Gerry Mulligan, Makoto Ozone, John Patitucci, Niels Pedersen, Jim Pepper, Zbigniew Seifert, Tommy Smith, Martial Solal, G.E. Stinson, Steve Swallow, Harvie Swartz, Toots Thielemans, Gary Thomas, McCoy Tyner, Miroslav Vitous, Bennie Wallace, Jack Walrath, Peter Warren, and Lenny White.

**LPs to Search For:** *East Meets West* (Blackhawk 533).

**Website:** www.johnscofield.com

---

# Andrew Scott
*b. Toronto, Canada*

A multitalented individual, Andrew Scott has emerged as one of Canada's top bop-oriented guitarists. He grew up in Toronto, singing in the Canadian Children's Opera Chorus and playing French horn in junior high school. Scott began playing guitar while in high school and discovered jazz through hearing his mother's records, which included Oscar Peterson, Junior Mance and Dave Brubeck. He went to Humber College of Applied Arts and Sciences, where his teachers included Charles Tolliver, Don Thompson and Pat LaBarbera.

While in college, he was part of One Step Beyond, a jazz group that recorded three albums, toured North America and was sometimes in the backup band for organist Merle Saunders. Scott also spent four months playing at the Hotel Eden in Arosa, Switzerland. In 1998, he moved to Boston to attend the New England Conservatory of Music, earning a master's in historical musicology. Scott earned a PhD at York University in 2006 and currently teaches at Humber College of Music, the University of Guelph and York University. Scott has written extensively for film and television and was the managing editor of *Coda* during 2007–08.

As a guitarist, he has recorded with pianist Jim Clayton in the Clayton/Scott Group, and been a sideman on a variety of sessions, having worked with David Sanborn, Grant Stewart, Randy Sandke, Dan Block, Tony Monaco, Bob James, Earl Klugh, Bob Moses, Mike Murley, Gene DiMovi, and Harry Allen. But Andrew Scott can be best heard on his own trio of CDs, which display a lot of potential for the future.

**Recommended CDs:** *This One's For Barney* (Sackville 2062), *Blue Mercer* (Sackville 2066), *Nostalgia* (Sackville 2073).

# Ari Seder
*b. August 26, 1978, Washington, DC*

A promising young guitarist based in Chicago, Ari Seder has been developing his own voice in modern mainstream jazz while sometimes stretching his music beyond jazz, particularly with Balkano. He began on guitar when he was 11 after a brief period of piano lessons. "I had a guitar teacher who started out teaching me rock but also steered me towards blues, and through that towards improvisation. He used to make me mix tapes of great rock and blues guitarists while slipping in some jazz recordings, including by Pat Martino. I also had a friend at school who was learning to play the drums around the same time. We used to jam together in his basement and his dad would sometimes join us on bass, introducing us to his jazz recordings." The three of them went to some jazz concerts in Washington, DC clubs, giving Seder an opportunity early on to see John McLaughlin, Mike Stern, Joe Zawinul, John Patitucci, and Joey DeFrancesco.

While attending the Oberlin Conservatory of Music, the guitarist played his first gigs at restaurants and coffee shops. After he graduated in 2001, he moved to Chicago. Although very impressed by the playing of Bobby Broom ("He managed to combine the melodic inventiveness of Keith Jarrett with the vocabulary of Wes Montgomery, George Benson and Pat Martino") and Kurt Rosenwinkel, Seder was determined to develop his own individual voice. He went often to see tenor-saxophonist Von Freeman play and subbed with his band on a couple of occasions.

"When I moved to Chicago, there seemed to be a glut of competent jazz guitarists. I decided to form my own group and focus on booking my own gigs. Having a regular trio has been important to my development as both a guitarist and a composer." Among his sidemen have been bassists Dan Thatcher and Cory Biggerstaff and drummers Ed Breazeale, Darren Scorza and Joe Chellman. Seder has also led a trio with organist Paul Mutzabaugh and worked with drummer Sharif Zaben's trio, trumpeter Curtis Black's quartet, and Balkano, a group that since 2007 has fused jazz with klezmer, Balkan wedding music, Turkish gypsy music and Latin American influences. "That allows me to express more of the rock-and-roll side of my musical personality. In my music, I try to strike a balance between elements of modernism and traditionalism. I feel that it is important both to know and reference the history and tradition of jazz, but equally important to try to extend it in some way and not just recreate the past."

**Recommended CDs:** Ari Seder has thus far led three CDs for his own label: *Ari Seder Trio*, *Ari Seder*

*Organ Trio* and *Time Well Spent*. Each is available through his website.

**Website:** www.ariseder.com

## Mitch Seidman
*b. November 27, 1953, Long Branch, NJ*

A flexible post-bop guitarist, Mitch Seidman is also an influential educator. "I was about ten when I started playing guitar and was first inspired by the music I heard on AM radio, especially the  guitar instrumentals that were popular then. My earliest memory of hearing jazz was of my sixth-grade teacher playing Louis Armstrong records for us. I don't remember the titles, but certainly the experience." Seidman first played in bands when he was in junior high and also played flute (which was his first instrument), electric bass, and a little bit of violin, trombone and clarinet in college, but guitar was always his main instrument.

"I met Attila Zoller in 1974. He started as my teacher but remained my close friend and inspiration until he passed away in 1998. Through Attila, I got to know and play with Jimmy Raney and Tal Farlow, who were both influential to me. Jim Hall, who I got to know later, has also been inspirational." Seidman attended Berklee during 1973–77, earning a composition degree and in 1993 a master's in music education from Boston University. He is a professor at Berklee.

In his career, Seidman has played in many different settings. "I really enjoyed the trio with saxophonist Charlie Kohlhase and trombonist Jeff Galindo from about 1999 to 2000. It was such a deep listening and responding experience, not to mention a real challenge for me as a guitarist. I also had an empathetic musical relationship with the late pianist Tony Zano that began in the middle 1980s." In addition, he has worked with Vera Auer, Harold Vick, Ted Brown, Alan Dawson, George Garzone, Herb Pomeroy, Hal Crook, Joe Beck, Michael Formanek, Holly Hofmann, Tyrone Brown, Billy Harper, and his own groups.

"Many of my recent musical activities have been in music education. I have been rather selective as a performer, focusing on performing situations that interest and inspire me. I would like to explore deeper into myself as an artist, and compose and improvise in a manner most natural to me."

**Recommended CDs:** *Fretware* (Brownstone 946), *This Over That* (Jardis 9816), *Congeniality* (Cadence 1118), *How 'Bout It?* (Jardis 20135), *Triangulation* (Kyran Music), *For One Who Waits* (Kyran Music).

**Website:** www.mitchseidman.com

## Bola Sete
**(Djalma de Andrade)**
*b. July 16, 1923, Rio De Janeiro, Brazil; d. February 14, 1987, Greenbrae, CA*

Bola Sete was a significant guitarist in the bossa nova movement, although he had been an established guitarist long before  that. Born Djalma de Andrade, he received the nickname of Bola Sete (meaning "Seven Ball") when he was the only black member of a jazz group. The seven ball in Brazilian billiards is the name for the lone black ball in the game.

Sete, who studied guitar at the Conservatory of Rio, was a professional musician as a teenager. He worked with composer Henricao at 17 and was a fixture in Rio for years. Sete worked for a time for Radio Transmissora and for three years was part of a major show at the João Caetano Theater. In the late 1940s, he led Bola Sete E Seu Conjunto. Sete spent 1952–54 living and working in Italy. In the mid-1950s, he toured Argentina, Uruguay, Spain and Peru. Sete moved to the United States in 1959 and, starting in 1962, had a regular job performing at several chains of the Sheraton Hotel.

By then, he had led a few albums, including 1960's *Bola Sete*, and was beginning to create a stir in the music world. In 1962, he was one of the stars at an influential Bossa Nova Festival held at Carnegie Hall. He recorded an album titled *Bossa Nova*, moved to San Francisco (playing at the Sheraton Palace), and met Dizzy Gillespie and Lalo Schifrin. Sete played with Gillespie at that year's Monterey Jazz Festival. He also recorded with the trumpeter and, during 1963–65, was a member of the Vince Guaraldi Trio. Sete's recordings for the Fantasy label, both with and without Guaraldi, were popular. He performed again at the Monterey Jazz Festival in 1966 (this time with his own trio) and, while having a lower profile, was active in the 1970s and the first half of the '80s. His later work was more introspective than earlier and had New Age elements to the music.

Bola Sete died in 1987 from lung cancer.

**Recommended CDs:** *Tour De Force* (Fantasy 24766) has all of the music from 1962's *Bossa Nova* and 1963's *Tour De Force*. *Voodoo Village* (Fantasy 24779) reissues performances originally on a pair of LPs from the mid-1960s (*The Incomparable Bola Sete* and *Autentico!*). *Vince & Bola* (Fantasy 24756) reissues two albums that Sete recorded with Guaraldi. Also excellent are *Bola Sete Live At The Monterey Jazz Festival* (Polygram 543379) and *Ocean Memories* (Samba Moon 890524); the latter has some of Sete's best late-period work.

**LPs to Search For:** *Aqui Está O Bola Sete* (Odeon 3005) from 1957 features Sete on electric guitar. Also quite worthy are a pair of largely straight-ahead recordings, *Bola 7 & 4 Trombones* (EMI-Odeon) and *E A Bola Da Vez* (Odeon), plus *The Solo Guitar Of Bola Sete* (Fantasy 8369).

## Marvin Sewell
*b. Chicago, IL*

Marvin Sewell is a modern yet bluesy guitarist who uses elements of the past (such as country blues) to create new sounds. He is best known for his association with Cassandra Wilson. Born and raised in Chicago, Sewell mastered both acoustic and electric guitars early on. Sewell played a wide variety of music in local bands including blues, rock, gospel and soul. He became interested in jazz while in high school, playing with the Malcolm X Community College Big Band. Sewell worked in Chicago with Von Freeman, Ramsey Lewis, Jody Christian, Big Time Sarah, Billy Branch and others, studying composition while attending Roosevelt University. After moving to New York in 1990, he toured with an Algerian pop band.

In 1992, Sewell performed with Jack DeJohnette's Special Edition, Diedre Murray and Fred Hopkins, also recording with Gary Thomas. He played blues slide guitar in Marvin "Hannibal" Peterson's *African Portraits* opera. He has since worked with David Sanborn, Marcus Miller, Greg Osby, Joe Lovano, George Benson, Jason Moran, Tom Harrell and Lizz Wright. Associated with Cassandra Wilson since 1995, Sewell has appeared on some of her recordings and gives an authentic sound to her explorations of country blues and vintage material. His versatility also allows him to sound quite at home on her most modern pieces too. Marvin Sewell has led his own band on an occasional basis, which put out a privately issued CD in 2005.

**Recommended CDs:** Marvin Sewell's self-released project, *The Worker's Dance*, matches his guitar with a rhythm section and two accordions; with Cassandra Wilson: *Traveling Miles* (Blue Note 54123), *Belly Of The Sun* (Blue Note 35072), *Silver Pony*

(Blue Note 29752); with Greg Osby: *Art Forum* (Blue Note 37319); with Yoron Israel: *Chicago* (Double-Time 145); with René Marie: *How I Can Keep From Singing?* (Maxjazz 109); with Jason Moran: *Same Mother* (Blue Note 71780), *Artist In Residence* (Blue Note 711).

**Website:** www.marvinsewell.com

## Eldon Shamblin
*b. April 24, 1916, Clinton, OK; d. August 5, 1998, Tulsa, OK*

A major force in Western swing, Eldon Shamblin was a pioneering electric guitarist and one of the stars of Bob Wills' Texas Playboys. Self-taught on guitar from an early age, Shamblin taught himself to read and arrange music, studying Eddie Lang's solos while a teenager. He picked up experience in Oklahoma City, played in nightclubs and had his own radio show as a solo singer-guitarist. Shamblin was a member of the early Western swing group the Alabama Boys during 1934–37 and was considered one of the two top guitarists based in Oklahoma during the period; the other one was Charlie Christian.

Shamblin joined Bob Wills' Texas Playboys in 1937; he was not only the band's first electric guitarist (after switching in 1938) but also their main arranger. He added a strong jazz element to the group's performances and recordings and participated on over 300 titles. Shamblin soloed on many of Wills' hits during the next decade, including "Bob Wills Special," which features his interplay with steel guitarist Leon McAuliffe.

He was drafted and saw active duty during 1942–46, serving under General Patton. After his discharge, Shamblin played with Leon McAuliffe's Western Swing Band before rejoining Bob Wills, with whom he worked for another eight years (1946–54) plus a few months in 1956. He was with Hoyle Nix's West Texas Cowboys during 1954–56 and then, after leaving Wills for the final time, retired from active playing, instead running a convenience store, teaching guitar in Tulsa, and becoming a piano tuner and organ repairman.

In 1970, Shamblin worked with Merle Haggard on a famous tribute album to Bob Wills, which led to him touring on and off with Haggard during 1973–83. His later musical activities included playing with Leon McAuliffe's Original Texas Playboys and recording on various projects with Joe Venuti, Tiny Moore, Asleep at the Wheel, Willie Nelson and others. One of the last major guitar pioneers of the 1930s, Eldon Shamblin retired in 1996, two years before his death at the age of 82.

**Recommended CDs:** Eldon Shamblin is on nearly all of the most important Bob Wills recordings. *Take*

*Me Back To Tulsa* (Proper Box 1032) has 100 performances dating from 1932–50. *Tiffany Transcriptions* (Collectors' Choice 991) has all 150 radio transcriptions that he made with Wills during 1946–47. Shamblin is also featured with Leon McAuliffe's 1946 band on *Take It Away Leon* (Harlequin 185). Merle Haggard's Bob Wills tribute album from 1970, *A Tribute To The Best Damn Fiddle Player In The World* (Koch 7900), led to a comeback for both Shamblin and Western swing. In 1976, Shamblin matched wits and creativity with violinist Joe Venuti, mandolinist Jethro Burns and steel guitarist Curley Chalker on *'S Wonderful—4 Giants Of Swing* (Flying Fish 70035), showing that he was quite comfortable playing jazz standards.

## Elliott Sharp

b. March 1, 1951, Cleveland, OH

A very adventurous improviser whose music reaches beyond jazz, Elliott Sharp says of his career, "I've never really considered myself to be a professional guitarist but rather a composer who plays guitar." He started off on piano at age six and played his first concert just one year later, performing Liszt's "Hungarian Rhapsody No. 2" at Carnegie Recital Hall. However, after suffering from severe asthma, he chose to give up the piano, switching to clarinet. Always interested in electronics, Sharp had built his own fuzz boxes by 1966, playing Jeff Beck solos on the clarinet in his band the Last Words. After hearing Jimi Hendrix, he started playing his father's acoustic guitar before saving the money for a new electric guitar. At a summer residency at Carnegie Mellon University in the summer of 1968, "I spent a lot of my lab time building effects boxes and playing with a seven-head Ampex tape deck. I also DJ'ed on the school radio station from midnight to 4 a.m., where I played all of the weirdest music I could find in their extensive library. I tried to translate a lot of what I was hearing to guitar."

Sharp picked up experience playing with blues and jug bands, playing solo country blues with a twist, exploring music with avant-garde rock groups, and presenting solo prepared guitar feedback concerts. He studied anthropology at Cornell University (1969–71) and composition, improvisation, ethnomusicology and electronics at Bard College (1972–73), where he earned a BA. Sharp earned a master's in composition and American studies while at SUNY Buffalo in 1977.

Since then, Elliott Sharp has played everything from free improvisations to contemporary classical music, from electronic explorations to blues. In addition to guitar, he occasionally plays mandolin, bass, banjo, piano, clarinet, bass clarinet, tenor-, alto- and soprano-saxophone, and various string and percussion instruments. Moving to New York in 1979, Sharp worked with Trio in Transit in 1980 (with bassist Jay Oliver and drummer Dennis Charles), 1981's Moving Info (a sextet with drummer Philip Wilson and bassist Bill Laswell), Carbon (off and on since 1983), the Soldier String Quartet (1986–96), and Oblique Ah Blue with Arthur Blythe, Oliver Lake and Ray Anderson (1996–98). As a significant part of the downtown New York experimental music scene, he worked with John Zorn, Wayne Horvitz and Butch Morris. He has also made music with such notables as his longtime friend drummer Bobby Previte, Hubert Sumlin, Billy Hart, Jack DeJohnette, Graham Haynes and Hamid Drake among many others. In 1991, he formed his blues group Terraplane.

Among the projects that Elliott Sharp named as most important are the release and performances of his solo electroacoustic project *Tectonics* (1993), the premiere of his orchestra piece "Racing Hearts" by the Radio-Sinfonie Frankfurt in 1998, "Synda-Kit" with Orchestra Carbon (1998), "Quarks Swim Free" with Orchestra Carbon (2003), and "Proof Of Erdös" by Ensemble Resonanz at the 2006 Witten Festival.

In recent times, Sharp has brought back Carbon for a new CD (*Void Coordinates*) and a European tour, has toured with both Terraplane and with various solo projects, created a new opera (*Port Bou*), premiered another one (*Binibon*), and continued writing compositions for orchestras and chamber groups. "I love not just jazz but all music, particularly the spirit of the unknown, the thrill of improvisation, and the beauty of form." He proves that consistently in his playing and very open-minded approach.

**Recommended CDs:** There are many Elliott Sharp recordings to choose from that cover a very wide area of music, beginning with six obscure LPs cut for the Zoar label during 1977–83. Ranging from solo guitar to work with string quartets, soundtracks, electronic noise, avant-fusion, blues and even standards, a partial list of Sharp's CDs includes *Nots* (Atonal 3011), *Spring & Neap* (Neos 40708), *Larynx* (Neos 40704), *Hammer, Anvil, Stirrup* (SST 232), *Datacide* (Enemy 116), *K!L!A!V!* (Newport 85504), *Tocsin* (Enemy 134), *Truthtable* (Homestead 202), *Amusia* (Atavistic 29), the blues-oriented *Terraplane* (Homestead 215), *Cryptid Fragments* (Extreme 20), *Dyner's Club* (Intakt 36), *Tectonics; Errata* (Neos 40702), *Interference* (Atavistic 61950), *Psycho-Acoustic* (Victo 26), *Blackburst Psycho-Acoustic* (Victo 44), *Field & Stream* (Knitting Factory Works 227), *Blues For Next* (Knitting Factory Works 285), *Suspension Of Disbelief* (Tzadik 7512), *Beyond* (Auditorium 004), *The Velocity Of Hue* (Emanen 4098), *Do The Don't*

(Intuition 34252), *Quadrature: Solo Electroacoustic Guitar* (Zoar 01), *Secret Life* (Intuition 3852), *Sharp? Monk? Sharp! Monk!* (Clean Feed), *Acoustic Guitar* (Cleanfeed), *Forgery* (Intuition 34112), *Concert In Dachau* (Intakt 149), *Octal Book One* (Clean Feed), *Tectonics—Abstraction Distraction* (Clean Feed), *Octal Book Two* (Clean Feed), and *Aggregat Trio* (Clean Feed).

**Website:** www.elliottsharp.com

## Sonny Sharrock
*(Warren Harding Sharrock)*
b. August 27, 1940, Ossining, NY; d. May 26, 1994, Ossining, NY

Sonny Sharrock was the first truly avant-garde guitarist in jazz. While Billy Bauer had recorded a pair of free improvisations with Lennie Tristano in 1949, when Sharrock burst upon the scene in the mid-1960s, he was not only free in his choice of notes but in his wide range of sounds and his use of feedback and distorted sounds. He preceded both Derek Bailey and Jimi Hendrix. During an era when few jazz guitarists even acknowledged rock, Sharrock was playing explosive solos that made him the Pharoah Sanders of the guitar.

Sharrock sang in doo-wop groups as a teenager. He first discovered jazz through Miles Davis' *Kind Of Blue*, and, inspired by John Coltrane, he wanted to play saxophone. But because he had asthma, he reluctantly played guitar instead of the tenor that he really wanted. He was already 20 in 1960 when he started, and it would not be until 1965 that he moved to New York and made his initial impact. Sharrock worked with Byard Lancaster and Babatunde Olatunji before making his recording debut with Pharoah Sanders (on *Tauhid*) in late 1966. He worked with Sanders during 1967–68 and was a logical foil for Sanders' emotional sound explorations. Less inevitable was his four-year stint with flutist Herbie Mann (1968–72). His free-form solos were definitely a contrast from Mann's melodic playing, but they helped to give Mann an audience among rockers, and that combination (along with David "Fathead" Newman's tenor) worked surprisingly well.

Sonny Sharrock made his debut as a leader with 1969's *Black Woman*, and that recording, along with a few others, also featured his wife Linda Sharrock's wordless singing. In 1970, Sharrock was a major part of Miles Davis' *A Tribute To Jack Johnson* but was not credited on the album. That same year, he turned down an offer to join Davis' group, which in retrospect was a major mistake.

After leaving Mann in 1972, years of obscurity followed. Sharrock was divorced and mostly worked outside of music, including jobs as a chauffeur and a caretaker for children with disabilities. Bassist-producer Bill Laswell emerged as his angel. Laswell's used Sharrock on a 1981 recording by Material called *Memory Serves*. In 1986, Laswell persuaded Sharrock to join Last Exit, a wild, sometimes violent and occasionally humorous freely improvising group that also included saxophonist Peter Brotzmann and drummer Ronald Shannon Jackson. Sharrock also worked with Machine Gun and led his own bands, making a full comeback and recording often. 1991's *Ask The Ages*, a reunion with Pharoah Sanders in which Sharrock was an equal, was one of the high points of his career. But it all ended in 1994 when Sonny Sharrock died suddenly from a heart attack at the age of 53.

**Recommended CDs:** *Black Woman* (Water Music 152), which has plenty of high energy playing and some unique vocalizing by Linda Sharrock, is the best early Sonny Sharrock CD despite its brief playing time. *Monkey-Pockie-Boo* (Sunspots 504), which has some moments, is a so-so effort unless one is dying to hear Sonny Sharrock play slide whistle, which he does at one point. *Guitar* (Enemy 102) from 1986 features Sharrock as the only performer, overdubbing two blistering guitars. *Seize The Rainbow* (Enemy 104) has the guitarist on a date that blends together heavy metal and avant-garde jazz. *Highlife* (Enemy 1919), an eclectic session with stronger melodies than usual, has no lack of passion. *Faith Moves* (CMP 52) is a set of mostly freely improvised duets with the string instruments of Nicky Skopelitis. But *Ask The Ages* (Axiom 848957) is Sonny Sharrock's definitive and most essential album. Teamed with Pharoah Sanders, bassist Charnett Moffett and Elvin Jones, Sonny Sharrock contributed all six originals, and his interplay with Sanders (who plays with more ferocity than he usually did during this era) is magical. Of the many Last Exit recordings, *Last Exit* (Enemy 101), *The Noise Of Trouble* (Enemy 103) and *From The Board* (Enemy 105) will certainly burn down the walls.

## Brad Shepik
*(Brad Schoeppach)*
b. January 1, 1966, Walla Walla, WA

An adventurous guitarist, Brad Shepik has long been interested not only in jazz but also in creative world music, particularly the modal music of the Balkans.

He grew up in Seattle and began on the guitar when he was ten. Shepik played both guitar and sax in school bands but soon chose to focus on the former. He earned a degree from Cornish College of the Arts and, after moving to New York in 1990, earned a master's in jazz performance composition from New York University.

Since relocating to New York, Shepik has been part of a large number of important post-bop and world music groups, including Dave Douglas' Tiny Bell Trio, Matt Darriau's Paradox Trio, Pachora, Babkas, Carla Bley's Escalator over the Hill, Charlie Haden's Liberation Orchestra, Paul Motian's Electric Bebop Band (he was a member for five years), Yuri Yunakov's Bulgarian Wedding Band, Simon Shaheen's Quantara, Joey Baron's Killer Joey, George Schuller's Circle Wide, Alexis Cuadrado Puzzles Quartet, Arthur Kell Quartet, Combo Nuvo, Bob Brookmeyer's Quintet East, Owen Howard, Andy Laster, Franz Koglmann and the Ken Schaphorst Big Band.

Brad Shepik has led and co-led several world music groups, including the Commuters, Triduga and Lingua Franca, and sometimes plays the Turkish guitar called the saz. His trio in 2000 included bassist Scott Colley and drummer Tom Rainey; they recorded *Drip* and *Short Trip*. In more recent times, he has had a trio with organist Gary Versace and Tom Rainey and expanded the group (adding trumpeter Ralph Alessi and bassist Drew Gress) to perform his "Human Activity Suite," a ten-movement piece about climate change.

**Recommended CDs:** *The Loan* (Songlines 1518), *The Well* (Songlines 1531), *Short Trip* (Knitting Factory Works 290), *Drip* (Knitting Factory Works 312), *Places You Go* (Songlines 1562), *Human Activity Suite* (Songlines 1576), *Across The Way* (Songlines 1586); with Paul Motian: *Paul Motian And The Electric Bebop Band* (Winter & Winter 919061); with Dave Douglas: *The Tiny Bell Trio* (Songlines 1504).

**Website:** www.bradshepik.com

## Jimmy Shirley
*b. May 31, 1913, Union, SC; d. December 3, 1989, New York, NY*

A fine electric guitarist who appeared on a lot of sessions in the 1940s and for a brief while in 1975, Jimmy Shirley had an attractive sound and a versatile style that fit in best in swing settings. Shirley, who grew up in Cleveland, took his first guitar lessons from his father. He played locally during 1934–36 in the bands of J. Frank Terry and Hal Draper. After moving to New York in 1937, Shirley was a member of the Clarence Profit Trio for four years. He made

his recording debut with trumpeter Wingy Carpenter in 1940 and appeared on one session the following year with Artie Shaw, Henry "Red" Allen and Benny Carter. Shirley was Ella Fitzgerald's accompanist during 1942–43, and he worked on and off in Herman Chittison's trio and in the studios with Phil Moore.

Associated with Blue Note during 1944–46 before it became a bop-oriented label, Jimmy Shirley is on sessions by James P. Johnson, Art Hodes and Sidney DeParis, showing how the electric guitar could sound natural in freewheeling Dixieland settings. Shirley, who also recorded during the era with Edmond Hall, Coleman Hawkins, Clyde Bernhart, Pete Johnson, Billie Holiday, Billy Kyle, John Hardee, Sid Catlett and Ram Ramirez among others, led two sessions of his own (one as an unaccompanied soloist), but only two duets with bassist Oscar Smith ("Star Dust" and "Jimmy's Blues") were ever released.

After 1946, much less was heard from Jimmy Shirley. He appeared on blues and jump records (including with Jimmy Rushing, Wynonie Harris and Screamin' Jay Hawkins), recorded rock and roll with Frankie Lymon & The Teenagers, and spent part of the 1960s as an electric bassist including working with Buddy Tate in 1967. While his swing style had long gone out of style, in the 1970s Shirley found an audience in Europe, particularly in 1975. During that visit, he made notable albums with Johnny Guarnieri, Slam Stewart and Stéphane Grappelli, and led his only full-length record, *China Boy*. But in the United States, Jimmy Shirley was merely a footnote in jazz history books by the time he passed away in 1989.

**Recommended CDs:** Jimmy Shirley fits in well on *Steff and Slam* (Black & Blue 863), a 1975 reissue co-led by Stéphane Grappelli and Slam Stewart.

**LPs to Search For:** Jimmy Shirley made his first jazz date on guitar in quite some time in 1970, sounding in excellent form on *A Portrait Of Julian Dash* (Master Jazz 8106). While Shirley can be heard taking brief solos on an impressive assortment of recordings in the 1940s, he received more of a chance to stretch out in 1975 when he recorded his lone LP as a leader, *China Boy* (Black & Blue 33.081), and he was well featured on pianist Johnny Guarnieri's *Gliss Me Again* (Classic Jazz 105).

## Yotam Silberstein
*b. January 6, 1982, Tel Aviv, Israel*

An up-and-coming bop-oriented guitarist, Yotam Silberstein (who recently has been going professionally by just his first name) has been very busy ever since moving to New York. Born and raised in Tel Aviv, Israel, he started playing guitar when he was ten. While he played rock and blues, Yotam studied jazz at the Alon High School of the Arts. At 18, he entered the Israeli Army for three years, playing music, being a musical director, and arranging for larger ensembles. The high point of his early career was playing at the Umbria Jazz Festival in Italy when he was 21.

After releasing his debut album and touring Europe, in 2005 Yotam gained a scholarship to study at the New School in New York City. Since moving to the US, he has worked with quite a list of major jazz artists, including James Moody, Benny Golson, Curtis Fuller, Louis Hayes, Jimmy Heath, Frank Wess, Al Jarreau, Junior Mance, Dee Dee Bridgewater, James Spaulding, Roy Hargrove, Pat Martino, Jon Faddis, Greg Hutchinson, Antonio Hart, Slide Hampton, Donald Harrison, Lew Soloff, George Cables, Eric Alexander, Avishai Cohen, Kenny Barron and, most recently, the Dizzy Gillespie Alumni All-Stars.

Yotam, who has thus far released four CDs as a leader, is a talented straight-ahead player who helps keep bebop alive in the modern jazz scene.

**Recommended CDs:** *Arrival* (Fresh Sound New Talent 185), *Next Page* (Posi-Tone 850), *Resonance* (Jazz Legacy 1008), *Brasil* (Jazz Legacy 1016); with the Dizzy Gillespie Alumni All-Stars: *I'm Beboppin' Too* (Half Note 924540).

**Website:** www.yotamsilberstein.com

## Ricardo Silveira
*b. October 25, 1956, Rio de Janeiro, Brazil*

One of Brazil's most popular jazz-oriented guitarists, Ricardo Silveira has long been interested in playing a wide variety of styles. Despite growing up in a musical environment, he did not begin playing the guitar until he was 16. But Silveira developed quickly, took classical guitar lessons, and earned a scholarship to Berklee. After a year at Berklee, he played with Marcio Montarroyos in Brazil for two months. Back in Boston, he worked in a salsa band and, on weekends in New York, with the Brazilian group Astra Carnival.

Silveira's big break was when he was noticed by Claudio Roditi, who recommended him to Herbie Mann. Silveira was part of Mann's group for two years and became in demand for session work with jazz artists. The guitarist worked with Sonny Fortune, Michael Brecker, Steve Gadd, Marcus Miller, Jason Miles, Naná Vasconcelos and others. After four years in the US, he returned to Brazil, working with Elis Regina, Hermeto Pascoal, Gilberto Gil, Gal Costa, Milton Nascimento, João Bosco, Ivan Lins, Nana Caymmi and other top Brazilian performers. He recorded his debut album, *Good To Play*, in 1984.

Since then, Ricardo Silveira has often recorded as a leader and, alternating between Brazil and the US, has worked with many musicians from different fields, including Sergio Mendes, Don Grusin, Dave Grusin, Oscar Castro-Neves, Dori Caymmi, Justo Almario, Toots Thielemans, Kevyn Lettau, Patti Austin, David Sanborn, Pat Metheny and Ernie Watts. Whether it is sambas, bossa nova, pop jazz, crossover, Brazilian-tinged R&B, or atmospheric improvising, Silveira (who considers Pat Metheny and Bill Frisell to be influences) fits in quite well.

**Recommended CDs:** *Long Distance* (Verve Forecast 835054), *Sky Light* (Verve Forecast 837696), *Amazon Secrets* (Verve Forecast 843602), *Storyteller* (Kokopelli 1307), *Noite Clara* (Adventure Music 1003), *Ao Vivo Tocam Milton Nascimento* (Universal 325912005302), *Live: Play The Music Of Milton Nascimento* (Adventure Music 1014), *Outro Rio* (Adventure Music 1033), *Até Amanhã* (Adventure Music 1057).

**Website:** www.ricardosilveira.com

## Roy Smeck
*(Leroy Smeck)*
*b. February 6, 1900, Reading, PA; d. April 5, 1994, New York, NY*

Roy Smeck was such a brilliant and futuristic musician when he emerged in the 1920s that he faced some of the problems that Rahsaan Roland Kirk did in the 1960s. He did not play three saxophones at once like Kirk, but Smeck was equally skilled on guitar, steel guitar, banjo and ukulele. As with Rahsaan, Art Tatum and Arturo Sandoval, his technique was so phenomenal that it made it easy for detractors to write him off as gimmicky or as a mere novelty act. Smeck could play each of his instruments at impossibly fast tempos and upside down, with the ability to jump effortlessly between several different styles and with a strong dose of his sense of humor. He fully deserved his title of "The Wizard of the Strings."

Largely self-taught, Roy Smeck grew up in Binghamton, New York. He dropped out of school after the fifth grade, working odd jobs while being very determined to make it as a musician. Once, he had a job in a shoe factory but was fired because he regularly brought his ukulele to work, playing for his co-workers. After a period of time, the eight to nine hours that he spent each day practicing started to pay off. He played banjo in a trio for local square dances, took up the Hawaiian steel guitar after being impressed by Sol Hoopii, and got work playing on the RKO Theater Chain. Smeck impressed Sam Warner, who featured him in a very early sound-film short in 1923, *Stringed Harmony*. In 1926 when Warner

Brothers made some highly publicized shorts to help introduce moviegoers to the idea of sound films (a year before *The Jazz Singer*), Smeck was picked as the only popular music performer to have his own feature, *His Pastimes*. The release of that pioneering film led to Smeck becoming popular for a time.

A hit on the vaudeville circuit, Roy Smeck's playing was full of unique effects and trick playing. He developed the talent (then unique) of being able to play ukulele and harmonica at the same time, playing the latter without a brace. Smeck also was on quite a few records in a variety of settings. He was one of the few white musicians to appear on classic blues recordings of the 1920s, with black singers including Bessie Brown, Edith Wilson and Maggie Jones. His steel guitar playing was considered so unusual that he was featured with King Oliver in the 1929 recording of "Everybody Does It In Hawaii," and he made a series of recordings with Clarence Williams' combos of 1933–35. His own records found him inspired by Sol Hoopii on steel guitar, guitarist Eddie Lang, banjoist Harry Reser and Sam Moore on the octachorda (an eight-string Hawaiian guitar). On ukulele and occasional harmonica, Roy Smeck sounded completely unlike anyone else. And on steel guitar, he was a major influence on Western swing and country musicians.

Smeck appeared in several films and shorts in the 1930s, so it is possible to see him getting an amazing amount of music out of a ukulele. While the death of vaudeville slowed him down, his showmanship and dazzling abilities kept him working. Smeck played at Franklin D. Roosevelt's inaugural ball in 1933, and he wrote a series of influential instructional books on how to play his instruments. Although largely overlooked by the jazz world, he continued playing quite well throughout the 1950s and '60s, appearing on such television variety series as *The Ed Sullivan Show*, *The Tonight Show* and *The Steve Allen Show*. A 1985 documentary on his life, *The Wizard Of The Strings*, was nominated for an Academy Award for Best Short Documentary and features Roy Smeck still joyfully playing hot jazz and unclassifiable music while in his mid-eighties. He lived to be 94.

**Recommended CDs:** *Roy Smeck Plays Hawaiian Guitar, Banjo, Ukulele And Guitar* (Yazoo 1052) has a cross section of Smeck's recordings as a leader, mostly from 1931–37 but also including 1926's "Tough Pickin'," 1928's "Laughing Rag," and "Ukulele Bounce" from 1949. Smeck contributes many remarkable moments on each of his instruments. A more comprehensive reissue of his work is long overdue, but this is a good beginning.

**LPs to Search For:** *Wizard Of The Strings* (Blue Goose 2027) has Roy Smeck in 1979 still sounding full of spirit, wit and brilliant musicianship during showcases for his guitar, ukulele, banjo and Hawaiian guitar.

## Floyd Smith
*b. January 25, 1917, St. Louis, MO; d. March 29, 1982, Indianapolis, IN*

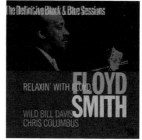

Floyd Smith is best known for recording an early if somewhat eccentric electric guitar solo with Andy Kirk's orchestra on "Floyd's Guitar Blues" in 1939. His odd improvisation on what was actually an amplified lap steel guitar hinted a little at the tonal distortions utilized by rock musicians 30 years later, and at Roy Smeck's more bizarre explorations on the Hawaiian guitar a decade before.

Smith played the ukulele before switching to guitar. He studied music theory in high school. Smith played acoustic guitar in such Midwest territory bands as Eddie Johnson's Crackerjacks, Dewey Jackson, the Jeter-Pillars Orchestra, the Sunset Royal Orchestra and the Brown Skin Models. He gained his greatest fame working with Andy Kirk's orchestra during 1939–46 except for a period spent in the Army. He took occasional solos with Kirk, but his only real showcase was "Floyd's Guitar Blues," recorded during the period right after he switched to electric guitar.

Floyd Smith left Kirk in 1946, led his own combo in Chicago, and in later years often played with organists including Wild Bill Davis, Bill Doggett, Johnny Hammond Smith, and Hank Marr. He also worked with Buddy Tate and Illinois Jacquet. Smith's last important musical association was a surprising one. In the 1970s, he became a record producer, founded a label based in Chicago, and produced singer Loleatta Holloway, transforming her from a gospel singer into a disco star. He married her a few years before his death in 1982.

**Recommended CDs:** Floyd Smith recorded a few singles as a leader for Hy-Tone, Chess, Decca and Mark during 1949–56, but these have not been reissued. He led one album in his career. *Relaxin' With Floyd* (Black & Blue 875) from 1972 has him playing basic material plus an inevitable remake of "Floyd's Guitar Blues" with Wild Bill Davis and drummer Chris Columbus. The original version of "Floyd's Guitar Blues" appears in several Andy Kirk collections, including *1939–1940* (Classics 640).

# Johnny Smith
b. June 25, 1922, Birmingham, AL

Johnny Smith, who never considered himself strictly a jazz musician but simply a guitarist, followed in the footsteps of George Van Eps in his ability to create and play beautiful chords. He is best remembered for his hit recording of "Moonlight In Vermont," but his decision to retire early led to him becoming obscure except to his fellow guitarists.

His father occasionally played a five-string banjo that Johnny Smith sometimes fooled around on. After short periods living in New Orleans and Chattanooga, his family settled in Portland, Maine. Smith was self-taught on guitar, and at one point, a local pawnshop let him play its guitars if he would be in charge of keeping them in tune. By the time he was 13, Smith was teaching guitar, frequently to adults, even though he did not actually own an instrument until he was 15. He played with the Fenton Brothers dance band and with the country group Uncle Lem & His Mountain Boys. By then, Smith was making enough money as a teenager to support himself, so he dropped out of high school. After leading the Airport Boys, a jazz trio comprised of two guitars and a bass for which he wrote the arrangements, he enlisted in the Army Air Corps in hopes of becoming a pilot. His faulty sight in one eye resulted in him having to forego that dream, and instead he joined the Air Corps Band. Because they had no openings for guitarists, Smith taught himself the cornet within two weeks. Later during his period in the service, he led a quartet comprised of two guitars, mandolin and bass.

After his discharge, Smith became a staff musician at an NBC station in Portland and, by 1946, at NBC in New York. Not only did he play as many as 35 radio programs a week, but he also guested with several symphony orchestras. During 1950–51, he was with Benny Goodman's big band and sextet. Smith was featured on three numbers on the Columbia LP *The Benny Goodman Trio Plays For The Fletcher Henderson Fund*.

In 1952, Johnny Smith signed with the Roost label, and his first session resulted in "Moonlight In Vermont." In addition to a spot for Stan Getz's tenor, the performance is notable for Smith's original and personal chord voicings, which were simply beautiful. He recorded a similar series of mostly easy-listening albums for Roost up to 1964, usually in trios or quartets, although 1962's *The Man With The Blue Guitar* is a set of unaccompanied solos. Rarely heard as a sideman on records, Smith was just on a few additional dates, including with the Hank Jones Trio, Johnny Richards, and singers Ruth Price, Beverly Kenney and Jeri Southern. Along the way,

Smith wrote "Walk, Don't Run," which the Ventures made into a pop hit in 1960.

In the 1950s, Johnny Smith appeared frequently at Birdland in New York, sometimes as much as 22 weeks a year. In 1958, Smith cut back on his activities to raise his daughter, moving to Colorado Springs in Colorado, where he ran a music store and taught. He recorded three final albums during 1967–68, although a set of solo performances from 1976 fill up half of a CD (*Legends*) that also includes some George Van Eps solos from 1994. In 1976, he toured with Bing Crosby and recorded with pianist Joe Bushkin, but that was his final main act. In 1991, Johnny Smith, who had been semi-active for decades, retired completely from playing.

**Recommended CDs:** The eight-CD box set *The Complete Roost Johnny Smith Small Group Sessions* (Mosaic 8-216), which has all of the guitarist's dates as a leader from 1952–64, is impossible to improve upon, but it was a limited-edition set and is now out of print. *Moonlight In Vermont* (Roulette 97747) has Smith's 1952–53 recordings not only with Stan Getz in his quintet but sometimes with tenors Zoot Sims and Paul Quinichette. *Walk Don't Run* (Roulette 60440) from 1954 and *The Sound Of The Johnny Smith Guitar* (Blue Note 31792), which collects together two of Smith's recordings from 1960–61, are both excellent reissues. *Legends* (Concord 4616) has Johnny Smith's final recordings along with unrelated solos by George Van Eps.

# Fabrizio Sotti
b. April 27, 1975, Abano Terme, Italy

Fabrizio Sotti has a dual career as a straight-ahead jazz guitarist and a hip-hop producer, although he has kept the two worlds separate. He started playing the piano at five, switching his focus to guitar four years later. "The earliest gig I can remember was a town parade when I was 11 years old, playing Pink Floyd and U2 songs. I started leading my own professional jazz groups at 15, playing all over Italy. I got introduced to jazz by older friends and a small collection of '40s and '50s vinyl I had found in my grandmother's house."

Sotti had a trio with bassist Ares Tavolazzia and drummer Mauro Beggio in Italy as a teenager. Since moving to New York, he has worked with Al Foster, Randy Brecker, John Patitucci, Steve La Spina and George Garzone. In 1998, he made his first American recording, *This World Upside Down*. Two years later he established a hip-hop label, Sotti Records. In 2003, he played, wrote and helped produce Cassandra Wilson's *Glamoured* CD. Most recently, Sotti recorded the music for an ironically titled project called *Against All Odds* with a trio, only to realize afterward that both the hard drive and backup that were used were defective. After some time off, he rearranged and re-recorded the music as *Inner Dance* with organist Sam Barsh and drummer Victor Jones plus some guests, considering the results (even though they are comprised of originals) to be a bit of a tribute to Wes Montgomery.

"My past, present and future goals have always been to make the best music I can. I see myself, in the near future, collaborating more with other artists for my own projects rather then just writing or producing for them."

**Recommended CDs:** *This World Upside Down* (BCI Eclipse 1701), *Inner Dance* (E1 Entertainment 2080); with Cassandra Wilson: *Glamoured* (Blue Note 81860).

# Les Spann
*(Leslie Spann, Jr.)*
*b. May 23, 1932, Pine Bluff, AK; d. January 24, 1989, New York, NY*

Les Spann's obscurity is a bit puzzling. A fine guitarist whose playing sometimes recalled Wes Montgomery, Spann was equally talented on flute. Very little is known about Spann's life beyond his recordings. He studied music at Tennessee State University off and on during 1950–57 and recorded with Phineas Newborn in 1957. After moving to New York, he worked with Ronnell Bright. He came the closest he ever would to finding fame when he was a member of the Dizzy Gillespie Quintet during 1958–59. He shared solo space (both on guitar and flute) with Gillespie and pianist Junior Mance, appearing on two of Dizzy's albums and touring.

During the next few years, Spann was quite busy. He was with the Quincy Jones big band that toured Europe; he is in fine form on a pair of records with a sextet that stars Johnny Hodges, Duke Ellington and Harry "Sweets" Edison; and Spann also recorded with Abbey Lincoln, Ben Webster, Randy Weston, Red Garland, Nat Adderley, Benny Bailey, Charlie Shavers, Curtis Fuller, Jerome Richardson, Charles Mingus, Sonny Stitt, Duke Pearson, Eddie "Lockjaw" Davis, Bill Coleman, Sam Jones, Billy Taylor, Charles Mingus (the Town Hall Concert), and Benny Goodman.

After recording with the Johnny Hodges/Wild Bill Davis group in 1967, Spann faded away, with alcohol contributing to his decline. Little was heard from him in the jazz world during the 20 years before his 1989 death.

**Recommended CDs:** Les Spann only led one album in his career, 1960s' *Gemini* (Original Jazz Classics 19482). He is heard on two quintet sessions with

Julius Watkins on French horn and pianist Tommy Flanagan, playing four songs apiece on guitar and flute. As a sideman, Spann is a strong asset on Dizzy Gillespie's *Have Trumpet, Will Excite* (Verve 549744) and Johnny Hodges' *Back To Back* (Essential Jazz Classics 55449) and *Side By Side* (Verve 21578).

# Melvin Sparks
*(Melvin Hamin Sparks-Hassan)*
*b. March 22, 1946, Houston, TX; d. March 15, 2011, Mount Vernon, NY*

A top-notch soul-jazz guitarist, Melvin Sparks had his own voice in the Grant Green/George Benson tradition. "When I was 11, I had a friend whose father bought him a guitar and taught him how to play 'Honky Tonk.' I was impressed and also wanted a guitar, so my father bought me one, providing I take lessons." Originally inspired by B.B. King and Chuck Berry, Sparks had an older brother, Danny Sparks, who was a professional drummer and urged him to listen to jazz and learn to read music. Sparks took his advice, writing arrangements for his high school band. He sat in with B.B. King when he was 13. At 17, he was part of an R&B show with the Upsetters that backed Jackie Wilson and Sam Cooke, he played in Texas with Hank Ballard and the Midnighters, and during 1966–67, he toured with Jack McDuff.

Sparks appeared on many soul-jazz dates during the late 1960s/early '70s, including sessions led by Dr. Lonnie Smith (also contributing arrangements to Smith's first two Blue Note albums), Idris Muhammad, George Benson (*Benson Burner*), Jimmy Witherspoon, Charles Kynard, Charles Earland, Sonny Stitt, Lou Donaldson, Rusty Bryant, Reuben Wilson and Johnny "Hammond" Smith, plus his own album *Sparks!* in 1970. While he recorded less often during 1975–95 due to soul jazz going out of style (although there were dates with Houston Person, Hank Crawford and Jimmy McGriff), Sparks continued working. He had a higher profile in his later years, often leading his own band and producing recordings by others (including Reuben Wilson and Bill Saxton).

"I enjoy performing as many concepts of American music as I can, especially jazz, blues, R&B and funk. Soul jazz is my favorite. I am very thankful to have met, performed and recorded with many great performers over the years."

Melvin Sparks died in 2011, a week short of his 65th birthday, from diabetes.

**Recommended CDs:** *Legends Of Acid Jazz* (Prestige 24171) has all of the music from the guitarist's first two albums as a leader (*Sparks* and *Spark Plug*) recorded during 1970–71, while *Texas Twister/75* (Beat Goes Public 92) is comprised of two of his

**Peter Sprague**

mid-1970s funk-oriented releases. *I'm A Gittar Player* (Cannonball 27101) was the guitarist's "comeback" album, directly preceding Melvin Sparks' finest work, his string of releases for the Savant label: *What You Hear Is What You Get* (Savant 2049), *It Is What It Is* (Savant 2057), *This Is It* (Savant 2065), and *Groove On Up* (Savant 2070).

**LPs to Search For:** One of Melvin Sparks' few recordings not currently available is his 1981 LP *Sparkling* (Muse 5248).

## Peter Sprague
*b. October 11, 1955, Cleveland, OH*

One of the top jazz guitarists from San Diego, Peter Sprague grew from his bop roots (Joe Pass was an early influence), keeping his music open to Eastern influences and developing his own individual voice. He began playing guitar when he was 12 because he liked rock music. "My dad is a jazz drummer, so he introduced me to the music through his record collection and love of jazz." During his last year of high school, he attended the Interlochen School of the Arts. "Right after my time at Interlochen, I was pretty sure that making music for my life was going to work. Both of my parents were very supportive, and that really helped. I connected with alto saxophonist Bob Mover, who was visiting San Diego, just having got off the band with Chet Baker. He had me come to NYC to record on his new record and also play gigs. That's how I met George Mraz, John Abercrombie and Tom Harrell and got a real experience of living in New York and hearing all of the incredible musicians."

Very important in his early development was his association with altoist Charles McPherson, which began in 1975 and included Sprague playing on McPherson's *Free Bop* album for Xanadu. That led to him getting his own record deal with the label and leading four of his own albums during 1979–82, followed by two for Concord. Also important in his development were a few guitar lessons with Pat Metheny in 1976.

In 1978 in Del Mar (near San Diego), Sprague formed the Dance of the Universe Orchestra, which included singer Kevyn Lettau. He also teamed up with Lettau in more recent years in a trio with her husband, percussionist Mike Shapiro, as BrazilJazz.

"Chick Corea has always been an important musical icon in my life, and it was a big moment when he asked me to play a series of concerts with him and his band around 1990. We recorded the soundtrack to a movie called *The Cat Chasers* and played a number of shows. He remains one of my biggest heroes." Sprague also worked with David Benoit in 1992 (recording *Letter To Evan* and *Shaken, Not Stirred*) and recorded *One Touch* with Eric Marienthal.

In 1995, he came off the road and resettled in Del Mar with his family. "A major turning point for me was when I started having hand problems. This led me to putting more time into my recording studio and learning engineering better. Now I have a full-fledged studio business of recording my own music as well as others. It's because of this balance that my hands are now doing well."

In recent times, Peter Sprague has been involved in a band, Blurring the Edges, that includes his brother Tripp Sprague on saxophones and flute and their father, Hall Sprague, on percussion. He formed a record company with his family called SBE (Strivin' to Break Even), recording quite a few CDs. He has also toured with Dianne Reeves, worked with pianist Geoffrey Keezer, written a guitar concerto that he performed with the San Diego Symphony, and recorded with the Peter Sprague String Consort.

**Recommended CDs:** Peter Sprague's recordings for his own SBE label include *Soliloquy*, *The Space Between Two Thoughts*, *You Make Me Want To Sing*, *Nikki's Rose*, *Songs Of Asaro*, *Pass The Drum*, *Friends For Life*, *Taking It All In*, *Peter Sprague Plays Solo*, and the debut of his String Consort on *The Wild Blue*.

**LPs to Search For:** *Dance Of The Universe* (Xanadu 176), *The Path* (Xanadu 183), the very intriguing *Bird Raga* (Xanadu 184), and *The Message Sent In The Wind* (Xanadu 193) are all unfortunately long out of print, as are *Musica Del Mar* (Concord 237) and the highly rated *Na Pali Coast* (Concord 277).

**Website:** www.petersprague.com

## Leni Stern
*(Magdalena Thora)*
*b. April 28, 1952, Munich, Germany*

Always an intriguing performer, Leni Stern had a period when she was primarily known as a jazz guitarist, but she has delved into other areas in recent years. She had classical piano lessons when she was six, taking up the guitar at 11, teaching herself to play jazz. However music took a back seat for some time. She spent 1969–77 primarily as an actress, being featured on a national television show in Germany and having her own acting company.

In 1977, Stern enrolled at Berklee, where she studied film scoring, and never returned to acting. In 1981, she moved to New York, where she played with both rock and jazz bands. In 1983, she had her own group with Bill Frisell (a mentor) and Paul Motian. During the next decade, she recorded nine instrumental albums, and although not considered a virtuoso on the level of her husband, Mike Stern, she was thought of as a very original player and a skilled composer.

1997 was a turning point in her career as Leni Stern, in recording *Black Guitar*, was reinvented as a singer-songwriter. While never completely abandoning jazz, her more recent efforts (recorded for her LSR label) are as much world music and pop as jazz.

**Recommended CDs:** Leni Stern's first CD as a leader, *Clairvoyant* (Passport 88015), is available through Stern's website, although *The Next Day* (Passport 88035) has not returned yet. *Secrets* (Enja 79602), *Closer To The Light* (Enja 79634), *Ten Songs* (Lipstick 8900) and *Like One* (Lipstick 8917) are also worthy recordings from Stern's "jazz years." *Words* (Lipstick 8928) features her as a lyricist-composer, while *Black Guitar* (LSR 419) has the debut of her singing. Her more recent recordings are mostly beyond the scope of this book.

**Website:** www.lenistern.com

## Mike Stern
*b. January 10, 1953, Boston, MA*

A powerful guitarist whose roots are in fusion, Mike Stern has developed in the years since into a very strong all-round player with an influential sound and style of his own. Stern started out on piano, switching his focus to guitar when he was 12. He grew up in Washington, DC, listening to blues, rock and soul, not discovering jazz until he was 18. After high school, he studied at the Berklee College of Music.

"Some of my musical influences are Jimi Hendrix, B.B. King, Albert King, Jeff Beck, plus lots of jazz guitarists like Wes Montgomery, Jim Hall and Joe Pass." He left Berklee when he was 22 to join Blood, Sweat and Tears. Stern was with Billy Cobham during 1979–80 and then gained recognition as an important part of Miles Davis' group during a period (1981–83) when the trumpeter was making his comeback. Davis nicknamed Stern "Fat

Time" and recorded a song with that title. Stern also worked with Jaco Pastorius' Word of Mouth band (1983–85), was back with Davis for a year, played with David Sanborn during the summer of 1986, and was a member of both the Michael Brecker band and Steps Ahead. Since that time, he has generally led his own groups, although during parts of 1989–92, he co-led a band with Bob Berg, and he also worked with the Brecker Brothers (1992) and the Yellowjackets (2007–08). Surprisingly, Mike Stern, who is married to Leni Stern, has yet to record with his wife.

"Over the last bunch of years, I've listened to more horn and piano players to try and get some of those ideas and phrasing in my guitar playing rather than other guitar players. I've been touring mainly with my own band, and I've been fortunate to do that for the last 20 years."

**Recommended CDs:** "I'm proud of all of my own 14 recordings as a leader because they represent me best. Some are more straight ahead (*Standards And Other Songs*, *Give And Take*), some are more electric (*Upside Downside*, *Odds And Evens*) and some have a few tracks of world music influences (*Voices*, *Who Let The Cats Out?*, and *Big Neighborhood*)." The guitarist's first CD, *Neesh*, was for the Japanese Trio label. He had a fine string of sets for Atlantic that could be considered funky fusion: *Upside Downside* (Atlantic 81656), *Time In Place* (Atlantic 81840), *Jigsaw* (Atlantic 82027), and *Odds Or Evens* (Atlantic 82297). *Standards And Other Songs* (Atlantic 82419) with Bob Berg and Randy Brecker was a bit of a departure and a surprise for listeners who had tended to think of Stern in only a certain way. *Is What It Is* (Atlantic 82571) and *Between The Lines* (Atlantic 82835) return to Stern's unclassifiable mixture of funk, fusion, rock and post-bop jazz, while *Give And Take* (Atlantic 83036) is a particularly rewarding set with bassist John Patitucci, drummer Jack DeJohnette, percussionist Don Alias and guests Michael Brecker (who steals the show on three numbers) and David Sanborn. *Play* (Atlantic 83219) teams Stern on some selections with Bill Frisell and John Scofield, while 2001's *Voices* (Atlantic 83483) uses wordless vocals on some selections. On *4 Generations Of Miles* (Chesky 238) Stern, along with tenor-saxophonist George Coleman, bassist Ron Carter and drummer Jimmy Cobb, performs songs associated with Miles Davis from a period long before Stern's stints with the trumpeter. *These Times* (Escapade 4911) is an all-originals session that includes altoist Kenny Garrett, bassist Richard Bona and banjoist Bela Fleck. *Who Let The Cats Out?* (Telarc 3115) and *Big Neighborhood* (Telarc 3157) find Mike Stern as eclectic as ever, featuring bassist-singer Richard Bona in a key role. His most recent recording is *All Over The Place* (Heads Up). Stern is also an important part of the Yellowjackets' *Lifecycle* (Telarc 3139) and is on Miles Davis' *Man With The Horn* (Sony 1234), *Star People* (Sony 9765) and (the best of the trio) *We Want Miles* (Sony 12356).

**Website:** www.mikestern.org

## Jimmy Stewart
*b. September 8, 1937, San Francisco, CA*

Throughout his career as a jazz and studio guitarist, Jimmy Stewart has shown that he can play in any style from Eddie Lang to bop, from Gabor Szabo to fusion. He was four when he started on piano, switching to guitar at eight. By the time he was 15, Stewart was working in Lake Tahoe as a professional guitarist. After studying at the College of San Mateo, the Chicago School of Music and Berklee, he was a guitarist, banjoist and singer for an agency called Fun Unlimited in 1957. Other important associations in Palm Springs were with Teddy Bunn, Earl Hines, and Ginny Simms (for whom he was the musical director). After serving in the military (during which time he played at variety shows), in 1960 Stewart moved back to San Francisco. He was the house guitarist at the Hungry I, worked in the studios, appeared on local television, and played shows with the San Francisco Civic Light Opera and the San Francisco Symphony.

During 1967–68, Stewart was an important member of the Gabor Szabo Quartet/Quintet. He often played acoustic classical guitar, which contrasted with Szabo's electric guitar. Stewart displayed his ability to sound just like Szabo at times, while other selections pushed Szabo toward straight-ahead jazz and Brazilian music. It was a classic band, the best regular unit that Szabo ever had.

After leaving Szabo and forming his own group, Stewart was the musical director for Lainie Kazan and Andy Williams, and performed with Rod Mc-Kuen. He also became one of the very first studio guitarists to be able to bring the sound of rock guitar to soundtracks and commercials, an important accomplishment. Stewart appeared on a countless number of recordings with pop artists, rock bands and famous names while primarily being known to his fellow musicians. His occasional jazz albums are rewarding but difficult to find.

In addition to his guitar playing (which includes playing classical guitar with symphony orchestras), Jimmy Stewart has made an impact as an educator. He wrote a column for many years in *Guitar Player*, has authored 27 books on guitar, and has composed classical works for electric guitar and solo violin.

**Recommended CDs:** The only Jimmy Stewart CD that is currently available, *Memorabilia* (J Bird 80079),

dates from 1977. It reissues most of his Blackhawk release *The Touch* plus previously unreleased material from the same period; with Gabor Szabo: *The Sorceror* (GRP/Impulse 211).

**LPs to Search For:** *Fire Flower* (Catalyst 7621).

**Website:** www.thecompletemusician.com

## Louis Stewart
*b. January 5, 1944, Waterford, Ireland*

Little known outside of Ireland and Europe, Louis Stewart is a superior bop-oriented guitarist who has a strong reputation among musicians. He grew up in Dublin, and after hearing Les Paul's music when he was 13, he took up the guitar. He was particularly inspired by hearing some of Barney Kessel's albums for the Contemporary label. Stewart began his career playing jazz locally, including with pianists Noel Kelehan and Jim Doherty and with saxophonist Jim Riley from Colorado, who operated a jazz club in Ireland (the Fox Inn).

Stewart gained some attention when he won a special jury prize at the 1968 Montreux Jazz Festival as the best soloist at that festival. He worked with Benny Goodman during 1969–72 and had long associations with both Tubby Hayes and Ronnie Scott. He began recording as a leader in the mid-1970s, performed with George Shearing's trio (with Niels Pedersen) during 1977–81, and was a member of Shearing's quintet during 1994–96. He also recorded with arranger Robert Farnon, including sets with Joe Williams and J.J. Johnson.

Louis Stewart, who is based out of Dublin, performs regularly throughout Europe and has made quite a few recordings (he lists *String Time, That Shearing Sound* and *Street Of Dreams* as his personal favorites), but since the Shearing days, he has rarely visited the United States.

**Recommended CDs:** *Louis The First* (Hawk Jazz 147), *Baubles, Bangles And Beads* (Wave 12), *Milesian Source* (Pye 18555), the unaccompanied *Out On His Own* (Jardis 9612), *Alone Together* (Livia 5), *Acoustic Guitar Duets* (Jardis 9613) with Martin Taylor, *Good News* (Villa 001), *String Time* (Villa 003), *Winter Song* (Jardis 9005), *In A Mellow Tone* (Jardis 9206), *Featuring Michael Moore* (Cecilia 9603), *Joycenotes* (Villa 004), *Overdrive* (Hep 2057), *I Wished On The Moon* (Jardis 20027), *Street Of Dreams* (Jardis 20243), *Core Business* (Villa 006), *Pardoxical Intervention* (Villa 007), *You've Changed* (Desert Island Jazz 0001); with George Shearing: *That Shearing Sound* (Telarc 83375).

**Website:** www.louisstewart.net

# Rick Stone
*b. August 13, 1955, Fairview Park, OH*

A solid bop-based guitarist, Rick Stone is reliable and always swings. After seeing a friend play guitar at a birthday party in 1963, the eight-year-old Stone convinced his mother to get him an electric guitar. "I played a lot of different styles at first, including country music, TV theme songs and rock. But around 1968–69, I started being drawn to blues guitar and listened to B.B. King. The thing that really drew me to jazz was a live broadcast of Sonny Stitt at the Smiling Dog Saloon in Cleveland in 1974. I think that was my first taste of bebop, and after hearing him on the radio, I went down there to hear for myself. It was definitely the turning point."

Prior to that, Rick Stone had played in a few blues-rock bands while in high school and, after his graduation, a psychedelic folk-rock band. He attended Cuyahoga Community College (1975–77) and had his first jazz gig during 1977–78, when he played every Sunday night at Genesis Vegetarian Restaurant in Cleveland with flutist Tom Moore's Compost. Stone attended Berklee (1978–80) and had opportunities to play duets with guitarist-violinist Alex Mitchell and guitarists Frank Sikora and Bruce Arnold. After finishing school in 1980, Stone moved back to Cleveland and played commercial gigs for a couple of years, saving his money. In 1982, he moved to New York and seriously started his jazz career.

Stone studied with Barry Harris (1982–87), Ted Dunbar, Jimmy Heath, Donald Byrd and Hal Galper, later earning a masters from Queens College in 1991. Since relocating to New York, Stone has sat in with Tommy Flanagan, Art Blakey and Lionel Hampton, recorded his debut LP in 1984, played with the Jimmy Robinson All Stars (1986–88), led his own all-star group that featured Junior Cook, performed many solo and duo concerts (including with Roni Ben-Hur, Peter Bernstein, Michael Howell, and Peter Leitch), and headed trios and quartets. He also worked with Irene Reid during 1998–2001 and swing clarinetist Sol Yaged (2002–05).

Rick Stone, who teaches at Hofstra University and Jazzmobile, is working on an instructional video. "I'm also currently archiving and digitizing tons of material that was recorded on live gigs and in my recording studio over the years and considering whether some of this material should be released or revisited. I'd like to see this stuff out there for people to enjoy."

**Recommended CDs:** Rick Stone is in excellent form on *Far East* (Jazzand 002), which also features Kenny Barron; *Samba De Novembro* (Jazzand 004); and *Fractals* (Jazzand 005). He is also well showcased on drummer Al Ashley's *These Are Them* (Jazzand 001), which also includes Dave Liebman.

**LP to Search For:** Stone's debut recording, *Blues For Nobody* (Jazzanne 001), has not been reissued yet.

**Website:** www.rickstone.com

# Jonathan Stout
*b. July 14, 1981, Northridge, CA*

An excellent swing electric guitarist inspired by Charlie Christian and other guitarists of the late 1930s/early '40s, Jonathan Stout leads the Campus Five and his own big band in the Los Angeles area, often performing at swing dances. Stout got his first guitar when he was 11. Although he heard some jazz, it was in 1996, when he was 15, that he became very interested in the music. "Our Spanish teacher organized swing dancing lessons as an extracurricular activity. I was hooked instantly. I went out and got some of the standard bearers of mainstream jazz: *Kind Of Blue*, some Cannonball Adderley and Coltrane. After that, I found Grant Green and Kenny Burrell and got hooked on the funky, hard-bop Blue Note sound."

Stout had a rock band throughout his school years. But after becoming a swing dancer, he also became involved in playing swing. "My first swing guitar lesson was with John Reynolds. I just watched in awe, and then stole as much as I could! Drummers Josh Collazo and Hal Smith were both very important, because it was through playing with them that I learned about real swing rhythm sections and the authentic swing feel—and not the straight-ahead jazz that is passed off everywhere as swing. I played with Josh in his New Orleans jazz band, the Feetwarmers. From there, I started my band, the Campus Five." He attended USC during 1999–2004.

Stout has led the Campus Five since 2002, he formed the Jonathan Stout Orchestra in 2004, and he recently joined the Bonebrake Syncopators. Stout has also guested with Mora's Modern Rhythmists, the Bill Elliot Swing Orchestra, Jim Ziegler's

**Dave Stryker**

Swingsations, Johnny Crawford, and steel guitarist Jeremy Wakefield. "Camp Hollywood, which is our singer Hilary Alexander's swing dance event, is probably the gig I look forward to most all year."

Jonathan Stout is doing his best to bring back swing. "I consider the straight-ahead-ification of traditional jazz to be a great tragedy. I've done lectures with the band about how the swing beat differs from straight-ahead jazz and from the two-beat feels that came before it. So many people are surprised by how different they really are. There's an energy and vitality to swing music—a joy that cannot be contained. The fact that I most often play for dancers is a special joy as well. I'm one of them, and when they are happy, I know I'm making music right."

**Recommended CDs:** *Jammin' The Blues* (Watch Out Now 001), *Crazy Rhythm* (Watch Out Now 002), and *Moppin' And Boppin'* (Watch Out Now 003) each feature Jonathan Stout's Campus Five (which is actually a two-horn sextet) and singer Hilary Alexander in excellent form, sounding very much as if it was 1940. Stout's big band has not thus far recorded.

**Website:** www.campusfive.com

## Dave Stryker
*b. March 30, 1957, Omaha, NE*

A versatile guitarist, Dave Stryker is perhaps best known today as co-leader with altoist Steve Slagle of the Stryker/Slagle Band. "I started playing guitar at age ten after hearing the Beatles on my older sister's record player. I was a pretty good rock player around Omaha. One day I went to a jam session at the Musicians' Union where some of the local jazz guys were playing tunes like Horace Silver's 'Song For My Father.' I sat in, and one of the older black guys came up and told me, 'You can't be playing those rock licks on this music.' The next day I went to the local record store, took home John Coltrane's *My Favorite Things* and George Benson's *Beyond The Blue Horizon*, and got hooked."

Stryker was playing gigs in Omaha at 13. In 1978, he moved to Los Angeles, learned from guitarist Billy Rogers (who was also from Omaha), sat in with organ groups, and met Jack McDuff at the short-lived Jimmy Smith's Supper Club. He moved to New York in 1980, freelanced on the local scene, and toured with McDuff during 1984–85 before beginning a ten-year association with Stanley Turrentine. "I was lucky to get the experience of playing with some of the masters of this music. Jack McDuff and Stanley Turrentine played with a lot of heart, soul and feeling. I hope some of that feeling comes through in my music as well and that it communicates with people and makes them feel good."

Dave Stryker started his adventurous post-bop group with Steve Slagle in 1987, has led a trio with organist Jared Gold and drummer Tony Reedus since 2004, heads the Blue to the Bone Band, and has also worked with Kevin Mahogany, Eliane Elias, Javon Jackson, Andy LaVerne and Trio Mundo.

**Recommended CDs:** Dave Stryker has led quite a few albums of his own. These include his debut, *First Strike* (for the Japanese label Someday), and 16 CDs for Steeplechase: *Strikezone* (Steeplechase 31277), *Passage* (Steeplechase 31330), *Blue Degrees* (Steeplechase 31315), *Full Moon* (Steeplechase 31345), *Stardust* (Steeplechase 31362), *Nomad* (Steeplechase 31371), *The Greeting* (Steeplechase 31387), *Blue To The Bone* (Steeplechase 31400), *Big Room* (Steeplechase 31426), *All The Way* (Steeplechase 31455), *Blue To The Bone II* (Steeplechase 31465), *Shades Of Miles* (Steeplechase 31480), *Changing Times* (Steeplechase 31510), *Blue To The Bone III* (Steeplechase 31524), *Shades Beyond* (Steeplechase 31559), *Strike Up The Band* (Steeplechase 31637), and *Blue Strike* (Steeplechase 31729). Asked to pick which ones he considers the most rewarding, Stryker named *Blue To The Bone*, *All The Way* and *Shades Of Miles*. In more recent times, he has recorded *Big City* (Mel Bay 06562); *The Chaser* (Mel Bay 10212), which is another of his personal favorites; *Guitar On Top* (Strikezone 8805), which is a reissue of a 1991 album for the Ken label; *Six String Santa* (Strikezone 8806); *Open Road* (Strikezone 8803); *Dave Stryker Quartet Plays Jobim* (Strikezone 8801); *Ballads* (Strikezone 8800) and *Live In Helsinki* (StrikeZone 8802). With the Stryker/Slagel Band, he is heard in top form on *Live At The Jazz Standard* (Zoho 200509), *Latest Outlook* (Zoho 200703), and *Keeper* (Panorama 400).

**Website:** www.davestryker.com

## Rory Stuart
*b. January 9, 1956, New York, NY*

A fine post-bop guitarist and educator, Rory Stuart was interested in jazz from an early age. "In seventh grade, a teacher exposed our class to Charlie Parker and John Coltrane. I did a report on Rahsaan Roland

Kirk in that class, and Rahsaan graciously played an afternoon set for us at the Village Vanguard, also answering our questions. Next year, the school got Jaki Byard to come and teach music to our class once a week. By ninth grade, I was buying records by Coltrane, Monk, and others. My mother got a guitar in which we shared ownership when I was in junior high. We took a few lessons together, and that got me started. By the end of tenth grade, I began to take classical guitar lessons with Leonid Bolotine, who I studied with for two years. I got an electric guitar, taught myself to play jazz that summer, and the next year at Stanford University, where I was fortunate to meet Tuck Andress, I decided to devote myself seriously to music."

Stuart lived in Boulder, Colorado for seven years, dedicating himself to working on the guitar. He played with Billy Tolles, organist Al "Hammond" Moore, Jerry Granelli's group Visions, Joe Keel's Action Orchestra, Carol Kaye, and in Parameters. During a few months spent in Paris, he had the opportunity to play with Steve Potts and Oliver Johnson, and he also went on the road with Brother Jack McDuff. In 1981, Stuart moved to New York, where he has worked with a wide assortment of top musicians in a variety of styles, including Charlie Rouse, Charles Earland, Vinny Golia, Michael Cochrane, Steve Nelson, Dr. Lonnie Smith, Ernie Krivda, Larry Coryell, Jeanie Bryson, Reggie Workman, Bill Doggett, Mike Richmond, Ronnie Burrage, Bill Saxton, the Errol Parker Tentet, Michael Vlatkovich, Joe Bonner, Billy Harper, Cecil Bridgewater, George Garzone, Sheila Jordan and others. Stuart has also performed in Europe with Steve Coleman's band, which at the time included Geri Allen, Graham Haynes, and Cassandra Wilson.

Rory Stuart put together his quartet in 1982, which originally consisted of Keith Copeland, Calvin Hill and Armen Donelian; it continues to this day. He has also co-led the Cadence All-Stars, had a longtime duo with baritonist Glenn Wilson, and recently has led two quartets with either John Ellis or Mark Shim on saxophones. In addition, he has taught at the New School for the past 15 years. For the future his goal is to "take the music to new places, explore some of the little-explored rhythmic and harmonic possibilities, and to advance artistically and creatively."

**Recommended CDs:** *Nightwork* (Cadence 1016), *Hurricane* (Sunnyside 1021), *Bittersweet* (Sunnyside 1057) with Glenn Wilson, *Lee's Keys Please* (Timeless 284) with the Cadence All-Stars, *So Rise Up* (Smart Cat Music 1001).

**Website:** www.rorystuart.com

## Monnette Sudler
*b. June 5, 1952, Philadelphia, PA*

Monnette Sudler has worked with such a diverse variety of major artists that it is surprising that she is not better known outside of her native Philadelphia. "My great-uncle Nathan introduced me to jazz. He played our baby grand piano when visiting our home. I would sit on the floor listening, wishing I could play like him. I started playing guitar at the age of 15 and took lessons with Carol Friedman at the Wharton Center in North Philadelphia." She also learned to play drums, plays a bit of piano, sings, and is a skilled arranger-composer and a poet.

One of Sudler's earliest musical jobs was with the Sounds of Liberation, a Philadelphia group led by vibraphonist Khan Jamal. She went to Berklee in the early 1970s, a decade  later attended Temple University's Ester Boyer College of Music and, after much time off, graduated in 2000 with a BA in music.

Since the mid-1970s, she has worked with many groups, including Hugh Masekela, the Change of the Century Orchestra (which included Leon Thomas and Odeon Pope), the Sam Rivers Big Band, Sunny Murray's Untouchable Factor with David Murray, Dameronia, Grover Washington Jr. (who played in her band), Kenny Barron, Cedar Walton, Reggie Workman, Trudy Pitts, Shirley Scott, Don Pullen, Hamiet Bluiett, Dave Holland, Cecil McBee, Arthur Blythe, Archie Shepp, Joseph Jarman, Freddie Hubbard, Sonny Fortune and Steve Turre. An adventurous guitarist, Sudler is versatile and fits easily into a variety of settings while displaying her own musical personality.

In recent times, she has worked with youth organizations, has plans to publish a music book on improvisation, and has led Quartet JAZZ and Monnette Sudler's Blues Express. "I have been very fortunate to have associated with diverse musicians who have in many ways changed and/or influenced the culture during their time. My music is a reflection of my experiences and personal ideas."

**Recommended CDs:** *Time For A Change* (Steeplechase 31062), *Brighter Days For You* (Steeplechase 31087), *Live In Europe* (Steeplechase 31102), *Other Side Of The Gemini* (Hardly 002), *Just One Kiss* (MSM 02), *Tenderly* (MSM 05), *Let The Rhythm*

*Take You* (Phillyinde), *Meeting Of The Spirits* (Phillyjazz), *Where Have All The Legends Gone?* (Heavenly Sweetness 018).

**Website:** www.monnettesudlermusic.com

## Nelson Symonds

b. September 24, 1933, Hammonds Plains, Nova Scotia, Canada; d. October 11, 2008, Montreal, Quebec, Canada

In some ways, Nelson Symonds was the Canadian Peck Kelley, a legendary performer who barely recorded, turning down opportunities that would have given him fame. Symonds grew up on a farm, teaching himself banjo at nine and guitar two years later. He never learned to read music. Symonds worked locally with his cousins Ivan and Leo Symonds, both of whom also played guitar. In 1951, he moved to Sudbury, Ontario, where he played with an uncle who was a saxophonist. Symonds spent a few years on the road, including three with a carnival band that toured throughout Canada and the US. After moving to Montreal in 1958, he became a major part of the local scene and later claimed that he had played at every local nightclub, often as part of the house band.

Top American jazz musicians went out of their way to see Nelson Symonds perform (including Miles Davis, Wes Montgomery and B.B. King), and he had opportunities to play with such visitors as Rahsaan Roland Kirk, Art Farmer, Sonny Red, Blue Mitchell, George Coleman, Jimmy Heath, Booker Ervin, Thad Jones, Pepper Adams, Benny Golson, Jack McDuff, Jackie McLean, Stanley Turrentine, Ray Charles and Sarah Vaughan. John Coltrane was one of several who offered him a job with his group, but Symonds preferred to stay home.

Instead, Nelson Symonds, who had his own conception of the Charlie Christian style (playing with a more intense sound), worked with the Stablemates, Dougie Richardson, the Montreal All-Stars (1985), the Vic Vogel Big Band (1988) and his own groups, especially duos and trios with bassist Charlie Biddle and occasionally drummer Norman Marshall Villeneuve. Amazingly, he made no appearances on records until 1990 and only led one album as a leader. After undergoing a quadruple bypass operation in 1996, he was forced into retirement, passing away a dozen years later from a heart attack.

**Recommended CDs:** *Getting Personal* (Justin Time 44) from 1992 was Nelson Symonds' only recording as a leader. Symonds can also be heard as a featured sideman with the Bernard Primeau Jazz Ensemble on *Reunion* (Amplitude 4019) and with Dave Turner on *Live* (Unidisc 3001) and *Pulse Brothers* (Unidisc 3006).

## Gabor Szabo

b. March 8, 1936, Budapest, Hungary; d. February 26, 1982, Budapest, Hungary

Gabor Szabo was one of the first guitarists to emerge after Charlie Christian who did not sound at all like him. He freely infused his jazz improvisations with the influences of Hungarian folk music while keeping his music open to rock and pop elements. While not all of Szabo's recordings are essential, he always had a unique voice on his instrument.

Szabo was given his first guitar by his father for Christmas when he was 14. Other than one free lesson, he was self-taught. Szabo learned about jazz by listening to Willis Conover's radio show on the Voice of America. He played with local groups for a few years and made one recording session (with Myrna Bell) in his native country. In November 1956, he fled Hungary with two friends, crossing over the Hungarian border into Austria, taking his guitar as his only possession. Over time, he made it to the United States. He played a bit with his own group in Los Angeles (the Three Strings) but also worked as a janitor, saving his money to go to Berklee. He was successful and attended Berklee during 1958–60.

The guitarist was part of the Newport International Jazz Band that played and recorded at the 1958 Newport Jazz Festival. He is also on two albums recorded by students at Berklee, *Jazz In The Classroom Vol. II* and *Vol. IV*. However, when money ran low, he was forced to drop out, returning to Los Angeles, where he worked a day job. The biggest break of his career was becoming a member of the Chico Hamilton Quintet, playing regularly with the drummer during 1961–65. The band, with Charles Lloyd on tenor and flute through 1963 and usually either George Bohanon or Garnett Brown on trombone, was a forward-looking hard-bop group that, with its lack of a piano, gave Szabo a lot of space in which to set moods during ensembles and solo. In 1965, he left Hamilton to become a member of the Charles Lloyd Quartet, also playing regularly with Gary McFarland. The following year, he began recording regularly as a leader, cutting *Spellbinder*, which mixed together his originals, standards and pop tunes. His *Jazz Raga* displayed his interest in Indian music, and it found him overdubbing his own sitar playing, although he was actually able to achieve a sitar-like drone sound on his own guitar.

During 1967–68, Szabo had his finest group: a quintet with fellow guitarist Jimmy Stewart (the interplay between the two guitarists was memorable), bassist Louis Kabok (also from Hungary), percussionist Hal Gordon and a few different drummers. Their work, featured on *The Sorceror* and *More*

*Sorcery*, was full of fire and creativity and was arguably the high point of Szabo's career.

But after that group ended, Szabo's recordings were often lightweight, poppish and not particularly inventive beyond his sound. He formed the Skye Recording Company with Cal Tjader and Gary McFarland, but its releases tended to be pretty commercial and dated. He teamed up with Lena Horne in 1969 for the popular *Lena & Gabor* album. Szabo's 1970 group featured vibraphonist Lynn Blessing and keyboardist Richard Thompson and was versatile enough to play both rock and jazz. However, that band did not last long, and he spent much of the rest of his career freelancing in projects that varied in quality.

Szabo recorded more rewarding dates for CTI, including *Mizrab* and Paul Desmond's *Skylark*. In 1974, he made his first visit to Hungary in 18 years. But back in the US, many of his other recordings were often forgettable and did not sell very well. However, he remained a major name who was always an attraction at festivals.

Gabor Szabo died in 1982 during a visit to Hungary from liver and kidney ailments. He was just 45.

**Recommended CDs:** *Gypsy '66* (Impulse 19129), *Spellbinder* (Impulse 19130); *Jazz Raga* (Light in the Attic 053); *The Sorceror* (GRP/Impulse 211); *Bacchanal/1969* (El 37); *High Contrast* (Verve 065406) with Bobby Womack, which has the original version of "Breezin'"; *Lena & Gabor* (El 42), *Macho* (CTI 512801); *In Stockholm* (Four Leaf Clover 2001/2), which teams Szabo with fusion guitarist Jan Schaffer; with Chico Hamilton: *Man From Two Worlds* (GRP/Impulse 127); with Charles Lloyd: *Of Course, Of Course* (Mosaic Select 1006); with Paul Desmond: *Skylark* (Sony/CTI 51293222).

**LPs to Search For:** *More Sorcery* (Impulse 9167), *Mizrab* (CTI 6026), *Rambler* (CTI 6035).

## Martin Taylor
*b. October 20, 1956, Collins Meadow, England*

Best known in the United States for his long period playing with Stéphane Grappelli, Martin Taylor is very highly rated by his fellow guitarists, particularly for his solo playing. His father was a bassist, and after hearing his dad's Django Reinhardt records, he started playing the guitar when he was four, being self-taught. His first gig was when he was eight, playing a dance with his father's band. Taylor worked regularly with his father until he was 15, leaving school to go on the road with a Scottish band.

Taylor first went to the US when he was 17. Back in London, he worked with guitarist Ike Isaacs, whom he considers his greatest influence on guitar. He also worked with bassist Peter Ind and made his recording debut on Ind's Wave label in 1978. During 1979–90, Taylor was a regular member of Stéphane Grappelli's group, touring the world, recording over 20 albums with the violinist, and playing with him on an occasional basis after leaving his band. He has also had opportunities to work with such fellow guitarists as Chet Atkins, Barney Kessel, Herb Ellis, Tal Farlow, and Joe Pass.

His 1992 album *Artistry* launched Taylor's career as an unaccompanied guitar soloist who is on the level of Joe Pass. In 1994, Taylor formed Spirit of Django, a group that has had several reunions since and pays tribute to Django Reinhardt. In addition to regular tours and recording, Taylor writes music for TV and film, penned *Autobiography Of A Traveling Musician* (Sanctuary Publishing), and has been very successful as an online educator with his Martin Taylor Fingerstyle Guitar School (www.martintaylorguitar.com).

**Recommended CDs:** *Taylor Made* (Wave 17); *Triple Libra* (Wave 24); *Sketches: A Tribute To Art Tatum* (P3 Music 70014); *Buddy DeFranco Meets Martin Taylor* (Hep 2030); *Sarabanda* (Gaia 139018); *Don't Fret* (Linn 014); *Change Of Heart* (Linn 016); *Artistry* (Linn 020); *Spirit Of Django* (Linn 030); *Portraits* (Linn 048); *Years Apart* (Linn 058); *Kiss & Tell* (Sony 62210); *Two's Company* (Linn 081); *I'm Beginning To See The Light* (Acoustic Disc 36) with Dave Grisman; *Gypsy* (Linn 090); *In Concert* (Milestone 9306), which is unaccompanied; *Nitelife* (Sony 85909); *Solo* (Sony/BMG 160); *The Valley* (The Guitar Label 11); *Gypsy Journey* (P3 Music 7); *Freternity* (The Guitar Label 16); *Double Standards* (P3 Music 319); *Celebrating Grappelli* (Linn 094); *Spirit Of Django: Last Train To Hauteville* (The Guitar Label 23); *Two For The Road* (Woodville 133), a set of duets with clarinetist Alan Barnes; with Stéphane Grappelli: *Vintage 1981* (Concord 4169), *Reunion* (Linn 022).

**Website:** www.martintaylor.com

## Thomas Tedesco
*b. February 2, 1943, Los Angeles, CA*

An adventurous guitarist best known on the West Coast, Thomas Tedesco bears no relation to studio guitarist Tommy Tedesco. Although he wanted to play guitar as early as seven years old,

Tedesco, who grew up in Omaha, Nebraska, did not get to start until he was in his late teens and living on his own. "I knew I would become a professional guitarist just days after I had purchased a guitar and started playing. It changed my life, gave me focus and direction. When I first started playing guitar in Omaha, I was listening to Calvin Keys, Billy Rogers and Don Archer (The Admiral), three wonderful guitarists who lived and played in the city. During 1964–67, there were many wonderful players living in Omaha who I would hang out with. And since Omaha was on the chitlin' circuit, I saw Miles Davis, George Benson, Grant Green, Jimmy Smith, Groove Holmes, Bill Evans, and many others. Ornette Coleman and Cecil Taylor had an influence on me as well. Interestingly, I went from the blues and Wes Montgomery to Ornette, and then filled in with swing, bop and hard bop."

After moving to Los Angeles, Tedesco became part of the local jazz scene. "An early gig for me was when I played at the Azz Izz Jazz Tea House in Venice during 1973–74. It was run by saxophonist Billy Harris and his wife, Carolyn (Cookie). That is where I met and established working relationships with many fine jazz players, including Horace Tapscott, John Carter, Roberto Miranda, Nate Morgan, and Bobby Bradford. I also had the opportunity to play with Frank Morgan, Ray Draper, Blue Mitchell, Arthur Blythe, and James Newton, to name a few. In Venice during the 1970s, there were always six to eight jazz clubs that I worked in. Some were within walking distance from where I lived, a block and half from the beach." He was a member of Bobby Bradford's quartet during 1975–78. Other associations included Roberto Miranda (starting in 1973), Garnett Brown and Henry "The Skipper" Franklin (from 1986). He played duets with Richard Aldorasi on tabla on an occasional basis during 1975–78, accompanied poets, and performed at solo concerts. Tedesco also taught guitar, theory and improvisation classes in the California prison system through Arts in Correction.

Thomas Tedesco was very active as a performer and educator up until 2009, when tendonitis forced his temporary retirement from public playing. "I've composed nine tunes for a future CD, and I have been teaching jazz guitar privately and at two elementary schools. The future holds for me a healed hand, many many gigs, and more rewarding teaching experiences. I also want to write a second jazz guitar instruction book to follow my first book, *Improvisational Concept For The Jazz Guitar*, which was published in 2002."

**Recommended CDs:** 1983's *Thomas Tedesco And Ocean* (Clarion Jazz 80508) and *Don't Ever Be Afraid To Be Scared* (Nine Winds 219) from 1999 are both fine sets that stretch the mainstream of jazz.

The former date has Tedesco leading a quintet with Bobby Bradford and Roberto Miranda, while the Nine Winds set has a group with trombonist Garnett Brown and pianist William Henderson. Most of the music on both CDs was written by Tedesco and ranges from hard bop to post-bop.

**Website:** www.thomastedesco.us

## Tommy Tedesco
*b. July 3, 1930, Niagara Falls, NY; d. November 27, 1997, Northridge, CA*

Tommy Tedesco has often been called "the most recorded guitarist in history." Jazz was only a small part of his career, but judging by the content of his solo albums, it was one of his true loves. A student of the guitar who combined natural ability with the desire to master his instrument, Tommy Tedesco seemed to spend most of his life in the studios. While attending Niagara University, he dropped out to tour with Ralph Marterie's orchestra for a year (1952–53), settling in Los Angeles. After entering the jazz scene, he became an extremely busy studio musician. Tedesco recorded constantly from the late 1950s until a 1992 stroke ended his career. In addition to his guitar playing, he played mandolin, ukulele, sitar and reportedly 28 other stringed instruments. He was on a countless number of pop, rock and vocal records in addition to recording for soundtracks of films and television shows. Tedesco was considered part of a group of constantly busy session musicians in Los Angeles who were dubbed "the Wrecking Crew."

A year after his career ended, Tommy Tedesco published his autobiography, *Confessions Of A Guitar Player.*

**Recommended CDs:** Although he spent most of his life playing music other than jazz, Tommy Tedesco's own solo albums, mostly recorded during 1978–86 for Discovery and its subsidiary Trend, are all jazz-oriented. *My Desiree* (Discovery 70959) is a quintet set, while *Carnival Time* (Discovery 70534) has Tedesco interacting with guitarists Jon Kurnick and Jimmy Bruno. *Hollywood Gypsy* (Discovery 70928) features Tedesco in a trio with Bruno and bassist John Leitham. One of Tommy Tedesco's last projects was recording *Roumanis' Jazz Rhapsody For Guitar & Orchestra* (Capri 75002), which really displays the depth and wide range of his playing.

**LPs to Search For:** Tommy Tedesco's Discovery and Trend CDs will most likely be difficult to find, but they will be easier to find than such worthy LPs as *When Do We Start* (Discovery 789), *Autumn* (Trend 514), and *Alone At Last* (Trend 517), the latter a set of unaccompanied solos.

# Marlina Teich

*b. December 23, 1953, Bayonne, NJ*

An important gui-tarist based in San Francisco who also sings, Marlina Teich grew up in New Jersey. "My grandmother gave me a ukulele when I was seven. I taught myself and gradu-ated to the guitar at nine. Louis Armstrong and Al Jolson were always playing in my house, along with Frank Sinatra. I loved any movie that had Louis Armstrong in it, such as *The Five Pennies*, the story of Red Nichols. After playing rock, funk and blues guitar, the progression to jazz seemed natural to me, particularly after hearing Miles, Monk and Wes Montgomery."

Teich moved to San Francisco when she was in her early twenties. She earned a teaching credential and taught in public schools for eleven years but always played music. "When I first moved to San Francisco, I found my mentor in Junius Simmons, who is my main inspiration on guitar. He was the guitarist in the 1950s and 1960s from the Fillmore District of San Francisco who played with Dexter Gordon, Dizzy Gillespie, Sonny Stitt, and others. In the '80s, we played some great private parties together as a duo all around San Francisco, and we still work together occasionally." She also co-led an all female band with saxophonist Yolanda Nichols, played guitar and bass with Richie Cole when he toured California, and worked with former members of the Charlie Barnet Orchestra in Bob Bissell's Swingin' Saxes in addition to playing with Mel Martin, Jules Broussard, Donald Bailey and other Bay area musicians.

In recent times, she has led a quintet in clubs and recorded *My Love Waits There*, which features her playing and arranging. Marlina Teich, who taught guitar at San Quentin Prison and spent a year tour-ing prisons in California, founded and works with the very worthy nonprofit organization Jazzheimers (www.marlinateich.com), which brings live jazz to Alzheimer's patients.

"My heart is in blues-based jazz. There is a certain feeling I get from blues-based music where I can feel relaxed and excited simultaneously. Playing with other musicians and creating an improvised event, feeding off each other's rhythm and harmony, is one of the most joyful feelings one could ever imagine."

**Recommended CDs:** Marlina Teich's 2009 recording *My Love Waits There*, which is available through her website, has her versions of standards, featuring her guitar playing, arrangements and occasional vocals.

**Website:** www.marlinateich.com

# Sister Rosetta Tharpe

*(Rosetta Nubin)*
*b. March 20, 1915, Cotton Plant, AR; d. October 9, 1973, Philadelphia, PA*

One of the top jazz guitarists of the early 1940s, Sister Rosetta Tharpe spent several years torn between play-ing secular music and gospel. While she ultimately decided on the latter, she was never ashamed of her roots in jazz, and even in later years, her guitar play-ing reflected her background in swing.

Her mother was a gospel performer, and Rosetta began her career as a singing evangelist. When she was six, she was already considered a fine guitarist. Her family moved to Chicago at that time, and she was influenced by many of the jazz performers she heard in the 1920s and '30s.

In 1938, Tharpe made her first recordings and gained a great deal of attention when she was fea-tured at John Hammond's From Spirituals to Swing concert at Carnegie Hall. During 1940–43, she starred with Lucky Millinder's orchestra as both a singer and a guitar soloist. Some of her material crossed over into religion, although those perfor-mances tended to be rollicking (including "Rock Me," "That's All," "This Train," "Rock Daniel" and "Shout Sister Shout"). A few of the numbers, particu-larly "I Want A Tall Skinny Papa," were definitely secular. In most cases, she also contributed hot guitar solos that, although acoustic, were full of electricity.

It could certainly be argued that, long before Ray Charles, Sister Rosetta Tharpe was the first to infuse secular music with the intensity and passion of gos-pel. However, it did not last long, for in 1943, she returned to gospel, soon having hits with "Strange Things Happening Every Day" and "Up Above My Head." During the next 25 years, she often worked as a solo performer, accompanying herself on electric guitar, or with small swinging combos, including the Sammy Price Trio. A 1957 tour of England had her joined by Chris Barber's flexible trad band. Her guitar playing by then was bridging the gap between swing and rock 'n' roll, always filled with enthusiasm and impressive musicianship.

Sister Rosetta Tharpe suffered a major stroke in 1970 but found that, although talking was difficult, she could still sing quite well. She stayed active until the end, carving out her own unique place in music history.

**Recommended CDs:** All of Sister Rosetta Tharpe's ear-ly recordings are on *1938–1941* (Document 5334) and *1942–1944* (Document 5335), including her first solo dates, her performances with Millinder's band (studio sides, radio appearances and V-Discs), "This Train" with Louis Jordan's Tympany Five, and the beginning of her return to gospel. A pair of exciting concert performances, *Live in 1960* (Southland 1007) and 1966's *Live At The Hot Club De France* (Milan 35624), contain plenty of fine guitar playing along with her spirited vocals.

## Toots Thielemans
*(Jean-Baptiste Frédéric Isidor Baron Thielemans)*
b. April 29, 1922, Brussels, Belgium

World famous as the greatest jazz harmonica player ever and the expert whistler who composed "Bluesette," Toots Thielemans was a highly rated guitarist in the 1950s, although he has gradually de-emphasized that instrument ever since. Thielemans began on the accordion when he was three, switching to guitar a few years later. While he started playing the harmonica for the fun of it as early as 1939, Thielemans was primarily known as a Django Reinhardt–inspired guitarist during the World War II years. He adapted easily to bebop in the mid-1940s, visiting the United States for the first time in 1947. At the 1949 Paris Jazz Festival, he was part of a jam session that included both Charlie Parker and Sidney Bechet. When Benny Goodman toured Europe in 1950, Thielemans was his guitarist. During that period, he made his recording debut with Zoot Sims.

In 1952, Thielemans moved to the United States. He worked in Philadelphia with a Charlie Parker all-star group and also gigged with Miles Davis and Dinah Washington. During 1953–59, he was a member of the George Shearing Quintet as a guitarist, occasionally getting a spot on harmonica. However, his two albums as a leader in the mid-1950s (*The Sound* and *Man Bites Harmonica*) emphasized his harmonica playing, and that would be his future direction. He continued playing guitar regularly in the 1960s and '70s ("Bluesette" in 1962 featured unison playing by his guitar and whistling), but as a greatly in-demand studio musician and jazz performer, his harmonica playing was more unique than his fine guitar solos. It was in the role of a harmonica virtuoso that he performed on a full album with Bill Evans; with such notables as Ella Fitzgerald, Elis Regina, Quincy Jones, Oscar Peterson, Jaco Pastorius, Paul Simon, and Billy Joel; and on soundtracks and television commercials.

Toots Thielemans, who turned 90 in 2012, has slowed down quite a bit during the past decade, but he still makes occasional appearances.

**Recommended CDs:** As a guitarist, Toots Thielemans can be heard with George Shearing and Dakota Staton on *In The Night* (Capitol 42311) and with Dizzy Gillespie in an odd trumpet-guitar-drums trio that includes drummer Bernard Purdie on *Digital At Montreux, 1980* (Original Jazz Classics 882).

**LPs to Search For:** *The Whistler And His Guitar* (ABC 482) from 1962 mostly has Toots whistling along with his guitar; it includes the original version of "Bluesette."

**Website:** www.tootsthielemans.com

## René Thomas
b. February 25, 1927, Liège, Belgium; d. January 3, 1975, Santander, Spain

René Thomas was one of the top European guitarists to emerge after World War II. He mastered bop early on and was open to freer and more unpredictable sounds as his career evolved. Many of today's guitarists have expressed admiration for his playing.

Thomas was mostly self-taught. In the late 1940s, he played with Bobby Jaspar and Jacques Pelzer in the Bop Shots, which was considered Belgium's first bebop group. In the early 1950s, he moved to Paris. Influenced by Jimmy Raney and Django Reinhardt, Thomas had a cool tone and an understated style that became more personal as he evolved. He worked with the major European musicians and with Chet Baker in 1955. During 1956–62, Thomas lived in Montreal. Sonny Rollins was impressed with his playing and used him on his recording *Sonny Rollins And The Big Brass*. Thomas also worked with Stan Getz, Toshiko Akiyoshi, Jackie McLean and even Miles Davis during this period.

After moving back to Europe in 1962, he gigged with Kenny Clarke, Lou Bennett, Han Bennink, Bobby Jaspar, Lucky Thompson, Sonny Criss and Eddy Louiss, among others. As a member of Stan Getz's band in Europe during 1969–72, Thomas (along with Louiss) really pushed Getz to stretch himself into freer territory.

René Thomas died of a heart attack while on tour with Lou Bennett in Spain in 1975. He was just 47.

**Recommended CDs:** René Thomas' most famous recording is *Guitar Groove* (Original Jazz Classics 1725), a 1960 album in which Thomas performs three originals by tenor-saxophonist J.R. Monterose and four standards in a group that includes Monterose and pianist Hod O'Brien. High point is the guitarist's six-minute feature on a trio rendition of "How Long Has This Been Going On." Other worthy sets include *Jazz In Paris: The Real Cat* (Verve 549400), which has the music from a pair of 1955–56 albums, *Meeting Mr. Thomas* (Universal 549812), and an encounter with altoist Pony Poindexter on *Blue Note Paris 1964* (Royal 512).

*Guitaristic* (Five Four 22), which has highlights from four albums dating from 1954–56 (three dates by Thomas and one led by Henri Renaud), is an excellent introduction to his playing along with *Guitar Groove*, while Stan Getz's *Dynasty* (Verve 1240802) is quite adventurous.

## Zvonimir Tot
*b. May 26, 1967, Novi Sad, Serbia*

A superior straight-ahead jazz guitarist, Zvonimir Tot's music is influenced indirectly by his Serbian heritage, although he fits in very comfortably with top American jazz musicians. He started on the guitar  when he was 14 and was mostly self-taught until his mid-twenties. "Some of my earliest memories involve hearing bossa novas on the radio. Also, there was an annual jazz festival in my city. This, along with hearing a few local players, provided my first live experiences in hearing jazz. For approximately three years, I played with Vojin 'Mališa' Draškoci, one of the best Serbian bassists. He was both a very strong jazz player as well as the principal bass at the Belgrade Philharmonic. He gave me my first professional opportunities as a jazz musician. I learned a lot from him about the music, interplay, musical (and human) integrity, and the need to find one's own path in life and music." He also worked with vibraphonist Carl Schulze during 1997–2000.

Tot earned a BA in jazz guitar performance and music education from the Franz Liszt Academy of Music in 1995 and a BA from the Amsterdam Conservatory (1999). After moving to the US, he earned a master's of music in jazz studies and composition from Northern Illinois University in 2002 and a doctorate of musical arts in jazz studies from the University of Illinois at Champaign-Urbana (2008). Tot is the Assistant Director of Jazz Studies at the University of Illinois at Chicago, where he teaches jazz guitar, harmony, ear training and ensembles.

As a guitarist, Zvonimir Tot has played with many top musicians, including Scott Hamilton, Peter King, Billy Harper, Johnny Frigo, Larry Novak, Larry Vuckovich, Philip Catherine, Henry Johnson, Paulinho Garcia, Joey DeFrancesco, Niels-Henning Ørsted Pedersen, John Clayton, Hein Van de Geyn, Jackie Allen, Carmen Lundy, Deborah Carter and the Chicago Jazz Philharmonic.

"As an educator, I strive to find better ways to help my students become able, creative professionals. As a musician, I want to keep writing my own music and play it with the people I admire. Also, I am interested in composing and performing larger-scale works for guitar, rhythm section and string orchestra. The main challenge for a jazz musician who was not born in America is one of identity. The American jazz tradition has to be thoroughly absorbed if one wishes to meaningfully interact with other musicians. But on the other hand, one's ethnic/cultural/geographic roots can become an expressive tool. My playing may not be literally influenced by my heritage (in the sense of arranging folk tunes, etc.), but it is probably fair to say that my jazz phrasing is inflected by the folk music of the Balkans."

**Recommended CDs:** *Travels And Dreams* (Groove Art 101), *Blue Quest* (Groove Art 102), *Unspoken Desire* (Groove Art 103), *Eloquent Silence* (Chicago Sessions 12717).

**Website:** www.zt-music.com

## Ralph Towner
*b. March 1, 1940, Chehalis, WA*

Nowadays, it is not that unusual for a guitarist in the jazz field to also be strongly influenced by classical and folk music or to concentrate on the acoustic guitar in folk/jazz settings. But in the late 1960s, that was quite innovative. Ralph Towner grew up in a musical family with a mother who taught piano and a father who played trumpet. He began playing piano when he was three and started trumpet lessons at five. But it was not until he was attending the University of Oregon as an art major that Towner purchased a classical guitar, studying for a time in Vienna. Still, piano was Towner's main instrument during much of the 1960s, being influenced by Bill Evans.

In 1968, Towner moved to New York to become part of the jazz scene as a guitarist. He initially worked with Jimmy Garrison and Jeremy Steig. He mastered the 12-string guitar as a member of the Paul Winter Consort, a pioneering group that utilized jazz improvisations on folk and world music. The other musicians included bassist Glen Moore, Collin Walcott on tablas, and the woodwind player Paul McCandless. In 1970, Towner, Moore, Walcott and McCandless broke away to form Oregon, a co-op group that gradually became very influential. The band has continued with the same personnel (other than Walcott, who died in 1984 and was succeeded by Trilok Gurtu, and since 1993, Mark Walker) up to the present time.

In addition to his work with Oregon, where he plays guitar, keyboards and, on a rare occasion, trumpet, Towner has had a steady solo career since the early 1970s. He signed with ECM in 1972 and has recorded regularly ever since, both as a leader and as a sideman. He has worked with Gary Burton (1974–75), guested with Weather Report (on the 1972 album *I Sing The Body Electric*) and on projects with John Abercrombie, Egberto Gismonti, Jan Garbarek, Gary Peacock and Keith Jarrett.

Towner, who lives in Rome, has stayed true to his musical vision up to the present time. Although Oregon has been less active during the last decade, their occasional reunions are happy affairs. And they would be unthinkable without the participation of the always inventive Ralph Towner.

**Recommended CDs:** *Diary* (ECM 1032), *Solstice* (ECM 1060), *Sounds & Shadows* (ECM 1095), *Batik* (ECM 1121), *Old Friends, New Friends* (ECM 1153), *Solo Concert* (ECM 1173), *Blue Sun* (ECM 1250), *City Of Eyes* (ECM 1388), *Open Letter* (ECM 1462), *Lost & Found* (ECM 1563), *Ana* (ECM 1611), *Anthem* (ECM 1743), *Time Line* (ECM 631202); with Oregon: *Music Of Another Present Era* (Vanguard 79326), *Distant Hills* (Vanguard 79341), *Winter Light* (Vanguard 79350), *In Concert* (Vanguard 79358), *Together* (Vanguard 79377), *Friends* (Vanguard 79370), *Out Of The Woods* (Elektra 154), *Moon and Mind* (Vanguard 79419), *Roots In The Sky* (Elektra 224), *In Performance* (Elektra 304), *Oregon* (ECM 23796), *Crossing* (ECM 1291), *Always, Ecotopia* (ECM 1354), *45th Parallel* (Portrait 44465), *Never And Forever* (Intuition 2073), *Troika* (Intuition 2078), *Beyond Words* (Chesky 130), *Northwest Passage* (Intuition 3191), *Oregon In Moscow* (Intuition 3303), *Live At Yoshi's* (Intuition 3299), *Prime* (CAM 7773), *1000 Kilometers* (CAM 7803), *In Stride* (CAM 7830), *Family Tree* (CAM 5046); with Paul Winter Consort: *Icarus* (Epic 31643); with John Abercrombie: *Sargasso Sea* (ECM 1080); with Gary Burton: *Matchbook* (ECM 1056), *Slide Show* (ECM 25038); with Glenn Moore: *Trios/Solos* (ECM 1025); with Gary Peacock: *Oracle* (ECM 1490), *Closer View* (ECM 1602); with Kenny Wheeler: *Deer Wan* (ECM 1102). Ralph Towner has also recorded with Arild Anderson, Horacee Arnold, Azimuth, Salvatore Bonafede, Bill Bruford, Mark Copeland, Larry Coryell, David Friesen, Jan Garbarek, Egberto Gismonti, Keith Jarrett, Vince Mendoza and Duke Pearson.

**Website:** www.ralphtowner.com

---

## James "Blood" Ulmer
b. February 2, 1942, St. Matthews, SC

Mix together the intense free-form sound explorations of Sonny Sharrock with Ornette Coleman's harmolodics and some futuristic blues and one has hints of what James "Blood" Ulmer sounds like. Certainly, it is unlike anyone else. Ulmer picked up early experience playing with soul-jazz and funk groups in Pittsburgh (1959–64), Columbus, Ohio (1964–67), and Detroit (1967–71). He made his recording debut with Hank Marr in 1964 and is on a pair of albums with Big John Patton from 1969–70. Ulmer moved to New York in 1971 and worked with Art Blakey's Jazz Messengers (an unlikely pairing that unfortunately was never recorded), Joe Henderson, Paul Bley, Rashied Ali and Larry Young. Most important for Ulmer was his association with Ornette Coleman's Prime Time in the 1970s. He was Ornette's first electric guitarist and his playing became very influenced by Coleman's free-funk ideas.

The unique guitarist began recording as a leader in 1977, and he made three widely heard albums for Columbia in the 1980s. He formed the Music Revelation Ensemble (which included David Murray and Ronald Shannon Jackson) in the '80s and co-led Phalanx with George Adams. Throughout all of this activity, Ulmer showed that he could hold his own with the fiercest saxophonist.

Ulmer surprised many by playing more blues-oriented music, starting in the 1990s. Judging him by his earlier work, one would never have expected him to take blues vocals, but typically his performances remained very unpredictable, passionate and free. As always, James Blood Ulmer found his own unique way of expressing himself.

**Recommended CDs:** *Revealing* (In & Out 7007), *Tales Of Captain Black* (DIW 403) with Ornette Coleman, *Are You Glad To be In America?* (DIW 400), *Odyssey* (Columbia 64934), *America—Do You Remember The Love?* (Blue Note 46755), *Blues All Night* (In & Out 7005), *Live At The Bayerischer Hof* (In & Out 7018), *Music Speaks Louder Than Words* (Koch 7833), *Reunion* (Knitting Factory Works 220), *Blue Blood* (Innerrhythmic 005), *Memphis Blood: The Sun Sessions* (Hyena 9310), *No Escape From The Blues* (Hyena 9312), *Birthright* (Hyena 9335), *Back In Time* (Pi 18), *Bad Blood In The City* (Hyena 9355), *Black Rock Reunion Live* (American Revelation 001), *In And Out* (In & Out 77100); with Music Revelation Ensemble: *No Wave* (Moers 1072), *Music Revelation Ensemble* (DIW 825); with Phalanx: *Got Something Good For You* (Moers 02046), *Original Phalanx* (DIW 801), *In Touch* (DIW 826).

---

## Phil Upchurch
b. July 19, 1941, Chicago, IL

A superior studio musician with a funky and soulful style, and a fine composer, in recent years Phil Upchurch has been concentrating on leading his own sessions. "My father was a jazz pianist in Chicago who often played the music of Duke, Bird and the Nat Cole Trio. He gave me a ukulele when I was 15, taught me how to play it, and later purchased a guitar for me. I played the guitar by ear for 25 years into my career when I decided it was time to learn to read music so I could compose arrangements for my bands."

Upchurch, who was mostly self-taught, began performing in clubs when he was 17, including with Porter Kilbert, the Dells, Otis Rush and Willie Mabon. "Working with Dee Clark as his music director and guitarist led to doing record dates with him. This opened many new doors for me to work with other arrangers and artists."

In 1961, Upchurch had a top-20 hit with "You Can't Sit Down." After serving in the Army during 1965–67, his career really accelerated, and he has not been out of work since then, becoming a first-call studio musician. He has appeared on over 1,000 recordings, led 25 albums of his own, playing jazz, funk, R&B, gospel, soul, and pop music, and recorded for movie soundtracks. He has also worked often as an electric bassist. "I was hired for many studio calls where they wanted me to play guitar and bass on the same tracks. In Quincy Jones' band on a Japanese tour, Ray Brown and I would take turns playing bass depending on what the tunes were."

Upchurch worked with the Staple Singers, became a session musician for the Chess label, and was on many George Benson recordings during 1974–81. Other important associations of the guitarist (who moved to Los Angeles in 1978) included Quincy Jones, the Crusaders, Jimmy Smith, Ray Charles, Ramsey Lewis, Carmen McRae, Eddie Harris, Jack McDuff, Joe Williams, Stan Getz, Cannonball Adderley, Herbie Hancock, Wynton Kelly, Grover Washington, Jr., and many artists in other fields.

In recent times, Phil Upchurch has been working on his first album of unaccompanied guitar solos (featuring his original compositions), putting together a book of his photography, and a book and film documentary on his life. "Too many musicians consider the blues unimportant and too basic. I have learned just the opposite. I stopped trying to impress with chops, slowed down, and learned to give the music more expression."

**Recommended CDs:** Some of Phil Upchurch's most rewarding recordings as a leader are *Feeling Blue* (Original Jazz Classics 1100), *Darkness, Darkness* (Universal 93418), *Lovin' Feeling* (Universal 93419), *Dolphin Dance* (Sound Service 6177), *All I Want* (Ichiban 1127), *Tell The Truth* (Evidence 2222), *Whatever Happened To The Blues* (Ridgetop 55566), *Rhapsody & Blues* (Go Jazz 6035) and *Truly* (private release).

**Website:** www.philupchurch.com

## George Van Eps
*b. August 7, 1913, Plainfield, NJ; d. November 29, 1998, Newport Beach, CA*

George Van Eps played the most beautiful chords imaginable. He designed a seven-string guitar in 1938 that made it easier for him to play bass notes simultaneously with melody lines and 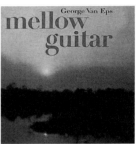 lush chords. His gentle playing was a part of a countless number of recordings over a 65-year period.

The son of the superb ragtime banjoist Fred Van Eps (it is a real shame that they never recorded together) and a mother who was a classically trained pianist, George Van Eps also had three older brothers (Bobby, Fred and John) who were musicians. He started on banjo at 11, switched to guitar the following year after hearing Eddie Lang play on the radio, and became a professional by the time he was 13 in 1926. He was heard regularly on the radio by 1927. Van Eps worked with Harry Reser's Junior Artists, the Dutch Master Minstrels, Smith Ballew, Freddie Martin (1931–33), Benny Goodman (1934–35) and Ray Noble (1935–36) but was primarily a studio guitarist. He was based in New York up until the mid-1930s, when he permanently moved to Southern California. Van Eps appeared on a huge number of movie soundtracks, commercials and jingles through the years, wrote several instructional guitar books, and was always available for jazz dates.

He was part of the Los Angeles area Dixieland scene in the 1940s and '50s, performing with many groups, including Matty Matlock's bands, Bob Crosby, the Rampart Street Paraders, and the Pete Kelly Seven. An influence on Bucky and John Pizzarelli (both of whom also mastered the seven-string guitar) and Howard Alden (one of his students), in his later years Van Eps was often in the spotlight, appearing in clubs where he played his beautiful chords while joined by a quiet rhythm section.

**Recommended CDs:** George Van Eps did not record a lot of albums in his career as a leader, but every one is well worth getting. *Jump Presents George Van Eps* (Jump 126) features Van Eps on four trio numbers from 1949 and on a hot session with tenor-saxophonist Eddie Miller and pianist Stan Wrightsman. *Mellow Guitar* (Sundazed 177) is a 1956 album originally put out by Columbia, featuring Van Eps with a rhythm section, a string orchestra and a nonet arranged by Paul Weston. During the mid-1960s,

**Frank Vignola**

Van Eps led a trio of albums for Capitol; *My Guitar* (Euphoria 182) and *Soliloquy* (Euphoria 193) have been reissued on CD. While *My Guitar* is melodic, tasteful and beautifully played, *Soliloquy* is particularly special, for it was Van Eps' only full album of unaccompanied guitar solos. During 1991–94, Van Eps teamed up with Howard Alden to co-lead three CDs. *13 Strings* (Concord Jazz 4464), which was actually issued under Alden's name, *Hand Crafted Swing* (Concord Jazz 4513) and *Keepin' Time* (Concord Jazz 4713) are all quartet dates, with the latter also featuring Alden on seven-string guitar. Howard Alden's respect and reverence for George Van Eps was well deserved. *Legends* (Concord Jazz 4616) is split between 11 Van Eps unaccompanied guitar solos and an unrelated but complementary session by Johnny Smith.

**LPs to Search For:** George Van Eps' *Seven String Guitar* (Capitol 2533), recorded in 1967, has yet to reappear.

## Frank Vignola
b. December 30, 1965, West Islip, NY

Best known for his swing and Django Reinhardt–inspired recordings, Frank Vignola is actually quite versatile and sounds credible playing fusion and other styles. He began playing the guitar when he was five. "When I was six, my father bought me a Django record and taught me the chords to 'Limehouse Blues.' I would play rhythm guitar for him and his banjo band." He studied at the Cultural Arts Center of Long Island and kept his mind open to a wide variety of styles, even beyond jazz. Rather than attend college, he moved to Manhattan and became quite busy as a musician. In the 1980s, Vignola worked extensively as a sideman, performing with Madonna, Leon Redbone and Ringo Starr. But it was in 1988 that he became known in the jazz world. "I walked right into Michael's Pub, the biggest cabaret room in Manhattan, and asked for a gig. In Manhattan, it takes balls to be a professional musician! I worked at Michael's Pub for 20 weeks performing the music of Django Reinhardt."

In 1993, Vignola recorded his first album for Concord, *Appel Direct*. He has recorded often since then as both a leader and a sideman. In addition to his own swing dates, he has worked with Mark O'Connor, Les Paul (2000–05), Donald Fagen, Queen Latifah, Wynton Marsalis, Bucky Pizzarelli, Jimmy Rosenberg, David Grisman and Australian guitarist Tommy Emmanuel. Vignola has also written 18 guitar instruction books. In recent times, he has toured regularly with his trio (which also includes rhythm guitarist Vincent Raniolo and bassist Gary Mazzaroppi), playing 200 shows a year.

"I love great melodies and songs. I believe that jazz should be about the song. I love performing songs that people know and doing something special with them."

**Recommended CDs:** Frank Vignola's versatility is reflected in his recordings, which include *Appel Direct* (Concord 4576); *Let It Happen* (Concord 4625); *Look Right, Jog Left* (Concord 4718); the relatively poppish *Déjà Vu* (Concord 4802); *Off Broadway* (Nagel Heyer 2006); *Blues For A Gypsy* (Acoustic Disc 43); *Vignola Plays Gershwin* (Mel Bay 10122); *Kong* (VMD 016), which has a rock repertoire played by an acoustic guitar and mandolin group; and the brilliant *100 Years Of Django* (Azica 72244). He has also recorded with Travelin' Light, Ken Peplowski, Jon-Erik Kellso, Susannah McCorkle, Vince Giordano, Bob Dorough, Charlie Byrd (*Du Hot Club De Concord*), Joey DeFrancesco, Frank Wess, John Bunch, and Joe Ascione (as "the Frank & Joe Show").

**Website:** www.frankvignola.com

## Randy Vincent
b. February 25, 1952, Rapid City, SD

Long considered one of the top jazz guitarists based in the San Francisco Bay area, Randy Vincent is also a well-respected educator. He began playing guitar when he was 15, inspired by a kid who lived across the street who played the top-40 hits of the time. He heard very little jazz as a teenager. "My earliest paid gigs were with garage rock-and-roll bands. In the early '70s, by chance, I got to hear George Benson sitting in with organist Clarence Palmer in Orlando, Florida, where I grew up. That was a major conversion point." Soon, Vincent was playing jazz with top local musicians, including three years with Ray Terry at Frank Wolfe's Beachside Motel in Cocoa Beach. At the third annual Space Coast Jazz Festival in 1977, the forward-looking hard-bop guitarist had opportunities to perform with Ira Sullivan, Plas Johnson, Terry Gibbs and Jack Sheldon.

After moving to the San Francisco Bay area in 1980, Vincent became a longtime member of the Mel Martin Quartet, also playing with Martin in several versions of Bebop and Beyond. In addition to his own groups and performing with the top local players, Vincent has worked with Mike Vax's Tpts, Bobby Hutcherson, Joe Henderson, Dizzy Gillespie (1990–91), Dave Eshelman's Jazz Garden Big Band, Benny Barth, Mel Graves, Peter Welker, Jeff Oster, the Mike Vax Jazz Orchestra and Leny Andrade. He has appeared at many jazz festivals (including Monterey) and taught at Sonoma State University since 1981; three of his former students are Julian Lage, Dave MacNab and Liberty Ellman.

As far as the future goes, Randy Vincent jokingly says, "I'd like to keep playing jazz as long as I can afford it."

**Recommended CDs:** Randy Vincent's two CDs as a leader, *Mirror Image* and *Nisha's Dream* (both of which are available through his website), feature his own quartets and examples of his writing. He has also recorded as a sideman with Larry Baskett, Mel Graves, Jeff Oster, Elaine Lucia, Mario Guarneri, Max Perkoff, Joey Schneider, Stephanie Ozer, Mike Vax, Dave Eshelman, Peter Welker, Vern Thompson, Steve Wolfe, the Turtle Island String Quartet, Bobby Hutcherson and Mel Martin's Bebop and Beyond (with guests Dizzy Gillespie and Joe Henderson).

**Website:** www.randyvincent.com

# Al Viola

b. June 16, 1919, New York, NY; d. February 21, 2007, Los Angeles, CA

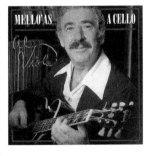

While Al Viola spent much of his career in the studios, he was always a superior swing soloist, best known for his associations with Page Cavanaugh and Frank Sinatra. During an interview on September 21, 1994, Viola remembered, "I had a big Italian family, and we had all kinds of musicians at the house. My brother played mandolin and needed someone to accompany him. Since I was the youngest child, he taught me some chords on the guitar when I was eight. I had an older brother who also played guitar for fun. We played Italian folk songs and some jazz standards. By the time I was in my teens, I was pretty advanced. I liked Eddie Lang, and there was a violinist in the neighborhood in Brooklyn. We would play like Venuti and Lang at a lot of Chinese restaurants for all of the

soup we wanted, $1.50 or $2 a night plus tips. My mother thought I was robbing the bank because I was bringing home over $22 a week in the Depression."

During 1942–45, Viola was in the Army, where he met pianist-singer Page Cavanaugh. "We were both in an Army band playing dances, and we met bassist Lloyd Pratt. When we were discharged, the three of us decided to stay together in Hollywood to see what would happen." During 1946–49, the Page Cavanaugh Trio was a popular attraction in Southern California, making records for RCA (which are long overdue to be reissued), appearing in five movies, and playing in a style not too different from the Nat King Cole Trio. Originally an instrumental group, the band was pressured to feature vocals and their whispered unison vocals on "The Three Bears" and "Walkin' My Baby Back Home" added to their popularity. Viola was never too happy about having to join in on the singing.

In 1949, he left Cavanaugh, worked around Los Angeles and studied music. When LPs came in, Viola found himself extremely busy. "For over 20 years, it seemed as if there were not enough skilled musicians in Hollywood. It was a great time, and of course we thought it would last forever. I lucked out and was recording constantly, as was Howard Roberts and later on Tommy Tedesco. I started in the mid-1950s, and by the time it got to the '60s, forget it, my book was filled. I had to turn down dates. The only time I would leave town was with Sinatra. I was his first call."

Viola had first met Frank Sinatra while with Page Cavanaugh when they accompanied the singer on some dates. Viola did all of the recordings with Sinatra during 1954–80 and occasionally afterward. In addition to his studio work, Viola recorded with the big bands of Harry James, Ray Anthony, Les Brown, and Nelson Riddle; played jazz with Bobby Troup, Buddy Collette, Red Callender, Terry Gibbs, Shelly Manne and Leroy Vinnegar; and accompanied such singers as June Christy (*Something Cool*), Julie London (he is the only other musician on her album *Lonely Girl*), Hadda Brooks, Jimmy Witherspoon, Helen Humes, Ella Fitzgerald, Anita O'Day and, in later years, Linda Ronstadt and Natalie Cole (most of her *Unforgettable* album).

Studio work slowed down in the 1970s, but Viola always played jazz at night. In 1989, he had a reunion with Page Cavanaugh, and until the late 1990s, he played regularly with Cavanaugh and usually bassist Phil Mallory at the Money Tree near Los Angeles two or three nights a week. He also worked with Buddy Collette, Sam Most and Richard Simon in his later years in addition to having his own trio.

"When I was in my late forties, Howard Roberts

interviewed me and asked what I was going to do when I was in my seventies. I said that if I'm still around, I hope that I'll be able to work regularly in a neighborhood bar and be a grandfather. And with the Money Tree, that happened!"

**Recommended CDs:** Al Viola led three albums in his career. He played unaccompanied solos on 1957's *Solo Guitar* (VSOP) and *Alone Again* (Legend 1002), which has only come out as an LP, and made a Frank Sinatra tribute album for PBR in 1978. *Mello As A Cello* (Starline 9010) has highlights from the latter two albums. Other fine examples of Viola on record are Julie London's *Lonely Girl* (Toshiba 6900); Page Cavanaugh's *The Digital Page: Page One* (Star Line 9001) and *Digital Page: Page Two* (Star Line 9006), which are from the 1990s; and a trio set with Sam Most and Richard Simon called *Pacific Standard Time* (UFO Bass 5).

## Ulf Wakenius
*b. April 16, 1958, Halmstad, Sweden*

Best known for his tours and recordings with Oscar Peterson and Ray Brown, Ulf Wakenius is often thought of in the United States as a top-notch bop-based guitarist. But

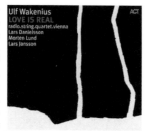

his career has also found him excelling at playing more adventurous music with the likes of Pat Metheny and Michael Brecker.

Born and raised in Sweden, Wakenius started on guitar when he was 11. Initially inspired by the top blues guitarists, he started listening to jazz after hearing John McLaughlin. He was a professional by the time he was 17, working mostly in Europe. Wakenius attended Gothenburg Music University for one year but had to quit due to his very busy touring schedule. During 1980–85, he often teamed up with Peter Almqvist as Guitars Unlimited. In 1985, they performed on television for the Melody Grand Prix before an estimated 600 million viewers.

As a member of the Oscar Peterson Quartet for ten years (1997–2007), Wakenius had the opportunity to tour the world. "That is by far my most important collaboration—a guitar player's dream! I first heard him when I was 15 years old. 25 years later, I was standing on the same stage with him." Much of the time, the bassist in the group was Niels Pedersen, who had recommended Wakenius to Peterson. Wakenius also worked in Pedersen's group and had opportunities to record with Ray Brown's trio.

Ulf Wakenius has also played and often recorded with such notables as Herbie Hancock, Michael Brecker, Joe Henderson, Phil Woods, Toots Thielemans, Clark Terry, Johnny Griffin, Jack DeJohnette, Dave Liebman, Chris Potter, Kenny Kirkland, Max Roach, Milt Jackson, Bobby Hutcherson, Jim Hall, Art Farmer, Benny Golson, James Moody, Hank Jones, Roy Hargrove, Jon Faddis, Joey DeFrancesco, Bob Berg, Randy Brecker, Kenny Drew, Benny Green and Michel Legrand. He toured and recorded with Graffiti, a group that utilized the rhythm section from John Scofield's band. In 2003, Wakenius performed a duo concert with Pat Metheny in Germany that was televised on German television.

"I have been blessed to have the opportunity to play with and get to know all of my idols. It is even more magical that I could come from a remote part of the world and get to play with them."

**Recommended CDs:** *Venture* (L&M 45052), *New York Meeting* (Bellophon 45082); *Enchanted Moments* (Dragon 278); *Dig In* (Sittel 9230); *Live* (Dragon 347); an unaccompanied set of guitar solos on *The Guitar Artistry Of Ulf Wakenius* (Dragon 373); *Forever You* (Stunt 3192); *Notes From The Heart: Music Of Keith Jarrett* (ACT 9435); *Love Is Real* (ACT 9459), which is a tribute to the late pianist Esbjörn Svensson; with Oscar Peterson: *Summer Night In Munich* (Telarc 83450); with Ray Brown: *Summertime* (Telarc 83430); with Niels Pedersen: *This Is All I Ask* (Verve 539695).

**Website:** www.myspace.com/ulfwakenius

## T-Bone Walker
*(Aaron Thibeaux Walker)*
*b. May 28, 1910, Linden, TX; d. March 16, 1975, Los Angeles, CA*

A master of straight-ahead and swinging blues, and an inspiration for both Chuck Berry and B.B. King, T-Bone Walker was one of the finest of all blues guitarists. His music frequently crossed over into jazz, although he was associated with blues throughout his life.

Walker grew up around music for his mother and stepfather were members of the Dallas String Band, and they were friends with Blind Lemon Jefferson. His stepfather, who was a bassist, taught him to play not only the guitar but also the banjo, ukulele, mandolin, violin and piano. Walker, who dropped out of school when he was ten, began playing professionally as a young teenager, working with Dallas string bands in the streets. In the mid-1920s, he was considered Jefferson's protégé and would go with him to his jobs. In 1929, he made his recording debut under the name of Oak Cliff T-Bone (the name of the town in which he lived plus an abstraction of his middle name).

During the 1930s, he moved to Los Angeles, got married, began raising a family, and started using the professional name of T-Bone Walker. Inspired by Charlie Christian, whom he knew well and played with in the mid-1930s, Walker switched to electric guitar near the end of the decade and developed a swinging style and an exciting stage show. His first recording since 1929 was 1940's "T-Bone Blues" with Les Hite, which featured him as a singer rather than a guitarist. However, in the early 1940s, he became a star in the blues world, beginning a lengthy series of impressive recordings in which he was usually featured with a jazz-influenced two-horn sextet. 1947 found him introducing his best-known song, "Call It Stormy Monday." Walker could play guitar behind his back, do splits, and even play guitar with his teeth (25 years before Jimi Hendrix). But, showbiz aside, he was a superb guitarist who could have held his own with any jazz guitarist of the time.

T-Bone Walker was in his heyday during the 1940s and '50s, when he recorded for Black & White and Imperial. While the rise of rock and roll overshadowed his career to an extent, Walker had success during several European tours in the 1960s and was in his musical prime until suffering his first stroke in 1974, a year before his death.

**Recommended CDs:** The four-CD set *The Original Source* (Proper Box 1038) does a very good job of reissuing Walker's 1929–51 recordings. *The Complete Imperial Recordings: 1950–1954* (Blue Moon 11259), a two-CD reissue, has some duplication while also covering Walker's work of 1952–54. *T-Bone Blues* (Atlantic 8020) from 1959 is also quite worthy.

## Kazumi Watanabe
*b. October 14, 1953, Tokyo, Japan*

A major fusion guitarist, Kazumi Watanabe has spent much of his life playing in his native Japan, where he has been an influential force. He started on piano when he was seven, switched to guitar at 12, and discovered jazz three years later when he heard Wes Montgomery's music. At 17, he debuted on records with *Infinite*, gaining a great deal of attention in Japan. Watanabe worked with the unrelated Sadao Watanabe, Masaru Imada and Isao Suzuki in the 1970s. 1977's *Olive Steps* gave him strong popularity in the fusion world. He led KYLYN in 1979 and toured with the Yellow Magic Orchestra. In 1980, he worked with Mike Mainieri, which alerted some notable American jazz musicians to his talent. Watanabe was part of the Japanese tours of Steps, the Brecker Brothers and Jaco Pastorius. He led the Kazumi Band and Mobo III. Watanabe also worked with Marcus

Miller, Jeff Berlin, Tony Levin, Bill Bruford, Peter Erskine and Wayne Shorter, touring the world with a variety of different fusion-oriented bands.

In the 1990s, Watanabe began to explore the acoustic guitar in addition to utilizing his intense electric playing. He has collaborated with such guitarists as John McLaughlin, Al Di Meola, Larry Coryell, Babik Reinhardt, Toninho Horta, Ralph Towner and Martin Taylor. Watanabe has also led Resonance Vox (1991–96) and the 32-piece Asia Fantasy Orchestra, recorded and performed duets with pianist Makoto Ozone (1998), and written a guitar suite, "Beyond The Infinite," that crosses many musical boundaries. In recent years, he has performed unaccompanied solos (documented on *Guitar Renaissance*), toured with the New Electric Trio (which includes bassist Richard Bona and drummer Horacio Hernandez), and in 2009, conceived his "Return to Jazz Project." That year, he toured China, fusing together jazz with traditional Chinese music. In addition, he has taught at the Senzoku Gakuen College of Music since 1996.

Kazumi Watanabe adds fire, creativity, passion and a furious power to every session on which he appears.

**Recommended CDs:** Although Kazumi Watanabe recorded for the American Gramavision label for a few years, many of his CDs are difficult to find outside of Japan. Some of the more important ones are *Infinite* (Toshiba Express 60001), *Endless Way* (Columbia 53292), *Milky Shade* (Tei-Union 5003), *Olive's Step* (Columbia 31637), *Lonesome Cat* (Columbia 31638), *Kylyn* (Columbia 53333), *Dogatana* (Sony 53337), *Mobo Club* (Gramavision 79419), *Mobo I* (Gramavision 8404), *Mobo II* (Gramavision 8406), *To Chi Ka* (Sony 53336), *Mobo Splash* (Gramavision 79418), *The Spice Of Life* (Universal 2430), *The Spice Of Life Too* (Gramavision 79416), *Kilowatt* (Gramavision 79415), *Pandora* (Gramavision 79472), *Dandyism* (IMS 557795), *One For All* (IMS 547803), *Beyond The Infinite* (Universal 2014) and *Guitar Renaissance* (WEA 74).

**Website:** www.kazumiwatanabe.net

## Mitch Watkins
*(Mitchell Watkins)*
*b. August 1, 1952, McAllen, TX*

Whether it is fusion, avant-garde explorations, or music that falls outside of jazz altogether, Mitch Watkins always plays with passion and constant inventiveness. He had piano lessons from the age of eight and began playing guitar when he was 12. "My first band (in Odessa, Texas) had three guitars, drums, and no bass or vocalist. We all played the chords (not the melodies!) to Beatles tunes at local dances. Later, I joined a band playing mainly Ventures stuff. The first jazz record I remember hearing was Barney Kessel, Ray Brown and Shelly Manne's *Poll Winners*. I knew then that there was more to this 'music thing.' Then I heard Hendrix, and nothing was ever the same."

Equally influenced by rock and jazz guitarists, Watkins attended Texas Christian University for a year on a choral conducting scholarship before dropping out of school to tour for two years with a rock group. He went back to school, earning a degree from the University of Texas (1974–78). "There was no guitar program, jazz or classical. I studied composition, with piano as my main instrument. What I learned there about jazz was presented on the piano; then, I would take it home and move the information from the keyboard to the fretboard. It was an interesting way to learn jazz theory. I never had a guitar lesson."

Watkins worked with organist James Polk (1976–80) and was in a fusion band called Passenger (1976–83). Passenger ended up as Leonard Cohen's backup group during 1979–80, touring Europe and Australia. Watkins has since worked with Joe Ely (1982–85), reunited with Cohen (1985), Jennifer Warnes, K.T. Oslin and Abra Moore. On the jazz side, he has had important associations with organist Barbara Dennerlein (1988–97), Bennie Wallace, Friedrich Gulda and Jack Walrath. "Each of them has had a unique and exciting musical experience."

Mitch Watkins has been a member of Lyle Lovett's touring band since 2000. He also teaches jazz guitar and digital audio at the University of Texas at Austin, produces projects by other artists, and performs locally. "In the immediate future, I look forward to collaborations with saxophone great Tony Campise and jazz mandolinist Paul Glasse. As I advance in years, it becomes more and more apparent that what is between the notes, what is not played, is at least as important as what is played."

**Recommended CDs:** Mitch Watkins still considers his first CD as a leader, 1988's *Underneath It All* (Enja 79603), to be his best jazz recording. He has also led four other stimulating recordings that display his strong interests in both jazz and rock: *Curves* (Enja 79649), *Strings With Wings* (Enja 79679), *Humhead* (Dos 7501) and *In The Time Of Long Shadows* (Viewpoint 0028). Also well worth checking out are his recordings with Barbara Dennerlein, including *Straight Ahead* (Enja 50772).

**Website:** www.mitchwatkins.com

## Chuck Wayne
*(Charles Jagelka)*
b. February 27, 1923, New York, NY; d. July 29, 1997, Jackson, NJ

One of the better jazz guitarists to emerge during the bebop era, Chuck Wayne had his own style within the Charlie Christian vocabulary while also being influenced by Charlie Parker and Lester Young. He was mostly heard as a dependable and stimulating sideman throughout his career.

Wayne not only learned guitar as a youth but also banjo, mandolin and the balalaika. He gained experience playing with small groups on 52nd Street in the early 1940s (including the trios of Clarence Profit and Nat Jaffe) before spending two years in the Army. After his discharge, he worked with Joe Marsala's group. Inspired by hearing Charlie Parker play in 1944, Wayne modernized his style and developed so quickly that he is on a Dizzy Gillespie session from January 1945 that resulted in "Blue 'N' Boogie" and the obscure original version of "Groovin' High." In 1946 Wayne was the guitarist with Woody Herman's First Herd, taking occasional solos. He wrote an original in tribute to trumpeter Sonny Berman, "Sunny," that was later renamed and claimed by Miles Davis as "Solar." He also worked during the era with Red Norvo, Jack Teagarden, Coleman Hawkins, Bud Powell, Lester Young and the Barbara Carroll Trio.

Wayne gained some recognition as the guitarist with the original version of the George Shearing Quintet during 1949–52. He kept busy in the 1950s, touring and recording with Tony Bennett (1954–57) and working with George Wallington, Brew Moore, Zoot Sims and the Gil Evans Orchestra. The 1960s were mostly spent doing studio work including as a member of the staff of CBS. Wayne was occasionally active in the jazz world during the 1970s and '80s, playing in the New York area, teaching, accompanying singers, and working with Broadway shows.

Chuck Wayne, who along the way recorded with Berman, Hawkins, Marsala, Bennett, Bill Harris, Tab Smith, Slam Stewart, Sam Most, Joe Bushkin, Frank Wess and Warren Chiasson, in his later years sometimes played guitar duets with either Joe Puma or Tal Farlow.

**Recommended CDs:** Although he never gained much fame, Chuck Wayne had occasional opportunities throughout much of his career to record as a leader. *The Jazz Guitarist* (Savoy 089) features Wayne in 1953 heading a quintet with either Brew Moore or Zoot Sims on tenor and the following year with pianist John Mehegan's quartet. *Tapestry* is a 1963 trio set (String 1017), as is 1964's *Morning Mist* (Original Jazz Classics 1097). *Interactions* (Choice 1004) is a tasteful set of guitar duets with Joe Puma while *Traveling* (Progressive 7008) has Wayne in 1976 showcased in a trio/quartet that sometimes includes vibraphonist Warren Chiasson. Chuck Wayne's last significant recording was on Warren Chiasson's *Point/Counterpoint* (Empathy 1007), a set of vibes-guitar duets from 1988.

## Lloyd Wells
b. April 22, 1938, Laurel, MS

In his career, Lloyd Wells has worked in Broadway pit orchestras, on television variety series and in Nashville, playing country music. However, his work with Mundell Lowe and his occasional entries into the jazz world have  revealed him to be a strong swing-oriented player. Wells was born and raised in Laurel, Mississippi, the same town in which Lowe was born 16 years earlier. "My dad gave me a small guitar when I was six or seven. He showed me a few chords and taught me a lot of tunes. Although he was musically illiterate, he sang well and would teach me the lyrics and melody to a song. Then, once I had memorized it, he would sing harmony with me. In Mississippi, in that era, the radios and jukeboxes constantly played country and blues. In Laurel, specifically, I came up under the influence of Mundell Lowe's reputation, although he had left Laurel by then. A bass player friend of mine gave me three records (78s) of Benny Goodman. As I was walking away from his house, he shouted 'That's Charlie Christian on those records.' I had no idea who Charlie was at that time, but quickly learned." Other guitarists whom he was in awe of include Tal Farlow, Jimmy Raney, Barney Kessel, Johnny Smith and George Van Eps.

Wells played early on with country singers and at square dances. He earned a degree from the University of Southern Mississippi in music education in 1960. After four years of teaching high school band, he was convinced by Mundell Lowe to move to New York. Wells soon landed a Broadway show, the first of 18. In addition, Wells worked on *The Ed Sullivan Show* and *Sesame Street*, subbed for Lowe on both *The Merv Griffin Show* and *The Tonight Show*, and worked with Peggy Lee, Rosemary Clooney and the Glenn Miller ghost orchestra.

In 1974, Wells moved to Nashville, starting a 17-year period working with Tennessee Ernie Ford, beginning long time associations with Porter Wagoner and Brenda Lee, and becoming the music director for Opryland USA (a show park) for 23 years, writing over 5,000 arrangements. He also got to conduct the Nashville Symphony on several occasions.

Of course, none of this had much to do with jazz. "But finally, I got to spend some serious playing time with Mundy. The CD we did together (*This One's For Charlie*) best represents me." And his wonderful collaboration with Lowe is the reason that Lloyd Wells is in this book.

"I hope to make a CD with Mundy and bassist Jim Ferguson, and possibly a duet CD with guitarist Mel Deal. I enjoy performing jazz because by nature it is the only musical form I constantly think about. Manipulating the harmonic changes is what intrigues me most."

**Recommended CDs:** *This One's For Charlie* (Azica 72213), a tribute to Charlie Byrd, features Lloyd Wells and Mundell Lowe playing good natured, easygoing and swinging duets.

## Mark Whitfield
b. October 6, 1967, Syosset, NY

A soulful guitarist, Mark Whitfield has displayed the ability to play soul jazz and hard bop plus R&B and pop music in his career. Originally a bassist, Whitfield switched to guitar when he was 15. He attend-  ed Berklee, graduating in 1987. George Benson, a musical influence and a friend, recommended Whitfield to Jack McDuff, an association that started the young guitarist's career. In 1990, he made his recording debut as a leader, *The Marksman*. Since then, Whitfield has frequently been a leader while also playing along the way with Dizzy Gillespie, Art Blakey, Clark Terry, Jimmy Smith, Carmen McRae, Herbie Hancock, Betty Carter, Shirley Horn, Joe Williams, Wynton Marsalis, Branford Marsalis, Stanley Turrentine, Roy Hargrove, Nicholas Payton and most recently Chris Botti, along with an assortment of R&B and pop musicians.

Mark Whitfield, who has had a lower national profile since his major label days, has continued to record and perform while also teaching at Berklee.

**Recommended CDs:** *The Marksman* (Warner Bros. 26321), *Patrice* (Warner Bros. 26659), *Mark Whitfield* (Warner Bros. 45210), *True Blue* (Verve 523591), *7th Avenue Stroll* (Verve 529223), *Forever Love* (Verve 533921), *Take The Ride* (Universal 559437), *Fingerpainting* (Verve 537856) with Nicholas Payton and Christian McBride, *Soul Conversation* (Transparent 50001), *Raw* (Transparent 50003), *Trio Paradise* (Vega 1020), *Mark Whitfield & The Groove Masters* (Vega 1030), *Featuring Panther* (Dirty Soap 100), *Songs Of Wonder* (Marksman 1790).

**Website:** www.markwhitfield.com

## Jack Wilkins
*(Jack Rivers Lewis)*
b. June 3, 1944, Brooklyn, NY

A very skilled straight-ahead guitarist who has been influential both as a musician and as a teacher, Jack Wilkins always keeps his playing open to new ideas. His mother and an older cousin played guitar for the fun of it. Wilkins, who also played vibes, piano and classical guitar, started on jazz guitar when he was ten, early on hearing recordings featuring Charlie Christian, Johnny Smith and Charlie Parker. "After high school I played in a lot of dance bands, including Les and Larry Elgart, Warren Covington, and Sammy Kaye. My first important gig was in 1972 when I was on Paul Jeffrey's recording *Watershed*, which also included Thelonious Monk, Jr., and Richard Davis."

Wilkins began to gain recognition during 1973–75 when he worked regularly with Buddy Rich's small groups, which gave him an opportunity to play with such greats as Dizzy Gillespie, Kenny Barron, Sonny Fortune, Zoot Sims, Lionel Hampton, Sonny Stitt, Sal Nistico, Jimmy McGriff, Frank Foster and Stan

Getz. Other associations since then include Michael and Randy Brecker, Bob Brookmeyer (late 1970s), Chet Baker, Albert Dailey, the Mingus Epitaph Orchestra, the Manhattan Transfer (1982–98), Phil Woods, Tom Harrell, Jack DeJohnette, Stanley Turrentine, Red Rodney, Ira Sullivan, Johnny Griffin, Mel Torme, Sarah Vaughan, Nancy Marano, Chris Conner, Cassandra Wilson, and Jay Clayton. "It's been a treat to play with all of these great musicians."

Jack Wilkins, who plays regularly in the New York area, teaches at the New School, the Manhattan School of Music, NYU, and LIU. He has encouraged and helped many younger guitarists through the years.

**Recommended CDs:** *Merge* (Chiaroscuro 156) reissues nine of the ten selections from a pair of brilliant hard-bop LPs (*The Jack Wilkins Quartet* and *You Can't Live Without It*) that team the guitarist with Randy and (on the second set) Michael Brecker. Also rewarding are *Call Him Reckless* (Music Masters 5019); *Alien Army* (Music Masters 5049); *Mexico* (CTI 7001481); *Keep In Touch* (Claves 1295) with pianist Kenny Drew, Jr.; *Trio Art* (Arabesque 135); *Cruisin' For A Bluesin'* (String Jazz 1005); *Heading North* (String Jazz 1014) with Jimmy Bruno; *Reunion* (Chiaroscuro 371) with Randy Brecker, Eddie Gomez, Jack DeJohnette and (on two numbers) Michael Brecker; *Christmas Jazz Guitar* (Mel Bay 20257); and the recent *Until It's Time* (Max Jazz 140606). *Just The Two Of Us* (Chiaroscuro 362) is a tasteful guitar duet set from 1998 that Wilkins shares with Gene Bertoncini.

**LPs to Search For:** Jack Wilkins' debut album as a leader, 1973's *Windows* (Mainstream 396), is a trio outing that remains out of print.

**Website:** www.jackwilkins.com

## Anthony Wilson
b. May 9, 1968, Los Angeles, CA

Anthony Wilson has achieved his greatest visibility as a well-featured member of Diana Krall's quartet during the past 11 years (where he has been her best guitarist since Russell Malone), but Wilson is also a significant arranger-composer who leads his own nonet. The son of the innovative bandleader Gerald Wilson, Anthony Wilson started on the guitar when he was eight. "Jazz has been in my life since the very beginning. In addition to seeing my father perform, my mother (Anita Leonard) always kept a huge collection of jazz records, which I could listen to at any time. And of course, they both had many friends who were also jazz musicians, so I encountered this culture extremely early. My first (and longest-running) professional association, and my first 'break,' has been my work with my father. I have played with him since 1984 and appeared on every recording since then except for one. I also benefited greatly from the encouragement of Harold Land, who hired me to play gigs with him at about that same time."

While attending Bennington College where he earned a bachelor of arts, Wilson studied with Bill Dixon, Allen Shawn and Milford Graves, and had opportunities to work with Ed and George Schuller. He attended summer sessions at the Tanglewood Institute in 1983 and Gunther Schuller's Festival at Sandpoint (1989 and 1990). He also gives strong credit to the guitar teacher Ted Greene for pointing him in new directions.

Anthony Wilson won the Thelonious Monk International Composers' Competition in 1995 (for "Karaoke"), which led him to put together a nonet that has since recorded four CDs. He has played with Bennie Wallace on an occasional basis since 1998 (including playing and arranging for Wallace's Coleman Hawkins Project in 2005) and has toured the world as a key part of Diana Krall's quartet since 2001. Wilson has appeared on all of Krall's recordings and DVDs of the past decade. In addition to his work with his nonet in the Los Angeles area, Wilson has recorded in recent times with Bobby Hutcherson, Mose Allison and Willie Nelson, and contributed an arrangement of "Love Dance" to the 2009 Barbra Streisand album *Love Is The Answer*.

Anthony Wilson is currently composing a suite for a guitar quartet to commemorate the "Four Seasons" quartet of guitars built by John Monteleone. Among his future goals is to form a big band to perform his repertoire of originals.

"Jazz music and jazz musicians must constantly expand, constantly learn, and evolve. We are most certainly 'servants' of the music, and we don't see the 'big picture' until later. That sense of keeping with the unknown (with the moment), staying present with one's collaborators, and trusting that the rhythm, melody, and harmony will take us where it needs to go is what keeps this music so exciting and gratifying for me."

**Recommended CDs:** The guitarist debuted as a leader on records in 1997. *Anthony Wilson* (Mama 1018), *Goat Hill Junket* (Mama 1022), and *Adult Themes* (Mama 1925) display his evolution as both a guitarist and an arranger-composer during 1997–99. *Our*

*Gang* (Groove Note 1008) and *Savivity* (Groove Note 1030) showcase Wilson's guitar playing in a trio with organist Joe Bagg. *Power Of Nine* (Groove Note 1035) features the nonet, while *Jack Of Hearts* (Groove Note 1046) has Wilson in a trio with keyboardist Larry Goldings. *Nova* (Goat Hill 1) finds him sharing the spotlight with Brazilian guitarist Chico Pinheiro. *Campo Belo* (Goat Hill 2) features Wilson performing with three Brazilians, while *Seasons* (privately released CD and DVD) has him interacting with fellow guitarists Steve Cardenas, Chico Pinheiro and Julian Lage. As a sideman, Wilson is heard at his best with Diana Krall on *Live In Paris* (Verve 440065), and he made very important contributions to Bennie Wallace's Coleman Hawkins tribute, *Disorder At The Border* (Enja 3327). In addition, he has recorded with the Gerald Wilson Orchestra, Dave Pike, Joe Henry, Jacintha, Joey Altruda, Mark Winkler, Elliott Caine, Chris Botti, Curtis Stigers, Eden Atwood, Terry Gibbs, Diane Schuur, Michael Bublé, Josh Nelson, Willie Nelson and Bobby Hutcherson.

**Website:** www.anthonywilsonmusic.com

## Jimmy Wyble
*b. January 25, 1922, Port Arthur, TX; d. January 16, 2010, Los Angeles, CA*

Jimmy Wyble was an important force in both jazz and Western swing. Born and raised in Texas, he worked early on at a Houston radio station. After gaining experience in a few Western swing bands, including one led by Foreman Phillips, he and fellow guitarist Cameron Hill were hired in the early 1940s to become part of Bob Wills and the Texas Playboys. Wills enjoyed their "twin guitars" sound, which can be heard on Wills' recording of "Roly Poly." Wyble served in the Army during 1942–46, and after his discharge, he continued working in a variety of Western swing bands into the early 1950s.

However Wyble was always strongly interested in bop and modern jazz. In 1953, he led his first album (*The Jimmy Wyble Quintet*), which featured a quintet that included accordion and clarinet, and also recorded with Barney Kessel. He had his greatest visibility during the late 1950s and early '60s, playing with Benny Goodman (1959–60 and 1963), Red Norvo, and Norvo's band during an Australian tour with Frank Sinatra.

By the 1960s, Jimmy Wyble was working as a studio musician, often performing on television shows and movie soundtracks. He studied classical guitar with Laurindo Almeida and in turn taught many younger guitarists, including Larry Koonse. In the 1970s, he worked with Tony Rizzi's Five Guitars. When his wife contracted muscular dystrophy in the mid-1980s, Wyble largely retired from music to take care of her. After her death in 2005, he began playing in public in the Los Angeles area, showing that he had lost little through the years. In 2007, Larry Koonse recorded an album of Wyble compositions mostly taken from his highly rated book of etudes, *What's In The Box?*

Jimmy Wyble continued teaching and playing until shortly before his death in 2010, nine days shy of his 88th birthday. He was considered a master of counterpoint, able to play simultaneous lines that moved in opposite directions.

**Recommended CDs:** Jimmy Wyble's most notable album as a leader has been reissued in Japan as *Diane: Jimmy Wyble Quintet* (3D 1057). He can be heard as a sideman on Red Norvo's *The Forward Look* (Reference 8), *Benny Goodman In Stockholm 1959* (Phontastic 8801) and Frank Sinatra's *Live In Australia* (Blue Note 37515). "Roly Poly" is included on Bob Wills' *King Of Lonestar Swing* (President 553). Larry Koonse's recording of Wyble compositions is available as *What's In The Box?* (Jazz Compass 1016).

**LPs to Search For:** Wyble led an unissued session in 1946. His other recordings as a leader, *Original Cast* (Jazz Chronicles 783), *Love Bros.* (Jazz Chronicles 773), *Etudes* (Jazz Chronicles 781) and *Classical/Jazz* (Jazz Chronicles 771/2), dating from 1974–77, have yet to be reissued.

## Richie Zellon
*b. December 28, 1954, Lima, Peru*

A talented guitarist and composer, Richie Zellon has infused jazz with his South American roots to develop his own style. "My mom, who was Brazilian, introduced me to my first jazz-related recordings through the music of Stan Getz and João Gilberto, which she constantly played at home during the early '60s. When I was nine, she took me to what I consider my first jazz-related concert, the Zimbo Trio with Elis Regina. I started playing after my parents brought me a guitar for my tenth birthday."

Zellon was originally a fan of the Beatles and the Ventures, and he played rock professionally when he was 12. At 15, he discovered recordings by Jimi Hendrix and Eric Clapton, which led him to B.B. King, Albert King and eventually Wes Montgomery. "At the time, I knew of no one else playing blues in Peru, let alone jazz, so there was no one I could go take lessons from. I had to rely solely on my ear. Eventually, I got frustrated and did not attempt to learn jazz until I came to the US in my early 20s." He worked as a studio and dance orchestra musician, playing a wide variety of music.

When he was 21, Zellon moved to San Francisco, spending a year as a disciple of Indian guru Sri Chinmoy. "I got to know Carlos Santana, who was also a member of this small community. Carlos took me to my first American jazz concert. We went to see Freddie Hubbard, Rahsaan Roland Kirk, McCoy Tyner, Ron Carter and Tony Williams all together! I was never the same thereafter."

Zellon attended the San Francisco Music and Arts Institute in 1974, going to Berklee during parts of 1977, 1982 and 1983. He also studied cello for a year, played mandolin in a bluegrass band and, after moving to Miami, worked regularly as a bassist for two years. Zellon worked in Orlando during 1989–92 with veteran pianist Jesse Stone and singer Evelyn McGhee, learning standards and getting opportunities to play with Sam Rivers. Since then, he has worked with multi-instrumentalist Richard Drexler, Alex Acuna, Oscar Stagnaro, Paquito D'Rivera, Jerry Bergonzi, Dave Liebman, Danilo Perez, Bob Moses, Abraham Laboriel, Justo Almario, George Garzone, Dave Samuels, Ignacio Berroa and Otmaro Ruiz on different projects.

In 1995, Zellon founded the Songosaurus label, which is devoted to documenting Latin jazz from South America. He produced over a dozen CDs for the label, for himself and others. He also co-founded the Pan-American Jazz Project (2003–07) with Carlos Averhoff, and as an educator, Zellon taught at the jazz department of the University of South Florida for three years and at Florida International University for four (2004–07).

"I consider myself a composer who happens to play guitar. When I entered the world of jazz as a guitarist, I realized early on that the world did not need another Wes Montgomery clone or another zillion recordings of the same standards. So I worked diligently on developing my own voice primarily through my writing and Latin-tinged adaptations of both jazz and rock standards. Even though I love to play mainstream jazz, when people ask me what kind of music I play, I tell them 'South American jazz.'"

**Recommended CDs:** Richie Zellon's first album as a leader, 1982's *Landologia* (Songosaurus 724786), is considered to be among the first recordings of Afro-Peruvian jazz. *Nazca Lines* (Songosaurus 724773), which has a tribute to Jimi Hendrix, and *Metal Caribe* (Songosaurus 724778), which includes unusual versions of such pieces as "Sunshine Of Your Love," Perez Prado's "Que Rico El Mambo," "Peter And The Wolf" and "The Twilight Zone," are eclectic yet unified releases that are full of surprises. Other fine showcases are *An Evening Of South American Jazz* (Songosaurus 724783); *Cafe Con Leche* (Songosaurus 724772), which matches him with such all-stars as Paquito D'Rivera, Jerry Bergonzi, Danilo Perez, Justo Almario, Abraham Laboriel and Bob Moses; and *Son De Las Americas* (Songosaurus 724785), a trio outing with Richard Drexler and Steve Davis. "My most representative recording is probably *The Afro-Peruvian Jazz Sessions* (Songosaurus 724784), a compilation of most of my work fusing Afro-Peruvian music and jazz during the '90s."

**Website:** www.richiezellon.com

## Attila Zoller
*b. June 13, 1927, Visegrad, Hungary; d. January 25, 1998, Townshend, VT*

A versatile guitarist who displayed his own musical personality (which included aspects of his Hungarian heritage) no matter what the setting, Attila Zoller's wide-ranging career ranged from swing and hard bop to

free jazz. Born and raised in Hungary, Zoller started out taking lessons in classical violin from his father, who played professionally. After stints on trumpet, flugelhorn and bass as a teenager, he settled on the guitar when he was 18, gaining experience playing jazz in Budapest clubs. Three days before the Soviets blockaded the Hungarian border in October 1948, he escaped Hungary on foot across the mountains to Austria, carrying only his guitar and some clothing.

Zoller worked in Austria for five years with Vera Auer (who played accordion and vibes) in a group that part of the time included the young Joe Zawinul on piano. After moving to West Germany in 1954, he worked with such major jazz musicians as Jutta Hipp (to whom he was engaged for a time), Emil Mangelsdorff and Hans Koller in addition to Oscar Pettiford and Lee Konitz. In 1959, Zoller moved to

the United States after he won a scholarship to the Lenox School of Jazz. Ornette Coleman and Don Cherry, who were at the school at the time, were his roommates, and Zoller had an opportunity to study with Jim Hall.

Zoller worked with Tony Scott (when Bill Evans was the pianist), the 1960 Chico Hamilton Quintet, Herbie Mann, Sonny Rollins and Stan Getz, and in 1965, he co-led an adventurous jazz group with pianist Don Friedman that sometimes played free improvisations. He also worked with Red Norvo and Benny Goodman. In 1968, Zoller led a group for a European tour that included Lee Konitz and Albert Mangelsdorff. He worked and recorded on several occasions with Konitz through the years. In the 1970s, he sometimes played unaccompanied solo guitar sets in clubs, preceding Joe Pass.

A teacher since the 1960s, in 1974 he founded the Attila Zoller Jazz Clinics, teaching at his second home in Vermont. In 1985, he incorporated his school as the Vermont Jazz Center, a local institution so strong that it has survived his death.

Attila Zoller, whose health began to fail in 1994, was active up until the end of his life.

**Recommended CDs:** *Zo-Ko-So* (Universal 8431072) from 1965 teams Zoller with Hans Koller and Martial Solal. *The Horizon Beyond* (Act 92112) is with Don Friedman in a 1965 quartet. *Gypsy Cry* (Collectables 6178) is an intriguing album from 1970 that is half commercial, half fairly free music, and all Zoller originals. Other gems from Attila Zoller's discography include *Common Cause* (Enja 3043), *Overcome* (Enja 5053), *When It's Time* (Enja 9031), the solo guitar CD *Lasting Love* (Acoustic Music 319 1131), and *The Last Recordings* (Enja 9349), which was recorded three weeks before the guitarist's death. A two-CD set, *Jim & I* (L&R 8002), has the music from three albums that Zoller co-led with Jimmy Raney.

**LPs to Search For:** *Conjunction* (Enja 3051) is a high-quality solo guitar set.

## Barry Zweig
*b. February 7, 1942, Detroit, MI*

When Barry Zweig was turning five and his parents asked him what he wanted for his birthday, he requested a banjo, having recently seen one played in a movie. Instead, he was given a ukulele, which he grew to love. Zweig had violin lessons for ten years, starting when he was eight, but switched his focus to guitar when he was 15 after hearing the Dave Pell Octet's recording of "Mountain Greenery" (which had Tony Rizzi on guitar). He soon bought his first guitar for ten dollars. In high school, Zweig played

**Barry Zweig**

with Bill Baldwin and the Seventeens, appearing on an album with the group. Matty Matlock provided the band's arrangements, and his son, Julian "Bud" Matlock, was Zweig's first guitar teacher.

In 1964, Zweig was drafted into the Army. By a stroke of luck, he was stationed in Colorado Springs, Colorado, where, in addition to playing with the NORAD Band, he took lessons with Johnny Smith for a year. Three weeks after he was discharged from the service, the guitarist got a call to join the Buddy Rich Orchestra. He worked with Rich for six months (recording two albums including Swingin' New Big Band) and with Sammy Davis, Jr., for a year.

After settling in Los Angeles in 1968, Zweig became a studio guitarist, worked with *The Dinah Shore Show* (1976–81), and appeared regularly in local jazz clubs. Among his associations have been Peggy Lee, Willie Bobo, Don Ellis, Henry Mancini, Ray Conniff (with whom he visited Brazil), Dave Pell, Natalie Cole, Bill Holman, Keely Smith, Frank Capp's Juggernaut, Bill Elliott, and Jackie Ryan. Zweig has also taught at UCLA, USC and the University of Texas at El Paso.

A superior straight-ahead guitarist, Barry Zweig, who survived a serious illness during 2009, is heard at his best in swing and cool-jazz settings.

**Recommended CDs:** Barry Zweig has only led one album in his career, the rather scarce LP *Desert Vision* (Jazz Chronicles 788). As a sideman, he is featured on Andrea Baker's *Table For One* (Danc 0003) and Al McKibbon's *Black Orchard* (Nine Yard Records), also appearing on sets led by Ron Kalina, Jackie Ryan, Anna Callahan, Keely Smith, Dave Pell, Bill Elliot, Ray Conniff, Frank Capp, Ray Anthony, Gene Estes, Bill Holman and Buddy Rich. But he really should be much more widely recorded as a soloist.

**Website:** www.barryzweig-guitar.com

# 44 OTHER HISTORIC GUITARISTS

**Elek Bacsik** (1926–93) was born in Budapest, a cousin of Django Reinhardt and skilled on both guitar and violin. A bop-oriented musician who moved to Paris in 1959 and settled in the US in 1966, he led some obscure sessions of his own. Bacsik's best-known recording was as a sideman with Dizzy Gillespie on *Dizzy On The French Riviera* (Verve 125560).

**Rolf Berg** was on many of the best cool jazz sessions that came out of Sweden in the 1950s, including dates with the great baritonist Lars Gullin. Gullin's *Danny's Dream* (Dragon 396) has several worthy Berg solos.

**Perry Botkin, Sr.** (1907–73), was Bing Crosby's guitar accompanist for 20 years, a top studio guitarist for decades, and worked with everyone from Al Jolson to Benny Goodman, Roy Rogers to the Boswell Sisters. Among his feats was playing ukulele with symphony orchestras. He can be heard on Jack Teagarden's *1941–1943* (Classics 874). His son Perry Botkin, Jr., is a very successful arranger-composer.

**Sam Brown** (1939–77) did not live long, but he made an impact with his jazz/rock playing during the late 1960s/early '70s. He recorded with Charlie Haden's Liberation Music Orchestra, Gary Burton, Carla Bley, Paul Motian, and most notably, Keith Jarrett on *Expectations* (Sony 65900).

**Mike Bryan** (1916–72) first worked with Benny Goodman's big band during 1940–41 but was not noticed because Charlie Christian was with Goodman's small groups. However, he got more attention when he was back with Goodman (1945–46), recording with BG's Sextet when it had Red Norvo and Slam Stewart. After 20 years as a studio musician, in 1962 he produced a series of half-hour jazz films for the Goodyear Tire Company, featuring jazz greats. He took the opportunity to lead a band of his own (the only one of his career) on one episode. The soundtrack from his film (which also features trumpeter Doc Severinsen and Georgie Auld on tenor) is on the LP *Mike Bryan Sextet* (Storyville 4015).

A valuable addition to many New Orleans jazz sets of the 1950s, **Joe Capraro** (1903–?) was valuable both as a soloist and an accompanist, often working with Sharkey Bonano and Armand Hug. He plays quite well on *The Out-Of-Towners* (GHB 79) and *Bob Havens In New Orleans* (GHB 126).

The musical talents of **Roger Chaput** (1909–95) are difficult to evaluate, for his most prominent role was as one of two rhythm guitarists who played behind Django Reinhardt and Stéphane Grappelli with the Quintet of the Hot Club of France during 1933–38. In later years, he became a cartoonist and an artist and ran his own music school.

**Pete Cosey** (1943–2012) was an explosive guitarist best known for touring and recording with Miles Davis during 1973–75. Prior to the Davis period, Cosey was a session guitarist for the Chess label. Since 1975, he was almost entirely off records for 25 years. He resurfaced to play quite well on the 2008 CD *Miles From India* (Times Square 1808). Some of his best playing with Miles Davis is on *Pangaea* (Sony 12323), which is full of fire, fury and passion.

**Jerome Darr** (1910–86) had such diverse musical activities in his life as playing with the Washboard Serenaders (1933–36), Charlie Parker, Buddy Johnson's R&B big band, Rex Stewart, Frankie Lymon and the Teenagers, and Jonah Jones. He was part of both Charlie Parker's *Cole Porter Songbook* (Verve 823250), which was Bird's final recording date, and Jonah Jones' *Back On The Street* (Chiaroscuro 118) from 1972.

**Sacha Distel** (1933–2004) was a popular singer and actor in France who, in the early part of his career, focused on being a top-notch jazz guitarist. The two-CD set *Jazz Guitarist* (Universal 980 692) features Distel in 1956 with mostly French and American musicians (including Slide Hampton, Kenny Clarke, and saxophonists Hubert Fol and Bobby Jaspar), showing what a fine bop soloist he was at the beginning.

A contemporary of Django Reinhardt, **Jean-Pierre "Matelo" Ferret** (1918–89) played musette music in Paris and swinging jazz with the likes of Eddie South, Benny Carter, Andre Ekyan, Alix Combelle, and the Quintet of the Hot Club of France. He did not record that often, making *Tziganskaia And Other Rare Recordings* (Hot Club 46) a valuable acquisition.

**Pierre "Baro" Ferret** (1908–78), the older brother of Jean-Pierre Ferret, also played with the Quintet of the Hot Club of France (as did a third brother, Etienne "Sarane" Ferret, and their cousin René "Challain" Ferret). Although considered a strong guitar soloist, he just played rhythm behind Reinhardt. In later years, his playing and composing were open to the influence of bop, but he is perhaps most significant as a composer, particularly of waltzes. His one LP as a leader, from the mid-1960s, is *Swing Valses D'Hier Et D'Aujourd'Hui* (Hot Club 45). Pierre Ferret is the father of Boulou and Elios Ferré. The four-CD set *Gypsy Jazz* (Proper Box 128), in addition to some well known selections featuring Reinhardt and Grappelli, features a strong cross section of gypsy-jazz guitarists from the 1930s through the '50s, including the Ferret brothers.

An early associate of Charlie Parker, **William "Biddy" Fleet** (1910–94) was an influence on Bird, particularly in his use of alternate chords and the higher interval of chords. They jammed often in 1939 in the back of Dan Wahl's chili restaurant in Harlem, and Parker was later quoted as saying that he "came alive" one night when they played "Cherokee." Fleet, who unfortunately never recorded with Parker nor made any significant recordings, was captured on a poorly recorded live session jamming with Jelly Roll Morton in 1938 ("Honeysuckle Rose" and "Melancholy Baby") and worked with Roy Eldridge's big band in 1946.

A studio guitarist for decades, **Tony Gottuso** was in the first Artie Shaw Orchestra in 1936, recorded with Ella Fitzgerald and Sarah Vaughan, and was still working steadily when he played banjo on Louis Armstrong's recording of "Hello Dolly" in 1963. Whether on acoustic guitar, banjo or electric guitar, Gottuso was a reliable craftsman. In 1937, he recorded six superb guitar duets with John Cali (who was better known as a banjoist), all of which are on *Guitar Rarities Vol. 2* (IAJRC 1018). Tony Gottuso's grandson is drummer Scott Amendola.

**Ted Greene** (1946–2005) was a much beloved and respected guitar teacher. He wrote four influential books, including *Chord Chemistry*. But a shy performer, he only recorded one album as a leader: *Solo Guitar* (Art of Life 1011).

A self-taught guitarist, **Albert Harris** (1916–2005) was born in London, moved to the US in 1938, and was well known in Hollywood as a classical composer and an orchestrator and composer for television shows and films. But back during 1935–36, he recorded six guitar duets with Ivor Mairants (including "Dedication To Eddie Lang" and "Yankee Doodle Had A Fugue") and one with Bert Thomas, which are included in the excellent *Guitar Rarities Vol. 1* (IAJRC 1017). There are also two Harris numbers with a slightly larger group on *Guitar Rarities Vol. 2* (IAJRC 1018).

**Jeff Healey** (1966–2008) usually played bluesy rock on guitar and, later in life, trad jazz on trumpet. His posthumous release *Last Call* (Stony Plain 1335) has him playing both guitar and trumpet on jazz standards and shows that he could have been a notable jazz guitarist too.

Now somewhat forgotten, **Carl Hogan** (1917–?) was an early influence on Chuck Berry (who used Hogan's solo on "Ain't That Just Like A Woman" for his opening on "Johnny B. Goode") and on Bill Haley's "Rock Around The Clock." His guitar playing with Louis Jordan during 1945–48 was a part of quite a few Jordan hits, setting the stage (a decade early) for

rock and roll. He is featured on Louis Jordan's *1945–1946* (Classics 921) and *1946–1947* (Classic 1010).

**Clarence Holiday** (1898–1937) was 16 when he became the father of Billie Holiday, and in the 1930s when she started to make it big, he was embarrassed to admit that he had a grown-up daughter, since he was in his mid-thirties. Holiday was Fletcher Henderson's rhythm guitarist and banjoist during 1928–33, appearing on many records but just as an accompanist.

**Ike Isaacs** (1919–96), not to be confused with the bassist of the same name, is undoubtedly the only guitarist in this book to have been born in Burma. He lived in England during much of his life (ending up in Australia) and is best known for playing acoustic rhythm guitar with Diz Disley's group when it accompanied Stéphane Grappelli on his world tours and recordings. Grappelli's *Shades Of Django* (Verve 825955) has good examples of Isaacs' rhythm guitar.

**Harry Leahey** (1935–90), who died from cancer, is best remembered for his association with Phil Woods (1977–80). In addition to being a member of Woods' quintet, Leahey was a teacher (Vic Juris was one of his students) and he worked with Gerry Mulligan, Al Cohn, Ira Sullivan and Mark Murphy. He plays particularly well on Woods' *Live From The Showboat* (BMG 37512).

**Ulysses Livingston** (1912–88) was on many swing records in the 1930s (including with Benny Carter, Coleman Hawkins, Billie Holiday and Lil Armstrong), toured with Ella Fitzgerald in the early 1940s, was part of the later version of the Spirits of Rhythm, popped up on R&B records in the 1950s, and was recording on both guitar and electric bass as late as the 1970s. He can be heard soloing on a couple of numbers on boogie-woogie pianist Pete Johnson's *1938–1939* (Classics 656).

**Billy Mackel** (1912–86), who led his own group during 1940–44, was with Lionel Hampton off and on from 1944 until 1978. He was a solid soloist on electric guitar whom Hampton always appreciated. In 1977, he led the only album of his career, the LP *Billy Mackel…At Last* (Black and Blue 33.117).

**Jack Marshall** (1922–73) had several overlapping careers in his life. He was a record producer for Capitol, an arranger-composer, and a conductor, did comedy records with Jack Sheldon, and played classical and jazz guitar. Some of his projects were outlandish or instantly dated, making use of odd sounds that probably sounded colorful on early hi-fi systems. On *Sounds* (Capitol 2610) and *Sounds Unheard Of* (Contemporary 9006), neither of which are available yet on CD, he plays classical guitar on duets with the drums and percussion of Shelly Manne.

**Charlie McCoy** (1909–50) and his brother Joe McCoy (1905–50) were best known for their guitar playing on blues records of the 1930s and '40s, including those of Charlie's wife, Memphis Minnie. However, they were also members of the Harlem Hamfats during 1936–39, an intriguing goodtime jazz/blues Chicago group led by trumpeter Herb Morand. Their playing on Morand's *New Orleans To Harlem* (Jazz Crusade 3015), which has both brothers on guitar with Charlie doubling on mandolin, is quite spirited, bluesy and swinging.

An underrated guitarist, **Eddie McFadden** (1927–92) helped establish the role of the guitar in organ-led groups. He was with Jimmy Smith when Smith hit it big in 1957 and also worked with Johnny "Hammond" Smith and Don Patterson, rejoining Smith for a time in the late 1960s. Jimmy Smith's two-CD set *Groovin' At Small's Vols. 1–2* (Blue Note 99777) features McFadden in a trio with drummer Donald Bailey, accompanying Smith and taking plenty of concise and soulful solos.

The older brother of cornetist Jimmy McPartland, guitarist **Dick McPartland** (1905–57) was also a member of the famed Austin High School Gang in mid-1920s Chicago. An acoustic rhythm guitarist who was a good soloist, he recorded with Irving Mills and Jack Teagarden and two sessions led by his brother in 1936 and 1939. But a heart attack resulted in him becoming semi-retired by the late 1930s, although he played as late as 1955.

**Lou Mecca** (1927–2003) was a chiropractor by day and a guitarist by night. He led two albums in his career, 1955's *Lou Mecca Quartet* (EMI 9228) and 2003's *Bridging The Gap* (Japanese Pony Canyon 1063). Part-time or not, he was a fine bop-based soloist whom Gil Melle used on some of his projects.

**Coleman Mellett** (1974–2009) was a young guitarist with a lot of potential who died in the same plane crash as saxophonist Gerry Niewood. He had gained some recognition for being in Chuck Mangione's band since 1999, had recorded his first CD as a leader, *Natural High* (standards and a few originals released on his own label), and was married to singer Jeanie Bryson.

**Johnny Moore** (1906–69), the older brother of Oscar Moore (who was best known for his work with the Nat King Cole Trio), played a brand of easygoing rhythm and blues throughout his life that bordered on and sometimes crossed over into jazz. He led the Three Blazers from 1944 until the mid-1960s, having his greatest success during 1945–48, when Charles Brown was the group's singer-pianist; many in the audience thought that Brown was Moore. The Three Blazers' early recordings are available under Charles Brown's name as *1944–1945* (Classics 894) and *1946* (Classics 971).

**Ronald Muldrow** (1949–2007) worked with Eddie Harris, was based in Los Angeles, and was a fine Wes Montgomery–inspired soul-jazz guitarist. Among his six recordings as a leader are the excellent *Facing Wes* (Kokopelli 1311) and *Freedom's Serenade* (Doubletime 159).

**Robert Normann** (1918–91) was considered by many to be Norway's finest jazz musician of the 1940s and '50s. He gained national fame with the Swing Strings in the late 1930s, was able to stay active during the German occupation of Norway, and continued playing swing in the post-war years, including a 1951 concert with Hot Lips Page. Later in the decade, he became a studio musician before drifting into semi-retirement. His musical legacy can be heard on *The Definitive Collection 1938–1941 Vol. 1* (Normann 3004) and *1942–54 Vol. 2* (Normann 3005).

**Kenny Poole** (1948–2006) was a strong and very technically skilled hard-bop guitarist who settled in Cincinnati after working with Richard "Groove" Holmes, Jack McDuff, Mark Murphy and many others. He recorded three CDs for the J-Curve label: *East Meets Midwest* (J-Curve 1054), which is a duo album with Gene Bertoncini; a quartet date co-led with Cal Collins called *Su's Four* (J-Curve 1064); and a tribute to George Van Eps, *For George: Tribute To A Master* (J-Curve 1007).

**Babik Reinhardt** (1944–2001) was the son of Django Reinhardt and was a fine player, even though he was not close to the level of his famous father. Babik actually learned the guitar from his mother, Naguine, while Django taught him a bit of piano. Just nine when his father died, in time Babik developed his own style on electric guitar. While he was naturally enlisted to participate in some tribute concerts to his father, Babik was actually more influenced by Wes Montgomery than by Django, and he also recorded fusion with Larry Coryell and Didier Lockwood. *Live* (DRG 8431) is a fusion date from the mid-1990s, recorded a few years before he passed away from a heart attack.

Considered one of Western swing's top guitarists despite making few recordings, **Jimmie Rivers** (1926–2003) was originally influenced by Barney Kessel and Charlie Christian. Because his trio, the Gadabouts, was making good money in Texas during 1946–53, he turned down offers to join both Spade Cooley and Bob Wills. After moving to Oakland in 1954, he formed the Cherokees (he was half-Indian), making a few recordings and working regularly until the band's breakup in 1964. Later in life, Rivers worked with the Fulton Street Jazz Band and had his own swing-oriented group. *Brisbane Bop* (Joaquin 2501) is his definitive CD.

**Dennis Sandole** (1913–2000) is best known as an important teacher in John Coltrane's life. As part of the Philadelphia jazz scene, he also taught James

Moody, Pat Martino, Michael Brecker and Matthew Shipp. While he played guitar on quite a few sessions prior to the late 1940s, he recorded very little after that. *A Sandole Trilogy* (Cadence 1102) has a 1958 session plus performances from two later sets of his compositions, although he only plays on the 1958 selections.

**Eugene Vees** (1915–77), a cousin of Django Reinhardt, was a loyal member of Reinhardt's bands during 1936–47, never soloing but rated highly for the steady rhythm that he kept. Although he recorded as a leader in 1956 (on obscure LPs), even then he was not considered that great a soloist, nor did he have the drive to continue much of a career after Reinhardt passed away.

**Frank Victor** was a talented guitarist but a minor figure in jazz history. He played and recorded with Joe Venuti and Adrian Rollini (when Rollini was playing vibes and leading a trio) during their less publicized periods in the 1930s and '40s. Venuti's *Performance* (Fuel 2000 839) has the guitarist as one of several soloists in a loose set of 1934 radio transcriptions.

Probably Victor's finest recordings are his guitar duets with the equally obscure **Harry Volpe** (1906–95). Volpe was an early studio musician and a composer who ran a music store, where his students included Johnny Smith, Sal Salvador and Joe Pass. The six guitar duets of Victor and Volpe are on *Guitar Rarities Vol. 1* (IAJRC 1017).

**Efferge Ware** worked with Harlan Leonard, Jay McShann and Julia Lee in the 1940s. Part of the Kansas City jazz scene and influenced a bit by Charlie Christian, Ware is included here because he

participated in a recorded jam session with Charlie Parker, probably from September 1943, playing rhythm guitar in a trio with drummer Phil Phillips (no piano or bass) while Bird performed four songs, including "Cherokee."

**Leonard Ware** (1909–74) was an early electric guitarist who appeared on records with Big Joe Turner, Don Byas, Buddy Johnson and Sammy Price. Most importantly, he was heard on electric guitar playing with Sidney Bechet in November 1938, predating Charlie Christian by nine months and playing in a viable swing style. That session is on Bechet's *1937–1938* (Classics 593). Ware dropped out of music by the late 1940s.

**Hy White** (1915–?) was a member of Woody Herman's orchestra during 1939–44, taking occasional solos, including those on "Red River Blues" and "Blues Upstairs." He also recorded with Coleman Hawkins and Ben Webster and played in the big bands of Les Brown, Gene Krupa and the Dorsey Brothers, working as a studio musician in the 1950s and accompanying many singers, including Ella Fitzgerald and Frank Sinatra. Woody Herman's *The Band That Plays The Blues* (Naxos 8120527) has some of his best early solos.

**Wayne Wright** (1933–2008) played rhythm guitar with the Ruby Braff–George Barnes Quartet during 1974–75, worked with many New York area swing combos, and recorded a pair of guitar duet albums (not yet reissued on CD) led by Marty Grosz: *Goody Goody* (Aviva 6003) and *Let Your Fingers Do The Walking* (Aviva 6004). Although he could solo well, Wright enjoyed playing rhythm guitar and inspiring other soloists.

# 175 OTHER JAZZ GUITARISTS ON THE SCENE TODAY

An intriguing guitarist from Norway, **Eivind Aarset** (www.eivindaarset.com) creates unusual electronic sounds and is influenced by both ambient music and ECM recordings. His music is thought-provoking and unusual, as can be heard on *Light Extract* (Universal 1025).

Originally from Pontiac, Michigan, **Paul Abler** (www.paulabler.com) gained experience playing music in Detroit and Los Angeles before moving to New York in 2003. He has been part of the post-bop scene ever since. His latest recording, *Fearless* (on Chesky's Bossa Nova subsidiary), features him in a quartet with drummer Cindy Blackman. Upcoming is a change of pace: a tribute to Jimi Hendrix titled *Only Cowboys Stay In Tune* (Bossa Nova).

**Steve Abshire** (www.steveabshire.com) was in the Navy for 24 years, playing with the Navy's main jazz band, the Commodores, for 18. He has since been based in Washington, DC, and Maryland, works as an educator, and has recorded a few mainstream swing-to-bop CDs. Recently, he made *Detour Ahead* (Patuxent Music) with fellow guitarist Paul Wingo, a tribute to Barney Kessel and Herb Ellis.

Best known as an explorative rock guitarist from Amsterdam who became well known in Europe with the group Focus, **Jan Akkerman** (www.janakkerman.nl) has often played fusion on his solo projects. A good example of his work in that idiom is on 1978's *Jan Akkerman* (Wounded Bird 9159), which also features Joachim Kuhn on keyboards.

**Glenn Alexander** (www.glennalexander.com) is a fine fusion guitarist whose sound and style sometimes hint at Pat Metheny. *Rainbow's Revenge* (Shanachie 5005) features him in passionate form with a band, while *Oria* (Palmetto 2015) is a laidback set of mood music.

A versatile guitarist based in Chicago, **Neal Alger** (www.nealalger.com) has worked with Patricia Barber on many occasions, appearing on four of her CDs and touring Europe. He has also worked and recorded with singer Typhanie Monique, including her *Intrinsic* (Blujazz 3331).

**Leonardo Amuedo** (www.myspace.com/leonardoamuedo) is from Uruguay, has spent time living in the Netherlands (where he worked with Laura Fygi, the Metropole Orchestra, Hermeto Pascoal and the Rosenberg Trio), and currently lives in Brazil, where he performs with Ivan Lins. 1994's *Dolphin Dance* (Challenge 70008) is the most readily available of his albums.

Based in Philadelphia, **Chuck Anderson** (www.chuckandersonjazzguitar.com) has been a music educator, a writer, and a guitarist who pioneered playing classical guitar with a pick. He is currently working on a recording project with Jimmy Bruno. *Freefall*, which is available on his own label, features the guitarist on his originals in a hard-bop trio with bassist Eric Schreiber and drummer Ed Rick.

**John Anello, Jr.** (www.johnanello.com), has run his own Cexton label in Orange County since 1983. An accessible player with an attractive sound and a versatile style, Anello is heard in top form on *Swing & Samba, Blues & Bossa* (Cexton 9999), which lives up to its title and is full of catchy melodies.

**Michael Anthony** (www.michaelanthonyonline.com) became a professional guitarist in 1960, worked in the L.A. studios, and eventually settled in New Mexico, where he plays regularly and teaches. *The Sands Of Time* (available from his website) features his straight-ahead trio with bassist Milo Jaramillo and drummer Andy Poling and is dedicated to his first guitar teacher, Jimmy Wyble.

**Marc Antoine** (www.marcantoine.com), who was born Marc Jean Roland Antoine Vouilloux in France, had classical guitar training and worked with Basia in London in the late 1980s. He was a session player in both Tokyo and Los Angeles before becoming a smooth star, beginning with the release of his first CD in 1994. His classical guitar playing is featured on nine CDs of his own, including *Foreign Xchange* (Peak 3094).

**Bruce Arnold** was raised in South Dakota, graduated from Berklee, and became a highly respected educator and guitarist. He has long been interested in improvising on modern classical music, leading such groups as Act of Finding and Spooky Actions at a Distance. *Two Guys From A Distance* (Muse Eek 121) is a set of guitar duets on standards with fellow guitarist Mike Miller, while *A Few Dozen* (Muse Eek 645) is one of a few of his CDs that utilize the 12-tone row as the basis for his solos with his trio.

**Erich Avinger** (www.heartmusic.com/erich/erich_home.html) has been part of the Houston jazz scene throughout much of his career as a guitarist and educator. Originally influenced by rock guitarists, he later became interested in Brazilian music, fusion, world music and Indian rhythms. Among his other instruments, he often plays a handmade ten-string acoustic guitar. *Poets, Misfits, Beggars And Shamans* (Heart Music 23) is a good example of his work.

**Mike Baggetta** (www.mikebaggetta.com) is an original post-bop guitarist who leads a quartet with tenor-saxophonist Jason Rigby and the duo Tin/Bag with trumpeter Kris Tiner. Based in New York, he is featured with his quartet on *Small Spaces* (Fresh Sound New Talent 339).

**Bob Bain** (b. 1924) has had a very long career as a studio musician. He worked with Freddy Slack in 1942, the Phil Moore Four, Frank Sinatra, Tommy Dorsey, Bob Crosby, and Harry James, and has worked in the studios since the 1950s. It is his guitar that is heard on Henry Mancini's famous *Peter Gunn* theme. Bain collaborated with Jack Marshall and Howard Roberts to form Guitars Unlimited, an easy-listening exercise for the top studio musicians in the 1960s. His handful of albums as a leader for Capitol is unfortunately all long out-of-print.

The founder and president of the Palmetto label, **Matt Balitsaris** (www.palmetto-records.com) has worked as a guitarist and producer with C'est What, Loose Shoes, Mino Cinelu, Cecil McBee, Dewey Redman and Fred Hersch in addition to the other artists on Palmetto. His own playing ranges from the avant-garde to fusion, post-bop to world music. *An Echoed Smile* (Palmetto 2022), which has duets with vibraphonist Jeff Berman plus some guest appearances, mostly focuses on Balitsaris' acoustic playing.

A major force in the Detroit jazz scene, **A. Spencer Barefield** (www.spencerbarefield.com) is the artistic and executive director of the Creative Arts Collective. He has worked with such avant-gardists as Lester Bowie, Roscoe Mitchell, Oliver Lake, Hugh Ragin and Andrew Cyrille in addition to leading his own groups. *Soul Steppin' Through The Fabulous Ruins* (CAC/Xenogenesis) is his most recent recording.

**Carl Barry** (www.carlandjoannebarry.com), who is based in Brooklyn, is a melodic bop-oriented player. He has often teamed up with his wife, singer Joanne Barry, and in his long career has also worked with Jack Wilkins, Don Friedman, Hal Galper, Helen Humes, Carrie Smith, Zoot Sims and Hank Jones. Most of his recordings are difficult to find, but *Holding On* (P-Vine 23293), a Stash album from 1982, was reissued.

**Robert Bell** (www.bellrobert.com) is a gypsy-jazz guitarist in Minnesota. He has led the swing septet Bellcats, organized Django Reinhardt tribute concerts, and formed the Twin Cities Hot Club, with whom he has recorded. He also plays with the Southside Aces and leads groups of his own. His *Gypsy Tendercies* CD is available from his website.

Around 2003, **Chris Bergson** (www.chris bergson.com) changed his musical direction from jazz to blues, having success since then with the Chris Bergson Band. Prior to that, during 1995–2002, he played jazz in New York with Annie Ross and Dena DeRose and as a leader of his own combos. His two jazz albums as a leader are *Blues For Some Friends Of Mine* (Juniper 102) and *Wait For Spring* (Juniper 107).

**Randy Bernsen's** (www.randybernsen.com) career started out strong. His debut recording *Music For Planets, People And Washing Machines*, originally released by Zebra in the 1980s but now available through Bernsen's website, has such sidemen as Herbie Hancock, Bob James, Jaco Pastorius and Peter Erskine. Since then, Bernsen has chosen to mostly stay in South Florida and work as a studio musician in addition to being a pilot, although he did tour with Joe Zawinul and work with a recent version of the Jaco Pastorius big band.

Originally from Cleveland, **Michael Bocian** (www.michaelbocian.com) had Bill DeArango as his mentor. After moving to New York in 1974, he worked with Rashied Ali, Dewey Redman, Richie Beirach, and led several groups, including Universal Language, which included his longtime friend Joe Lovano, and Wood, a group in which the musicians only utilize acoustic wooden instruments. *The Five Elements* (released on his Ulua Music) is a set of thoughtful unaccompanied acoustic guitar solos.

A very popular smooth guitarist, **Norman Brown** (www.normanbrown.com) often sounds very similar to George Benson, both in his guitar playing and in his singing. His eighth CD, *Sending My Love* (Concord 31327), is similar to his previous seven, pleasing his fans but not converting anyone else to his mildly soulful easy-listening music.

**Dale Bruning** (www.jazzlinkenterprises.com) has been a lyrical guitarist since the 1950s and a teacher to over 1,000 students, including Bill Frisell and Margaret Slovak. Among his recordings is *Reunion* (Jazz Link), which teams him with Frisell on standards.

South African **Jonathan Butler** (www.jonathan-butler.com) is a smooth and R&B/pop guitarist and singer who is sometimes heard in pop/jazz settings. *So Strong* (Rendezvous 143) is one of several of his CDs that find him strongly influenced by George Benson in his post-*Breezin'* period.

**Al Caiola** (born 1920) has had one of the longest careers of any guitarist, still being active at the age of 92 at this writing. He was a professional by the early 1940s, became a studio musician, and appeared on all types of recordings, some of which are jazz. He had pop hits in the 1960s with his versions of the themes of *The Magnificent Seven* and *Bonanza*, and appeared on many easy-listening albums. He still works with Frank Sinatra, Jr., and Steve Lawrence. *Deep In A Dream* (Savoy 205) and *Serenade In Blue* (Savoy 232), which suffer from poor packaging, feature Caiola playing melodic jazz in the mid-1950s.

An up-and-coming jazz guitarist from Southern California who is now in New York City, **Brent Canter** is impressive on his *Soundscape* CD, which was privately released and is available at www

.brentcanter.com. His CD features his BC3 organ trio. Canter seeks to invigorate and update the classic guitar-organ-drums trio beyond its usual roots in soul jazz.

**John Carlini**'s roots are in bluegrass, but like David Grisman, with whom he has worked on an occasional basis for the past 40 years, Carlini (www.johncarlini.com) also explores jazz on a part-time basis. His 1995 duet album with Tony Rice (a major bluegrass guitarist also involved in the "new acoustic music" movement), *River Suite For Two Guitars* (Sugar Hill 3837), crosses many stylistic boundaries and is quite jazz-oriented, while *Angel Eyes* (Blue Night 216) is an exploration of jazz standards that teams him with mandolinist Don Stiernberg.

**Deirdre Cartwright** (www.deirdrecartwright.com), who originally hid from nuns at her convent school the fact that she wanted to play guitar (and was secretly practicing), has been a top British post-bop guitarist for the past 20 years. She co-runs the Blow the Fuse jazz club in England, and her current group is featured on *Tune Up Turn On Stretch Out* (Sam 0707).

A popular figure in the trad-jazz circuit, **Katie Cavera** (www.katiecavera.com) is a fine rhythm guitarist who also takes occasional solos, sings well, and is an excellent string bassist and banjoist. She plays with such artists as the Reynolds Brothers, Clint Baker, drummer Hal Smith and pianist Ray Skjelbred. *Who's Foolin' Who?* (Burgundy St) features her and Clint Baker overdubbing most of the instruments with Cavera on guitars, banjo, ukulele, kazoo and vocals.

A fine guitarist based in San Diego, **Mike Cea** (www.mikecea.com) is an excellent straight-ahead player. *Java Jazz* (available from Cea's website) features his trio plus guest Holly Hofmann on flute and singer Debbie Cea.

**Emmett Chapman** (www.emmettchapman.net) was a jazz guitarist who constantly experimented with his instrument years before he invented the Chapman Stick. After he mastered tapping on the guitar in the early 1970s, he built the first Chapman Stick in 1974. Chapman, whose early inspiration was Barney Kessel, became more influenced by John McLaughlin by that time. Surprisingly, Chapman (who is still active at the age of 74) has made few recordings, making *Parallel Galaxy* (Backyard 1) a valuable acquisition.

Considered one of Tunisia's top jazz musicians, **Fawzi Chekili** (www.myspace.com/fawzichekili) has been an important part of his country's music scene since the mid-1970s. Although he has played in Canada, the US and Russia, most of his work has been in his native country, combining together the influence of Tunisian folk music with jazz. He has

performed with Jimmy Gourley, Didier Lockwood, Russell Malone and Deborah Brown. Of his three CDs as a leader, *Echihem* (Blue Jasmin) is his most recent.

**John Chiodini** (www.johnchiodini.com) has always been in great demand to accompany singers, having worked for years with Peggy Lee. He has also accompanied Natalie Cole (for eight years), Diane Schuur, Nancy Wilson, Al Jarreau, Lainie Kazan, Celine Dion, Monica Mancini, Barry Manilow, Rosemary Clooney, Michael Bublé and even Barbra Streisand. As part of Affinity (with is comprised of Natalie Cole's rhythm section), he is well featured on *Route 66* (Rhombus 7052).

**Joe Cinderella** (b. 1929) made records in the 1950s with Vinnie Burke, Chris Connor and Gil Melle and spent decades as a studio musician, recording with everyone from the Beach Boys and Judy Garland to John Cage. He did not make his lone album as a leader until 2002, when he cut the privately released *Concept*, which features him playing standards and originals on an eight-string guitar.

**Doug Clarke** (www.dougclarkemusic.com), who studied with Tal Farlow, is a talented hard-bop guitarist. He often teams up with bassist Gary Mazzaroppi. On *Beware Of Doug*, he leads a quartet with Mazzaroppi, saxophonist Paul Carlon and drummer Scott Latzky through modern swinging originals and a few fresh versions of standards.

**Greg Clayton** (www.gregclayton.com) was born in Montreal, where he has been based for his whole career thus far. He has mostly worked with local performers, including singers John Labelle and George Evans. *Live At Boomers* (String Jazz 1013) gives listeners excellent examples of his playing with a trio.

As a guitarist and a singer, **Joyce Cooling** (www.joycecooling.com) has long shown the potential to be a significant jazz performer. She even played early in her career with Joe Henderson, Stan Getz and Charlie Byrd. However, she has since mostly performed smooth music, having a great deal of commercial if not artistic success. Her 1990 recording debut, *Cameo* (P-Vine 8808), is her most jazz-oriented recording.

**Laurie Dameron** (www.lauriedameron.com) has been based in Colorado for 40 years. She leads Laurie D. and the Blues Babes and plays jazz, blues, pop and country. *I Can't Wait To See You Again* (Windchime) shows how strong a jazz player she can be.

**Mike DeMicco** (www.mikedemicco.com) has worked with the Brubeck Brothers Quartet for quite a few years, and has played with the Dolphins (which he co-led with drummer Dan Brubeck), Jack DeJohnette, Nick Brignola and Warren Bernhardt. He has also led an organ trio with Pete Levin. DeMicco is in fine form on *As The Sun Sets* (Blue Forest 5701).

**Tom Dempsey**

**Tom Dempsey** (www.tjdmusic.com) is based in New York, performs hard bop and post-bop jazz, and has worked with such notables as George Coleman, Kenny Barron, Jack McDuff and Roy Haynes. Of his four CDs as a leader, his most recent one is *What's Going On?* (City Tone 701), a set of duets with bassist Tim Ferguson that includes modernized standards and inventive originals.

**Mike DiBari** (www.mikedibari.com), who plays regularly in Boston, performs blues, swing and bop with equal skill and understanding. In 1996, he formed the Mike DiBari Swingtet and he has since also led a trio. The Swingtet is heard in spirited form on *Jumpin' The Blues* (Palomino Jazz), while the trio has several CDs, including *Music Of The Spheres* (Palomino Jazz).

**Eddie Diehl**, who is now 75, has had a productive career since the late 1950s, recording with Jack McDuff, Gene Ammons, Sonny Stitt, Johnny "Hammond" Smith, Hank Mobley, Reuben Wilson and others. A soulful bop-based guitarist, he finally made his recording debut as a leader when he was 69 in 2006 with *Well Here It Is* (Lineage 101), a swinging quartet date with pianist Hank Jones.

**Pat Donohue** (www.patdonohue.com) has been part of Garrison Keillor's *A Prairie Home Companion* house band since 1993, being featured each week on the popular NPR show. He is expert at playing early jazz, blues, ragtime, folk and R&B, infusing the music with both creativity and joy. *Two Hand Band* (Blue Sky 916) features his solo versions of such tunes as "High Society," "The Mooche," "Yardbird Suite" and "Royal Garden Blues."

**Lars Edegran** not only plays guitar but also piano, banjo, mandolin, and on rare occasions, clarinet and saxophone. Born in Stockholm, he moved to New Orleans in 1966 and has always played early jazz. He founded and leads the New Orleans Ragtime Orchestra and wrote the music for the show *One Mo' Time*. Edegran has recorded a string of worthy albums for the GHB label, including *Shim Sham Shimmy Dance* (GHB 323).

**Howard Elkins** has been the guitarist and banjoist with the Jim Cullum Jazz Band since 1978. Each week, he is heard on Cullum's *Riverwalk Jazz* public radio series, and it is his song "Nightspell" that is used as the Cullum band's opening theme. He is prominent on clarinetist Allan Vaché's quartet set *One For My Baby* (Audiophile 255).

**Charles Ellerbee** was one of the two main guitarists (along with Bern Nix) who was featured in Ornette Coleman's explosive Prime Time during 1975–87, playing harmolodic music that utilized free-funk rhythms and joyfully overcrowded ensembles. Although he has continued leading groups up to the present time, Ellerbee has maintained a surprisingly low profile and has yet to lead a CD of his own. He can be heard creating a musical storm with Ornette and Nix throughout 1976's *Body Meta* (Verve 531916).

**Tommy Emmanuel** (www.tommyemmanuel.com) is considered one of Australia's finest guitarists. His fingerstyle way of playing, which utilizes all ten of his fingers, has long impressed other guitarists. While much of his career has found him playing country (inspired by Chet Atkins), rock, and pop music, he explored smooth after visiting the US in 1997. *Happy Hour* (Original Works 0206) features his concise versions of a variety of standards, some from the swing era.

**Gene Ess** (www.jazzgenemusic.com), who was raised in Okinawa, Japan, started his career in the US on top, attending Berklee and making his debut in New York in a quartet that also included Rashied Ali, Reggie Workman and Eddie Henderson. He has since played with Ravi Coltrane, Danilo Perez, Archie Shepp and Cindy Blackman among others. Among his rewarding post-bop recordings is *Sandbox And Sanctum: Song Cycle For Guitar* (Simp 50701).

**Dan Faehnle** (www.danfaehnle.com), a native of Ohio, toured with Diana Krall during 2000–03 and has worked along the way with such notables as Leroy Vinnegar, Joey DeFrancesco, Eddie Harris, Terry Gibbs, Clark Terry, Zoot Sims, Dave Frishberg, Pink Martini, and Rebecca Kilgore. *Ohio Lunch* (Heavywood 7884) teams him with a trio plus guest guitarist John Stowell, playing swing tunes and originals.

**Julio Fernandez**, who was born in Cuba, came to the United States when he was eight. He is best known for being a member of Spyro Gyra since 1984, where his guitar work adds to the band's grooves. While he has appeared on other pop/jazz dates, Fernandez has never led a CD of his own. *Down The Wire* (Heads Up 53361315429) is a good example of his work with Spyro Gyra.

**Ed Fila** (www.edfila.com) is based in Madison, Wisconsin, where he performs with his band Next Exit, a group that he co-leads with saxophonist Anders Svanoe called the Ed Anders Quartet, the Stella Novas and the Caravan Gypsy Swing Ensemble. With the latter group, which is a modernization of gypsy swing, he and Chris Ruppenthal trade off playing lead and rhythm guitar while joined by bassist Kevin Tipple and occasional guests. Their debut CD is simply called *Caravan Gypsy Swing Ensemble* (Hot String Swing).

A skillful fusion guitarist who can also play straight-ahead jazz, **Carl Filipiak** (www.carlfilipiak.com) has worked with Bob Berg, Gary Thomas, Victor Wooten, and Dennis Chambers. While most of his CDs are on his own Geometric label, *I Got Your*

*Mantra* (Art of Life 1029) is an exception. Filipiak is quite passionate yet versatile throughout.

**Jamie Findlay** (www.jamiefindlay.com), who is based in Los Angeles, specializes in the acoustic guitar. He has played in both poppish and straight-ahead jazz settings. In 1999, he formed the Acoustic Jazz Quartet, which also includes saxophonist David Sills, bassist Zac Matthews and drummer Dean Koba; they recorded *Acoustic Jazz Quartet* (Naxos 86033). Also of strong interest is Findlay's set of guitar duets with Duck Baker that explores mostly vintage material, *Out Of The Past* (Day Job).

**Barry Finnerty** (www.barryfinnerty.com) has primarily played commercial music in his career. After working with Chico Hamilton, Flora Purim & Airto, Joe Farrell, and the Crusaders, he became a top session player in the 1980s and '90s. *Straight Ahead* (Arabesque 116) from 1995 is a change of pace, a fine set that features Finnerty mostly playing originals but in a hard-bop style in a combo with pianist David Kikoski.

The French acoustic guitarist **Marc Fosset** spent most of the 1980s and part of the 1990s playing regularly with Stéphane Grappelli, sometimes as a duo and at other times as part of a quintet. The Grappelli-Fosset duo is featured on swing standards during *Stephanova* (Concord 4225) and *Looking At You* (JMS 033).

As the founder and longtime leader of the Rippingtons, **Russ Freeman** (no relation to the pianist of the same name) has long been a major attraction on the smooth circuit. In addition to the many recordings by the Rippingtons, Freeman occasionally leads a CD under his own name. *Drive* (Peak 8511) from 2002 puts the emphasis on his guitar playing, which is as melodic and pleasant as usual, as close to R&B and pop as to jazz.

A sound improviser, **Fred Frith** (www.fredfrith.com) has a background in rock (having led Henry Cow) and has worked with such groups as Massacre, Skeleton Crew and Keep the Dog. While he has worked with John Zorn, much of his work is outside of jazz. *Digital Wildlife* (Winter & Winter 71) gives one an example of Frith's highly original and very abstract music.

**Gabor Gado**, who is from Hungary, studied classical violin and guitar before discovering jazz. He splits his time between Budapest and Paris, playing post-bop jazz that is influenced by Hungarian folk music, modern classical music and his interest in free improvisations, as can be heard on *Homeward* (BMC 56).

The husband of singer Kate McGarry (whom he frequently works with), **Keith Ganz** (www.keithganz.com) is a lyrical folk/jazz guitarist who often plays acoustic. In addition to his recordings with his wife,

Ganz has recorded with Sean Smith, Melissa Walker, and Hayes Greenfield, and as a leader on the thoughtful *Music For People* (K&K Verlagsanstalt 96001).

Equally skilled on electric bass as he is on guitar, **Al Garcia** (www.myspace.com/algarciamusic) is a powerful fusion musician who has no difficulties with complex chord changes or time signatures. Influenced by Allan Holdsworth, he is also a solid straight-ahead jazz player when that is the context. Garcia's two recordings as a leader are *Make It So* (Al Garcia 8018) and *Alternate Realities* (Wandlar).

**Dick Garcia** (born 1931) in his career has worked with many jazz greats, including Charlie Parker, Tony Scott, George Shearing, Joe Roland, Milt Buckner and Kai Winding. The cool jazz guitarist's lone recording as a leader is *Message From Garcia* (Blue Moon 108), which has clarinetist Scott and Bill Evans among the sidemen.

Based in Baltimore and Washington, DC, **Mike Gellar** (www.mikegellar.com) is a fine bop guitarist who is also adept at playing swing tunes. *Perdido* features him in several settings, including two duets with guitarist Steve Abshire, while *Got The World On A String* teams him with singer Christina Drapkin. Both CDs are available through his website.

In her career, **Jane Getter** (www.janegetter.com) has worked with Jack McDuff, Joe Lovano, Richie Beirach, Kenny Barron, Regina Carter and Cindy Blackman. But much of her solo output has thus far been in the smooth/lite fusion area. *See Jane Run* (Alternity 5694) is likable but only hints at her potential.

**Joe Giglio** (www.joegiglio.com) studied under pianist Sal Mosca, has performed guitar duos regularly (including with Bucky Pizzarelli) and occasionally sings. Based in New York, where he has been a significant teacher, the bop-based guitarist is in fine form on *Sound Scapes* (Bella Firenze 1865), a set of duets with saxophonist Jimmy Halperin, and *3 Spirits* (available from his website) with his regular trio.

The world-famous and highly influential **João Gilberto** is the definitive bossa nova guitarist and singer. While his playing rarely crosses over into jazz, no book on guitarists would be complete without this understated yet masterful musician. *Getz/Gilberto* (Verve 68545) is the classic best-selling album with Stan Getz, while *The Legendary João Gilberto* (World Pacific 93891) focuses on bossa nova at its very beginning.

**David Gilmore** (www.davidgilmore.net) is an adventurous and versatile guitarist who has performed with such greats as Wayne Shorter, Dave Douglas, Muhal Richard Abrams, Sam Rivers, Steve Coleman, Don Byron, Cassandra Wilson and David Sanborn. In the late 1980s, he was part of the M-Base Collective; a few years later, he was in the fusion group

**Steve Giordano**

Lost Tribe. He has also appeared in rock and pop settings. 2006's *Unified Presence* (RKM 1124) features Gilmore with an all-star group that includes Ravi Coltrane, Christian McBride and Jeff "Tain" Watts, performing his complex originals.

**Steve Giordano** (www.stevegiordanoguitar.com) is a fine Philadelphia-based guitarist who has worked with Chico Hamilton, Richard "Groove" Holmes and Willis Jackson. He recorded an early album for Muse and, in recent years, has been leading the Steve Giordano Spacetet, a pianoless quintet that is featured on *TimeLine* (Dreambox Media 1112).

**Jeff Golub** (www.jeffgolub.com) spent years as a sideman to rock and pop acts, including Rod Stewart. His solo career since the mid-1990s has mostly found him playing smooth and R&B-ish music, often with his own Avenue Blue band. *Blues For You* (Koch 4540) is a bit different, a blues-based album that is rockish but with some jazz-oriented playing.

**Torsten Goods** is a German post-bop guitarist who also sings. He considers his inspirations to be George Benson, Biréli Lagrène and Wes Montgomery, although he is also open to pop music. Born Torsten Gutknecht, he was given his name of "Goods" by Les Paul. His CD *1980* (Act 97192) features music composed during the year of his birth.

Best known as an influential teacher in Wisconsin, **Jack Grassel** (www.jackgrassel.com) is a versatile musician equally at home playing jazz standards and adventurous originals. He has recorded with Tal Farlow, his own trio, and his wife, Jill Jensen. *Live At The Uptowner* (Frozensky 2012) finds Grassel and Kirk Tatnall both playing the Superax (which has guitar and bass strings, allowing them to continually switch roles) in a trio with drummer Ernie Adams, while *Guitar Smoke* (Frozensky 2008) features his expertise as an unaccompanied guitar soloist. In recent years, Jack Grassel has often teamed up with his wife singer Jill Jensen as a duo known as Jack & Jill. *Live At The Carleton Orange Pub* (FS 2017) has swinging, tender and often exquisite performances by the very appealing couple.

Born Gregory Green, the oldest son of Grant Green uses the name of his younger brother, **Grant Green, Jr.** (www.myspace.com/grantgreenjr), in his music career. He has a style that is influenced by George Benson and his father's later R&B period. Green has worked with the Masters of Groove and the Godfathers of Groove, groups that also feature organist Reuben Wilson. *Introducing G.G.* (Jazzateria 310) has some good examples of Green's playing, as does the Godfathers' *3* (18th & Vine 1061).

Since he is the professor of jazz guitar at the University of North Florida in Jacksonville, the playing career of **Barry Greene** (www.barrygreene.com) has been somewhat overshadowed by his teaching. A fine

post-bop guitarist, he has worked with Tim Hagens, Kenny Drew, Jr., Scott Wendholt, Danny Gottlieb, Jack Wilkins and others, leading six CDs of his own. *The Trio* teams Greene with bassist Dennis Marks and drummer Peter Miles on jazz standards, while *The Other Side* puts the emphasis on funkier music; all of his recordings are available from his website.

**Fred Hamilton** (www.fredhamilton.com) teaches at the University of North Texas and has been a member of drummer Earl Harvin's trio, which has recorded four albums. He also plays banjo, acoustic guitar and the Hindustani slide guitar in a mixture of Indian, Arabic and Balinese music and jazz with the Brahma. Hamilton teams up with David Friesen and drummer Ed Soph on *Looking Back On Tomorrow* (Heart 9), a set of originals that alternates between introspective explorations and rockish romps.

The music of guitarist-composer **Joel Harrison** (www.joelharrison.com), although it contains advanced improvising, often stretches beyond jazz into fresh and unusual looks into modern classical music, Appalachian folk music, country, and traditional African songs. *Urban Myths* (Highnote 757104), which features violinist Christian Howes and altoist David Binney, and *The Music Of Paul Motian* (Sunnyside 281273) are two of his most jazz-oriented sets.

**Jimmy Herring** (www.jimmyherring.net) has spent much of his career with rock groups and jam bands, including Aquarium Rescue Unit, the Dixie Dregs and Widespread Panic. He has also appeared in all-star tribute recordings on the Abstract Logix label that pay homage to the Mahavishnu Orchestra and Miles Davis' electric period. *Lifeboat* (Abstract Logix 13), a fusion-ish set, features him stretching out with top-notch musicians, including saxophonist Greg Osby.

Although apparently still active, not much has been heard from **Michael Howell** since the 1980s. He worked with Art Blakey, the Bobby Hutcherson–Harold Land band, Ella Fitzgerald, John Handy, Woody Shaw, and five years with Dizzy Gillespie. His lone album as a leader, *Alone* (Catalyst 7615), has yet to be reissued on CD.

Best known as a writer about jazz guitarists (including a book on Wes Montgomery) and an educator, the British-born **Adrian Ingram** (www.adrianingram.com) is also a fine straight-ahead guitarist. *Introducing The Jazz Guitar Of Adrian Ingram* (Just Jazz Guitar 2509298) is an excellent trio date from 1995, while *Homage* (String Jazz 1012) matches him in a set of duets with John Pisano, paying tribute to many of his predecessors.

**Enver Izmailov**, who was born in Uzbekistan in 1955 and has long lived in the Ukraine, developed the tapping technique independently of anyone else. His music includes jazz, classical and Eastern

(Balkan, Turkish and Crimean) folk music. *Minaret* (Boheme Music 902037) teams him with a saxophonist and a percussionist as a trio, playing music that sounds unique.

**Sid Jacobs** (www.sidjacobs.com), who started on guitar when he was seven, was an instructor at the University of Nevada, Las Vegas when he was only 18. He has since taught at the Dick Grove School and the Musicians Institute. He has played with Harold Land, Eddie Harris, Buddy Montgomery, Brad Mehldau and Javon Jackson but surprisingly has only led one CD so far: *It's Not Goodnight* (Best 9192).

**Tomas Janzon** (www.tomasjanzon.com) was born in Stockholm, was originally a cellist, and worked in Sweden and Northern Europe as a guitarist and a composer for television and films. He moved to Los Angeles in 1991, studied at the Guitar Institute (where he has taught since 1994), and has worked regularly in the Los Angeles area ever since. *Coast To Coast To Coast* (Changes 2516) is the post-bop guitarist's most recent recording.

**Bill Jennings** (b. 1919) came up after the rise of Charlie Christian. He made a strong impression playing with Louis Jordan in the late 1940s and has been cited as an early influence by B.B. King and Wes Montgomery. Jennings also recorded music that led the transition from early R&B to soul jazz with Bill Doggett, Wild Bill Davis, Jack McDuff, and in the 1960s with Willis "Gator" Jackson, although little has been heard from him since that era. On his *Legends Of Acid Jazz* (Prestige 24234), Jennings performs with Jack McDuff's group during 1959–60.

**Barbara Jungfer** (www.barbara-jungfer.de) is a significant post-bop guitarist from Germany who is based in Munich. She has worked with John Tchicai, Ed Schuller, pianist Peter O'Mara and Passport and recently toured as a duo with fellow guitarist Margaret Stowe. Her two CDs, *Berlin Spirits* (Minor Music) and *Going Places* (Phonector 100 388), are worth searching for.

London-born **Ronny Jordan** (www.ronnyjordan.com) was an important force in mixing together jazz with hip-hop in what for a little while was known as acid jazz. His recordings have since veered off into smooth. His 1992 debut, *The Antidote* (4th & Broadway 444047), remains his most interesting recording.

Born in Germany, **Dirk K.** (www.diprecords.com) has studied at the Musicians Institute and Berklee. He has worked with Randy Brecker, Peter Erskine, Toots Thielemans, Dave Weckl, Brandon Fields, Alan Paqua and others, appearing on over 30 albums. He has recorded music ranging from hard bop to smooth, many on his own DIP label, including *When Sunny Gets Blue*, a set of mostly standards.

**Jackie King** plays both jazz and country music with equal credibility. In the late 1960s, he was in the fusion band Shades of Joy. He performed with Sonny Stitt, Chet Baker and Jimmy Witherspoon and has jammed with everyone from Stevie Ray Vaughan to Big Joe Turner. Willie Nelson is a longtime friend and his guest on the charming standards-oriented *The Gypsy* (Free Falls 7014).

**Jerry Krahn** (www.jerrykrahn.com) was raised in Wisconsin, lives near Nashville, and often appears at classic jazz festivals. A founding member of Four Wheel Drive, and a veteran of rock and country groups, for the past 15 years Krahn has been a member of the Titan Hot Seven, matching wits on vintage jazz tunes with pianist Jeff Barnhart. Krahn's wide repertoire and diverse musical tastes are displayed on *Midwest Dreams* (Heartdance Music) and *Tell Me I'm Crazy* (Pick Song 005).

**Fapy Lafertin** (www.hotclub.nl) is a top guitarist in the Django Reinhardt style. Based in his native Belgium, he has played with the Piotto Orchestra, WASO, Bob Wilber (with whom he recorded) and, since 2001, his Lafertin Quintet. Among his recordings are *Star Eyes* (String Jazz 1010) and *Fleur D'Ennui* (Timeless 457).

**Steve Laury** (www.stevelaury.com) was the original guitarist with Fattburger and has shown versatility in his career, being able to play blues, in a Wes Montgomery vein, post-bop jazz or more commercial music with credibility. *Vineland Dreams* (CTI 67239) is an example of his playing in the mid-1990s.

Although not a household name, **Michael Leasure** (www.michaelleasure.com) has been quite busy throughout his career. He has composed over 1,000 pieces, performed regularly in Florida in many settings, and has mastered the guitar synthesizer while playing in many different styles including jazz. He has released 17 CDs on his MTL Productions, including *The Michael Leasure Band*, which is a good place to start.

**B.D. Lenz** (www.bdlenz.com) was originally a rock guitarist until he discovered the music of Mike Stern and Pat Metheny. Developing into an excellent fusion player, Lenz has recorded seven CDs thus far for the Apria label, including *Hit It And Quit*.

An adventurous post-bop guitarist, **Rob Levit** (www.roblevit.com) is never shy to stretch himself as a player or a composer, ranging from electronic music to free jazz. On *Uncertain Path* (Symbol System 0401), Levit's music includes a calypso, a Sting ballad, a rockish piece and "Footprints."

A fine soul-jazz guitarist, **O'Donel Levy** was on quite a few records during the first half of the 1970s, including with Groove Holmes and Jimmy McGriff, but has had a much lower profile since that period. *Simba* (P-Vine 23459) features soulful guitar solos and fine arrangements by Manny Albam.

**Vince Lewis** (www.vincelewis.com) has long been based in Virginia, where his swing-to-bop style makes him and his trio regulars at festivals and clubs. *Charlotte Swing: The Gift* (Redstone 4505) is one of his many fine recordings.

**Ed Littman** (www.edlittman.com) started with rock and blues, went through fusion, explored New Age, and developed into a strong post-bop guitarist. Based in New York, he has led several adventurous groups, including Splatt, a trio with bassist Danny Zanker and drummer John Bollinger that is featured on *Splatt* (Yeahman 8012).

A fixture in Detroit since the 1970s, **Robert Lowe Jr.** (www.myspace.com/guitaristrobertlowe) originally discovered jazz through Wes Montgomery and George Benson. He has worked with Houston Person, Lonnie Smith, Charles Earland, Richard Groove Holmes, Jimmy Smith, Joey DeFrancesco, Kenny Garrett and others. *Double Dip* (Lowe Down) is a soulful jazz set from 2001.

**Reggie Lucas** made a strong impression playing with Miles Davis during 1972–75, creating ferocious solos influenced by Jimi Hendrix. Within a few years of leaving Davis, Lucas disappeared from the jazz world but not from music, becoming a successful songwriter and arranger who wrote for Madonna, Phyllis Hyman and other pop and R&B acts. He has barely recorded on guitar since the late 1970s. Miles Davis' *Get Up With It* (Sony 9741/2) from 1974 features Lucas and fellow guitarist Pete Cosey in several intriguing jams.

Born in Norway, **Lage Lund** (www.lage-lund.com) is an up-and-coming post-bop guitarist. Lund has recorded with Seamus Blake, Jaleel Shaw, Kendrick Scott, Carmen Lundy, David Sanchez and Jimmy Greene. *Early Songs* (Criss Cross 1307), one of his three Criss Cross releases as a leader, features Lund sounding quite forceful and purposeful in a quintet, carving out his own musical path.

**Janet Marlow** (www.janetmarlowmusic.com), who was born in London, was classically trained on guitar (taking a class with Segovia), violin and piano. After moving to New York, she became influenced by Bill Evans and Joe Pass, both of whom she knew. She mastered the ten-string guitar and recorded some jazz sessions before becoming more involved as an educator and one who records mood music, including relaxation music for pets. One of her earliest sets, 1987's *Outside The City* (Chase 8003), teams her with pianist Renee Rosnes and saxophonist Dave Mann.

**Yoshiaki Masuo** (www.ymasuo.com/eng) was born in Tokyo, worked with altoist Sadao Watanabe (1967–70), and moved to New York in 1971. He played with Lenny White, Michael Brecker, Chick Corea, Elvin Jones (with whom he recorded), Lee Konitz and Sonny Rollins (1973–76 and 1981–84). He also led his own fusion group. Masuo has also spent long periods in which he primarily worked as a producer rather than a guitarist. *Are You Happy Now* (Sunnyside 1083) features him playing hard bop and soul jazz in 1998 with organist Larry Goldings and drummer Lenny White.

**Rick Matle** (www.myspace.com/rickmatle) is best known for his work in the Midwest with the inventive jazz singer Sheila Landis, which has resulted in quite a few recordings. A strong blues player also influenced by Joe Pass and Kenny Burrell, Matle also does projects on his own. *Riding The Round Pool* (Shelan 1019) is one of his better collaborations with Ms. Landis.

The rhythm guitarist with the Count Basie Orchestra since 1996, **Will Matthews** (www.willmatthews.com) was born in Kansas City and grew up as part of the scene, inspired by George Benson and Wes Montgomery. He also plays with the 18th Vine Street Big Band led by Bobby Watson. Matthews—who, unlike his predecessor Freddie Green, also solos—recently recorded *Count On Swinging*, a set with organist Mel Rhyne, for his Weebop label.

**Peter Mazza** (www.petermazza.com) is an excellent hard-bop guitarist based in New York. *Through My Eyes* (Late Set 62474) is a fine quartet date with Will Vinson on alto and soprano. Mazza has worked in many guitar duos (including with Jonathan Kreisberg, Peter Bernstein, Kurt Rosenwinkel and Jack Wilkins) and leads a trio with organist Brian Charette.

Based in Chicago, **John McLean** (www.johnmcleanmusic.com) has worked with Kurt Elling, Patricia Barber, Dr. Lonnie Smith, Randy Brecker, Mose Allison, Jane Ira Bloom and Dave Douglas, among others. His CD *Better Angels* (Origin 82486) is full of variety, with McLean ranging from Pat Metheny to modern pop and modernized swing standards, sounding comfortable in each genre.

**Chris Mello** (www.chrismello.com) earned a master's from the University of North Texas, toured with the Dallas Jazz Orchestra, and currently directs the guitar program at El Camino College. Based in Los Angeles, he has worked with the top local musicians plus Ernie Watts and Kenny Wheeler. His recording debut, *The Global Village* (available from his website), features the guitarist mixing together Cuban and Brazilian music, turning it all into modern jazz.

Born in Serbia, **Rale Micic** (www.ralemicic.com) has long been based in New York without forgetting his Balkan roots. While influenced by Jim Hall, Micic's style is all his own. He has recorded three rewarding sets for the CTA label, including *Serbia* (CTA 004), which features trumpeter Tom Harrell.

A talented young guitarist from New Orleans, **Davy Mooney** (www.davymooney.net) has already had many diverse musical experiences. He won third place in the Thelonious Monk guitar competition in 2005, played with the Hot Club of New Orleans, spent two years working with the Thelonious Monk Institute Septet, performed with Nicholas Payton, toured Japan, and visited India as part of a State Department delegation. He recently recorded a seven-string guitar duet album with John Pizzarelli, *Last Train Home* (Challenge 73273).

**Juarez Moreira** (www.juarezmoreira.com.br) is a major Brazilian guitarist who has worked with pianist Wagner Tiso, Milton Nascimento, Toninho Horta and other top Brazilians. While most of his recordings are only available in Brazil, he gained some international attention for his work on singer Ithamara Koorax's *Bim Bom: The Complete João Gilberto Songbook* (Motéma Music 30), a set of exquisite duets.

**Mike Moreno** (www.mikemoreno.com) clearly has a great future. A talented hard-bop and post-bop guitarist, he has worked with such major names as Joshua Redman, Nicholas Payton, Terence Blanchard, Greg Osby, Wynton Marsalis, Kenny Garrett, Jeremy Pelt and Gretchen Parlato, and his career is still just getting started. Of his four recordings as a leader, the quartet outing *First In Mind* (Criss Cross 1338) is an excellent place to start in exploring his music.

**Scotty Morris** is the guitarist and singer with Big Bad Voodoo Daddy (www.bbvd.com) in addition to being one of its founders. The group, one of the very best of the retro swing bands, was formed in 1992, solidified its personnel and size within a few years, and has been a popular attraction ever since. Morris is on all of the band's recordings, with *Big Bad Voodoo Daddy* (EMI-Capitol 72434-93338) and the recent Cab Calloway tribute *How Big Can You Get?* (Big Bad/Vanguard 79925) being particularly enjoyable and fun.

Guitarist-educator **John Moulder** (www.johnmoulder.com) is based in Chicago. He has been part of the Paul Wertico Trio for 15 years and performed with such notables as Kurt Elling, Eddie Harris, Bob Mintzer and Gary Burton. *Bifrost* (Origin 82546) is an intriguing set that successfully mixes the passion of Moulder's guitar with the much cooler playing of his sidemen, some of whom are from Norway.

**Jim Mullen** (www.jimmullenjazz.co.uk), born in Scotland and based out of London, worked with Brian Auger's Oblivion Express, the Average White Band and, most importantly, saxophonist Dick Morrisey in an important British fusion band during 1975–90. He recorded three albums with singer Claire Martin and has performed with such visiting American players as Jimmy Smith, Mose Allison,

Gene Harris, Jimmy Witherspoon, Plas Johnson and Teddy Edwards. Mullen's most recent CD as a leader is *Smokescreen* (Diving Duck 005), performed with an organ trio and ranging from swing standards to "Walk On By" and "Aja."

**Doug Munro** (www.dougmunro.com), an excellent guitarist, is nearly as busy as an arranger, composer, producer and educator. He has played with Michael Brecker, Dr. Lonnie Smith and his own groups, while his writing and producing often take him far beyond jazz. Munro's *Big Boss Bossa Nova* (Chase 8071) and *Big Boss Bossa Nova 2.0* (Chase 8078) feature the guitarist in combos that utilize bossa nova rhythms but frequently stretch the music into hard-bop and post-bop explorations.

**Ron Murray** (www.ronguitar.com) not only plays jazz but also classical and flamenco. He does a solo guitar presentation called the Flamenco Influence, is a music contractor for the Mohegan Sun Hotel and Convention Center, and has arranged and recorded guitar parts for Broadway shows. *Romanza* (Whaling City Sound 26) has Murray combining together all of his influences on a jazz set with a trio, displaying both his impressive technique and his creativity on a variety of melodic tunes.

**Wolfgang Muthspiel** (www.materialrecords.com), from Austria, attended the New England Conservatory and Berklee. He first gained attention with Gary Burton's band and has since played with Dave Liebman, Paul Motian, Bob Berg, John Patitucci, Brian Blade and singer Rebekka Bakken (from Norway). In 2002, he moved back to Vienna, where he founded the Material record label. He has recorded prolifically since the mid-1980s, including *From A Dream* (Material 024), which is a guitar trio album with Ralph Towner, and a collaboration with Mick Goodrick called *Live At The Jazz Standard* (Material 029).

The Florida-based **Nate Najar** (www.natenajar.com) has played both straight-ahead jazz and smooth during his career thus far. His trio has performed with Clark Terry and Ken Peplowski and recorded boppish sets, but in recent times, he has been exploring more pop-oriented jazz and has been a member of Eric Darius' band. 2004's *Like Coolsville* (Orchard 0204) is more inventive and jazz-oriented than the recent *Until Now*.

**Randy Napoleon** (www.randynapoleon.com) has worked with the Benny Green Trio (1999), the Clayton-Hamilton Jazz Orchestra, Michael Bublé (2004–07) and most recently Freddy Cole. The excellent bop-based guitarist is heard in top form on 2006's *Between Friends* (Azica 72236), which features either pianist Green or organist Jared Gold, displaying the influence of Wes Montgomery but also showing glimpses of his own emerging musical personality.

**Ken Navarro**

A commercial pop/jazz player with excellent technique who is a regular on smooth radio, **Ken Navarro** (www.kennavarro.com) was a session musician in Los Angeles before starting his solo career in 1990 on his own Positive Music label, which he still runs. One of his better sets is 2008's *The Grace Of Summer Night* (Positive Music 77793).

**Calvin Newborn**, the younger brother of the great pianist Phineas Newborn and the son of drummer Finas Newborn (who played with Jimmie Lunceford's Chicasaw Syncopators before Lunceford made it big), has played in Memphis throughout much of his life. He picked up early experience working with his brother in R&B and blues bands (including B.B. King's), was on some of Phineas' recordings, and played with Wild Bill Davis, Jimmy Forrest and Earl Hines. He also appeared on records by Charles Mingus, Sun Ra, Hank Crawford and others. But Calvin Newborn was never that famous and became a teacher. *New Born* (Yellow Dog 1159) features Newborn as he still is: an excellent soul-jazz guitarist whose playing falls between jazz and blues.

A fine rhythm guitarist whose initial background was in folk music and blues, **Paul "Dutch" Newman** has developed into a gifted songwriter and lyricist who writes tunes that sound like they were from the 1920s. He is the leader of the Musical Melodians, a top-notch 1920s group based in Los Angeles that features cornetist Corey Gemme, Dan Weinstein on trombone and violin, pianist Bob Mitchell and singer Mikal Sandoval. *Lowdown Man* (available through www.musicalmelodians.com) has Newman's vocals, rhythm guitar and memorable songs in the spotlight.

**Robin Nolan** (www.robinnolan.com) is a gypsy-jazz guitarist based in Amsterdam who sometimes stretches the style into hard-bop areas. He has been one of the first to teach gypsy guitar formally, and he has worked with his trio (which includes his brother Kevin Nolan on rhythm guitar and bassist Paul Meader) in several countries, including the US. *Boulevard Of Broken Dreams* (Refined 1005) is a change of pace for the group, for they are joined by singer Randy Greer (drummer Sonny Greer's grandnephew) for a repertoire that is as reminiscent of Nat King Cole as Django Reinhardt.

**Brian Nova** (www.briannova.com), who studied and toured with both Joe Pass and Herb Ellis, is a fine swing and bop guitarist who is also an excellent singer a bit influenced by Nat King Cole. Based in Seattle, Nova has recorded several very rewarding CDs, including 2005's *I Could Have Told You* (Vivify Music), which also features Eddie Harris and trombonist Fred Vesley.

Born in Stockholm, **Andreas Oberg** (www.andreasguitaruniverse.com) has often played in the United States. His Andreas Oberg Guitar Universe is an online guitar instructional site. *Six String Evolution* (Resonance 1015) finds him holding his own with keyboardist David Kikoski, bassist John Patitucci and drummer Lewis Nash on a variety of modern jazz styles, ranging from funky to explorative.

From Toronto, **David Occhipinti** (www.davidocchipinti.com) studied in New York with Jim Hall, spent two years in the 1990s in Italy, played duos with saxophonist Mike Murley, and has recorded several stimulating post-bop sets. *Duologue* (Cornerstone 121) documents his duets with Murley, while *Forty Revolutions* (Occdav 005) features the guitarist in a quartet with Murley, bassist Andrew Downing and drummer Terry Clarke.

A smooth guitarist and singer, **Steve Oliver** (www.steveolivermusic.com) plays upbeat music that is open to the influence of other cultures. His songs are frequently heard on smooth radio. *3D* (Koch 9583) is typical of his pleasant output.

**Jeff Parker** (www.jeffparkersounds.com) attended Berklee, worked with Antonio Hart, and moved to Chicago in 1991, where he has become a permanent part of the creative music scene. He helped form the Chicago Underground Trio, the Chicago Underground Orchestra and Isotope 217. He has also worked with the rock group Tortoise, the New Horizon Ensemble, Uptightly, the Aesop Quartet, Tricolor, Joshua Redman, Brian Blade, Fred Anderson, Ken Vandermark and Lin Halliday. A creative guitarist who ranges from hard bop to free, Parker's *The Relatives* (Thrill Jockey 12) features the guitarist with an adventurous quartet.

**Ricardo Peixoto** is closely associated with singer Claudia Villela, whose website (www.claudiavillela.com) he shares. They were both born in the same neighborhood in Rio de Janeiro, although they did not meet until 1984, when they were in San Francisco. They have been working together regularly since 1995, with Peixoto (frequently on acoustic guitar) playing beautifully behind the singer and also contributing arrangements. He has also toured with Flora Purim & Airto and worked with Bud Shank, keyboardist Marcos Silva, Dom Um Romão and his own group Terra Sul. He interacts closely with Claudia Villela on *Inverse Universe* (Adventure Music 1002).

**Evan Perri** is best known as the guitarist and leader with the Hot Club of Detroit (www.hotclubofdetroit.com). He did not begin on the guitar until he was 16 and was unfamiliar with Django Reinhardt until his twenties, but in 2005, he was motivated to form the Hot Club of Detroit, one of the best American gypsy-jazz groups. The band, with two guitars (including Perri as the soloist), bass, accordion and sax, has thus far recorded three excellent albums that update the Hot Club tradition while staying attached to its roots: *Hot Club Of Detroit* (Mack Avenue 1030), *Night Town* (Mack Avenue 1041), and *It's About That Time* (Mack Avenue 1051).

Born in Czechoslovakia and a longtime resident of Germany, **Lorenzo Petrocca** (www.petrocca.de) started on guitar when he was 18 and developed into a highly respected swing stylist. He works with the European Swingstars, with his siblings in the Petrocca Brothers, and with his own quartet. Along the way he has gigged and often recorded with Monty Alexander, Scott Hamilton, Tony Scott, the Heath Brothers, Peanuts Hucko, Jeff Clayton, Harry Allen, Howard Levy and many others. *Milan In Minor* (Jardis 20136) and *On A Clear Day* (Jardis 20146) are his most readily available recordings.

A consistently inventive guitarist, **Frank Portolese** (www.frankportolese.com) started out as a Jimi Hendrix fan before Joe Pass and George Benson won him over to jazz. Based in Chicago as both a player and an educator, he is heard with a pair of combos on *Last Call* (Southport 72) and playing unaccompanied on the recent *Plectrum Jazz Guitar Solos* (available through his website).

An excellent fusion guitarist, **Brad Rabuchin** (www.myspace.com/bradrabuchin) toured with Ray Charles for five years (1999–2004) and has worked with Stevie Wonder, Willie Nelson, David "Fathead" Newman, Louie Bellson and Roy Hargrove. He plays frequently in the Los Angeles area and is featured on *Cats Have Edges* (Manasus Music 06060) in a quartet with bassist Dean Taba, drummer Kendall Kay and saxophonist Andy Suzuki.

**Aurell Ray** played with Sonny Rollins (*Don't Stop The Carnival*), Freddie Hubbard, Charles Earland, Roy Haynes, Jack McDuff and Lonnie Liston Smith in the 1970s and '80s. However, not much had been heard from the guitarist in years when he recorded his debut as a leader, *Smile And Smile Again* (Seven Venues 1001), in 1997. Switching to acoustic guitar, Ray holds his own with the all-stars in his hard-bop combo and makes one wonder why he has been in obscurity in Cincinnati for so long.

**Vernon Reid** (www.myspace.com/vernonreid) gained fame with Living Colour and as the co-founder of the Black Rock Coalition. An explosive guitarist, much of his career has been spent playing rock, R&B and funk, but during 1980–83, he played avant-garde jazz/free funk with Ronald Shannon Jackson's Decoding Society. *Mandance* (Antilles 846 397) features Reid as one of the main stars, adding a great deal of fire and intensity to the passionate ensembles.

Originally from Norfolk, Virginia, **Paul Renz** (www.paulrenz.com) graduated from Berklee and the New England Conservatory and has been the head of the Department of Jazz Studies at Minneapolis'

West Bank School of Music. An excellent post-bop guitarist, Renz has recorded six CDs for his Gabwalk label, including the well-rounded *Beyond Blues* (Gabwalk 0601), which features him on four standards and three originals with a quintet of talented local musicians.

**Jeff Richman** (www.jeffrichman.net) first recorded with Ray Barretto in 1978. After moving to Los Angeles the following year, he toured with Ronnie Laws and Doc Severinsen and became part of the local studio and fusion scene, working with Ernie Watts, John Klemmer, Henry Mancini and others. Richman has produced several tribute albums for the Tone Center label, playing guitar on homages to Santana, the Mahavishnu Orchestra, Steely Dan, Miles Davis, Jeff Beck and John Coltrane. He has led 16 CDs of his own thus far, including *Aqua* (Mascot Music 7263).

**Reuben Ristrom** (www.reubenristrom.com), who plays both guitar and banjo, has worked in music for 40 years while based in his native Minnesota. He has gained some recognition for his appearance on swing recordings by pianist John Sheridan and singer Connie Evingson. His own CDs, which include a solo guitar outing on *Sunday Afternoon* and a quartet set with his wife, Diane Ristrom, on vocals (*Songbook*), are available through his website.

**Jim Robitaille** (www.jimrobitaille.com) is a guitarist and educator based in Massachusetts. Most of his recordings thus far are a bit obscure, but *To Music* (Whaling City Sound 21) gained some recognition for his originals and post-bop playing with his quintet, which includes Dave Liebman.

**Romane** is a gypsy guitarist who was classically trained before deciding to devote his career to playing Django Reinhardt–style jazz. His string of recordings for Iris are excellent, including *Ombre* (Iris Musique 943), which matches him with violinist Florin Niculescu, and *Double Jeu* (Iris Musique 1883), which teams him with the brilliant Stochelo Rosenberg in a quartet with bass and drums.

**Brandon Ross** (www.myspace.com/brmuse) has a long resume of top musicians (most in the avant-garde) with whom he has worked, including Cassandra Wilson (*Blue Light 'Til Dawn*), Henry Threadgill's Very Very Circus, Leroy Jenkins, Butch Morris, Bill Frisell, Archie Shepp, Muhal Richard Abrams, Don Byron, Ron Miles, Oliver Lake, and Wadada Leo Smith. He also has a real feel for country blues and aspects of early jazz. While currently working with several groups, including the acoustic quartet Blazing Beauty, his electric trio Harriet Tubman (with bassist Melvin Gibbs and drummer JT Lewis) is the best showcase for his passionate and extroverted solos, as can be heard on *I Am A Man* (Knitting Factory 228).

**Thom Rotella**

**Thom Rotella** (www.thomrotella.com) has played both music influenced by Wes Montgomery and more pop-oriented jazz. A studio musician since the 1970s in both Los Angeles and New York, Rotella has mostly been behind the scenes, although he has recorded eight CDs as a leader. *Out Of The Blues* (Four Bar 001) is a straight-ahead set that is one of his best jazz recordings.

Along with Ed Fila, **Chris Ruppenthal** (www.gypsyswing.com) alternates playing lead and rhythm guitar with the Caravan Gypsy Ensemble, an excellent gypsy-jazz group consisting of two guitars and bass plus occasional guests based in Madison, Wisconsin. The band began in 2002 when Ruppenthal, who was more of a bop player, heard Jimmy Rosenberg and decided to explore Django Reinhardt's music. *Caravan Gypsy Swing Ensemble* (Hot String Swing) is their debut recording.

A fine modern jazz guitarist, **Bruce Saunders** (www.brucesaunders.com) has taught at Berklee since 1992. He has recorded with Michael Cain, the New York Guitar Trio (with Ben Monder and Steve Cardenas), Dave Pietro, Barbara Sfaga, and Alan Ferber. *8 X 5* (Mel Bay 9802) shows off his warm tone on eight of his complex originals played with a quintet that includes tenor-saxophonist Adam Kolker.

**Karl Schloz** (www.karlschloz.com) calls his music "contemporary swinging jazz." Born in St. Louis, Schloz studied with Bucky Pizzarelli and spent time living in New York. Now based in Berlin, he has worked with top German jazz musicians and mainstream swing artists and recorded with Sarah Partridge, Mark Murphy and the Berlin Voices. *A Smooth One* (Nagel Heyer 2012) features Schloz playing swing tunes with a trio plus guest Harry Allen.

An excellent gypsy-jazz guitarist, **Tchavolo Schmitt** was born in Paris, started playing guitar at six, and was in Hot Club da Sinti in the 1980s and Gypsy Reunion the following decade. *Miri Familia* (Le Chant du Monde 2741629) is a bit unusual, for Schmitt plays swing standards and a few originals while backed by a bass and no less than four rhythm guitarists.

**Joachim Schoenecker** (www.joachimschoenecker.com) is an excellent hard-bop guitarist from Germany who has worked as a sideman with Toots Thielemans, Patti Austin, Paquito D'Rivera and the WDR Big Band. He has recorded as a leader since 1997, including *Dialogues* (Parashoot), a set of guitar duets with Peter Bernstein, and a quartet set with Chris Potter, pianist John Goldsby and drummer Adam Nussbaum, *In The Moment* (Nagel Heyer 2009).

**Karen Segal** (www.karensegal.com) has played a wide variety of jazz, from fusion to post-bop and the avant-garde. Born in Boston and part of the San Francisco jazz scene since 2002, she worked with Marilyn Mazur and Suzanne Fasteau in Copenhagen when she was a teenager. Her acid-jazz group Red Clay was active in Los Angeles in the early 1990s. In San Francisco, Segal has worked with Marcus Shelby, Babatunde Lea and other local greats. She has recorded two trio CDs for her Lilleskat label: *In The Moment* and *The Mystery Of Life*.

**Ben Sher** (www.bgirecords.com) blends together hard-bop jazz with Brazilian music. Originally from Pittsburgh, he has been in New York since the mid 1990s. Originally inspired by George Benson and Kenny Burrell, after visiting Brazil he formed TudoBem, a Brazilian jazz group. *Please Take Me To Brazil* (BGI 103), which also features Kenny Barron and Luciana Souza, is a good example Sher's brand of Brazilian jazz.

**James Silberstein** (www.jamessilberstein.com) has been active in New York since the late 1970s, with time also spent in Georgia and Miami. A straight-ahead player, he worked with Attila Zoller, Peter Leitch, Carter Jefferson and Norah Jones (before she switched to pop music) in addition to his own groups. *Song For Micaela* (Consolidated Artists 978) is an excellent quartet date with guest spots for Eric Alexander, Randy Brecker and singer Carla Cook.

A lyrical and thoughtful improviser, **Margaret Slovak** (www.margaretslovak.com) is originally from Denver, began playing guitar at 11, spent 1988–93 playing in New York (including with Fred Hersch, Joel Weiskopf, Michael Formanek and the Peruvian jazz group Antara) and led her own group. She moved to Portland in 1994, toured with a band that included drummer Bob Moses, and played in Europe with a quintet and as a solo artist. Health problems slowed down her career for some time, but she has been making a comeback, having moved back to New York in 2008. Margaret Slovak has three CDs out, including *From The Moment* (Slovak Music), a 1989 quartet set that also features Fred Hersch.

One of the top guitarists in smooth music, **Richard Smith** (www.richardsmithguitar.com) has musicianship that is widely respected even by those not into his melodic and mildly soulful music. Originally inspired by hearing Chick Corea, he played with Dan Siegel's band when he was 19, worked with Richard Elliot's group for ten years, and became the department chair of the Studio/Jazz Guitar Department at USC before he was 30. Smith began recording as a leader in 1989 and all of his recordings have been popular in the smooth world, including *Soulidified* (A440 Music Group 4029).

**Bob Sneider** (www.myspace.com/bobsneidermusic) grew up in Rochester, New York, toured with

Chuck Mangione for four years, and has worked with Nat Adderley, Don Menza, Houston Person, Etta Jones, Nnenna Freelon, Freddie Cole, and Jon Faddis. He has taught at the Eastman School of Music since 1997. Sneider is involved in the Film Noir project with vibraphonist Joe Locke, recording music from film noir soundtracks in jazz settings with an octet. *Nocturne For Ava* (Origin 82523) honors actress Ava Gardner.

**Chris Standring** (www.chrisstandring.com) plays smooth music that has as much rock, blues and R&B in its mixture as it does jazz. Born in England, he studied classical guitar, wrote music for the BBC, moved to Los Angeles in 1991, where he worked as a session player, and made his first of six smooth CDs in 1998. *Blue Bolero* (Ultimate Vibe 002) is his latest recording.

**John Stein** (www.johnstein.com) grew up in Kansas City, teaches at Berklee, and is a fine bop-based guitarist who has a traditional but fresh style. Among his recordings are *Green Street* (Whaling City Sound 039), which also features tenor-saxophonist David "Fathead" Newman, and *Turn Up The Quiet* (Whaling City Sound 051) with singer Ron Gill.

A German gypsy who made his recording debut at the age of 20, **Joscho Stephan** (www.joscho-stephan .de) is an outstanding gypsy-jazz guitarist who at this point is much better known in Europe than in the US. *Swinging Strings* (Acoustic Music 31911952) was his impressive first recording, while *Django Nuevo* (Acoustic Music 31914372), his most recent set, has five original songs plus other tunes that turn Latin, classical and pop into gypsy jazz.

**Margaret Stowe** (www.margaretstowe.com) from Toronto is an eclectic jazz guitarist who is also open to playing world music, folk, funk, ambience and blues. She has primarily played in Canada and Europe, including working in musical theater, guesting with symphony orchestras, teaching, and performing her S'Women in Blues shows. *Adventures Of The Red Guitar* (available from her website) has fine examples of her jazz and blues playing.

**Andy Summers** (www.andysummers.com) is world famous for his work with the Police during 1977–84, but since beginning his solo career, he has often played and recorded jazz. *Green Chimneys* (RCA 63472) finds him exploring the music of Thelonious Monk with a group that includes Joey DeFrancesco, while *Peggy's Blue Skylight* (RCA 63679) features Charles Mingus pieces. Summers comes to jazz on its own terms rather than sounding like a moonlighting rocker, and he fares quite well on these CDs.

**Ewan Svensson** (www.esm-prod.com) is a significant guitarist from Sweden. His original playing on his own CDs, although mostly documented by

the Dragon label, is more reminiscent of some of the music heard on ECM, with its use of space and gradual development. However, he has been versatile enough in his career to also play with Art Farmer, Clark Terry, Maria Schneider, Johnny Griffin, Scott Hamilton, Toots Thielemans, Ken Peplowski and Monica Zetterlund. *Figures* (Dragon 367) is a fine release from 2002.

**Ed Taylor** (www.edtaylormusic.com) is an accessible guitarist and singer whose music ranges from straight-ahead to R&B-ish. George Benson and Wes Montgomery were early influences. After a period as a session musician in Los Angeles, he settled in Tacoma, Washington, forming the TaylorMade band, a group that is sometimes as large as a septet. *TaylorMade* is an excellent set of soulful originals, available from Taylor's website.

**David Torn** (www.davidtorn.net) is an avant-garde sound explorer who has come up with new sounds on his instrument. Along the way he has worked with Jan Garbarek, the Everyman Band, Mark Isham, Bill Bruford, Dave Douglas and many major performers from the rock world in addition to writing quite a few soundtracks. *Prezens* (ECM 1877) teams him with most of Tim Berne's Science Friction band to create some wild music.

**Mark Towns** (www.marktowns.com) plays Latin jazz that has a bit of flamenco and music from the Middle East. He performs most often in Houston and in Southern California, and his gentle blend of styles (which includes straight-ahead jazz) is lively and melodic. *Passion* (Salongo 2922) is a fine set that has guest appearances by flutist Hubert Laws.

The son of Lennie Tristano, **Bud Tristano** (www .budtristano.com) is actually more of a rock guitarist than a jazz guitarist at this point, more influenced by Led Zeppelin than by Billy Bauer. However, his first CD, *Primal Elegance* (New Artists 1038), teams him with pianist Connie Crothers for a set of free improvisations and has the spirit of jazz and of his father.

**David Tronzo** (www.myspace.com/tronzo), a master of the slide guitar, is unusual in that he utilizes his blues-associated technique in a variety of settings, including jazz, rock, funk and avant-garde. He has appeared on many sessions and worked with Spanish Fly at the Knitting Factory. Tronzo interacts in a trio with saxophonist Peter Epstein and bassist J.A. Granelli to create passionate and free improvisations on *Crunch* (Love Slave 1101).

From the 1970s on, **John Tropea** (www.john tropea.com) has appeared on a countless number of sessions, ranging from Deodato, Hubert Laws, and Billy Cobham to Paul Simon, Roberta Flack, and Van Morrison. Always a funky and soulful player, Tropea loves soul-jazz organ combos. In recent times, he has recorded an excellent CD in that genre, *Take Me*

**Jaime Valle**

*Back To The Ol' School* (STP 1000), which includes Ronnie Cuber and Steve Gadd in the lineup.

A fine straight-ahead guitarist who also plays Latin music, writes music for commercials, and books local clubs, **Jaime Valle** (www.myspace.com/jaime .valle) is an important musical force in San Diego. In addition to recording with flutist Bradley Leighton, Valle has led several CDs of his own through the years, including *Vital Signs* (Bluport 012).

**Jesse van Ruller** (www.jessevanruller.com), the winner of the Thelonious Monk Guitar Competition in 1995, is from Holland and has performed with such notables as Joe Lovano, Pat Metheny, Mike Stern, Tom Harrell, Toots Thielemans, Roy Hargrove, the Metropole Orchestra and the WDR Big Band. He has recorded hard bop and post-bop on his nine CDs as a leader, including *Views* (Criss Cross 1273), which co-stars saxophonist Seamus Blake and organist Sam Yahel.

**Rick Vandivier** (www.rickvandivier.com) was born in Ohio, went to Berklee and settled in San Francisco. He has long been a fixture on the Northern California scene as a guitarist and educator and has worked with John Handy, Mose Allison, David Grisman, Richie Cole and Dr. Lonnie Smith. His most recent CD is *Vandivier* (Avatar Productions), an inventive straight-ahead set.

When it comes to playing ragtime guitar, early blues or classic jazz, **Craig Ventresco** (www.craigven tresco.com) is one of the best around today. He revives early obscurities from his 78 collection (sometimes as early as the 1910s), and in many cases his versions are superior to the original ones. His guitar was used on the soundtrack CD to the documentary *Crumb*, he led the trio Bo Grumpus shortly after he moved to San Francisco in 1988, and these days he often plays duets with pianist-guitarist-singer Meredith Axelrod. *The Past Is Yet To Come* (Origin Jazz Library 2000) shows just how talented he is as a musician and an archivist.

**Ricardo Vogt** (www.myspace.com/ricardovogt), who was born in Brazil, plays and sings bossa nova and Brazilian jazz. He came to the US in 17, studied at the University of Wisconsin–Green Bay and Berklee, and has made a strong impression ever since. He has toured with Toots Thielemans, works with Eliane Elias, and has been a member of the Esperanza Spalding Quartet since 2008. Vogt has not yet led his own CD but can be heard on Spalding's *Chamber Music Society* (Telarc 31810).

**Matthew Von Doran** (www.matthewvondoran .com) was born in Germany and grew up in Washington, DC, in Canada and near Los Angeles. He began on guitar at 15, originally played rock, and became interested in fusion while in college. After attending the Guitar Institute, he worked for years with top-40 bands, and was a member of the Don Miller big band during 1986–2002. Surprisingly, he did not pursue a solo career until recently, playing with fusion with the New Trio of Doom, which evolved into his own trio. His debut CD, *In This Present Moment* (BCRT 1001), is a fine post-bop date with saxophonists Bob Mintzer and Bob Sheppard helping out.

Born and based in England, **Mike Walker** (www .mike-walker.co.uk) has played with Mike Gibbs, Kenny Wheeler, the fusion band Some Other Country, Julian Arguelles, Tommy Smith, Tal Farlow, George Russell, the Creative Jazz Orchestra, Norma Winstone, Dave Holland and many top British players. The adventurous guitarist's debut album as a leader, *Madhouse And The Whole Thing There* (Egea 01), features Walker with a large orchestra.

Relatively little is known about **Quentin Warren**'s life, and even whether he is still alive or not. Warren was Jimmy Smith's guitarist during 1960–65, appearing on many of his recordings. Although overshadowed by Wes Montgomery and Kenny Burrell (both of whom also appeared on Smith's records of that era), Warren was in the organist's working group and gave him what he wanted: concise bluesy statements and rhythmic comping behind his solos. *Crazy Baby* (Blue Note 84030) features Smith's 1960 trio with Warren and drummer Donald Bailey. He is the uncle of bassist Butch Warren.

**Peter White** (www.peterwhite.com) started playing acoustic guitar in his native England, moved to the US, and worked as a featured backup musician for many acts, including Basia. He released his first solo album in 1990 and has since become a major attraction in the smooth world, playing with Richard Elliot, Warren Hill, Rick Braun, Kirk Whalum, Everette Harp and as part of Guitar and Saxes. All of his releases have been strictly in the smooth genre, including the recent *Good Day* (Peak 31006).

No one could accuse **Lew Woodall** (www.lew woodall.com) of rushing into jazz. Although he loved hearing it when he first started playing guitar at the age of 14, he spent years playing with rock, top-40 and blues groups, took 12 years off from playing altogether, and did not start playing jazz gigs until 2000 when he was 60. Influenced by Wes Montgomery, he has since recorded four excellent CDs, including *Simply Cooking* (Philology) and *Second Time Around* (Philology), both with quartets featuring the great bop pianist Hod O'Brien.

Born in Paris, **Stephane Wrembel** (www.stephane wrembel.com) was trained to be a classical guitarist, but discovering the music of Django Reinhardt when he was 14 caused him to go in a different musical direction. He studied at Berklee, moved to New

York, and formed the Django Experiment, a quartet similar to the Quintet of the Hot Club of France except without a violin. Wrembel also writes film scores and plays with other types of groups, including with David Grisman. *Gypsy Rumble* (Amoeba 3) features him playing swing tunes, both standards and originals.

**Rick Zunigar** (www.rickzunigar.com) was originally inspired by Wes Montgomery and Joe Pass. A professional by the time he was 17, the L.A.-based musician has worked with Freddie Hubbard, Cal Tjader, Jimmy Smith, Willie Bobo and many others. His own projects have ranged from fusion to soul jazz, including *Organ Trio* (Jazzuni 002).

# THEY ALSO PLAYED JAZZ GUITAR

The 36 performers in this section have little in common except that none of them tried for long to earn a living strictly as a jazz guitarist, yet all of them have played jazz guitar to at least a small extent sometime in their careers.

The great country guitarist **Chet Atkins** could have been a jazz performer if that had been his goal. Some of his recordings were of swing standards, but his concise versions during his many years for RCA stuck strictly to country. However, he liked jazz and recorded two albums in the 1970s with Les Paul (*Chester And Lester* and *Monster Guitars*), which have been reissued as *Masters Of The Guitar Together* (Pair 1230).

In the trad-jazz festival circuit, it would be easy to think that there were three or four **Clint Baker**s, since he plays trumpet, trombone, bass, tuba, drums, banjo, and probably several other instruments in addition to guitar. Actually, guitar is probably Baker's fourth- or fifth-best instrument, but he is good enough to be on clarinetist Paul Cosentino's *Linger Awhile* (Biograph 155).

**Al Bowlly** was the British Bing Crosby, the most popular singer in England during the 1930s and one who had many hits with his renditions of ballads. In addition to singing, Bowlly was also a rhythm guitarist, particularly during the 1920s, when he played with dance bands. He largely gave the guitar up after 1931.

One of the top jazz drummers of the past decade, **Brian Blade** has played acoustic guitar on records on rare occasions. Those include albums by Dianne Reeves and Lizz Wright plus his own *Perceptual* and most notably his folk/pop Verve Forecast album *Mama Rosa* (Verve Forecast 1261302), which also features his singing and lyrics.

**Glen Campbell** in a jazz book? Before he became a very popular country singer, Campbell was a studio guitarist who, among other recordings, took some worthwhile jazz solos on *Dylan Jazz* (GNP/Crescendo). While Dylan's songs may not have all that much potential as vehicles for jazz improvisations, the five musicians on this album from 1967 (which include saxophonist Jim Horn) play decent instrumental versions of such tunes as "Blowin' In The Wind," "Mr. Tambourine Man" and "Like A Rolling Stone."

A warm, sensuous singer from Brazil, **Ana Caram** effectively accompanies her own vocals on guitar. Her American debut, *Rio After Dark* (Chesky 28) from 1989, is a good place to start in exploring the music of this Antonio Carlos Jobim protégée.

One of the most famous country performers of the 1970s and '80s, **Roy Clark** may have featured cornball humor in his act, but he was a world-class guitarist. It has long been an open secret that the best Nashville guitarists play jazz in their off-hours. In 1994, he matched wits and swinging ideas successfully with Joe Pass on *Roy Clark And Joe Pass Play Hank Williams* (Buster Ann Music).

An important and influential New Orleans jazz–style cornetist in Great Britain, **Ken Colyer** also enjoyed playing guitar in a "skiffle" band taken out of his larger jazz group. Colyer's brand of skiffle was a mixture of old blues, folk and jazz tunes and, although he was not a major guitar soloist, he certainly had fun bringing back the vintage tunes. *Somewhere Over The Rainbow* (Upbeat 170) features Colyer on both guitar and trumpet.

While **Ry Cooder** has spent much of his life playing folk, Cuban, Latin, ethnic music, blues and rock, he did record *Jazz* (Warner Bros. 12696), a respectful and educational revival of tunes by Bix Beiderbecke, Jelly Roll Morton and other vintage jazzmen. There should have been sequels, for he displays a real feeling for the older tunes.

**Lonnie Donegan**, who played occasional solos on acoustic guitar and banjo while with Chris Barber in 1953–54, was at first an intermission favorite when he sang skiffle songs. After he had a giant hit with "Rock Island Line," he was a major attraction as a singer for much of the pre-Beatles era. The three-CD set *Midnight Special: The Skiffle Years* (Acrobat 9013) is a fine overview of his career.

The grandson of Duke Ellington, **Edward Ellington II** was briefly in his father Mercer Ellington's band. He is on the Duke Ellington Legacy Band's *Thank You Uncle Edward* (Renma 6400) with such top players as Virginia Mayhew, Wycliffe Gordon, Norman Simmons and Nancy Reed for a fine set of Ellington music.

**Brick Fleagle** played rhythm guitar with a few 1930s big bands but was more notable as an arranger for such orchestras as Chick Webb, Jimmie Lunceford, Duke Ellington and Fletcher Henderson. A good friend of cornetist Rex Stewart, Fleagle appeared on and wrote for many of Stewart's sessions. His guitar is part of an all-star group during four numbers reissued as *Rex Stewart And The Ellingtonians* (Original Jazz Classics 1710).

**Peter Frampton**

**Peter Frampton**? The rock star can be heard playing Thelonious Monk's "Work" in a quartet with Marcus Miller on the eclectic and often remarkable Monk tribute set *That's The Way It Is* (Verve 543 514) in 1984. He apparently never felt tempted to play jazz again.

The J. Geils Band was a very popular rock group during 1970–85. Decades later, **Jay Geils**, whose first love was Charlie Christian–style jazz, finally returned to his real roots, playing with Duke Robillard and Gerry Beaudoin in New Guitar Summit and leading his own jazz albums. *Jay Geils Plays Jazz!* (Stony Plain 1306) is an excellent modern swing album with guest spots for tenor-saxophonist Scott Hamilton.

One of the top singers of 1920s, '30s and '40s tunes since her debut in 1981, **Banu Gibson** leads the New Orleans Hot Jazz, an exciting septet. At her many performances at classic jazz festivals, Banu lets her band cut loose on instrumentals (perhaps one-third of the songs) while she sits down and enthusiastically plays rhythm guitar. She does not take solos, humorously calling herself a "21st-century Eddie Condon." While one should not acquire her highly enjoyable recordings looking for guitar solos, she can be heard in some of the ensembles on *Let Yourself Go* (Swing Out 103) and *You Don't Know My Mind* (Swing Out 104).

A major arranger whose charts for the Casa Loma Orchestra in the early 1930s predated and helped set the stage for the swing era, **Gene Gifford** was also the band's rhythm guitarist and banjoist during 1929–33 before he gave it up to concentrate on writing. The Casa Loma's *Maniac's Ball* (Hep 1051) has some of Gifford's best arrangements, and he plays rhythm guitar on most of the numbers.

One of the most lyrical cornet players of all time, **Bobby Hackett** could always be counted on to play beautifully and to sound relaxed, even during the hottest Dixieland ensembles. Few remember that he was originally a guitarist who often doubled on the instrument up until the mid-1940s. In fact, when he was hired by Glenn Miller in 1942, it was as a guitarist, although his cornet solo on "A String Of Pearls" was much more notable. Hackett takes a rare acoustic guitar solo on a date led by jazz critic Leonard Feather, which is included on Feather's *1937–1945* (Classics 901).

**Jeff Healey**, who had big success as a rock performer in the 1990s, was a record collector who loved early jazz and blues. Later in his life, he often performed trad jazz, usually on cornet but also guitar. *Among Friends* (Stony Plain 1312) features fine playing by Healey on both of his instruments.

**Diane Hubka**, a fine jazz singer currently based in Los Angeles, has always loved the sound of the guitar. She often accompanies herself on a seven-string guitar and features other guitarists on her recordings. Her album *You Inspire Me* (VSO Jazz 5173) has seven different guitarists on various tracks: Romero Lubambo, Bucky Pizzarelli, Frank Vignola, John Hart, Paul Bollenbeck, Jack Wilkins and Gene Bertoncini. She accompanies herself during "Manha De Carnaval" from her more recent CD *Diane Hubka Goes To The Movies* (18th & Vine 1054).

One of the greatest vibraphonists of all time, **Milt Jackson** on rare occasions played piano, at very rare times (fortunately) took vocals, and just once played guitar on record. During a Ray Charles jazz combo set (itself a rare occurrence), Jackson is heard on vibes and piano, and showcased during "Bag's Guitar Blues," not sounding bad. The two Charles/Jackson albums from 1957–58 have been reissued as the two-CD set *Soul Brothers/Soul Meeting* (Atlantic 89851) and also feature some of Ray Charles' best alto-sax solos.

A superb songwriter who made bossa nova a worldwide phenomenon, **Antonio Carlos Jobim** wrote dozens of wonderful melodies. He also played piano, sang and sometimes accompanied himself on guitar, although his composing was on a much higher level than his performances. The mostly instrumental *Wave* (A&M 9411) has some examples of Jobim's guitar and piano playing.

While **Joyce** is primarily known as a very skilled Brazilian singer who has led 21 albums of her own at this writing, she is also an excellent guitarist who occasionally supports her vocals with her playing. *Music Inside* (Far Out 34), which features her originals, has her guitar playing in a more prominent role than usual.

One of the most rewarding interpreters of swing-era songs, during the past 20 years singer **Rebecca Kilgore** has been heard with the all-stars of mainstream swing. She has recorded over a dozen CDs as a leader and collaborated with Dan Barrett, Eddie Erickson and bassist Joel Forbes as B.E.D.; recently, the group has been renamed the Rebecca Kilgore Quartet. She usually plays guitar on stage, sticking to playing rhythm with her knowledge of chords resulting in her seeming to always know the perfect note to sing at the perfect moment. *Get Ready For Bed* (Blue Swing) is one of many fine Rebecca Kilgore recordings.

**Oscar Klein** was a very good Dixieland trumpeter from Austria who also occasionally played swing guitar. *Big Four/Jazz For Two* (Lino Patruno 01) has Klein on trumpet for the first half in a quartet that includes guitarist Lino Patruno. The second half is a set of Klein-Patruno duets, some of which have Klein on electric guitar, playing in a style reminiscent of Tiny Grimes.

**Hugh Leal** ran the Parkwood label in the 1980s/'90s and has been an important swing/trad-jazz record producer and promoter. He has also played acoustic guitar and banjo in Canada for the past 40 years, led the Motown Classic Jazzband, and is heard on several albums, including clarinetist Dave Bennett's *100 Years Of Benny Goodman* (Arbors 19389).

A significant bandleader and a facilitator of recording projects in England for decades, **Vic Lewis** evolved from playing Dixieland to being a leader of orchestras that were influenced by Stan Kenton. In addition to occasionally playing cornet and trombone, Lewis was often on rhythm guitar through the mid-1940s, as can be heard on *Singin' The Blues* (Upbeat 163).

As a pianist, composer, arranger and bandleader, **Jelly Roll Morton** was one of the giants not only of early jazz but of jazz history. So what is he doing in a book on guitarists? Morton played guitar at an early age before discarding it. In 1938, when he recorded extensively for the Library of Congress, before the final sessions, he was injured in a fight and temporarily could not play piano. For the only time on records, Morton can be heard on guitar, accompanying his storytelling on a few selections. But of course, the reason to acquire the eight-CD *The Complete Library Of Congress Recordings* (Rounder 1898) is for Jelly Roll Morton's stories and brilliant piano.

**Willie Nelson**, the beloved country singer, always liked Western swing and swing music in general. He knows a fair number of Charlie Christian licks and fares well on his unlikely but successful meeting with Wynton Marsalis, *Two Men With The Blues* (Blue Note 4454).

**Jackie Paris** should have made it big, for he was one of the first bop singers, a superior interpreter of ballads, and was active during the 1950s, when male singers were in strong demand. Paris is now thought of as a cult figure. In his career, he occasionally accompanied himself on guitar, as can be heard on *The Intimate Jackie Paris* (Hudson 1001), a late 1990s program in which his only other accompanist is bassist Mike Richmond.

The older sister of John Pizzarelli and the daughter of Bucky Pizzarelli, **Mary Pizzarelli**, a classical guitarist, makes appearances on two of Bucky's albums. On *Green Guitar Blues* (the LP Monmouth 7047), she duets with Bucky on "Chicken A La Swing" in 1972; she was 14 at the time. Two years later on *Bucky Pizzarelli Plays Beiderbecke/Challis and Kress/McDonough* (Audiophile 238), she plays "Stage Fright" and "Danzon," also in duets with her father.

**Jimmie Rodgers**, "The Singing Brakeman," in his six-year career, was the first major star of country music. His music (recorded during 1927–33) often included blues that swung, and even his yodeling was somewhat jazz-oriented. One selection, "Blue Yodel No. 9," has Louis and Lil Armstrong as his accompanists. Rodgers' guitar playing not only backed his singing, but his solos were related to those of Lonnie Johnson and Eddie Lang. The five-CD set *Recordings 1927–33* (JSP 7704) contains his entire musical legacy.

A superior singer with a haunting voice and a real feel for lyrics, **Kendra Shank** has sometimes played guitar behind her own vocals, particularly earlier in her career. She made a guest spot on guitar on an Abbey Lincoln record (*Over The Years*) and her 1994 debut recording, *Afterglow* (Mapleshade 2132), has a few examples of her guitar playing.

**Bobby Sherwood** was a multi-talented individual. He played very good swing trumpet, also recorded on trombone, took occasional vocals, led an excellent big band during 1942–47 (having a hit with "The Elks' Parade"), and was a studio musician for years, an actor and a disc jockey. His rhythm guitar playing was also excellent. Sherwood was Eddie Lang's successor as Bing Crosby's accompanist (on and off during 1933–42) and had a brief stint with Artie Shaw.

**George M. Smith** was the first staff guitarist at Fox and Paramount Studios, appearing on a countless number of movie soundtracks in the 1930s and '40s. While widely respected by many who followed him, Smith made very few recordings in the jazz world. *Guitar Rarities Volume 1: 1934–46* (IAJRC 1017) has six numbers by George M. Smith with a string quartet, bass and drums that hint at his talent.

**Daryl Stuermer** is a rock guitarist best known for his work with Genesis and Phil Collins. Just prior to that work, Stuermer played regularly with violinist Jean-Luc Ponty during 1975–77, showing that he was a very good fusion guitarist too. Ponty's *Aurora* (Atlantic 19158) is a good example from Stuermer's brief fusion period.

A top swing violinist who had a rediscovery and renaissance later in his life, **Claude Williams** originally doubled on rhythm guitar. He was with Andy Kirk's 12 Clouds of Joy in the late 1920s and was Freddie Green's predecessor with the Count Basie Orchestra. Williams was replaced only a short time after the band came East, because producer John Hammond apparently did not like his violin solos. Williams managed to make it through many decades of obscurity, started to gain prominence as a violinist in the 1970s, and had the last laugh by outliving every musician in the original Basie band. He was still an active musician when he passed away in 2004 at the age of 96 as the last survivor of 1920s jazz.

# JAZZ GUITARISTS ON FILM

The birth and rapid expansion of YouTube (www .youtube.com) has resulted not only in an excess of cute pet videos but also in a remarkable number of rare jazz film clips becoming easily available online. This is true of both early jazz and current groups, with many jazz guitarists being represented by films, long-lost television appearances and live performances. Spend a few hours (or months) exploring YouTube, and you will be amazed at what can be found. One can even find clips featuring Oscar Alemán.

This section is not about that, or about the work of guitarists on instructional videos, but instead gives a sampling of significant on-screen appearances by jazz guitarists. Unlike with my previous book *Jazz On Film*, there is no attempt here to list everything, but these are performances that should be of great interest to fans of jazz guitarists.

## Jazz Guitar DVDs

John Abercrombie: *Solos: The Jazz Sessions* (MVD)
Howard Alden: Ken Peplowski's *Live At Ambassador Auditorium* (Concord)
Gerry Beaudoin: New Guitar Summit's *Live At The Stoneham Theatre* (Stony Plain)
George Benson: *Absolutely Live* (Pioneer)
Peter Bernstein: *Live At Smoke* (Mel Bay)
Lenny Breau: *The Genius Of Lenny Breau* (Guitarchives)
Kenny Burrell: *Legends Of Jazz Guitar Vol. 2* (Vestapol)
Charlie Byrd: *Great Guitars Of Jazz* (Vestapol), *Legends Of Jazz Guitar Vols. 2 & 3* (Vestapol), *Jazz Masters Vol. 2* (Vestapol)
Charlie Christian: *Solo Flight: The Genius Of Charlie Christian* (View Video), a documentary, but unfortunately, no footage exists of Christian
Eddie Condon: *Jazz Festival Vol. 1* (Storyville)
Larry Coryell: *Making Of The Spirits* with John McLaughlin and Paco de Lucía (MVD)
Al Di Meola: Return to Forever's *Returns* (Eagle Rock Entertainment)
Herb Ellis: *Detour Ahead* (Vestopol), *Great Guitars Of Jazz* (Vestapol), *Legends Of Jazz Guitar Vols. 1 & 3* (Vestapol), *Jazz Masters Vol. 2* (Vestapol)
Tal Farlow: *Great Guitars Of Jazz* (Vestapol), *Legends Of Jazz Guitar Vol. 3* (Vestapol), *Jazz Masters Vol. 2* (Vestapol), Red Norvo's *Jazz At The Smithsonian* (Kultur Films)
Boulou and Elios Ferré: *Gypsy Guitar: The Legacy Of Django Reinhardt* (Shanachie)
Bruce Forman: *Cool Summer: Stan Getz & Richie Cole's Alto Madness* (MVD)

Bill Frisell: *Jazz Masters Volume One* (Vestapol)
Mick Goodrick: Charlie Haden and the Liberation Music Orchestra's *Live In Montreal* (Image Entertainment)
Grant Green: *Legends Of Jazz Guitar Vol. 2* (Vestapol)
Jim Hall: *Jazz Casual: Sonny Rollins* (Rhino), *Jazz Casual: Art Farmer/Jim Hall* (Rhino), *Art Farmer* (Jazz Icons), *A Life In Progress* (Rhapsody), *Legends Of Jazz Guitar Vol. 3* (Vestapol)
Allan Holdsworth: *Allan Holdworth & Alan Pasqua* (MVD)
Stanley Jordan: *One Night With Blue Note* (Blue Note Video), *Live In Montreal* (Image Entertainment), *Live From Velocity Studios* (Mack Avenue)
Vic Juris: *Live At The Smithsonian Jazz Cafe* (Mel Bay)
Barney Kessel: *Rare Performances 1962–1991* (Vestapol), *Legends Of Jazz Guitar Vols. 1–3* (Vestapol)
Steve Khan: *Jazz Masters Vol. 1* (Vestapol)
Biréli Lagrène: *Gypsy Guitar* (Shanachie), *Django: A Jazz Tribute* (View Video)
Jon Larsen: *Jon & Jimmy* (Euforia)
Pat Martino: *Legends Of Jazz Guitar Vol. 3* (Vestapol), *Jazz Masters Vol. 1* (Vestapol)
John McLaughlin: *Making Of The Spirits* with Paco de Lucía and Larry Coryell (MVD)
Pat Metheny: Creative Music Studio's *Woodstock Jazz Festival* (Pioneer Artists), *DeJohnette/Hancock/ Holland/Metheny* (Pioneer), *We Live Here* (Image Entertainment)
Wes Montgomery: *Live In '65* (Jazz Icons), *Legends Of Jazz Guitar Vols. 1 & 2*
Jordan Officer: Susie Arioli's *Live At The Montreal International Jazz Festival* (Justin Time)
Joe Pass: *Genius Of Joe Pass* (Vestapol), *Legends Of Jazz Guitar Vols. 1 & 2* (Vestapol)
Les Paul: *Chasing Sound* (Koch)
Bucky Pizzarelli: *Favorite Solos* (Mel Bay)
Django Reinhardt: Stéphane Grappelli's *A Life In The Jazz Century* (Music on Earth)
Emily Remler: *Jazz Masters Vol. 1* (Vestapol)
Duke Robillard: New Guitar Summit's *Live At The Stoneham Theatre* (Stony Plain)
Jimmy Rosenberg: *Gypsy Guitar* (Shanachie), *Jon & Jimmy* (Euforia)
Stochelo Rosenberg: *Gypsy Guitar* (Shanachie), *Symphonic Django* (Anet)
Mike Stern: *New Morning* (In-Akustik)
Martin Taylor: Stéphane Grappelli's *Live In San Francisco* (Storyville)
Jack Wilkins: *Jazz Masters Vol. 2* (Vestapol)
Anthony Wilson: Diana Krall's *Live In Paris* (Eagle Rock Entertainment)

## Videotapes Not Yet Reissued on DVD

Howard Alden: *Ruby Braff Trio In Concert* (Storyville)

Charlie Byrd: *Live In New Orleans* (Leisure Video)

Eddie Durham: *Born To Swing* (Rhapsody)

James Emery: The String Trio of New York's *Built By Hand* (Rhapsody)

Barney Kessel, Herb Ellis and Charlie Byrd: *Great Guitars—Jazz At The Maintenance Shop* (Shanachie) and *Jazz At The Maintenance Shop 1979* (Rhapsody)

## 10 Memorable (if Brief) Appearances by Jazz Guitarists in Hollywood Films

Dave Barbour: *The Secret Fury* (1950)

Jack Bland: *The Opry House* (1929), a film short, with Red McKenzie's Blue Blowers

Herb Ellis: *Pete Kelly's Blues* (1955)

Jimmy Gourley: *Round Midnight* (1986)

Eddie Lang: *The King Of Jazz* (1930), for a glorious minute with Joe Venuti

Eddie Lang: *The Big Broadcast* (1932), with Bing Crosby

Les Paul: *Sarge Goes To College* (1947)

Alvino Rey: *Sing Your Worries Away* (1942)

Roy Smeck: *His Pastimes* (1926), a film short

Al Viola with the Page Cavanaugh Trio: *Romance On The High Seas* (1948)

## The Best Ghosting by a Jazz Guitarist

Howard Alden playing for Sean Penn: *Sweet And Lowdown* (1999)

# OTHER BOOKS ON JAZZ GUITARISTS

Barker, Danny, and Alyn Shipton. *A Life In Jazz*. Oxford University Press, 1986.

Condon, Eddie, and Thomas Sugrue. *We Called It Music*. Da Capo Press, 1947.

Coryell, Julie, and Laura Friedman. *Jazz-Rock Fusion*. Delta, 1978.

Delaunay, Charles. *Django Reinhardt*. Da Capo Press, 1961.

Gregory, Hugh. *1000 Great Guitarists*. GPI Books, 1994. (Not strictly jazz, but informative.)

Hadlock, Richard. *Jazz Masters Of The Twenties*. Da Capo Press, 1965. (Recommended for its chapter on Eddie Lang.)

Ingram, Adrian. *Wes Montgomery*. Ashley Mark Publishing Co., 1985.

Jordan, Steve, with Tom Scanlan. *Rhythm Man*. University of Michigan Press, 1991.

Niles, Richard. *The Pat Metheny Interviews*. Hal Leonard Books, 2009.

Shaughnessy, Mary Alice. *Les Paul—An American Original*. William Morrow & Co., 1973.